JUSTICE ANTONIN SCALIA
AND THE CONSERVATIVE REVIVAL

JUSTICE ANTONIN SCALIA AND THE CONSERVATIVE REVIVAL

Richard A. Brisbin, Jr.

THE JOHNS HOPKINS UNIVERSITY PRESS
Baltimore and London

© 1997 The Johns Hopkins University Press
All rights reserved. Published 1997
Printed in the United States of America on acid-free paper

Johns Hopkins Paperbacks edition, 1998
9 8 7 6 5 4 3 2 1

The Johns Hopkins University Press
2715 North Charles Street
Baltimore, Maryland 21218-4363
The Johns Hopkins Press Ltd., London
www.press.jhu.edu

Library of Congress Cataloging-in-Publication Data

Brisbin, Richard A.
    Justice Antonin Scalia and the Conservative revival / Richard A.
Brisbin Jr.
        p.   cm.
    Includes bibliographical references and index.
    ISBN 0-8018-5432-6 (alk. paper)
    1. Scalia, Antonin. 2. United States. Supreme Court.
3. Political questions and judicial power—United States.
4. Conservatism—United States. 5. United States—Constitutional
law—Interpretation and construction.
    KF8745.S33B75 1997
    347.73´2634—dc20
    [347.3073534]   96-22883
                                                                                CIP

ISBN 0-8018-6094-6 (pbk.)

A catalog record for this book is available from the British Library.

To my family—
Mom, Jim, and Matt

Contents

viii

CONTENTS

Preface and Acknowledgments

Antonin Scalia can be blunt. He has alleged that his colleagues on the Supreme Court want to be a "junior varsity Congress."[1] He has complained that his colleagues "rattle off a collection of adjectives that simply decorate a value judgment and conceal a political choice." He has asserted that his colleagues propose an American politics in which "unelected judges . . . [are] leading a Volk."[2] Despite his claim that he wants the Court to do "lawyer's work" and stay out of policy controversies, the frankness of Scalia's language seems atypical of the penchant of lawyers and Supreme Court justices to use, in Scalia's phrase, "words that would make people look at you funny if you used them at a cocktail party."[3] The frankness appears more like the rhetoric of the militant political activist. Indeed, Scalia's opinions often ring with phrases like those spoken by the politicians and pundits of the recently revived conservative movement. They sound like the middle-class homilies and slogans about taxes and the Soviet Union made by Ronald Reagan, the simple nativist political formulas offered by conservative spokesman and candidate Patrick Buchanan, or the "lessons" about American "culture" and "civilization" offered by House of Representatives Speaker Newt Gingrich. Scalia's comments about his own Court rival in directness the criticisms of the Court's policymaking voiced by the conservatives of past decades—the southern agrarians opposed to the nationalism of Chief Justice John Marshall's Court, the industrial elites critical of economic regulation in the first three decades of the twentieth century, and even the anticommunist and segregationist critics of the Warren Court of the 1950s and 1960s. The primary aim of this book is to explore how and in what ways Justice Scalia's reputedly conservative vision offers a politically important message in the revival of American conservatism.

Although a superficial analysis would dismiss Scalia as merely an outspoken fellow traveler in the contemporary conservative movement, I claim that there is much more in his conservative message. His message is one—but not the only—argument against the politicians who have governed America since the New Deal. And yet, it is a message of great consequence because of the American reliance on law and the Supreme Court's interpretations of the Constitution to define the boundaries on public and private power. Thus, although Scalia normally votes in the conservative direction because of his political attitudes, he *advocates* his conservative ideology through a mode of jurisprudential discourse—what legal scholars call "Reasoned Elaboration"—that tends to value order and stability over pragmatism and experiment. This book, however, is designed to be more than the exposition of Scalia's jurisprudence. It also offers an analysis of the meaning of Scalia's discourse about the normative political order in modern America. What I call his "constitutive" discourse attempts to formulate a disciplinary regime and contributes to the uneven distribution of political and economic power and personal liberty in the United States.

It was my friend and critic Edward V. Heck, of San Diego State University, who encouraged me to undertake a study of Scalia. As my thoughts on Scalia began to take a new interpretive turn in 1992, Ed reacted with doubt, but he continued to provide a very detailed critique of my manuscripts and saved me from numerous errors. John C. Kilwein, my colleague at West Virginia University, reacted to my ideas, read and commented on my manuscripts, generated the raw data used to construct several tables, and made me sharpen my language on the connection between judicial attitudes and opinions. The book was completed during a sabbatical leave granted by West Virginia University for the academic year 1994–95. Allan S. Hammock, chair of the Department of Political Science at the university, ensured that I had the means to complete my work on Scalia. Several graduate assistants of the department—Jennifer Apple, Ken Knelly, Randy Moffett, Joe Patten, and Deborah Wituski—performed valuable services related to my earlier writing on the Supreme Court and Justice Scalia. Joseph Stewart Jr., of the University of New Mexico, and Robert DiClerico and Robert Dilger, of West Virginia University, assisted my scholarship at critical stages. Melissa A. Butler, chair of the Department of Political Science at Wabash College, made it possible for me to undertake editorial work on a first draft of the book in the quiet of Crawfordsville, Indiana. Justice Scalia kindly allowed me to use excerpts from one of his unpublished speeches.

This book is not a compilation of articles, but bits and pieces of the argument have appeared in articles I published in other forums. I thank the editors of the journals in which they appeared for permission to reprint segments of these articles: "The Conservatism of Antonin Scalia," *Political Science Quarterly* 105 (1990): 1–29; "Justice Antonin Scalia, Constitutional Discourse, and the Legalistic State," *Western Political Quarterly* 44 (1991): 1005–38; "'Administrative Law Is Not for Sissies. . . .': Justice Antonin Scalia's Challenge to American Administrative Law," *Administrative Law Review* 44 (1992): 107–29; "The Rehnquist Court and the Free Exercise of Religion," *Journal of Church and State* 34 (1992): 57–76; "Antonin Scalia, William Brennan, and the Politics of Expression: A Study of Violence and Repression in the Law," *American Political Science Review* 87 (1993): 912–27; and an article I wrote with Edward V. Heck, "The Battle over Strict Scrutiny: Coalitional Conflict in the Rehnquist Court," *Santa Clara Law Review* 32 (1992): 1049–1105.

These publications and this book also derive from papers I presented at the Western Political Science Association meeting, March 1987; the Midwest Political Science Association meeting, April 1987; the Western Political Science Association meeting, March 1988; the American Political Science Association meeting, September 1990; the Southwestern Political Science Association meeting, March 1991 (with Edward V. Heck); the Southwestern Political Science Association meeting, March 1992; the Southwestern Political Science Association meeting, March 1993; the Law and Society Association meeting, May 1993; and the West Virginia Political Science Association meeting, 1995. The participants at these meetings provided valuable advice about my interpretations of Justice Scalia's political message.

JUSTICE ANTONIN SCALIA
AND THE CONSERVATIVE REVIVAL

ANTONIN SCALIA AND THE NEW AMERICAN CONSERVATISM

If you attend a revival meeting, you will hear preachers wailing against the sinfulness of society. Through their performance, they seek to convince their listeners of the truths they derive from passages in their textbook, the Holy Bible. They also want to convince their listeners of the wonders of a postapocalyptic Second Coming and the resurrection of believers. Today American conservatives are conducting a political revival meeting. Through their performance, they want to convince the public of the political sins of post–New Deal American liberal politics and to revive the value of what they allege to be the true American political creed. Their meeting place is not a tent or a church but public forums such as the floors of legislatures, the press conference, the political banquet, the television and radio talk show, the newspaper, the Internet, and the courtroom. Their texts are selected passages in the Constitution, the writings of its Framers, and political thinkers from Aristotle to Russell Kirk. If the nation does not adhere to their faith and seek a better world through consent to conservative dogmas, their eschatology predicts an apocalypse.

A journalist once called him the "Leader of the Opposition," but Justice Antonin Scalia of the Supreme Court of the United States is a leading preacher in the conservative revival that is rapidly becoming the creed of the American political majority.[1] Very bright, with an intellect honed at Jesuit institutions and Harvard Law School, he has, in his opinions and speeches, sliced away at what he regards as heretical assumptions in the legal methodology of late-twentieth-century American liberals. Just as the Republican majority elected to Congress in 1994 assaulted long-established public policies, Scalia has condemned the sins of the post–New Deal Supreme Court's legal legacy. At times engaging and witty in his criticism, he has at other times been sarcastic, barbed, and demeaning in his comments about the legal analysis of his colleagues and the legal work of Congress and administrative agencies. Through trenchant criticism he also has promoted an alternative faith about the function of Constitution and law in the American polity, a conservative vision of the future of national public life.

Scalia's decisions and his political vision are important because Americans rarely search for guidance about the nature of politics in the writings of political philosophers of the past or academic thinkers of the present. Instead, the writings and speeches of lawyer-politicians provide many of the cardinal statements about the American political persuasion and the practice of politics. The writings and speeches of lawyer-politicians such as Thomas Jefferson, George Mason, John Adams, James Madison, Alexander Hamilton, and John Marshall first established an American vision of a competitive political order. In the nation's first century the interpretations of politics in the writings of John Taylor of Caroline, James Kent, John C. Calhoun, Joseph Story, Thomas Cooley, and Stephen J. Field, and in the speeches of Abraham Lincoln and Daniel Webster, inspired American political thought.

During much of the twentieth century the "liberal" political convictions of Franklin Delano Roosevelt and the many lawyer-politicians of the New Deal dominated political discussions.[2] Also, during this century some of the most lucid discussions of the nature of politics came from the ranks of the lawyer-politicians serving as justices of the U.S. Supreme Court—Louis Brandeis, Oliver Wendell Holmes Jr., Harlan Fiske Stone, Felix Frankfurter, Hugo Black, William O. Douglas, Earl Warren, William Brennan, and Thurgood Marshall. Most of these justices had some political connection to Roosevelt, the New Deal, or post–New Deal liberalism. Nevertheless, in the past two decades the political ideas and policies of New Deal and post–New Deal liberal lawyer-politicians have come under increasing criticism. A revitalized American conservatism personified by President Ronald Reagan challenged the New Dealers' assumptions about the conduct of politics.

Part of the Reagan challenge was an effort to alter post–New Deal liberal interpretations of the Constitution and law by appointing conservatives to the federal judiciary. To that end, in 1986 Reagan appointed Antonin Scalia as associate justice of the Supreme Court. Since his appointment Scalia has emerged as an articulate and visible member of the lineage of American lawyer-politicians. Because of his position and his vigorous denunciation of some aspects of post–New Deal liberalism, he is now regarded as a leading conservative legal voice in the nation. Scalia's *vision*, or conception of what American politics ought to become in the future, appears to offer a new, conservative direction for the role of American government and a new interpretation of Americans' personal rights and liberties.[3]

THE POLITICAL VISION OF CONTEMPORARY CONSERVATISM

Commentators can label Scalia a conservative, but the extent to which he assents to the political tenets of the contemporary conservative revival is crucial in the analysis of his political vision. Like any faith, contemporary American conservatism is an intellectually fragmented movement that employs diverse and sometimes contradictory political concepts. Although central themes in contemporary conservatism revive nineteenth-century ideas of state's rights, laissez-faire economics, religious moralism, and nativism, almost all American political conservatives share an aversion to the political vision that evolved from the New Deal of the 1930s and the Democratic control of Congress for much of the period from 1940 to 1994. Many conservatives agree with Scalia's statement that "the real birth of the administrative state in this country dates from the New Deal."[4] They argue that a bureaucratic state emerged from New Deal efforts to devise national laws and regulations to control economic inequality, to protect the public against market failures, and to establish a powerful national executive to implement laws protecting the public welfare and regulating the economy. They are especially troubled by the philosophy of what Michael McCann calls "public interest liberalism." Since the 1970s, building on the reform tradition of the New Deal, public interest liberals have voiced criticisms of corporate power, economic "corruption," and the interconnection of corporate and political power. They have combined these criticisms with a reform program that relies on pragmatic governmental strategies for attacking self-interested uses of economic power.[5] In contrast, the conservative political movement contends that the Democratic party, the post–New Deal American left, and public interest liberals have created three problems that have prevented a good or just society from flourishing in America.

First, the contemporary conservative movement contests the New Deal and public interest liberal definition of legitimate state power and private rights. Especially, the movement reacts to the threat that bureaucratic regulation and the emergence of a central administrative state pose to liberty of property and choice in economic markets.[6] Conservatives contest the expansion of administrative rulemaking to govern private market decisions that were once ordered by common law, and the development of bureaucratically administered policies that affect the distribution of wealth. Often conservatives regard the result of post–New Deal institutional redesign, the creation of a "welfare state," as the assignment of political authority to bureaucratic experts. They complain that the bureaucratic state is unsympathetic toward business and creates unwarranted overhead costs associated with administrative procedures, administrative favoritism toward selected clientele, inertia on emerging policy problems, unnecessary litigation and administrative hearings, and uncontrolled discretion in enforcement of regulations in ways that penalize technological innovation. Thus, contemporary conservatism associates the New Deal redesign of American politics with what it calls the *bureaucracy problem.*[7]

Besides criticizing the institutional design of contemporary American policies, modern conservatism also contests changes in interest group roles in American political and social life. Since the New Deal, interest group participation in the political process has expanded for various reasons, including increased regulatory and distributive policy activity in Washington that spurred the organization of groups to influence Congress and agencies; statutory changes that protected labor unions; judicial decisions that expanded freedom of association and group participation in agency decisionmaking; the cost of electoral campaigns; and the organization of influence on government by corporations seeking economic gain from the expansion of federal expenditures on defense. Many conservatives find that the expansion of interest group politics or political pluralism creates costly regulations and causes economic redistributions from traditional economic elites and corporations to new entries in the political arena, such as racial minorities and the poor. Conservatives maintain that only those organized interests long supported or protected by law, especially corporations and trade associations, have a legitimate role in politics. Also, the participation of business interest groups has escaped conservative criticism because of the assumption that increased business income somehow helps most citizens. Therefore, conservatives interested in the preservation of a political equilibrium fear the expansion of pluralism because it portends challenges to the power of vested interests. They especially dislike efforts by advocates of the new public interest liberalism who during the past three decades have organized to counter the social and economic costs of lightly regulated markets or who have tried to impose ecological or social ethics on corporations. Therefore, fearful of the potential critical power of adversarial interests, conservatives complain about increased group participation in politics, and about "pluralism." They discern a *problem of expanded political pluralism.*[8]

Related to the expansion of the political pluralism problem is what American conservatives might label as the *problem of moral discord*. American conservatives view New Deal pragmatism and respect for the claims of multiple interests as frustrating the development of a moral consensus or a shared religious vision of social and political life. They sense a loss of shared moral traditions and virtues centered on the perceived certainty of selected normative values. Going beyond politics, they also fault the modernist penchants for individual awareness, respect for variations in sexual practice, respect for variations in ethical practice (i.e., ethical relativism), and psychological therapy for debasing the importance of individual moral responsibility and of religious traditions that emphasize the paternalistic guidance of God and community over individual desire.[9] These conditions are fostered, some conservatives argue, by post–New Deal public welfare policies that make persons dependent on the state, or by judicial decisions such as the Supreme Court's ban on prayer in public schools, which are assumed to undercut the ethical basis of American life by disestablishing moral education. By creating dependency and moral discord and by responding to interest groups challenging social traditions in court, conservatives claim, post–New Deal American government has eroded any principled basis for politics and has allowed the emergence of threats to the social and political stability of the nation. They fear a society without a normative anchor in a world where moral chaos threatens political order.

Although this brief summary only encapsulates the primary challenges of contemporary conservatism to New Deal politics, the conservative movement rests its criticism on a majoritarian democratic argument. Most conservatives believe that there is a public virtue— patriotic, traditional, and conservative in ideology—possessed by the majority. Thus, majority values, or even the "silent" majority as defined by the Nixon administration, ought to construct public policy and guide elites in the establishment of a better government. It is the genius of the majority, not the desires of bureaucratic experts, emerging interest groups, or moral relativists, that should give direction to politics. Conservatives accept the legitimacy of the institutional processes of politics, but because of their commitment to the political virtue of the majority they contest constitutional interpretations and policies that provide protection for the interests of minorities and social outsiders.

This perspective creates a tension between contemporary conservatives and some of the views of the Founders. For example, James Madison doubted the virtue of the majority and of many minority "factions" because they might be "united and actuated by some common impulse of passion, or of interest, adverse to the rights of other citizens, or to the permanent and aggregate interests of the community." Therefore, majority and minority interests or "passions" had to be checked by institutions in which the virtue of representatives "whose wisdom may best discern the true interest of their country" would prevent the betrayal of the interests of all of the people by government.[10] Contemporary conservatives largely lack a sense that a majority can be "factional" or practice a passionate politics lacking in wisdom and antagonistic toward the liberties of minorities.

THE CONSERVATIVE VISION OF ANTONIN SCALIA

Popular and scholarly commentators have made a series of claims about the conservative direction of Scalia's case votes and the ways in which his normative legal theory, or jurisprudence, coincides with contemporary conservative values.[11] The initial studies of Scalia's votes as a Supreme Court justice showed that he voted in a conservative direction, or voted for the claims of government in criminal procedure, civil rights, First Amendment, due process, and privacy cases, and against unions and the extension of federal judicial power. Also, he immediately closely aligned his voting behavior with that of Chief Justice Rehnquist and Justice O'Connor, the other Reagan administration appointees to the Court.[12] However, studies of the arguments in Scalia's opinions have found that he has rarely embraced many varieties of conservative thought, such as the classical conservative thought of Edmund Burke and the contemporary conservative legal motifs of "originalism," or reliance on the Founders' definitions of constitutional terminology, natural law, or religious traditionalism.[13] Consequently, Scalia's judicial votes have appeared to be less a result of philosophical conservatism than reaction against Warren Court (1953–69) and Burger Court (1969–86) decisions in cases involving criminal procedural due process, abortion rights, free speech, free exercise of religion, the Establishment Clause, and the Equal Protection Clause.[14] Also, some scholars argue that the opinions Scalia has written are an effort to mask the political character of his choices from criticism by a legal profession that expects choices to be made on the basis of the application of legal texts, such as the Constitution, statutes, and precedent-setting cases, to the facts of discrete cases.[15]

Pursuing the argument about the political basis of Scalia's decision-making in a different direction, a few studies have attempted to identify his conservatism as a unique, personal political philosophy. For example, George Kannar has linked Scalia's childhood experiences, including his exposure to his father's scholarship and to pre–Vatican II Roman Catholicism, to his legal and political ideas.[16] Other commentators have argued that Scalia is less a political conservative than a devotee of a "formalist" and a "new textualist" jurisprudence.[17] A legal formalist is presumed to make judicial decisions on the basis of the words in legal texts rather than to pursue policy goals. Scholars who regard Scalia as a formalist depict him as a legal craftsman who searches through the Constitution, enacted law, and case law to decipher and then apply rules of law to concrete circumstances. New textualist arguments about Scalia also stress that he, more than most other justices, refuses to evaluate the context in which a legislature drafts a statute and instead applies the "plain meaning" of statutory language. The formalist and allied new textualist interpretations of Scalia's behavior posit that his votes and opinions are caused not by his politics but by his hostility to active judicial policymaking and to pragmatic or results-oriented legal theories that ignore texts and appropriate practice of the legal craft. By demonstrating his use of precedent-setting cases, statutory language, legislative history, and procedural and substantive administrative rules, commentators have usually attempted only to illustrate the importance of a pattern of legal argumentation in Scalia's opinions.[18] They then have assumed that his formalist, new textualist methodology and related jurisprudential concepts have contributed to his decision about the claims of liberal and conservative litigants. Alternatively, a few scholars have tried to trace the source of Scalia's formalism to his exposure to the jurisprudence of Justice Felix Frankfurter and to the jurisprudence and method of legal analysis called "Reasoned Elaboration," developed by professors at Harvard Law School from some of Frankfurter's ideas.[19] However, these scholars also have assumed that Scalia's legal method determines his preference for the claims of liberal or conservative litigants. They usually have not found politics at work in his choice of the legal method or in the normative values expressed in his opinions. They have chosen not to question how his neglect of the "social facts" of cases—the social and political reality in which a case is embedded—and his political attitudes contribute to his message.[20]

Given various commentators' different perspectives on Scalia's politics and on the linkage of his politics to his opinions, exactly what kind of conservative—if any kind of conservative—is he? To answer this question we need to analyze Scalia's vision of the American *regime*. That is, how does he understand the complex of sociopolitical practices that divides power between the public sector—the "state," or the permanent aggregate of career officials and administrators—and private sector institutions such as the market, commercial enterprises, churches, and the home, as well as the autonomous individual.[21] In culling Scalia's ideas from his votes, opinions, and off-the-bench speeches and publications, I shall attempt to explain his *discourse,* or a special use of words, signs, and actions—such as votes and opinions—that defines proper action in present time and the future.[22] His discourse on specific topics contributes to the construction of a story, or *narrative,* bearing a message about the meaning of law and politics in the American regime.[23]

As a baseline for evaluating the conservatism of his political vision, I want to compare Scalia's narrative and message with the central themes of the contemporary conservative revival. I also want to ask three additional questions: Is Scalia just a judge who votes against economic regulation by bureaucracy, the political claims of liberal interests (including minorities and criminal defendants), and efforts to isolate religion and other moral values from the public arena? Do his opinions offer a consistent critique of post–New Deal politics and the alleged problems of bureaucracy, expanded political pluralism, and moral discord? Is his political narrative a twist on the basic principles of a constitutional democracy relying on the rule of laws made by representatives, or does he propose a redefinition of the Constitution and the political character of America?

To answer these questions, I examine the sources and development of Scalia's political and legal ideas. The foundation of his political and jurisprudential ideas came in two stages. His early academic and political life provided an opportunity to develop an expertise in administrative law and public management. Then, at age forty-six, he became a federal appellate judge and was forced to decide on a wider range of policy issues. Chapters 1 and 2 recount these foundational experiences, which affected his political discourse, the origins of his political vision, and his early participation in the conservative revival. After examining the foundation of his politics and jurisprudence, chapter 3 posits three propositions about how Scalia's experiences before his appointment to the bench might have affected his Supreme Court career. It presents some preliminary data for a definition of his message—a summary of his overall pattern of voting on cases, and a discussion of the political presuppositions of the jurisprudential arguments used by the Supreme Court in the late twentieth century. Chapters 4 through 9 scrutinize Scalia's opinions and public addresses to provide an understanding of his political vision with regard to the specific issues that appear on the Court's docket. Chapter 10 considers his commitment to the value of the rule of law and his assumptions about the general nature of justice and political order. It might be that Scalia's conservatism accepts the fundamental reliance of American politics on the notion that human life, and the conflicts that mar human life, can be regulated by rules of law. This is fundamentally an Enlightenment conception of politics, a concept often called liberal. It points to a possible interpretation of Scalia's constitutive discourse as a species of the liberal genus. If his constitutive discourse is liberal, he might be less the reactionary or less the conservative visionary. Chapter 10 discusses whether a rule-based theory of politics is embedded in Scalia's constitutive opinion discourse. And chapter 11 presents a consideration of criticism of Scalia's political narrative and a commentary on the importance of his politics and political thought in the revival of conservatism.

To explore dimensions of Scalia's politics, I have used information including his recorded votes, public statements, publications, and judicial opinions to 1 November 1995. Unusually direct and forceful in their prose, Scalia's opinions provide a record of their author's political message.[24] The opinion, in particular, is a "document that catches and freezes for a moment the legal mind at work."[25] It is a means by which a justice tries to validate or authorize one policy and one way of looking at the political world. With a focus on Scalia's political ideas, this book does not purport to offer a psychoanalysis of his decisionmaking, a detailed analysis of the role of the Scalia nomination in the judicial selection politics of the Reagan administration, a micro-level description of the internal politics of the Supreme Court, or an analysis of the impact of Scalia's decisions on his colleagues or the wider politics of the nation.[26] It does not examine the implications of Scalia's gregarious personality, personal warmth, and humor.[27] It does not examine his apparent disquiet with the Court's operational practices.[28] Also, it does not explore claims about the tensions that reportedly affect his relations with some of his colleagues, his possible influence over Justice Clarence Thomas, or the implications of the professorial way in which he has sometimes grilled counsel during oral argument.[29] Studies offering such analyses contribute to an understanding of Scalia and the

Court; however, the issue addressed here is the contribution of Scalia to the definition of the principles of American governance. I do not attempt to explain Scalia's political behavior, but I explore his political ideas and his construction of a normative meaning for politics and life in modern America. In this exploration I assume that his use of jurisprudential argument, what some scholars call his legal methodology, is a written statement of his instrumental political aims or a vehicle for the expression of what some scholars call his attitudes or ideological and political commitments.[30] Together, his votes, opinions, and off-the-bench dialogues communicate his critical statements of principles for the solution of the public policy problems raised in cases and provide evidence of the nature of his commitment to the conservative revival in American politics.

Chapter One

FROM PROFESSOR
TO PUNDIT

American religious revivalism is Protestant and historically a rural phenomenon. From Jonathan Edwards through Billy Sunday, and from
Billy Graham to Jerry Falwell and Jimmy Swaggart, religious revivalism
has flourished in the social and intellectual periphery of America. The
contemporary conservative revival is far different. Although it wins its
greatest allegiance from voters in the rural South and West, some of its
most important preachers—men such as William F. Buckley and Patrick Buchanan—are Roman Catholics raised in upper- and middle-
class families in the suburban Northeast. They are men whose political
vision was shaped by the Catholic emphasis on the reasoned explication of binding moral absolutes and respect for institutional authority.
Scalia fits this mold.

Antonin Gregory Scalia was born in Trenton, New Jersey, on 11
March 1936. Raised in the psychological security and academic rationality of a bourgeois Roman Catholic family during the 1940s and
1950s, he had the life of an exceptional child of the East Coast Roman
Catholic intelligentsia. Whatever his political leanings during his for-
mative years, he was exposed to a world in which merit derived from
adherence to formal rules of behavior, and rebellion was rational dissent, best expressed through the spoken and written word. His early
life isolated him from the economic uncertainty facing working-class
America throughout the post–World War II cycles of boom and re-
cession. His education in elite urban Roman Catholic institutions
distanced him from confrontations with nativist hostility to Italian-
American Catholics. And he matured before the onset of the political
activism of the civil rights and Vietnam War eras. These patterns of
elite contacts would mark much of his life, and they would contribute
in subtle ways to his perception of law and politics as he moved from
success to success as lawyer, professor, federal official, and academic
pundit.

Antonin was the only child of Catherine Panaro Scalia, an elementary school teacher, and Samuel Eugene Scalia, who when his son was
born was thirty-six years old and soon to become a professor of Ro-

mance literature at Brooklyn College of the City University of New York. S. Eugene Scalia had immigrated to the United States from Italy at age fifteen. For a youthful immigrant, Eugene's academic success was astounding. He earned a bachelor's degree from Rutgers University and a doctorate at Columbia University.[1] Catherine Scalia was a first-generation American. Her brother, Vincent, was an attorney, county prosecutor, and Democratic politician. Antonin spent his early childhood living in a cluster of houses belonging to the Panaro family in suburban Trenton and spent his school years in what was then the middle-class Irish-Italian neighborhood of Elmhurst, Queens, New York City. He attended Public School 13 in Queens and graduated as class valedictorian from an all-male Jesuit preparatory school, Saint Francis Xavier Military Academy, in Manhattan. His schooling included concentrated study of ancient languages, and he learned to play the piano and acted in dramatic productions. Continuing his education in Jesuit institutions, he received his A.B. degree in 1957 from Georgetown University. He was again valedictorian of his class. He also studied abroad, at the University of Fribourg, in Switzerland. He then proceeded to earn his LL.B. degree, magna cum laude, from Harvard Law School in 1960. At Harvard he was note editor of the law review and received a Sheldon Fellowship for international travel after graduation. The September after his graduation from Harvard he married Radcliffe graduate Maureen McCarthy. They have raised nine children.[2]

George Kannar contends that this education, training, and early family life, or "socialization," explain Scalia's jurisprudence. Kannar's thesis is that the scholarly ideas of Scalia's father and his Catholic education fostered a textualist methodology of legal interpretation which is revealed in the criminal due process opinions of the adult justice. In tune with other evaluations of the justice, Kannar finds that Scalia's methodology emphasized reliance on the plain meaning of language and scorned reliance on unwritten fundamental rights or policy values not contained in the language of the Constitution or statutes. Like the background studies developed by political scientists, Kannar assumes that selected stimuli in Scalia's past contributed to his adult personality traits and his political and legal choices. Thus, his socialization predicted his "deep theoretical commitments" as an adult judge. His cultural identity as a person became "fused" into his constitutional theory.[3]

In depicting Scalia's socialization to the law, Kannar relied on assumptions about Scalia's Catholic education and family life. From the testimony of other Catholics raised during World War II and the 1950s, Kannar inferred the religious experiences of Scalia in his youth. According to Kannar, part of the experience was the inculcation of a "linguistic essentialism" and "obsessional textualism," or the special pre–Vatican II attention of Catholic religious education to the use of words to define rules of moral conduct. Consequently, the practice was close reading of texts, such as the Baltimore Catechism, to find their one true meaning. There was no acknowledgment of the effect of the reader's values on the meaning of the text. A second part of Catholic socialization in this era, according to Kannar, was an effort by individuals to diminish the conception of Catholic difference from a historically Protestant American culture. Thus, Catholics often tried to compartmentalize their religious duties and their secular legal obligations as American citizens. In establishing the division, the duty to obey secular law as written was a paramount consideration. Catholic values and natural law were a personal preference for the private realm of being.[4]

Furthermore, Kannar inferred that Scalia's jurisprudential ideas originated in the justice's family and school experience. He noted that Scalia's father confronted the problem of the interpretation of language throughout his academic career. The elder Scalia thought that "literalness is . . . one of the chief merits of a translation, especially when the translation is the product of a conscientious worker and not of a born poet." He also believed that literalness "prevents the translator from yielding to the temptation of following the line of least resistance, that is, the temptation of translating what is unique in the poet of another language by the poetically conventional and stereotyped of his own language." However, he thought that a really good translator of a work needed to do more than reconstruct with a dictionary at hand. Superior translation required "a man of great poetic qualities."[5] Kannar inferred that the elder Scalia had passed along his ideas about the importance of the text and the craft of interpretation "at the dinner table forum." Also, Kannar noted that young Antonin assiduously studied classical Greek for five years and Latin for six years and thus apparently learned about the problem of translation. As described by Kannar, Scalia's Supreme Court opinions replicated the future justice's training in the interpretation of language. Scalia's world view thus found enshrined in the text of law a single vision of moral virtue which could be located without the interference of the views of the reader.[6]

Kannar's socialization explanation of Scalia's jurisprudence rests heavily on undocumented assumptions and on a very few facts about Scalia's education, his Catholicism, and his relationship with his father. Yet despite the guesswork about Scalia's socialization, Kannar has raised an important issue: How does a justice develop his jurisprudential philosophy? Church, school, and family undoubtedly contribute to the process, but not always in the same way for every individual. Despite Catholic education's emphasis on tradition and order, Donald Beschele has found little to support Kannar's conclusion that such an education would make a judge a positivist and textualist. Beschele pointed out that Catholicism did not have the same effect on Scalia as on other Catholics of Scalia's generation. Also, he indicated that social science survey data refute Kannar's notion of Catholics as "more rigorist in their analysis of moral, social, and political issues than Protestants."[7] Beschele pointed out that Kannar's argument about the separation of secular positivism and the sacred in the political life of Catholic American elites lacks any empirical reference in social psychology, sociology, or the study of political elites. Likewise, Kannar's assumption of the effect of a father upon a son's theory of textual interpretation lacks supporting evidence. Did the Scalia family really talk about literary interpretation over dinner?

In addition to the problems identified by Beschele, Kannar ignored a conspicuous source of Scalia's jurisprudence, the justice's education in the craft of the law at the Harvard Law School.[8] In the late 1950s several Harvard faculty members engaged in the formulation of jurisprudential arguments to counter the effects of Legal Realism. Legal Realism, a product of American thinking of the 1920s and 1930s, was at its core a pragmatic and policy-oriented legal discourse resting on the same normative basis as New Deal liberal political thought.[9] Legal Realists implied that any interests feeling the negative sting of the law could pressure for pragmatic changes in the law by criticism, especially "scientific" criticism, of law's policy biases. The political process thus could be improved by political debate and compromise among plural interests.

Criticism of Legal Realism took several directions. However, the criticism of greatest influence was offered by "Legal Process," or "Reasoned Elaboration," methodology. This methodology found its intellectual stimulus in the opinions of Justice Felix Frankfurter. Frankfurter's political vision proposed that representative leaders would be responsible for evoking and maintaining a democratic consensus. In the late 1950s and early 1960s scholars at Harvard Law School, including Henry Hart Jr., and Albert Sacks, Paul Freund, Lon Fuller, and Louis Jaffe, expanded the rudimentary jurisprudential themes and the political vision of Frankfurter into a more comprehensive jurisprudential system.[10] The emphasis of their work was on curtailing the remedial judicial policy action proposed by Realists through procedural rules encouraging judicial passivity in policy conflicts. The political course of the nation was to be charted by elected representatives who considered and refined public sentiments, not by an unelected judiciary or a tumultuous interest group conflict.

Since the Reasoned Elaborationists sought procedurally induced judicial passivity, like the Realists they did not concern themselves with inculcating a transcendent morality into the law. In the words of Herbert Wechsler of Columbia University, an ally of the Harvard movement, judges were to apply "neutral principles" in constitutional cases. A neutral principle was a reason that transcended "any immediate result that is involved." This transcending principle could be discerned by judges on the basis of "sustained, disinterested, merciless examination" of the reasons for a decision offered by the litigants in a case. Relying on their expertise and craftsmanship, judges could locate in legal texts the neutral principle that could decide that case while preventing the Court from becoming a "naked power organ."[11] The implication of the neutral principles argument was that the moral content of law depends on the neutral principles located by judges: law did not have a necessary connection to a specific ethical theory. As a top student at Harvard Law School between 1957 and 1960, Antonin Scalia heard these themes about the ethical content of the law, as well as the criticism of Legal Realism and the argument for Reasoned Elaboration as he read the materials on the legal process compiled by Hart and Sacks and as he attended the classes of Fuller, Freund, and Jaffe. Evidence exists that Scalia accepted many of the jurisprudential precepts taught by the Reasoned Elaborationists on the Harvard faculty.[12]

Regardless of whether family or law school was the primary source of his outlook, life experiences had exposed Scalia to issues such as the interpretation of texts, the ideas of principled interpretations of law, the value of rules, and the alleged dangers of an overtly policy-oriented jurisprudence. Education had steered him to elite institutions and away from contacts with social and intellectual circles outside the academic realm of elite East Coast institutions. Scalia experienced the way in which academic merit, as defined by evaluations by faculty members at prestigious institutions, was the gateway to a career and influence in public life.

THE ADMINISTRATIVE LAWYER AND PROFESSOR, 1960–1971

Harvard Law School retains its elite status by placing its graduates in the best of the nation's law firms. Antonin Scalia followed the accepted procedure for Harvard graduates. The year of his graduation, he accepted a position as an associate with the firm of Jones, Day, Cockley, and Reavis (now called Jones, Day, Reavis, and Pogue) in Cleveland, Ohio. When he joined Jones, Day, it was a firm with about fifty-five attorneys in Cleveland and a small Washington, D.C. office, but it added about thirty positions during Scalia's six-year tenure. The largest firm in Cleveland, it had a string of major corporate clients, including American Greetings, Anchor Hocking Glass, Cleveland-Cliffs Iron, Ernst and Ernst accountants, General Motors, Gray Drug Stores, M. A. Hanna Company, Midland-Ross, the National City Bank of Cleveland, Ohio Bell Telephone, Sherwin-Williams, Tappan appliances, Westinghouse Electric, and two of northeastern Ohio's largest corporate employers—Jones and Laughlin Steel and Republic Steel.[13] At Jones, Day, Scalia reportedly handled real estate, corporate finance, and labor matters.

Reputedly stimulated by "broader" interests and an "urge to teach,"[14] in 1967 Scalia left Jones, Day to join the faculty of the law school at the University of Virginia. During his tenure at Virginia he taught commercial law, contracts, and comparative law, and he began writing about administrative law. Although some of his articles displayed the traditional mode of academic legal scholarship, he more frequently wrote about the practical problems of judicial administration and case management. For example, he published a study of the appellate judicial caseload in Virginia with Graham Lilly, a colleague on the Virginia law faculty. They examined the caseload and procedures of the Virginia Supreme Court to conclude that the appellate process had reached a situation detrimental to the interests of parties and the public. Scalia and Lilly then methodically reviewed alternative options for the relief of the crisis and concluded that an intermediate appellate court was necessary. They rejected as insufficient the use of procedural rules and practices to stem the expanding tide of appeals.[15] The article had little immediate effect; Virginia did not establish an intermediate court of appeals until 1985. Another more practical article addressed the structure of federal administrative justice under the federal Administrative Procedure Act (APA), the statute that standardized basic rules for federal agency rulemaking and adjudication. As adopted in 1946, the APA (§ 3344) permitted agencies to loan their hearing examiners (now called administrative law judges) to other agencies that had case backlogs or staff shortages. Concerned about the expertise of examiners who were shifted from the legal issues raised before one agency to the issues considered by another agency, Scalia proposed a "loan corps" of examiners—a special body of existing hearing examiners whom a service agency had especially trained to qualify them to hear claims in several agencies.[16]

Scalia wrote his major single-author article during this period for the prestigious *Michigan Law Review*. It was a study of how sovereign immunity doctrine placed procedural restraints on the judicial review of administrative agency actions in public lands cases. Much of the article described the development and erosion of case law that prevented suits against federal government agencies and their employees (the "sovereign") in disputes about the taking of private land for public purposes. Structuring his argument about the rise and decline of common law concepts on the model of University of Chicago law professor Edward H. Levi's *Introduction to Legal Reasoning*,[17] Scalia provided an elaborately documented legal history of his topic, together with comparisons of sovereign immunity in public land cases with immunity doctrine affecting federal taxation and the post office. In his conclusion, he made three points. First, he stated that from passing references in past cases, judges created a rule of law that later worked to impede judicial review. Second, he stressed that the "existential" development of case law creates many discrete and independent compartments in the law, each of which has its own special internal consistency. These compartments, he noted, are known to the legal profession—a comment that implies the importance of professional craftsmanship in the interpretation of law. Third, he recommended that the interpretation of case precedents in the public lands cases should be derived from the case law rather than imposed on it; and that judges should attend to the text of discrete decisions in order to understand the essence of the law rather than impose concepts on a mass of cases.[18]

During this period, the articles and addresses that Scalia wrote had nothing to do with constitutional law or jurisprudential theory and, with the exception of obscure cases on sovereign immunity, little to do with the U.S. Supreme Court. Yet they voiced some important themes. Respect for legal expertise is evident in three of the articles. Procedure or legal process and access to courts is always Scalia's concern, just as they were the concern of Harvard legal scholars of the late 1950s.

SERVING THE EXECUTIVE BRANCH, 1971–1976

Apparently Scalia had long favored the more conservative policies associated with the Republican party. Now that he had the contacts and prestige associated with a professorship at Virginia, he became known by members of the Nixon administration. He took leave from Virginia from 1971 to 1974 to serve as general counsel in the Office of Telecommunications Policy in the Executive Office of the President. In this position he helped develop presidential policy and administrative procedures about the telecommunications industry.[19] Scalia made a few public statements on administrative matters when serving in the Office of Telecommunications Policy. He addressed the Federal Communications Bar Association on the Fairness Doctrine and other aspects of the Communications Act of 1934. The act requires the Federal Communications Commission (FCC) to consider applications for communications licenses in light of how the licensees' practices will serve the general public interest. It also forbids the FCC to practice censorship or interfere with the right of free speech.[20] As evidenced by the number of complaints about fairness filed with the FCC, Scalia noted that tensions between these two provisions had dramatically escalated in the 1960s. He also noted more complexity in the issues raised in some of the complaints and suggested that the increasing number of complaints reflected a desire for an individual right of access to the media. He went on to characterize free access to the media as an "undesirable . . . imposition on the viewer." He also rejected any policy that required paid advertisements, especially on political matters, to be rebutted by unpaid replies. He only wanted the paid time to be sold on a nondiscriminatory basis. Finally, he argued that the FCC might need to consider giving broadcasters the option to present paid commercial messages, especially on political issues, free of any legal liability.[21] His suggestions tended to favor the messages of those persons and interests with the resources to buy air time. Also, his liability argument implied that purchasers of air time might have some opportunity to broadcast claims—such as, possibly, assertions that tobacco use is not harmful to a person's health, or outrageous racist political claims—subject only to later libel or defamation action. Traditionally the Fairness Doctrine allowed rebuttal time but not broadcaster control of the responsibility of such messages. Consequently, his speech can be read as saying: If you pay for it, you can broadcast what you want.

The next year President Nixon nominated Scalia to a five-year term as chairman of the Administrative Conference of the United States. In 1972 the Administrative Conference consisted of a chair, a small staff, a council of eleven, appointed by the president, that advised the chairman, and an assembly of from seventy-five to ninety-one members, who were the top legal officers in federal agencies or prominent academic and private practice attorneys. Its mission was to develop improved legal procedures for federal agencies by setting an agenda for the study of procedural problems, employing persons to conduct the studies, and providing recommendations for executive action. It also was to share information among agencies and respond to agencies' requests for procedural advice. The chair was to manage the agenda, contract with attorneys and academics for studies, and preside at meetings of the council and the assembly. Because the conference's mission was research and consultation, the conference chairmanship isolated Scalia from the Nixon administration's Watergate crisis.[22] However, he met nearly all of the nation's experts in administrative law, as well as members of Congress and many executive agency administrators.

During Scalia's tenure as chairman, the Administrative Conference staff considered American Bar Association recommendations that the Administrative Procedure Act be revised. Less significantly, it conducted seminars for the legal staff of the Environmental Protection Agency and administrative law judges, consulted with the White House on a trade bill, and studied the labor certification of aliens and offshore port facility legislation.[23] Scalia testified before Congress about changes in the Federal Parole Board, proposed amendments to the Freedom of Information Act (FOIA), the proposed Consumer Protection Act, the creation of a federal consumer protection agency, and agency reform in general.[24] The written product of his conference service was a study of the Consumer Product Safety Act, which had been recently passed; the study was written with Frank Goodman, research director of the conference. Aimed more toward the practicing administrative lawyer than toward the scholar, the article emphasized the act's establishment of inventive procedures for the formulation of agency rules on product safety. Preferring to avoid premature judgment, the article offered few conclusions about the value of the inventive procedures, including procedures requiring the agency to use private expertise, to encourage industry and consumer participation in rulemaking, to establish an "attorney general" to represent consumer interests, to allow access to information about products, and to maintain independence of the executive.[25] Scalia made his position on innovations in administrative procedure more definitive in a letter to Congressman John Dingell. He noted a "visible and steady erosion of standardized administrative practice, through individualized provisions contained in new pieces of regulatory legislation where no real reason for individualized treatment exists." Although he admitted that some operational variations among the procedures of agencies might be necessary, he argued that uniform practice served "several important values." The benefits of uniform practice which he listed included the virtues of procedures fathomable to the nonexpert and the facilitation of broadly applicable precedent when agency decisions were subject to judicial review. Also, because he believed that in most legislative debates Congress attended to substantive policy issues rather than procedures for administration, he thought that including in every legislative act standard procedures would be "significantly more sound" than leaving them to development by an agency.[26]

Resigning from the University of Virginia in 1974, Scalia accepted an appointment as assistant attorney general in charge of the Office of Legal Counsel. His appointment to this prestigious position by President Gerald Ford occurred during the tenure of Attorney General Edward Levi. In this position Scalia supervised many activities, including the drafting of the opinions of the attorney general, the review of presidential orders and proclamations for legal form, the provision of legal advice to presidential staff, especially on legal issues about the agencies, the legal counseling of Executive Office agencies and the attorney general, and the coordination of Department of Justice drafting of treaties and other international agreements. In particular, Scalia supervised staff members involved with the disposition of the papers and tapes of Richard Nixon and the legality of intelligence gathering within the United States.[27]

As assistant attorney general, Scalia addressed a forum on oversight and review of agency decisionmaking sponsored by the Section on Administrative Law of the American Bar Association. His comments challenged the constitutionality of the legislative veto, the requirement that federal agency regulations be submitted to one or both houses of Congress for approval before they can take effect. It was his first major public statement about a constitutional issue. Noting the absence of judicial decisions on the practice, Scalia presented an elaborate argument against the constitutionality of the legislative veto. Using case law and the arguments and notes of James Madison from the Constitutional Convention of 1787, he argued that both the language of the Constitution and the general principle of separated powers forbade the legislative veto. Despite the long history of its use, the legislative veto was an illegitimate gloss on the Constitution. "Custom or practice may give content to vague or ambiguous constitutional provisions, but it cannot overcome the explicit language of the text, especially when that text is supported by historical evidence that shows it means precisely what it says," he wrote.[28]

Scalia also questioned the views of Justice Byron White of the Supreme Court on the constitutionality of the legislative veto. In *Buckley v. Valeo* White wrote a concurring and dissenting opinion in support of a one-house legislative veto of independent agency regulations.[29] He argued that the Court ought to defer to pragmatic congressional judgments about "the corrosive effects of money in federal election campaigns" and the legal rules best suited to control those effects. Scalia thought White's justification to be imprecise and, in part, "contrived." He thought that White had introduced into the judicial evaluation of the validity of Congress's veto power an unnecessary technical distinction between the veto power as a requirement for the approval of a regulation and the veto power when used for the invalidation of a regulation. Scalia then turned to critique the practical political consequences of the legislative veto. He argued that it permitted Congress to avoid potential disputes when drafting statutes delegating authority to agencies, to make policy without majority approval from both houses, and to avoid responsibility for hard choices about the distribution of resources or the regulation of interests. Relying on the constitutional principle of separation of powers, he concluded that the legislative veto deprived the executive of its primary duty to enforce the laws and of revered institutional roles granted to it by the original plan of the Founders. In response to a comment from another participant, he also stressed that he wanted a Congress that took much more responsibility for creating statutes with "clear and well-defined standards," not a Congress that spent its time second-guessing executive branch policies.[30] The congressional check on the executive was to occur primarily before, not after, executive action.

During his service as assistant attorney general, Scalia testified before Congress to state the Ford administration's views on a variety of issues. Many of the hearings addressed the legal aspects of executive power during a period in which the Watergate scandal had called claims of executive independence and privilege into question. He defended the administration's position against a legislative veto of executive agreements with other nations, a broad legislative veto of agency actions, and legislative power to force agency action.[31] He spoke for the administration's definition of executive powers in times of national emergency, for executive privilege, especially in the area of intelligence operations, and for the administration's conception of the application of the Twenty-fifth Amendment of the Constitution to presidential successions.[32] Finally, he presented to Congress the Ford administration's positions about legislation on municipal bankruptcy reform, nondiscrimination in overseas job assignments, the Arab boycott of American businesses trading in Israel, news reporters' right to refuse to testify in federal trials, election campaign law, and his office's budget.[33]

Between 1971 and 1976, Scalia received an education in executive branch politics, expanded his contacts with important figures in Washington political circles, and began to refine his ideas about public policymaking. He also began to articulate a concern with the congressional management of administration. In the letter to Congressman Dingell and the address on the legislative veto, he spoke of the need for uniformity in federal administrative procedures and for policy implementation uncluttered by the special treatment afforded some agencies by Congress. Uniform procedures would keep Congress from legislating special procedures for a particular agency and its clientele, and the demise of the legislative veto would keep Congress from intervening to protect specific interests, policies, or constituents. He seemed to want to curtail the responsiveness of Congress to the political aims of interest groups. This was the beginning of Scalia's response to the problems of bureaucracy and expanded political pluralism, and his identification of Congress as the creator of ineffective public policies hostile to majority interests.

PROFESSOR SCALIA AND PUBLIC AFFAIRS, 1977–1982

Left without a government position at the end of the Ford administration, Scalia accepted a position as a scholar in residence with the American Enterprise Institute for Public Policy Research (AEI), in Washington, D.C., in January 1977. At AEI he participated in a daily brown-bag lunch with other AEI scholars, several of whom then espoused a conservative or neoconservative ideology.[34] Among the participants were Robert Bork and Laurence Silberman, both later nominated for the U.S. Court of Appeals for the District of Columbia Circuit by President Ronald Reagan; James C. Miller III, later Reagan's director of the Office of Management and Budget; Jeane C. Kirkpatrick, a Reagan administration ambassador to the United Nations; Jude Wanniski, whose writings became a basis for the Reagan supply-side economic policy; and Herbert Stein, the former Nixon administration chairman of the Council of Economic Advisors. All of these individuals have had public careers during which they criticized the bureaucratic and expanded political pluralist themes of post–New Deal liberalism. However, their political criticism of liberalism differed from that of Ronald Reagan, Dan Quayle, Newt Gingrich, William Bennett, Jerry Falwell, and Pat Robertson in that ethical or moral discord never emerged as its central focus.

During his stay at AEI, Scalia served as a visiting law professor at Georgetown University for the 1977 spring term. Although he returned to traditional academic duties as a professor at the University of Chicago Law School in the fall of 1977, he continued to be the editor of AEI's journal, *Regulation;* an adjunct scholar with AEI; and a proponent of extensive deregulation. As a highly visible administrative law scholar, Scalia was a natural choice to become the chairman of the American Bar Association's Section on Administrative Law for 1981–82. The chairmanship brought him special visibility within the community of administrative law scholars and practitioners.[35] In addition, he consulted with prominent Chicago law firms, conducted seminars for firms, including American Telephone and Telegraph (AT&T), and served as a visiting professor at the Stanford University Law School for the 1980–81 academic year.

Commentary on Administrative Law

In the years 1977–82, Scalia published a considerable number of articles. The most systematic of these dealt with legal aspects of administrative law and regulation, but mostly he wrote articles about the
politics of administration for *Regulation*. When serving as chairman of
the American Bar Association section, he also published some of his
views in the *Administrative Law Review*. The tone of most of his articles
of this period differed markedly from the legalistic tone of the articles
and speeches of his early career. Pithy, humorous, and sarcastic, they
attempted a critique of American public administration from the vantage point of administrative law. They were the writings of an academic
pundit.[36] At the heart of the critique was a call for a curtailment of
the influence of interest group politics on administrative policymaking. His articles identified four significant problems in administrative
policymaking:

Judicial Hard Looks. First, Scalia argued that the courts had departed from the scheme of the APA and interposed themselves in
agency rulemaking by elaborating on the procedures that agencies
should follow. He found that judicial evaluation of rulemaking procedures allowed judges and interest groups the opportunity to question
rules and rulemaking. This judicial practice, justified by the procedural
and substantive "hard look" doctrines, especially forced an agency to
justify the way in which it made its rules and to respond to every public
comment and justify its choices in a manner not explicitly required by
the APA. Congress had contributed to the expansion of judicial intervention for some agencies, he argued, by requiring adjudication within
the agency for the development of standards and imposing a tougher
test, called the "substantial evidence test," on agencies' justifications of
their choices when judicial review of agency actions occurred. He regarded this "judicialization" of rulemaking as subversive of legislative
and executive power and, ultimately, the will of the people because it
increased the political power of interest groups. It allowed minority
interests to seek adjudication of many stages of the development of the
rules prescribing administrative policy and could potentially frustrate
efficient and organized policymaking.[37] Scalia wanted to get courts to
refrain from procedural innovation. Congress, he thought, ought to
determine the public interest and address whether the views of interest
groups are accommodated in legislation or in agencies' application of
legislation under legislatively established guidelines for public par-

ticipation in rulemaking.[38] To this end, he outlined some legal standards for the control of judicial consideration of agency rules. These remedies included keeping the cases out of court by a reversion to rules of ripeness and standing, rules that prevented suits against the agency before enforcement of agency rules occurred. Also, his remedies included giving agencies greater freedom from judicial oversight in the control of their agendas and their decisions not to act; using a standard for judging the legality of agency choices—the "arbitrary and capricious" test—which was more favorable to agency discretion in rulemaking than was the substantial evidence requirement; and giving agencies more opportunity to engage in confidential rulemaking away from interest group scrutiny.[39]

Imprecise Statutes. Despite his hostility to trends in judicial oversight of rulemaking, Scalia faulted Congress for problems of public management which he associated with expanded pluralist politics. In commentary on the Health Professions Educational Assistance Act of 1976, which required American medical schools to use federal financial assistance to expand admissions to accommodate foreign medical students, he addressed the incapacity of Congress to draft statutes that delegated precise powers to federal agencies. In drafting the provision on foreign physicians he contended that a congressional conference committee had sought to accommodate the divergent interests of foreign medical students, some of whom were American citizens; the interests of American medical schools; and its own desire to control the number of physicians in the country. According to Scalia, the result was a statutory provision "devoid of meaning" because it was "*meant to be unclear.*" Congress had delegated to the secretary of health, education, and welfare any decisions about foreign medical students. The Department of Health, Education, and Welfare would make policy through negotiation and adjudication with medical schools and other interests. Also, interest groups would eagerly try to affect regulations because they wanted a share of federal funds. They would, he argued, subject themselves to regulation and involvement in regulatory politics because of the potential for economic gain.[40]

Scalia's solution for the lack of statutory clarity in the delegation of power to agencies was a judiciary that actively resisted "standardless legislation." His specific cure was a revitalization of the doctrine of "unconstitutional delegation," which considered it to be unconstitutional for Congress to delegate unspecified lawmaking powers to the executive branch. If applied by the Supreme Court to more standardless legislation, Scalia thought, the doctrine would curtail "the danger of government by bureaucracy supplanting government by the people."[41]

Concerns about the imprecise delegation of authority to agencies caused Scalia to launch a campaign against delegation and the legislative veto. Reiterating his earlier objections to the legislative veto, he proposed, as an alternative solution to standardless delegatory legislation, that the judiciary find the legislative veto unconstitutional. Extending his earlier political criticism of the veto, he argued that the veto encouraged rather than curtailed bureaucratic government. His concern was not the veto's creation of a constitutional imbalance between the executive and legislative branches. Rather, he charged that the legislative veto encouraged legislators to delegate powers to agencies with the promise that Congress could police any policy standards or decisions that the agencies developed under unspecified legislative mandates. However, he contended that Congress would not intervene and police agencies if it found that review and possible veto of agency standards would be politically controversial. Instead, congressional committees' members and staff and agency personnel would resolve the direction of agency policy behind the scenes. No pressures would force Congress to stop delegating "vague and standardless rulemaking authority" to agencies or intervening in international policies of the executive. Therefore, as he claimed in an article containing a make-believe letter from a member of Congress to constituents, congressional proposals to expand the use of legislative vetoes would not resolve the problem of extensive, largely unsupervised agency rulemaking power. As he stated in congressional testimony on the veto, the legislative veto attended to narrow interests and disregarded the problem of "iron triangles" of agency, agency clientele, and congressional committee—alliances that failed to bring "to bear the entire national concern" in policymaking.[42]

The solution for this balkanized regulatory and foreign policy review process dominated by special interests, he argued, was greater presidential involvement in the regulatory process and a bar to congressional vetoes of foreign assistance pledged by the executive. He thought that an alternative proposal for a separate congressional committee to review all regulations and possessed of a veto power—an arrangement common in state government—could not handle the work and that staff would make the decisions. He made it clear that by encouraging specialized policy review by selected interests, the veto hampered the executive power to manage the agencies and the ability of the entire Congress to act on matters of public concern.[43]

Scalia brought his themes of the dangers of judicial intervention and faulty congressional lawmaking together in his most traditional scholarly article of the 1977–82 period, an analysis of the Supreme Court's decision in *Vermont Yankee Nuclear Power Corporation v. Natural Resources Defense Council.*[44] The *Vermont Yankee* article questioned the ability of the Supreme Court to "establish coherent principles" of administrative law unless guided by a revision in the text and the assumptions of the APA. After discussing the flexibility and choice of procedures afforded to agencies under the APA, he recounted how the U.S. Court of Appeals for the District of Columbia Circuit (commonly called the D.C. Circuit) had imposed additional procedural requirements on Atomic Energy Commission rulemaking in its *Vermont Yankee* decision. The supplemental procedure required by the D.C. Circuit demanded that "hybrid" hearing procedures be added to the informal rulemaking process defined by the APA. However, the Supreme Court justices rejected the creation of the supplemental procedure. Scalia applauded the way in which the Supreme Court had made "meticulous reference to the text" of the APA, while the D.C. Circuit had relied on "'basic considerations of fairness' and 'the interest of justice.'" Yet despite his approval of the Supreme Court's reliance on the text of the APA, his support of the decision was muted. He evidenced concern about lack of previous control by the Supreme Court over D.C. Circuit doctrine. He seemed surprised that litigants, including agencies and the solicitor general, had not argued the previous position of the Supreme Court to the circuit judges. Also, he questioned *how* the justices read the text of the APA. Fundamentally, his argument was that the justices had misread some of the legislative compromise worked into the APA and read into the act a procedural rigidity not sought by Congress. But he went on to argue that these faults stemmed from the inherent inadequacy of the procedural specifications of the APA, from changes in the substantive duties of agencies not comprehended by the statute, and from congressional failure to employ APA procedures in new legislation. In conclusion, he did not see *Vermont Yankee* as a case that worked a revolution in administrative law. A single opinion could not change the path of congressional legislation, nor could it replace other decisions that allowed for some technical judicial justifications for departure from the text of the APA. A single opinion could not guarantee change in interpretive practice by the D.C. Circuit. Instead, he offered an outline of another solution. The APA should be revised by Congress so that it would contain more detailed alternative agency procedures. The expansion of procedural detail and options would, he thought, curtail judicial improvisations of procedures like the innovations imposed by the D.C. Circuit. A revised APA also might induce Congress to avoid creating for new agencies new procedures not limited by APA practice. Uniform standards could replace the politically motivated creation of special practices in the regulation or provision of services to special interests by Congress, agencies, and courts.[45] Thus, pragmatic procedural evolution would be replaced by more neutral rules of procedure. Interest groups could no longer be empowered by judges, agency allies, or congressional committees.

Freedom of Information Legislation. During this period Scalia addressed a third problem affecting the politics of American public management: legislative efforts to expand public knowledge about governmental activity through freedom of information legislation. He regarded the FOIA amendments of 1974 as costly for the agencies and ineffective in the promotion of public knowledge about government. The FOIA, he argued, required agencies to spend enormous financial resources accommodating requests for documents rather than addressing policy priorities. The act required courts to give preference to FOIA cases, contained provisions for courts to compel agencies to pay the attorney fees of requesters, and required courts to delay other litigation at a cost to the parties in the other litigation. He thought these provisions unfair or costly. The FOIA allowed requesters to gain access to information about the private persons, firms, and associations regulated by government; according to Scalia, this had the negative effect of reducing "their privacy, and hence autonomy." His solution was to abandon the premises of the FOIA, especially the idea "that the first line of defense against an arbitrary executive is do-it-yourself oversight by the public and its surrogate, the press." Against this "romantic notion" he claimed that responsible government is best achieved through the institutionalized system of checks and balances. Therefore, control of the executive would depend on effective congressional oversight.[46]

The Limitations of Administrative Law Judges. Finally, Scalia sought to address the problem of the limited expertise of administrative law judges. He wanted improvement in the entry requirements for administrative law judges, the introduction of a multi-grade structure to provide prestige and economic rewards in return for special judicial competency, and changes in the discipline and removal of incompetent judges.[47]

Summary of Scalia's Solutions to Public Management Problems. Scalia's solutions to the four problems of public management asserted that the informed use of agency discretion by administrators should be controlled primarily through precise legal rules and procedures adopted by Congress. Extensive judicial review, judicially and legislatively advanced public participation in or oversight of agencies, and congressional second-guessing of agency uses of discretion only muddied the policymaking process. In Scalia's world, after extensive public debate Congress would pass a specific law that delegated specific duties to an agency. The agency, freed of bothersome judicial and public or interest group intrusions, would use its expertise and make rules detailing the enforcement of the specifically stated aims of Congress. Congress might revise the law at a later date if agency rules were deemed ineffective, but it could not micromanage agency policy implementation through the creation of special procedures for specific agencies or the use of the legislative veto.

Because it could help achieve these goals, Scalia supported the deregulatory policy of the Reagan administration. He was less concerned about the substantive policy implications of reform than was the administration, but he nonetheless applauded the administration's attention to and especially Congress's interest in the revision of agency procedures under the APA.[48] In *Regulation* he set forth proposals for Reagan administration changes in the Federal Trade Commission (FTC) and the FCC. At the FTC he did not envision any radical change in personnel affecting the philosophical direction of the commission's rulemaking. However, he did argue that some changes in statutory directives might curtail "activist" or pro-consumer economic regulation by the FTC by limiting its ability to undertake rulemaking initiatives, to make rules in the antitrust field, and to restrict adjudications by consumer interests. To foster communications deregulation, he also wanted to rewrite statutes to induce more competition among communications technology industries.[49] He continued to argue for regulatory change by encouraging the administration to seek repeal of the Bumpers Amendment that gave federal judges authority over FTC policy on deceptive practices, to repeal FTC rulemaking procedures, to try to abolish the legislative veto, and to add cost-benefit analysis requirements to evaluate the utility of new rules. With these changes, he predicted that Republican executive appointees committed to deregulation would have a freer rein to carry out their objectives. The executive, Scalia argued, would no longer be enfeebled in carrying out its electoral promises.[50] A year later he assessed the administration's efforts and backed off from his earlier statement about the utility of cost-benefit analysis for assessing the value of new regulations. Instead, he regarded the administration's requirement for Office of Management and Budget (OMB) review of new rules as a significant accomplishment. Also, he argued in support of legislation making OMB regulatory-impact or cost-benefit analysis permanent and confirming OMB authority to clear new regulations. However, he was concerned that Republicans in Congress supported a more judicialized rulemaking process and greater judicial authority to interpret the statutes governing agencies, which promised less respect for agency expertise and more interest group involvement in rulemaking.[51]

Commentary on Other Constitutional Issues

During his professorial years, Scalia rarely spoke about other constitutional or political issues. However, appearing before a House committee to support a bill providing criminal penalties for the disclosure of the identity of American intelligence agents, he indicated that legislation of limited scope requiring evidence of intent to harm should pass muster as a national security exception to the First Amendment freedoms of speech and press.[52] And in a published speech he considered the importance of federalism in the American constitutional system. After noting that conservatives had largely opposed greater federal involvement in policymaking since the New Deal, he made the argument that a conservative policy of market freedom might benefit from federal rather than state policymaking. Implicitly relying on his hostility to expanded pluralist politics, he contended that multiple local standards, such as those facing the cable television industry, imposed unnecessary costs on economic activity. National economic regulation therefore could be beneficial in some instances, especially when the "economic mood in Washington" was conservative.[53]

His comments on affirmative action and the Establishment of Religion Clause of the First Amendment of the Constitution were far more controversial. In an address at Washington University in St. Louis, later published in the university's law review, he sarcastically denounced affirmative action policies. He opened his comments with a reflection on the Supreme Court decision in *Regents of the University of Califor-*

nia v. Bakke.[54] Noting that the Court was badly divided on affirmative action, he went to characterize Justice Powell's opinion "as an excellent compromise between two Committees of the American Bar Association on some insignificant legislative proposal. But it is thoroughly unconvincing as an honest, hard-minded, reasoned analysis of an important provision of the Constitution." He also characterized governmental regulations and the arguments of some defenders of affirmative action as "full of pretense or self-delusion."[55]

Scalia argued that affirmative action was "based on concepts of racial indebtedness and racial entitlement rather than individual worth and individual need; that is to say, . . . it is racist." He attempted to reinforce the logic of his position by a professorial use of hypothetical argument, the description of a "Restorative Justice Handicapping System." Turning to the utility of affirmative action policies, he made several points: Affirmative action did not change but instead reinforced concepts of racial difference. Affirmative action cheapened the achievements of successful individual blacks. Affirmative action frustrated those blacks who could not satisfy the merit-based requirements of the educational institutions that had admitted them because of legal requirements. Affirmative action hurt the economic status of blacks. He thought that sex-based affirmative action was an "equally poor idea." However, he stated that he strongly favored programs to help the "poor and disadvantaged."[56] Underlying his position was an acceptance of institutional definitions of merit, the notion that individuals should bear primary responsibility for their successes or failures, a distrust of pragmatic efforts to cope with the effects of the institutionalized racism of the past, and a belief that equal rules and procedures would allow persons to realize their aspirations.

Three times Scalia appeared before congressional committees to support tuition tax credits for the parents of students in religious schools. When he testified, he commented on the Supreme Court's Establishment Clause precedents. He made two arguments. First, Congress did not have to accept the judgment of the Supreme Court as binding, especially if the decisions of the justices cannot be regarded as conclusive on a specific issue. Second, he recapitulated the Establishment Clause cases about tuition credits and other aid to religious schools and found the Court's reasoning irrational. He labeled the Court's holdings as "utter confusion" and as "confusing, bewildering, positively embarrassing."[57] In particular, he faulted the Court for its effort to develop a principle of neutrality and a clear legal rule on religious establishment. Contending that the Free Exercise Clause gave religion "special privileges," he claimed that it was "impossible to interpret the Establishment Clause in such a fashion as to provide no favor whatever to religion."[58] One privilege accorded to religion could be a tax credit for the costs of exercising the religious "practice" of separate education.

CONCLUSION

In 1982 President Reagan nominated Scalia to fill a vacancy on the U.S. Court of Appeals for the District of Columbia Circuit. Until his appointment to the court of appeals, he had thrived on conditions that rewarded his academic talents and sociability. Intellectual brilliance, the application of his brilliance in his assigned tasks, a practicality in his academic scholarship that brought him to the attention of public officials, and the development of contacts with influential persons, as well as his gregarious personality, had carried him into a position of political importance and esteem. His appointment to the D.C. Circuit was in keeping with the standards of merit used in the selection of American political elites—standards that rewarded conformity to academic expectations; intellectual expertise in a specialty; hard work that went beyond assigned tasks; the making of favorable impressions on professors at elite institutions, federal officeholders, and colleagues; and a political position comforting to elites. It is no wonder that Scalia objected to efforts to change the standards of merit by introducing affirmative action programs. They countered the principles that governed his life, and they questioned the value of elite education, expertise, networking, and conformity to the concerns of influential persons.

Scalia was always articulate and direct, but his ideas tended to be legal elaborations of established themes seen in the Nixon, Ford, and Reagan administrations' reaction to the New Deal. Even in his writings as a pundit, he had only begun to set forth his vision of a revived conservative American politics. He had criticized the post–New Deal political regime along two dimensions. First, he had taken aim at Congress's role in creating bureaucracy and fostering expanded political pluralism by including new and nontraditional interests in policymaking. He saw the "bureaucracy problem" as one generated by congressional interference with federal bureaucratic discretion. The problem was not bureaucrats or bureaucracy per se, but congressional unwillingness to let the executive function under clear rules governing the use of expertise. He had redefined the "bureaucracy problem" into a "Congress problem," or the problem of inadequate congressional statutory control of bureaucratic discretion.[59]

Second, Scalia accepted a pluralist debate about policy before Congress but not the participation of interest groups in agency decision-making or judicial review of agency action. Judges were to be restrained and were to restrain themselves from intervention in the judgments of policymakers, a position of Reasoned Elaboration. Moreover, judges were not to expand opportunities for groups—especially "public" interest groups—to participate in agency decisions. Scalia regarded judicial intervention and greater interest group access as only compounding the Congress problem. Thus he redefined the conservatives' problem of expanded political pluralism as the problem of interest group efforts to influence or control the implementation of public policy by the executive agencies. However, the problem of moral discord and the lack of consensus on moral values which troubled many conservatives had hardly ever surfaced in his public statements. He had not taken a boldly creative step toward the establishment of a political narrative justifying a moral or philosophical vision for American politics.

Chapter Two

REWIRING THE
D.C. CIRCUIT

On 15 July 1982, President Ronald Reagan nominated Antonin Scalia to serve as a judge of the U.S. Court of Appeals for the District of Columbia Circuit. The D.C. Circuit is a unique federal appellate court. It hears initial appeals of cases arising in the District of Columbia—cases in which the federal agencies located in Washington are frequently parties. Consequently, it has long heard more appeals about federal regulatory and distributive policies than have other federal appellate courts, and its judges have won recognition as leading exponents of innovative interpretations of the APA and the statutes governing specific federal administrative agencies.[1] The Reagan administration, committed to a policy of deregulation, wanted expert Republican judges on the D.C. Circuit who could undo some of the innovations in administrative law developed by the Court's Democratic appointees. Given his reputation, experience, and published criticism of trends in administrative law, Antonin Scalia was an obvious choice to "rewire" some of the decisions of the Circuit and empower the conservative revival.

Scalia's nomination hearings before the Senate Judiciary Committee, then under Republican control, took only a few hours on 4 August. The chairman of the Senate Judiciary Committee, Strom Thurmond (R-S.C.), examined Scalia as part of a hearing on several judicial nominees. As a result of the questions asked by Thurmond, two-thirds of Scalia's brief testimony was about his views on the Freedom of Information Act. Scalia reiterated his objections to the costs of the FOIA, the trial de novo of FOIA cases, the authorization of federal payment of attorney fees for FOIA litigants, and the preference given FOIA cases on the judicial docket. Thurmond then asked a question about Scalia's perception of conflicts of interest. Finally, Thurmond, the former states'-rights governor of South Carolina, asked about Scalia's definition of federalism and the Tenth Amendment. Scalia replied with a statement that the federal government had "specified powers . . . affirmatively granted" while other powers remained in the states. The potential tension between this position and his published address on federalism was not examined. Thurmond wished Scalia "a nice service on the bench." Although it was the briefest recorded appearance Scalia ever made before a congressional committee, it was typical of the hearings for federal judgeships in that period.[2] The Senate confirmed the nomination, and on 17 August 1982 Scalia began what became almost exactly four years of service with the D.C. Circuit.

SCALIA'S VOTING RECORD ON THE D.C. CIRCUIT

Scalia came to the D.C. Circuit as an expert in administrative law, and his labors for the Circuit enhanced his expertise. While on the Circuit he wrote 133 opinions that were published in the *Federal Reporter*.[3] As table 2.1 reveals, slightly over two-thirds of these dealt with either agency powers under regulatory statutes or the standing of parties to challenge agency action. During his service on the D.C. Circuit, Scalia had infrequent opportunities to write on freedom of expression, criminal justice rights, and civil rights issues, and he never wrote about school desegregation, state action issues, abortion, gender, voting rights, or economic equal protection claims, freedom of religion and the Establishment Clause, the Interstate Commerce Clause, most federalism issues, and most civil rights, bankruptcy, taxation, and antitrust statutes.

Scalia's D.C. Circuit opinions included 104 opinions for the court (78.2% of his total opinions), 6 concurring opinions (4.5%), 15 dissenting opinions (11.3%), 6 "concurrence and dissent in part" opinions (4.5%), and 2 statements on a denial of a rehearing of a case (1.5%). The D.C. Circuit, meeting *en banc,* or with all judges, overruled his decisions for a panel on only three occasions. However, these figures only partially reveal his position with regard to his colleagues. Like the other federal courts of appeals, the D.C. Circuit considers most cases before panels of three judges. On occasion, judges from other circuits of the U.S. Court of Appeals or trial judges from the federal district courts will serve on a panel for the D.C. Circuit. Table 2.2 contains a record of Scalia's voting agreements and disagreements with the other judges. Agreements are votes cast by another judge in favor of an opinion by Scalia or by Scalia in favor of the opinion of the paired judge. Disagreements are votes cast by the paired judge against Scalia's opinion and vote on the merits of the case, or cast by Scalia against the opinion and vote on the merits by the paired judge. The middle column contains cases in which Scalia voted on the merits with the paired judge but one of the pair expressed disagreement with some of the

Table 2.1   Published Opinions of Antonin Scalia for the District of
Columbia Court of Appeals

Topic	Number	Percentage
Administrative law, including APA, FOIA, agencies' statutory powers, and justiciability cases with agency party	90	67.7
Foreign affairs, judicial powers abroad	6	4.5
Exclusive power of Congress or president	6	4.5
First Amendment issues	5	3.8
Criminal procedure	8	6.0
Equal protection and civil rights statutes	5	3.8
Federal judicial rules and jurisdiction	11	8.3
Other	2	1.5
Total	133	100.0

Source: Compiled by the author from *Federal Reporter,* 2d ser.

other's reasoning, usually through the issuance of a concurring opinion. The cases include all decisions containing an opinion on the substantive merits of a case and all procedural decisions containing any opinions, mostly on requests for all the judges of the Circuit to review the decision of one of its panels (to hear a case en banc). The panel assignment process worked so that Scalia served on panels less often with some of his colleagues—especially Chief Judge Spottswood W. Robinson III—than with others. Robinson's administrative duties removed him from most panels, and those cases in which he participated with Scalia were almost exclusively cases about whether to hear a case en banc or about the merits of a case heard en banc.[4] Also, Scalia sat less frequently with judges who had senior status (i.e., were semi-retired).

As reported in table 2.2, Scalia's mean rate of agreement with all of the other D.C. Circuit judges was 75.2 percent. His agreement rate with seven of these judges stood above his mean. Four of these seven had been nominated by Ronald Reagan—Robert Bork, James Buckley, Laurence Silberman, and Kenneth Starr. Scalia knew Bork and Silberman from his days at AEI, and Buckley was a former U.S. senator and brother of the famous conservative commentator William F. Buckley. The other judges with whom he had an agreement ratio above his mean were Kennedy appointee Carl McGowan, Johnson appointee George

Table 2.2   Pairwise Voting Record of Antonin Scalia and Other D.C. Circuit Judges, 1982–1984

Judge, and Party of Nominating President	Votes, with Percentages in Parentheses		
	Agree with Scalia	Partially Agree with Scalia	Disagree with Scalia
Judges and Senior Judges of the District of Columbia Circuit			
Bazelon, D. (D)	12 (70.6)	1 (5.9)	4 (23.5)
Bork, R. (R)	51 (91.1)	0 (0.0)	5 (8.9)
Buckley, J. (R)	13 (100.0)	0 (0.0)	0 (0.0)
Edwards, H. (D)	53 (74.6)	7 (9.9)	11 (15.5)
Ginsburg, R. B. (D)	49 (83.1)	4 (6.8)	6 (10.2)
MacKinnon, G. (D)	36 (90.0)	2 (5.0)	2 (5.0)
McGowan, C. (D)	11 (91.7)	1 (8.3)	0 (0.0)
Mikva, A. (D)	38 (63.3)	8 (13.3)	14 (23.3)
Robinson, S. (D)	15 (41.7)	7 (19.4)	14 (38.9)
Silberman, L. (R)	12 (92.3)	1 (7.7)	0 (0.0)
Starr, K. (R)	38 (86.4)	2 (4.5)	4 (9.1)
Tamm, E. (D)	26 (68.4)	2 (5.2)	10 (26.3)
Wald, P. (D)	43 (61.4)	9 (12.9)	18 (25.7)
Wilkey, M. (R)	28 (73.7)	2 (5.3)	8 (21.1)
Wright, J. S. (D)	50 (64.1)	7 (9.0)	21 (26.9)
Federal Judges on Temporary Assignment to the District of Columbia Circuit			
Friedman, D. (D)	7 (100.0)	0 (0.0)	0 (0.0)
Gasch, O. (D)	6 (100.0)	0 (0.0)	0 (0.0)
Gesell, G. (D)	11 (100.0)	0 (0.0)	0 (0.0)
Greene, H. (D)	0 (0.0)	1 (33.3)	2 (66.7)
Haynesworth, C. (R)	3 (100.0)	0 (0.0)	0 (0.0)
Harris, S. (R)	2 (100.0)	0 (0.0)	0 (0.0)
Hogan, T. (R)	1 (100.0)	0 (0.0)	0 (0.0)
Lumbard, J. E. (R)	3 (75.0)	1 (25.0)	0 (0.0)
Markey, H. (R)	2 (100.0)	0 (0.0)	0 (0.0)
Richey, C. (R)	4 (100.0)	0 (0.0)	0 (0.0)
Swegert, L. (D)	7 (70.0)	1 (10.0)	2 (20.0)
Van Deusen, F. (D)	5 (83.3)	1 (16.7)	0 (0.0)
Van Pelt, R. (R)	4 (100.0)	0 (0.0)	0 (0.0)
Weigel, S. (D)	5 (83.3)	0 (0.0)	1 (16.7)
Williams, D. (R)	9 (100.0)	0 (0.0)	0 (0.0)
Total	544 (75.2)	57 (7.9)	122 (16.9)

Source: Compiled by the author from *Federal Reporter,* 2d ser.

MacKinnon, and Carter appointee Ruth Bader Ginsburg. He was paired in agreement at a ratio below his mean with eight judges of the Circuit, seven of them appointed by Democratic presidents—judges Harry T. Edwards, Abner J. Mikva, Spottswood Robinson, Edward A. Tamm, Patricia Wald, J. Skelly Wright, and senior judge David Bazelon—and one a Nixon appointee, senior judge Malcolm Wilkey.

Like the rest of the D.C. Circuit, Scalia supported a majority of the claims of agencies. When voting in cases raising issues of agency action which were decided by any action of the Circuit, Scalia voted for the agency position in 59.6 percent of the cases (93 votes); he voted to support in part the claims of the agency in 13.5 percent of the cases (21 votes), and against all aspects of the agency claim in 26.9 percent of the cases (42 votes). Another study examining only the votes of three-judge panels on specific points of law (as opposed to cases) found that Scalia evidenced the greatest support for federal agencies of all the judges of the Circuit, a rate of 77 percent for the agency claim (50 of 65 votes).[5]

SCALIA'S D.C. CIRCUIT OPINIONS AND OTHER PUBLIC STATEMENTS

The data on Scalia's voting shows his support for the decisions of agencies of the Reagan administration and his ideological conformity with other Reagan appointees to the Circuit. However, during his D.C. Circuit service Scalia supplemented his vision of the problems with bureaucracy, Congress, and expanded political pluralism.[6]

The Management of the Regime and the Problems with Bureaucracy and Congress

Most of Scalia's D.C. Circuit opinions on administrative law matters involved the consideration of allegations of agency or district judge errors in the application of precedent, statutory language, or administrative rules. In evaluating allegations of administrative error, Scalia was not a fan of the "procedural hard look" doctrine developed by the D.C. Circuit, which allowed judicial specification of agency procedures to ensure "adequate consideration" of issues.[7] Scalia also disliked its counterpart, the "substantive hard look," which required a judicial assessment of agency expertise and the rationality of an agency's policy choices.[8] In opinions on cases raising questions about the lawfulness of agency actions, Scalia considered only whether procedures were "arbitrary and capricious" and when an agency failed to consider evidence properly. In cases raising questions about whether agency actions disclosed a lack of fidelity to plain statutory language expressing the will of Congress about agency operations, Scalia normally deferred to agency expertise. He decided against agency discretion primarily when the agency's procedures violated the procedural requirements or when the legal standards adopted by the agency contradicted the text of a statute.[9]

For example, in a case challenging automobile bumper standards set by the National Highway Transportation Safety Administration (NHTSA), he accepted as a matter consigned to agency discretion the agency's use of cost-benefit analysis in the establishment of the standards. However, he did closely examine the conduct and reasoning of the agency's analysis to test whether the assessments of the NHTSA were arbitrary or capricious. Thus, he took less of a hard look at the logic of discretionary agency policy—the decision to use the cost-benefit test for deciding whether to establish a rule—and more of a hard look at whether the agency's evaluation of evidence for a regulation provided overall support for its rule. His test of the legality of agency action was whether the agency drew conclusions "within the range of those a reasonable person could derive from the evidence presented."[10] He did not second-guess the substantive agency decision or the agency's procedures in the use of cost-benefit analysis.

In addition to showing a general respect for agency procedural practice and expertise, some of Scalia's D.C. Circuit opinions disclosed a more comprehensive vision of the arrangement and management of American political institutions. It was those opinions in particular that addressed how a strong executive might direct public policy and control aspects of the bureaucracy problem—which was, from Scalia's viewpoint, the Congress problem. His statement of a vision of good political management had three aspects: presidential control, restricted congressional participation, and judicial restraint, especially in granting interest groups a right to participate in or challenge agency procedures and rules.

Executive Direction of Administration

Although the D.C. Circuit's caseload did not afford frequent opportunities to speak about executive power from a constitutional vantage point, Scalia supported the independence of executive policy decisions. In a speech he posed his central concern. The constitutional decisions of the Supreme Court on executive matters had given the president policy control over all federal administrative institutions, including the independent agencies as well as the traditional executive departments. Subsequent court decisions had impeded executive control of all agencies. In particular, the judiciary had induced the president "to leave policy control of the independent agencies to congressional committees."[11] Since Scalia saw this situation as a source of the bureaucracy problem, especially the unresponsiveness of bureaucrats to public opinion, his opinions expressed a desire to return to more direct political control of agencies by the president. In particular, he wanted to free presidential foreign policy and national security policies from judicial and congressional interference, and he wanted more presidential direction of agency rulemaking.

Scalia's few opinions on foreign affairs assigned an inherent and exclusive authority over foreign policy issues to the president. With regard to foreign affairs, he wrote that he did not want courts to interfere "inappropriately" in "matters that judges know little of, and that are preeminently the business of another Branch." In dicta, he commented that it was not the "special mission" of the judiciary to keep the president or Congress "in line," unless there was a need to "protect individuals against unlawful private action" by these officials.[12] He made these statements when the D.C. Circuit, en banc, overruled his opinion for a panel deciding whether a case on uncompensated American military taking of property in Honduras was justiciable in federal courts. Scalia held that the case raised the justiciable issue of the constitutionality of the taking. However, the court could not provide equitable relief for the taking and enjoin military occupation of the land. Such an injunction would violate the separation of powers and intrude on the presidential conduct of foreign affairs. Any relief would have to be for money damages, and the case would have to be lodged, per a statute called the Tucker Act, in the U.S. Claims Court, a special legislative court.[13]

When the Circuit overruled him en banc, it afforded equitable relief from the federal courts for the occupation of the property. Scalia's response was that, because his court had professed an "elegant agnosticism" toward the Tucker Act and judicial interpretations of the act that serve as a limitation on the general jurisdiction of federal courts, it had erred. In addition, he thought that the majority's contention that some of the stockholders of a Honduran corporation could, as individuals, sue the United States was "highly undesirable." Such suits, he contended, opened the federal judiciary to all sorts of suits over shareholder rights never before considered justiciable. Turning to the issue of executive power, he concluded that injunctive relief against the executive would violate the separation of powers. Injunctive relief complicated the use of the military and foreign affairs powers of the president, and it permitted American courts to impugn "the integrity and fairness of a friendly nation, at the instance of a plaintiff who has not sought judicial relief in the country where the real estate in question is located." Therefore injunctive relief, or the majority opinion's alternative equitable remedy of a declaratory judgment that stated the property rights of the Hondurans, would usurp the executive duty to handle foreign and military affairs with a friendly nation.[14]

Litigation about covert U.S. military operations in Central America resulted in another opinion on the foreign and military powers of the presidency. The suit was complex and involved three classes of appellants and two classes of appellees. Using doctrines of standing to sue, Scalia disposed of Nicaraguan citizens' claims against the executive branch, including allegations of violations of constitutional rights, injury to personal constitutional rights by federal officers ("constitutional tort" or "*Bivens*" claims),[15] breech of four American statutes, and violations of international law. He concluded that the parties had simply failed to set forth a claim on which relief could be granted. Also, he noted that the extent of executive involvement in the issues raised by the parties precluded any discretionary relief by the court. He chose the path of restraint on a matter dominated by executive policymaking. The case also featured a complaint by members of Congress who alleged that covert action in Nicaragua violated statutory restrictions and usurped the power of Congress to declare war. Scalia dismissed the complaint by noting that the expiration of the statutory restriction made aspects of the claim moot and that the question regarding the purported declaration of war was not justiciable before American courts.[16]

Scalia voted for presidential authority to conduct warrantless wiretaps in national security matters. His argument for presidential authority had two parts. First, the executive possessed a qualified immunity from judicial enforcement of civil judgments for harms caused by electronic eavesdropping done for national security purposes. And second, if questions about his qualified immunity arose, a "reasonableness" standard, not tougher evidentiary standards, could be used to evaluate the propriety of a presidential action.[17]

When addressing statutory and administrative law issues, Scalia worked to secure a preeminent presidential role in administration based on the president's constitutional authority to execute the laws. In an opinion supporting a National Highway Traffic Safety Administration decision to reduce automobile bumper standards in response to White House influence, he wrote: "There seems to us nothing either extraordinary or unlawful in the fact that a federal agency opens an inquiry into a matter which the President believes should be inquired into. Indeed, we had thought the system is supposed to work that way . . . It would be a different matter if the President directed the agency . . . to disregard the statutory criteria controlling its actions."[18] From his perspective, executive direction, when coupled with the proper use of agency rulemaking powers, made an agency choice responsive to public sentiments.

The Reagan administration policy of deregulation raised new legal questions for the federal judiciary. Scalia addressed the question of courts' standards for the review of agency deregulatory actions. In a panel discussion at the Judicial Conference of the D.C. Circuit, he discussed the implications of the deregulation movement with Judge Stephen Breyer, then of the U.S. Court of Appeals for the First Circuit, and two leading private attorneys in administrative law practice, James Fitzpatrick, of the firm of Arnold and Porter; and William H. Allen, of Covington and Burling. Scalia introduced the participants and posed questions about their approach to the review of deregulation efforts. Only toward the end of the session did Scalia offer his own telling assessment of deregulation, stating, "It seems to me that the impetus for deregulation is largely the very antithesis of expertise. In a way, deregulation is an antiexpertise movement. The felt fault with the existing system was . . . [that] the sum of those individually expert decisions doesn't make sense . . . So I think you have to regard the deregulation movement as to some extent a reaction to conferring too much power upon the expertise of individual agencies at the expense of the overall picture."[19] The implication was that deregulation was an executive policy decision to limit agency power. Extending this theme in another speech, he contended that there is a constitutional dimension to deregulation litigation. The decision to deregulate, to react against the power of agency expertise, is a "political choice . . . left to the executive branch." Judges should treat this judgment using the same standards of review and deference to the executive that they employ in rulemaking. Further, echoing his previous opinions, he indicated that regulation and deregulation properly should be affected by political compromise and not just expert choices by administrators.[20]

Scalia also addressed another administrative practice linked to the control of bureaucratic power—agency inaction, or the executive's refusal to regulate. When the Food and Drug Administration (FDA) refused to adopt a rule requiring the drugs used by the states for the lethal injection of convicted capital criminals to meet Congress's requirement that drugs be "safe and effective," the D.C. Circuit held that the FDA had to proceed with rulemaking. Scalia dissented for reasons associated with the separation of powers, stating, "Generally speaking, enforcement priorities are not the business of this Branch, but of the Executive—to whom, and not the courts, the Constitution confides the responsibility to 'take care that the Laws be faithfully executed.'" Further, he argued that the APA (§ 702[a][2]) recognized this principle and left enforcement decisions "committed to agency discretion." He considered that case law, contrary to the views of his panel's majority, reaffirmed the principle. Therefore the FDA could use its discretionary authority to decide whether to regulate the use of drugs for lethal injection. Since he held that specific statutory language required the FDA to control only "the sale and distribution of drugs rather than their use," the law confirmed the agency's discretion to chose inactivity.[21] His dissenting opinion in this case, as well as a statement issued when the D.C. Circuit refused to consider the case en banc, indicated that he was not willing to accept judicial intrusion and "hard looks" at agency inaction or other discretionary actions of deregulation by agencies. These actions were matters of political discretion.[22]

Despite this decision, Scalia believed that there were limits to judicial deference to the executive agencies. Deference was the norm when courts were sorting out the effect of competing interpretations on the policy aims of a statute, when the statute assigned vague duties to the agency, or when there was a longstanding administrative interpretation of a statute relied on by the public. But agency discretion could not contravene the ordinary meaning of statutory language. Specific congressional assignment of duties was always a restraint on agency discretion which judges had to respect.[23] Therefore, in an opinion dissenting from the interpretation of a deregulatory statute, the Staggers Rail Act, Scalia rejected a panel's acceptance of Interstate Commerce

Commission (ICC) efforts to use ambiguous language in the act to support ICC deregulatory standards against challenge from a state governmental regulatory body. He thought that the ICC had taken statutory language containing a legislative compromise about the commission's ability to review the exemption of freight from state regulation and had applied the language against the clear standards that he thought the statute imposed on the agency.[24] The result of the panel's vote for the ICC was something that worried him greatly—agency redirection of the purposes of a deregulatory action by president and Congress.

Congress's Role in Administration

Scalia's system of interbranch relations encouraged Congress to make specific laws for executive enforcement. His standard on the congressional role in administration specified that Congress should draft statutes in precise language that assigns discrete duties to federal agencies. Vague statutes without a "clear purpose" only trigger administrative discretion and occasional judicial review of the exercise of that discretion or encourage congressional intervention in administrative decisions.

To provide guidance to agencies and to limit later congressional intervention in administration, Scalia relied on the use of the "plain-meaning," or common usage, approach to the construction of statutory language. He did not seek to infer the meaning of the words of a statute from the general purpose of the legislative act. He believed that a plain-meaning approach discouraged the introduction of external instrumental political and social demands into the judicial analysis of a statute. Repeatedly, he emphasized that judges should be true to the "ordinary meaning" of the text of statutes and of the constitutional and treaty language having a bearing on public administration.[25] Scalia lectured those administrators and judges who ignored the plain meaning of language or who reconstructed legislative and administrative intent using questionable sources.[26] Also, he disapproved of the use of committee reports and legislative history as guides to statutory interpretation because he believed that congressional staff drafted these materials with little oversight by legislators.[27] In concurring in a decision about the Equal Access to Justice Act, he averred, "I frankly doubt that it is ever reasonable to assume that the details, as opposed to the broad outlines of purpose, set forth in a committee report come to the attention of, much less are approved by the house which enacts the committee's bill." Instead, he wanted the court to judge on the basis of the text and "the most rational reconciliation of the relevant positions of law Congress had adopted."[28] He also thought that sources such as legislative debates only confounded the application of statutory texts by courts and administrators. Thus, only amendments that had been defeated on the floor served clearly to signal legislative intentions about what the statute did not mean.[29]

To ensure certainty in the meaning of statutes, Scalia wanted Congress to refrain from intervention in agency affairs. In 1983 the Supreme Court had held that the legislative veto, long opposed by Scalia, was unconstitutional.[30] Also, while on the D.C. Circuit he participated in a per curiam decision that held as unconstitutional parts of a scheme to ensure a balanced budget.[31] The legislation—the Budget and Emergency Deficit Control Act of 1985, or Gramm-Rudman-Hollings Act— provided for a maximum yearly federal budget deficit. Each year the Congressional Budget Office, an arm of Congress, and the Office of Management and Budget, an executive agency, would estimate the deficit. Their estimates would be reviewed by the comptroller general, who would then report to the president if any spending cuts were needed. The president was then to put the cuts into effect unless Congress met the deficit in other ways.

The per curiam opinion granted two parties standing to challenge the act. It deemed that the retirees of the National Treasury Employees Union would suffer a real injury from the executive's elimination of cost-of-living increases in their pensions to meet deficit maximums. Members of Congress who had voted against the act also had standing because they had suffered a specific and cognizable injury to their Article I, section 7, constitutional duty to enact appropriations measures. Turning from jurisdictional to substantive issues, the opinion discussed whether the act improperly delegated congressional authority to the executive. Although Scalia had questioned delegation practices of Congress in his articles and speeches,[32] he agreed with the court's judgment that the act's delegation was valid. Indeed, the opinion rejected six arguments for the invalidity of the delegation. Scalia's court deemed that the delegation was not functionally different from delegations upheld in precedent cases, was not unduly broad, was necessary, was not improperly contingent on events such as the appearance of a deficit, was not imprecise in specifying the duties of the agency, and appropriately defined how it would be reviewed by courts.[33]

Despite the court's general support for the delegation doctrine and the delegation of spending-control powers to the executive, the unconstitutional aspect of the act was its delegation of executive authority to administer expenditures to the comptroller general, a legislative officer. This conclusion about improper delegation hinged on the president's power to remove public officials. After a review of removal powers precedents, the opinion concluded that the comptroller general was neither an executive agent nor a quasi-executive director of an independent regulatory agency.[34] Instead, the power to remove the comptroller general rested in Congress. Because "powers conferred upon the Comptroller General as part of the automatic deficit reduction process are executive powers, which constitutionally cannot be exercised by an officer removable by Congress, those powers cannot be exercised and therefore the automatic deficit reduction process cannot be implemented."[35] This decision kept congressional officers from having direct control of the spending decisions of the executive and his agencies. Although the opinion smacks of Scalia's rigid view of the separation of powers, the standing and delegation sections of the opinion cannot be fully squared with his earlier views on these topics. Perhaps he would have distinguished these positions if he had signed the opinion as sole author. Perhaps he muted his positions to accommodate other judges and to produce a consensus judgment on an issue of national political significance.

Overall, Scalia's version of federal administration leaned toward executive dominance in the relations among the branches. Separated powers did not mean equal participation by each branch in the policy process. Since each branch had exclusive powers, separated powers did not mean an aggressively political process of checking and balancing of executive policy choices by Congress. But it did mean that Congress was to confine its role to drafting precise statutes so that the judiciary would rarely be invited to review the boundaries of administrative authority.

Judicial Review of Administrative Decisions

Scalia did not want the judiciary to impair the ability of agencies to accommodate the executive's political concerns. This consideration led him to develop standards to restrain the judicial checking and balancing of agency policy choices. First, unless agency exercise of discretion went beyond the intent discernable by any reasonable interpretation of statutory language, he rejected the substantive hard look and judicial inquiry into the policy choices of agencies.[36] He recognized that an agency statement of justification for a rule might not indicate the real reason for the adoption of the policy choice or rule, but he was willing to accept the record as a plausible justification for the agency action. Scalia's rejection of the substantive hard look rested on his reading of the Supreme Court's decision in *Chevron v. Natural Resources Defense Council*.[37] According to his reading of Justice John Stevens's opinion for the Court in *Chevron*, the judge first should ascertain whether clear statutory language permits agency action. If the statutory language is not plain, courts should not overrule a "reasonable" executive agency interpretation of any statutory ambiguities about agency authority. Judges were to afford "considerable weight" to an executive agency's construction of an ambiguous statute and to avoid judgments of the wisdom of agency policy. Following this guidance, Scalia would allow a court to rule that an agency had abused its discretion only if the agency's actions were clearly unreasonable. The court need not engage in a detailed review or "hard look" at agency procedures or at substantive choices involving judgments within the agency's area of expertise. This standard of deference evoked trust of, but not blind devotion to, agency discretion in questions of fact and policy.[38]

Second, Scalia supported what he believed were valid statutory constraints on judicial review of executive agency processes and enforcement decisions.[39] Third, he believed that recent changes in the doctrine of standing had made it possible for litigants to challenge the executive for broad policy reasons rather than because of the reason traditionally embedded in the doctrine of standing: a particularized injury to an individual's rights of person and property. He put his passive conception of the judiciary, a cardinal principle of Reasoned Elaboration jurisprudence, into a broader context in an academic article that was an expansion of a lecture on separation of powers and standing to sue which he had presented at Suffolk University Law School. In the article, he provided general commentary on the powers of judges and the "overjudicialization of the process of self-governance." He especially sought a reconsideration of the stakes required to stand before a court to challenge the operations of the executive branch and see that the agencies satisfied the legislative purposes of Congress. He argued that the Supreme Court had split the doctrine on standing to sue into two parts: a "prudential" rule defined by the Court but subject to legislative revision and judicial reinterpretation, and a "core" constitutional doctrine about the scope of judicial power.[40]

Examining the development of "prudential" standing, Scalia perceived a new eagerness of federal courts to interpret statutes so as to "discern a congressional elimination" of the barriers "to challenges of federal executive action." The doctrinal change by the judiciary included a willingness to accept the standing of parties who alleged harm to their environmental, recreational, and aesthetic interests, and a willingness to liberalize the judicial review provisions of the APA by allowing suits about a grievance despite the lack of a legal right created by the legislature or specific statutory language affecting a party. Scalia's dislike of changes in prudential standing doctrine led him to advance alternative standards to create judicial passivity in administrative matters.[41]

Turning to examine "core" standing doctrine, Scalia adopted a position similar to one developed by Professor Alexander Bickel, an exponent of Reasoned Elaboration jurisprudence. Bickel argued that courts had to practice passivity because of the limited authority and resources assigned to them by the Constitution. Passivity thus would enable the courts to avoid provoking challenges to the constitutional legitimacy of their actions by legislators and other external political critics.[42] Drawing on Bickel's ideas, Scalia lamented changes in the "core" doctrine of standing. He charged that the Court had revised the core doctrine (in *Flast v. Cohen*),[43] and that because of the Court's revisions the doctrine was now "only meant to assure that the courts can do their work well, and not to assure that they keep out of affairs better left to the other branches."[44] He contended that the doctrinal change in *Flast* had modified the function of standing as a support for the constitutional principle of the separation of powers. Standing, he argued, had once restricted courts "to their traditional undemocratic role of protecting individuals and minorities against impositions of the majority" and excluded them from "the even more undemocratic role of prescribing how the other two branches should function in order to serve the interest *of the majority itself.*" Changes in standing moved the courts from inquiry into concrete injuries to plaintiffs into inquiry into the effect of governmental policies on ill-defined groups whose interests were allegedly harmed by the policy. Thus, the revised doctrine permitted judges to define what was good for the people.[45]

The thrust of his idea of "core" standing was a reduction in judicial power to recognize the claims of certain kinds of interest groups. If a doctrinal barrier was in place, courts could not respond to the claims of social and environmental interest groups. These groups lacked the kind of property rights that corporate interests held under the tradi-

tional doctrine of standing. Instead, judges should consider corporations' traditional policy claims, in suits about material damage to property or person, breach of contract, or violation of rights granted by the
Constitution or other legal texts. Standing would support the theory of
separated powers and leave the recognition of the claims of social
and environmental groups to Congress and the executive. The courts
would be excluded from involvement in the politics of administration
and the second-guessing of administrative expertise.

Scalia used his conception of the core doctrine of standing in his
administrative opinions. He used the injury-in-fact rule (a person must
suffer a direct physical or psychological harm or loss of legal rights) and
the requirement of available judicial relief (a court must be able to
remedy the harm or loss of rights by awarding money damages or ordering a change in actions) to encourage judicial passivity in claims about
the constitutional definition of judicial power. He desired that parties
use the courts for specific relief for specific problems. Thus, parties
should not be allowed to sue agencies about light-truck fuel economy
standards that might harm the nation at some time in the future, about
whether rules on the importation of films might cause harm to theaters
by dissuading persons from spending money to view them, and about
fears of surveillance by intelligence agencies and fears of injury to
rights of association.[46] Also, he refused to grant standing in a dispute
among members of Congress which also, tangentially, involved the
executive. To involve the judiciary in this matter would violate a proper
understanding of the separation of powers.[47] Thus, his opinions refused judicial relief in public claims against administrators when a
litigant

- failed to assert consequential harm that was in violation of a
  statute,[48]
- was not an aggrieved party in the rulemaking process it challenged,[49]
- sought to litigate a frivolous suit that would waste judicial resources,[50]
- failed to proceed with its statutory claim,[51]
- made a claim of a remedy not available from a court, especially a
  benefit for society at large rather than the party before the
  court,[52]
- violated finality rules defining the end of an action between
  parties,[53]

- made a moot claim,[54]
- made a claim not ripe for judicial resolution because of unsettled preliminary disputes,[55]
- attempted to restart litigation in a case that had failed to satisfy the criterion for monetary loss required to lodge a claim in a federal court,[56]
- sought to litigate attorney fees from the government when a case was not alive during the period when fees were statutorily available,[57]
- failed to meet the injury-in-fact standard necessary to permit pre-enforcement judicial review of agency rulings,[58] or to permit civil actions against third parties for harms resulting from a criminal acts,[59]
- was barred from legal relief by language in a treaty or statute.[60]

Scalia also narrowly construed provisions of the FOIA, a practice that has often but not always made it more difficult for private parties to obtain the information necessary to litigate against policy choices by agencies.[61] He only supported standing for a group when he encountered cases in which a potential "substantial" personal harm affected a group or when a public institution, a state governmental counsel, was acting on behalf of an interest group.[62]

Consequently, Scalia's administrative law decisions sought to free public management from political and social interests' conflicting claims about administrative affairs. He was not a supporter of the "interest representation model" of administrative operations or of increased clientele and citizen participation in the various stages of the administrative process.[63] He did not want courts to expand such participation, and he distrusted the ability of courts to respond to public or interest group challenges to the fairness of agency procedures and agency expertise. Underlying his disquiet with interest group participation was a fear of judicial entanglement in evaluating the wisdom of the policies and politics of administration.

Summary of Scalia's D.C. Circuit Opinions about Public Management

The opinions and speeches that Scalia wrote during his D.C. Circuit service expanded his political narrative about his view of proper institutional roles in public management and, indirectly, his solutions to conservatives' "bureaucracy problem" (or as he defined it, the "Congress problem") and to the problem of expanded political pluralism. According to Scalia, after considering the claims of interests Congress should legislate to furnish clear policy standards for the executive branch. The president and his appointees should direct the agencies toward the political objectives specified by Congress or assigned to the executive by the Constitution. The courts should defer to agency procedural practices and expertise in the setting of the policy agenda, the formulation of rules, and the implementation of rules and other standards. The courts should avoid cluttering the use of agency discretion with judicially mandated intervention by interests. Little of this argument differs from the statements of Professor Scalia. The significant difference was that as a judge Scalia was able to make his views influence the rules that governed federal administrative decisionmaking. Case by case, he attempted to provide an incremental cure for the problems of bureaucracy and expanded political pluralism by addressing the behavior of Congress. His solutions to the bureaucracy problem (a reduction of congressional interference in agency decisions) and to the problem of expanded political pluralism (the use of rules of standing to control interest group challenges) promised a different national political regime, one in which law would confine political struggle.

Rights and the Problem of Expanded Pluralism

During his service on the D.C. Circuit, Scalia extended his political narrative about personal rights and equality issues. Because of his court's limited docket and the fact that he had few opportunities to speak in public, he could only partially elaborate his vision of the political function of rights. He had little to say about most freedom of speech and press issues, religious liberty and the Establishment Clause, substantive due process rights to property and personal privacy, equal protection of the laws, and criminal justice rights.[64]

Near the end of his service on the D.C. Circuit, Scalia spoke on the general meaning of the First Amendment at Macalester College, in Minnesota. The title of the speech, "A House with Many Mansions," indicated that he assumed that consistency and uniformity could not be expected in First Amendment law because the courts responded to "concrete and fact-bound" wrongs. Therefore, the Supreme Court could not employ or develop a uniform theory of the First Amendment. Examining precedent, he set forth categories of wrongs against freedom of expression which the Court had considered, rank-ordering forms of expression on the basis of how highly protected they were, along six dimensions. An examination of precedent regarding the subject matter of expression, which was his first dimension, showed political speech meriting the greatest protection, followed by expression on "philosophical, social, artistic, economic, literary, or ethical matters— to take a nonexhaustive list of labels." At the lower end of the ranking was commercial speech. On the dimension of truth, he noted the difference between opinion and fact enunciated by the Court, and the preference shown for opinion and true facts. On the third dimension, the identity of the speaker, he noted the preference shown for expression by adults, especially those outside of governmental service or prison. His fourth dimension was the nature of the audience. He explained how speech to a voluntary audience of adults ranked higher in protection than speech to other audiences. On the fifth dimension, the location of the act, he found that a preference was shown for speech in public forums, as opposed to closed governmental facilities or private places. Finally, he noted that verbal speech had stronger constitutional protection than did symbolic speech and speech plus conduct.[65]

In his Macalester College speech, Scalia offered little personal assessment of specific First Amendment decisions or doctrines. He accepted a case-by-case judicial construction of the meaning of the First Amendment rather than any uniform value for expressive freedom, and he accepted judicial construction of responses to disputes about expression in varying factual situations. Quoting Justice Felix Frankfurter, who thought that an informed weighing of interests by judges, rather than dogma, ought to mark First Amendment decisionmaking, Scalia asserted that the judicial weighing of interests might theoretically produce perfect justice in the individual case. But it might make "equivalent justice in the whole body of cases impossible." Nonetheless, he concluded that "uniformity does not seem worth the cost of uniform foolishness."[66]

While serving on the D.C. Circuit, Scalia applied this weighing-of-interests approach and the related ranking of interests which he discerned in First Amendment precedent. What he called the first and fourth dimensions of expressive rights figured in *Block v. Meese*. At issue was the constitutionality of a law that classified as political propaganda three Canadian films on the topics of acid rain and nuclear proliferation and that required reports on their dissemination to audiences. Because he regarded the classification of the films to be criticism of them as "propaganda," and because the defendants did not argue that the classification was governmental control of expression, he concluded that the classification did no harm to the freedom of political speech. Also, he judged that the dissemination reports did not classify audiences in a manner violative of freedom of association. The audience still could voluntarily attend the showing of the films in anonymity. The policy affected no special category of audience in any way.[67]

Employing what he called his second dimension of First Amendment analysis, Scalia supported some claims of expressive freedom in libel cases. Libel law reduced the protection of false speech only, not of opinion or true speech. In *Ollman v. Evans* the D.C. Circuit en banc faced the problem of defamation in a libel action about the statements of fact and opinion in a newspaper column attacking the professional reputation of a University of Maryland professor. Judge Wald ruled that one particular statement about the professor's reputation was not a constitutionally protected statement of opinion. Concurring, Judge Bork argued that a "totality of circumstances" test should replace any distinction between statements of fact, which were subject to legal challenge if false, and constitutionally protected opinion.[68] Scalia dissented. Most of his dissent addressed the totality of circumstances test offered in the Bork opinion. Taking a position at variance with the Macalester College speech, he claimed that the test was fraught with the subjective judgment of the balancing of interests. There was "really no mechanism to gauge how much defamation is a decent amount." In its place he argued for the retention of a definition of defamation that excluded opinions about professional reputation; such a definition would be "ample protection against the entire list of horribles confronting the defenseless modern publicist." Any further protection of press commentary against libel action, he thought, ought to come through legislative action. Correction of the problem that Bork saw in large awards of monetary damages for libel was not a judicial function and thus should not be accomplished by judicial evolution of doctrine.[69]

In another libel action, one brought by a right-wing organization against a publisher and reporters, Scalia considered the malice standard required for proof of libel against a public figure. He defined the criterion for malice as clear and convincing proof that a statement had been made with the knowledge it was false or with reckless disregard of whether it was true.[70] This placed a distinct burden on the person alleging a libel, especially since Scalia ruled that evidence of malice consisted of specific and verifiable facts. Applying this standard to the evidence of the case, he first eliminated from consideration nondefamatory allegations and opinions, per the panel opinion in *Ollman*. Then he concluded that eleven allegations required summary judgment for the publisher, although "a jury could reasonably conclude [that other allegations had been] made with actual malice" or with "a disregard for . . . truth or falsity that constituted actual malice."[71] Thus, Scalia still retained a respect for judicial enforcement of precedential standards in libel cases, but he wanted it done at trial. This burden did not have to be met during the pretrial stages of the cases.

In the case of *In re Reporters' Committee for Freedom of the Press*, Scalia upheld a district court decision permitting a reporter's postjudgment access to discovery documents about related suits between the president of Mobil Oil Company and the *Washington Post* and between the Mobil president and a reporter.[72] The Reporters' Committee questioned a court order prohibiting disclosure of documents about summary judgments on aspects of the cases not used as evidence to support the final judgment. Scalia's opinion considered constraints on expression based on what he called the fifth dimension of free speech and press standards: the location of the act. In this case, the location was the court. Using precedent, he concluded that it was constitutional to postpone full access to the documents until final judgment. First, he argued that historical practice had not permitted absolute access. He could not "discern an historical practice of such clarity, generality, and duration as to justify the pronouncement of a *constitutional rule* preventing the federal courts and the states from treating the records of private civil actions as private matters until trial or judgment." Second, he asserted that access in this setting would not play "an essential role in the proper functioning of the judicial process." He did not see the prejudgment release of documents as having functions such as safeguarding the integrity of factfinding, ensuring fairness and due process, or providing public oversight of the judicial process. Other functions of the release of documents to the public could be accomplished after judgment.[73]

Scalia weighed symbolic and speech-plus-conduct free expression against governmental regulation of the "mode of expression," which he called the sixth dimension of free speech doctrine, in his dissenting opinion in *Community for Creative Nonviolence [CCNV] v. Watt*.[74] In *CCNV* a group sought a permit to conduct a sleep-in protest in a national park to protest the problem of homelessness. The National Park Service denied the permit, citing a threat to the natural environment of the park. Scalia read the permit denial as reasonably aimed at protecting the quality of a park, and he determined that the park service had applied its rules in an even-handed fashion. In support of this conclusion, he used a ranking of the value of expressions akin to the ranking along the sixth dimension which he presented in his later Macalester College speech. At the highest-protection end of his ranking was the communicative act of speaking. A restriction on communicative speech could be justified only by a "substantial showing of need," especially the need to preserve order. However, according to his reading of various precedent cases, especially *United States v. O'Brien*,[75] expressive physical conduct such as sleep-ins ranked lower and could be regulated. From his viewpoint, the government had to permit only conduct that had a communicative character. Other regulations (such as criminal laws) "proscribing conduct for a reason having nothing to do with its communicative character need only meet the minimal requirements of the equal protection clause." His argument was that, despite the incidental control of a form of expression, the rules at issue in this case were not directed against demonstrations or against communication. The purpose of the statute empowering the National Park Service to regulate camping in federal parks, and the purpose of the rule derived from the statute by the park service, had to do with the substantial governmental interest in the prevention of injury to the parkland. The primary objective of the rule was not to unreasonably curtail expression, and the burden on CCNV was no greater than was essential to preserve the land. Thus, the regulation was valid. However, the Park Service could not curtail all expressive actions in the park, only those that might harm the substantial interest in park preservation.[76] Despite the hostility expressed toward an outsider political interest in *CCNV*, Scalia's First Amendment decisions, like his Macalester College address, contained little consideration of whether rights ought to expand political pluralism or limit it. He applied precedent and avoided any new directions in doctrinal arguments.

Scalia's Equal Protection Clause opinions accepted the three-tier "strict," "intermediate," and "reasonableness" scrutiny of discrimination against various classes of persons elaborated by the Supreme Court during the 1970s.[77] In *United States v. Cohen* he followed the three-tier formula in deciding an equal protection claim by a District of Columbia criminal defendant who had been automatically committed to a mental institution after successful assertion of an insanity defense. Scalia's reasoning relied on precedents defining the "higher" or "stricter" two tiers of scrutiny. The defendant argued that he had been denied equal protection because Congress required automatic commitment only for federal defendants who successfully asserted the insanity defense in the District of Columbia. Automatic commitment procedures did not exist in other United States district courts. Scalia held that the United States had only to convince the court that the automatic commitment procedure used in the District of Columbia had a rational basis and was reasonable. Questions of the inequity of punishment or commitment did not require any form of more intensified scrutiny. They involved no fundamental interest or liberty recognized by the Supreme Court, and residents of the District of Columbia were not a "suspect class" whose claims were recognized by the Supreme Court as requiring strict scrutiny.[78] Turning to the rationality of the differences in federal commitment procedures, he concluded that Congress had rational reasons for the distinction because of its reasonable assumption that outside the District of Columbia the states could act to commit federal defendants found criminally insane. However, in the District, Congress had to act to establish some form of commitment procedure. It had done so, he concluded, in a rational manner.

The interpretation of equal protection and civil rights statutes led Scalia into commentary about judicial interpretation of the evidentiary standards of civil rights statutes. In *Carter v. Duncan-Huggins* his dissent urged the court not to find a violation of civil rights laws before they had acquired evidence of intentional racially motivated discrimination. He clearly wanted to keep the court out of the business of promoting equality unless it had strong evidence of a distinction in the way an employee was treated and "some evidence that would enable a reasonable person to conclude that the *basis* for the discriminatory treatment was *race*." Evidence of discrimination absent "race-related treatment as circumstantial evidence of racial animus" would not satisfy his understanding of the proof necessary to find a violation of federal civil rights laws.[79] In another employment discrimination case he determined that the party had failed to provide even prima facie evidence of acts of racial discrimination that might merit relief.[80] Scalia would put the burden on minorities to show racism in acts of discrimination against them. He also found no equal protection violations in the refusal of the Federal Bureau of Investigation (FBI) to hire a Cuban American because he had family still resident in Cuba, and in a decision not to appoint an attorney in an employment discrimination case against the FBI.[81]

These equal protection decisions fit with the opinions of the more conservative members of the Supreme Court. With the exception of Rehnquist, these justices had rarely objected to the three-tier scrutiny formula, and they demanded more direct and substantial evidence of racial discrimination than did their liberal colleagues. Scalia did not offer any reconsideration of the political pluralism recognized by the three-tier formula or the special protective character of civil rights laws.

During his service on the D.C. Circuit, Scalia made few comments on substantive due process or extratextual constitutional rights. His comments on due process came in a speech at the Cato Institute. His theme was "economic liberty under the judiciary," but for the most part he commented on the elimination of economic interests' substantive constitutional rights against governmental regulation. The elimination of the substantive protection of economic rights had been the great jurisprudential victory of the New Deal. Scalia thought that the victory was "good," but not because of its policy consequences or because it fit with history. Instead, he thought it good for three other reasons related to the effective functioning of the judiciary. First, the substantive protection of economic rights encouraged judicial intervention in the business of the other branches and in complex federal and state policy disputes. He wanted a "more restricted view of the court's role in a democratic society." In addition to taking this passivity position based on separated powers theory, he claimed that courts lacked the expertise to make "sensible" decisions about economic rights. Finally, he argued that the "constitutionalizing" of economic rights would raise issues about the nature of those rights. Should the rights be affirmative, like a right to employment; or negative, like constraints on governmental regulation? He contended that courts were too distant from popular sentiment to make such choices. Instead, they should distance themselves from the contest of political interests over economic policy and rights.[82]

During his D.C. Circuit years, Scalia offered only one commentary about the problem of moral discord. In a published speech given before the Federalist Society, he seemed to accept the premise of a morally pluralist American society. For example, he stated that "it is impossible to say that our constitutional traditions mandate the legal imposition of even so basic a concept of distributive justice as providing food to the destitute," and that "fortunately . . . the overwhelming majority of issues of public policy do not rise to a moral level." Unlike religious conservatives, he seemed to regard moral discord as a minor public problem. Except with regard to moral controversies already affected by the courts, such as capital punishment and abortion, he thought that judges ought to ignore "polemicized" moral claims and apply the written law in a utilitarian fashion. Further, he opined that government response to policy demands from moral interests should be "prudential."[83] He did not recognize the problem of moral discord in the same way as many other conservative revivalists.

CONCLUSION: THE FOUNDATION OF A CONSERVATIVE POLITICAL VISION

During his D.C. Circuit service, Scalia continued to develop his political narrative in his opinions and published speeches. Judging and speaking as a judge mellowed the polemical style and the professorial methodology of combative confrontation that had marked his earlier essays and public statements; however, the nature of judging and the caseload of his court restricted his opportunity to write on many aspects of American politics. He continued his redefinition of the "bureaucracy problem" into a "Congress problem." To this argument he added more on the "problem" of an active judiciary that second-guessed agencies and frustrated effective policymaking. He continued to discredit expansive interest group participation in federal administration, and he tried to "rewire" D.C. Circuit efforts to expand interest group participation in administration and interest group challenges to agencies in the courts. However, his opinions about rights did not present anything like a detailed position on the problem of rights as a source of expanded political pluralism or as a resource for interest group influence on the policymaking process. His brief comments on morality contradicted the postulates of conservatives who worried about moral discord and the loss of a national consensus on religious and family values. However, he had yet to speak on the great issues about the value of human life and human freedom which were embedded in the controversies about the freedom of expression, capital punishment, and abortion.

Chapter Three

SCALIA AND THE CONSERVATISM OF THE REAGAN ADMINISTRATION

In 1986 Chief Justice Burger retired from the Supreme Court. To many conservatives his leadership of the Court seemed like a failure. Except on criminal justice issues, William Brennan had been the intellectual leader of the Court: in case after case, Brennan had evolved pragmatic doctrines that derailed conservative attacks on minorities and public interest liberals, federal governmental power, and the secularism of the state. To replace Burger, President Reagan, adopting a strategy used successfully only by Presidents William Howard Taft and Franklin Roosevelt, nominated a sitting associate justice, William Rehnquist, to be chief justice. He then nominated Scalia to fill the vacancy to be created if Rehnquist won Senate confirmation. Not a single Republican voiced any criticism of Scalia's nomination to the press. The nomination almost certainly was intended to push the Court to attend to the policies of the conservative revival, for Rehnquist and Scalia appeared to be more able and loyal conservatives than the often pompous and intellectually pliable Burger had been.

Christopher Smith contends that Scalia had also been expected to lead the undoing of the judicial doctrines and policies of post–New Deal liberalism, but the public statements of President Reagan and the defenders of the nomination present a less clear-cut picture of Reagan's intent. In his initial remarks on the nomination, Reagan read a statement praising Scalia's "personal energy, the force of his intellect, and the depth of his understanding of our constitutional jurisprudence." The theme of Scalia's expertise continued in later presidential statements on the nomination, but Reagan also stressed Scalia's Italian ancestry.[1] Reagan hardly ever used code words about Scalia's ideological or political leanings. In Congress, the initial comments on Scalia by Senator Pete Domenici (R-N.M.) and Congressman Mario Biaggi (D-N.Y.) focused on Scalia's Italian ancestry.[2] Additionally, since Scalia's nomination was paired with the promotion of Rehnquist, a justice with a distinctive commitment to the conservative revival, it is doubtful that Reagan intended Scalia rather than Rehnquist to be the leader of a conservative judicial revolution. Nonetheless, Scalia satisfied three

Reagan administration concerns. He appeared to be at least as conservative as Warren Burger, he wrote in a more forceful prose, and he was from a group of ethnic Catholics important to the electoral success of the Republican party.

Scalia testified before the Senate Judiciary Committee on 5 August 1986. After opening statements of praise from the Republican majority and expressions of concern about some of his past writings from Democrats, Scalia began to answer questions. In questioning spread over six hours, Scalia reiterated his desire for more specificity in congressional actions delegating power to the agencies; expressed his views on the selection of administrative law judges, the legislative veto, standards for the review of agencies, the reliability of legislative history, and executive privilege; and explained his role in the evolution of the FOIA and his views on the statute. He attempted to clarify his opinion in the *CCNV* sleep-in case in response to questions from Senator Joseph Biden (D-Del.) and his opinions in the *CCNV, Ollman,* and *Liberty Lobby* cases in response to questions from Orrin Hatch (R-Utah) and Paul Simon (D-Ill.).[3]

Scalia refused to answer a question posed by Senator Edward Kennedy (D-Mass.) about his position on the *Roe v. Wade* abortion decision. When he indicated that he regarded some precedents as weaker than others, he generated further questions implicitly related to the value of *Roe* as precedent. However, despite later testimony, his exact standard for evaluating the strength of precedent remained unclear. He refused to address specific questions about affirmative action, the constitutional right of privacy, and unresolved FOIA issues, because he thought that doing so might impair his impartiality as a justice. A brief comment on religious liberty barely touched on the positions expressed in his prior congressional testimony on the topic. When he did state a position on affirmative action, it was only to say that he disagreed with affirmative action "solely on racial or ethnic grounds, and not on the basis of poverty or disadvantage." The only ethical issue, raised by Senator Patrick Leahy (D-Vt.), concerned Scalia's requalification to hear cases about AT&T, a firm to which he had been a consultant. Scalia indicated that he thought the period of disqualification, three years, had effectively separated him from the firm.[4] A few senators also asked about his former membership in an all-male club.

The following day the committee considered testimony from interest groups and individuals. Scalia received the highest evaluation of the American Bar Association Standing Committee on the Federal Judiciary. Distinguished persons testified for him, including Dean Gerhard Casper of the University of Chicago Law School; Lloyd N. Cutler, former counselor to President Carter and at that time a Washington attorney; former solicitor general Erwin Griswold; former secretary of housing and urban development Carla Hills; and President Paul Verkuil of the College of William and Mary, an administrative law expert. Spokespersons for conservative interest groups and individuals also supported the nomination and sought to defend Scalia's record on women's issues. The AFL-CIO raised "concerns" about his positions on executive power and individual rights but did not oppose the nomination.[5]

Because of his Washington University address on affirmative action and his decisions in employment discrimination cases involving women, opposition to the Scalia nomination came from liberal organizations, including the National Organization for Women. Joseph Rauh of Americans for Democratic Action vociferously attacked Scalia's jurisprudential and civil liberties positions. Audrey Feinberg of the Nation Institute provided a statement thoroughly criticizing almost all of Scalia's positions as "extremist." Other opposition came from Kate Michelman of the National Abortion Rights Action League, Robert L. Maddox of Americans United for Separation of Church and State, and Peter Weiss of the Center for Constitutional Rights. A pair of disgruntled litigants also testified against him.[6] The committee voted unanimously to support his confirmation.

Senate debate on the nomination of Scalia was perfunctory. The Senate first attended to the Rehnquist nomination. During the Rehnquist debate, Howard Metzenbaum, a liberal Democratic senator from Ohio, and Jeff Bingaman, a senator from New Mexico, announced that they would vote for Scalia because of his "fitness." They refused to consider his conservatism. When the Senate took up the Scalia nomination, twelve senators spoke. Strom Thurmond and Orrin Hatch provided a detailed recounting and defense of the Scalia record. The only doubts expressed about Scalia came from Joseph Biden, who questioned Scalia's reluctance to answer doctrinal questions during his hearing and questioned whether Scalia would adhere to "settled doctrine"; and from Edward Kennedy. Kennedy thought Scalia "insensitive" to women's rights and was "concerned" about the nominee's positions on the constitutionality of independent agencies and on the delegation doctrine. However, he thought it "difficult to maintain that Judge Scalia is outside the mainstream." Carl Levin (D-Mich.) expressed satisfaction about Scalia's personal letters to him which had cleared up doubts about an ethical situation. With every Democratic senator voting yea, the vote for confirmation was 98 to 0.[7]

The ease of Scalia's confirmation should come as no surprise, because the conditions commonly associated with failed or difficult nominations did not exist. Reagan was popular. The Republicans controlled the Senate. Scalia had the expected experience and connections, and his political activity elicited none of the racial charges heard during the divisive Rehnquist nomination hearings. The interest groups objecting to Scalia did so only on ideological grounds, but the Senate Democrats could not consider Scalia's ideology as relevant in light of their disavowal of ideological hostility to Rehnquist.[8]

THREE PROPOSITIONS ABOUT SCALIA'S JURISPRUDENCE

Regardless of the political reasons affecting Reagan's nomination of Scalia and the Senate's acquiescence in the nomination, the meaning of the nomination for American politics and political thought can only be discerned by a close examination of the justice's political message. However, as noted in chapter 2, above, at the time of his appointment to the Supreme Court Scalia had not spoken on many of the most contentious civil rights and liberties issues in modern American politics. To explain how he drew upon his pre-Court experience to construct a more comprehensive personal narrative with a distinctive conservative political vision, I draw upon his previous experience to formulate three propositions to explain his political message as a Supreme Court justice:

First—as might be predicted from his connections to conservative interests, his service to Republican administrations, and his voting behavior as a D.C. Circuit judge—Scalia's voting behavior as a Supreme Court justice can be expected to indicate a robust allegiance to the principles of the contemporary conservative revival, especially the principles stated by Ronald Reagan. His votes would thus be instruments that he might use to advance his conservative political ideology or attitudes.[9]

Second, when writing legal opinions for the Court, Scalia can be expected to offer reasons also based on his conservative attitudes. Because of his exposure to Reasoned Elaboration jurisprudence at Harvard Law School and his reliance on this mode of legal discourse in some of his D.C. Circuit opinions, his Supreme Court opinions might feature a modification and expansion of Reasoned Elaboration as a means of expressing his conservative attitudes. Thus, my second proposition is that he is likely to use Reasoned Elaboration as an instrument to communicate his conservative policy choices, to construct opinions to legitimate his conservative attitudes, and to provide legal doctrines to guide the solution of similar future political problems by judges and other legal decisionmakers. Also, his use of Reasoned Elaboration jurisprudence—a discourse—should convey his presuppositions about the proper conduct of American politics which *add* a special meaning to his general attitudinal conservatism, thereby enriching his political vision.

Third, Scalia should offer more than votes and arguments that define instrumental solutions to contemporary political conflicts. His votes and opinions also might assume the legitimacy and propriety of a regime that functions under the rule of law. Thus, he might offer a rule-based theory of politics. Additionally, he might use law to discipline inappropriate uses of liberty, in order to advance his preferred vision of political order. Yet he might never question the use of legalities as means for the expression of power and the constitution of order in the regime. Seeing political problems and defining his attitudes through the law could be part of his political vision. Therefore, he would accept the proposition that law "constitutes" politics or is an effective means by which a regime can structure, interpret, and control political conflicts.

SCALIA'S VOTING BEHAVIOR

Does Scalia's voting behavior as a Supreme Court justice indicate a robust allegiance to the conservative revival? Votes provide a measure of a justice's preference among possible instrumental outcomes for cases and are an indicator of the justice's self-conscious, strategic choices to create a legal legitimacy for the political interests of a litigant. Although tactical voting to advantage personal power in transactions with other justices is not unknown, justices most commonly vote to send a message about the propriety of a litigant's actions to other persons in the regime. Votes thus tell the story of a justice's attitudes about the allocation of valued interests among the parties in a case. Also, because decisions of the Court often have a broad political impact, the vote signals a justice's support for a vision of the institutional structure of politics and a pattern of relations between state and indi-

Table 3.1   Supreme Court Justices Ranked by Percentages of Liberal Votes, 1986–1992 Terms

Justice(s)	Total	Criminal Process	Civil Rights	First Amendment	Due Process	Privacy	Attorneys	Unions	Economic Activity	Judicial Power	Federalism	Taxes	No. of Votes
Marshall	77.2	88.7	94.0	86.2	76.5	70.0	82.4	69.0	69.3	52.7	65.0	60.0	692
Brennan	75.3	87.6	91.6	85.2	80.6	62.5	86.7	61.9	66.7	46.8	63.3	66.7	580
Blackmun	64.6	63.4	82.2	72.0	70.0	57.1	81.8	56.3	56.9	50.0	63.0	76.7	934
Stevens	64.3	72.5	69.9	68.0	70.7	64.3	77.3	50.0	63.4	50.0	53.7	51.6	936
Souter	50.1	40.2	49.1	76.2	37.5	40.0	42.9	36.4	51.5	54.5	57.1	75.0	341
White	43.7	29.5	41.6	32.0	46.3	21.4	39.1	40.6	52.2	48.1	69.1	93.5	939
Kennedy	41.6	28.9	39.8	48.1	32.0	25.0	50.0	27.3	49.6	46.2	52.5	77.3	700
Powell	40.8	27.3	56.0	46.2	50.0	100.0	0.0	60.0	50.0	13.3	66.7	80.0	157
O'Connor	39.3	29.5	39.7	42.7	43.9	42.9	34.8	31.5	41.9	43.2	53.8	54.8	933
Thomas	38.8	22.6	27.5	35.7	20.0	33.3	33.3	33.3	41.8	50.0	66.7	60.0	214
Scalia	37.8	27.7	32.8	35.1	29.3	33.3	30.4	37.5	46.2	36.9	61.8	77.4	932
Rehnquist	33.0	19.4	26.8	21.9	29.3	25.0	30.4	34.4	47.2	36.1	52.7	80.6	938
Court mean	52.9	45.5	53.9	53.3	51.9	43.0	53.3	44.9	53.3	45.4	61.3	72.4	8296

Source: Data from Harold J. Spaeth, "United States Supreme Court Judicial Database, 1953–1992 Terms" [computer file], 5th release (East Lansing: Michigan State University, Department of Political Science [producer]; Ann Arbor: Inter-University Consortium for Political and Social Research [distributor], 1994.
Note: Nonparticipations and cases not classified in the United States Supreme Court Judicial Database are excluded from the calculation. Cases are defined by citation number.

viduals. More specifically, by examining his votes, one can reach preliminary conclusions about my first proposition.

After his appointment to the Supreme Court, Scalia quickly established himself as a justice inclined to act in accord with the contemporary popular definition of a conservative justice.[10] This definition measures conservatism by the extent to which justices' voting patterns are critical of the political aims of the New Deal and the newer public interest liberalism. Therefore, a conservative vote is a vote against the claims of "outsider" or "underdog" litigants, including criminal defendants, civil liberties claimants, racial or ethnic minorities, women seeking equal protection, the poor, and economic underdogs such as employees, debtors, bankrupts, consumers, and unions. A conservative vote also is one cast against the national government in federalism cases, against the extension of federal judicial power, in favor of attorney regulation by government, or against the federal government in taxation cases. These patterns, defined in the United States Supreme Court Judicial database coding scheme, have been used to evaluate the ideological direction of Scalia's votes. Table 3.1 presents the liberal percentage of Scalia's vote for the 1986 to 1992 terms in all cases decided by signed opinion or lengthy per curiam opinion, with or without oral argument.[11]

As table 3.1 discloses, in all votes and in each specific category of votes—except federalism and federal taxation cases—Scalia has cast his votes in a conservative direction. Although Chief Justice William Rehnquist has been the Court's most conservative voter overall, Scalia has been the second most conservative overall, and the most conservative, second most conservative, or third most conservative voter on criminal procedure, civil rights, First Amendment, due process, privacy, attorney-related, economic, and judicial power issues. His voting has been more conservative, both overall and in these categories, than has that of Thurgood Marshall, William Brennan, Harry Blackmun, John Stevens, David Souter, Byron White, Anthony Kennedy, Lewis Powell, and Sandra O'Connor. However, Scalia has not been nearly as conservative a voter on federalism and taxation issues. On these issues he has been slightly more liberal than the average for the Court as a whole. His votes on federalism have indicated a commitment to federal power over state power in about three of every five cases. This has put Scalia at odds with the many conservatives hostile to the nationalization of policymaking associated with the New Deal and public interest liberalism. He also has been slightly less conservative in voting on federalism issues than have the Reagan administration Court appointees O'Connor, Rehnquist, and Kennedy. In about three of every four votes on taxation issues Scalia has supported the federal government and the decisions that its Internal Revenue Service has made against taxpayers.

Scalia's voting patterns have aligned him closely with the other Reagan and Bush administration appointees to the Court. From the start of the 1986 term through the end of the 1992 term, he served on five "natural courts"—each defined by a period in which the membership of the Court was stable.[12] Tables 3.2 through 3.6 contain matrices of the percentage of interagreement among pairs of justices in votes on cases decided by the Court. The cases include those decided with signed opinion, by equally divided vote, or by lengthy per curiam decision, with or without oral argument, during the period of the natural court. The matrices are constructed from the "United States Supreme Court Database" according to procedures developed by John Sprague. First, the pair of justices having the highest percentage of agreement is identified. Then a third justice having the highest agreement score with either of the original pair is located. Positions two and three from the left of the table are assigned, respectively, to the justice from the original pair who has the highest agreement percentage with the third member and to the third member. The other justice in the original pair occupies the first position from the left. The next position is allocated to a remaining justice with whom the third justice has the highest

Table 3.2   Supreme Court Interagreement Percentages, 1986 Term

Justice	Br	Ma	Bm	Sv	Wh	Rh	Sc	O'C	Po
Brennan (Br)	—	94.4	83.4	74.2	49.1	40.6	51.3	50.3	57.2
Marshall (Ma)		—	80.3	71.1	47.2	39.4	49.4	47.2	55.3
Blackmun (Bm)			—	74.4	62.8	54.1	59.5	59.2	67.9
Stevens (Sv)				—	61.4	49.1	60.6	58.2	60.1
White (Wh)					—	84.9	81.9	76.6	81.0
Rehnquist (Rh)						—	86.5	84.3	83.0
Scalia (Sc)							—	79.4	78.1
O'Connor (O'C)								—	81.6
Powell (Po)									—

Source: Data from Spaeth, "Supreme Court Judicial Database."
Note: Court cohesion = 67.1 percent; Sprague criterion = 83.6 percent.

Table 3.3   Supreme Court Interagreement Percentages, Early 1987 Term

Justice	Rh	Wh	Sc	O'C	Sv	Bm	Br	Ma
Rehnquist (Rh)	—	100.0	95.7	91.7	87.5	87.5	73.9	70.8
White (Wh)		—	95.7	91.7	87.5	87.5	70.8	70.8
Scalia (Sc)			—	95.7	82.6	82.6	69.6	62.5
O'Connor (O'C)				—	87.5	87.5	73.9	70.8
Stevens (Sv)					—	91.7	87.0	83.3
Blackmun (Bm)						—	87.0	83.3
Brennan (Br)							—	95.7
Marshall (Ma)								—

Source: Data from Spaeth, "Supreme Court Judicial Database."
Note: Court cohesion = 84.0 percent; Sprague criterion = 92.0 percent.

Table 3.4   Supreme Court Interagreement Percentages, Middle of 1987 Term through 1989 Term

Justice	Br	Ma	Bm	Sv	Wh	Kn	Sc	Rh	O'C
Brennan (Br)	—	95.8	83.3	78.5	60.8	58.5	58.1	52.9	55.3
Marshall (Ma)		—	80.3	77.0	58.0	54.4	53.5	49.3	52.1
Blackmun (Bm)			—	74.6	68.9	67.0	61.7	62.5	64.1
Stevens (Sv)				—	69.7	64.4	63.3	50.4	65.9
White (Wt)					—	84.8	80.2	84.4	78.5
Kennedy (Kn)						—	91.1	88.3	87.1
Scalia (Sc)							—	88.1	86.0
Rehnquist (Rh)								—	86.4
O'Connor (O'C)									—

Source: Data from Spaeth, "Supreme Court Judicial Database."
Note: Court cohesion = 70.4 percent; Sprague criterion = 85.2 percent.

agreement percentage; this procedure continues until all justices are positioned. Consequently, the matrices represent interagreement, not a left-to-right ideological spectrum of the Court.[13] As can be seen in tables 3.2 to 3.6, Scalia agreed most frequently with Rehnquist during the 1986 term and the 1990 term, with Kennedy during the period from the middle of the 1987 term through the 1989 term, and with Rehnquist, White, and O'Connor during the eight-justice Court that operated at the beginning of the 1987 term. He agreed least with

Table 3.5   Supreme Court Interagreement Percentages, 1990 Term

Justice	O'C	So	Kn	Sc	Rh	Wh	Bm	Ma	Sv
O'Connor (O'C)	—	91.1	87.7	80.6	83.2	76.8	67.2	59.2	60.0
Souter (So)		—	86.5	84.7	85.7	82.1	70.0	59.8	59.8
Kennedy (Kn)			—	86.8	86.1	74.0	63.9	59.0	59.8
Scalia (Sc)				—	87.1	78.2	62.1	58.1	54.8
Rehnquist (Rh)					—	81.6	59.2	54.4	52.8
White (Wh)						—	72.8	68.0	65.6
Blackmun (Bm)							—	87.2	80.0
Marshall (Ma)								—	86.4
Stevens (Sv)									—

Source: Data from Spaeth, "Supreme Court Judicial Database."
Note: Court cohesion = 72.6 percent; Sprague criterion = 86.3 percent.

Table 3.6   Supreme Court Interagreement Percentages, 1991—1992 Terms

Justice	Sc	Th	Rh	Kn	So	Wh	O'C	Bm	Sv
Scalia (Sc)	—	89.4	85.7	83.5	80.9	77.6	78.1	57.2	57.4
Thomas (Th)		—	85.6	81.0	76.7	75.9	80.6	60.0	56.0
Rehnquist (Rh)			—	85.2	78.0	83.5	79.7	64.0	57.4
Kennedy (Kn)				—	83.9	82.3	81.0	70.0	67.5
Souter (So)					—	81.4	78.4	79.1	70.8
White (Wh)						—	73.4	69.5	65.0
O'Connor (O'C)							—	70.8	66.7
Blackmun (Bm)								—	85.2
Stevens (Sv)									—

Source: Data from Spaeth, "Supreme Court Judicial Database."
Note: Court cohesion = 74.9 percent; Sprague criterion = 87.5 percent.

Marshall during the 1986 through 1989 terms and least with Stevens during the 1990 term.

To identify bloc voting within the Court, Sprague applied a criterion that measures the strength of agreement among the justices. It is calculated by averaging the percentage of agreement for all pairs of justices serving on a natural court. To this average, which he called a court cohesion percentage, one-half the difference between that score and 100 is added to determine the "Sprague criterion." When a subgroup of pairs of justices have a percentage of cohesion greater than the Sprague criterion for a natural court, a bloc is presumed to exist.[14]

The application of the Sprague criterion to the cohesion averages for subgroups of the interagreement matrices indicates that Scalia joined blocs with Rehnquist and White and a separately identifiable bloc with O'Connor and Powell during the 1986 term. During the brief eight-person natural court early in the 1987 term, Scalia joined a bloc with O'Connor, Rehnquist, and White. In the next natural court, from the mid-1987 term through the 1989 term, Scalia joined a majority bloc with Kennedy, O'Connor, Rehnquist, and White. During the 1990 term, he joined in bloc behavior only with Rehnquist, as a separate bloc comprising Kennedy, O'Connor, and Souter formed. In the natural court that existed during the 1991 and 1992 terms, a very conservative court but one with factions that realigned themselves differently on different issues, he joined a bloc with the newly appointed Clarence Thomas. Scalia has never joined blocs with Blackmun, Brennan, Marshall, or Stevens. His votes thus normally have aligned him with other appointees of Republican presidents.[15]

Christopher Smith has argued that Scalia's pattern of voting with the other conservative justices did not always result in victories for a conservative political agenda. Smith contends that Scalia often has written opinions containing language that other conservatives could not accept or that personally irritated them. Consequently, the justice could not lead a conservative revival inside the Court. Nevertheless, despite frequent opinions concurring with his fellow conservatives rather than offering them his outright support, he has remained an ally of the Reagan and Bush administration appointees: Rehnquist, O'Connor, Kennedy, Souter, and Thomas. Also, as the overall pattern of voting in the Court indicates, Scalia has not contributed to what Smith has called "conservative disappointment."[16] The Republican appointees allied together, isolated Brennan, Blackmun, and Marshall in a majority of cases, and directed overall Court voting toward the conservative pole. Scalia might not have led a conservative Court or voted conservative in every case or on every issue, but he certainly has helped make a conservative Court.

Consequently, Scalia's voting record has often restricted the instrumental use of judicial power while expanding governmental discretion. His votes, in tune with the Reagan administration's political agenda, present a tale of opposition to the extension of personal expressive rights and the rights of criminal defendants, and to legislative and judicial efforts to promote minorities' rights to the equal protection of the laws. Although cases involving combinations of issues, as well as his personal preferences and support for the federal government in federalism and taxation issues, sometimes have caused Scalia to cast liberal votes, he far more frequently has joined Rehnquist and Thomas as the most stalwart conservatives of a conservative court. Scalia thus has contributed to the Rehnquist Court's pattern of moving American law to the side of the state and away from support for groups seeking greater access to the political process or greater judicial defense of their political liberties claims. However, the voting data tell little about whether his votes against economic regulation reflect his discernment of a "bureaucracy problem" as opposed to a "Congress problem" in American politics. Also, on the question of federalism, he has not sided with the conservative position in a majority of the cases in which he cast a vote. According to the data, and in support of the first proposition, he has used his votes as an instrument for the advancement of some but not all of the policy objectives of contemporary political conservatism.

THE INSTRUMENTAL DIMENSIONS OF LEGAL DISCOURSE

William F. Harris II began a recent study of constitutional interpretation by stating, "American constitutional interpretation takes for granted the elemental preposterousness of its subject—the presumption that a political world can be constructed and controlled with words."[17] My second proposition, above, is that Scalia's words, particularly his use of Reasoned Elaboration jurisprudential arguments in his opinions, are the vehicle he has used to communicate his conservative policy choices and to legitimate his conservative attitudes about the control of the political world to others, especially to lawyers and political elites. In Scalia's words, judicial opinions are the "central forum of current legal debate," and transform the Court's reports "from a mere record of reasoned judgment into something of a History of American Legal Philosophy with Commentary."[18] However, the legal context in which he has developed his arguments has been framed by his attitudes. His opinions are arguments that bear "the impress of social ideologies."[19] Because opinion writing is a sociopolitical process of writing for others, the logic of legal argumentation—or discourse—is a political variable affecting how other persons understand the political vision offered by a judge. Opinion or discourse analysis recognizes the instrumental dimension of the words in judicial opinions—the use of language as part of a self-conscious, strategic effort by a justice to justify his attitudes and to present doctrines that offer specific directions to other persons, especially the legal elites, in the regime. The instrumental argument in an opinion, therefore, is the vehicle that tries to shape various political, social, and economic relationships and gives order to society.[20] It is political in its use of words as a tool to regulate (by defining crime and civil wrongs), to define a status or legitimate a status (e.g., married, mentally ill), and to define rational behavior (such as the principles of "due care" in personal injury law or *mens rea* [intent] in criminal law). As a kind of tool for ordering society, instrumental opinion argument defines the propriety of specific rules that govern conflicts or episodes in the lives of persons and that penalize those who fail to conform to the rules. In the words of Peter Goodrich, "It is the visible surface or icon of a more complex source of belief, order and unity."[21] Therefore, the aim of judicial opinions is to change behavior toward a political vision of what is "good" or just for society.

Besides having an instrumental goal, the arguments in judicial opinions have a special temper. As suggested by the social theorist Pierre Bourdieu, the opinions of a justice are a function of the specialized discourse of a "field of practice." The legal profession, or what Bourdieu labels the "juridical field of practice," is a partially autonomous political space filled with the institutions, professional personnel, and special language of the law, a field of relations relatively independent of external pressures and determinations. "Practice," or the physical and verbal relational acts of legal professionals, features an instrumental discourse distinct from that used in the general political universe, a discourse developed from texts such as the Constitution, precedent, statutes, legislative records, case briefs, and academic arguments about the role of courts. Knowledge of the special discourse gives power to legal professionals when political conflicts center on legal and constitutional rules. Thus, the legal struggles about the language of the law within the professional field of practice represent a specialized form of political struggle about the construction of an instrumental definition of the roles of the state and individuals.[22]

The writing of an opinion by a supreme court justice is a specialized practice by which the justice, with relative autonomy from external politics, crafts the rules of law to accomplish personal political goals such as stability or change in the political power of the legal profession, the institutional structure of politics, and the pattern of relations between governments and individuals. However, because of the intellectual constraints stemming from their professional education, the justices use professional legal arguments to emphasize a need for the certainty of legal rules as a control on self-interested political behavior. From their vantage point, rules of law seem to offer a reliable, efficient, and simplified method for the management or discipline of interests and the encouragement of cooperation among the officials of the state. Consequently, the justices and other officeholders in the constitutional regime associate rules of law with a fair political process and a better political future.[23]

Despite the justices' willingness to accept the instrumental use of law, since World War II they have struggled over differences of belief regarding the best way to use law, especially constitutional law, to improve life in the regime. Despite the unique modes of legal argumentation offered by some of the individual justices and academics, two pivotal discourses about the certainty of the Constitution and the rule of law emerged.[24] Several scholars have examined the connection of judicial arguments and democratic theories, and they have described how pragmatic political philosophy and the reaction to it from more rationalist circles conditioned the development of streams of jurisprudential thought.[25] One stream of pragmatic legal thought, identified here as "pragmatic liberalism," accepted the value of human autonomy or liberty as the foundation of American politics, but it also assailed the idea that legitimate laws had to be unquestionable and certain. Reacting against pragmatic liberalism, Reasoned Elaboration posited a more rule-bound politics governed by precise and unassailable legal principles.

Pragmatic Liberalism and the Legacy of the Warren Court

Pragmatism is an American philosophy that appeared in the early twentieth century, but not all pragmatists agree on a common dogma. Nevertheless, sharing a faith in the principle of individual autonomy or liberty, they normally believe in the importance of action and experimentalism rather than idealism or deductive reasoning. Pragmatists find that the essential principles necessary for the good life for humans are not known. Principles are uncertain and should be discovered by experience, observation, experiment, or the evaluation of proposals and projects. Therefore, pragmatists construct the good life by a political process in which competent and autonomous citizens are important. Pragmatists thus regard public life, democratic political argument, open participation and fair deliberation, and egalitarian processes as essential in order to define the morality, economic arrangements, and role of the state.[26]

These values worked their way into the political thought and practice of the New Deal, into recent public interest liberal thought, and—through Legal Realist jurisprudence—into American legal discourse.[27] Pragmatic liberal jurisprudence refused to identify law with any foundational ethical principles other than the recognition of human autonomy and dignity. It sought, through empirical study, to disclose the functions of law in a way that might generate the information necessary for the progressive improvement of the legal and political order. In addition to rejecting a formal certainty for law, pragmatic liberal law rested on four supporting principles:[28]

First, pragmatic liberals viewed the law as an instrument for use in furthering the enhancement of personal dignity. Through an instrumental law that guided judicial choice, pragmatists sought change toward an "improved" or "reconstructed" regime that would eliminate political practices blocking the achievement of its foundational goals of equal dignity and the protection of personal autonomy under law for all groups in society. Government was to correct the unfair or imbalanced exercise of power by some interests which adversely affected other interests.[29] Pragmatic liberal law was an essential instrument in helping public officials achieve social justice. Second, pragmatic law approached moral principles with uncertainty. Dubious of the theoretical certainty of any principle, it was instead a method for discerning ethical standards that might be used in the improvement of specific, "local" problems confronting the conditions of some person or group. Therefore, law was to be a contextual instrument for problem resolution rather than a fixed rationale governing human conduct across a range of specific contexts.

Third, pragmatic liberalism held that law was best appreciated through an empirical methodology or inductive logic. Thus, finding solutions to case conflicts meant experimentation and tinkering with the materials of the law. Law was not a bundle of abstract principles or formal rules, ascertainable through a deductive logic, that could be applied to a specific conflict. Pragmatic law rejected any commitment to essential truths; it sought justice for individuals. Finally, the pragmatic liberal approach was practical.[30] For pragmatic liberals, truth or

meaning in legal conflicts was found in individual and social consequences, not in the "correct" application of procedures or rules. Thus,
rather than apply rigid procedural rules and look to established rules of
law for guidance in the resolution of conflicts, pragmatic liberals focused on devising conventional rules of decisionmaking to resolve legal
cases. In particular, they were conscious of how law might generate
outcomes that satisfied positive popular aspirations and educate persons in the skills deemed essential for democratic citizenship.[31]

The introduction of pragmatism into American legal thought did not
mean the abandonment of a reliance on law as a force for social and
political order. This is most explicit in the legal writings of pragmatist
philosopher John Dewey.[32] Order was no longer to depend on a command theory of law; rather, law was to provide "working hypotheses" to
be "constantly tested by the way in which they work out in application
to concrete situations." Dewey's hypothesis was that law could grow
and improve through human action toward the achievement of the
foundational goal of individual autonomy. Yet, as Dewey noted, a theoretical uncertainty in the law did not mean a practical uncertainty. A
theoretically certain or determinant law meant that the law should be
assumed to be a fair, neutral, intelligible, and comprehensive expression of a representative political choice and should be applied in a
stable and predictable manner. Law required interpretation only if it
had been written in unintelligible or contradictory language. A belief in
practical certainty regarded the law as less determinant. Law might be
changed to accommodate the need to address social problems rather
than "flow with formal logical necessity from antecedently known
premises." Although law still needed to have a regularity "to enable
reasonable persons to foresee the legal import of their acts,"[33] a devotee
of practical certainty such as Dewey refused to recognize that the interpretation of law entailed a deductive process resulting in an intelligible
rule. Instead, the law was to be an empirical discipline devoted to
"experiments" with laws or the consideration of alternative interpretations toward a social need—an emancipated and self-reliant people and
practical rules of conduct for everyday life.[34] Therefore, although it
rejected the need for a logical rationale and a certainty based upon a
series of philosophical premises, pragmatism sought a law with a *practical certainty.*

Originating in Justice Harlan Stone's *Carolene Products* footnote 4,
pragmatic liberal legal arguments found their way into the opinions of
Chief Justice Earl Warren and of Justices William Brennan and Thur-

good Marshall on matters of constitutional law.[35] Pragmatic liberalism matured in Warren's proposition that American constitutional politics could progress only if there was progressive cooperation among
equals.[36] Warren, Brennan, and Marshall adopted pragmatic liberal
arguments to reach a transcendent outcome, a vision of an egalitarian
society, when they interpreted the Constitution.[37] This vision assumed
that political leaders should not adopt policies or practices that fail to
treat people with equal dignity and respect or that prevent citizens
from participating in political decisionmaking.

To promote their vision, these justices' instrumental arguments
placed a priority on rights. The attention to rights had a dual character.
They wanted to eliminate from the American political process systemic
bias against disadvantaged groups or interests. Therefore, they criticized the failure of American politics to include some disadvantaged
groups, and they sought judicial remedies—a kind of experimentalism—for political failure. Also, they wanted to build a future society on
the transcendent value of human dignity, which they found was a basic
principle expressed in the text of the Bill of Rights and the Equal
Protection Clause. Consequently, in their opinions they expressed
skepticism that unregulated markets would be truly competitive, and
they thought that personal rights should have priority over the efforts
of elected leaders or a majority to enforce a definition of the good life.[38]
The measure of good law was how effectively it protected and encouraged human dignity. Concern with theoretical certainty in law thus was
replaced by concern with the creation of practical measures to expand
personal autonomy.

To this end, Warren, Brennan, and Marshall aimed at a reconstruction of law to protect certain rights as well as equality, which they saw
as fundamental for achieving greater personal dignity.[39] Any limitations
upon or disadvantages to the fundamental rights of a classifiable group
of people should be closely examined by courts, or given "strict scrutiny." The interference will be presumed to be invalid unless the state
bears the burden of proving that the limitation on rights was "compelling," or necessary to meet a critical governmental objective using the
least restrictive means available. Brennan and Marshall endeavored to
use the "compelling state interest" standard to protect—as fundamental First Amendment rights—rights of voting and participation in politics, and the equal protection of various disadvantaged groups.[40] Brennan and Marshall held that a state could justify affirmative action
legislation or limitations on freedom of speech when such legislation

would both advance the fair treatment of a disadvantaged minority and protect their transcendent right to human dignity and autonomy from the effect of majoritarian policies.[41] Although generally supporting strict scrutiny standards, they sometimes used a less stringent standard of scrutiny in majority opinions supporting the rights claims of women and some other distinctive minorities.[42]

Brennan and Marshall joined their emphasis on reconstruction of law to protect rights and equality, and the contextual or "local" resolution of the scope of rights and equality, using the tiers of scrutiny doctrines with a respect for legal experimentalism in the name of the protection of rights and equality. Warren, indeed, was something of the godfather of the experimental approach through his development of the *Miranda* requirement to protect the rights of persons subjected to custodial interrogation.[43] Also, these justices favored experimental or creative applications of rights and equality doctrine, as with their opinions or votes in critical cases about the application of scrutiny doctrine to gender classifications, legitimacy of birth classifications, school desegregation, public and private affirmative action programs, the incorporation of Bill of Rights guarantees into Fourteenth Amendment due process, and the fundamental right to privacy and other substantive due process rights.[44] Finally, all three justices concerned themselves more with consequences and the future than with orderly procedures. In racial segregation cases and legislative apportionment, Warren found no reason to maintain doctrines that he thought created harmful consequences for the regime. He and his two like-minded colleagues wanted to use legal argument as an instrument in the development of the more egalitarian society that they envisioned.[45]

Reasoned Elaboration

No sooner had pragmatic liberalism affected legal interpretation than it attracted criticism. From neo-Aristotelian sources and then from rationalists with an affinity for the value of the certainty of ideals or faith in principle, the pragmatic roots of Legal Realism and allied approaches to constitutional law came under immediate attack. Based on a modification and elaboration of the traditional concern with legal certainty, an alternative vision of courts as a less active instrument of policy change and as an instrument for the legitimation of a stable political consensus emerged. It became especially influential in the academic legal community in the later 1950s as law professors, especially at Harvard Law School, examined Supreme Court decisions opposing racial segregation and developed the jurisprudential arguments of Reasoned Elaboration.[46] The intellectual tension between pragmatic liberal and Reasoned Elaborationist arguments soon became a central part of the conflict within the Court. Indeed, there were several dimensions to the conflict between the two modes of legal argument, a conflict that Scalia was to enter in 1986.

Many of the central principles of Reasoned Elaboration argumentation emerged from conflicts between Justice Felix Frankfurter and early proponents of aspects of pragmatic liberalism such as Chief Justice Stone. Frankfurter assumed that the good life should be defined by the majority through the political process. Expounding on democratic majoritarianism, he stated, "Our scheme of society is more dependent than any other form of government on knowledge and wisdom and self-discipline for the achievement of its aims."[47] Frankfurter based his view of the judicial role on his understanding of political structure of the regime. He wrote, "Courts are not representative bodies. They are not designed to be a good reflex of a democratic society. Their judgment is best informed, and therefore most dependable, within narrow limits. Their essential quality is detachment, founded on independence."[48] Moreover, "they are confined by the nature and scope of the judicial function in its particular exercise in the field of interpretation."[49] To ensure that courts did not act in a fashion that threatened the policy choices of elected leaders, he proposed that courts rely on the "passive virtues." "Reliance for the most precious interests of civilization . . . must be found outside of their vindication in courts of law. Only a persistent positive translation of the faith of a free society into the convictions and habits and actions of a community is the ultimate reliance against unabated temptations to fetter the human spirit."[50]

Thus, Frankfurter encouraged checking and balancing of the other branches by the Court only in those instances in which there was a breach of specific constitutional rules or clear statutory language and in which there was grievous misconduct that offended the sense of justice embodied in constitutional provisions.[51] Judges had to avoid making policy. Although he admitted that the line between the judicial function and the legislative function was uncertain, he argued that the "only safeguard against crossing the line between adjudication and legislation is an alert recognition of the necessity not to cross it and instinctive, as well as trained, reluctance to do so."[52] Frankfurter feared that courts could displace competent decisionmaking by other institu-

tions of representative government and encourage civic lethargy, dem-
agoguery, and corrupting factional interests. He held that the choices
of experts and leaders should not be easily challenged by groups or
private parties. Courts did not need to open administrative actions to
participation or legal intervention by groups and private parties.[53] He
thought that experts schooled in science and scientific management
should set the policy agenda along the single best course and should
then implement policy, retaining the discretion to adjust it to new
problems. His principles for the organization of the state thus favored
leadership of administration by elected leaders. In the 1930s, James
Landis, a student of Frankfurter who became his coauthor and dean of
the Harvard Law School, applauded the development of a professional
administrative process, expressing the hope "that policies . . . could
most adequately be developed by men bred to the facts" rather than the
"casual office-seeker." He contended that professional administrators
would "fill the need for [the] expertness" that legislatures and courts
lacked.[54]

In their interpretation of economic liberties, Frankfurter and Landis
encouraged competitive markets. However, they desired the policing of
markets by expert administrative bodies to ensure that less virtuous
interests did not corrupt the neutral "laws" of supply and demand
governing the marketplace. Also, they believed that courts should defer
to agency judgments about market policing and should avoid interfering with the market to achieve redistributive policy ends.[55] In market
regulation, Frankfurter generally assumed the supremacy of national
institutions over state and local governmental regulation. However, he
retained a belief in the benefits of some independence in state governments' policymaking.[56]

Since Frankfurter viewed the public good as the community's sense
of virtue, individual actions could not be allowed to threaten the good
life, as defined by the majority. Personal freedom was most secure
when it was "ingrained in a people's habits," or when it was part of the
history and common experience of a people.[57] Under his constitutional
standard, rights were not a resource to be used to permit diverse theories of the good life to flourish. Rights could be used to change the
effect of "habits and the feelings they engender" only when the enforcement of rights taught the public to respect each other and the
community's sense of right, or when the enforcement of rights prevented arbitrary actions detrimental to constitutional governance.[58]
Thus, rights were to be used by courts to reaffirm community con-

sensus. Rights were to foster consent rather than choices among diverse values.

Although Frankfurter and Landis had close connections to the New Deal, their principles of public management and personal rights did not square with the view of the New Deal's pragmatic liberal supporters. In the 1950s a group of legal scholars employed the arguments of Frankfurter and Landis to criticize pragmatic liberalism. In their influential unpublished materials on the legal process, Henry M. Hart Jr. and Albert M. Sacks, both of the Harvard Law School, formulated the interpretive discourse or mode of argument called Reasoned Elaboration.[59] Their understanding of Reasoned Elaboration rested on an antipragmatic faith in the value of a range of ethical principles, and a subordinate faith that the law and the legal process were reasonable expressions of ethical principles that could effectively coordinate society. In their view, law was part of a community member's "understandings about the kinds of conduct which should be avoided if cooperation is to be maintained . . . [and] understandings about the kind of affirmative conduct which is required if each member of the community is to make his due contribution to the common interest."[60] This manifestation of ethics in popular sentiment and consensus, these rules of law, were to act as a control on judicial discretion "so the answer will be the same in all like cases." These rules of law would also "respect . . . the position of the legislature in the institutional system" rather than allow pragmatic policy choices.[61] A similar foundational proposition about the function of law guided other scholars of the era, including Harvard faculty members Paul Freund, Lon Fuller, and Louis L. Jaffe—all of whom were Scalia's teachers—as well as Alexander Bickel of the Yale Law School, and Herbert Wechsler of the Columbia University School of Law. In the late 1950s and early 1960s their ideas would be disseminated across the academic legal community.[62]

From the perspective of most representatives of Reasoned Elaboration, law demanded argument from central propositions rather than a pragmatic, experimental search for legal principles. Its essential or foundational proposition was that judges should avoid value judgments about substantive political outcomes by committing themselves to the rules of law devised through a lawmaking procedure defined by the democratic majority, and by employing traditional modes of judicial decisionmaking established in precedent cases. The assumption was that if judges reasoned from law created by settled institutional procedures, "the answer will be the same in all like cases."[63] This stable rule of law would be an instrument to protect human dignity and autonomy, the same political goal sought by the pragmatic liberals. However, procedural regularity would prevent variations in substantive law and its ethical basis. As explained by Alexander Bickel and Herbert Wechsler, the objective of Reasoned Elaboration was *theoretical certainty* in the law, and the political stability that such certainty provided.[64]

As the 1960s unfolded, Bickel expressed fear of "unvarnished populism" and unrestrained majorities or interests advancing moral claims. He regarded morality as the duty to obey the law of the "manifest constitution" of legal structure and process and related judicial precedents and statutes.[65] A reliance on fixed legal procedures could offset such the pressures he feared and benefit the long-term interests of the majority. Again, the foundational assumption of Reasoned Elaboration is stated by Bickel: "Law is more than just another opinion; not because it embodies all right values, or because the values it does embody tend from time to time to reflect those of a majority or a plurality, but because it is the value of values. Law is the principal institution through which a society can assert its values."[66] If it is made through a popular process, law will reflect and reiterate social and political consensus and accommodate diverse interests.

To support the foundational proposition about the special value of legal processes as a means for the coordination of social and political consensus, defenders of Reasoned Elaboration relied on several subsidiary postulates. The first of these was that a popular consensus of purpose existed in the general social and moral arrangements stated in legal precedents and statutes.[67] They tended to regard law as a coordinated and functioning whole containing substantive agreements and procedures of community collaboration established by prior interaction of interests in representative decisionmaking processes.[68] Society needed "directive" arrangements or understandings which were "authoritative" for the society, and "general" or basic for all in a society.[69] Law rested upon principles, with judgment resting "on analysis and reasons quite transcending the immediate result that is achieved."[70] The principles were to have a "workable clarity" and generality and neutrality that would permit their use as legitimate guides for a category of conflicts. The assumption was that the state's processes, especially legislative action or popular consensus developed through benign pluralist interplay of interests, determined how law could control the range of public and private decisions.[71]

The second subsidiary postulate was that, by reconciling discordant decisions or sorting out problems with legal arrangements when private processes of settlement failed, judges applying Reasoned Elaboration were to settle conflicts rationally. To advance the larger purposes of society the judge would use law and legal procedures to enforce the certain, authoritative standards of the law. The term adopted by Freund for the judicial role, at least in federalism cases, was "umpire."[72] Judicial discretion was to give way to a double "test" or practice. The judge "must elaborate the arrangement in a way which is consistent with other established applications of it. And he should do so in a way which best serves the principles it expresses. If the policy of the specific arrangement is in doubt, the official should interpret it in the way which best harmonizes with more basic principles and policies of the law."[73] Thus, judicial decisionmaking was to be mostly a rational, deductive craft centering on the application of rules derived from existing texts. "Institutional competence," or the application of allegedly neutral craftsmanship by judges, would settle legal conflicts. Underlying this craft or practice was concern with the dangers of human discretion. If the regime was to attain the ideal of justice as fairness and to avoid the "counter-majoritarian difficulty" of pragmatic judicial determination of public policy, it needed limits on official—especially judicial—power.[74]

Also, Reasoned Elaboration proponents held that rational judicial decisions depended on a process allowing reasoned arguments to be made to the judge. In the words of Fuller, "Adjudication is . . . a device which gives formal and institutional expression to the influence of reasoned argument in human affairs." A litigant must "present proofs and reasoned arguments," "assert some principle or principles by which his arguments are sound and his proofs relevant," avoid "naked" demands and expressions of emotion, and assert a claim of right or accusation of fault. Consequently, reasoned decisionmaking depended on partisan advocacy of principles by lawyers, on due process, and on independent judges who wrote reasoned judicial opinions developed in response to the arguments of parties. To the same end, courts should not confront "polycentric tasks" or engage in other social ordering activities that do not involve the judge as a neutral decisionmaker in a bipolar conflict.[75]

Reasoned Elaboration jurists regarded rational legal deduction within an adjudicatory process as a satisfactory method for the dynamic control of some aspects of human behavior. However, they recognized that law had limits and was different from political decisionmaking. Politics was "interested," or not neutral. Politics neglected the enduring value of principled legal judgment.[76] Reasoned Elaboration, according to one of its critics, held that "law and politics must be kept apart as much as possible in theory no less than in practice. The divorce of law and politics is, to be sure, designed to prevent arbitrariness, and that is why there is little argument about its necessity." Additionally, the argument maintained, "Politics is regarded not only as something apart from law, but as inferior to law. Law aims at justice, while politics looks only to expediency. The former is neutral and objective, the latter the uncontrolled child of competing interests and ideologies. Justice is thus not only the policy of legalism, it is treated as a policy superior to and unlike any other."[77]

In their third subsidiary postulate, Reasoned Elaboration jurists rejected the role of science in the development of legal principles. Experimentalism was not needed, especially if it would introduce politics into the evaluation of legal arrangements. There was no need for empirical information and the study of "social facts" about inequality.[78] In the interpretation of case law and statutes, the primary task of the judge was to apply the law as written without regard to political, economic, or social conditions or social facts that contributed to inequality. The judge was not to experiment with the law in light of the social facts or circumstances of the case. When confronting a conflict governed by case law, the judge was to use precedent to reduce uncertainty about the outcomes of conflicts and clarify the principles of law governing social behavior. Rules of law were not to be reformulated or created to address the facts of a particular case.[79] Likewise, the judge was to treat statutes with respect because they were the rules preferred by a democratic majority. Frankfurter argued for the need for judges to rely first on "plain meaning," or "popular meaning, as used in the common speech of men," to define statutory language and protect the majority's political choice. His use of this technique discouraged the introduction of external instrumental political and social demands into the judicial analysis of a statute. But if statutory language was not plain, he was willing to use carefully evaluated legislative history and other sources of information about the intent of the legislature to determine the meaning of the statute.[80]

Reasoned Elaboration jurisprudents also questioned judicial reliance on agency expertise and policy experimentalism. Moving away from the arguments of Landis and the early administrative law opinions of Frankfurter, Louis Jaffe raised questions about agency expertise. He feared that problems such as capture of agencies by the interests they regulated, administrative power-seeking, bias toward stasis in policy, and internal tensions frustrated expert judgment by agencies. Despite doubts about agency expertise, he still thought that expertise was needed for systematic regulation. Therefore, he adopted two positions to foster a "strategic control" of administrators. First, the legislature had to establish the bounds of regulation through the construction of laws that defined precisely the realm of administrative competence. The legislature had to consult with the agency, intervene and settle disputes about agency choices, and insist on precision in agency rules. Second, there had to be comprehensive, simple, and predictable judicial remedies for alleged administrative malfeasance or error. These remedies should be in the hands of a "discreet judge . . . who constantly is aware and respectful of the limits of his role. He feels free only in a rarely appropriate occasion to make a positive contribution toward the fulfillment of statutory objectives." Then Jaffe delineated a series of doctrinal limitations for use by a judge considering judicial review of expert agency decisions. These included statutory limitations on judicial review, the ripeness doctrine, the exhaustion of remedies requirement, the doctrines of standing, the law-fact distinction on reviewable issues, and various common law and statutory rules of jurisdiction. Consequently, any policy experimentalism had to be a decision of the people's representatives, the legislature, rather than the choice of expert administrators or judges.[81]

As a fourth subsidiary postulate, Reasoned Elaboration jurists implied that law should be disciplined in its application. Courts were to abet this goal by institutional resolution of uncertainty using general, directive legal rules. In addition, judges should curtail their discretion in the resolution of uncertain legal arrangements by respecting checks and balances on their power, including procedural rules of decision, precedents in case law, statutes binding their discretion, craft techniques and accepted ideas of official behavior, political checks, and a general prohibition against arbitrary decision.[82] Through these practices, which Bickel called "passive virtues," judges would produce decisions and then explain the reasons for their resolution of the conflict. Failure to consider cases closely and explain the principled nature of their decisions would undermine the legitimacy of their effort.[83]

Reasoned Elaboration argumentation, with its reliance on its initial proposition, on written or positive law, and on a rule-governed judiciary, attempted to inculcate both a theoretical and a practical certainty in law and politics. A legal process functioning through appropriate procedures would respect democratic consensus and laws that guaranteed the fundamental values of democracy. Reasoned Elaborationists assumed that these practices would keep judges out of tense situations of conflict with the political majority and would defend the elite status of the judiciary from involvement in the distasteful features of ordinary political debate. By creating boundaries on permissible judicial decisionmaking, the subsidiary principles of Reasoned Elaboration argumentation assumed that judges would be left to apply relatively clear legal rules to mostly private two-party disputes. These "easy cases" would be decided without a judicial inquiry into the social facts surrounding the case and without discretionary judgments about the meaning of the law.[84]

Despite these claims, Reasoned Elaboration jurisprudence had a political content. In its original form, it was an attempt to use rules, judicial procedures, precedent, and passivity to conserve democratic traditions and majority preferences from assaults by emerging pluralist factions and interests. At its core, Reasoned Elaboration demanded political consent rather than encouraged political choice. Also, its defenders dignified elite jurists with professional expertise, and those with credentials that avouched their "merit." These expert jurists had an advantage in arguing the neutrality of their positions to a court and tended to become the holders of judicial office. Moreover, Reasoned Elaboration was a jurisprudence that preserved the political advantages of the bar and tried to avoid threats to the legitimacy of its power and knowledge from various interests. Yet, despite its professional paternalism, it was not a form of conservative political theory that demanded moral unity in the community or the enforcement of a single set of cultural values. It was not a conservatism that attacked the bureaucratic state or that demanded a rule by elites in a way that foreclosed a politics of interests and personal economic and political opportunism.[85] Therefore, many of the initial proponents of Reasoned Elaboration could feel comfortable with the 1950s and 1960s struggles for civil rights and the battle against McCarthyism.[86] Yet, as chapters 1 and 2 indicate, prior to his service on the Supreme Court Scalia had deployed Reasoned Elaborationist ideas about statutory analysis, respect for the judgments of elected politicians and for agency expertise, and the concept of judicial passivity as a vehicle for the legitimation of conservative politics. Consequently, an examination of the linkage of his often-conservative votes and his modification of Reasoned Elaboration jurisprudence is essential in understanding his political vision as a Supreme Court justice.

Chapter Four

PRESIDENTIAL LEADERSHIP AND THE SEPARATION OF POWERS

Many persons might find the legal dimension of federal policymaking "pale and dull," but Antonin Scalia half-jokingly called it a "field of enormous glamour and excitement; there's blood about it, on every hand."[1] Glamour might not characterize the technical debates about the powers of the branches of the federal government or the powers of federal administrative agencies, but during recent decades the debates have had a bloodiness about them. To gain an advantage in the direction of national politics in an era when neither conservatives nor liberals could gain complete control of national institutions, politicians in one branch have used law as a rapier to slice away the power of the other branches. Antonin Scalia entered this contest to defend the Nixon and Ford administrations against the legal tactics of their critics in Congress, and as a Supreme Court justice he has continued to defend the executive and his earlier thrusts at the problems created by Congress.

Scalia's votes and opinions about the structure of federal governmental institutions have emphasized executive leadership of policymaking. He wants the executive to lead the conservative revival. He has rejected participatory, cooperative, and populist modes of democratic choice as instrumental solutions to the problems of bureaucracy, the Congress, and the loss of political and moral consensus. Although his opinions have indicated a confidence in the expertise of the president and executive administrators, he has found these officials capable of arbitrary and capricious action and subject to undue influence by interest groups. Likewise, he has indicated that executive administrators and Congress can make errant decisions. But his faith in the wisdom of these officials—within their sphere of constitutional authority—has usually been greater than that of most pragmatic liberal judges and the general public.

Scalia's political vision has prioritized the construction of rules of law to promote an efficient state and provide order in the regime. In particular, his conception of the Constitution's schema of separate but competitive branches of government has three distinctive aspects.

First, he has drawn a legal line between the powers of courts and the powers of the other branches. Second, he has been exceedingly protective of executive and administrative agency discretionary powers. Third, he has emphasized that legislative power is confined to the drafting of precise statutes. Because his reading of aspects of the separation of powers has emphasized the need for rules of law to circumscribe power, his position has corresponded with what Louis Fisher called a "formalistic model" of separate powers rather than with a "functional, pragmatic approach."[2] Scalia's opinions in cases centering on governmental powers have reflected a faith that properly designed rules of law can and must order or discipline the governmental sector of the regime. In his definition, the good society is a function of law, as implied by Reasoned Elaboration jurisprudence, rather than a function of the civic virtue of public officials or officials' reliance on normative perspectives not explicitly included in the Constitution or other law.[3] For Scalia, law can make a regime with separated powers work to protect liberty, and law can make the government work effectively for the public.

THE COURTS

In reading the constitutional provisions about the public sector of the national government and its system of separated branches, Scalia has relied on propositions associated with Reasoned Elaboration jurisprudence. Like other proponents of Reasoned Elaboration, Scalia has asserted that judges should avoid value judgments about substantive political outcomes by committing themselves to the rules of an institutional settlement procedure and a substantive legal text democratically defined by the majority. In particular, they should avoid concern with values, for "the Constitution, like a statute, is an authoritative text, and it may well require dispositions that the particular judge, or all judges, or even the vast majority of the citizenry, do not approve."[4] He has also assumed that procedural regularity can prevent variations in substantive law, including those variations that are designed to control imbalances in the power of *some* minority interests and that affect the policies adopted by political institutions. He has adopted the techniques of Reasoned Elaboration argument to elevate procedural concerns, and he has relied on *stare decisis,* or the use of precedents in case law and canons of statutory construction, as well as on a neutral law, and passivity by courts. All of these techniques rest on political values demanding that judges exercise limited personal discretion in construing the language of the Constitution and of statutes. His use of these techniques has permitted the establishment of general rules that restrict political conflict and reproduce the political status quo in the regime. Additionally, four subsidiary postulates of Reasoned Elaboration legal argument—on textual construction and precedents, procedural regularity, neutral law, and judicial passivity—have found their way into his opinions.[5]

Textual Construction and Precedents

Reasoned Elaboration legal argument relies on the postulate that the law pursues popularly established social or moral ends, purposes expressed in the general directive provisions of four kinds of legal texts: the Constitution, statutes, precedents or previous judicial conclusions about the meaning of the law, and administrative agency rules and adjudicated judgments. According to the discourse of Reasoned Elaboration, a regime needs directive arrangements that are authoritative for all persons within it. The methodology that Scalia has used in reading constitutional and statutory texts affirms this postulate. Time and again he has emphasized that judges must be true to the "normal meaning" of the text of the Constitution, treaties, or statutes.[6] Although he has not precisely defined how a judge can determine the normal meaning of the Constitution or a statute, he has lectured those judges and parties who ignore the plain or usual meaning of language and those judges who search for the meaning of statutory texts by reconstructing legislative or administrative intent on the basis of questionable sources.[7] Indeed, because he believes that legislative staff members have often drafted such materials with little oversight by the elected representative, in cases requiring statutory interpretation he has often refused to give credence to legislative sources such as committee reports. He has argued that sources such as legislative debates and legislative history only confound the use of clear statutory text.[8] Rejecting the cautious use of legislative history counseled by Justice Felix Frankfurter and by Henry Hart and Albert Sacks, he once stated in a solo opinion that "the greatest defect of legislative history is its illegitimacy. We are governed by laws, not by the intentions of legislators."[9] Finally, he has sought the abandonment of tests of the constitutionality of claims which required judges to use a technique of analysis demanding inquiry into "subjective" legislative motives.[10] He has rejected these techniques because they often let judges develop general rules of law in a fashion potentially violative of a formal separation of powers. Only in a few disputes over the meaning of constitutional—not statutory—text has he extensively examined historical materials.[11] In statutory interpretation, he only has employed historical documents when he thought that the Court used the legislative history of a statute in an inaccurate fashion.

On a related topic, Scalia has taken a "normal meaning" approach, and often a literal approach, to the reading of administrative law. He has argued that the rulemaking and adjudicatory powers of agencies should conform to the language of the Administrative Procedure Act or other applicable statutes. The APA, he has commented, "means what it says," and it should not be compromised by legal arguments not based on germane language in its text. For example, in a concurring opinion he rejected allowing the retroactive imposition of a rule that would have imposed a cap on hospital wages. He could not locate such a power for the federal agency seeking to impose the rule—the Department of Health and Human Services—in the Medicare statutes. "The issue is whether it is a permissible form of agency action under a particular structure established by the APA," he wrote. Because he thought that the APA did not allow retroactive rulemaking, he concluded that it was not.[12]

Although not an unconditionally loyal to the practice of stare decisis, in dissent Scalia has stated that decisions should respect long-established interpretations or interpretations that are embedded in precedent cases, in order to protect the rule of law, check judicial power, and "prevent the destruction of predictability" in law.[13] Judges should read statutes in ways that attend to precedents, especially precedents elaborating on constitutional provisions or clarifying established interpretations of statutes.[14] For example, in one case he refused to allow the retroactive application of a statute (28 *U.S. Code* § 1961) so a party could collect interest on damages awarded at trial while awaiting the resolution of an appeal in the case because the application had no basis in general precedents and he found no congressional intent to create a special rule.[15] In addition, he used the lack of statutory text as a reason to reject claims of retroactivity for sections of the Civil Rights Act of 1991.[16] However, because he thought that precedent on the retroactive application of constitutional doctrine in case doctrine about federalism supported a flexible evaluation of retroactive state legislation, he offered a solo concurring opinion to a decision allowing the retroactive application of a state law taxing federal retirees.[17] Also, joined by Kennedy and O'Connor, he rejected a majority position on the plain meaning of a criminal forgery statute because it bypassed the meaning of the statutory words "falsely made" established in common law at the time of the legislation and reestablished in later cases applying the statute.[18] Even in negative or dormant Commerce Clause cases, in which an alleged lack of constitutional justification for the "balancing of burdens and benefits" standard made him unwilling to apply it to new kinds of state regulations, he accepted past precedents employing the standard by a "sort of intellectual adverse possession."[19] In a speech he once stated that to neglect precedent would "leave citizens without guidance as to what the law requires." The statement echoed Hart and Sacks's respect for courts' institutional duty to introduce certainty into the law through the clarification of common law.[20]

However, Scalia has abandoned precedent in at least five types of situation: First, he has forsaken precedent in situations in which he thought that the decision in the precedent case was based on a misreading of statutory text. For example, he argued that the permissibility of private affirmative action programs established in *United Steelworkers v. Weber* disregarded the text of Title VII of the Civil Rights Act of 1964. Despite congressional quiescence about the Court's construction of the statute, he considered invalid any precedent that seemed to change the meaning of statutory language as he understood it.[21] He made the same contention in *United States v. Johnson,* when challenging the value of the *Feres v. United States* ruling which prohibited personal injury suits by servicemen and their estates against the federal government.[22] He thought *Feres* wrong because it ignored the "unambiguous text" of the Federal Tort Claims Act. Also, he urged the overruling of a previous decision requiring provisions of the Federal Arbitration Act to be applied by state courts. Agreeing with O'Connor's contention that the prior decision was an erroneous construction of the act, he stated that the practice of stare decisis did not prevent the correction of error.[23]

Second, as will be discussed in greater detail in chapter 9, below, he has disdained precedents employing substantive fundamental liberties drawn from the Due Process Clause of the Fourteenth Amendment. He has regarded these liberties as a judicial creation lacking a basis in the text of the Constitution. When the Court, in *Pacific Mutual Life Insurance Company v. Haslip,* considered whether due process provided a fundamental liberty to obtain punitive damages in personal injury cases, he wrote a solo concurring opinion to separate himself from the use of a fundamental liberties argument in Justice Blackmun's majority opinion. He thought that an Alabama procedure permitting unlimited awards of punitive money damages by jurors did not violate well-established principles of cases at common law preceding the Fourteenth Amendment. He thought that the majority's effort to make the jury's award of damages subject to a Fourteenth Amendment rationality test indiscriminately changed the traditional meaning of constitutional due process to afford "fundamental fairness" to all sorts of new kinds of rights claims. Unlike the majority, which upheld the Alabama practice, he did not apply a constitutional test of the reasonableness of the substantive award. The reasonableness of damage awards was a state legislative matter, and, absent state legislation, "punitive damages assessed under common-law procedures are far from a fossil, or even an endangered species. They are (regrettably to many) vigorously alive. To effect their elimination may well be wise, but it is not the role of the Due Process Clause."[24] When the Court reconsidered the punitive damages issue in a slander of title case (a case about a malicious, disparaging statement about title to property) which centered on ownership of coal lands in West Virginia, Scalia, joined only by Thomas, again argued that punitive damage amounts did not raise substantive due process problems. Courts, he contended, could only eliminate any unfair procedures used in the calculation of damages; they could not define a substantive award as correct. Since the West Virginia jury had followed appropriate instructions on the award of damages, instructions that had passed muster with the trial judge and had been upheld on appeal, he saw no need to enter into an extratextual debate about substantive rights and fundamental fairness to reinforce the *Haslip* precedent. He wanted to "shut the door" on litigation about the fairness of damage awards.[25]

Likewise, Scalia has refused to accept as precedent the cases that draw on the "fundamental liberties" of privacy and personal choice which a majority of the Court has occasionally recognized. Although he has evidenced concern about judicial competency to address privacy rights and abortion, he has been most concerned about fundamental liberties precedents expanding the powers of the judiciary in the separated powers scheme. Therefore, in solo opinions he has opposed applying the precedents that protected a fundamental right to privacy encompassing a woman's decision to obtain an abortion. From his perspective, abortion is a political matter best left to majoritarian decisionmaking in the electoral and legislative arenas, both because "the answers to most of the cruel questions posed are political and not juridical" and because many citizens conceive it to be a political issue.[26] Also, Scalia has been unwilling to reject certain statutes, such as those defining paternity, because of the demand of parties for the protection of a fundamental liberty interest. Because he could not locate a liberty interest "rooted in history and tradition" to permit either a claim by the alleged biological father of a child or a claim by the child to contest legal records that stated, on the basis of parentage definitions in state law, that her mother's husband was her legitimate father, he refused standing to allow a party to employ judicial power to create a right and abrogate a rational state law.[27] He rejected a reading of the Due Process Clause of the Fourteenth Amendment which created standing to assert a right to avoid medical treatment. He found that no substantive due process right "historically and traditionally protected against State interference" to permit judicial discernment of such a right.[28]

Third, Scalia has been willing to overrule any precedent of recent vintage "before state and federal laws have been adjusted to embody it." Thus, contrary to the Court's majority, he has voted to overrule decisions excluding from the penalty phase of a capital criminal case victim impact testimony made at trial and prosecutorial presentation of victim impact statements. Because the precedents were but four and two years old, respectively, because he thought that they lacked a basis in the common law antecedent to the Eighth Amendment and in long-standing societal tradition, because they had been adopted by narrow 5-to-4 margins, and because contemporary opinion supported the inclusion of the statements, the Court could readily reverse the precedents. Thus, he refused to agree that "a constitutional decision with plainly inadequate support *must* be left in place for the sole reason that it once attracted five votes."[29]

Fourth, Scalia has voted against precedent that was contrary to his construction of the historical intent of the Constitution. His rejection of the Court's definition of double jeopardy is evidence of this practice.[30] And fifth, Scalia's use of stare decisis has permitted the overruling of precedents with unacceptable consequences, consequences that cannot be avoided by judges. For example, he sought to overrule a precedent holding that federal criminal law penalizing false statements to federal officers applied to statements made in trials. He argued that the precedent case had the unacceptable consequence of deterring vigorous representation by counsel of a defendant's claims in adversarial criminal proceedings.[31]

The situations in which Scalia has abandoned precedent have offered him the opportunity to adjust precedent to square the law with several contemporary conservative political objectives. The problems he discerned in "liberal" precedents about civil rights laws, abortion and other fundamental liberties, and capital punishment cases illustrate a common practice of the other justices of the Court in the late twentieth century. Like Scalia, they use precedent as an instrument to legitimate their positions to external legal authorities, but they abandon precedent when it conflicts with their ideology or instrumental policy objectives.[32]

Procedural Regularity

Scalia has elevated the examination of procedural concerns as an analytical technique because he wants judges to promote the law as a closed and autonomous system whose development is directed by its own inner rational dynamic. To allow the judge to be a fair umpire, this dynamic would be independent of external political and social power constraints and pressures. Consequently, as he stated in a speech, judges should apply proper process and law, "for in judging, process is a value unto itself, and not (except in a very remote sense) merely a means to achieving a desirable end. The result is validated by the process, not the process by the result."[33] For him, making good or bad policy is the province of the other branches. Scalia has wanted the judiciary to adopt regular procedures to govern its authority. These procedures have to be rationally grounded either in the specific Article III constitutional duties of courts in a separated powers system (as he stated in a solo concurring opinion and a dissenting opinion) or in the authority granted to the judiciary by specific statutory language (as stated in a concurring opinion).[34] Consequently, he dissented when the majority extended the Article III powers of federal courts to penalize parties for bad behavior under Rule 11 of the Federal Rules of Civil Procedure. Although he has recognized that the courts have some inherent powers to regulate litigants, he thinks that there are recognizable limits to the inherent powers of the courts to impose penalties. Although courts might use these powers in ways that exceed the authority granted by Congress to "protect the integrity of their proceedings," as he indicated in a solo dissenting opinion, they cannot use the power outside the confines of the conduct of trials or in consideration of agreements made as part of the parties' withdrawal from litigation.[35] Also, Scalia has not wanted federal courts to use statutory or case management powers to extend suits beyond the initial adversary parties.[36] He objected to a ruling extending the authority of United States magistrates to jury selection, even with the consent of both parties, because it had no statutory basis.[37] Also, unless congressional intent is clear in the statutory text, he has not accepted implied rights of action enabling private litigants to try to enforce statutes in court without governmental intervention. He has refused to imply any private rights of action to challenge governmental law enforcement decisions, and he has refused to allow a court to imply a statute of limitations on an implied private right of action.[38] When he joined Kennedy, O'Connor, and Rehnquist in writing a dissenting opinion about habeas corpus procedures, he indicated that, unless dealing with subjects assigned to the Court's authority by Congress, the Court should not make adjustments in the federal judiciary's procedural rules which create exceptions or diminish the rules' uniformity.[39] Finally, he has argued that only cases between "the government and others" could be assigned to agencies rather than federal courts.[40]

Neutral Law

Reasoned Elaboration employs the analytical technique of reading law as "status neutral" in an endeavor to diminish differences among litigants. The objective of neutrality is to strip political discretion from the judiciary and confine the range of possible judicial experiments with the law. Scalia's treatment of affirmative action issues has contained a reliance on the logic of neutrality.[41] For him, neutrality has meant that distinctive treatment of minorities could only be justified by finding some specific damage to equal treatment or other constitutional rights.[42] Legal remedies can give preference to a group only with evidence of a concrete harm in the past. Relief is not available because "societal attitudes . . . have limited the entry of certain races, or a particular sex, into certain jobs" or because the government or judiciary wishes to change those attitudes.[43] He has stated that the judiciary would damage the idea of equality through almost any use of racial, ethnic, religious, and gender categories.[44] It would "effectively replace the goal of a discrimination-free society" or a status-neutral

world "with the quite incompatible goal of proportionate representation by race and sex in the workplace."[45] The general lesson of his
argument is that law functions best when it ignores the social fact of
cognizable differences among persons.

Judicial Passivity

Finally, in the tradition of Reasoned Elaboration jurisprudence, Scalia
has utilized a variety of standards to induce judicial passivity on policy
matters. He has wanted procedures to free legal analysis from considering the claims of political interests. Relying on many of the techniques of passivity offered by Alexander Bickel, he has tried to limit the
authority of the judiciary. For example, he used techniques of passivity
in some statutory and administrative law matters, such as when finality rules were violated, when Congress amended laws to make a case
moot, when suit was barred because there was no "unequivocal" waiver
of the sovereign immunity of the United States from suits, or when the
case or controversy rule was not satisfied.[46] According to his reading
of constitutional language, the judiciary should not check and balance actions assigned to the other branches—for instance, by ruling in
disputes about issues such as requirements regarding the legislative
house of origin of federal legislation or (as stated in a solo concurring
opinion) the president's liability for his official executive actions such
as the enumeration of persons in the decennial census.[47] His decisions
on standing to sue have sought to limit judicial power in order to
prevent a variety of suits in which individuals have attempted to use the
courts to prescribe constitutional rights, choices that he deems to be
within the province of the legislative or executive branch. Scalia's approach in abortion cases, in which he has argued that the Court has no
business making policy, typify his practice of passivity.[48]

　　Besides citing legal and constitutional reasons for judicial passivity,
Scalia has supported statutes that curtail judicial power. He has supported jurisdictional limitations on the participation of parties in an
appeal when they were not named in the filing.[49] Therefore, he argued
against giving the federal district courts, rather than the U.S. Claims
Court, jurisdiction in a case about the availability of remedies for Medicare disallowances. The majority of the Court had expanded federal
district court power, but Scalia believed that their decision threw readings of statutes about federal Claims Court personal injury jurisdiction
into "chaos."[50] He has wanted to curtail litigation under criteria con-

tained in statutes, as in aspects of a claim of attorney fees made under provisions of the Equal Access to Justice Act, as well as in civil actions under the Racketeer Influenced and Corrupt Organizations (RICO) chapter of the Organized Crime Act of 1970 (as indicated in a solo concurring opinion).[51] In the civil RICO case, he determined that the alleged harm did not fall into the "zone of interests" covered by the statute. Finally, he has argued against the expansion of precedent to justify the judicial consideration of a greater variety of antitrust claims under the Sherman Act.[52] In *Finley v. United States* his opinion for the majority held that precedents and the text of the Federal Tort Claims Act did not extend the Claims Court's jurisdiction to the owner of electric transmission lines as a "pendent party" in a suit alleging that Federal Aviation Administration (FAA) maintenance of an airport caused a fatal aircraft crash. The injured party could only adjudicate the claim against the electric company in state court or—if satisfying diversity of citizenship requirements (i.e., if parties are from different states)—in federal court under state law.[53] Scalia has also refused to grant standing for a federal agency, the Office of Workers' Compensation Programs (OWCP), to appeal a decision on the disability of a worker made by a second federal agency, the Benefits Review Board, because Congress had not specifically assigned standing to the OWCP in cases considered by the Benefits Review Board and because the OWCP could not prove that it had been "adversely affected or aggrieved."[54]

In other efforts to control judicial power, Scalia voted for an opinion of Chief Justice William Rehnquist which held that the Senate's procedures during an impeachment of a judge were not justiciable because choice of procedures was assigned to the Senate by sections of Article I of the Constitution.[55] Scalia voted for an opinion that prevented, for separated powers reasons, litigation to stop governmental payment of appropriated funds.[56] He also supported Rehnquist's majority opinion that treaty language permitted executive officers to abduct a Mexican national for criminal prosecution in the United States.[57] He cast a vote in favor of the justiciability of a suit challenging the method Congress used to assign the number of congressional seats to each state. However, he agreed with sections of Stevens's majority opinion which deferred to the reasonableness of the assignment method used by Congress.[58]

However, Scalia has not seized every opportunity to deny access to the courts. Less in character with his effort to restrict litigation was his vote for Justice Clarence Thomas's majority opinion about standing to challenge governmental benefits programs. A group of white contractors had sued to overturn a Jacksonville, Florida, program setting aside certain public contracts for minority-operated enterprises. After litigation and appeal, the City of Jacksonville revoked the ordinance establishing the program. Despite a claim of mootness, Thomas concluded that the white contractors had suffered a potential injury to their guarantee of constitutional equal protection of the laws because they, at a point in time, could not compete equally for the governmental benefit of a contract.[59] The opinion potentially encouraged the federal courts to assume the justiciability of constitutional challenges to all sorts of benefit and transfer payment programs. In addition, Scalia joined the Court to declare that when parties assert federal rights in state cases, including an equal protection claim about voting rights, the case becomes justiciable in federal court.[60] These votes signaled a willingness to grant limited access to disadvantaged minority interests and public interest groups. However, in each case the final judgment denied the minority or group claims. He thus favored expanded access to the courts as a tactic for the promotion of conservative policies.

Writing for the Court, Scalia limited the application of penalties for frivolous suits under Federal Civil Rule of Procedure number 11 to the offending attorney, not his firm, through a reading of the plain meaning of the rule. He refused to expand the Act of State Doctrine, which prevented suits about the acts of foreign officials, to thwart civil RICO suits against American firms that had bribed Nigerian officials. He determined that statutes permitted federal court litigation against the Republic of Argentina when it defaulted on bond interest payments. He used the constitutional concept of due process to uphold a limitation on the standing of lawyers to challenge fee arrangement restrictions contained in the Black Lung Benefits Act. He dissented when the Court dismissed the applicability of the Sherman Antitrust Act to certain extraterritorial acts. He contended that the law of nations and the language on boycotts in the act gave jurisdiction to federal courts. Conversely, he has expanded the potential of litigants to challenge government corporations for "state action" violations of rights and of equal protection of the laws. For the Court he held that Amtrak, the National Railroad Passenger Corporation, was a governmental entity. In the act creating Amtrak, Congress had placed language that indicated that the corporation was not a governmental entity. After examining the rest of the statute, the history of government corporations, and precedents, he concluded that Amtrak was a governmental unit subject to litigation for alleged infringements of First Amendment rights of commercial speech. Overall, his opinions have implied that he would avoid the use of judicial power when he could find a textual justification for his passivity.[61] Therefore, his Reasoned Elaboration methodology has left disputes about political processes and rights to the executives, legislators, and experts who then can monopolize the writing and reading of the law.

THE EXECUTIVE BRANCH

In addition to using Reasoned Elaboration arguments to justify a restrained judicial role, Scalia has offered another standard for governance of the state: the president should identify, define, and proclaim policies in the community interest, subject to public electoral consent. Executive experts can then determine what is the best course for the implementation of presidential policy and communicate their views to executive and legislative officials. The public can respond to the president's positions, especially at election time, and support or reject the agenda set by the president and refined by executive experts. In executive policymaking, the public thus serves as a sporadic checker rather than as a participant.

The Boundaries of Executive Power

Scalia's assumptions about the Constitution's provisions on separated powers have found their most direct expression in his opinions on the appointment and removal powers of the president, especially his solo dissenting opinion in *Morrison v. Olson*,[62] a case about the authority of Congress to establish special prosecutors to inquire into alleged misbehavior in the executive branch. His dissenting opinion was multifaceted and often digressive, but at the heart of it was a guiding principle. Scalia wanted the law to define sharply the boundaries of these powers of the branches of the federal government in a manner favorable to exclusive executive management of administration. As he wrote in concluding his opinion: "A government of laws means a government of rules. Today's decision on the basic issue of fragmentation of executive power is ungoverned by rule, and hence ungoverned by law."[63]

In asserting the need for a law that formalizes interbranch relations, Scalia's dissenting opinion in *Morrison* scorned the balancing test employed by Rehnquist in the Court's opinion.[64] Because case-by-case balancing of constitutional presidential powers with modifications in these powers made to ensure honest administration did not provide fixed rules to govern political conduct, he found that it made the meaning of executive power uncertain. Unlike James Madison, who found the effort "to mark with precision and boundaries of these departments in the Constitution of the government" to be "greatly over-rated" as a security against political abuses, Scalia wanted positive and certain legal rules.[65] After calling for a positive law of interbranch relations, Scalia's *Morrison* opinion endeavored to define the content of such a law. From the "plain meaning" of Article II, section 1, clause 1, of the Constitution, which states, "The executive Power shall be vested in a President of the United States of America," Scalia deduced that the Constitution provided a realm of exclusive legal powers for a "unitary executive." He wrote, "A system of separate and coordinate powers necessarily involves the acceptance of exclusive power that can theoretically be abused."[66] The argument thus relied heavily on the assumption of exclusive executive prerogative over removals of executive officers, a prerogative defined by Chief Justice William Howard Taft in *Myers v. United States.*[67]

Having discussed the legality of exclusive executive administrative power, Scalia's *Morrison* opinion described how prosecutorial power in criminal cases is exclusively executive because "governmental investigation and prosecution of crimes is a quintessentially executive function."[68] Nevertheless, apparently thinking that this was part of the plain meaning of Article II, he cited no constitutional or statutory support for this position. He then considered whether the statutory provision of a special prosecutor offended the principle of exclusive executive control over an executive task. He decided that it did, stating, "It is ultimately irrelevant *how much* the statute reduces presidential control. The case is over when the Court acknowledges, as it must, that '[i]t is undeniable that the Act reduces the amount of control or supervision that the Attorney General and, through him, the President exercises over the investigation and prosecution of a certain class of alleged criminal activity.'"[69] Because prosecution was an exclusively executive task, the Court had no business trying to consider presidential controls on prosecution. He declared, "It is not for us to determine, and we have never presumed to determine, how much of the purely executive powers of the government should be within the full control of the President. The Constitution prescribes that they *all* are."[70]

In *Morrison* Scalia concluded that the Court does not convincingly establish that the special prosecutor is an "inferior officer" subject to congressional control, performing certain limited duties, and holding an office of limited tenure and authority. He did not find that the statute made special prosecutors inferior or subordinate to other executive officers whom the Constitution permits to be removed through statutory procedures.[71] Relying on a reading of *Humphrey's Executor v. United States*, which permitted congressional control of independent agency officers who had mixed executive, judicial, and legislative duties, he stressed that the special prosecutor's office is constitutionally executive in character and should be subject to presidential removal powers because it did not perform any legislative or judicial duties.[72] The statute had assigned the approval of removal to Congress. Therefore, the law's removal provisions allowed Congress to interfere unconstitutionally with what were defined by the Court in *Myers* as exclusive presidential removal powers.

After reaching these conclusions, Scalia's *Morrison* opinion strayed into extraneous commentary on the threat the act posed to exclusive presidential prerogative. He rejected the pragmatic approach to interbranch relations—focusing on checks and balances rather than rules defining the powers of each branch—that had been approved by both Congress and the president when they adopted the Ethics in Government Act. In addition, he contended that the threat of prosecution by one of Congress's special prosecutors could intimidate executive staff in their advocacy of executive interests, and that it could permit erosion of popular support for executive policy efforts before any official was convicted.[73] Further, he drifted into dicta about the fairness of the process of investigation by special prosecutors. In his comments he did not refer to constitutional concepts of due process of law. Rather, he commented on how the special prosecutor was not subject to popular control because he or she was selected by a panel of appointed judges and not by the elected executive.[74] Scalia failed to note that the special prosecutor's discretion to prosecute, like that of any other federal prosecutor, is conditional upon both the approval of a grand jury and the satisfaction of the evidentiary standards set by judges.

Finally, Scalia's opinion criticized the act's "distortion" of the idea of a unitary executive. He found that it permitted subordinate officers to go about questioning executive actions. He wanted subordinate executives such as the special prosecutors to use their discretion only to further the objectives of their director. Scalia presented a command-and-control model of the executive branch. In his judgment, the president was to have the prerogative to run the executive branch without external interference. Any checks were to come through another branch's use of its specific exclusive powers (such as the congressional power to impeach the president) or through the electoral process and popular pressures on the executive. Congress was not to impose restrictions within the exclusive realm of executive authority, to breach the bright legal line separating executive power from that of the other branches, or to fragment executive authority, for "all purely executive power must be under the control of the President."[75]

Although *Young v. United States ex rel. Vuitton et Fils S.A.*, a case in which a district court judge had appointed a special prosecutor to try a case of criminal contempt, was not a case about presidential powers, Scalia's solo concurring opinion attempted to define further the boundary between executive and judicial power.[76] He found that precedent cases and history held the prosecutorial power to be exclusively executive in nature, and he argued that the judiciary could not interfere with this power. Also, he interpreted precedent cases to support his conclusion that the appointment in question was not a special exception to the executive nature of prosecution because the case involved the judiciary's contempt power. The exception sought would simply confer on the court powers not necessary to ensure the orderly conduct of its business, and that would breech the idea of a judiciary with limited power. For Scalia the judicial power to prosecute a contempt of court was a fundamental threat to liberty because it violated the bright line separating powers, a protection for liberty built into the Constitution.[77]

In his solo dissenting opinion in *Mistretta v. United States*,[78] Scalia addressed the constitutionality of the creation of the United States Sentencing Commission as an independent body within the judicial branch. The commission was charged with issuing guidelines on the imposition of criminal sentences. In an opinion by Justice Blackmun, the Court's majority upheld this delegation of authority as an intelligible, constitutional delegation of power and as a useful way to create judicial policy. Although Scalia agreed that Congress had used intelligible standards in delegating authority to the commission, he wanted to hold that Congress had erred because the authority was granted to a body that was not executive in either its power or its control, because "the Commission neither exercises any executive power on its own, nor is [it] subject to the control of the President who does."[79] He admitted that the Court had permitted agencies to exercise executive powers independent of the control of the president in *Humphrey's Executor*.[80]

Nevertheless, he found that it had never agreed to what had occurred in the *Mistretta* conflict—the delegation of legislative and judicial power to an independent body lacking other judicial or administrative functions. The act thus commingled powers in an unconstitutional fashion. Second, he regarded the Constitution as only allowing the legislative and judicial power to be exercised personally by constitutional officers. Consequently, the majority had permitted the "creation of a new Branch altogether, a sort of junior-varsity Congress . . . And in the long run the improvisation of constitutional structure on the basis of currently perceived utility will be disastrous."[81] It could result in expert decisionmaking insulated from the political process. Scalia thought that the majority had violated the bright lines defining the exclusive powers of the branches and establishing the authority of constitutional officers over subordinates by using a functional and pragmatic rather than a textual analysis of constitutional definitions of the separate powers of each branch. They had, he argued, removed governmental authority from the controls of the Constitution.

In *Freytag v. Commissioner of Internal Revenue*,[82] the Court considered whether a statute allowing the appointment of special trial judges by the chief judge of the United States Tax Court violated the Appointments Clause of the Constitution. Joined by Kennedy, O'Connor, and Souter, Scalia concurred in part with Blackmun's opinion that the statute did not violate the clause. Scalia's reasoning, however, was quite different. He concluded, using selected historical materials and a few case references, that the Tax Court was one of "the Courts of Law" referred to in Article II, section 2, clause 2, of the Constitution. Therefore, the Tax Court had the character of an executive department. Its head, the chief judge, possessed an appointment power assigned by Congress through a statute pursuant to language in Article II, section 2, which allowed Congress to vest the appointment of subordinates in courts of law.[83] However, Scalia did not end his opinion at this point. Instead, he went on to examine the phrase "the Courts of Law." Using historical materials, case law, and statutory references, he concluded that the courts of law of the third branch were defined not by the function of adjudication or by their mode of decisionmaking but by the identification or naming of their judges in the Constitution or a statute. He wrote that "it is the identity of the officer—not something intrinsic about the mode of decision making or type of decision—that tells us whether the judicial power is being exercised."[84] Thus, he rejected a functional definition of the separate powers of the branches in favor of one based on the words of the Constitution. Consequently, the chief judge was the head of an executive department and not an independent officer insulated from presidential control.

In another Appointments Clause case, Scalia concurred with a decision allowing military officers to serve as judges of military courts without having received specific presidential appointments to such posts. Because he thought that the new duties were "germane" to service as an officer, he agreed there was no need for specific appointments. However, he urged the Court to give close attention to germaneness because Congress might be lodging "the appointment power in any other person than those whom the Constitution specifies."[85]

Although his opinions on the executive's appointment and removal powers have presented a formal and legalistic description of executive powers, Scalia has considered other issues about the executive role in governmental administration. In a paragraph of a concurring opinion in *James B. Beam Distilling Company v. Georgia,* a case raising the issue of the application of a new decisional rule by courts, he objected to judicial activity that decreed what a law should be "changed to" and to the improper use of executive power in areas of private conduct. Both, he contended, joined by Marshall and Blackmun, violated constitutional language assigning powers to the branches. Additionally, he said that "if the division of federal powers central to the constitutional scheme is to succeed in its objective, it seems to me that the fundamental nature of those powers must be preserved as that nature was understood when the Constitution was enacted."[86] However, as indicated in his *Morrison* opinion, this criterion meant applying the text of the Constitution and not conducting a historical inquiry into its original intent.

In *Plaut v. Spendthrift Farm* Scalia wrote for the Court's majority in a case about the power of Congress, through an amendment to the Securities Exchange Act, to force courts to reopen securities fraud actions undertaken by the executive in which judgment had been rendered. He held that the amendment violated a fundamental principle of separation of powers: the judicial power to render dispositive judgments in cases and controversies as defined under Article III of the Constitution. His decision rested on a historical analysis of the intent of the Framers, a few cases from the early national period, and nineteenth-century treatises. These sources, he concluded, defined separation of powers as requiring that there be no retroactive legislative interference with the specific judgments of courts.[87] In this case he found that Congress had retroactively rescinded an individual final judgment. Although courts might order retroactive change in judgments through the appeals process, Congress could not do so without overstepping its constitutional authority under Article I.

Scalia has not wanted the judiciary to impair agencies' ability to make internal managerial decisions. For example, he offered a solo dissenting opinion when the Court's majority let an intelligence agent litigate the reasons for his dismissal. He thought that the dismissal was not reviewable on constitutional or statutory grounds. He argued that the former agent had a constitutional remedy, but not a remedy in the federal district court. The constitutional remedy was to petition the executive branch, in this case the director of the Central Intelligence Agency, for the protection of constitutional liberties. Scalia wanted to retain the assumption that there are "executive decisions that cannot be hauled into courts" and to free the executive branch from the potential checking and balancing of every one of its decisions.[88] He later reiterated this position when litigants challenged the procedures used during the 1990 census. Unlike the Court's majority, which held that the challenging parties had no statutory cause of action against the president or the secretary of commerce, Scalia argued that the Constitution prevented action against the president. The president's constitutional immunity—a stronger protection of his independence from litigation—was "implicit in the separation of powers established by the Constitution" and recognized by historical practice. More critically, the judiciary had no authority to remedy presidential actions, for, he concluded, "unless the other branches are to be entirely subordinate to the Judiciary, we cannot direct the President to take a specified executive act or the Congress to perform particular legislative duties."[89]

Echoing several of his D.C. Circuit opinions, Scalia's opinions on foreign affairs have assigned to the president an exclusive authority over the administration of foreign policy issues. For example, his very first Opinion of the Court supported executive definitions of treaty terms when he upheld a reading of taxation language in the Panama Canal Treaty.[90] The exclusive power of the executive to make treaties having provisions enforceable in the courts has also drawn Scalia's attention. As he stated in a case about the meaning of the Warsaw Convention, a treaty providing remedies for international airliner accidents: "We must thus be governed by the text—solemnly adopted by the governments of many separate nations—whatever conclusions might be drawn from the intricate drafting history the petitioners and the

United States have brought to our attention."[91] Going further in a solo concurring opinion in a case about Internal Revenue Service application of the 1942 United States–Canada Convention Respecting Double Taxation, he gave preference to executive branch interpretations of treaty text. He refused to consider various Senate debates and committee reports about the meaning of the treaty because only the president had the constitutional power to make treaties. Only if the president and "other contracting Parties" acceded to Senate resolutions about the conditions of a treaty during the advise-and-consent process would the senators' interpretations have any legal value. "Moreover, if Congress does not like the interpretation that a treaty has been given by the court or the President, it may abrogate or amend it as a matter of internal law by simply enacting inconsistent legislation."[92] Again the idea of a bright legal line delimiting the exclusive powers of the branches appeared, and again the result favored executive independence from external checks and balances.

As might be predicted from his position on the legislative veto and his interpretations of the foreign affairs power of the president, Scalia's most significant vote on separated powers issues countered pragmatic institutional designs for policy formulation and implementation. He joined the Court's majority and voted against an act of Congress that created a board of review comprising nine members of Congress with the power to veto decisions of the Metropolitan Washington Airports Authority. Justice John Stevens, for the Court's majority, held that the board of review placed legislators in a position of executing and administering the airports.[93]

The Executive and Administration

In a speech at Duke University in 1989, Justice Scalia jokingly prefaced his remarks with the statement "Administrative law is not for sissies— so you should lean back, clutch the sides of your chairs, and steel yourselves for a pretty dull lecture."[94] Although the statement exemplifies the Scalia wit, it prefaced a speech in which the justice conveyed a serious and strong-minded perspective on the powers of federal agencies. In many opinions he has presented a straightforward challenge to the other justices and to the administrative law community: Your design of the administrative system and administrative law has not adequately addressed the bureaucracy problem. In place of the traditional standards he has offered an alternative vision of the administrative system which expanded upon themes present in his D.C. Circuit opinions. He has assumed that administrative law is about the constitutional propriety of the institutional roles of the president, agencies, courts, Congress, and the public in the policy process. And he largely has discounted the idea that administrative failings result less from inadequacies in bureaucrats' use of information, interagency communications, and internal bureau controls on discretion—the lesson of studies of the policy implementation literature—than from institutions' performing tasks that are not included in their constitutional roles.[95] Therefore, as in his D.C. Circuit opinions on administrative issues, his treatment of the bureaucracy problem has implied the existence of a Congress problem, or a failure of Congress to produce laws that effectively guide the use of agency discretion.

His solution to this institutional problem has several elements. First, he has indicated his support for executive policy development by expressing a fundamental confidence both in extensive presidential control of purposeful and rational agency rulemaking and in agency discretion in "factual" decisionmaking. Second, he has sought to constrain judicial intervention in the interpretation of questions of the lawfulness of agency policymaking. He wants to give agencies an important role in the resolution of "questions of law."[96] Third, because post-legislative interventions by interest groups only muddy the fairness of agency rules, adjudications, and implementation actions, he has sought to limit public efforts to use legal remedies to correct alleged errors by administrators. The pattern of management resulting from his standards has emphasized both the concentration of administrative authority in the executive agency, and judicial passivity.

Presidential Leadership of Agencies

Justice Scalia has promoted presidential political control of the decisions of administrative agencies. In making nonfactual discretionary judgments about policy implementation and policy evaluation, he has anticipated that agencies should follow the popular will as conveyed by the executive. He has wanted an executive that takes charge of the federal bureaucracy. He has supported vigorous executive efforts to command the machinery of government, to control deregulation, and to control agency policy actions. Consequently, as he stated in a concurring opinion joined by O'Connor,

> It is ordinarily no proper concern of the judge how the Executive chooses to exercise discretion, so long as it be within the scope of what the law allows. For that reason, judicial dicta criticizing unintelligent (but nonetheless lawful) executive action are almost always inappropriate. The context changes, however, when the exercise of discretion relates to the integrity of the unitary adjudicative process that begins in an administrative hearing before an administrative law judge and ends in a judgment of this or some other federal court. Agency action or inaction that undermines that process undermines and dishonors the legal system—undermines and dishonors the courts. Judges may properly protest, no matter how lawful (and hence irreversible) the agency action or inaction may be.[97]

The lesson he has taught is that the separated powers system required presidents and their subordinates to act with discretion, and to undergo checking and balancing—by law or public criticism—only when they violate the law or impinge on the integrity of another branch of government. In particular, as he stated in a speech, executive agencies possess considerable discretion in making factual judgments within the boundaries of a statute and in making fact-related decisions. These decisions include choices about the social policies they pursue, estimations of the probable effects of a policy, evaluations of policy costs and benefits, and judgments about evidence concerning a regulated party's adherence to agency rules. These decisions, he has commented, are "political ones—made by institutions whose managers change with each presidential election and which are under constant political pressure of congressional authorization and appropriations processes."[98]

Judicial Deference to Agency Discretion

Building on the logic of executive independence, in a unanimous opinion by Justice Stevens in *Chevron U.S.A., Inc. v. Natural Resources Defense Council*,[99] the Supreme Court held that federal courts should defer to reasonable and legitimate agency constructions of statutes and to the agency policy choices predicated upon such constructions. Courts should not second-guess agency judgments about questions of law when the administrative determination "represents a reasonable accommodation of manifestly competing interests and is entitled to deference."[100] Like the rest of the Court, Scalia has presumed that *Chevron* requires a two-step test to determine if the agency choice is entitled to deference.[101] First, if the statutory text is plain, clear, and unambiguous, the agency should follow the text. If it does not, then courts can require the agency to follow the text. Second, if the text is not clear and contains ambiguity, the courts should allow the implementation of any "reasonable" agency interpretation of the statute. Therefore, courts cannot restrain an executive agency's discretion under a statute unless the agency's discretion is somehow unreasonable.[102] The aim of this approach, he once wrote, is not to protect the separation of powers. The courts are not denied a role in checking and balancing agency power, but their duty is confined to "questions of law" or to the interpretation of ambiguous statutes, and they must defer to the agency interpretation of the statute.[103] Thus, the logic of Scalia's decisions on administrative agency powers has conformed with Louis Jaffe's use of a Reasoned Elaboration conception of the Court as a fixer of boundaries or an implementer of strategic controls on agency expertise. Nevertheless, the two steps comprising the *Chevron* test, although designed to curtail judicial construction of statutes bounding agency powers, pose two problems.[104] First, how can courts determine whether a statutory text is clear and unambiguous? Second, in situations of ambiguity, what is reasonable in an administrative interpretation of the procedural or substantive policy language of a statute?

Scalia provided his most direct response to the first problem raised by *Chevron* in a solo opinion concurring with a decision about the Equal Employment Opportunity Commission's (EEOC's) extension of its guidelines to protect U.S. citizens from discrimination by U.S. employers in international operations. He stated that the

> EEOC was entitled to deference on the particular point in question. But deference is not abdication, and it requires us to accept only those agency interpretations that are reasonable in light of the principles of construction courts normally employ. Given the presumption against extraterritoriality that the Court accurately describes, and the requirement that the intent to overcome it be "clearly expressed," it is in my view not reasonable to give effect to mere implications from the statutory language as the EEOC has done.[105]

Therefore, as indicated in his speech at Duke, ambiguity is "not just when no interpretation is even marginally better than any other, but rather when two or more reasonable, though not necessarily equally valid, interpretations exist."[106] Using this standard, Scalia refused to use judicial powers to interfere with the Immigration and Naturalization Service's (INS's) application of explicit congressional standards on the naturalization of aliens, or with Interstate Commerce Commission interpretation of congressional policy on negotiated rates for shippers.[107]

However, as in a case about the meaning of the Civil Service Reform Act of 1978, he rejected agency interpretations of statutes when they ignored the plain meaning of the statute. He made this clear in a solo concurring opinion chiding an agency for pushing the language of a statute to extremes because of excessive judicial deference to the agency. Similar language faulting the National Labor Relations Board (NLRB) for an enforcement order "not within the range of reasonable interpretation of the statutory text" appeared in a case about the remedies available in suits under Title VII of the Civil Rights Act of 1964. Likewise, he found that the Environmental Protection Agency (EPA) had gone "beyond the scope of whatever ambiguity" the statute contained, in his opinion for the Court in a case about the meaning of the Resource Conservation and Recovery Act. Agencies could not alter the plain meaning of a text to aggrandize their discretion, especially if their reading made "fundamental changes" in the statutory scheme, he argued in a case about the authority of the Federal Communications Commission over long-distance telephone carriers. In a solo concurring opinion in a case about INS hearing procedures, he refused to defer to the agency interpretation of a statute when the agency relied on the ambiguous legislative history of the statute rather than the statute's plain meaning. Finally, in a dissenting opinion joined by Rehnquist and Thomas, he rejected a Department of the Interior regulation of property usage made pursuant to the Endangered Species Act. He held that three aspects of the regulation, made to protect the spotted owl, were not based on statutory text and, additionally, had been incorrectly construed by the Court's majority. His opinion featured an especially detailed effort to define and decipher the definition of words and the meaning of legislative passages in order to construct legislative intent.[108]

In response to the second problem raised by *Chevron*, Scalia has defined unreasonableness in agency interpretation of a statute as a decision "inconsistent with a clearly expressed congressional intent."[109] Unreasonableness in agency interpretations of statutes becomes manifest, he argues, when an agency ignores reasonable interpretations of procedures or substantive standards in its analysis of an ambiguous statute. Otherwise, as stated in a solo dissenting opinion, "deference is appropriate where the relevant language, carefully considered, can yield more than one reasonable interpretation, not where discerning the only possible interpretation requires a taxing inquiry. *Chevron* is a recognition that the ambiguities in statutes are to be resolved by the agencies charged with implementing them, not a declaration that, when statutory construction becomes difficult, we will throw up our hands and let regulatory agencies do it for us."[110]

Unreasonable agency discretion includes procedural errors contrary to statutory guidelines, such as acting in an arbitrary and capricious manner, failing to consider evidence properly, using improper procedures, or violating plain statutory language about procedures. However, Scalia has supported constraints on the judicial scrutiny of rule-making procedures. He has not been a fan of the "procedural hard look" doctrine. In opinions on cases raising questions about whether agency actions had been "arbitrary and capricious" and whether an agency had failed to consider evidence properly or used improper procedures, and in cases raising questions about whether agency actions disclosed a lack of fidelity to plain statutory language expressing the will of Congress about agency operations, Scalia normally has deferred to agency procedures. For example, he wrote for the Court and permitted the ICC to refuse to clarify an earlier decision because the statutory requirement of "material error" for further proceedings had not been met. Also, he concurred, in a solo opinion, in deferring to Federal Energy Regulatory Commission (FERC) jurisdiction over ratemaking for electrical generation and the procedures FERC used to establish the rates. In an unpublished concurring opinion, he argued that the time limits for administrative action contained in the Clean Air Act were directive and not mandatory. He read the statute as giving the EPA administrator the discretion whether or not to review state air pollution control plans within the time limit.[111]

He also has objected to agency procedural discretion when the agency's procedures violate the facial requirements of a statute. Thus, he wrote for the Court to require the INS to satisfy evidentiary procedures on the record according to statutory requirements.[112] His opinion for the Court in a case about agency discretion to set the eligibility criteria for disability benefits for black lung disease sufferers also demanded adherence to procedures defined in a statute. Although he thought that the statute contained some ambiguity about the procedure for assessing evidence of disability, he sorted through the text of the statute to arrive at a conclusion that the agency procedure for the evaluation of evidence was not consistent with a reasonable reading of the statute.

Instead, the agency had inaccurately used legislative history to define its procedures.[113] In a dispute questioning the clarity of FERC's statutory jurisdiction over rate setting because of another statute conferring some potentially overlapping powers on the Securities and Exchange Commission (SEC), he relied on "long-time understanding and practice" to foreclose a procedural role for the SEC.[114] Even when he doubted the Court's definition of agency procedural discretion, he required parties to meet procedural standards such as the requirement that they have a prima facie case before having a hearing on their claim.[115]

To determine that there has been unreasonable agency discretion in applying the substantive language of a statute, Scalia held that a judge need not engage in a detailed review or "substantive hard look" at agency choices involving judgments within the agency's area of expertise.[116] Instead, his prudential standard of deference was designed to decrease judicial intervention in agency policy choices and placed responsibility on the agency for resolving ambiguities in the law or establishing standards drawn from its statutory authority. Although the agency standard could increase executive power, he justified his position by arguing that Congress cannot always avoid statutory ambiguity. Also, he assumed that the agency, because of its expert knowledge of the consequences of various statutory interpretations, is better placed than the courts to resolve the ambiguity. For example, as he stated in a concurring and dissenting opinion joined by Blackmun, O'Connor, and Rehnquist in a case about a U.S. Customs Service regulation about the importation of goods with a domestic trademark, the agency's reading of an ambiguous term in the law should not be overturned by the Court "to burden the agency with an interpretation that it not only has never suggested, but that is contrary to ordinary usage, to the purposes of the statute, and to the interpretation the agency appears to have applied consistently for half a century." However, he would afford deference about the interpretation of ambiguities only to the agency that had initially drafted a regulation in dispute.[117]

Consequently, his standards on the scope of judicial control of administration which have rejected the substantive hard look have placed responsibility on the agency for the initial resolution of "questions of law," the ambiguities in statutes which should be resolved to establish standards for administrative action.[118] Also, because the Court is to intervene only when the agency's statutory interpretation is less than reasonable, the scope of judicial control of the agency has been narrowed in questions of law as well as questions of fact. Following his reading of the second part of the *Chevron* test, Scalia has relegated the courts to double-checking agency decisions in matters of law and has allowed agencies to engage in text-based speculation about ambiguous statutory language. His rationale for this approach has been that judicial interpretations or "substantive hard looks" that depart from statutory language can embolden an agency to press the judicial interpretation to "the limits of its logic." The result is a judicially sanctioned agency deviation from the statute. This practice, he has argued, undermines both the value of a statute as a representative act of Congress and the duty of courts in a separated powers system of governance. Thus, he has regarded text-based agency action to be a critically important discretionary practice in the political regime.[119]

Public Control of Administration

Justice Scalia's conception of separation of powers attempts to guarantee presidential control of the discretionary choices of administrative agencies. He also has assumed that agencies, in making nonfactual discretionary judgments about policy, will follow the popular will as expressed through the enactment of clear statutes by the peoples' representatives. Additionally, to combat the problem of expanded political pluralism in contemporary politics, he has wanted to control interest group or individual efforts to secure access to government or to criticize government administrators by instituting legal action to question the lawfulness of agency activity. He has defined several controls on public and interest group participation which he favors in his opinions about the Freedom of Information Act and about standing to sue government administrators.

First, Scalia has narrowly construed provisions of the Freedom of Information Act and has made it more difficult for private parties to obtain the information necessary to litigate policy choices by agencies. With several categories of exceptions, the FOIA opened agency procedural and policy documents, procedural manuals, and records to the public. The aim of the FOIA was to facilitate knowledge of governmental processes and deter political corruption, but it had several "exceptions" to prevent the release of some kinds of documents. When confronting a FOIA case about the release of information on Haitian boat people who had been returned to Haiti after seeking political asylum in the United States, Scalia stressed the limited scope of the act. Inter-

preting exception 6 of the FOIA, which prevents the release of personnel and medical records, he construed the act as barring the consideration of "derivative uses" when courts assessed the effect of the release
of information. Information release decisions were to balance personal
privacy against the immediate public interest in the information and
were not to consider the "intrinsic public value" of the information, or
any potential uses.[120]

Scalia has sought to have exception 5 of the FOIA and related statutes read so that persons can only inspect, not copy, pre-sentence
reports compiled by the Department of Justice. In one opinion he
expressed a concern that the FOIA might be used by individuals interested in legal action for personal gain rather than by citizens who, in
the spirit of the act, wanted to become informed about agency action.
Although the Court's majority rejected his inspection standard, Scalia
also indicated that an increase in the number of FOIA requests for
copies of documents might impede agency efficiency and effective-
ness.[121] Although both the impediment to challenges to government
and the danger of copying might seem to be slight, Scalia viewed the
majority's evaluation of the act as facilitating interest group and individual challenges to public policies in the courts. In unpublished memoranda in a case in which he did not write an opinion, he further
challenged any broadening of exceptions to the FOIA. He regarded any
such change as extending an unwise policy of allowing persons to make
costly demands for government documents and as generating more
litigation over exemptions to the disclosure of information. However,
sometimes these policy concerns were offset by his desire to read the
FOIA literally. Thus, in a case about the exception of law enforcement
records from FOIA requests, he reasserted his belief that the act had to
be narrowly construed even if a narrow reading resulted in the disclosure of information. Reasonable narrow construction meant, "if
anything, construing ambiguous language of the exemption in such a
fashion that the exemption does not apply." Reliance on text, rather
than speculation about the meaning of language, was the way to produce the benefits of the release of general information and perhaps to
signal to Congress about the need to change the act.[122]

Second, Scalia has tried to minimize interest group efforts to impose
judicial control on agency activity. He has not supported the "interest representation model" of administrative operations which emerged
from public interest liberal political thought.[123] He has distrusted the
ability of courts to resolve the public challenges to agency expertise and

to the fairness of agency procedures which result when plural interests find it easy to litigate their demands. Underlying his disquiet has been his fear that courts will become entangled in judging the wisdom of the policies and politics of administration. From his point of view, judicial passivity is essential if the Court is to avoid challenges to the legitimacy of its actions coming from external political critics of its competency and craftsmanship.

Scalia has adopted judicial passivity themes in many administrative claims. He proposed "further limiting principles" in the Court's rules about the finality of judgments, to control the possible readjudication of issues before federal courts.[124] He made it clear that parties have to exhaust administrative remedies established by statutes before they can seek a judicial remedy. Parties should exhaust all of these administrative remedies before the judiciary can review the agency action.[125] As he stated in a concurring opinion in a case about a mine safety inspection rule, there is strong precedent against preenforcement judicial review of an agency rule.[126] As indicated above, he has supported what he believes to be valid statutory constraints on judicial interference with or review of executive agency processes and enforcement decisions, such as the Central Intelligence Agency's dismissal of a homosexual employee.[127] This position implied that constitutional claims against an agency, such as the CIA employee's claim of a denial of equal protection, might not be subject to judicial remedy. He dissented when the Court's majority supported the litigation of a claim under the Education of the Handicapped Act by a litigant who was no longer a student and was older than the age group protected by the statute. The majority thought that the harm to the litigant was capable of repetition despite the inability of the Court to afford a remedy to the litigant, a doctrine long applied in abortion cases. Scalia argued that the time for action had not been too short and that the litigant could never suffer the same harm in the future. These facts, he argued, distinguished the question of standing in this case from the problem of standing in abortion cases.[128] He upheld the use of the military contractor defense found in the Federal Tort Claims Act to prevent personal injury litigation in a state court against a federal military contractor.[129] He rejected "constitutional tort" or *Bivens* doctrine personal injury litigation regarding the service-connected disabilities of former soldiers who had been subjects in a civilian-operated LSD experiment.[130] He supported as "reasonable" a qualified immunity of FBI officers from damage suits for warrantless searches that they had thought to be lawful.[131] On occasion he opposed some precedent-based passivity doctrines (e.g., the *Feres* doctrine) related to the concept of the sovereign immunity of United States administrators from suits. However, the reason for his rejection of the *Feres* doctrine, which made it impossible for military personnel to sue the government for injuries suffered in the line of duty, had little to do with his concern about judicial meddling in executive affairs. Rather, as stated in his solo dissenting opinion, he thought that the use of sovereign immunity to prevent personal injury claims against a federal government air traffic controller by the family of a Coast Guard pilot allegedly killed by controller error contradicted the text of the Federal Tort Claims Act.[132] Here, as in a later Clean Water Act case, his practice was to read statutes as conferring limited jurisdiction on federal courts. He indicated that federal courts should not attempt to define jurisdiction more broadly than it was defined in the plain text of a statute.[133] Also, he accepted statutory language and a statutory scheme in the Civil Service Reform Act which prevented the judicial review of an administrative personnel decision.[134]

Regarding issues of judicial review of litigation against agencies, he voted for Justice Souter's opinion that the Court could consider questions of the ripeness of litigation, drawn from Article III and prudential concerns, even if the questions had not been raised by the parties. Thus, he signaled that a party had to take affirmative steps to seek a benefit from the INS before the party could challenge rules about the benefit.[135] In joining a concurring opinion by Rehnquist, he supported *Bivens* challenges of harms to constitutional rights by federal prison officials prior to the exhaustion of administrative remedies.[136] However, he agreed with an opinion recommending denial of *Bivens* action against an agency rather than a person and denial of *Bivens* relief when a statute offered an avenue for remedy.[137] He also voted for a plurality opinion by Justice O'Connor which limited civil rights actions against individual state and local government administrators.[138] As a result, only discrimination suits against policymakers, not subordinates, could result in relief drawn from the "deep pockets" of the public treasury. Yet, his position soon underwent modification when he voted with a majority of the Court to permit civil rights challenges to state policymakers who had breached the limitations on state governmental power established by the Commerce Clause.[139]

Finally, Scalia ruled against public interest groups that sought standing to challenge agency environmental regulatory decisions promulgated by the Bush administration's secretary of the interior, Manuel Lujan. For example, when the National Wildlife Federation sought to initiate a class action suit to challenge a Bureau of Land Management land withdrawal review program, a policy designed to regulate the private acquisition of federal land, Scalia rejected their plea. His Opinion of the Court made two points. First, under the APA and the Federal Rules of Civil Procedure, he could not find that National Wildlife Federation members were alleging any "specific facts" about the injury or grievance that they had suffered. Second, he could not locate any final agency action that had been a cause of injury adversely affecting or aggrieving the members. Failing to satisfy both the "injury in fact" and the causation requirements he had discovered in precedents, he refused to allow the class action suit. In addition, the land withdrawal review program was not an agency action but a descriptive label covering a series of agency actions. So, even if the National Wildlife Federation could show an injury, it had to locate the harm in a specific action and not in the program in general.[140]

When the Defenders of Wildlife, an environmental group, sought to challenge a Department of the Interior rule limiting the scope of the Endangered Species Act so that it did not apply to activities that received federal funds but that affected species in other nations, he also denied standing. Again writing for the Court, he could not find an "injury in fact" as required by precedents about standing. First, he asserted that American travelers' claims to have been injured by observations of possible harm to endangered species in Sri Lanka and Egypt were "simply not enough" to establish the potentiality of injury that would justify an injunction against the enforcement of the Interior Department rule. He thought that related claims of injury as a result of harms to the world ecosystem, or to the interests of persons or professionals who desired to study or see world wildlife, went "beyond the limit, and into pure speculation and fantasy" about the injury suffered. He could locate no injury in fact. Second, he did not find a way to redress any injury. Although the Court could have the rule revised, the suit did not address the cause of the alleged injury, the funding decision made in Congress which ultimately affected wildlife in the world ecosystem. Because the group did not challenge the actual source of the harm, they had sought judicial jurisdiction over a conjectural issue. Precedent, he noted, does not allow standing based on conjectural interests. Finally, he concluded that the group had not suffered a "procedural injury" or a harm recognized by the Endangered Species Act.

Although correct statutory procedures had not been followed by the Interior Department, he dismissed this claim. Instead, he held that a procedural injury claim must be connected to a direct injury. A procedural injury for which standing to sue is granted by a statute does not grant standing unless it satisfies the case or controversy precedents created pursuant to Article III of the Constitution. Congress cannot create "prudential" standing in this situation. Therefore, he concluded that "vindicating the *public* interest (including the public interest in government observance of the Constitution and the laws) is the function of the Congress and the Chief Executive."[141] In effect, his reading of the powers of the separate branches kept the courts out of interest group efforts to influence administration.

CONGRESS

In Scalia's formal system of interbranch relations, Congress is to make specific laws and is to refrain from checking the executive through political interference in agency operations. Unlike most justices, he has wanted the primary restraint on the executive branch to be the establishment, by Congress, of uniform administrative procedures and precise language about agency authority. Thus, his reading of the structure of separated powers in the Constitution has tilted toward executive dominance of the relations among the branches. His version of the separation of powers has meant that a potentially powerful Congress can exist, but it is a Congress that interferes with other branches only in ways sanctioned by a formalistic interpretation of separated powers. From Scalia's viewpoint, courts are to defer to congressional policies—but only when Congress has done its job.[142]

Scalia has envisioned statute writing as the exclusive power of Congress, but he has regarded Congress as a peculiar kind of statute writer. Its duty is to draft constitutional, precise, rational, and purposeful statutes that assign discrete duties to federal agencies. Judges should defer to such statutes. Although judges should consider the meaning of imprecise language, Scalia believes that vague statutes only trigger administrative discretion and judicial review of that discretion.[143] Only when there is vagueness should the judiciary try to impute a meaning to statutes, and it should do so using a very specific set of techniques.

To constrain congressional powers, Scalia has revised Frankfurter's argument about the need for judges to rely first on "plain meaning" to define statutory language. Scalia has agreed that such a technique discourages the introduction of external instrumental political and social demands into the judicial analysis of a statute. Repeatedly, he has emphasized that judges should be true to the "ordinary meaning" of the text of statutes as well as to the constitutional and treaty language having a bearing on public administration.[144] But, departing from Frankfurter, he has been more hostile to the use of other resources to determine the meaning of statutes. Although he has used the grammar and structure of a text to decipher its meaning, he has often lectured those judges who search for the meaning of statutes in ways that direct them into false reconstructions of legislative and administrative intent.[145]

One reason for Scalia's concern with the use of legislative history has been his commitment to what Professor William Eskridge called "formalism," or a belief that judges should be "constrained by the objectively determinable meaning of the statute."[146] Based on the purposeful approach to law advocated by defenders of Reasoned Elaboration, formalism places the justice in the role of an umpire officiating among competing definitions of words in a statutory text. Summarizing his "formal" views about statutory interpretation in his solo concurring opinion in *Green v. Bock Laundry Machine Company,* a case about congressional intent in the creation of a section of the Federal Rules of Evidence, Scalia wrote,

> The meaning of terms on the statute-books ought to be determined, not on the basis of which meaning can be shown to have been understood by a larger handful of the Members of Congress; but rather on the basis of which meaning is (1) most in accord with context and ordinary usage, and thus most likely to been understood by the whole Congress which voted on the words of the statute (not to mention the citizens subject to it), and (2) most compatible with the surrounding body of law into which the provision must be integrated—a compatibility which, by a benign fiction, we assume Congress always has in mind. I would not permit any of the historical and legislative material discussed by the Court, or all of it combined, to lead me to a result different from the one that these factors suggest.[147]

Following this logic in other cases, he used dictionary definitions to resolve the meaning of the word *representatives* in the Voting Rights Act and the meaning of the word *marketing* in the Plant Variety Protection Act.[148] The search for meaning in surrounding language induced him to offer a concurring opinion, joined by Kennedy, examining the style of statutory phrases, and to rely on grammatical standards for the analysis of statutory text of 18 *U.S. Code* § 209.[149] On one occasion he drew on several statutes—"the body of both previously and subsequently enacted law"—using a term or similar language to define a use of words in a case before him.[150] He refused to rely on the notes of the Advisory Committee, which had assisted in the preparation of the Federal Rules of Evidence, to decipher the meaning of a section of the Rules; he stated, "The Rule says what it says."[151] Finally, he issued a concurring opinion in a federal taxation case to argue against what he regarded as the majority's misstatement of unequivocal statutory language.[152]

A second reason for Scalia's hostility to the use of legislative history has been what Eskridge calls "realism," or skepticism about the accuracy of any historical evidence of collective legislative intent.[153] Scalia indicated in a solo concurring opinion that the use of legislative history was a relatively new phenomenon without longstanding interpretive guidelines.[154] Consequently, in statutory interpretation he has often refused to give much credence to such legislative sources as committee reports and other extratextual sources because he believes that the staff drafts these materials with little oversight by legislators or because sources such as legislative debates can only confound the use of clear statutory texts by courts and administrators.[155] Unlike Frankfurter and Legal Process scholars, who cautioned against the search for legislative intent but did consider "the known temper of legislative opinion," Scalia has thought that contextual perspectives on statutes subject courts to the possible machinations of unrepresentative interest groups or even the conspiratorial efforts of congressional staff.[156] As he stated in a solo concurring opinion about the discussion of district court decisions in a House committee report, he rejected legislative history because

> I am confident that only a small proportion of the Members of Congress read either one of the Committee reports in question . . . As anyone familiar with modern-day drafting of congressional committee reports is well aware, the reference to the cases was inserted, at best by a committee staff member on his or her own initiative, or at worst by a committee staff member at the suggestion of a lawyer-lobbyist; the purpose was not primarily to inform the Members of Congress what the bill meant . . . but rather to influence judicial construction.[157]

Scalia later stated a policy concern, rooted in a conception of the proper role of Congress and the Court in a separated powers system, that appeared to motivate his statutory literalism and rejection of the use of legislative history. At the conclusion of a dissenting opinion, joined by Kennedy and Rehnquist, that criticized the Court's majority for reasoning that judges were "representatives" within the meaning of the Voting Rights Act of 1965 as amended in 1982, he stated,

> When we adopt a method that psychoanalyzes Congress rather than reads its laws, when we employ a tinkerer's toolbox, we do great harm. Not only do we reach the wrong result with respect to the statute at hand, but we poison the well of future legislation, depriving legislators of the assurance that ordinary terms, used in an ordinary context, will be given a predictable meaning. Our highest responsibility in the field of statutory construction is to read the laws in a consistent way, giving Congress a sure means by which it may work the people's will.[158]

A related concern, expressed in a concurring opinion by Scalia, Kennedy, and Thomas about penalties provisions in the Juvenile Delinquency Act, has been that the ambiguous text of the act, rather than legislative history, should be used to "support a more lenient reading" of the statute which was advantageous to a criminal defendant.[159] In an opinion about the interpretation of the National Firearms Act, Scalia used this "rule of lenity," the rule of construction of penal statutes in favor of the defendant, to limit the application of ambiguous statutory language and prevent penalization of a person for selling a firearm conversion kit.[160] Since he also objected to other readings of legislative history which ignored the rule of lenity and disadvantaged minorities and criminal defendants, his argument conveyed a greater concern for the proper roles of judicial and legislative power than for the policy outcome of favoring governmental efforts to convict criminals.[161]

Also, he has disputed efforts to change the construction of a statute when circumstances changed. For example, he refused to follow Justice Brennan and reconsider the meaning of trademark laws enacted in the early part of the century. He believed that for a judge "to support the power of a court to disregard the plain application of a statute when changed circumstances cause its effects to exceed the original legislative purpose," two conditions had to be met. These were that the changed circumstances were unknown to and not envisioned by the enacting legislature, and that the new circumstances had caused "the challenged application of the statute to exceed its original purpose."[162] Also, as he pronounced in a solo concurring opinion, he refused to consider post-enactment legislative history of a statute, stating that it "should not be taken seriously, not even in a footnote."[163]

Thus, Scalia believes that the regime is best served by clear and concise congressional policymaking. Looseness of statutory language—as he expressed in a concurring opinion, joined by Kennedy, O'Connor, and Rehnquist, in a case about the imprecise statutory text discussing civil RICO actions—can be a danger to liberty.[164] Unclear text, he has argued, lets judges draw on the imprecise but traditional canons of statutory interpretation. Also, imprecise text abets the growth of agency power and makes judicial review of agency actions more difficult. Imprecise statutes generate a diversity of agency procedures and rules that prohibits easy and comprehensive oversight of the propriety of agency action by Congress. Imprecise language threatens legislative power because it introduces uncertainties of statutory meaning resolvable only in court. Consequently, problems in Congress, including uncontrolled staff power to create legislative history, then have to be corrected by the unelected federal courts.[165] He almost seems to have thought that the Court, to resolve aspects of the "bureaucracy problem" and the "Congress problem," had to teach Congress to become a coherent statute writer.

SCALIA'S VISION OF THE AMERICAN STATE

Antonin Scalia's vision of the state or public sector is conveyed by the application and extension of the principles of Reasoned Elaboration legal arguments. The general formalism of his approach to separate powers, as seen in cases about the boundaries of institutional power such as *Morrison, Mistretta, Young, James Beam Distilling, Plaut,* and *Freytag,* resembles the primary proposition of Reasoned Elaboration jurisprudence. He has assumed the law to be the primary means for asserting the popular consensus about policy and defining the use of political power. This position has led him to conclusions consistent with Reasoned Elaboration.

First, in cases about institutional power he has favored the application of his understanding of plain statutory text as the best statement of public purpose. He has regarded it as more trustworthy than potentially countermajoritarian judicial interpretations derived from extratextual constitutional language about fundamental liberties, the legislative history of statutes, and some judicial precedents. Second, especially as has been evident in his reading of *Chevron* tests, he has regarded the courts as Freund's umpires in conflicts among the branches. In the language of Jaffe, he has indicated that the courts are to exercise a kind of rational, strategic control over agencies and, by implication, over the entire policymaking process. Third, he has stressed that courts are to avoid policy experimentalism by applying legal texts without concern for their overt policy consequences. Therefore, judges should not second-guess the logic of executive policy or try to correct the surface meaning of acts of Congress. As he stated in *James Beam Distilling*, "I am not so naive (nor do I think our forebears were) as to be unaware that judges in a real sense 'make' law. But they make it *as judges make it*, which is to say *as though* they were 'finding' it—discerning what the law *is*, rather than decreeing what it is today *changed to*, or what it will *tomorrow* be."[166] Finally, in applying and extending the concept of the judicial role favored by Bickel, he has urged that courts are to try to reinforce their own passivity in the operations of the state. This means that judges are to restrict the range of conflicts they consider and the kinds of judgments they render. Also, judges are to avoid inviting interest groups to use litigation as a means of affecting public policy.

Unlike pragmatic liberals, Scalia has been greatly concerned with process. As he stated in a speech, "In judging, process is a value unto itself, and not (except in a very remote sense) merely a means to achieving a desirable end. The result is validated by the process, not the process by the result."[167] Like Bickel's, Scalia's law has not been a pragmatic means to an outcome such as equality, greater personal liberty, or creative controls on the state. Also, according to Scalia, judges cannot condone what he has regarded as experimental variations in the boundaries of the separate powers of the branches, such as the special prosecutors law, nor can they, in evolution of doctrines such as the "hard look," neglect process to achieve pragmatic outcomes. Experiments, he has implied, cause the law to lose its neutrality and encourage courts to start making overt policy choices. This practice becomes even more egregious when judges ignore the plain text and start rummaging through legislative history and ambiguous statutory phrases to construct a law serving judicial or interest group aspirations. If judges are to play their proper role in the regime, he has urged that they be true to their craft. Judges are to practice their special expertise or, as he has put it, their "specialized field, fully comprehensible only to the expert."[168]

Although Scalia's opinions about the instrumental duties of national governmental institutions have emphasized the need for public officials to perform legally assigned duties, his Reasoned Elaboration argument has promoted an additional instrumental political end—executive dominance in the relations among the branches. His interpretation

of separated powers has not meant equal participation by each branch
in the policy process. He has envisioned executive discretion as extensive—because of the Constitution, as in *Morrison,* and because of congressional action, as in his exposition of the *Chevron* test. Additionally,
since in his view Congress and the judiciary have limited and specific
exclusive powers, his vision of national institutional politics has not
meant an aggressively political checking and balancing of executive
administrative choices by Congress or the courts. It has meant that
Congress is to confine its role to drafting precise statutes and creating
certainty in the law. Consequently, the judiciary will not have to review
the boundaries of executive and legislative power unless Congress invades the executive domain.

Because Scalia has derived his executive-dominant vision of the
state from Reasoned Elaboration jurisprudential discourse, his opinions contain two important premises about political management in
modern America. His first premise—the need for a strong federal executive—is one that is not completely in tune with all contemporary
conservative visions of the organization of the public sector. Even prior
to his appointment to the Court, his use of Reasoned Elaboration
arguments forced him to pay special attention to the Congress problem
and the expanded political pluralism problem rather than to the bureaucracy problem. Because Congress and expansive political pluralism frustrated the tenets of his Reasoned Elaboration jurisprudence,
they were more significant for him. An irresponsible Congress concerned with reelection or other interests tended not to make precise
statutes and therefore thrust the judiciary into a policymaking role.
And the unchecked pluralism and interest group entrée into the policy
process which were encouraged by public interest liberalism undercut
a stable, neutral rule of law based on choices made by majoritarian
institutions. Bureaucracy and executive power were less of a problem,
especially if the bureaucracy was under strong executive and statutory
direction and if it was free to use its lawful, expert discretion. These
views are coupled with Scalia's respect for majority rule and legal text,
again a postulate of Reasoned Elaboration jurisprudence. Unlike Congress, the president is a single representative of the majority. Moreover,
the Constitution assigns the president generous discretionary powers.
Scalia has recognized that the representative and constitutional dimensions of the executive branch place limitations on the power of
courts or interest groups.

Therefore, despite his conservative reputation, he adopts an administrative theory that relies on ideas about executive management and agency expertise closely associated with Franklin Delano Roosevelt and the New Deal. Writing during the New Deal and in obvious sympathy with Roosevelt, the administrative scholar Luther Gulick urged "unity of command" as a central principle for the avoidance of confusion, inefficiency, and irresponsibility in administration. Gulick emphasized that the executive needed to develop central coordination and stronger central administrative staff units to assist him. He and his colleagues did not want participation by the governed, or checks and balances on bureau power by nonexecutive officials or interests.[169] Likewise, the New Deal insider James Landis emphasized the need for expert control of public affairs and powerful executive sanctions over miscreants both in his writings and in his role in the creation of the Securities and Exchange Commission.[170] Analyzing New Deal politics, Cass Sunstein argued that the New Dealers wanted increased presidential power, judicial review only when agency behavior raised "questions of law," constraints on legislative checking and balancing of the executive agencies, reduced autonomy of state governments, and enhanced agency discretion.[171] With the possible exception of reduced state governmental powers, all are part of Scalia's vision of executive-centered public sector administration.

Scalia's second premise about American political management calls for the rejection of the continuation of the radically pluralistic and politicized public sector offered by public interest liberalism. His belief has been that the "bureaucracy problem" can be solved simply by rules of law that promote executive political control of agencies. He has aspired to constitutional standards, standards of statutory interpretation, and standards of judicial practice which limited the control of agency behavior by external judicial review and interest group participation. His use of legal standards, the "Rule of Law," rests on the proposition that a low-cost, efficient state is a reasonable goal. It is a goal achievable through the proper design of laws that encourage "synoptic"—or rational, executive-centered—decisionmaking.[172]

Scalia's two premises about American public management ignore the Madisonian system of factional and institutional conflicts as a means for directing and controlling the definition and implementation of public policy.[173] Also, his aspirations have caused him to ignore the model of an uncertain and contingent world offered by empirical research in public administration and policy science. The findings of this empirical research do not fit his legalistic paradigm of what good governmental management should be. Reasoned Elaboration analysis has prevented him from considering other instrumental means of addressing the problems of bureaucracy and expanded political pluralism. Consequently, not every conservative political proposition has been satisfied by his definition of the public sector and the power of the branches of government. Rather, he has wanted to keep the courts from fostering a political environment in which Congress encourages bureaucratic discretion, interest groups constantly attempt to redefine policy, the stability of policy is at a minimum, and bloody battles occur about institutional authority. His use of Reasoned Elaboration arguments thus has led him to restate the conservative vision. The bureaucracy problem became a problem with congressional lawmaking and its susceptibility to expanded political pluralism. Adherence to legal texts, controls on interest group intervention in policy processes, and, especially, enhanced executive policymaking power would resolve these problems, prevent political bloodshed, and animate the conservative revival. His vision has been that what would make for a better America is not a nonbureaucratic state but, rather, precise law representing popular sentiments and a responsible Congress.

Chapter Five

THE TRICK OF HARNESSING FEDERAL POWER

According to Antonin Scalia, former attorney general William Saxbe once hypothesized that the basic goal of "the Republican party is not to govern, but to prevent the Democrats from doing so." In the wake of the New Deal, the Supreme Court legitimated the constitutional supremacy of federal governmental policies and federal legislative or judicial oversight of state policy in nearly every political arena. Judicial efforts to protect a residue of state governmental independence in the control of internal operations have ended up stillborn.[1] Since the New Deal, Republican presidents, as part of an attack on the bureaucracy problem, have pledged to reverse the drift of policymaking authority to Congress and the federal agencies. Richard Nixon and Ronald Reagan both endorsed a "New Federalism," but they achieved little more than marginal adjustments in a pattern of creeping extension of federal regulatory and fiscal power.[2] Recently, congressional Republicans have tried to promote the conservative revival by preventing the national Democratic party from ever governing effectively in many policy arenas by shifting some administrative and policymaking duties to state governments. In a more extreme fashion, especially in the rural West, conservatives have attempted to use state and local initiatives to void federal administrative rules on land use and environmental protection. However, Scalia has evidenced mixed support for the curbing of federal power by the reassignment of policymaking duties to the states. Indeed, he once remarked that "the federal government is not bad but good. The trick is to use it wisely."[3]

During his service on the Court, Scalia's opinions and votes have fleshed out a distinctive narrative about federalism. As indicated in table 3.1, his position has been noticeably more favorable to the exercise of federal power than have the positions of most other justices appointed by Republican presidents, including Chief Justice Rehnquist and Justices Kennedy, O'Connor, Souter, and Stevens. Scalia has constructed a jurisprudential narrative that some commentators have characterized as "lukewarm support for federalism."[4] It has contained a political vision not supportive of a radically weakened federal govern-

ment. Additionally, his opinions about federalism and intergovernmental relations have drawn upon a very personal reading of the Constitution and precedent, an interpretation that has continually questioned
whether the Constitution's language justified the Court's doctrines
about federal-state relations. Even though he often supported federal
governmental power, his opinions have placed him in frequent conflict
with the premises of the national supremacist discourse of Justice John
Stevens and the Court's majority. His interpretive process has spared
not even longstanding doctrines from critique if the text of the Constitution implied a different conclusion. In his opinions he specifically has called for the reconsideration of four aspects of federalism
jurisprudence: preemption doctrine, the negative or dormant Commerce Clause, relations between federal and state courts, and interstate relations.

THE SUPREMACY OF NATIONAL LAW, AND FEDERAL PREEMPTION OF STATE SOVEREIGNTY

Article VI of the U.S. Constitution defines the supremacy of the Constitution and laws of the United States over state constitutions and
laws. The related doctrine of preemption permits the justices of the
Supreme Court to void state governments' statutes or regulations when
the federal government has adopted laws, under the General Welfare
Clause or the Interstate Commerce Clause of Article I of the Constitution, that "occupy the field" or address a policy issue. Alternatively,
state and local officers can elect preemption by voluntarily accepting
federal governmental restrictions on their power in exchange for federal monies. By the end of the Burger Court era, only a limited zone
of state authority potentially remained outside the scope of federal
preemption.[5]

The Rehnquist Court first addressed the nature of national supremacy in *South Dakota v. Dole*,[6] which was the most significant constitutional case about federalism on which Scalia did not write an opinion.
For a 7-to-2 majority of the justices in *Dole*, Rehnquist sustained a
provision of federal law that decreased the dispersal of federal grant-in-
aid monies to states that did not ban persons under age twenty-one
from the purchase or possession of alcoholic beverages. Scalia voted
for the Rehnquist opinion, an opinion that held that Congress had
made its spending decision in conformance with the General Welfare
Clause of the Constitution; that no personal rights had been violated;

that the Twenty-first Amendment's repeal of Prohibition did not create an "independent constitutional bar" to the federal requirement of the ban; and that the Tenth Amendment's grant of reserved power to state governments was not infringed by the condition placed on dispersal of federal money.

In *South Carolina v. Baker*,[7] Justice Brennan explicated national supremacy doctrine by holding that the federal income tax could be imposed on the interest earned from bearer bonds issued by state governments. He reasoned that Congress had not restricted a state's powers because of an extraordinary defect in its lawmaking process or singled out the government of South Carolina and left it politically isolated and powerless. Consequently, he refused to let the federal judiciary use the Tenth Amendment to second-guess the substantive basis of congressional legislation. The decision effectively decreased the willingness of potential purchasers to invest in what had been a tax-exempt instrument, and it forced the states to raise capital by issuing more tax-exempt registered bonds. Scalia's solo concurring opinion was brief but significant. He refused to accept the premise that the national political process was the only constitutional protection of state governments' power. However, he provided no detailed comment and did not identify how the constitutional structure placed "affirmative limits" on "federal action affecting the states under the Commerce Clause" or why the constitutional structure did not prohibit the federal government from taxing the interest on the bearer bonds.[8]

Despite his votes and his agreement with national constitutional supremacy over state policy in *Dole* and *Baker*, Scalia later voted for two majority opinions written by O'Connor which protected the range of the fundamental duties of state governments from federal control. In *Gregory v. Ashcroft*,[9] he supported an opinion stating that "sufficient ambiguity" in the language of the Age Discrimination in Employment Act afforded the Missouri judiciary an exemption from the act. Pursuant to Commerce Clause powers, a federal intrusion on a state government's regulation of the retirement age of its employees required a plain statement in the federal statute so that the Court could be "absolutely certain" that Congress had intended the intrusion. In *New York v. United States*,[10] he voted for O'Connor's majority opinion about the application of the Low-Level Radioactive Wastes Policy Amendments Act of 1985. O'Connor held that the law was a mandate that compelled the state governments to enact and enforce a federal program and did not offer the kind of choice that existed in incentive programs such as

the minimum-drinking-age incentive addressed in *Dole*. Thus, by requiring states to enact and enforce a policy devised by Congress, Congress had effectively interfered with the fundamental independent processes of state government protected by the Guarantee Clause and the
Tenth Amendment. Scalia also voted in support of Rehnquist's majority opinion in *United States v. Lopez*.[11] Rehnquist's opinion held that
Congress had no authority to enact the Gun-Free School Zones Act
under its Commerce Clause power. The legislation, he concluded, addressed a criminal act that had no "substantial effect" on interstate
commerce and sought to replace state police power with an unprecedented federal police power. In addition, Scalia voted with the dissenters when the Court upheld federal control of the number of terms a
member of Congress can hold. He joined Justice Thomas's dissenting
opinion arguing that the Constitution had no text preventing states
from imposing term limits as a restriction on the qualifications of
members of Congress.[12]

However, in opinions in preemption cases, Scalia has failed to spell
out any affirmative constitutional limits to federal power over state
governmental operations or to impede policy choices made by state
governments. Instead, he has applied precedents and engaged in statutory analysis to sort out whether federal or state law regulated various
acts of private parties. In *California Coastal Commission v. Granite
Rock Company*,[13] O'Connor upheld California's imposition of a permit
requirement for a private firm seeking to mine on federal forest land.
She concluded that various federal laws regulating mining in the forest
and the Property Clause of Article IV of the Constitution did not preempt the state permit regulation. Because the Property Clause did not
conflict with all state regulation of federal lands, and because the federal laws contained no specific preemptive language and concerned
land-use planning, the state permit process, which she read as an environmental regulation, could stand. Scalia, dissenting with White,
argued that O'Connor had made a fundamental mistake. The state
permit law was "plainly a land use statute," not an environmental law.
Illustrating his contention through a section-by-section commentary
on the plain meaning of the state law, Scalia concluded that it controlled land use in the same way as did federal laws regulating mining
in the forest. Therefore, the federal land-use law preempted the state
land-use law. In addition, the federal law provided a procedure by
which California could have its environmental concerns accommodated by the federal government, a procedure that California had ne-

glected to utilize. This fact reinforced his conclusion that the California permit process aimed at land-use control and not environmental goals.[14]

In *Boyle v. United Technologies Corporation*, Scalia's opinion for the court affirmed and extended precedents favoring federal preemption. Preemption precedents, he held, normally required a "clear statutory prescription," or "a direct conflict between federal and state law." Preemption could also occur when state law affected the contractual obligations of the United States or the civil liability of federal officials for actions taken in the course of their official duty. These four standards served as the basis of his analysis in *Boyle* and subsequent cases.[15]

Considering whether a state product liability action initiated by the estate of Boyle, a military helicopter pilot, could proceed against the federal contractor who had manufactured the helicopter, Scalia extended the last of these sets of precedents. He held that federal authority preempted state judicial jurisdiction over the dispute because the state's determination of the liability of the private contractor would directly affect the federal government in the course of its official duties. He justified the extension of precedent because a state decision could impose greater financial liability on the federal government than was permitted under a federal statute.

In a case about whether a Federal Energy Regulatory Commission proceeding and order requiring a utility company to purchase power from a nuclear power plant at a set rate preempted Mississippi's utility-rate-setting powers, he again avoided analysis of federalism issues. Instead, in his solo concurring opinion he sought "to discuss more fully" FERC jurisdiction. Assuming federal preemptive authority because of precedent cases on the clear intent of Congress to preempt interstate power regulation, he turned to the *Chevron* test to ensure that the FERC had satisfactorily construed the scope of its preemptive power under the Federal Power Act.[16] The next term, the justices considered whether a federal court could decline to exercise jurisdiction in equity over the Mississippi state utility regulation agency's subsequent application of the FERC order. For the Court, Scalia held that precedents restricting federal equitable jurisdiction because the cases in question raised difficult state law questions, required an effort to set state policy, or interfered with constitutional state judicial action did not apply. He concluded that, once a state action has been preempted by a federal regulation, the federal court cannot deny jurisdiction over the issue.[17]

In *Owen v. Owen*,[18] he held for the Court that federal Bankruptcy
Act language preempted a Florida law exempting property that was
under a judicially imposed state lien from seizure by the federal bankruptcy court. The direct conflict of federal and state law, he reasoned,
had to be read to favor federal governmental preemption. Scalia offered a solo concurring opinion in *Wisconsin Public Intervenor v. Mortier,* a case about whether the Federal Insecticide, Fungicide, and Ro-
denticide Act preempted a Casey, Wisconsin, ordinance governing the
aerial spraying of pesticides. Justice White had used legislative history
to determine that Congress had not intended to preempt the local
pesticide usage ordinance. Scalia devoted most of his opinion to a
critique of the use of legislative history. But he discerned enough in the
text of the statute to conclude that the act was primarily a sales and
labeling act rather than a sweeping, or "field," preemption of local
police powers about pesticide use.[19] Likewise, his Opinion of the Court
in *Morales v. Trans World Airlines* deciphered language in a statute, the
Airline Deregulation Act of 1978, to determine whether the act clearly
preempted state efforts to regulate deceptive airfare advertisements.[20]
Contending that the words *relating to* permitted extensive federal regulation of practices connected to airfares, he held that the statute
preempted the state regulations on deceptive practices.

In an extensively publicized case brought by the estate of Rose Cipollone, which was attempting to attribute to tobacco companies the responsibility for her death from lung cancer, Scalia issued a concurring
and dissenting opinion that elaborated on the theme of *Morales,* the
"broad" construction of "clear" preemptive statutes in favor of federal
authority. Stevens's plurality opinion held in part that the Federal Cigarette Labeling and Advertising Act of 1965 did not preempt all state
tort claims against tobacco companies. Rather, the act had to be construed as creating a "narrow" federal preemption applying only to litigation about the duty of cigarette companies to warn users of the
hazards of smoking. Scalia, joined by Thomas, argued that a clear
statement of intent to preempt by Congress had to be read without a
judicial second-guessing of the narrowness of its scope on the basis of
"sheer implication." In addition, he contended that the Court's interpretation of preemptions had to allow them to sweep as broadly as
indicated by Congress. The Court could not read sweeping but ambiguous statutory language about federal authority in a way that preserved
state power. Instead, it had to accord the language its "ordinary" mean-

ing as evidence of intent to empower federal jurisdiction on the matter. The application of these principles caused him to reject any notion of only partial federal preemption of the state claims, as well as a limited definition of federally protected expressive rights to advertising and promotion, a definition that restricted federal preemption.[21] The case thus was, he concluded, a federal matter.

Voting but not writing an opinion, Scalia also agreed with the Court majority's decision to void state laws forbidding the disposal of wastes from other states in state-regulated landfills and hazardous waste disposal sites. The majority concluded that the national governmental control of interstate commerce under the Commerce Clause preempted the state laws.[22] These votes, like the thrust of the opinions in *Granite Rock, Morales,* and *Cipollone,* short-circuited state governmental efforts to protect the environment and consumers and forced the issue into the federal judicial arena.

However, Scalia's readings of his precedent-based standards on preemption have not always favored the federal government. In a majority opinion in *Lukhard v. Reed,* a case about a Virginia regulation on a person's eligibility for partially federally funded Aid to Families with Dependent Children benefits, he avoided constitutional issues. Concluding that the Virginia regulation was a reasonable interpretation of the powers assigned to state governments under the federal statute providing the funds, he deferred to the state policy.[23] There was in the federal law a clear effort *not* to preempt, he maintained.

During a crisis in the savings and loan business, the Federal Savings and Loan Insurance Corporation (FSLIC) became the receiver of FirstSouth, F.A., a savings and loan firm in Texas. A creditor of First-South, Coit Independent Joint Venture, had already sued the savings and loan in state court under state law, but the FSLIC had the case removed to federal court. The federal judge then ordered that the case had to be first adjudicated under Administrative Procedure Act procedures before an FSLIC administrative hearing could occur. The FSLIC, its docket packed with savings and loan default cases, reached no decision on the claim. Coit, the creditor, then went back to federal court to secure a remedy. For the Court, Justice O'Connor held that preemption by a federal court required the exhaustion of federal administrative remedies. However, she concluded that the federal judge had erred by assigning the case to FSLIC for the administrative hearing when FSLIC had not yet established effective claims procedures.

Thus, the creditor could proceed to federal court for determination of its state law claims. Scalia's solo concurring opinion argued that the case was unduly complicated by O'Connor's argument requiring the exhaustion of available federal administrative remedies before a federal court preempted a state court action. Claiming O'Connor's argument to be a "novel doctrine," he refused to accept it. Relying on his textual mode of statutory analysis, he asserted that Congress ought to manifest a clear intent to preempt state legal claims by providing specifically for the administrative adjudication of the case. Federal preemption of state judicial power when the federal government had neither required preemption by statute or devised rules for action on the claim was a "distortion" of existing law.[24]

When Stevens found no preemption by federal authority of a North Dakota regulation on the labeling of liquor sold on federal military bases in the state, Scalia concurred. Most of the concurrence addressed Stevens's determination that there had been no state interference with federal authority because the regulation had not created economic costs for the federal government or its employees. Scalia refused to involve the Court in weighing and balancing the economic effects of legislation on federal power, and he refused to consider the North Dakota regulation to be a tax imposed on the federal government. Rather, he proposed a formal rule that federal regulatory authority under the Twenty-first Amendment preempted state liquor laws only when the facts of the case revealed unconstitutional discrimination against the United States.[25]

Scalia dissented from Stevens's Opinion of the Court in *Summit Health, Ltd. v. Pinhas,*[26] a case about the preemptive implications of the Sherman Antitrust Act. A California ophthalmologist filed a Sherman Act claim that his denial of staff privileges at a hospital was part of an effort by physicians at the hospital to drive him out of business and gain a greater share of the total ophthalmology practice. Stevens permitted the suit because he determined that the hospital's action had a potential effect on interstate commerce. Scalia disagreed, primarily because Stevens had not used a "substantial effect on interstate commerce" test to judge whether the case involved the required federal harm for preemptive Sherman Act litigation in a federal court. Claiming that precedent cases until 1980 had mandated the substantial effect criterion, Scalia argued that Stevens's modification of this test to permit a suit when the party had not alleged any substantial effect on interstate commerce only muddied the legal standards used to determine when federal antitrust law preempted state antitrust laws and laws on restraint of trade.[27]

Scalia found that a Wisconsin law taxing out-of-state businesses was only partially preempted by a federal statute. Sorting through the text of the federal law with the aid of dictionary definitions of statutory terms, he determined that the federal law had not preempted some state taxation of business activities.[28] In another case, he found neither clear preemptive intent in various federal laws nor any direct conflict of federal and state law to prevent a federal agency, the Federal Deposit Insurance Corporation, from suing under California professional liability (malpractice) law to recover damages from a law firm for its role in the default of a savings and loan association.[29] Also, Scalia wrote a majority opinion finding no clear federal purpose to override state law on fraudulent transfers of funds. A federal agency, the Resolution Trust Corporation, had contended that the state law was preempted by federal bankruptcy law.[30]

At issue in one of Scalia's opinions was the control by state law of activity on Native American lands. Interpreting the Indian General Allotment Act of 1887, he concluded that it permitted the imposition of an ad valorem tax by a county, acting under state law, on the land owned by a tribe and its members. However, he concluded that statutory text preempted a state excise tax, a deed transfer fee, when the land was sold.[31]

Finally, Scalia wrote for the Court to conclude that federal admiralty law did not preempt a Louisiana court from using the procedural doctrine of *forma non conveniens* ("not a convenient court") to dismiss a case. To cut litigation costs, the federal Jones Act permitted an allegedly injured seaman to file his case against his employer, in this case the American Dredging Company, in state court. Although the alleged injury had occurred in the waters between New Jersey and Pennsylvania, the seaman filed in state court in Louisiana. Scalia concluded that the determination of whether Louisiana was a convenient forum was a matter of trial court discretion and judicial housekeeping. The state court did not impede uniformity in substantive federal admiralty law or interfere with the Jones Act's preemption of the substantive state law of personal injury.[32]

The *Parker v. Brown* doctrine of 1943 is related to the preemption issue. Chief Justice Harlan Fiske Stone's *Parker* opinion employed a balancing test to provide state and local governments with the authority to regulate anticompetitive interstate commercial practices despite the preemption of this authority by Congress in the Sherman Act and in later antitrust statutes.[33] In two opinions, Scalia affirmed this special state governmental exemption from federal law. In *City of Columbia v. Omni Outdoor Advertising, Inc.*,[34] he upheld a city ordinance (adopted under state government authority) that directly restricted new billboard construction and ensured the continued control of billboards by a firm already in control of 90 percent of the billboards in the city. After reaffirming the *Parker* doctrine that the direct involvement of a municipal government in an anticompetitive scheme precluded an antitrust challenge, he dismissed an effort by Omni, a firm seeking to enter the billboard business, to claim that an exception to the *Parker* rule might cover what it deemed to be a conspiracy against it. He thought that Omni's proposed exception was, for several reasons, too impracticable to implement. However, Scalia concurred when Kennedy determined that two states' laws regulating the price of title insurance did not prevent antitrust action against the firms selling the insurance. Kennedy held that there was no "active" supervision by the state and no direct state legislation on the prices, and Scalia agreed. However, in a brief concurring opinion Scalia went on to indicate that he was skeptical about Sherman Act exemption for "state programmed private collusion" and about the logic of *Parker*.[35] Whether he would apply his general standards of preemption and eliminate the judicially created *Parker* exemption, thus achieving an even more precise and direct set of preemption rules, remains in doubt.

In these statutory interpretation cases affecting preemption, Scalia's aim has not been the conservative goal of aggrandizing state governments' powers. He offered only a hint of some unknown range of state reserved powers in *South Carolina v. Baker*. However, other preemption cases *(Boyle,* the Mississippi nuclear power rate cases, *Morales,* and *Cipollone)* have caused him to deploy a principle: when Congress clearly preempts or where there is a clear conflict of law, federal preemption should be deferentially or broadly read by the Court. This principle can be qualified if constitutional language or congressional legislation leaves authority in state governmental institutions (as in *Lukhard, Summit Health, Coit,* and *Mortier)* or if the state action has no direct effect on federal power (as in the North Dakota liquor regulation case and *American Dredging).* His federalism opinions thus have rested on the concept of federal supremacy, but he has not indicated that federal supremacy should encroach on all state powers.

THE "DORMANT" INTERSTATE COMMERCE CLAUSE

Scalia has campaigned to eliminate "negative" or "dormant" Commerce Clause doctrine. Developed by Chief Justice John Marshall in the 1820s, this venerable doctrine allows federal courts to void a state government's legislation that has a negative or discriminatory effect on interstate commerce—even when Congress has expressed no interest in lawmaking on the topic subjected to state legislation. Subsequent development of the doctrine has required the justices to balance the extent of the state regulation's "facial discrimination" or the "undue burden" on interstate commerce with the regulation's value for state interests.[36] Therefore, unless the state has shown that a law serves a substantial health, safety, or moral interest that cannot be adequately served by nondiscriminatory alternatives, a protectionist state law is normally "facially discriminatory" or "unduly burdensome."[37] The Court has tended to use the facial discrimination criterion when addressing a single law promulgated by a state to protect a local commercial activity, while it has used the undue burden criterion to assess state laws that were in conflict with those of other states. Complicating these doctrines, in *Complete Auto Transit v. Brady* the justices developed a four-factor test to evaluate the "practical effect" of state taxes alleged to interfere with interstate commerce. The justices have to consider whether the "tax is applied to an activity with a substantial nexus with the taxing State, is fairly apportioned, does not discriminate against interstate commerce, and is fairly related to the services provided by the state."[38] This test, like facial discrimination and undue burdens tests, has required the justices to engage in a process of sifting through evidentiary claims and making judgments based on the direction or balance of the evidence.

Scalia's distaste for the pragmatic process of balancing and the unbounded discretion it affords judges, an attitude apparent in his opinions on separated powers cases such as *Morrison v. Olson,* has provided a justification for an assault on the dormant Commerce Clause doctrine in cases in which the Court used a discrimination criterion or addressed a protectionist measure. In *CTS Corporation v. Dynamics Corporation of America* he inaugurated his assault in a concurring opinion. His opinion argued that federal law and the Commerce Clause did not prevent the state of Indiana from imposing regulations on the sale of "control shares" of stock in corporations it had chartered, to prevent corporate mergers potentially detrimental to both shareholders and employment in the state. Justice Powell's majority opinion asserted that Indiana had a substantial interest in the protection of shareholders and that the regulation would not have a detrimental effect on interstate commerce in securities. Scalia concurred with the conclusion that the law was discriminatory and protectionist, but he rejected Powell's application of a balancing test to assess discriminatory effects. Because Powell's balancing test weighed the burden on commerce against putative local benefits, Scalia feared that "such an inquiry is ill suited to the judicial function and should be undertaken rarely if at all."[39] Instead, he called for a brighter legal line less subject to judicial interpretation, a simple determination of whether the law discriminated against out-of-state interests.

In *Tyler Pipe Industries v. Washington State Department of Revenue*,[40] the Court considered state taxation of firms engaged in interstate commerce. The case centered on a Washington state business and occupation (B&O) flat tax on wholesaling and manufacturing, and the exemption of in-state but not out-of-state firms from aspects of the tax. Stevens's majority opinion struck down the taxation exemption scheme both as facially discriminatory and as containing "multiple burdens" to interstate commerce. Scalia did not accept Stevens's mixture of facial discrimination and undue burdens assessments. His concurring and dissenting opinion, joined in part by Rehnquist, argued that the B&O tax was "not facially discriminatory." Scalia contended that in its application the tax exemption was only relieving in-state manufacturers from double taxation. Despite the "discriminatory appearance" of the tax, he endeavored to illustrate that the tax on all manufacturers could not be imposed on out-of-state manufacturers. Thus, an exemption for tax on in-state goods reduced the in-state firms' taxes to a level like that paid by non-exempted out-of-state firms.[41] The Court, Scalia alleged, did not see the lack of facial discrimination because it was concerned with the "internal consistency" of the tax. The concern with internal consistency, originating late in the Burger Court era,[42] required that the tax rate be the same for all firms. Scalia stated that the internal consistency doctrine was "nowhere to be found in the Constitution. Nor is it plainly required by our prior decisions." He went on to critique the lack of textual support for the internal consistency and dormant Commerce Clause doctrines more generally. Concerned that the Court was "expanding its beachhead in this impoverished territory, rather than being satisfied with what we have already acquired through a sort of intellectual adverse possession," he thought that the justices should not extend any dormant Commerce Clause doctrine and should confine their judgments to "rank discrimination against citizens of other states."[43]

In subsequent opinions Scalia has elaborated on his concern with limiting dormant Commerce Clause doctrine to facial discrimination and topics covered by precedent. For a unanimous Court in *New Energy Company of Indiana v. Limbach*,[44] he held that an Ohio state tax credit to Ohio ethanol producers and to ethanol producers in states granting a reciprocal tax credit to Ohio producers was facially discriminatory. Besides finding the "cardinal requirement of nondiscrimination" violated, he dismissed Ohio's claim that the credit was not a governmental act but the act of a "market participant" and that the state government had adopted the credit to encourage a reasonable public policy aimed at improving the environment.

Kennedy's majority opinion in *Bendix Autolite Corporation v. Midwesco Enterprises* used a balancing test to determine whether an Ohio tolling statute interfered with interstate commerce.[45] The Ohio statute tolled, or suspended the counting of elapsed time toward, a four-year statute of limitations when a firm, such as Midwesco, was not headquartered in or did not have an agent located in Ohio. Balancing the interests of the parties, Kennedy determined that the statute impermissibly affected interstate commerce by forcing Bendix Autolite to sue in Illinois, Midwesco's location, or to have Midwesco sit in perpetual potential liability if Midwesco did not locate in Ohio. The Ohio interest in securing jurisdiction over out-of-state defendants did not outweigh these harms. Scalia concurred, but stated in his solo opinion, "I cannot confidently assess whether the Court's evaluation and balancing of interests in this case is right or wrong." He thought that the interests on either side were "incommensurate." Moreover, weighing state governmental interests against the needs of interstate commerce was "a task squarely within the responsibility of Congress." Instead, he reiterated his facial discrimination rule: "A state statute is invalid under the Commerce Clause if, and only if, it accords discriminatory treatment to interstate commerce in a respect not required to achieve a lawful state purpose." However, such facial discrimination did occur in the application of the Ohio tolling statute because it was "a disadvantageous rule against nonresidents for no valid state purpose."[46]

Scalia concurred with Blackmun's majority opinion that found facial discrimination in a Connecticut law requiring that brewers post Connecticut prices on beer no higher than the prices in bordering states.[47] However, Blackmun's analysis additionally found the statute unconstitutional because it attempted to control, indirectly, the prices of beer in the adjoining states. Scalia refused to accept this analysis, contending that it involved the Court in the "dubious and unnecessary" evaluation of the economic effects of a law.[48] He did not want the Court entering into the realm of policy analysis or the assessment of policy outcomes.

However, Scalia did not find facial discrimination against interstate commerce in some situations. For example, because Illinois taxed intrastate and interstate telephone calls at the same rate, he concluded that this taxation imposed no facial discrimination against interstate commerce.[49] Also, he concluded that a New Jersey tax on money paid to the federal government as a windfall profits tax on crude oil producers did not facially discriminate against interstate commerce. Further, the New Jersey tax did not violate the Fourteenth Amendment's Due Process Clause.[50] The same themes appeared in his concurring opinion in a case about a Michigan business tax that required interstate firms to calculate their tax obligations using a formula that measured the value added to a product during the part of the production process occurring in Michigan. Scalia agreed with Kennedy's majority opinion, which held that the tax did not violate due process. But Scalia opted for a facial discrimination test to evaluate the effect of the tax on interstate commerce. Kennedy had used the more complex assessing process of the *Complete Auto Transit* test to reach a similar conclusion: the tax was not protectionist.[51]

Scalia has used a similar rule-oriented approach to bypass the use of the "undue burdens" balancing criterion in cases about conflicting state laws. However, rather than just applying a facial discrimination rule hostile to balancing, he has considered precedents governing similar situations. In his dissenting opinion in *American Trucking Associations v. Scheiner,*[52] he disagreed with the Court's conclusion that a Pennsylvania axle tax and marker fee on motor carriers was unduly burdensome and unconstitutional because it lacked internal consistency. The Pennsylvania legislation imposed no marker fee on out-of-state carriers. It did impose marker fees on Pennsylvania residents, but in-state carriers received a reduced rate of axle taxation for paying the marker fee. Scalia concluded that, because the axle tax was imposed uniformly and the marker fee was not imposed on out-of-state vehicles, there was no facial discrimination against interstate commerce. Also, in addition to the facial discrimination analysis, he could not find any precedent opposed to the Pennsylvania tax system. Thus, a determination of facial discrimination required evidence of an overt protectionist act by a state which was costly to interests *external* to the state.

When considering the State of North Dakota's effort to impose a sales use tax on mail order and common carrier sales by an out-of-state office supplies firm, the Quill Corporation, Justice Stevens's majority opinion reversed precedents that had used the Due Process Clause to hold that a firm had to be physically present in a state to be subject to its laws. However, he allowed North Dakota to tax Quill because the tax satisfied the four criteria of the *Complete Auto Transit* test. In reaching this conclusion, Stevens also reaffirmed precedent stating a bright-line rule requiring that parties be physically present in the state in order to be subject to sales and use taxes. He then tried to reconcile this rule with the *Complete Auto Transit* test.[53] Scalia's concurring opinion agreed with Stevens on the due process issue, but he did not accept Stevens's reconsideration of the bright-line test. Because he believed that the bright-line rule on sales and use taxes had engendered substantial reliance as a precedent, following the doctrine of stare decisis he favored using the bright-line rule rather than attempting to reconcile it within the *Complete Auto Transit* test.[54] He reiterated this point in a brief concurring opinion in a case about state taxation of interstate bus tickets and contended that the *Complete Auto Transit* test should be replaced by an explicit congressional definition of facial discrimination against interstate commerce.[55]

Also, joined by Thomas in *West Lynn Creamery v. Healy*,[56] Scalia concurred with Stevens's majority opinion voiding the undue burdens caused by a Massachusetts law that subjected all milk, much of it produced in other states, to an assessment that was then distributed to Massachusetts dairy farmers. Scalia's concurring opinion argued that the Massachusetts law could not satisfy precedent. However, he thought the situation to be a close one. If the subsidy for Massachusetts farmers came from the state's general revenue fund rather than from a discriminatory tax, he thought that precedents indicated that it could stand. This reading of case law, he contended, would draw a "clear, rational line at the limits" of dormant Commerce Clause doctrine and avoid a balance struck by the Court which he thought too greatly expanded judicial power over in-state production.[57]

Related to the balancing, four-factor (*Complete Auto Transit*), and undue burdens tests of protectionism is the "speak-with-one-voice" test. This test defines state laws that prohibit the United States from speaking with one voice in international commerce as facially discriminatory.[58] Scalia disagreed with the use of this test in a case about Tennessee's taxation of cargo containers used for international shipments of products. He thought that the speak-with-one-voice test forced the Court to make "policy judgments" about whether state regulatory interests had to be weighed against the national interest. This, he argued, was properly a congressional decision:[59] the Court should confine its decision to a judgment about any facial discrimination by the law. He reiterated this position in a case about California's requirement that a firm provide a worldwide reporting of its income in order for California to calculate its state corporate franchise tax. Justice Ruth Ginsburg used the four-factor test and the speak-with-one-voice test to determine that the statute did not violate the Commerce Clause. Scalia concurred with a brief opinion rejecting the use of the speak-with-one-voice test for the same reason as in the Tennessee container case. He claimed that facial discrimination had not occurred and that no precedent existed that made the tax unconstitutional.[60]

In addition to arguing for more formal rules and for less balancing in dormant Commerce Clause cases, Scalia has attempted to control the situations in which the Court could apply any dormant Commerce Clause doctrine. In a challenge to an Oklahoma law that required coal-fired power plants to use 10 percent Oklahoma-mined coal, the majority permitted the state of Wyoming to lodge a complaint. Scalia dissented, joined by Rehnquist and Thomas, because he read precedent as confining dormant Commerce Clause cases to private litigants whose business had suffered a direct injury from the protectionist policies or undue burdens imposed on their enterprise by a state government. Returning to his frequent use of the rules of standing to restrict litigation, he argued that Wyoming had not suffered an injury-in-fact when it contended that its coal severance tax revenues might be diminished by the Oklahoma law. He deemed the harm speculative and potentially generative of "endless" state-against-state battles about the effect of state regulatory schemes.[61]

Finally, there are two important exceptions to the practice of balancing discrimination or undue burdens against state governments' interests in dormant Commerce Clause cases. The first exception is when the state acts as a "market participant," and the second is when the Privileges and Immunities Clause of Article IV is used to assert fundamental rights that offset state regulation.[62] Scalia did not issue an opinion that stated his position on either of these exceptions.

Scalia's assault on the dormant Commerce Clause and its application through a balancing test has reflected his commitment to a goal of Reasoned Elaboration jurisprudence: constrained judicial power. Rather than impede the majoritarian decisions of state governments through judicial evaluation of the extent to which those decisions impose a burden on commerce, he has sought a precise and rational doctrinal standard spelling out the judicial role in a selected set of facially discriminatory situations and situations governed by longstanding precedent. The political effect of his position on the dormant Commerce Clause can be somewhat beneficial to state governments because it tries to restrain the Court, a national institution, from developing rules that could control state legislative initiatives. At the same time, he never has abandoned the New Deal's legacy of federal judicial preeminence in the establishment of boundaries between federal and state governmental power.

ISSUES OF JUDICIAL FEDERALISM

Justice Scalia has addressed a number of cases about the relationship of the federal and state courts. In part, his opinions have attempted to sort out the independent authority of state courts as constitutional institutions of state governments and the nature of federal judicial supremacy in three legal arenas: the Eleventh Amendment, the "diversity of citizenship" provision of Article III of the Constitution as elaborated by federal judiciary acts, and the use of state law to elaborate federal judicial procedural rules.

Eleventh Amendment Interpretations

The Eleventh Amendment, a response to the Supreme Court's 1793 decision in *Chisholm v. Georgia*,[63] was intended to eliminate suits in federal court against a state government "by Citizens of another State, or by Citizens or Subjects of any Foreign State." Nearly a century later, in *Hans v. Louisiana*,[64] the Court extended the meaning of the Eleventh Amendment to prevent suits in federal court against a state government by the state's own citizens unless the state government consented. The *Hans* extension of the Eleventh Amendment has troubled the Rehnquist Court. In *Welch v. Texas Department of Highways and Public Transportation*,[65] Justice Powell used the *Hans* doctrine to bar a federal suit brought by a Texas state employee against the State of Texas, for injuries suffered while working on a ferry dock. The federal Jones Act permitted dockworkers to sue for personal injuries in federal court, but Powell held that *Hans,* the lack of language in the Jones Act limiting the application of *Hans* in the circumstances of this case, and federal admiralty law required Welch to seek relief in state court, if Texas consented. In a brief concurrence, Scalia agreed that *Hans* prevented the federal suit and should be relied upon because of its value as a longstanding precedent. Additionally, he argued that Article III contained an implicit limitation on federal jurisdiction over suits brought by individuals against states.[66]

In three opinions Scalia has spelled out in detail his views on *Hans.* He has accepted congressional authority to develop statutory provisions that overrode the *Hans* limitation in certain circumstances. He concurred with Justice Brennan's opinion for a plurality of a badly divided court about the meaning of provisions in the Comprehensive Environmental Response, Compensation, and Liability Act as amended by the Superfund Amendments and Reauthorization Act. Brennan let a private party, the Union Gas Company, a Pennsylvania firm, sue the Pennsylvania state government to pay for the costs of an environmental cleanup on land over which the state had acquired an easement. However, joined by Rehnquist, O'Connor, and Kennedy, Scalia dissented from Brennan's use of language that reduced the power of the states to consent to suits. In defense of state judicial power he concluded that *Hans* served a valuable function in the preservation of state sovereignty and the system of federalism. Therefore, the Court could not restrict the *Hans* doctrine just because an act of Congress used the Commerce Clause to regulate the disposal of wastes shipped from state to state and to eliminate bothersome state sovereign immunity from suits seeking money to operate the disposal process. Congress should not be allowed to let private parties challenge a state in federal court. This would be an unconstitutional restriction on the immunity from suit which was afforded by state sovereignty. Instead, Scalia thought that the restriction on state sovereign immunity or on state power to forgo that immunity was justified only if it came under Article III. Thus, to become liable for the cleanup costs, Pennsylvania had to consent by voluntarily assuming liability and waiving its immunity. Because Pennsylvania had independently waived immunity by conducting cleanup actions in conformity with the federal laws, Scalia concluded that it had consented and could be sued in federal court.[67] However, if Pennsylvania had chosen not to act, and thus not to waive immunity, congressional acts based on Article I powers could not restrict the state's decision to remain immune from the suit.

Scalia applied the logic of *Hans* in a case about whether the Bankruptcy Act abrogated the sovereign power of states to consent to their citizens' suits against them. His concurrence stressed that Congress never had the power to restrict states' decisions to be immune from suit, and that any restriction on immunity must be the result of a state's independent consent to a suit.[68] Finally, he refused to let Native American villages sue the Alaska state government to compel the payment of money allocated to them but not fully appropriated by state law. For the Court, he ruled, first, that the state power to consent to suits against it extended not just to suits by its individual citizens but to suits by tribal groups having some aspects of sovereignty; and second, that federal statutory provisions did not abrogate the authority of the state to consent to suits against it.[69]

Diversity Jurisdiction and Related Issues Affecting Federal Judicial Power

When private parties in a suit are citizens of different (diverse) states and are engaged in a live civil conflict that satisfies the jurisdictional amount of alleged economic damages fixed in the amended Judiciary Act, they can sue in federal rather than state court. Since the Court's decision in *Erie Railroad Company v. Tompkins* in 1938,[70] the federal court in such a suit is to resolve the case using the law of the state in which it sits. Before *Erie* there was a federal common law that differed from state common law in its substantive content, in its requirements for the admission and evaluation of evidence, and in the remedies available to winning parties. Therefore, plaintiffs could shop for a favorable federal or state forum in which to file their case. However, the *Erie* requirement on the federal use of state law has discouraged the practice of forum shopping.

Scalia has sought to further the *Erie* effort to curtail forum shopping. For example, he dissented from Justice Thurgood Marshall's holding that federal law determined the validity of the effort of a photocopier manufacturer and its dealers in other states to place language in a contract that would determine the forum for suits if the contract was breached. Scalia disagreed with Marshall's conclusion that a federal statute could be interpreted as resolving the validity of the contract's forum specification clause. He thought that Marshall gave the statutory language "novel scope" by twisting both its plain meaning and its meaning in the context of federal jurisdictional practice. Additionally, he refused to consider a "judge-made" federal rule to govern the question. Considering the aims of *Erie* to be the equitable administration of laws and the reduction of forum shopping, he concluded that the federal statute did not displace state courts' jurisdiction over the case.[71]

In another case, Scalia wrote for the Court to hold that federal jurisdictional rules required that all parties in a limited partnership be from different states if they are to meet federal criteria to initiate an action based on diversity of citizenship. Although the Court has long considered a corporation to be a single person for diversity determination, he concluded that a limited partnership was not similar to a corporation. The decision made it more difficult for this business entity to seek relief in federal court.[72] Finally, in *American National Red Cross v. S.G.*,[73] he dissented from an opinion by Souter which construed the congressionally issued charter of the American Red Cross as mandating the exclusive jurisdiction of federal courts in cases in which the Red Cross was a party. Scalia argued that the charter should be read as only creating the capacity for the Red Cross to choose federal jurisdiction, a sort of special grant of jurisdictional choice to the organization.[74]

Scalia has tried to frustrate the efforts of parties in disputes to manipulate forum selection rules. In a dispute about which state's law was to be applied in a federal court when, for the convenience of the party, a case had been transferred from Mississippi to Pennsylvania, his dissenting opinion took a dim view of party efforts to use Mississippi law to circumvent a Pennsylvania statute of limitations that would have prevented action in the long-delayed case. Taking a more formalist view of *Erie* than was used in Kennedy's majority opinion, he argued that, even if the case first arose in another state, the federal court was required to apply the law of the state in which it sat.[75]

Finally, Scalia has resisted efforts to curtail state judicial power. In *Tafflin v. Levitt*,[76] O'Connor's majority opinion held that the federal courts and a state court had concurrent jurisdiction over civil RICO suits because there was no clear indication that state jurisdiction was incompatible with the federal RICO law. Thus, unless prohibited by Congress or the Constitution, a party in a diversity of citizenship case could use state rather than federal courts to pursue a civil action made available by federal law. Scalia concurred, offering a caution. He indicated that Congress should expressly act to deprive the state courts of concurrent jurisdiction over civil diversity cases arising under federal laws such as RICO. Exclusion of state jurisdiction over federal civil law cannot be on the basis of implication from legislative history or on the basis of allegations of the incompatibility of state jurisdiction with "federal interests"; it had to be spelled out in an act of Congress.[77]

The Use of State Law

A third judicial federalism issue involves the "borrowing" of state statutes of limitations and their use as federal rules of procedure by federal courts. In *Agency Holding Corporation v. Malley-Duff and Associates*,[78] the Court considered the federal judicial practice of borrowing statutes of limitations for civil diversity actions from similar state law when no federal statute of limitations existed. This practice of borrowing state procedural rules and rules of decision, designed for an era when Congress afforded little procedural guidance to federal courts, was over 150 years old.[79] O'Connor's opinion in *Agency Holding*, building on decisions of the Burger Court, carried borrowing in a new direction. At issue was whether a statute of limitations existed in a civil RICO diversity action about an alleged insurance company fraud. RICO offered no statute of limitations, and O'Connor could find no similar state statute from which a federal district judge could borrow a statute of limitations. Therefore, she turned to federal law and borrowed a four-year statute of limitations from the Clayton Act, an antitrust law. Scalia concurred. Opening his solo opinion with a history of borrowing practice, he concluded that borrowing rested on a general theme in American federalism: federal courts should apply state law in diversity cases when congressional acts had not preempted state law. But he thought that what O'Connor had done was something quite different. Without any expressed congressional attempt to preempt state statutes of limitations in RICO, he concluded that she had gone "prowling hungrily through Statutes at Large for an appetizing federal limitations period, and pounc[ed] on the Clayton Act." Her "hunt" had departed from borrowing's origin as a principle of federalism. It had also enhanced the Court's power to locate and apply rules of decision when Congress had not done so. Scalia desired to retain borrowing as doctrine rooted in concerns of judicial federalism, so he argued that when a federal statute of limitations was lacking and no similar state rule of decision

existed, there was simply "none to apply."[80] Later, when the Court
allowed a federal court to borrow a North Carolina statute of limitations after finding none in the federal Labor Management Reporting
and Disclosure Act, Scalia issued a paragraph-long concurring opinion
reiterating that borrowing from federal rather than state law, indicated
as a possibility in the opinion of O'Connor, should not be practiced.[81]
In another case, he counseled against the judicial development of federal statute of limitations standards when there was no state statute of
limitations from which borrowing could occur. If there was no federal
statute of limitations in the statute, he wanted a uniform practice to
govern the use of state statutes of limitations.[82]

Summary of Scalia' Opinions on Judicial Federalism

Scalia's opinions on the various dimensions of judicial federalism have
evidenced his concern with the constitutional basis of existing doctrines. His opinions in *Welch* and *Union Gas,* on diversity in general,
and in *Agency Holding* have rested on a constitutional argument that
attempted to restrain federal judicial authority through the use of federalism. Thus, Scalia has been less concerned about judicial federalism
in the abstract than he has been concerned that federal courts could
transform congressional acts into a source of federal judicial power in
suits between state governments and their citizens (see his opinions in
Welch, Union Gas, and the dispute between Native American villages
and Alaska), reconstruct diversity standards to permit more federal
adjudication of conflicts, and alter precedent on borrowing to permit
more federal judicial specification of their own rules of decision (see
his opinion in *Agency Holding*). What has bothered him has been the
trend toward a more active federal judiciary. Thus, it has been his fear
of pragmatic liberal jurisprudence more than a conviction about the
shape of American federalism that has driven his decisionmaking in
judicial federalism cases. He has preferred to apply the Reasoned Elaboration postulate of judicial passivity to ensure judicial deference to
state governments' policies.

INTERSTATE FEDERALISM ISSUES

Scalia has written opinions in a smattering of cases about intergovernmental relations.[83] "Full faith and credit," the constitutional requirement in Article IV that a state should respect the laws and legal

decisions of other states, governed his opinion in a case about the applicable statute of limitations. In a case about interest on suspended gas royalty payments which was tried in Kansas but involved parties and properties in Kansas and other states, he held that the Kansas court had only to give full faith and credit to the substantive law of the other states. Kansas courts could use their own procedural law, such as a statute of limitations. Moreover, Kansas courts had to give full faith and credit only to the law of other states which was brought to their attention by the litigants. Full faith and credit thus was like a personal protection of liberty that litigants had to activate.[84]

The extradition of criminals from one state to another, also required by Article IV of the Constitution, was at issue in *Puerto Rico v. Branstad*.[85] In this case, the Court reversed a Civil War era doctrine holding that the mandatory duty of a state to return a criminal suspect could not be enforced in federal court.[86] Scalia concurred that a federal commonwealth such as Puerto Rico could use the federal court to compel the extradition, but he did not want to extend the doctrine beyond the facts of the case and impose federal jurisdiction over state-to-state extraditions.[87]

Due process standards of the Fifth Amendment also affect relations among the states. For the Court, Scalia held that California did not violate due process standards of fair play and substantive justice by serving process on a New Jersey resident temporarily visiting California. The service of process was related to a divorce action initiated by the California-resident wife of the New Jersey resident. Brennan's dissenting opinion argued that the service of process violated a due process standard of fairness based on the totality of the circumstances. Scalia countered that precedent required his decision and that Brennan's approach was too subjective and violated traditions of procedural due process.[88]

Altogether, Scalia's opinions on intergovernmental relations have conveyed a message of caution if not skepticism about the development of federal judicial standards. A theme of judicial passivity has marked his attitude toward federal judicial development of intergovernmental relations doctrine (*Branstad*), toward rules on the invocation of full faith and credit rules (the Kansas case), and toward due process criteria affecting state procedures (the California service of process case). Again, his decisions have displayed less interest in the political-constitutional value of federalism than in applying the passive and deferential methodology of Reasoned Elaboration.

CONCLUSION

Scalia's opinions on federalism, like his opinions on the powers of the branches of the federal government, have addressed the need for specific rules and the control of balancing and related pragmatic judgments by judges. Therefore, he has applied the principles of Reasoned Elaboration jurisprudence to construct what he deems to be a viable process of judging in federalism cases. With clear standards, the process of judging can proceed with few value judgments by judges. The test of facial discrimination in preemption cases and dormant Commerce Clause cases *(Boyle Technologies, Mortier, Morales, Summit Health, Tyler Pipe, American Trucking, New Energy, West Lynn Creamery)*, reliance on long-established precedent and the *Hans* doctrine *(Welch, Union Gas)*, and the requirement of statutory specificity in the borrowing cases *(Agency Holding)* have illustrated his desire for a neutral law. Also, his arguments against judicial doctrinal creativity, especially in the cases about the dormant Commerce Clause and borrowing, have moved the Court closer to the umpire role envisioned by Reasoned Elaboration jurisprudence. His reliance on precedent and statutory text has reinforced the opposition to experimentation and the consideration of social facts which appears in his separated powers opinions. Finally, he has voiced the message of judicial passivity by attempting to locate a constitutional basis for precedent, and he has discouraged the use of precedent without a logic rooted in a respect for the constitutional sovereignty of the states. Consequently, he has tried to prevent courts from evolving on their own a new federalism favorable to *either* federal or state governmental interests.

Scalia's application of Reasoned Elaboration arguments in federalism cases has not always advanced the conservative vision of a weaker federal government. By focusing on the constraint of judicial choice, which is the aim of Reasoned Elaboration, he has sometimes left Congress free to engage in policymaking inimicable to independent state power. In particular, his *South Carolina v. Baker* and *Morales* opinions left Congress free to use the Commerce Clause to advance federal interests. They signaled that the Court ought to defer to statutory language empowering federal regulatory efforts. As in the separated powers cases, he has indicated that the constraint on the federal government should come from congressional decisions. Consequently, his opinions have demanded that Congress defend state governmental power. Congressional statutes, made in response to popular majorities, should reinforce the constitutional sovereignty of the states.

With their emphasis on limiting the role of courts in politics, Scalia's opinions about American federalism have neglected the larger issue of the independence of the states in American governance. His instrumental use of a Reasoned Elaboration construction of law has harnessed judicial interrogation of the division of governmental power and brazen efforts by courts to use federalism doctrine in new ways. But he has failed to pursue a conservative vision that, in the spirit but not the practice of Nixon and Reagan's New Federalism, aggressively seeks to move power from Washington bureaucracies to the states. Like the Nixon and Reagan New Federalism proposals, Scalia's opinions have not worked a revolution in American federalism. All that he has done is to advance the use of formal rules as a trick that might harness the scope of federal supremacy and curtail pragmatic interpretations of the Constitution that promise even more centralization of government power. If his instrumental use of Reasoned Elaboration arguments has been conservative, it is only because he conserves a status quo marked by extensive state governmental dependence on Washington's definition of the powers of the states.

Chapter Six

EQUALITY THROUGH THE PANACEA OF NEUTRAL LAW

Professor Antonin Scalia once remarked that it was an "embarrassment" to teach Supreme Court opinions about the Fourteenth Amendment's Equal Protection Clause. Finding a "trivialization" of the Constitution, he thought that the Court had neglected "hard-minded, reasoned analysis" in an effort to provide experimental and discriminatory remedies for racial and gender discrimination. His remedy was simple: the application of neutral rules of law would leave persons to rise or fall on their own merit. The pathologies of racism and sexism would submit to this antidote, an antidote without the side effects of the "racist principles" that marked affirmative action and other judicial remedies for the pathologies.[1] His neutral-rule formula thus adopted a tenet of the conservative revival: inequality is cured by neutral laws and not by governmental remedies that compel attention to race in employment, education, and other economic and social decisions.

In the 1830s Alexis de Tocqueville, writing about Americans, recognized that "nothing can satisfy them without equality, and they would rather perish than lose it."[2] In a general sense, equality is a core element in Americans' political vision; however, the political meaning of American equality has become legally defined as "equal protection of the laws." After the Civil War, the federal government made two key decisions to codify equality, decisions that still delimit legal definitions of the concept. First, Congress wrote the Thirteenth, Fourteenth, and Fifteenth Amendments to suppress racial inequality. The initial Supreme Court interpretations of the Fourteenth Amendment read it only as a legal protection for African Americans. Second, the Court confirmed Fourteenth Amendment language confining relief to state laws or "state action" violating the amendment's Privileges and Immunities, Due Process, and Equal Protection Clauses. The amendment did not require equal protection in the private sector.[3]

Not until after the New Deal did Fourteenth Amendment doctrines undergo significant modification. In the period from 1938 to 1978, the justices developed the "tiers of scrutiny" approach to the Fourteenth

Amendment, Congress enacted civil rights legislation in conformity with the amendment, and the justices expanded the meaning of state action. Central to the contemporary interpretation of the Equal Protection Clause was the *strict scrutiny* of governmental action that resulted in discrimination against disadvantaged racial, ethnic, national, or religious groups. Under strict scrutiny doctrine, the government had to show the Court that a policy affecting a disadvantaged group served a "compelling governmental interest," was a substantially effective means of furthering the compelling governmental interest, and was a necessary and least restrictive alternative for achieving the governmental interest. Any restrictions upon the fundamental rights of a disadvantaged group of people had to be closely examined by courts, or given "strict scrutiny." Through the strict scrutiny of the legislation, the restriction on rights would be deemed unconstitutional if there was evidence that it could ultimately be traced to an unconstitutionally discriminatory legislative purpose or if there was evidence of intentional acts of discrimination by government.[4]

During the early years of the Burger Court (1969–78), the justices made it clear that constitutional equal protection meant the strict scrutiny of governmental acts of racial, national, ethnic, and alienage discrimination and impediments to a right to vote and a right to travel.[5] A state had to provide evidence of a "compelling governmental" interest in order for a court to permit use of the state's police power in ways that created racial and related forms of discrimination or that imposed restrictions on the rights of racial and national groups. Also, the majority of the justices required *intermediate scrutiny* of governmental acts that restricted rights on the basis of gender and legitimacy of birth; they sought proof by the state that the restriction served "important governmental objectives" and was "substantially related to achievement of those objectives."[6] A standard requiring *"reasonableness"* in governmental action ("nondeferential rationality review" or "deferential rationality review")[7] protected other groups against discrimination. With these latter categories of persons, the Court examined less closely whether the government, in responding to the public, discriminated. Also, a deferential consideration of the reasonableness of governmental acts of economic discrimination and age discrimination permitted many of these forms of regulatory legislation to survive judicial inquiry.[8] Also, most private acts of discrimination, remained outside the zone of governmental regulation, unless they occurred with significant state involvement or "under color" of state law, or violated congressional civil rights acts adopted pursuant to the Interstate Commerce Clause and the Thirteenth and Fourteenth Amendments.[9]

During the Rehnquist Court the justices continued to employ the levels of scrutiny criteria and the state action formula to determine the legally enforceable definition of equality. Most of the Rehnquist Court's decisions elaborated on existing standards defining equal protection of the laws, especially in cases about the level of scrutiny to be used in the evaluation of legislative affirmative action programs designed to remedy discrimination against minorities; about the authority of courts to remedy racial discrimination; about racial discrimination in jury selection; and about the interpretation of civil rights and voting rights laws legislated by Congress under the enforcement sections of the Thirteenth, Fourteenth, and Fifteenth Amendments. Scalia has written very few Opinions of the Court on equality issues, and his dissenting opinions rarely have provided an elaborate argument expressing his vision of the role of equal protection in American political life. His actions have implied a reluctance to enter into the continuing controversy about race, gender, and equality in American life. Instead, as indicated by the tabulation of civil rights votes in table 3.1, he simply has chosen to vote against about seven of every ten civil rights claimants. And when he has written on equality, he has focused his discussion on the errors of pragmatic liberal civil rights decisions, including the author's neglect of purposeful and rational text and precedents or the author's definition of evidence of discrimination. Nonetheless, his opinions have worked against legal rules protecting the equal treatment of disadvantaged groups and the capacity of these groups to play an equal role in contemporary American politics.

LEVELS OF SCRUTINY AND LEGAL NEUTRALITY

In *City of Richmond v. J. A. Croson Company*,[10] the Rehnquist Court considered a policy of the city of Richmond, Virginia, which designated 30 percent of the subcontracts on city business for award to minority business enterprises. Scalia concurred with the majority. The effect of Reasoned Elaboration argumentation on equal protection law was visible in the opinions of the majority justices. They asserted the theoretical certainty of a race-blind reading of the Equal Protection Clause. Through brief reference to history and more extensive discussion of strict scrutiny, Justice O'Connor's Opinion of the Court concluded that the clause must mean the same thing in all situations, for to read it otherwise carries a "a danger of stigmatic harm." Thus, in a few pages she transvalued strict scrutiny from its initial form—in which it was a pragmatic instrument for the pursuit of equality—into a rule requiring government to avoid considering race in public policymaking.[11] Her logic was that the law could only target explicit discriminatory acts by employing a simple, allegedly neutral rule. Consequently, affirmative action programs could be used only to discipline pathological inequality.

When she turned to evaluate evidence of discrimination and the appropriateness of remedies in the Richmond setting, O'Connor sought a practical certainty in the law. She argued that evidence of an injury must be specific and that a specific party must come forward with direct evidence of personal injury. Only such evidence could provide a reason for deducing that the general rule had been violated. She rejected the remedy of the contract set-aside because it was not narrowly tailored; she wanted a specific remedy for a specific harm or a sure solution to a sure injury. O'Connor regarded quotas, a part of the program in question, as an arbitrary policy choice unrelated to the specific remedy of a specific discriminatory act against a specific individual. In addition, she disregarded statistical evidence of probable harms and the general empirical judgments of injury by local officials. There was no room for experimentation with contingent remedies for discriminatory inequalities and no room for a law searching for better policy outcomes.[12] Justice Kennedy's brief concurring opinion restated the idea of neutrality: "The moral imperative of racial neutrality is the driving force of the Equal Protection Clause."[13] However, because it was generally consistent with the idea of neutrality and was supported by precedent, he agreed that the "less absolute rule" of strict scrutiny was acceptable.

In a lengthy solo concurring opinion, Justice Scalia bypassed O'Connor's transvaluation of strict scrutiny. Instead, he presented a requirement that the Court practice racial neutrality. Relying heavily on the argument of Alexander Bickel in *The Morality of Consent*, he started with the premise that only one pragmatic or "benign" reason could ever be compelling enough to justify state governmental action using a racial classification. That reason, illustrated in decisions about remedies for school desegregation, was the need to eliminate the maintenance of a system of unlawful racial discrimination. In *Croson* the contracting provisions did not apply to unlawful racial classification by law (de jure segregation), so there could be no use of remedial racial classifications in the assignment of contracts. Thus, Scalia rejected dicta in O'Connor's opinion implying that some benign governmental use of racial classifications might survive strict scrutiny. The rationale offered for this position was that racial preferences designed to overcome the effects of past discrimination did not eradicate the *source* of discrimination, "the tendency—fatal to a nation such as ours—to classify and judge men and women on the basis of their country of origin or the color of their skin."[14] He assumed that racially neutral laws would contribute to the elimination of this evil.

The adoption of this position posed a problem. Some precedent validated congressional acts allowing benign racial classifications in affirmative action programs. Scalia chose to distinguish the Richmond case from these cases for two reasons. First, he argued that precedent cases allowed the use of congressional powers "explicitly enhanced" by the Fourteenth Amendment to address "egregious and persistent unlawful discrimination." This situation, he concluded, did not exist in Richmond because a remedial contracting policy had been adopted by the local government and because there was no de jure segregation affecting the award of contracts. Second, he contended that historically the struggle for racial justice was a "struggle by the national society against oppression in the individual States," or a struggle of a national interest favoring racial equality against factional racist political interests in the states, especially in the South. Although this conclusion greatly oversimplified the history of racial politics in the United States, he used it to justify federal judicial application of a neutral rule of equal protection against any "dominant" racial faction—such as the blacks of Richmond—benefiting from state or local policies. Thus, a fear of expanded political pluralism helpful to long-suppressed interests marked his opinion, as evidenced by his remark that "blacks have long been on the receiving end of the injustice. When injustice is the game, however, turn-about is not fair play."[15]

Finally, Scalia suggested that the racial quotas in the Richmond program violated a somewhat different principle, the idea of equal treatment of *individuals* by government. More than O'Connor or Kennedy, he saw the city's program as an affront to personal autonomy. He quoted Bickel to argue that the practical effect was the establishment of blacks as a subject caste and the derogation of individuals by their assignment to that caste. This practice, he argued, violated an undefined "American principle" of individual treatment. Therefore, individual "actual victims" of racial discrimination had to prove the need for a remedy for their disadvantage. Programs for the relief of cumulative discrimination against an aggregate class did not eliminate thinking in terms of race.[16] He did not confront the social fact that blacks are already a caste and that neutral laws will not address many of the power relationships that have placed them in a separate caste. He simply assumed that neutral laws would erase culture and history.

The pragmatic liberal counterargument to the rule of racial neutrality appeared in Justice Marshall's dissenting opinion. Using language from his earlier opinion in the *Bakke* medical school admissions case,[17] Marshall applied an intermediate scrutiny or substantial capacity test to race-conscious remedial policies of governments. He was unwilling to apply a racially blind rule and a compelling governmental interest test for two reasons. First, he argued that the need to break down barriers caused by past discrimination ought to be a paramount objective, occurring not just when the evidence of discrimination was compelling. Second, he argued that the affirmative action plan was designed to avoid the danger of "perpetuating the exclusionary effects of past discrimination."[18] His evaluation of discrimination thus aimed more at the goal of rooting out both overt and more subtle exercises of discriminatory power which prevented the fulfillment of the idea of equality for blacks as a distinctive bloc or class.

Marshall then considered the evidence in support of a finding of "purposeful" discrimination. Unlike the majority's, his evaluation of the evidence was a wide-ranging impact analysis. It included the use of social facts such as historical statistics, past events, and the testimony of local officials to construct a history of racial discrimination in the city's contract process. Turning to the construction of the remedy, he adopted an approach different from that of O'Connor and Scalia. Unlike the majority, he refused to limit remedial efforts to "narrowly tailored" remedies, which he likened to "steps that lead nowhere." He was willing to let Richmond experiment with its set-aside program as a remedy for past racial discrimination. Clearly he feared that without such governmental experimentation with class- or bloc-oriented remedies for racism, a racist status quo would be frozen in American politics.[19] From this logic, he developed the notion that the rules instituted by affirmative action programs can be instrumental in the pursuit of racial equality. The practical certainty of such rules would serve to establish his desired outcome or aspiration, an egalitarian society.

Marshall disagreed with Scalia's conclusion that benign use of racial classifications to eliminate the effects of past discrimination was racist. He especially took issue with Scalia's "artful distinction" separating the legality of the Richmond remedy from that of the remedy offered in school desegregation cases. Marshall read the history of the Fourteenth Amendment as evidencing no constitutional inhibition on state governmental policies consistent with class-oriented rather than individual-oriented federal efforts to end racial discrimination. He rejected the idea that the amendment charged the federal government alone with the power to remedy discrimination and its effects.[20]

The deep division in *Croson* illustrates the commitment of Scalia to the instrumental political aims of Reasoned Elaboration jurisprudence. None of the pragmatic arguments made by Marshall were acceptable to him. He could not accept that a benign racial classification was not necessarily racist against some individual, and he thought that by ignoring race the law could automatically provide a society of equals. He tended to undervalue the cumulative effect of race on blacks as a class with a distinctive cultural identity, and he saw sinister motives in black efforts to win some group-oriented compensation for centuries of discrimination.[21] Finally, he adopted questionable perspectives on the history of legal efforts to end racial discrimination. Although the bitter sarcasm of his Washington University address was absent in his *Croson* concurring opinion, the notion of legal rules providing the basis for advancement on the basis of individual merit remained. But in his reliance on rules, he never considered that merit is a social construction tinged by the social acceptance of racial stereotypes. His reading of the rule of racial neutrality into the equal protection standard of strict scrutiny precluded any governmental empathy with disadvantaged classes. It obviated most uses of law to end stigma against classes long subject to a majority prejudice against their equality. Instead, it was an extremely individualistic construction of equality which underlies his approach to legal issues related to equal protection, including the judicial and legislative power to relieve recognized discriminatory acts.

In 1995, when the Court, in *Adarand Constructors, Inc. v. Pena,*[22] voided a federal set-aside program that gave financial incentives for federal contractors to hire minority subcontractors, Scalia wrote a brief opinion concurring with O'Connor's plurality opinion. In her argument to void the program, O'Connor used a strict scrutiny test akin to her *Croson* argument. Scalia's opinion reasserted his opposition to the use of strict scrutiny analysis in racial discrimination cases. Neglecting the caveat about one permissible use for racial classifications which he had stated in his *Croson* opinion, he implied a rejection of the post–*Carolene Products* strict scrutiny of most governmental racial classifications in favor of a nondiscretionary rule that any governmental racial classification was unconstitutional. His reason for this clear rule was that "to pursue the concept of racial entitlement—even for the most benign of purposes—is to reinforce and preserve for future mischief the way of thinking that produced race slavery, race privilege, and race hatred. In the eyes of government, we are just one race here. It is American."[23] His rule thus would prevent almost any governmental remedy for the legacy of racism, surely the most politically divisive problem in the American regime. Unlike Justice Marshall, Scalia implied that racism will end if government neglects the legacy of racism.

When Scalia voted but did not write opinions in cases considering affirmative action remedies for previous discrimination, the vote was always against the affirmative action program. He joined a dissenting opinion by Rehnquist arguing that a plan to further the elimination of discriminatory promotion practices in the Alabama state police was not narrowly tailored. Rehnquist contended that the court-ordered changes in promotion practices could have achieved their goal without the use of a quota plan "trammeling on the rights of nonminority troopers."[24] Scalia's other important vote without opinion in an affirmative action case was in *Metro Broadcasting v. FCC*.[25] For the Court, Justice Brennan upheld FCC policies that enhanced the opportunity for minority ownership of broadcast licenses. Strangely, Scalia joined both O'Connor's and Kennedy's dissenting opinions. O'Connor found no compelling state interest to justify the policies and no narrowly tailored remedy substantially related to the elimination of racial discrimination.[26] Kennedy argued for neutral rules as the lawful means to end racial discrimination.[27] Scalia also voted with a Rehnquist opinion allowing white firefighters to enter a suit and challenge an affirmative action program established in a consent decree arranged between a city and African American groups.[28]

Consistent with his affirmative action opinions and votes, Scalia has given other indications that he is reluctant to extend the use of intensified scrutiny to nonracial groups. He joined a 5-to-4 majority that refused to consider a challenge to the use of deferential rationality analysis in a case about Kentucky's involuntary mental illness commitments because the legality of the rationality analysis had not been ruled on when the case was before lower federal courts.[29] He also joined the Court's opinion requiring the use of a deferential rationality review to resolve a claim of discrimination in a governmental acquisition-value taxation scheme.[30] He supported O'Connor's 5-to-4 majority opinion in *Kadramas v. Dickinson Public Schools*,[31] which held that the denial of free bus transportation to public schools had to be evaluated under a deferential rationality test. It confirmed earlier Court rulings refusing some form of more intensified scrutiny of claims of economic discrimination in public education.[32] He voted with the Court to uphold Hawaii's restriction on write-in voting and to reject the claim that all restrictions on the right to vote deserved strict scrutiny. Justice Byron White had applied a balancing test and judged that write-in voting could be abolished because the dangers of "unrestrained factionalism" outweighed the right to vote for a candidate of one's choice.[33] In cases about economic classifications, Scalia agreed with the Court's majority when it used a deferential rationality analysis to evaluate claims against discrimination in governmental property tax assessment practices and claims of unequal treatment in cable television regulation.[34] The Rehnquist Court applied intermediate scrutiny, originally used in gender discrimination cases, to discrimination against persons of illegitimate birth.[35] Scalia was a participant in this unanimous decision by the Court. However, he agreed with a unanimous Court and used strict scrutiny analysis to void laws banning primary election endorsements by a party and subjecting party organizations to various restrictions.[36]

JUDICIAL REMEDIES FOR SCHOOL SEGREGATION

In 1955, the year after the justices' momentous *Brown v. Board of Education* decision to end racial segregation in the public schools, they permitted federal courts to employ remedial orders containing a wide variety of procedures to force local school districts to desegregate with "all deliberate speed." After over a decade of delay, Brennan's Opinion of the Court in *Green v. New Kent County* changed the stipulation of "all deliberate speed" into a mandate to desegregate *"now."* Later decisions explicated the measures that could be undertaken to satisfy this mandate.[37] However, even into its 1991 term, the Court continued to define the scope of judicial remedies for school segregation. Scalia did not fully support its choices.

In *Freeman v. Pitts* the Rehnquist Court, with Justices Brennan and Marshall in retirement, approved the partial withdrawal of judicial supervision from the DeKalb County, Georgia, school system even though racial segregation had reoccurred after the implementation of a desegregation plan in 1969.[38] No justice objected to the relaxation of remedial control. Kennedy's Opinion of the Court granted partial dismissal of a desegregation decree and asserted that judicial control over local schools could only be temporary. Kennedy was willing to lift some requirements of the desegregation decree, believing that judicial oversight was no longer necessary to alleviate the initial constitutional violation and that the school district had made a good-faith commitment to enforce the original order. He deemed the resegregation associated with population shifts among school zones after the remedial consent decree to be the result of private choices of residence not closely linked to any intentional state action in violation of the original order.

Instead of the use of Brennan's *New Kent County* allocation of the burden of proof to defendant school districts in educational segregation cases, Scalia's solo concurring opinion recommended a return to traditional concepts of placing on plaintiffs the burden of proof of intentional discrimination. The effect of his recommendation would be a rule that plaintiffs bear the burden of proving segregative intent, not just social facts about racial disparity, to win a desegregation remedy. The primary reason given for his willingness to abandon *New Kent County* was that "it is now 25 years later" and that the "temporary" standard of *New Kent County* was no longer necessary. He introduced no empirical evidence or other facts to indicate why the "temporary" necessity of *New Kent County* could be abandoned. Rather, he simply concluded that "the percentage of the current makeup of school systems attributable to the prior, government-enforced discrimination has diminished with each passing year, to the point where it cannot be realistically be assumed to be a significant factor."[39]

The instrumental result of his abandonment of *New Kent County* would be a curtailment of opportunities for judicial decrees and other outcome-oriented judicial uses of discretionary power, a result that is in keeping with Reasoned Elaboration jurisprudence. Scalia suggested that his standard would permit parents and school boards to have "free choice" to assign students to schools in their own neighborhood. Thus, without judicial interference, local majorities, probably reflecting the predominant race in a racially segregated population, could define the racial composition of a school. This outcome, he believed, was an acceptable result of majority rule at the local level and of the constitutional rule he reads as "equal racial access to schools, not access to racially equal schools." However, his standard was a restricted construction of *Brown*, a standard that neglected the instrumental aim of

Brown to provide a remedy for the effect of segregation on the "hearts and minds" of black children. Equal racial access in a regime characterized by private housing discrimination and by the Court's own approval of local boundaries as a restriction on remedies for school desegregation efforts was little more than the assignment of power to local "majority factions," to use James Madison's definition.[40] It allowed black children's hearts and minds to continue to be isolated from the experiences of white America. Finally, when considered in light of his *Croson* and *Adarand Constructors* opinions, Scalia's decision seemed to discourage further governmental efforts to provide a place for disadvantaged classes or factions in the regime. It allowed majority rule, even if the majority acts as a self-interested faction to preserve its own advantage and disadvantage the equality and rights claims of discrete and insular minorities.

In *United States v. Fordice* Justice White wrote for a majority of the Court when it considered remedies for racial segregation in the eight institutions of the Mississippi college and university system. First, White found a continuing violation of *Brown v. Board of Education.* Despite the *New Kent County* decision, racial discrimination in the system had not been eradicated. Then, displaying a willingness to go behind the allegedly neutral admissions and operational rules adopted by the Mississippi system of higher education, he found various vestiges of the regime of de jure segregation which necessitated continuing judicial supervision of the system's policies. Despite efforts by the state to eliminate overt de jure discrimination in admissions to the schools, and twelve years of efforts to reach a consensual resolution with black plaintiffs, he concluded that the state had not met the burden of proving that it had dismantled the dual system of education of the races. The state had not shown that its practices and procedures in the use of admission tests for automatic admission into the schools, its failure to consider student grades, and its current institutional funding and definition of the programs and missions at the institutions had replaced discriminatory practices traceable to the prior segregated system. Even if race-neutral justifications could be offered for these practices and procedures, the policies were judged to lack sufficient educational justification.[41]

Scalia reacted to White's conclusions in a concurring and dissenting opinion that criticized the application of *New Kent County* to higher education, boldly stating that the case "has no proper application in the context of higher education, provides no genuine guidance to States and lower courts, and is as likely to subvert as to promote the interests of those citizens on whose behalf the present suit was brought." In his opinion Scalia first addressed his "no general guidance" criticism. Although he criticized the Court for establishing two conflicting tests for determining compliance with *Brown*, he concluded that both tests were so ambiguous and lacking in substance that they created unbounded judicial discretion. Relying again on the postulates of Reasoned Elaboration, he concluded that the conflicting tests left the remediation of school segregation unbounded by the rule of law and afforded the states no way to defend any educational decisions in any judicial challenge to their policy choices.[42]

Second, Scalia turned to the scope of *New Kent County*. Much of his argument used precedent cases to show that the Court had not applied standards for desegregation used in public elementary and secondary school cases to public higher education. However, finding that cases about higher education had required "discontinuation of discriminatory practices and the use of a neutral admissions policy," and that Mississippi's use of a test to determine admissions was a racially exclusionary practice, he concurred that at least in some respects Mississippi was still practicing de jure segregation. However, he located no evidence and no precedent to support the Court's specification of other discriminatory practices.[43]

Finally, Scalia discussed the "unanticipated consequences" of the Court's decision, a political commentary alien to his use of the discourse of Reasoned Elaboration. As in *Freeman*, his concern was that freedom of educational choice would be undermined by a judicial policy requiring racial balance. In particular, he thought that such a policy of compulsory integration threatened the congressional desire to strengthen historically black colleges. Additionally, Scalia thought that the Court's opinion would result in "litigation-driven confusion and destabilization in the university systems of all of the formerly *de jure* states." He thus expressed a Reasoned Elaborationist's fear of a world without the ordering force of rules of law.[44]

The pattern of Scalia's voting was the same in cases in which he did not write an opinion. Scalia agreed with Rehnquist's opinion in a case about the extent of federal judicial supervision of formerly segregated schools, a case in which Rehnquist provided a reasonableness standard to guide the decision to withdraw judicial oversight of a school board, rather than a standard requiring an elimination of all effects of past racial discrimination.[45] Also, Scalia voted for Justice Anthony Ken-

nedy's concurring opinion in *Missouri v. Jenkins I.*[46] In the last-named
case, the majority limited a federal judge's power to impose a tax increase to pay for school desegregation unless all less costly remedies
would plainly leave the violation without remedy. Kennedy considered
taxation a wholly legislative matter, and he argued that no judicial
power to impose a tax increase existed. In a reprise of the case, Scalia
voted for Rehnquist's majority opinion that restricted school desegregation remedies to the district in which the violation had occurred and
to remedies that addressed the specific, judicially determined violation, and that required measures of the achievement of desegregation
related to the numbers of students of each race in schools or school
programs rather than measures of student accomplishment such as
achievement test scores for students of different racial groups.[47]

OTHER CIVIL RIGHTS ISSUES

In other cases about discriminatory actions, Scalia voted for Rehnquist's Opinion of the Court in *Spallone v. United States.*[48] In this case a
federal judge had imposed contempt sanctions on city council members who refused to vote to implement a plan to end racial discrimination in the location of public housing. Rehnquist held that contempt
sanctions should have been first leveled at the city; a citation of council
members for contempt demanded a continuing extreme recalcitrance
by them. In another case, despite a general hostility to most parties
seeking innovative remedies for civil rights violations, Scalia did vote
with the unanimous court to allow abortion clinics to use unambiguous provisions of the Racketeer Influenced and Corrupt Organizations
law to obtain monetary remedies against abortion protestors.[49] He also
voted to allow federal adjudication of age discrimination complaints
after state agencies had dismissed the complaints.[50] In these cases a
respect for statutory language marked the willingness of the opinion
writer to offer the remedy.

EQUAL PROTECTION AND JURY SELECTION

In *Batson v. Kentucky* the Court's opinion, written by Justice Lewis
Powell in 1986, held that equal protection forbade a prosecutor to use
voir dire, or preemptory or discretionary challenges during jury selection, "to challenge potential jurors solely on account of their race or on

the assumption that black jurors as a group will be unable to impartially consider the State's case against a black defendant."[51] Justice Rehnquist and Chief Justice Warren Burger dissented. During the Rehnquist Court, litigants sought additional clarification of the scope of this decision and the rule against discrimination that it contained. In subsequent cases, the majority of the Rehnquist Court, on the basis of an empirically derived sense of the effects of racial discrimination on minority criminal defendants, favored a rule to curtail prosecutorial discretion in the use of preemptory challenges. Although several of these decisions addressed less consequential issues such as the retroactivity of *Batson,*[52] Justice Kennedy's opinions for the Court extended *Batson* remedies to preemptory challenges of jurors not of the same race as the defendant and to preemptory challenges solely on the basis of race in civil cases because the challenges were permitted by state action and imposed an unconstitutional racial stigma on jurors.[53] Justice Blackmun wrote for the Court that racially discriminatory preemptory challenges were a form of state action subject to equal protection remedies, regardless of whether they were made by criminal prosecutors or defendants.[54] Additionally, the Court applied *Batson* logic and an intermediate scrutiny test to determine the unconstitutionality of preemptory challenges that used gender as the sole criterion to exclude persons from jury service.[55] Although a majority agreed to these extensions of the judicial power to provide equal protection using a three-part test derived from *Batson,* the Court allowed use of peremptory challenges to eliminate Spanish-speaking jurors as a rational means of ensuring that jurors heard only one version of the testimony of a Spanish-speaking defendant.[56] Justice Stevens, joined by White and Marshall, dissented. Stevens argued that the application of the *Batson* doctrine did not necessitate the acceptance of such preemptory challenges. Objecting to the rationality rule used by the Court, he wanted the Court to scrutinize closely the objective and subjective intent of the prosecutor's challenge and to consider practical techniques for preventing the exclusion of Latino jurors.[57] Regardless, in the preemptory challenge cases most of the justices recognized the empirical reality that race often colored jury decisionmaking.

In the *Batson* doctrine cases, Scalia objected to the use of state action doctrine to ban any race-based or gender-based preemptory challenges in the selection of juries. His dissenting opinion in *Powers v. Ohio* is the most complete expression of his position. The opinion opened with a detailed discussion of precedent to justify his claim that *Batson* and cases based upon *Batson* did not establish a constitutional standard granting standing for a defendant to challenge the exclusion of jurors of another race through the use of a prosecutor's preemptory challenges. Concentrating on the issue of third-party standing, he argued that a defendant could not argue that an injury had occurred to a juror, a third party, because no evidence of an injury-in-fact to the third party was presented. Thus, the majority of the Court had failed to adhere to traditional constraints on judicial power, the passive virtues of his Reasoned Elaboration approach.[58] Beyond this point, his opinion lapsed into dicta critical of the policy implications of the majority decision. As in *Miranda v. Arizona*,[59] he found that the Court had used "its key to the jail-house door not to free the arguably innocent, but to threaten the release upon the society of the unquestionably guilty unless law enforcement officers take certain steps that the Court newly announces to be required by law." Thus, he regarded the decision as a "self-satisfying" blow against racism by the Court's majority and a "tragedy" for later victims who "may pay the price for our extravagance."[60]

In his dissenting opinion in *Edmonson v. Leesville Concrete*,[61] Scalia made few comments on the question of standing when the Court's majority disallowed race-based preemptory challenges in civil cases. Rather, he concentrated on the "unfortunate consequences" of the case. He claimed that the instrumental aim of the Court's decision, racially diverse juries for minority litigants, would actually suffer a "net hindrance" because of the decision. Minority litigants, he contended, could no longer seek to seat as many jurors of their own race as possible through the use of preemptory challenges, increasing the likelihood of more all-white juries. Second, he argued that these preemptory challenge rules increased the complexity of litigation and encouraged appeals. More energy would be devoted to "sideshows and less and less to the merits of the case" because of a decision that "neither follows the law nor produces desirable concrete results."[62] This conclusion assumed a finite boundary to available judicial time and resources. Additionally, in a brief dissent issued when the Court decided to bar racial preemptory challenges by the defense, he added another item to his list of criticisms of *Batson* doctrine cases. In the interest of a supposed improvement of race relations, these decisions, he claimed, destroyed the "ages-old right of criminal defendants to exercise preemptory challenges as they wish."[63] When the Court extended the range of the *Batson* doctrine decisions to cover gender-based use of preemptory challenges, he reiterated his objections—on the basis of standing, "net hindrance," cost in judicial resources, and history—to the Court's position. Clearly he thought that a parade of horribles leading to gender and racial tests of all trial strategies of counsel might result from the continued extension of *Batson*.[64]

Although not raising equal protection constitutional issues related to *Batson*, in *Holland v. Illinois* Scalia held that a white criminal defendant's Sixth Amendment right to an impartial jury had not been violated by the prosecutor's preemptory strikes of potential black jurors to produce an all-white jury.[65] In reply to a dissenting opinion by Marshall, Scalia also reiterated that his opinion applied only to Sixth Amendment claims not advanced by Holland, and he refused to incorporate an equality standard into the Sixth Amendment provision requirement of an impartial jury.

STATE ACTION AS A CRITERION FOR ILLEGAL DISCRIMINATION

For discriminatory action to be considered illegal, the Court had long held that the Fourteenth Amendment and related scrutiny standards required that there be governmental or "state" action that either discriminated or enforced private discrimination.[66] Although passing references to state action requirements appeared across the range of his equal protection and civil rights laws opinions, Scalia voted against three efforts to extend state action doctrine. In *National Collegiate Athletic Association v. Tarkanian*,[67] he joined the Court's 5-to-4 majority to rule that the NCAA, which regulated sports at public and private colleges and universities, was not a state actor that might unlawfully discriminate by having its sanctions of a basketball coach enforced by a state university. And despite special commercial and promotional authority granted to the United States Olympic Committee by Congress, he agreed with the Court to hold that the committee was not a state actor covered by the Equal Protection Clause.[68] Finally, he voted for the Court's opinion by Rehnquist in *DeShaney v. Winnebago County Social Services Department*.[69] Rehnquist had concluded that a state *inaction* to protect a child from an abusive parent did not constitute the state action required for a Fourteenth Amendment challenge of the city. Since due process limited state power and did not empower governments to intrude into family matters, no claim of a deprivation of liberty could be lodged on behalf of the child.

CIVIL RIGHTS STATUTES

The fifth section of the Fourteenth Amendment and the second sections of the Thirteenth and Fifteenth Amendments provide that Congress can pass civil rights statutes to enforce equal protection of the laws, due process of law, the privileges and immunities of citizens, and an end to slavery and involuntary servitude, and can ensure racial equality in voting. Judicial interpretation of the meaning of these statutes has become an essential part of the determination of the scope of equality in the nation. The pragmatic liberal approach has treated civil rights statutes as a command to executive branch and state and local officials to achieve racial or gender equality using any rational means available, including the imposition of equality-inducing practices on private firms and persons. Reasoned Elaboration jurisprudence has encouraged a closer analysis of the adherence of governmental action to the language of these statutes.

Title VII of the Civil Rights Act of 1964

Johnson v. Transportation Agency,[70] the first major civil rights statutory case decided by the Rehnquist Court, addressed the conformity of a governmental affirmative action plan to the dictates of Title VII of the Civil Rights Act of 1964.[71] Title VII bars discrimination on the basis of race, national origin, gender, and religion in the employment practices of public agencies and of private firms engaged in interstate commerce. Using a pragmatic liberal methodology, Brennan held that a "flexible" plan for the promotion of minority and female employees over non-minority male employees with higher test scores adopted by the Transportation Agency in Santa Clara, California, was a legitimate use of governmental power in pursuit of the legislature's objective of ending workplace discrimination. Also, he concluded that the legitimacy of the plan was supported by evidence that the agency examined the overall qualifications of a female who was selected for a promotion ahead of a male with a higher test score, gave a nondiscriminatory reason for the promotion, explained how the promotion plan was individualized, did not promote a quota of members of any disadvantaged group, and identified the way in which the plan was not an absolute bar to white men who applied for similar jobs.[72]

Dissenting in *Johnson,* Scalia resorted to ridicule of Brennan's reading of Title VII, use of precedents that Scalia interpreted as hostile to affirmative action remedies, and construction of a standard for the evaluation of evidence of discrimination. First, Scalia charged that Brennan's opinion and a concurring opinion by O'Connor converted the purpose of Title VII from the "goal of a discrimination-free society" into "the quite incompatible goal of proportionate representation by race and sex in the workplace." He buttressed this claim by arguing that the language of the Santa Clara plan indicated that it was not a remedy for unlawful past acts of discrimination but a policy "in defiance of normal expectations and laws of probability," to "give each protected racial and sexual group a governmentally determined 'proper' proportion of each job category." Further, he interpreted the facts of the case to illustrate that plaintiff Johnson had been denied a promotion to a position because he was white and not in a category to be awarded a proportion of positions in the agency.[73]

Second, Scalia claimed that Brennan had converted Title VII from a protection against employer discrimination into an instrument for attacking "societal attitudes that have limited the entry of certain races, or of a particular sex, into certain jobs."[74] He argued that precedent indicated that Title VII could be used for relief when evidence of conscious discrimination by an employer was found by a court. Findings of past societal discrimination could not be used to justify a remedial program. This was especially true with the Santa Clara plan, a program that Scalia thought addressed a harm not firmly established by judicial decision, administrative hearing, or conclusive evidence supporting an admission of wrongdoing by the agency.

Third, he argued that Brennan's construction of the statute and precedent to distinguish between private and public affirmative action programs was not legally justified. The effect of the Brennan approach was to reaffirm precedent about the legality of "discriminatory" voluntary private sector affirmative action programs and to extend such precedent, without consideration of the implications of "discriminatory" state action under the Equal Protection Clause, to the public sector. Scalia thought that Title VII prohibited any public or private "discriminatory" racial or gender preference programs. Thus, he sought to eliminate precedent allowing voluntary private affirmative action plans.[75]

Scalia's questioning of the reasonableness of Brennan's use of legal text and procedures for the evaluation of evidence followed the jurisprudential framework of Reasoned Elaboration. However, Scalia accompanied it with a conclusion that overtly attacked the political basis of governmental efforts to eliminate discrimination against disadvantaged groups. The result of Brennan's opinion, Scalia claimed, would be not a "color-blind and gender-blind workplace" but a discriminatory system "practically compelled" by the threat that lawsuits would be brought when a workforce did not include a proportionate number of members of disadvantaged classes. This outcome, he contended, would please public officials desirous of pleasing minority interests and corporate interests willing to promote less costly, less highly skilled workers and eager to use numerical means to avoid costly Title VII litigation. It would only penalize "predominantly unknown, unaffluent, unorganized" white males such as Johnson.[76] Scalia's argument held that governmental efforts to empower previously disadvantaged interests will harm a member of a faceless class. Scalia implied that this faceless class was without political power or was "unaffluent, unorganized." However, governmental support of the freedom of private organizations to make hiring decisions and to arrange seniority systems that have long rewarded the majority of a predominantly white, male workforce and have made American white male workers and managers among the most highly paid in the world escaped his attention. Indeed, he had dubiously tried to convert a predominant faction in the regime into a disadvantaged class suffering from the adverse effects of affirmative action. Yet he did not, and perhaps could not, explain why the denial of an increase in income was equivalent to the stigma suffered by the victims of the racism and sexism that Title VII sought to eliminate.

In a series of decisions from the 1988, 1989, and 1990 terms of the Court, all later modified by the Civil Rights Act of 1991,[77] the Court attempted to restrict the availability of statutory remedies for discrimination. In two of these cases the postulates of Reasoned Elaboration counseled Scalia to write opinions denying executive branch and state and local officials the discretion to address discriminatory acts. In these opinions he employed methods used in his general practice of statutory interpretation, including the search for a single meaning for the text based on the ordinary construction of words; the refusal to use information sources such as legislative debates and committee reports to determine the meaning of the text, although these often implied that the text possessed multiple meanings; and the avoidance of the consideration of the consequences of court decisions.

Because he could not find definite words in statutory language or precedent to justify an action by the Equal Employment Opportunity Commission, in *EEOC v. Arabian American Oil* the search for legal certainty caused Rehnquist to refuse to apply Title VII to extraterritorial acts of discrimination against American workers by American firms.[78] Scalia offered a brief concurring opinion. He accepted much of Rehnquist's analysis of a lack of congressional intent to make Title VII apply abroad. However, using the *Chevron* doctrine, he disagreed with Rehnquist's construction of the EEOC's discretion. Although he believed that the EEOC was normally entitled to deference in its construction of Title VII, he argued that the agency had exceeded its discretion by constructing Title VII contrary to the accepted law and precedents against extraterritorial application of American law.[79]

In *Lorance v. AT&T Technologies*,[80] the Court considered a challenge to a statutory restriction (42 *U.S. Code* § 2000e-5[e]) specifying 180 days (in some cases, 300 days) as the period of time within which a Title VII case against an allegedly discriminatory seniority system can begin, even though originally the seniority system was not facially discriminatory and the adverse effects of the system had not become manifest. Female employees of an AT&T plant filed the claim after being selected for demotion from better-paid positions during production reductions at the plant. They filed the claim about four years after the seniority system had taken effect. They contended that the seniority system under which they had been demoted was a product of an intent to discriminate. Scalia's Opinion of the Court upheld the time restriction on the filing of the challenge. In large part, his opinion consisted of a rejection of the women's claim that there was a continuing violation of Title VII and that they did not have to file a claim within the 180-day or 300-day limits. The rationale for his decision was precedent that required discriminatory acts, not effects, to trigger filing periods. Since the discriminatory act, the critical issue for evidentiary evaluation at trial, was the date of the start of the system, the suit could not be maintained. In dicta, Scalia also indicated that if the discriminatory nature of the system was overt, or "facial"—for instance, if there were a rule accruing seniority differently for men and women—it could be challenged at any time. However, a system without such overt discriminatory language, or "facially neutral," had to be challenged within the statutory time period, otherwise the suit would "disrupt those valid interests that [the law] was meant to protect." The interests especially protected, he illustrated, included the freedom of the employer from being subject to lawsuits every time an employee was demoted or had some other grievance.[81]

When the Civil Rights Act of 1991 changed some of the statutory language and interpretive guidelines for reading Title VII and other aspects of the Civil Rights Act of 1964 and 42 *U.S. Code* §§ 1981 and 1983, affecting how the courts should consider evidence of discrimination, Justice Stevens wrote for a majority including Rehnquist, Kennedy, O'Connor, and Souter in opposition to making two of the changes retroactive. Scalia, with Thomas, concurred with the refusal to make the new standards retroactive. The change, he argued, violated precedents on retroactivity which required a clear statement of retroactive intent. Then, relying on a Reasoned Elaboration argument, he went beyond the civil rights issues in the case to challenge a venerable doctrine that permitted the retroactivity of substantive legal changes unless they affected a vested right. Instead, he wanted a clear statement of retroactive intent in a statute to replace the vested-right doctrine and control policymaking by courts.[82]

In addition, Scalia wrote opinions on other Title VII issues not affected by the Civil Rights Act of 1991. Writing for the Court in the Title VII attorney fees case, *International Federation of Flight Attendants v. Zipes*,[83] he refused to allow a court to require losing third-party intervenors to pay the attorney fees of other parties, because the intervention had not been frivolous or without foundation. At issue was a challenge by a group of pregnant or formerly pregnant female flight attendants of Trans World Airlines (TWA) to the airline's policy of termination of pregnant flight attendants. The group and TWA settled out of court, but the flight attendants' union intervened, contending that the settlement contained provisions that illegally altered the seniority provisions in the union contract covering all TWA flight attendants. After a court rejected the intervenor union's challenge, class members sought legal fees from the union under a provision of the Civil Rights Act of 1964 (42 *U.S. Code* § 2000e-5[k]). Scalia sorted through legislative text and precedent on the award of attorneys' fees to impose a boundary on fee shifting in Title VII cases. Deducing that fee shifting was a policy designed "to vindicate the national policy against wrongful discrimination by encouraging the victim to make the wrongdoer pay at law," and to penalize interventions that were "frivolous, unreasonable, or without foundation," he then considered the claims of the parties. Concluding that the intervenor union was not a wrongdoer who had to be deterred from discriminatory practices, since TWA had admitted to the wrong, and that the intervenor union had a good-faith desire to protect the contractual rights of its members, he held that the class had not established that the union satisfied the statutory requirement to allow fee shifting.

Marshall dissented from Scalia's decision. Much of his opinion focused on how the majority had misread the text of the law and ignored the statutory rule that a prevailing plaintiff can collect attorney fees against any losing defendant charged with discrimination or any losing intervenor. Also, he averred great concern about the consequences of the decision. He thought that the decision allowed the defendants in discrimination cases to use intervenors to assist them in arguing against Title VII claims without fear of having to pay the costs of plaintiffs' attorney fees, and that, "as a result, injuries will go unaddressed and the national policy against discrimination will go unredeemed."[84]

A Title VII dispute resulting in an opinion for the Court with pragmatic liberal overtones was *United Auto Workers v. Johnson Controls*.[85] In this case, Blackmun rejected claims of business necessity and business concern about the health of female employees and their fetuses as rationales for the exclusion of all females of child-bearing age from jobs exposing them to lead. Title VII allowed the exclusion of women from some jobs if gender was a bona fide qualification for the occupation (e.g., the job of men's room attendant). Because a complete ban on the employment of females in their child-bearing years lacked empirical support as an effective, reasonable protection of workers—in part because exposure to lead also could harm males and their future children—and because the threat of civil liability by the company for the lead exposure resulted only in the exclusion of women from the jobs because of their ability to become pregnant, Blackmun held the policy to be facially discriminatory.

Scalia concurred. His criticism of the majority made four points about the logic of its opinion. First, he saw no reason why the majority opinion had considered facts about the effects of lead exposure on men, arguing that the company simply discriminated against women because they could become pregnant. Second, he regarded as irrelevant the Court's conclusion that Johnson Controls had failed to show that the women could perform the job safely. Title VII, he concluded, left it to the women, not Johnson Controls, to decide whether they could perform the job safely. Third, he disagreed with some language on when or whether Title VII preempted state tort litigation of the case; and fourth, he disagreed with a statement that economic costs alone might not provide a reason for a bona fide occupational qualification that eliminated all members of a particular gender from a position.[86]

In *St. Mary's Honor Center v. Hicks*,[87] Scalia read the precedents about the "trier of fact" or evidentiary requirements in Title VII cases in which disadvantaged plaintiffs sought relief for alleged discriminatory discharges. He held that minority plaintiffs must offer direct evidence of discrimination even though the trier of fact rejected the employer's claim that their act of discharge was nondiscriminatory. For example, St. Mary's Honor Center, a division of the Missouri Department of Corrections and Human Resources, had failed to provide evidence that legitimate, nondiscriminatory reasons justified the discharge of Hicks, an African American. However, Scalia concluded that this failure was not a default or a refusal to contend the case. Thus, the center's failure did not set aside the requirement that Hicks prove intentional discrimination by introducing for judicial consideration his own admissible evidence of a Title VII violation.[88] Souter, with Blackmun and White, dissented from the standard about the burden of proof. He sought a standard that allowed judgment for the plaintiff without the plaintiff bearing the burden of proving the discriminatory intent of employer behavior.[89] Scalia replied with a criticism of Souter's application of precedent to justify his position and Souter's assessment of "dire practical" consequences flowing from Scalia's opinion. With regard to the practical argument, Scalia commented that Souter's contention that placing the burden of proof on employees would give special favor to employers, especially those in a position to conceal direct evidence of discrimination, was in error. Instead, he argued that judicial procedures provided ample opportunities to gather evidence and test its veracity. Litigants in Title VII cases had to adhere to these procedures, as did any other federal civil litigant.[90]

Because of language in Title VII, in *Harris v. Forklift Systems, Inc.* the Court unanimously supported the introduction, as evidence of gender discrimination, of testimony about various forms of psychological harm to a woman caused by abusive and hostile sexual innuendo and related actions on the part of her employer.[91] O'Connor held that such evidence, not definable by "a mathematically precise test," could indicate the creation of "an abusive work environment" as part of an intentional effort to discriminate against members of a disadvantaged class. Scalia concurred. The "vague statutory language" such as *abusive* in Title VII forced him to conclude by allowing the introduction of various forms of evidence of abuse, rather than direct or tangible harm, in workplace discrimination cases. In reluctant tones, he stated that this would let "unguided juries" determine liability for sex-related con-

duct engaged in or condoned by employers.[92] Yet his concern illustrated a constant theme in his Title VII opinions, a desire for explicit
statutory language and a desire for explicit rules to govern statutory
remedies for discrimination. It was coupled with a demand for evidence of specific, individualized harm caused by action of law or defined by law. His decision rejected, as proof of discrimination, both
statistical associations of harm with a generalized class of persons, and
descriptions of harm not clearly defined in a statute.[93] The pragmatic
liberal concern for implementing policies designed to promote a less
discriminatory society never surfaced in his Title VII opinions.

42 *U.S. Code* § 1983

Designed by Congress to enforce the Fourteenth Amendment, the
1871 Civil Rights Act contained language, later codified as 42 *U.S.
Code* § 1983, that permitted federal civil litigation of alleged injuries to
a person's federal constitutional rights and privileges and immunities
committed under "action of law" or "color of law" by state and local
governmental entities. In *Jett v. Dallas Independent School District*,[94]
Scalia concurred with O'Connor's opinion that limited the liability of a
municipality for actions of subordinate officers—a black principal and
a school superintendent—who had dismissed a white football coach,
Norman Jett, for allegedly racially discriminatory reasons. O'Connor
concluded that Jett had to seek relief under § 1983 "action at law"
language. She disallowed his effort to sue the district under another
civil rights law (42 *U.S. Code* § 1981), because the history of the adoption of § 1981 did not disclose a congressional effort to create a cause
of action for suits against municipalities and their officers. Instead, she
found that history revealed a congressional intent to provide relief for
public discrimination under § 1983 and to allow § 1981 to be a source
of relief for private discrimination. Scalia's brief concurring opinion
only questioned her opinion's use of legislative intent about remedies
for discrimination.[95]

Other § 1983 cases with opinions by Scalia addressed claims of the
violation of civil rights by officials of state criminal justice systems. In
Hewitt v. Helms,[96] Scalia wrote for a 5-to-4 majority and ruled against a
state prisoner's petition for the award of attorney fees, under 42 *U.S.
Code* § 1988, a provision that made attorney fees available to prevailing
parties in § 1983 litigation. Helms, the prisoner, was released on parole, but he pursued his § 1983 case, alleging that his discipline by

prison officials without a hearing violated his civil rights. After a series of actions, the court of appeals decision recognized a violation of
Helms's constitutional rights during the prison's disciplinary proceeding. However, because of Helms's counsel's failure to take the steps
necessary to secure relief from a court, the appeals court agreed that
Helms could be awarded no damages or other relief. All the courts had
found was liability for the harm to his civil rights; they had not issued
a declaratory judgment or provided damages according to his literal
reading of § 1988. Because Helms did not recover relief, Scalia concluded that the "ordinary language" of § 1988 also precluded recovery
of attorney fees for his § 1983 claim. Some form of redress, he argued,
was essential if a litigant is to recover attorney fees. In a related case
about the availability of § 1983 relief, Scalia wrote for the Court and
held that to seek relief under § 1983 an inmate named Heck, convicted
of manslaughter, had to prove the reversal, expungement, or invalidity
of his conviction or challenge the issuance of a writ of habeas corpus by
a federal court.[97] His opinion turned on a reading of precedent cases
about finality and the availability of § 1983 relief. Although Scalia
concluded that § 1983 relief required no exhaustion of relief for the
suit, in these circumstances he held that the defendant had not yet
been harmed. Since the inmate had an appeal of the conviction pend-
ing, he had yet to suffer a final, unconstitutional conviction or sentence that was actionable under § 1983. Therefore, the action had to
be dismissed.

However, Scalia sided with two defendants who sought § 1983 relief. In a case about whether a physician had acted "under color of law"
when providing part-time, contractual services at a state prison, he
concurred with Blackmun's conclusion that the physician had been
acting within the meaning of § 1983. Nevertheless, Scalia briefly
stated that he did not accept Blackmun's argument that a physician
simply treating patients could inflict punishment as defined by the
Eighth Amendment. Rather, he stated that any physical harm to prisoners caused by deliberate indifference was a violation of the Fourteenth Amendment Due Process Clause and subject to § 1983 relief.[98]
In an Opinion of the Court in a case raised by a descendent of a man
who had crashed a speeding, stolen car into a police roadblock and
died, he ruled that the police had acted under color of law. First, he
held that the police roadblock had constituted an effort at a seizure
within the meaning of the Fourth Amendment precedent. Further, he

ruled that, according to longstanding principles of the law of torts, the roadblock was the proximate cause of the death. Therefore, he remanded the case to the District Court to determine whether the roadblock had been a reasonable action or a violation of § 1983.[99]

In another display of willingness to extend § 1983 relief, Scalia wrote a concurring and dissenting opinion, joined by Blackmun and Marshall, to qualify state prosecutorial immunity from § 1983 suits. Justice White held that the prosecutor was absolutely immune from a § 1983 suit for participation in a probable cause hearing about the admission of evidence about the multiple personalities of a murder suspect derived from questioning under hypnosis. However, since such advice was not part of the legal duty of prosecutors, the prosecutor had only qualified liability for any advice given to police about the questioning of the hypnotized suspect. Therefore the defendant could sue and contend that the advice had given rise to a violation of her civil rights, including her constitutional protection against self-incrimination.[100] Scalia's argument for qualified prosecutorial immunity from all § 1983 suits rested on his reading of precedent cases. His construction of precedent led to the conclusion that the common law had not recognized any absolute immunity for prosecutors, especially in 1871 when § 1983 was adopted. Further, even if under later Supreme Court decisions prosecutors could receive absolute immunity for duties intimately associated with the criminal process, the advice to police at the probable cause hearing was outside the judicial phase of the criminal process.[101]

Scalia's § 1983 opinions all turned on his construction of precedent cases, especially precedents about standing to sue. They evidenced a reluctance to offer new or more flexible rules of standing. Thus, traces of the passive-virtues theme of Reasoned Elaboration arguments have marked his treatment of civil rights claims under § 1983.

42 *U.S. Code* § 1985(3)

In *Bray v. Alexandria Women's Health Clinic*,[102] a group of abortion clinics and supporting organizations in the metropolitan Washington, D.C., area sought an injunction under 42 *U.S. Code* § 1985(3) against Bray and other abortion protestors who had obstructed access to the clinics. Originally, § 1985(3) was a provision of the Civil Rights Act of 1871 designed to permit federal litigation against alleged conspiracies, such as the Ku Klux Klan, bent on depriving persons or classes of persons of the equal protection of the laws and privileges and immunities. Scalia's plurality opinion approached § 1985(3) with much greater certainty about the meaning of the section and with a narrower reading of the facts of the case than did the dissenting opinions of Justices Stevens and O'Connor.

First, Scalia argued that § 1985(3) had been designed to provide relief for conspiratorial acts based on an invidious discriminatory animus against some disadvantaged class of persons. But he found that the Alexandria Women's Health Clinic made no effort to claim that women seeking abortions, a partially constitutionally protected class, were an invidiously injured party. Rather, he argued that the clinic had argued that "women in general" had been injured. This argument, he contended, assumed that opposition to abortion was sex-based. However, the clinic provided no direct evidence of intentional, invidious sex-based discrimination against women by the protestors. Second, Scalia rejected the clinic's argument that a right to interstate travel by women seeking abortions had been violated by a conspiratorial act engaged in by Bray and others. He found no action by Bray intentionally aimed at barring interstate travel or discriminating against persons from other states. Any effect that the protests had on the travel rights of women was deemed incidental. Third, he argued that precedent indicated that § 1985(3) did not apply to rights protected against state interference, such as First Amendment or abortion rights, but applied only to rights protected against state *and* private interference, such as the right to be free from involuntary servitude or the right to interstate travel. Fourth, despite the claims of dissenting justices, he concluded that the clinic had not presented a "hindrance" claim for review. Such a claim had to rely on § 1985(3) language allowing action against persons preventing or hindering governments from securing equal protection of the laws. He concluded that the clinic had not argued this claim and that there was no evidence that a conspiracy had hindered governmental protection of rights.[103]

Scalia then went on to lecture the dissenters and Justice Souter, who wrote a concurring and dissenting opinion, about their use of precedents and their alleged expansion of the issues under review. Their opinions apparently were inconsistent with his Reasoned Elaboration practices of relying on established legal categories and specific language of precedents and with his sense of judicial restraint, and touched on the edges of judicial lawmaking. Evidence of this pattern of instrumental discourse appears in phrases such as "Our precedents establish . . ." and "the term unquestionably connotes . . . " which marked Scalia's discussion of intent. They revealed his assumption that he could establish a singular meaning of precedent and that there was in the language of precedents a certainty and rationality that precluded the need to examine the context in which precedent cases appeared.[104] Using this logic, he denied relief and left the women's clinic to find relief in the state criminal and civil courts.

The Voting Rights Act

Congress adopted the Voting Rights Act of 1965 to enforce the Fifteenth Amendment's bar on racial discrimination in the exercise of the right to vote. Later acts amended and extended the act pursuant to the enforcement section of the Fifteenth Amendment. Scalia has written opinions in three important cases about the act. In *Chisom v. Roemer*,[105] Stevens applied § 2 of the Voting Rights Act to judicial elections in Louisiana. A class action by black voters alleged that the construction of a multimember state supreme court district for the greater New Orleans area was a state action to dilute and cancel their voting strength and prevent the creation of a voting district with a black majority. Stevens determined that Congress had not excluded judicial elections from coverage by the act, that elected judges are representatives, and that violations of the act would be determined by an evaluation of the results of the judicial districting process. In *Houston Lawyers' Association v. Attorney General of Texas*,[106] decided at the same time as *Chisom*, Stevens applied § 2 of the Voting Rights Act to judicial elections in Texas. The Texas scheme for electing trial judges let several judicial candidates from the same district run for specific, predesignated seats, with the winners being the candidates who received the highest number of votes for the predesignated seat they sought. For example, in a hypothetical district with five seats, candidates chose to run for seats one, two, or three. The winners were those who received the plurality of votes for their seat; they were not the candidates who won the most votes in the district. Stevens concluded that this scheme violated § 2 of the act because it made it harder for nonwhite candidates to win a seat.

Scalia wrote a dissenting opinion in *Chisom* which he also applied to the *Houston Lawyers'* case.[107] The opinion attempted to rebut the argument that judges were representatives within the meaning of the Voting Rights Act. Using the "ordinary meaning" of the word *representatives* as defined by the dictionary and applied in other cases—albeit none of them cases about judges—he concluded that the act should not have been applied to judges. Thus, his use of a favorite practice of Reasoned Elaboration argumentation, reliance on the plain or literal readings of statutes, resulted in a rejection of a pragmatic and commonsense definition of the representative role of judges in acting for the peoples' Constitution and for their rights against "ill humours" caused by political factions.[108] Later, in *Growe v. Emison,*[109] Scalia's opinion for a unanimous court reiterated precedents explicating "vote dilution" under the Voting Rights Act, especially those precedents requiring statistical rather than anecdotal evidence of dilution under a state legislative apportionment plan.

In a North Carolina apportionment and Voting Rights Act case in which he did not write an opinion, Scalia joined O'Connor's Opinion of the Court, in which O'Connor held that an apportionment plan creating an irregularly shaped district created a claim under the Equal Protection Clause because the plan was so irrational that it could only be understood as an effort to segregate voters into separate voting districts because of their race. The theme of O'Connor's argument—that the implicit discrimination shown by a legislative district's shape, not an individualized act of discrimination against a voter, justified further adjudication of the case—apparently satisfied Scalia.[110] Two terms later, Scalia supported Kennedy's Opinion of the Court when the majority determined that parties might rely on evidence other than the shape of the district to establish race-based districting.[111]

In another important Voting Rights Act case, Scalia voted for Kennedy's majority opinion that changes in the county commissioner selection process by the white commissioners in two Georgia counties did not require preclearance by the federal Department of Justice. The changes, according to Kennedy, were more in the function of government than in voting.[112] Scalia also joined a concurring opinion written by Thomas which refused to support the evaluation of changes in the number of members of a county commission under the language of § 2 of the Voting Rights Act. Rejecting past interpretations of § 2, Thomas found judicial review of the size of the commission unsupported by statutory language, resulting in a "misadventure in judicial policy-making."[113]

CONCLUSION: SCALIA AND THE MEANING OF EQUALITY

In equal protection cases and related cases about civil rights statutes, Scalia has employed themes of Reasoned Elaboration and has sought neutral legal principles and the application of less flexible standards of statutory construction and evidence. Especially in affirmative action cases, his use of Reasoned Elaboration arguments has led him to attempt to apply neutral laws to mandate racial equality. He has attempted to avoid the messy political business of sorting through empirical information to discern the best policies for the attainment of some measure of racial and gender equality in a regime filled with patterns of implicit racial and gender bias. Legal text and doctrine, he had assumed, can offer a nondiscretionary, purposeful, and rational rule for the scrutiny of policies affecting equality. In cases involving juror challenge and in civil rights statutory cases he has sought procedural certainty in traditional legal problem-solving techniques rather than any form of egalitarian outcome. He has not just wanted justices to craft reliable legal rules conducive to equal protection or to concern themselves with subjective aspirations. He has been committed to the theoretical certainty of law, including precedent and the use of ordinary language to discern legislative meaning in the statutory civil rights cases. This practice has been buttressed by his opinions that relied on detailed evidence of intent to discriminate, evidence he regarded as more certain than social scientific evidence about the discriminatory effect of a defendant's behavior. Thus, in his opinions, discussion of rules and neutral procedures and standards of passivity has masked his allocation of power among interests.

Scalia's use of Reasoned Elaboration has aimed at bolstering a political vision that constrains the special protection of the interests of disadvantaged classes. By accepting legal equality among individuals as the goal of the Equal Protection Clause and of civil rights laws, he could void experimental policies such as affirmative action which sought more equality among segments or blocs of citizens. He has refused to encourage expansive pluralist political competition for equal political and socioeconomic resources. His assumption that equal protection law and policy require rules mandating equal treatment of individuals has challenged the argument for the special protection of disadvantaged classes, the implication of the concern in *Carolene Products* for "discrete and insular minorities." Also, he has neglected the social facts contributing to the deeply rooted, bloc-oriented racism embedded in American life. Instead, he has assumed that rules of law can induce a consensus of values as long as the rules *appear* neutral or consensus-based. Then, all a passive judiciary need do is enforce rules requiring equal treatment for individuals.[114]

Scalia's rule-oriented interpretation of the Equal Protection Clause and civil rights laws has scorned the expansive political pluralism abetted by pragmatic programs that treat disadvantaged classes of persons differently or that the efforts of such classes to realize their political and economic equality. Especially in his *Croson, Adarand Constructors,* and *Johnson v. Transportation Agency* opinions, he has asserted that these programs are pathological. They divide Americans, award special privileges, and undercut majority rule. However, he has provided no evidence that neutral rules rewarding socially constructed ideas of merit can really cure the pathologies inherent in existing racial and gender-based political pluralism. Thus, either it has been naive of Scalia to assume that a cure of racial or gender divisions can be achieved by law, or he simply has expressed a political vision hostile to governmental action against racial and gender subordination.

Chapter Seven

ORDERING THE CHAOS
OF EXPRESSION

The expression of ideas and the practice of religious faith are inherently fraught with conflict. People who speak their minds and worship as they wish introduce chaos into political life. They undermine consensus and order. Justice Scalia has recognized that what he calls the "problem of disuniformity" also affects the Court's effort to provide a rational set of rules to promote orderly expression. Indeed, as this chapter recounts, he seems to have abetted the disuniformity. Rather than attempting to impose a single rationale on the interpretation of the First Amendment, he has accommodated himself to the problem of disuniformity. He has sought the uniformity promised by Reasoned Elaboration only *within* what he calls the "existential categories of common First Amendment cases." Additionally, his refusal to adopt a single legal criterion to guide his First Amendment decisions allows him to make choices that convey a distinctly conservative message about expression and public order. [1]

Defenders of the American regime presuppose that discussion contributes to the generation of ideas and consideration of policy choices by the public and its representatives, or has a value in itself as an attribute of individual freedom. These presuppositions are reflected in the First Amendment's statement that "Congress shall make no law respecting an establishment of religion, or prohibiting the free exercise thereof; or abridging the freedom of speech, or of the press, or the right of the people peaceably to assemble, and to petition the Government for a redress of grievances." By 1958 the Supreme Court had recognized that all First Amendment rights were incorporated into the Fourteenth Amendment Due Process Clause and served as a protection against state governmental actions. [2] However, since the second decade of the twentieth century most of the justices have acknowledged that some restrictions on these rights must exist to ensure orderly discussion and prevent factional domination of politics. Thus, when assembling their opinions about the First Amendment the justices have considered two questions: the meaning of the text of the amendment, and the decisional standard used to evaluate governmental restrictions on the rights protected by the amendment.

In keeping with his reticence on other constitutional law issues, Scalia had only partially exposed his position on the First Amendment before he joined the Court. As indicated in table 3.1, from 1986 to 1993 he generally opposed litigants seeking First Amendment protection for their expressive actions. Although not nearly as hostile to First Amendment claims as Chief Justice Rehnquist, Scalia voted against 65 percent of the claims. He opposed First Amendment claims more frequently than ten of the eleven justices who served with him.

Scalia's opinions on expression have displayed a reliance on the postulates of Reasoned Elaboration jurisprudence. First, to define the "generality," scope, or range of actions protected by rights, he has adopted a practice akin to his textual approach to statutory interpretation. Second, his opinions on First Amendment claims have elaborated on his views on the use of various intensified scrutiny doctrines and other decisional guidelines in First Amendment cases. However, to curtail the political discord that he has associated with expanded political pluralism, Scalia has recommended that courts should moderate the application of some of the intensified scrutiny standards used to resolve First Amendment rights controversies in certain contexts. Finally, despite the dangers posed by majority factions' prejudices, in his Establishment Clause opinions he has iterated deference to majority policy decisions and powerful interests. He has treated Establishment Clause questions as a unique issue, and his theme has been that the boundaries of the clause must be set by the majority of the people's representatives in the legislature and not by the judiciary. His views on generality, strict scrutiny and other forms of intensified scrutiny, and the Establishment Clause have used Reasoned Elaboration arguments as an instrument for the construction of a narrative that confirms the existing political and social relations among groups and the existing consensus of values in the regime. He has not envisioned a political order marked by fewer restrictions on individual speech and related expressive acts, greater public access to the media, controls on the use of economic power to affect political communications, or a change in the power of traditional American religious groups and the influence of their values.

THE GENERALITY, OR SCOPE, OF THE FIRST AMENDMENT

In First Amendment cases the first question faced by a justice is the generality, or scope, of the meaning of the amendment's text. This "central substantive question of modern constitutional law" is how literally or abstractly to construe the amendment.[3] Although Justice Black argued that the sentence that begins, "Congress shall make no law" banned any restriction of speech, press, and religion narrowly defined,[4] most friends of the First Amendment have relied on a pragmatic liberal approach and treated the amendment as a principle protecting the individual against a variety of governmental intrusions into personal beliefs and expressive acts. Justice William Brennan best summarized this approach, writing, "I have always thought that one of this Court's most important roles is to provide a formidable bulwark against governmental violation of the constitutional safeguards securing in our free society the legitimate expectations of every person to innate human dignity and sense of worth."[5]

During the Rehnquist Court, the scope of the Free Exercise Clause of the First Amendment became a central issue. At question was whether all speech and religious expression was covered by the protection of the clause or whether, according to precedent, some expressive behavior, although associated with speech, association, assembly, or religion, fell outside the protection afforded by the First Amendment. At the outset of the Rehnquist Court, the only types of expressive action or material *always* outside the protection of the First Amendment were child pornography and actions or material judged obscene by a court.[6]

In *Employment Division v. Smith*,[7] Scalia's opinion for the Court provided a definition of his construction of the generality of the amendment. At issue was whether the use of a mild hallucinogen—peyote—as part of a religious ceremony by a member of the Native American Church was protected by the Free Exercise Clause. Alfred Smith and Galen Black, Native American Church members, had been fired from jobs as drug counselors because of their religious use of the drug. Subsequently, when they applied for unemployment benefits, an official of the state unemployment compensation agency determined that their dismissal for the use of peyote had been due to "misconduct." According to a state statute, misconduct required a determination of ineligibility for unemployment compensation. After extensive preliminary litigation, the Oregon Supreme Court determined that the Free Exercise Clause exempted the use of peyote by members of the Native American Church from prosecution under Oregon laws against possession and use of controlled substances. Therefore, the use of peyote was not misconduct and Smith and Black could obtain the unemployment benefits. The state then obtained review from the U.S. Supreme Court.[8]

Scalia opened his opinion with a discussion of the text of the Free Exercise Clause, and he very quickly moved to read the text as protecting religious conduct as well as religious belief.[9] With little discussion of the history of the clause, he then considered the scope of the clause as defined in cases in which the clause had been used to protect categories of religious belief, profession, and action or refusal to act. He distinguished the precedents from his position that even though the drug use had been part of a religious ceremony it could not be excused, since it was a violation of neutral, generally applicable criminal laws not specifically directed at the religious practice in question. The Free Exercise Clause, he argued, prohibited only laws directly burdening religious belief and conduct. Therefore, he concluded that physical acts, such as peyote consumption, performed for religious reasons could be regulated by laws "not specifically" designed to prohibit a religious practice. According to Scalia, "We have never held that an individual's religious beliefs excuse him from compliance with an otherwise valid law prohibiting conduct that the State is free to regulate."[10] An incidental burden on free exercise by a general criminal law or a general tax law thus was constitutionally valid.

He continued by noting that the Court had made exceptions to this incidental-burdens standard only when a neutral, generally applicable law involved free exercise of religion in conjunction with freedom of speech or freedom of the press. Such an exception would deem unconstitutional laws that banned charitable solicitation by religious groups, prohibited religious rather than state-directed education of children, and placed a flat tax on actions related to the dissemination of religious ideas, displays, or materials. Except for these "hybrid" situations, which he chose to distinguish from simpler claims regarding the protection of religious conviction under the Free Exercise Clause "unconnected with any communicative activity or parental right," he made it clear that laws established by the democratic majority to prohibit socially harmful conduct could restrict the scope of the Free Exercise Clause guarantee.[11] Provided that the specific conduct of a specific religious association was not singled out for restriction or penalization, he left the definition of socially harmful conduct to the legislature. The Oregon law, he concluded, had neither singled out a specific religion nor impeded any communication of religious ideas or religious education.

Scalia supplied two additional reasons for his refusal to exempt Smith's exercise of religion from the general criminal law. To exempt a religion from the criminal law, he said, "contradicts both constitutional tradition and common sense." Through his constitutional tradition argument, Scalia asserted that Smith's claim was not comparable to the claims in those race and speech cases in which strict scrutiny and the compelling governmental interest test had been applied in the past to exempt persons from governmental control. "What [the test] produces in those other fields—equality of treatment, and an unrestricted flow of contending speech—are constitutional norms; what it would produce here—a private right to ignore generally applicable laws—is a constitutional anomaly."[12] Previous cases had applied the compelling interest test in free exercise claims against state efforts to deny unemployment compensation to persons who refused to work on their sabbath or to perform other actions inconsistent with their religious beliefs. Indeed, he had twice voted with the majority in concluding that freedom of religious belief, even if a person was not associated with an established church or sect, prevented the state from denying generally applicable unemployment benefits to individuals who had been fired for refusing to work on their sabbath, or who had refused employment that required them to work on their sabbath.[13] Also, he had joined a dissenting opinion of O'Connor which deemed unconstitutional an IRS rule on charitable contributions. O'Connor argued that the rule, affecting payments to the Church of Scientology for goods and services used in the practice of the religion, placed a burden on the central practice of the religion. The payments for the goods and services (a biofeedback device and counseling) were not regulable "incidental" benefits given to the church.[14] However, in *Smith* Scalia argued that these decisions "have nothing to do with an across-the-board criminal prohibition on a particular form of conduct."[15] The compelling governmental interest test, he held, was inapplicable to challenges that do not require—as occurred in the unemployment compensation cases—an examination of specific individual beliefs protected by the First Amendment. The result was that the compelling interest test did not apply to free exercise of religion claims in cases in which general criminal laws curtailed practices that an individual or religious association contended were religiously commanded.

His commonsense argument was that allowing exemptions under a compelling interest test would afford "the prospect of constitutionally required religious exemptions from civic obligations of almost every conceivable kind." Exemptions would threaten the rule of law and would court "anarchy." He also claimed that exemptions would force judges into the unsound practice of deciding whether a religious practice was so central to a faith that governments had no compelling interest in regulating it. Instead, he concluded, it was better to leave some religious conduct and belief relatively disadvantaged than to leave religions to become either privileged and a law unto themselves, or subjected to judicial consideration of the merits of their beliefs.[16] Thus, common sense was the result of the application of Reasoned Elaboration postulates about the limited capacity of the judiciary and the necessity of judicial passivity in the face of legislative choice. Scalia's argument left religious exercise to legislative whim.

In *Smith* Scalia barely achieved five votes for his argument against the claim of Smith. O'Connor concurred in the 6-to-3 decision, contending that settled doctrine required strict scrutiny of all free exercise claims. Although in an earlier opinion she had indicated a desire to limit the categories of governmental actions subjected to strict scrutiny under the Free Exercise Clause, in *Smith* she wrote that "recent cases have instead reaffirmed that [the compelling interest] test [is] a fundamental part of our First Amendment doctrine" and that "the cases cited by Court signal no retreat from our consistent adherence to the compelling interest test." Despite loyalty to the application of the strict scrutiny standard to a broadly defined category of religious exercise or conduct, she upheld the ban on peyote consumption. She found that the ban was necessary to promote the government's compelling interest in controlling the harms of drug use and drug trafficking.[17] In several footnotes to his opinion, Scalia rejected her argument that the compelling interest test should be applied in this case, arguing that her test created a private right to challenge almost any legislation having an incidental effect on religious belief and introduced courts into the business of evaluating the religious burdens in almost all regulatory laws.[18]

Brennan, Marshall, and Blackmun concurred with O'Connor's justifications for the use of the compelling governmental interest test over a broad range of religious activity claims, but they dissented from her assessment of the harm of peyote use. Writing for these justices, Blackmun found that the state had simply not provided enough solid documentary evidence about the harms of peyote use to prove a compelling interest. Blackmun also criticized Scalia's assumption that allowing an exception to the criminal law to permit peyote consumption would oblige a host of other exemptions to the criminal law. Calling such argument "speculative," Blackmun argued that the courts still should be able to distinguish claims based on sincere religious belief from false claims that might endanger public health and safety or promote drug trafficking. Scalia replied in his opinion that this encouraged the dangerous exercise of judicial choice via a balancing test.[19] Despite the objections, Scalia's opinion determined that some religious exercises were not a fundamental right at all. The right to the free exercise of religion was defined as narrower in its scope, or generality, than some parties desired. Therefore, religious conduct could be regulated by reasonable state criminal or tax laws or by the policies and practices of federal and state agencies. It need not be subject to First Amendment protection.

In *Barnes v. Glen Theatre*,[20] Scalia's concurring opinion extended the logic of his *Smith* opinion on the narrow scope, or generality, of the First Amendment to another form of expression. The *Barnes* plurality upheld an Indiana regulation penalizing nude dancing and other acts of public indecency. The Court used a four-part intensified scrutiny analysis derived from *United States v. O'Brien* to justify its conclusion.[21] However, Scalia upheld the ban on nude dancing because the dancing violated a traditional public immorality statute, a law he deemed to be "a general law not specifically targeted at expressive conduct." First, he argued that the law was part of a long tradition of laws, had a long history in common law, and had never been regarded as an infringement on freedom of speech. This historical argument allowed him to conclude that the indecency law was a criminal law of general applicability akin to the rule at issue in *Smith*. He then argued that the statute was constitutional because it was "not specifically targeted at expressive conduct." Only when a statute prohibited "conduct *precisely because of its communicative attributes*"—as in the case of flag burning or silent sit-ins—would it be unconstitutional. Referring back to *Smith*, he again indicated that unless the government directly denied individuals the ability to convey a message, restrictions of an "incidental" nature on expressive conduct, if they were framed as criminal laws of general applicability, would be immune from constitutional challenge. In these cases, variations of intensified scrutiny tests such as that used in *O'Brien* need not be applied because the conduct was beyond any kind of protection under the First Amendment. He concluded that "the State is regulating conduct, not expression, and those who choose to employ conduct as a means of expression must make sure that the conduct they select is not generally forbidden."[22] However, he did not consider that legislative regulations of conduct might sweep so broadly as to foreclose most avenues for the public expression of political and other ideas.

In *Church of the Lukumi Babalu Aye v. City of Hialeah,*[23] the Court considered a city ordinance banning the possession of animals for "sacrifice" and "ritual" slaughtering. Adherents of Santeria, an Afro-Caribbean religion, who practiced outdoor animal sacrifice at the Church of the Lukumi Babalu Aye contended that the law violated their free exercise of their religious beliefs. Kennedy distinguished the case from *Smith* by arguing that the city had not adopted a facially neutral criminal law. Rather, he found evidence of an effort to single out and penalize Santeria adherents, linked with a deliberate effort by the city to enact provisions that went beyond those necessary for the protection of public health. As a biased law affecting free exercise, the ordinance could be evaluated through strict scrutiny. Applying the test, he found no compelling interest justifying the ordinance.

Scalia concurred. His primary difference with Kennedy was with Kennedy's effort to separate out the issues of the neutrality and the general applicability of the ordinance. Scalia thought that these categories, derived from his *Smith* opinion, substantially overlapped and did not require separate evaluation. Especially, he demurred from the separate evaluation of the general applicability of the law because it led Kennedy to inquire into legislative motivations. Scalia argued that inquiry into legislative motivation might be acceptable in some circumstances, but not in First Amendment cases. The reason to neglect motivation, he argued, was that the text of the amendment required analysis of the effect of the law and not determination of whether it had been created with "evil motivation."[24] His opinion simply ignored the critical issue of *Smith* and *Barnes* by accepting Kennedy's argument that the ordinance was neither neutral nor of general applicability because its text was created to control religious practices.

In *Waters v. Churchill,*[25] O'Connor's plurality opinion adopted a rule for the protection of the speech of public employees during work hours. Cheryl Churchill, a nurse at a public hospital, had been fired for allegedly making disruptive statements to a superior in front of coworkers. O'Connor stated that any restriction or penalization of Churchill's speech could occur only after a reasonable and adequate investigation of the allegedly disruptive incident. If the hearing generated evidence that the speech had harmed reasonable governmental interests in the effective and efficient provision of a public service, the government could dismiss the employee.

Scalia's concurring opinion argued that the investigation was unnecessary. He argued that the previous rule—which held that a public employee could be disciplined for words spoken while at work unless the speech was on a matter of public concern—ought to apply. He rejected the expansion of a procedural protection of First Amendment rights because it was "unprecedented," "unnecessary," and "unpredictable." The decision was unprecedented, he argued, because O'Connor had created "new First Amendment rights," including a right to speech for public employees. Previously, public employees had only possessed a protection against retaliation for speech on matters of public concern, not a general right to free speech while at work. In addition, Scalia contended that O'Connor's expansion of the generality of substantive speech rights of public employees and her creation of the procedural protection of the investigation were superfluous and unnecessary for the resolution of Churchill's claim. He claimed that Churchill's constitutional rights had been reasonably investigated and that a constitutional analysis of this question could have been avoided. Finally, he asserted that O'Connor's decision created "intolerable legal uncertainty" by not offering a clear line between protected and unprotected speech by public employees. Decisions about harms to the free speech rights of public employees would be left to jury assessments of the reasonableness of speech, a vague standard from his perspective.[26]

When coupled with the approach used in the other cases about the generality, or scope, of the First Amendment, Churchill's case confirms Scalia's hostility to the construction of the First Amendment in ways that introduce a wider array of substantive and procedural challenges of the law and of governmental procedures. He has attempted to beat back these new First Amendment claims—claims that could ultimately generate expanded political pluralism and less social consensus—by reference to the instrumental discourse of Reasoned Elaboration. Consequently, he has used Reasoned Elaboration arguments about the need for stability and rationality in law, the worthiness of the majority preferences enshrined in purposeful legislative policies, the dangers of judicial lawmaking, and the value of judicial passivity to legitimate his votes. Although this method advantaged the Santeria adherents, it did not result in a First Amendment bulwark that protected all forms of expression.

STRICT SCRUTINY AND OTHER STANDARDS FOR
THE EVALUATION OF FIRST AMENDMENT CLAIMS

Most of Scalia's First Amendment opinions have not questioned the generality, or scope, of protection under the amendment. Rather, they have offered instrumental rules for the application of strict scrutiny to First Amendment claims. His treatment of strict scrutiny doctrine in First Amendment issues, like that of most of the other justices of the Rehnquist Court, has apparent inconsistencies. Additionally, his choice of what level of scrutiny to apply appears to have a connection to the kind of group claiming a disadvantage. His opinions about the First Amendment have illustrated especially clearly a political preference for expression by majorities and established interests rather than a concern with extending the expressive freedom of political and moral groups long disadvantaged by the regime. His use of strict scrutiny or other standards to evaluate rights claims has generated a distinctive pattern of empowerment, one consistent with his preference for a legal order founded on the principles of Reasoned Elaboration, the idea of majority rule, and conservative political aims.

Although Scalia has applied strict scrutiny to control governmental regulation of speech, he also has recognized that the majoritarian nature of the structure of decisionmaking processes has meant that some compelling governmental interests can restrict claims to expressive rights. His speech at Macalester College demonstrated his acceptance of a variety of restrictions on freedom of speech, the press, and assembly, and his opinions as a justice have specified his reasons for accepting six exceptions to the use of strict scrutiny of First Amendment claims.[27] These exceptions refer to occasions when the content of speech is restricted for a neutral reason such as the prevention of fighting words or obscene forms of expression; when there is a compelling interest in controlling the context or the time, place, and manner of the expression; when the expression is commercial in nature and the government presents a substantial interest for its control; when the expression is made on the job by public employees; when the expression is affected by neutral taxation statutes; and when the expression is libelous or defamatory. However, he also has defended freedom of expression through the application of overbreadth doctrine, or the requirement that laws be precisely written so that they do not encourage governmental infringements on rights.

Content-Based Governmental Restrictions on
First Amendment Rights

The Supreme Court has generally rejected content-based regulations of expression as a violation of the First Amendment. In the 1930s, Justice Stone called for strict scrutiny of controls on First Amendment rights in *Carolene Products,* and the Court developed the rule of no prior restraint to protect freedom of the press from prepublication censorship.[28] After decades of discussion about the possible preferred position of First Amendment rights and the use of "absolutes" and "balancing" techniques, by the end of the Burger Court a majority of the justices accepted some form of intensified scrutiny of content-based regulations of pure speech, symbolic expression, and some aspects of free exercise of religion.[29] The major Rehnquist Court decisions about content-based regulations of speech used strict scrutiny and the compelling interest test, an approach that Scalia supported in many cases, even though he gave it an interesting twist.[30]

In *Austin v. Michigan Chamber of Commerce,*[31] in an opinion by Marshall, the Court upheld a Michigan law permitting the state government to control corporation-funded but legally independent political campaign expenditures funneled through political action committees (PACs). Employing strict scrutiny, Marshall concluded that the law served a compelling state interest in preventing political corruption.[32] In his dissenting opinion, Scalia also used the strict scrutiny standard, but he construed strict scrutiny doctrine to defend corporate participation in pluralist politics. Unlike the Court's majority, which found that Michigan had a compelling interest in regulating independent corporate expenditures in state electoral campaigns, he disputed the conclusion that the state's interest was compelling. In particular, he attacked the majority's conclusions that corporations had been granted special legal advantages placing them in a special category with regard to First Amendment rights and that corporate expenditures induced a form of special advantage or corruption. These conclusions allowed the Court's majority to conclude that the state had a compelling interest permitting its control of corporate political contributions.[33]

Scalia regarded the Court's conclusions as erroneous because they suspended the rights of a definable group in political matters without defining the compelling need to regulate. He especially noted that the harm of corporate spending is only "potential" and is not "compelling."

The participation of corporations in elections, he judged, must be proven to be corrupting before speechlike activities can be regulated by government. He rejected the idea that the government had greater authority to regulate speech by a corporation because the corporation had been given special advantages by the state. Speech, he contended, cannot be more readily restricted because the speaker has special advantages. Special advantages were not identical to corruption. Also, special advantages did not establish a harm so significant and compelling that governmental regulation was necessary.

Scalia found that the majority had tried to "equalize" political debate by preventing disproportionate expressions of corporations' values. However, he concluded that this was an unsound effort to let the government manage political debate. He argued at length that the massive wealth of corporations did not automatically make them likely to corrupt politics and generate a sufficient compelling state interest in the regulation of their political contributions. By declining to view great wealth as a "potential" source of corruption and wrongdoing, he again countered the compelling interest argument of the majority. Unless a harm occurred, he stated, strict scrutiny demanded the protection of corporate expression through political contributions. Corporations' speech acts, he argued, deserved protection unless clear evidence of actual harm emerged.[34]

Scalia not only rejected the pragmatic arguments of the majority regarding the effect of wealth on politics but also concluded with praise for corporate participation in pluralist politics. Arguing that the majority had redefined corruption to limit the role of a class of participants in political debate, he contended that corporate participation through PACs supplied information from associations "owning and operating a vast percentage of the industry of the State, and employing a large number of its citizens." This was not an evil to be prevented; rather, it was constitutionally protected speech. And if corporate money gave the corporation's views prominence, this also was no evil. Instead, as he concluded, "the premise of our system is that there is no such thing as too much speech—that the people are not foolish but intelligent, and will separate the wheat from the chaff."[35]

Scalia's reconstruction of scrutiny doctrine in *Austin* obviously did not aim at the protection of the interests of traditionally disadvantaged persons. Although he appeared to defend speech, his opinion reaffirmed an advantage in communication afforded to a privileged class because of its wealth. His instrumental use of scrutiny doctrine and the compelling interests test contained themes of Reasoned Elaboration jurisprudence—neutrality in the application of law to rich and poor, the refusal to make pragmatic adjustments in the concept of corruption, and the refusal to allow a legislative experiment in equalizing political resources. His opinion was conservative in its preservation of the status quo; it opposed a law that restricted political practices favorable to a wealthy faction.[36]

In a conflict about the constitutionality of the St. Paul, Minnesota, Bias-Motivated Crime Ordinance punishing the expressive display of symbols known to arouse "anger, alarm or resentment in others on the basis of race, color, creed, religion, or gender," Scalia's Opinion of the Court addressed the conflict between free speech and governmental efforts to prevent racially discriminatory acts. R.A.V. v. St. Paul centered on an incident in which juveniles had burned a cross on the lawn of an African American family.[37] One of them, R.A.V., claimed that the ordinance banning the burning interfered with his freedom of expression. The Minnesota Supreme Court upheld the ordinance as a permissible, content-based restriction on "fighting words" which was narrowly tailored to serve a compelling governmental interest.

Scalia first considered whether the statute was a restriction of fighting words. Although, as he noted, First Amendment doctrine generally opposes any content-based ban on speech, the Court has recognized an exception to the ban for words about to incite fights or physical violence and injury.[38] After a detour into a discussion of the scope of the First Amendment ban on content-based restrictions on free speech, he concluded that any exception to the ban had to serve a comprehensive, neutral goal unconnected to the message being communicated. Therefore, through nondiscriminatory legislation the state could control the effects of messages. However, he determined that the St. Paul ordinance was not permissible because it was an action that did not penalize all fighting-words messages, only fighting words aimed at certain racial, religious, and gender groups. Therefore, the ordinance contained viewpoint discrimination and was an unconstitutional content-based regulation of speech.[39]

Scalia rejected the city's argument that the statute was a narrowly tailored regulation of speech designed to further a compelling state interest in protecting the right of disadvantaged classes to live in peace. However, he argued that this interest might be served by other, content-neutral means. But because the ordinance "distinctively served" the city's interest by expressing hostility to particular ideas, it had enforced an unconstitutional content-based restriction on speech. A valid compelling state interest was thus offset by an unconstitutional method for the defense of the state's interest. Although Scalia's opinion did not allow the city to repress the vicious expression of a hateful viewpoint, it left the potential for the city to repress other categories of expression because of a compelling interest, through broadly designed, "neutral" controls on content such as bans on fighting words, fraudulent commercial speech, or prurient publications.[40]

Although Scalia used strict scrutiny doctrine to repudiate governmental restrictions on expression in *Austin* and *R.A.V.*, his reliance on principles of Reasoned Elaboration has qualified strict scrutiny doctrine in two ways. First, like O'Connor in *Croson*, he has used strict scrutiny and the language of neutrality to offset legislative efforts to defend members of disadvantaged groups against the social reality of their mistreatment. His "neutral" application of the compelling interest test, coupled with his refusal to accept legislative assessments of the harm directed at minorities in *R.A.V.* or less affluent citizens in *Austin*, and his traditional constructions of concepts such as "corruption" and "fighting words," have allowed him to use strict scrutiny and its compelling governmental interest component to defend advantaged PACs and racists. By insisting that strict scrutiny doctrine should be neutral and denuding it of the *Carolene Products*, note 4, objective of ending discrimination against minorities, he has transvalued the doctrine.

Second, despite rulings that countered Reasoned Elaboration dictates and rejected laws made by legislative majorities through active, countermajoritarian judicial evaluation of legislative policy choices, Scalia's use of scrutiny doctrine has echoed the hostility of Reasoned Elaboration to legal experimentalism and doctrinal creativity. Using this truncated conception of scrutiny doctrine, he has countered compelling interest arguments made in state efforts to defend disadvantaged classes and expand political discussion. The result of the decisions, especially language in *Austin* and the ban on most content-based regulations of speech in *R.A.V.*, has been a confirmation of established pluralist political divisions. For example, when he recognized that content-based discrimination against expression was not absolute in *R.A.V.*, he confirmed both his practice and the Court's practice of reading the First Amendment to defend the existing equilibrium among interests rather than to protect the voices of the politically disadvantaged.[41]

However, Scalia has acquired a notoriety among conservatives for his votes in support of the constitutionality of symbolic speech in cases about the burning of the American flag. He supported Brennan's opinions that the flag burning was expressive conduct and, although offensive to a national symbol, did not create a dangerous context that might invite a governmental restriction on the manner of the expression. Instead, the ban on flag burning was an unconstitutional content-based regulation.[42] Scalia also protected speech in some electoral settings. For example, he voted with a unanimous court to strike down a Colorado law prohibiting the payment of persons to circulate petitions in connection with a ballot initiative. Stevens held that the state's prohibition of the action did not offer a compelling interest to satisfy strict scrutiny analysis. Also, Scalia agreed to support freedom of expression in some other public forums and contexts using strict scrutiny analysis. Thus, he voted for striking down a blanket ban on solicitation, and canvassing by groups in the central terminal of a public airport and a ban on protest activity near foreign embassies and legations in Washington, D.C. as content-based regulation of speech serving no compelling governmental interest.[43]

Scalia voted for Stevens's Opinion of the Court in *City of Ladue v. Gilleo*.[44] The opinion struck down a local ordinance that banned certain kinds of signs in residential areas. A sign protesting the Persian Gulf intervention by American military forces was held to be protected by the First Amendment against content-based discrimination by the city. Scalia also supported Souter's opinion in a case about the state regulation of the contingents permitted to march in a privately sponsored St. Patrick's Day parade. Souter held that the parade was a protected form of expression and that efforts forcing the parade sponsors to admit a gay and lesbian contingent, which it wanted to exclude, forced a specific content into the sponsors' expression. This form of content-based interference with an expressive act was unconstitutional, he concluded.[45] Finally, when a state university failed to assist financially a religiously oriented student group despite financial assistance granted to other kinds of student groups, Kennedy found content or viewpoint discrimination and violation of the First Amendment. Scalia voted for Kennedy's opinion.[46]

Four times, Scalia wrote opinions to protect the content of expression more extensively than the majority of the justices. The first of these opinions was a concurrence with the Court's definition of the scope of governmental licensing and time-place-manner restrictions on charitable solicitations, in a case in which the Court ruled that North Carolina restrictions on the fees charged by professional fund-raisers chilled the North Carolina Federation of the Blind's ability to speak about its needs. The Court also ruled that requirements compelling the disclosure of professional fundraisers' activities and the licensing of their solicitations did not serve a compelling governmental interest. Scalia's only objection to the Court's opinion concerned language in a footnote to the Court's opinion. His objection signified his reluctance to allow states to impose an even more narrowly tailored disclosure requirement on professional solicitors.[47]

In the second of these opinions, Scalia concurred when Marshall held unconstitutional, as a violation of freedom of the press, a Florida judicial decision based on a statute that permitted the imposition of civil damages against the *Florida Star,* a publication that had printed the name of a victim of a sexual assault.[48] Scalia did not consider the Florida law a valid contextual limitation on the manner of expression because of just one of three reasons offered by Marshall—it did not protect "an interest 'of the highest order.'" Scalia could not find a compelling or substantial state interest that justified a restriction on truthful speech unless more substantial evidence of its capacity to prevent damage could be shown.[49]

In the third of his opinions, Scalia concurred when the Court unanimously overturned a Florida law forbidding a witness to ever disclose testimony given to a grand jury.[50] For the Court, Rehnquist held that control over disclosure during a grand jury term was a reasonable contextual restriction to prevent the subornation of witnesses. But once the term ended, Florida had insufficient interest to ban speech about testimony. Scalia's concurring opinion agreed with Rehnquist about the unconstitutionality of the ban on the post-term discussion of personal testimony, but he pointed out that he could find substantial reasons for a ban on witnesses' discussion of grand jury proceedings and of the statements and actions of others on or before the grand jury.[51]

In *Madsen v. Women's Health Center, Inc.,*[52] Chief Justice Rehnquist upheld, as a valid contextual limitation of expression, an injunction establishing a "buffer zone" and other spatial restrictions on the location of picketing by antiabortion protestors at a clinic providing abortion services. Writing for the majority, he characterized the injunction on the antiabortion pickets as content-neutral and as imposing reasonable restrictions with but an incidental effect on expression. Also, because there was evidence of the expression of fighting words by the protestors, he allowed a large buffer zone around the residences of clinic staff.

Scalia dissented. Rejecting Rehnquist's categorization of the case as centering on the context of expression, he called the injunction a content-based regulation of the speech and assembly of the protestors. The injunction was improper because the court lacked a compelling governmental interest to justify it. To reach this conclusion, he first argued that, although the Court had not employed either strict or intermediate scrutiny because the situation involved an injunction rather than a statute, the situation demanded strict scrutiny analysis. In making this judgment, he examined precedent and determined that prior restraints on speech, such as the injunction, required evidence of a compelling governmental interest. He argued that the majority's use of a "significant governmental interest" standard to assess the burden was a new legal creation outside the boundary of existing authority. Second, he contended that the injunction was "content-based (indeed, viewpoint based, to boot)," not a contextual restriction on the location of pickets. The injunction, he contended, aimed at the restraint of the expression of a viewpoint about abortion. Turning to reconstruct evidence about the protest, he argued that there had been no unlawful conduct or effort to use unlawful conduct on the part of the picketers. Therefore no significant interest as defined by the majority—let alone a compelling interest—existed. He concluded by arguing that the majority had so burdened expression that it had left "a powerful loaded weapon lying about today," a weapon empowering sweeping judicial restraints on free speech.[53]

Despite his objections to government controls on the content of free speech, Scalia has voted to support some governmental restrictions alleged to affect the content of speech. In *Rust v. Sullivan* the Court considered congressional restrictions on federally funded family-planning services, including restrictions on the discussion of abortion with women, on legal or political activity or the dissemination of information by the services, and on physical separation of facilities and records related to abortion at the services. He joined Rehnquist's Opinion of the Court, which focused on the suppression of speech of employees of the services. Rehnquist held that the controls on the discussion of abortion were not an unconstitutional form of discrimination by government based on the content of the expression. There had been no effort to disfavor a group on the basis of speech content; instead, there was a case of governmental refusal to fund an activity. Therefore, governments might fund programs or subsidize a private institution to encourage some forms of expression and to discourage expression of "alternate goals."[54]

In *Alexander v. United States,*[55] a RICO proceeding, Scalia agreed with Rehnquist's majority opinion permitting a seizure of theaters, bookstores, and publications. Alexander alleged that the seizure had been an unconstitutional prior restraint on his First Amendment expressive freedom, but Rehnquist concluded that the publications were assets and could be seized as assets regardless of their content and constitutionally protected status. Also, Scalia voted for a Rehnquist opinion that permitted Wisconsin to increase the penalty of a person convicted of aggravated battery who had spoken racial epithets during his crime. Rehnquist concluded that harsher sentencing for crimes in which the content of speech had given evidence of racist or sexist bias was constitutional. The harsher sentence targeted conduct that was unprotected by the First Amendment and was more socially and individually harmful than other assaults. Additionally, the sentencing rule was not an overbroad restriction on expression.[56]

Scalia voted for a Rehnquist opinion that permitted the penalization of an attorney for public statements whose content created the substantial likelihood of material prejudice in a case. Even though the speech was political in content, it could be regulated if, using a balancing test, the substantial state interest in due process at trials was affected.[57] Scalia also voted for O'Connor's Opinion of the Court upholding the constitutionality of a New York law requiring accused or convicted persons to turn over to a state agency income from their publications about their crimes. Although this was not judged a law of general applicability, O'Connor argued that the law served a compelling state interest in compensating crime victims and was narrowly tailored to serve that interest. It did not impose a content-based restraint on publication.[58] Finally, although the general rule is that government can impose no prior or prepublication restraint on the press, Scalia voted to exempt high-school students' publications from the doctrine of no prior restraint, and he allowed content-based regulation of their stories by school officials.[59]

He also voted to support O'Connor's opinion in *Frisby v. Schultz.* The case was about a ban on residential picketing focused in front of a particular residence. O'Connor concluded that strict scrutiny applied to the content of expression in such settings but that the content-neutral restraint on the picketers was "narrowly tailored" to serve a "significant government interest" in protecting the privacy of private residences.[60] When Kennedy upheld a restriction on the loudness of musical concerts in New York's Central Park, Scalia voted for his conclusion that the restriction was content-neutral and narrowly tailored, was the least restrictive means to serve an important but not compelling governmental interest in noise control, and did not prevent the expression from occurring, albeit in a lower decibel range.[61]

Obscenity and Sexually Oriented Expression

Because its content is "utterly without redeeming social importance," the Supreme Court has placed obscene speech and publications into a category of expression that is not afforded constitutional protection.[62] However, the definition of the proscribed content—the speech and publication that is obscene—has long troubled the Court. In *Miller v. California*, Chief Justice Burger drew on previous definitions to establish a three-part test to determine obscene content: "whether the 'average person, applying contemporary community standards' would find that the work, taken as a whole, appeals to the prurient interest"; "whether the work depicts or describes, in a patently offensive way, sexual conduct specifically defined by the applicable state law"; and "whether the work, taken as a whole, lacks serious literary, artistic, political, or scientific value."[63] This test in effect required a version of intensified scrutiny of governmental decisions that labeled publications or acts as obscene.

Scalia has accepted the doctrine that obscene material is utterly without redeeming social value and is not protected by the First Amendment. However, he has expressed unique views about the definition of obscenity and the applicable level of scrutiny to be used when courts are called on to judge the constitutionality of governmental allegations of obscenity. In *Pope v. Illinois*,[64] White's Opinion of the Court held that the literary, artistic, political, or scientific value of allegedly obscene material required reference to a "reasonable person" standard, not the specific standards of ordinary members of a given community. Concurring with the use of the reasonable person standard, Scalia nevertheless expressed doubts about the value of the "literary or artistic value" prong of the *Miller* test of obscenity as used by the Court. He suggested that the standard lacked enough precision to forewarn publishers. According to Scalia, and reflecting his preference for articulate legal rules, an obscenity test using the literary or artistic value standard relied too much on undefinable standards of taste. But rather than propose a more precise legal standard, Scalia simply indicated a need to consider excluding disputes about taste from the evaluation of obscenity law.[65]

Scalia also used a reasonableness standard to curtail some forms of sexual expression. In *FW/PBS v. Dallas,* a case about the constitutionality of the restrictive application of an ordinance defining the location and licensing of sexually oriented businesses, he concurred in part with and dissented in part from O'Connor's plurality opinion.[66] O'Connor's opinion provided a complex answer to the question of the validity of elements of the Dallas ordinance. She granted the sexually oriented businesses standing to challenge the licensing law and found that the law's provisions did not afford due process in the awarding of licenses and the appeal of adverse licensing decisions. However, she concluded that the city could nevertheless label motels renting rooms for less than ten hours "sexually oriented businesses" subject to the licensing provisions of the ordinance. Also, the labeling of these motels did not injure the freedom of association rights of the occupants of the motels' rooms.

In a concurring and dissenting opinion, Scalia opted for a First Amendment standard to validate the controls on obscenity found in the Dallas ordinance. Finding that limitations in the application of the *Miller* test fostered local governmental control of sexually oriented businesses "by reason of the very stringency of our obscenity test," and finding "oblique methods" such as the use of zoning laws and RICO actions "less than entirely effective in eliminating the perceived evil at which they are directed," he sought another solution.[67] Resurrecting the pandering standard of Brennan's opinion in *Ginzburg v. United States,*[68] he sought to construe the Dallas ordinance as a valid, narrowly drawn, and reasonable effort to prevent directly the unconstitutional distribution of sexual material through salacious appeals. In *Ginzburg* Brennan held that pandering, or the deliberate purveying, presentation, or dissemination of material with the sole purpose of appealing to the erotic interest of potential customers, "may be decisive in the determination of obscenity," especially if the purveyor "deliberately emphasized the sexually provocative aspects of the work, in order to catch the salaciously disposed."[69]

Scalia contended that the *Miller* test did not alter the validity of the prior *Ginzburg* rule. Thus he argued that the state could directly regulate the sexually provocative aspects of the advertising, sale, or distribution of the material. Turning to the Dallas ordinance, he concluded that it was a narrowly drawn effort to control and prevent salacious appeals by businesses intending to present live nudity or sell hardcore sexual material. It was not an overbroad regulation of a wide variety of constitutional expressions; it restricted only those enterprises that sold materials with a salacious appeal. Also, he argued that his use of the pandering standard avoided the evidentiary difficulties with satisfying the intensified scrutiny of the *Miller* test. Rather, since the regulation was "not directed to particular works or performance, but to their concentration, . . . the constitutional analysis should be adjusted accordingly." The regulator did not have to find the material obscene and without constitutional protection. Material or acts presumably constitutionally protected under *Miller* could be controlled if presented for sale through a salacious appeal. The clear implication was that a form of lower-tier scrutiny, an evaluation of the reasonableness of restrictions on the licensing of businesses engaged in pandering, was a constitutional method for the control of expressive activity "patently objectionable to large segments of our society."[70]

Scalia's use of a reasonableness test rather than the more intensified scrutiny demanded by the *Miller* test also appeared in his concurring opinion in *Sable Communications v. FCC*, a "dial-a-porn" case. Despite the fact that dial-a-porn, or indecent telephone messages, might be accessed by juveniles, the Court refused to uphold a federal statute denying access to erotic telephone messages deemed indecent but not obscene. Scalia agreed that the ban on all adult access to indecent speech was unconstitutional. However, he determined that a more narrowly tailored and reasonable ban on indecent speech, one that was aimed at minors, might survive his analysis, although such a ban was presently not technologically possible.[71]

Scalia's opinions about sexually oriented materials and businesses have reflected his disquiet with the capacity of policymakers to deal with the trade in erotic materials. Working at the edges of *Miller*, he has attempted to carve out aspects of the sex business for which governmental regulations only had to survive a reasonableness test. His effort thus has supported both content-based control on obscene material and also indirect controls that regulate such material through controls on its salacious appeals or on the content of a vendor's effort to sell both obscene and salacious but constitutional material.[72]

Time, Place, and Manner Restrictions on
First Amendment Rights

The Supreme Court has long recognized that restrictions might be placed on expressions made in selected contexts. Governments can enact neutral time, place, and manner restrictions of expression in public forums to ensure public order and enable the use of public places by all citizens.[73] Such "reasonable" time, place, and manner restrictions on expression must be a narrowly drawn effort to control harmful conduct and must be applied in an evenhanded manner. However, they do not have to satisfy strict scrutiny and the compelling interest test. Scalia's treatment of time, place, and manner restrictions on rights of expressive conduct has evidenced a pattern of controlling selected social harms on the basis of a personal assessment of the degree of harm and the reasonableness of the regulation.

In *McIntyre v. Ohio Elections Commission*,[74] the Court concluded that Ohio's imposition of penalties for the distribution of anonymous election campaign material was unconstitutional. Scalia, joined by Rehnquist, dissented. His argument was that the governmental regulation of anonymous campaign literature was justified by a legal tradition justifying regulations to secure public order at election time which stretched back to the early national period and which reflected the judgments of legislatures in forty-nine states. This history and legislative evidence indicated that the regulation of anonymous campaign material bore a "strong presumption of constitutionality." Absent a clear text, historical practice, or constitutional interpretation to the contrary, he refused to establish a constitutional protection where none had existed.[75] Even though Scalia considered this argument sufficient, he moved to offer an alternative analysis. He then argued that the Court had recognized that the government had a compelling interest in protecting the electoral system and that this interest was not offset by a previously unrecognized compelling interest to protect a right to anonymity in speech. No only did the right not exist but "common sense" suggested that it was not a right essential to "protecting and enhancing democratic elections." Therefore, he regarded the Ohio law against anonymous distribution of election material to be a valid contextual restriction on speech and press designed to deter campaign falsehoods, promote "civil and dignified" campaign debate, and provide information about candidates.[76]

Scalia concurred with the Court when it upheld the application of

New York City's Human Rights Law to force an end to gender discrimination by an allegedly private club. He agreed with the equal protection analysis but differed on the Court's rejection of the club's claim that the law interfered with its First Amendment rights. Using precedent, the Court held that, as a valid place and manner restriction on free association, governments could impose regulations on private clubs that assisted commercial business transactions. Also, the Court concluded that it was reasonable for the city to exempt benevolent and religious associations from the regulations. Although he accepted the regulation of the club because the club assisted commercial transactions, Scalia argued that the Court had not shown an adequate lower-tier reason for the exemption of the benevolent and religious organizations. Thus, he wanted analysis to round out the Court's argument and justify all aspects of the city's regulation.[77] He also supported a state civil rights law that barred all-male clubs from discriminating against women. The Court held that government had a compelling state interest in eliminating discrimination against women and that this interest was sufficient to require a change in the association's rules. Further, the law did not unduly interfere with the aims, activities, or membership selection process of the association.[78]

In related matters, Scalia voted with the majority to uphold a decision to limit certain dance halls to juveniles because no right to association of a disadvantaged group was infringed and the regulation was a reasonable effort to control the behavior of minors. He voted for an opinion of White which withheld food stamp benefits from striking workers as a reasonable decision to avoid favoritism in a conflict among associations. Finally, in a case about the free exercise of religion and rights of association, Scalia agreed with Rehnquist's majority opinion that it was reasonable for prison officials to prevent prisoners from attending an Islamic service. Rehnquist rejected the application of strict scrutiny analysis and the corollary proposition that the officials, to justify their decision, were obliged to demonstrate that they had a compelling interest; he regarded the decision as a reasonable regulation designed to ensure order and security in the context of the prison.[79] However, Scalia voted for a majority opinion by Rehnquist that held that membership in a white racist association and information about the abstract beliefs of the association could not be introduced in the penalty phase of a capital criminal trial unless it was relevant to the commission of specific acts or might be relevant as an indicator of aggravating circumstances during sentencing.[80]

In a concurring opinion to a decision to curtail expressive activities on the streets near polling places, Scalia rejected the strict scrutiny approach of the majority. He simply found the curtailment to be a reasonable control of time, place, and manner of expression. Reciting the history of election day restrictions of the space adjoining polling places, he concluded that the street near the polls was not a "traditional public forum." Instead, a long history of legislation indicated that the street was a space subject to time-place-manner regulations on election day. Since the street was not a public forum, according to precedent the regulation on the use of the street for expressive purposes had only to satisfy a reasonableness test.[81]

Taking this restrictive position further, Scalia supported Rehnquist's conclusion for the Court that airports were not a "traditional" public forum. Instead, they were places subject to "designation" as public forums. A designated public forum was one in which government had a specific proprietary interest that implicitly limited the use of that forum to certain functions deemed reasonable. In *United States v. Kokinda* Scalia voted for O'Connor's plurality opinion using a reasonableness test to evaluate restrictions on protestors using a sidewalk at a post office. O'Connor regarded the post office sidewalk to be a special form of governmental property designated for certain business purposes and lacking the character of a traditional public forum, unlike a sidewalk beside a business or residence.[82] Also, Scalia voted for Rehnquist's dissenting opinion in a case about a parade permit ordinance in Forsyth County, Georgia. Although the majority held that the ordinance created arbitrary standards and allowed administrators to set fees so as to discourage some speech on the basis of its content, Rehnquist argued that precedent supported the reasonableness of the ordinance.[83] Also, Scalia agreed with Rehnquist's plurality opinion for the Court and special separate opinion that concluded that a public airport could ban, as a reasonable contextual restriction of expression, both the solicitation of funds and the distribution of literature by a religious group. The majority favored as reasonable the ban on solicitation of funds but not the ban on the distribution of literature.[84]

Scalia's opinions about limitations on expression contain a political message. He has not made a concentrated effort to distinguish legally the logic of his decisions supporting contextual restrictions—including also his *CCNV* decision while on the D.C. Circuit, the *McIntyre* opinion on anonymous electoral material, the New York club case, the polling place restriction, and the rape-shield law—from his decisions stating that the *Madsen* injunction and the prohibition of flag-burning were content-based restrictions. Although he used a reasonableness scrutiny approach in most contextual cases, he has never clearly defined the line between content and contextual limitations on expression. Thus, the questions are: If *Madsen* is about a content regulation, why are the other laws treated under standards about contextual limitations on speech? Why is not the issue in *Florida Star* the content of a news report, the issue in *McIntyre* the protection of all forms or content of electoral materials, the issue in *Burson* the content of speech near the polls, the issue in the New York club case the content of club policies about women? The answer to these questions seems to be that Scalia has differentiated content and context restrictions, and the level of scrutiny appropriate in expression cases, on the basis of his personal predilections about whether the interest deserved protection and whether rights of expression ought to be expanded to include a group's ideas in the pluralistic politics of the regime. The result of his opinions and votes thus has been greater protection for established or conservative interests, such as abortion protestors, interests that can pay to people to disseminate their ideas, and the interests of the media as opposed to the interests of women. When coupled with his decisions in *R.A.V.*, *Austin*, the peyote case, *Barnes*, and other content cases, his practice has been to use the First Amendment to deny the liberal legislative effort to support the politically disadvantaged and outsiders. However, with respect to this answer, his votes in the flag-burning cases appear to be an anomaly. Whether these votes reflect a "libertarian" streak in his political attitudes or whether the argument to the Court in support of the restriction on the burning was legally deficient and violated his Reasoned Elaborationist understanding of the Constitution's clear ban on content-based regulations of expression cannot be discerned.[85] Although his votes in the flag-burning cases make him look liberal, the vast majority of his votes and opinions about expression have favored conservative, vested, or governmental interests.

Governmental Restrictions on Commercial Speech

In *Central Hudson Gas Company v. Public Service Commission* the Burger Court evolved a special, four-part, intermediate scrutiny test for the evaluation of governmental regulation of advertising and other forms of commercial expression.[86] In *Board of Trustees of State University of New York v. Fox*,[87] Scalia wrote for the Court in a case in which the campus police of the State University of New York (SUNY) at Cortland had enforced a regulation prohibiting the use of school property for commercial purposes and removed from the campus a person holding a Tupperware party in a dormitory room. Fox, a student attending the party, claimed that the regulation was an overbroad limitation on the use of a public facility or forum for commercial purposes and was in contravention of the fourth prong of the *Central Hudson* test. The prong required that a regulation be the "least restrictive means available" to control commercial speech. Scalia held that the regulation of the party as commercial speech did not have to satisfy the least restrictive means available test to survive as a regulation of commercial speech. Reconstructing this prong of *Central Hudson*, he concluded that the school's regulation was legitimate if the government's goal was "substantial, and the cost to be carefully calculated."[88] Despite precedent, he judged that his was a more precise standard for guiding the regulation of commercial speech. Additionally, since the validity of the statute had not been decided, he refused to determine whether the regulation was more generally overbroad as a regulation of noncommercial speech until the trial court had ruled on the issue.

In cases in which he voted, but did not write opinions, about commercial speech, Scalia's votes were not as deferential to regulatory concerns as were those some of his more conservative colleagues. In *Lakewood v. Plain Dealer Publishing Company,*[89] he joined Brennan's plurality opinion allowing a challenge to a local ordinance that required licenses for the location of newspaper vending racks on public property. Brennan held that the licensing law created the possibility of content-based or viewpoint discrimination against selected newspapers, especially because the ordinance posed no controls on administrative discretion in the award of licenses. Extending his support for this position to commercial speech issues, in *City of Cincinnati v. Discovery Network,*[90] Scalia voted for Stevens's majority opinion that overturned a local restriction on the location of news racks for the distribution of commercial handbills, but not newspapers. Scalia agreed that the local law did not reasonably advance a substantial governmental interest as defined in prong 3 of the *Central Hudson* test. Also, he agreed with an opinion of Kennedy that struck down a ban on advertising by certified public accountants in Florida, on the ground that it did not advance a substantial governmental interest per *Central Hudson's* third prong. He later voted against an effort by Florida to impose modified controls on accountants' advertising.[91]

However, in *United States v. Edge Broadcasting*,[92] Scalia supported White's majority opinion that a ban on the advertising of nonstate lotteries served a substantial government interest and was necessary and effective. He also voted for a dissenting opinion by O'Connor in a case about representations on the commercial letterhead of an attorney. O'Connor objected to the rote inclusion of the letterhead under commercial speech doctrine and the restriction of the state's "inherent authority" to police the professional ethics of its lawyers.[93] Later Scalia voted for O'Connor's opinion when she wrote for the majority to conclude that *Central Hudson* analysis allowed the Florida bar to restrict direct mail solicitation of potential personal injury and wrongful death clients within thirty days of an accident.[94] And finally, he agreed with an opinion by Kennedy which stated that intermediate scrutiny, not strict scrutiny, ought to be applied to evaluate content-neutral federal regulations of the information carried by cable communication services. Kennedy concluded that FCC "must-carry" provisions regulating the channels carried on a cable system served an important governmental interest and were substantially related to that interest.[95]

Regulation of Public Employees' Speech

Scalia has argued that public employers can regulate the speech of employees on matters of public concern when the need for effective policy implementation outweighs expressive rights. Thus, speech can be regulated because of the status of the speaker. In *Rankin v. McPherson*,[96] the Court determined that a First Amendment right to make a statement on a matter of public concern outweighed any reasons for the dismissal of McPherson, a clerk in a Texas constable's office who had been fired because of a remark made in front of other employees indicating that she hoped that someone might assassinate President Ronald Reagan—"If they go for him again, I hope they get him."

Scalia dissented. First, he considered that McPherson's statement failed to satisfy the threshold requirement to qualify as speech on a matter of public concern. He argued that in its content the statement was dissimilar to other statements the Court had deemed to be on matters of public concern, and that it was closer to statements the Court had judged to be entitled to no First Amendment protection. In making this judgment, Scalia refused to inquire into the context in which McPherson had made the statement, and he treated it as "only one step removed" from statements similar in content but made in an environment of imminent disorder, as in the "fighting words" cases. Second, he assessed the weight of the constable's reasons for dismissal differently from the majority of the Court. Scalia thought that the constable's interest in "maintaining both an esprit de corps and a public image consistent with his office's law enforcement duties outweighs any interest his employees may have in expressing on the job a desire that the President be killed, even assuming that such an expression addresses a matter of public concern." It is not protected by the First Amendment from suppression.[97] This balancing test, atypical of Scalia's opinions but drawn from precedent on the subject, avoided any form of scrutiny analysis. Later he voted for a dissenting opinion written by Rehnquist in a case in which the majority determined the unconstitutionality of a ban on the receipt of honoraria by federal employees. Echoing the Scalia dissent in *Rankin v. McPherson*, the Rehnquist opinion concluded that "the weight" given governmental justifications for the ban was not properly considered in judging—through a balancing test—the validity of what Rehnquist deemed a contextual regulation of speech.[98]

Taxation as an Impediment to Expressive Freedom

When a state tax singled out newspapers for a special use tax on ink and paper, the Burger Court applied strict scrutiny analysis to void the tax.[99] However, when the Court's majority in *Arkansas Writers' Project, Inc. v. Ragland* used strict scrutiny and refused to allow a selective, content-based taxation of some magazines,[100] Scalia dissented because he believed that the Court should not have applied strict scrutiny criteria to evaluate the constitutionality of subsidies administered through exemptions from the tax. Such indirect subsidization of publication was not a direct restriction or prohibition on freedom of the press, he claimed, and it did not have a coercive effect on protected rights. Fearful that the use of strict scrutiny would cause free expression challenges to direct or indirect governmental subsidization of bulk mail, the arts, and public broadcasting, he preferred the use of a rational basis test. Reasonable subsidies encouraging expression might then survive, he concluded.[101]

In *Texas Monthly v. Bullock*,[102] the Court considered the constitutionality of the exemption of religious periodicals from a state sales tax. The primary issue in the case was whether the exemption violated the

Establishment Clause of the First Amendment. However, in his dissenting opinion Scalia also considered the freedom of the press. He argued that the exemption on the periodicals was content-based but that it was a reasonable exemption because it accommodated the constitutional interest in "freedom of religious expression."[103]

In several cases on taxation as an impediment to expressive freedom, Scalia did not write an opinion. He voted to support an opinion by O'Connor which held that distinctions in the sales taxation of various classes of media—for instance, a difference between the taxation of cable television and that of print media—were constitutional as part of a law of general applicability. The practice of classification for taxes was general in nature and did not single out a particular group of ideas or viewpoints for penalty, O'Connor concluded.[104] In *Cohen v. Cowles Media*,[105] Scalia voted for an opinion by White which permitted the award of damages to a person who had been promised but not provided confidentiality by a newspaper. White reasoned that a law of general applicability which did not target the press was at issue. In addition, he joined a unanimous decision that extended the proposition that laws of general applicability can regulate publications firms and that created a standard holding that tax laws of general applicability can apply to sales of religious materials so long as there is no significant burden on religious practices or beliefs.[106]

Overbreadth Doctrine

The Warren Court developed the rule that the First Amendment is violated when a regulation sweeps unnecessarily broadly and thereby invades the area of protected freedoms.[107] In *City of Houston, Texas v. Hill*,[108] Justice Brennan ruled that a Houston ordinance prohibiting various verbal and physical challenges to police who were performing their duty was overbroad and facially invalid. Hill had been arrested after shouting at police and diverting their attention during an interrogation of another person. Brennan reasoned that the ordinance allowed the penalization of Hill's constitutional act of speech. Thus, the ordinance improperly permitted broad discretionary impediments to the exercise of a constitutional right. Scalia concurred, and joined most arguments in a concurring opinion written by Powell. Powell argued that the ordinance improperly regulated any type of interruption or verbal molestation of police. Despite his effort to carve out a context for the regulation of expression directed at police, Scalia agreed that the Houston ordinance was overbroad because it regulated some of the content of expressions.[109]

Despite some judicial efforts to limit the situations in which overbreadth claims can be made, Scalia has supported the use of such claims. When a criminal conviction under a Massachusetts law that prohibited adults from posing children for nude photographs or exhibiting nude photographs of children was held to be invalid because the law was an overbroad restriction on expression, the state amended the law to apply to nude photographs made or displayed with "lascivious intent." The state then prosecuted and again convicted the accused. A plurality of the Court, in an opinion by O'Connor, permitted the conviction on retrial to stand. In a concurring and dissenting opinion, Scalia argued that O'Connor's approach made it "cost-free" for a legislature to enact overbroad laws and chill free speech. He thought that the amendment of the statute did not automatically preclude a defense of overbreadth. Turning to the amended statute, he concluded that it was not overbroad because it did not sweep into protected expression. Rather, it controlled material—child pornography—that according to precedent could be legitimately banned.[110] Therefore, Scalia, in keeping with Reasoned Elaboration ideals, used overbreadth doctrine when it forced legislatures to draft precise statutes. Overbreadth doctrine, however, was not primarily a means for the protection of expressive rights.

First Amendment Claims Involving Privileged Private Institutions

Governmental authority over expression does not always impose restrictions on private parties or groups. Often, as in *Texas Monthly*, government tries to assign privileges, subsidies, or other benefits to some communicators or groups. Typical of other governmental benefits are privileges assigned to political parties and labor unions. The question is whether these privileges and protection burden the First Amendment rights of some members of the association or of other individuals.

Generally, Scalia has rejected the use of strict scrutiny when individuals sought to challenge established organizations benefiting from governmental assistance. In *Tashjian v. Republican Party*,[111] Scalia dissented from an Opinion of the Court which used the compelling interest test to strike down a closed primary law requiring that to vote in a Republican party primary election voters become registered members of the Republican party. The Court determined that the law unconstitutionally burdened the right of the Republican party to decide for itself whether to admit nonmembers to its candidate selection process, and that the state offered no compelling reason for the burden. Scalia thought that the Court had "exaggerated the importance of the associational interest at issue, if indeed it does not see one where none exists." Instead, he read the associational contact to be casual and the regulation to pose no burden on this brief encounter between a private person and a private organization. Indeed, the state did not have to honor "a party's democratically expressed desire" to have its candidates selected as it chose.[112] His argument thus implied that states can assist the party in maintaining its institutional integrity, through the protection of its candidate selection practices against external and internal freedom of association claims.

In *Norman v. Reed*,[113] the court considered state rules on the placement of a new political party on the Illinois ballot. Using strict scrutiny, Souter's Opinion of the Court held that the state had failed to provide evidence that the provisions of the law regarding the name of the party, and the requirement that the party provide a petition signed by 25,000 persons in each political subdivision to earn a spot on the ballot for all of its candidates in one subdivision, served a compelling interest. However, another signature provision requiring a given number of signatures from a subdivision for a party to earn a spot on the ballot in that subdivision was sufficiently supported by a governmental interest. Scalia dissented, contending that "no proper basis has been established in this case for interfering with the State of Illinois' arrangement of its elections." He argued that the provisions all advanced a legitimate state interest in the defense of the role of parties in elections. Refusing to apply any form of intensified scrutiny, he reviewed the practice and concluded that the provisions, all of which protected and privileged the existing party system, were reasonable.[114]

The same rejection of the use of strict scrutiny marked his dissenting opinion regarding a decision about the use of party affiliation as a criterion for the promotion of governmental employees. In *Rutan v. Republican Party*,[115] Brennan's Opinion of the Court held that political party membership was not a permissible factor in the dispensation of government jobs, except for a category of confidential policymaking jobs. Brennan determined that the constitutional right to freedom of association could not be set aside when the government failed to prove a compelling interest in the maintenance of the partisan hiring practices required by a patronage system of public employment. Scalia's dissenting opinion attacked the majority, and a series of earlier Court decisions against the patronage system, by arguing for the use of a deferential rational basis test to evaluate the rights of association at issue. The reason he gave for diminished scrutiny was that governmental employment has long featured restrictions on employee speech and behavior which are subject to a rationality test analysis different from the standards applied when government regulates private conduct. Further, he contended that either on the basis of a rationality test or on the basis of the Court's balancing test, patronage employment should survive as a privilege of elected officials. It was a traditional practice long deemed reasonable, and it played a useful purpose in fostering parties, the two-party system, and electoral participation. In a footnote, Brennan had dismissed this argument by arguing that the interests that Scalia thought were promoted by patronage are not interests that government has in its capacity as an employer. "Therefore, even were Justice Scalia correct that less-than-strict scrutiny is appropriate when the government takes measures to ensure the proper functioning of its internal operations, such a rule has no relevance to the restrictions on freedom of association and speech at issue in this case." However, Scalia recognized that government can assign the use of the privilege of patronage to elected representatives of parties, not merely to foster these interests but also to establish its own version of good public management. He closed his opinion with a theme of Reasoned Elaboration argumentation—the assertion that the creation of doctrine in this case would lead to confusion and more litigation. He deemed a passive stance by the Court and deference to legislative judgment about the criteria for public employment to be a more reasonable course of action.[116] He did not examine the way in which this legislative assessment of public employees, which introduced politics as a factor in addition to experience or academic knowledge as a measure of merit, was a different kind of discrimination than the introduction of race or gender through affirmative action rules (as in *Johnson v. Transportation Agency*).

In *Lehnert v. Ferris Faculty Association*,[117] a group of dissident union members challenged various acts of political spending by their elected union leadership. They claimed that the spending violated their First Amendment rights of association. The Court decided that union members' dues could be used only for expenditures "germane" to the union's primary function of collective bargaining or other statutory duties. Scalia agreed with the Court's conclusion but not with the three-part legal test of germaneness it had used to reach that conclusion. Instead, he proposed a simple evaluation of whether the union had made its expenditures in the performance of its statutory duties. Unlike his arguments in the cases about political parties, his test made it easier to challenge institutional decisions. These included the decision of the union to use its most powerful tool in contractual disputes, the strike.[118]

The Scrutiny of the Regulation of Expression: A Summary

Scalia's opinions about laws regulating free expression and laws supporting the control of expressive rights by private associations have melded Reasoned Elaboration argument into opinions that largely constrain expression by litigants critical of the political status quo and governmental authority. The standards of Reasoned Elaboration, such as deference to the legislature, antiexperimentalism, and judicial passivity, appear in his opinions. He has approved of any expressive regulations as long as the government imposed them as clear rules not aimed at the content of the expression. However, the thrust of Scalia's opinions about free expression has also advantaged existing centers of political power and social consensus. His opinions did not aim at including in American pluralist politics the political outsider and the less wealthy or organized participant. The centers of power whose expression might benefit from his opinions—such as corporations, governments, and antiabortionists—were not the disadvantaged classes that Brennan and Marshall attempted to defend through strict scrutiny. Thus, he wrote against liberal efforts to control PACs in *Austin,* to prevent hate speech in *R.A.V.,* and to control abortion protests in *Madsen.* His standards have, or could have, facilitated the achievement of conservative policy goals such as the control of obscenity (*Pope, FW/PBS, Sable*). Also, he wrote for strong administrative control—of subordinate bureaucrats in *Rankin;* of—indirectly—campus speech in *SUNY v. Fox;* of liberal union leaders in *Lehnert;* and for the interests of established party leaders or party policies in *Tashjian, Norman v. Reed,* and *Rutan.* Despite some exceptions to this pattern, such as his votes in the flag-burning cases, he has thus tried to limit judicial protection of expression and the presence of more voices in the regime.

LIBEL AND DEFAMATION

The Court has recognized that judicial actions resulting in findings of libel or defamation can result in post-expression recovery of damages. Although the regulation is indirect, the message of a libel decision conditions and controls future expression. The Court distinguishes between the evidence required to prove libel against public officials and public figures, and the evidence required for proof of libel against private persons.[119] In *Harte-Hanks Communications, Inc. v. Connaughton*,[120] the Court considered whether a reviewing court had properly evaluated the "actual malice" of a published statement about a candidate for public office—that is, determined whether the statement had been made with "knowledge that it was false or with reckless disregard of whether it was false or not." The Court concluded that the candidate was a public figure whose evidence sufficiently proved actual malice. Scalia concurred, agreeing with the Court that "'highly unreasonable conduct constituting an extreme departure from ordinary standards of investigation and reporting'" is evidence of actual malice. However, he disagreed with the Court's restriction on the facts that the jury could use to reach judgment. Rather than limiting the consideration of the plaintiff's claim of malice to "adequately supported favorable facts" found by the jury, he would have allowed the jury to consider all facts that it could reasonably have found that were favorable for the party seeking relief. Although in this case his standard for the evaluation of facts led to the same conclusion as that of the majority, it opened libel trials to more forms of evidence of malice and potentially more decisions against publishers.[121]

In libel cases Scalia voted to support the proposition that defamation actions should apply identical constitutional analysis of truth and malice to published statements of events and to opinions.[122] These standards, requiring proof of falsehood and "actual malice," underwent explication in *Masson v. New Yorker Magazine.* Scalia supported White's concurring opinion in *Masson* which argued that a material alteration of a speaker's words was actual malice. The Court, in an opinion by Kennedy, considered the alteration to be malicious only if it created a different rational interpretation of the words. Also, Scalia joined the Court in a unanimous decision to protect nonmalicious printed parodies from tort actions and to protect musical parodies as a "fair use" of copyrighted materials.[123]

THE ESTABLISHMENT CLAUSE

In 1971 Chief Justice Burger drew on the Court's previous decisions about the "No Establishment of Religion" Clause of the First Amendment and developed a three-part test for judging claims arising under the clause. His *Lemon* test had three prongs: first, "the statute must have a secular legislative purpose; second, its principal or primary effect must be one that neither advances nor inhibits religion; finally, the statute must not foster an 'excessive government Entanglement with religion.'"[124] With its three prongs imposing on governments the burden of justifying laws affecting religious organizations, the test invited but did not necessarily compel an approach to standards of review and burdens of proof directly parallel to strict scrutiny.[125] However, *Lemon* occasioned considerable debate within the Court. Because of his constant questioning of both the meaning of the test's prongs and, at times, the value of the entire standard, Scalia's position on *Lemon* has typified one side of this debate.

In *Edwards v. Aguillard*,[126] the Court held that a Louisiana law requiring the teaching of "creation science," a theory of the development of mankind based on accounts in the biblical book of Genesis, was unconstitutional. The Court rejected the argument that the act promoted academic freedom and instead held that it violated the first, or secular purpose, prong of *Lemon*. Relying on legislative history, the opinion illustrated that the primary aim of the act was to advance a religious idea and "to restructure the science curriculum to conform with a particular religious viewpoint."[127]

Scalia dissented. First, he attempted to define the nature of the evidence required, under the secular purpose prong, to prove compliance with the Establishment Clause. The thrust of his interpretation was that a law only had to serve *some* secular purpose. Also, incidental effects of a law beneficial to a religion, like "the fact that creation science coincides with the beliefs of certain religions, . . . does not itself justify invalidation of the Act."[128] Citing precedent, he argued that governments could pass some laws that benefit religious claims to free exercise or that accommodate religious practices. Citing Justice Frankfurter, he indicated that the Court ought to defer to these legislative judgments and not assume unconstitutional motives on the part of the state. Adding to this argument, with its echoes of Reasoned Elaboration principles, was his subsidiary position that the Court had erroneously located a religious purpose in the adoption of the law. Reviewing the majority's reading of legislative history, he recited at great length language and events to contend that the Louisiana legislators and other officers primarily bespoke a secular purpose in their debate about the law. And closing his opinion with a theme from Reasoned Elaboration jurisprudence, he remarked that this decision, like other Establishment Clause cases, had "made such a maze" that "conscientious governmental officials can only guess what motives will be held unconstitutional." Also, the decision left the Court unguided by a precise rule and the clause open to subjective judicial interpretation in the future. To avoid such flexibility and pragmatic judgment, he concluded that it would be best to abandon the first prong of *Lemon*.[129] Only then might a reasonable Establishment Clause jurisprudence emerge.

As indicated above, in *Texas Monthly v. Bullock* the Court considered the constitutionality of the exemption of religious periodicals from a state sales tax.[130] Brennan's Opinion of the Court applied the *Lemon* test and concluded that the exemption failed to satisfy the secular purpose prong of the test. "Texas' sales tax exemption for periodicals published or distributed by a religious faith and consisting wholly of writings promulgating the teaching of the faith lacks sufficient breadth to pass scrutiny under the Establishment Clause."[131] The exemption did not present a compelling interest requiring the granting of a special preference to religious publications.

In dissent, Scalia found "no basis in the text of the Constitution, the decisions of this Court or the traditions of our people for disapproving this longstanding and widespread practice." He made three points. First, he cited cases in which the Court had supported state policies that exempted religious organizations from taxes and might entangle government and religion. He contended that Brennan had misdescribed these cases and indirectly overruled them. Second, he argued for an application of an "accommodation principle" in the relations of church and state, citing cases to indicate that the exemption was an accommodation and not a governmental promotion of religion. Finally, he disagreed with Brennan's assessment that the exemption did not serve a secular purpose. Scalia argued that the exemption was not a direct diversion of public money; its primary effect was not to sponsor religion. Moreover, it did not entangle government in the operations of a religion.[132]

Revisiting the Establishment Clause three years later, Scalia moved away from a use of Reasoned Elaboration arguments and away from a legalistic critique of *Lemon*. In *Lee v. Weisman*,[133] the Court, in an opinion by Justice Kennedy, held that, because of its coercive effect on religious belief, a state-imposed prayer at a public school graduation ceremony had violated the secular purpose prong and other prongs of *Lemon*. Again Scalia dissented, but in the first part of his opinion he switched to a historical attack on the majority's argument. He argued that the Court had invented a test of psychological coercion to create a *Lemon* violation. However, in so doing it had slighted a practice with "deep foundations in the historic practices of our people."[134] After an illustrative review of the history of prayer at graduation events, he turned to challenge the notion that high-school graduates were readily subjected to psychological coercion because of the prayer. Finally, he commented that the school had not designated the content of the prayer, and therefore that the state had not chosen to advance a specific viewpoint. Instead, the state had only accommodated a longstanding historical practice.

In the remainder of the opinion Scalia launched into a general argument for the abandonment of *Lemon*. Arguing that "long-accepted constitutional tradition" ran counter to *Lemon* and decisions based upon it, he called the case a "jurisprudential disaster." Historical evidence, he argued, only demanded that direct governmental coercion of religious practices or support of religion not occur. Counter to what he believed the Court had said in reading *Lemon*, incidental exposure to religion, such as hearing a graduation prayer, was not coercive. *Lemon* had afforded the Court a basis for such flexible and pragmatic constructions of the Establishment Clause that constitutional tradition could be ignored. The result, he claimed, would be more contention, and less exposure to and understanding of religious difference. In short, the application of *Lemon* created expanded political pluralism and moral discord, not the political and moral unity encouraged by reliance on a common tradition.[135]

Scalia's hostility became even more polemical in *Lamb's Chapel v. Center Moriches Union Free School District*.[136] Justice White wrote for the Court to permit the after-hours use of school property for a religious meeting. He concluded that banning the meeting would be a form of unconstitutional content-based suppression of freedom of speech and that showing a religious film at the meeting was not an endorsement of religion in violation of a modified construction of the second prong of the *Lemon* test. Scalia concurred but commented, "Like some ghoul in a late-night horror movie that repeatedly sits up in its grave and shuffles abroad, *Lemon* stalks our Establishment Clause jurisprudence once again, frightening little children and school attorneys of Center Moriches Union Free School District." He argued that *Lee v. Weisman* had "conspicuously avoided using the supposed 'test,'" and that "five of the currently sitting justices have, in their own opinions, personally driven pencils through the creature's heart." His citations especially singled out Kennedy, O'Connor, and White for repudiating and then resurrecting *Lemon*. He then lambasted his colleagues for keeping the monster around "at least in a somnolent state; one never knows when one might need him." Instead, he thought, the Court needed to finally kill *Lemon* and apply a test that determined whether there was discrimination against or in favor of a religion.[137]

Despite his effort to point out the inconsistency of his colleagues in *Lamb's Chapel*, the justices voted to prevent the State of New York from establishing a school district with boundaries coterminous with those of a neighborhood inhabited by members of a Hasidic Jewish religious denomination. Souter's Opinion of the Court found that the state action was a nonneutral decision that benefited the religious group. Kennedy, O'Connor, and Stevens wrote concurring opinions. Scalia dissented, again citing the Court for abandoning "text and history as guides." He argued that the creation of the school district for the sect was a permissible accommodation of religion. It was not, as Souter claimed, a use of civil authority to advantage a religion. Contending that Souter had too readily allowed "unelected judges" to set aside "democratically adopted laws," Scalia illustrated the way in which he thought the New York law was similar to other laws establishing school districts. In addition, he pointed out that the law was little different from other laws accommodating specific religious practices which the Court had upheld. Turning to the concurring opinions, he simply labeled Stevens's opinion "less a legal analysis than a manifesto of secularism." Kennedy's standard, he argued, was similar to that of the Court, while O'Connor had tried to replace *Lemon* "with nothing." Together with Souter's, these opinions all worked toward the repeal of "our Nation's tradition of religious toleration."[138]

In *Capitol Square Review and Advisory Board v. Pinette*,[139] Scalia wrote for the Court's plurality in a case about a governmental board's refusal to allow the Ku Klux Klan to place a Latin cross in a public plaza surrounding the Ohio statehouse. After its refusal to permit the erection of the cross was enjoined by a court, the board permitted the placement of the cross. In his opinion, Scalia first chose to ignore any free speech dimensions of the case because the petitions from the parties and prior litigation of the case had not considered the board's decision as a time, place, or manner contextual regulation of speech.[140] Proceeding to the Establishment Clause issue, he relied on the majority position in *Lamb's Chapel* and *Widmar v. Vincent* to hold that the state could not regulate the placement of the cross in an open public forum.[141] There was in the erection of the cross no governmental endorsement, encouragement, favoritism, or assistance that in any way established an official preference for one religious symbol. Rather, the cross had been erected by a private organization in a place long recognized as a public forum. Concluding his opinion, he addressed suggestions by Stevens, O'Connor, Souter, and Breyer which recommended a form of public notice that would inform persons that the cross was a private display and did not represent the government's views. Scalia argued that this effort, to prevent a misplaced attribution of private religious views to the government, was discriminatory if directed only toward acts of religious expression. Also, he reasoned that it would create new complexities for governmental regulation of the incidental benefits of religious expression in public places.[142]

Scalia also voted, without opinion, against other applications of the three-part test of *Lemon v. Kurtzman* in cases involving the Establishment of Religion Clause.[143] Thus, he joined Kennedy's concurring and dissenting opinion in *County of Allegheny v. American Civil Liberties Union*,[144] which favored latitude in religious displays on public property during the Christmas and Chanukah seasons and which questioned but did not offer an alternative to the Court's use of a modified second part of the *Lemon* test. He joined Kennedy's concurring opinion in a case in which a school district had denied access to school facilities to a Christian club. Supporting access for the club, Kennedy also argued that the accrual of incidental benefits to a religion as a result of a governmental activity did not violate the Establishment Clause; the clause was only violated by the coercion of persons to participate in a religious activity.[145] Scalia agreed with Kennedy's concurring opinion in a case about a law that afforded grants to religious organizations as part of a general program of grants for counseling adolescents about sexual activity and pregnancy. For Kennedy the issue was not whether the program satisfied *Lemon* criteria. Rather, the issue was whether a religious organization had spent granted funds to foster or coerce a religious belief.[146] In addition, Scalia supported the Court's majority when it ruled that a public school district did not violate the

Establishment Clause by providing government-funded sign language interpreters for deaf students at a religious school because the benefit neutrally benefited a broad class of citizens without reference to religion.[147] However, Scalia voted for an opinion by White that upheld the exemption, in Title VII of the Civil Rights Act of 1964, of religious organizations from compliance with the title's ban on religious discrimination in employment. White concluded that the exemption satisfied the *Lemon* test because it did not advance religion, and it respected free exercise by a religion.[148]

In these cases, as in most other Establishment Clause cases, Scalia could not shake the Court away from its post-*Lemon* questioning of laws providing special protection for religion. The other justices simply favored more separation of church and state than Scalia's accommodationist arguments would permit. Like a good exponent of Reasoned Elaboration jurisprudence, he embraced the decisions of the legislative majority. Although sometimes legislators have approved a practice probably favored by a majority, such as the graduation prayer, in other cases legislative bodies have used their authority to privilege a minority religious faction, such as believers in creation science, a religious publisher, or the residents of Kiryas Joel. These distinctions have not mattered for Scalia. Further, history and tradition—which he has construed as a kind of political consensus from the past—provide supplemental support for such legislative choices. More flexible or pragmatic constructions of doctrine, let alone the implied intensified scrutiny required by the *Lemon* test, have upset him because they allow claimants of rights to veto a majority decision of the legislature—regardless of whether the legislature has advantaged a popular majority, as allegedly occurs in the graduation prayer case, or a religious minority, as with creation scientists, religious publishers, or the Hasidic Jews in Kiryas Joel. From his perspective, judicial passivity in the face of laws *protecting* religion is the path for the Court to follow.[149]

CONCLUSION

Scalia's instrumental discourse in his First Amendment opinions confirms what David Schultz has concluded—"the Justice is not a friend of individual expression and criticism. Instead, he supports numerous restrictions endorsing what he perceives to be a majoritarian position in society."[150] By employing the central tenets of Reasoned Elaboration—as he has done in most of his opinions about context-based, commercial speech, and taxation restrictions on First Amendment claims—Scalia has encouraged "reasonable" policymaking by the legislature. His limitations on the use of strict scrutiny have promoted a passive judiciary that involves itself in close analysis of laws only on rare occasions, an involvement especially focused on those laws designed to serve liberal purposes such as controlling the influence of corporate wealth and preventing hate speech. He has treated judicial standards under the Establishment Clause as a kind of experiment— a deviation from traditional methods—with possible adverse consequences, such as increased religious conflict and controversy. Consequently, his opinions have contained a message about the value of a set of doctrinal standards hostile to expanded political pluralism and supportive of existing powerful interests. His deference to legislative majorities under reasonableness criteria and his avoidance of aggressive review under the *Miller* and *Lemon* tests have meant that he affords less legal protection to pluralist political actions that threaten majority rule and the influence of corporations in political debates.[151]

Only in the event of grossly unreasonable governmental mistakes, such as the failure of government to appreciate the content-based nature of its regulation of speech in the flag-burning and abortion demonstration cases or to avoid overbroad regulations, would Scalia let the judiciary defend expression. However, the "disuniformity" of these votes and opinions indicate that he has done more than just employ the themes of Reasoned Elaboration to decide about expressive freedoms. His opinions have had a decidedly conservative ideological cast. By restricting the generality of the First Amendment, he has established the potential for public officials to use the criminal law to curtail disadvantaged groups' nontraditional political and social messages that afford a threat to a majority's vision of social order. For example, the use of peyote was a symbol of the unique character of the values of native American peoples, and its suppression was a mark of the political dominance of Western religious and moral values about personal purity, abstinence, and mortification of the flesh. Nude dancing ran counter to the same Western moral tradition, a tradition frequently converted into statutes by the political majority, because it allegedly encouraged erotic thought and sensualism. Although the acts of peyote eating and nude dancing might appear superficially to be nonpolitical, a state that permitted them would encourage moral discord by not enforcing traditional Western and Judeo-Christian values. Although in First Amendment cases Scalia's discussion of tradition—for instance, "constitutional tradition" in *Smith,* or the "traditions of our people" in Establishment Clause cases—has often been ill-defined, his application of tradition has implied an advantage for Western moral and religious ideals. Consequently, in concert with the conservative revival, his message has been that the First Amendment should not encourage moral discord.

By interpreting the First Amendment to prevent the expansion of political and moral discord, Scalia has sought to reduce the legitimacy of discussion and actions that promote difference and alternative visions of the political future of the regime. Although his curtailment of discussion and action undermines the kind of experimentalism and evaluation of alternatives which are a part of the pragmatic liberal vision, Scalia's narrative has not just applied Reasoned Elaboration jurisprudence to aid the conservative revival. His opinions have called into question a more fundamental tenet of American constitutionalism—the value of dissent against the decisions of the state.

Chapter Eight

CRIME AND THE POWER
OF THE STATE

In keeping with the conservative revival, Antonin Scalia believes in social virtue and social responsibility. In a speech, he once illustrated how the constitutional right to the writ of habeas corpus could be suspended when "the public safety may require it." The public good, as defined by the state, must outweigh personal rights. To that end, Scalia's criminal rights message has often derided the liberal defenders of personal freedom and encouraged the state to respond to popular demands to reduce legal barriers to conviction and wield pain and violence against the criminal.[1] Moreover, his message rejects some aspects of the late-twentieth-century revolution in suspects' and defendants' rights sponsored by the pragmatic liberal justices.

During the later years of the Warren Court (1961–69), the justices worked a revolution in criminal procedure. The Warren Court nationalized the exclusionary rule corollary to the search and seizure provision of the Fourth Amendment of the Constitution, which prohibited the use, at trial, of evidence obtained without a warrant, and "incorporated" or included the provisions of the Fifth, Sixth, and Eighth Amendments, except for clause on the right to a grand jury indictment, into the Due Process Clause of the Fourteenth Amendment to make them applicable in state criminal proceedings. Also, the justices required federal and state law enforcement officers, prior to interrogating suspects in custody, to inform them of their Fifth Amendment protection against compelled self-incrimination.[2]

Most Burger Court criminal procedure decisions limited the scope of defendants rights decisions made by the later Warren Court. The Burger Court beset the warrant requirement and exclusionary rule with exceptions to permit warrantless searches by police, and limited the contexts for the application of the *Miranda* rule. Despite popular views and media presentations of courts as liberal and "soft on crime," the justices moved to adopt many more limits on criminal procedural rights and to let states adopt mandatory sentencing as part of the substantive criminal law.[3] The ideological direction of their decisions pleased many contemporary conservatives' who demanded less restrictive procedural constraints on the prosecution of criminal suspects and harsher discipline of criminal offenders by the state. The Rehnquist Court continued the Burger Court's approach to the rights of criminal defendants.

Although Scalia had not written many criminal due process opinions while on the Court of Appeals, when on the Supreme Court he supported fewer than three of every ten criminal defendants' claims (see table 3.1). Although not as hostile to defendants as Chief Justice Rehnquist and Justice Thomas have been, Scalia has been far less inclined to vote for defendants than the other justices. In addition, he has become a prolific author of criminal law opinions. Most of his opinions have conveyed a vision about proper criminal procedures akin to the vision of his more conservative colleagues. His opinions also have tried to control discretion in the criminal process. In his search for a criminal law that provides for reliable evidence and a more certain conviction of defendants, he has deployed Reasoned Elaboration argumentation in ways that support the contemporary conservative vision of a retributive criminal process.[4]

FOURTH AMENDMENT ISSUES: SEARCHES AND SEIZURES

In 1961 the U.S. Supreme Court incorporated the Fourth Amendment's procedural protection against "unreasonable searches and seizures" and made them applicable in state criminal cases. In addition, since 1961 the Court has required that state courts follow a corollary to the Fourth Amendment—the exclusionary rule, which barred the use of evidence secured through an unreasonable search or seizure from the judicial process.[5] From the last terms of the Warren Court and throughout the Burger Court, the justices developed more than twenty exceptions to the general rule that searches without warrants were unreasonable and that the evidence from such searches had to be excluded at trial.[6] This issue has continued to challenge the Rehnquist Court.

The Scope of the Fourth Amendment Protection

The Fourth Amendment protects "persons, houses, papers, and effects" against "unreasonable" searches and seizures. Therefore, the first question in Fourth Amendment interpretation is, What is a search or seizure? In *County of Riverside v. McLaughlin,*[7] a defendant, arrested without a warrant and held in jail without a hearing on probable cause for his arrest, challenged his seizure without warrant or prompt hearing under a construction of the Fourth Amendment offered in *Gerstein v. Pugh.*[8] Because of the *Gerstein* rule, O'Connor held that seizures of persons require prompt determinations of the probable cause for the warrantless seizure. However, she used a flexible standard of promptness and concluded that "the Fourth Amendment permits a reasonable postponement of a probable cause hearing while the police cope with the everyday problems of processing suspects through an overly burdened criminal justice system." Scalia dissented to support the defendant's claim. After a quick historical review illustrating that the English common law rules on seizure of persons and later American cases supported the *Gerstein* rule "that the period of warrantless detention must be limited to the time necessary to complete the arrest and obtain the magistrate's review," he concluded that the Court had ignored these "plain statements" of law. Challenging the Court's "novel" provision of flexibility and experimentalism in the timing of the hearing, he sought a prompt hearing "as soon as [the] arrest was completed and the magistrate procured." *Prompt,* he later indicated, ought to be after the steps connected to arrest, or within twenty-four hours of arrest. Otherwise, "a law-abiding citizen may be compelled to await the grace of a Dickensian bureaucratic machine, as it churns its cycle for up to two days—never once given the opportunity to show a judge that there is absolutely no reason to hold him, that a mistake has been made."[9]

Scalia's Opinion of the Court in *California v. Hodari D.* considered the issue of defining when a person and evidence had been seized.[10] The juvenile Hodari D. had fled police officers, dropping a rock of crack cocaine as he ran through streets and alleys. Hodari D. contended that the police had seized him at the beginning of the chase and that subsequent seizures had been unreasonable. Therefore, the crack should be excluded as the fruit of an illegal seizure. Relying on a definition of seizure as "a laying on of hands or the application of physical force to restrain movement," Scalia found that the Fourth Amendment's language could not "remotely apply."[11] Also, he saw no reason to "stretch the Fourth Amendment beyond its words and beyond the meaning of arrest," especially given the understanding of those terms in precedent cases. Thus, the crack could be admitted because the fleeing suspect had not yet been seized. As in *McLaughlin,* Scalia relied on the historical meaning of legal texts to avoid novel or experimental construction of the amendment—a practice associated with the jurisprudence of Reasoned Elaboration.

Exceptions to the Warrant Requirement

When he reached the Supreme Court, Scalia surprised some commentators who had expected him to use textual or plain-meaning analysis to critique judicial corollaries to the text of the Constitution, such as the exclusionary rule. Instead, Scalia has recognized the exclusionary rule as valid precedent. However, he has set forth some guidelines on when he thinks the warrant requirement need not be satisfied to allow the admission of evidence at trial. Especially, he has considered whether probable cause existed to allow the warrantless search, or whether the search could be conducted on the basis of any reasonable suspicions by police.

Despite the exclusionary rule, in several categories of cases the late Warren Court and the Burger Court upheld warrantless searches as reasonable, and allowed the admission of evidence obtained from these searches at trial. One category of permissible warrantless search occurred when the evidence was located in an open field and outside the curtilage, or the area around a domicile to which the privacy of home life extends.[12] Scalia confirmed the validity of this exception to the warrant requirement in his opinion for the Court in *United States v. Dunn*.[13] His opinion allowed Drug Enforcement Agency investigators to obtain a warrant to search Dunn's barn after they had established probable cause to believe that illegal drug manufacturing activities occurred there. To establish probable cause, the officers had conducted aerial surveillance of Dunn's property to locate the barn, approached the barn by climbing over several fences, and observed a probable drug laboratory through a barn window. Applying precedent cases on searches of open fields, Scalia concluded that the barn was outside the curtilage of Dunn's domicile. The barn was more than fifty yards from the home and was outside the privacies of domestic life. It was not protected from observation by persons standing in the open fields around it. Also, applying the text of the amendment, he concluded that the barn area was not a "house" or an "effect." Therefore, the observation had not been an unreasonable search, and the observation could provide the probable cause required for the issuance of a warrant to search the inside of the barn.

Another category of cases in which the Burger Court upheld "reasonable" warrantless searches involved law enforcement officers' observation of evidence of a crime "in plain view."[14] In *Arizona v. Hicks*,[15] Scalia's Opinion of the Court confirmed this exception to the warrant requirement. After a shooting in the apartment below resulted in a bullet entering through the floor of Hicks's apartment, police had entered Hicks's apartment. Spotting stereo equipment that seemed out of place, an officer had moved the equipment, checked one component's serial numbers against a list of stolen items, and discovered that it had been stolen during an armed robbery. Officers seized the component for later use as evidence against Hicks. Scalia first concluded that the movement of the stereo components to check serial numbers had been a search—an action to gain information—and not the passive observation of an item in plain view. To conduct this warrantless search, he argued, the officer needed probable cause to believe the stereo components were stolen. But probable cause had not been shown. "Reasonable suspicions" that an item had been stolen, he held, are not probable cause and do not justify warrantless searches unless "the seizure is minimally intrusive and operational necessities render it the only practicable means of detecting certain types of crime."[16] He concluded by challenging the dissenting opinions by O'Connor and Powell, joined by Rehnquist, which argued that the police action had been a cursory inspection and not a search.

However, when police searched a warehouse without a warrant and saw marijuana in plain view, Scalia's Opinion of the Court upheld the admission of the marijuana as evidence after a judge, uninformed of the illegal entry but informed of other illegal acts of the defendant, then issued a warrant for a lawful search of the warehouse.[17] Again relying on precedent, he found that the judge had relied on an "independent source" or on facts learned from sources and events other than the illegal entry to ascertain probable cause for the warrant. Thus, the search warrant was valid. Also, the admission of the marijuana was then permissible because it had been in plain view when the warrant was executed at the warehouse. Scalia dismissed defense contentions that his ruling would encourage warrantless searches. He argued that the ruling did not give police an incentive to search illegally and risk suppression of the evidence.

A related exception to the warrant requirement exists when a person invites police to enter a private place and observe illegal activity in plain view. However, the Burger Court ruled that the police had to believe that the person inviting them in had common authority, or joint control, over the premises.[18] Scalia has confirmed and extended this "consent" exception to the warrant requirement. In *Illinois v. Rodriguez*,[19] he held that police could be invited into a residence by a woman claiming common authority and possessing a key to the residence, even if it was later determined that she did not possess common authority. The evidence thus obtained was admissible. His decision turned on his assessment that the search had been reasonable. Because the woman claimed common authority and held the key, police could reasonably assume that she had the authority to invite them into the residence. The Fourth Amendment did not require "factual accuracy" in police judgments, only responsible inquiry. Courts could assess the reasonableness of police inquiries under an "objective standard"—a finding that, after inquiry, the facts available to police at the moment of the entry allowed cautious officers to conclude that a person who was inviting them in lived in or controlled the premises.[20]

An opinion by Blackmun in *California v. Acevedo* provided a general exception to the warrant requirement for automobile searches based on probable cause.[21] Previously, the automobile search exception had included counterexceptions for locked containers and selected places within the vehicle. Scalia concurred with Blackmun because the latter was "more faithful to the text and tradition of the Fourth Amendment" than the previous cases about automobile searches. Indicating that he considered previous decisions about searches requiring a warrant to be inconsistent, Scalia argued that a warrantless search can occur if it is reasonable.[22]

Scalia's emphasis on the Fourth Amendment's phrase prohibiting "unreasonable searches" rather than on the phase "probable cause" as the key to granting or denying approval for exceptions to the warrant requirement matured in his concurring opinion in *Minnesota v. Dickerson*.[23] At issue was the admissibility of evidence found in a suspect's jacket during a frisk. In *Terry v. Ohio* the Warren Court had allowed police to conduct warrantless frisks of suspects who they had reason to believe were about to commit a crime, to locate weapons that might threaten public or police safety. Concealed weapons located by the frisk could be used as evidence of a crime.[24] In *Dickerson* Justice White held that other contraband located during the warrantless frisks was admissible—but only if it had been discovered by touch and not by intrusion into or manipulation of items of apparel or of items in or under them. Scalia began his concurring opinion with a "fundamental principle": "the terms in the Constitution must be given the meaning ascribed to them at the time of their ratification." Using this originalist argument, he concluded that the search had to meet a traditional common law standard of reasonableness. He then determined that the historical standard of reasonableness did not permit searches on mere suspicion and that the evidence from the frisk was to be excluded. In applying the standard of reasonableness, Scalia admitted that he called the stop-and-frisk exception to the warrant requirement into question. However, since the constitutionality of the frisk was not challenged, he assumed that the search was lawful.[25] Curiously, while calling the idea of an exception to the warrant requirement into question on historical grounds, he did not challenge the exclusionary rule on the same grounds.

Drawing on language from his *Arizona v. Hicks* opinion and other precedents, Scalia recognized that there is a category of warrantless but minimally intrusive or "special circumstances" searches that require only reasonable suspicion, not probable cause. During the late Burger Court era the justices had permitted reasonable suspicion searches of a high-school student's purse and a prisoner's cell because of the special circumstances of the search.[26] In *O'Connor v. Ortega*,[27] Justice O'Connor's plurality opinion allowed the warrantless search of a physician's office located in a public hospital. The search turned up information about misconduct on the job and evidence of criminal acts in Dr. Ortega's private practice. Citing special circumstances and needs, including the special need to secure government property in Ortega's office and to protect materials related to his status as a government employee, she permitted the search as a reasonable effort to deter work-related misconduct and loss of government property.

Scalia concurred. His opinion differed from O'Connor's on several points. First, O'Connor's opinion required a case-by-case assessment of the reasonableness of warrantless special circumstances searches. Scalia preferred a clear rule. Second, he disagreed with O'Connor's argument that expectations of privacy were less in a government office than in a private office. The same standard should exist for both, he argued. Third, he argued that a warrantless "special circumstances" search could occur, but that, to be reasonable, the search must be to "retrieve work-related materials or to investigate violations of workplace rules."[28] O'Connor's opinion allowed the use of materials discovered during the search for the prosecution of criminal acts in Ortega's private practice, but Scalia countenanced a less extensive judicial use of materials from a warrantless search. However, he agreed to remand the case to determine whether the validating purpose for the use of the work-related materials existed.

Although he did not allow the search of the home of a probationer under a Wisconsin law permitting warrantless searches of a probationer's domiciles on "reasonable grounds," Scalia ruled that probable cause was not necessary to legitimate a search in circumstances in which the state had determined that there were "special needs" for searching a probationer's home to ensure the effective operation of the probation system. Drawing on *Ortega* and related precedent, he concluded that the operation of a probation system, "like the operation of a school, a government office or prison, or [the] supervision of a regulated industry likewise presents 'special needs' beyond normal law enforcement that may justify departures from the usual warrant and probable-cause requirements." In this case, the special need was Wisconsin's need to enforce the restrictions on probationers' liberties. A warrant requirement, Scalia argued, would "interfere to an appreciable degree with the probation system" by creating delays in responses to potential misconduct and undermining the deterrent effect of supervision.[29]

Voting but not offering an opinion, Scalia has supported the expansion of the scope of warrantless searches. He voted for opinions that permitted police to conduct warrantless searches of

- a junkyard already "closely regulated" by the government;[30]
- garbage placed for disposal near a street;[31]
- contraband in plain view in a home, when the police were executing a search warrant for other items;[32]
- a home, when police had reason to believe that a protective sweep of it was necessary to see whether it harbored a person dangerous to them;[33]
- the property of illegal aliens which was located in another nation;[34]
- a person in a public place, when the police had reasonable suspicion but no probable cause or warrant, and believed that the person was engaged in wrongdoing;[35] and
- enclosed containers located inside automobiles.[36]

Also, he voted to allow, as reasonable, police stops of automobiles based on anonymous tips about illegal activity by occupants; police checkpoints to stop automobiles without probable cause to locate intoxicated drivers; and police stops and random questioning of selected, racially identifiable bus and train passengers which included requests to inspect luggage.[37] He agreed with the admission of evidence obtained by police acting in good faith and following a statute authorizing warrantless searches, even though the statute was later found to be unconstitutional.[38] Finally, he supported, as reasonable and not demanding probable cause, mandatory warrantless drug and alcohol testing of transportation employees who became involved in accidents.[39] Evidence located through these actions on the part of police or other officials was admissible at trial.

The only significant example of a vote cast by Scalia to protect a criminal suspect in a Fourth Amendment case was his vote with a unanimous court to conclude that the seizure and towing away of a suspect's mobile home, without entry into the home, required a warrant.[40] His only opinion in support of the warrant requirement was in *National Treasury Employees Union v. Von Raab*.[41] In this case, Justice Kennedy upheld regulations authorizing the U.S. Customs Service to conduct, without warrant or probable cause, the urinalysis of employees seeking transfer or promotion to positions involving drug interdiction or drug law enforcement tasks, requiring the use of firearms, or involving the handling of classified material. Using a balancing test, he concluded that the Customs Service had a special need to test employees in order to ensure their fitness and probity. The special need outweighed the privacy interests of employees. Scalia dissented because he did not think that the government had presented "real evidence" that special circumstances for the test existed. Although he agreed that special circumstances might permit warrantless searches based on reasonable suspicions, his difficulty was the justification of special circumstances. He argued that the Customs Service had not provided evidence of "*even a single instance* in which any of the speculated horribles actually occurred" or evidence of incidents in which agents' drug use had compromised agency interdiction, enforcement, firearms use, or secrecy. Examining precedents on special needs, he found that in past cases the Court had taken "pains to establish the existence of a special need for the search or seizure." The majority had not done so in this case. Instead, he thought that the Court and the Customs Service had simply sought to make a symbolic point about the evils of drugs. However, "the impairment of individual liberties cannot be the means of making a point; that symbolism, even symbolism for so worthy a cause as the abolition of unlawful drugs, cannot validate an otherwise unreasonable search."[42]

However, in *Vernonia School District 47J v. Acton*,[43] Scalia wrote for the Court and clarified his *Von Raab* vote. In *Vernonia* he allowed warrantless drug testing of student athletes in a public school. As in *Von Raab*, he treated the drug testing under a reasonableness criterion. Under this criterion he concluded that the critical difference between the testing in *Von Raab* and the student athlete testing was the establishment of a special need for the testing of the athletes by the school district. In his *Von Raab* dissenting opinion, he found that the evidence of a special need was lacking. However, the school district's testing was reasonable because of several interconnected considerations. First, previous cases had established that public school students had a diminished expectation of privacy. Second, student athletes further diminished their privacy by voluntarily choosing to use public shower rooms and to submit to the rules and regulations of the school and school personnel which affected their participation in a sport. Third, the collection of urine samples for drug testing was managed in a discrete fashion, and its results were known only by a limited number of school personnel. The minimally invasive nature of the testing was, Scalia contended, important. Thus, his fourth consideration was that the test addressed an evil that might do special harm to those who play sports. Citing a limited amount of medical literature, he concluded that in this case there existed evidence of a specific problem that satisfied the evidentiary requirement he had sought in his *Von Raab* dissent.[44] On the basis of these considerations, he concluded that the testing program was a legal warrantless search that could result in the removal of a student from a sports team.

Interpretations of the Fourth Amendment: A Summary

In Fourth Amendment cases Scalia has disclosed a penchant for trying to establish the textual language of the amendment as a basis for opinions providing a clear set of legal directions for police. Consequently, he has spent time interpreting the words of the amendment on the basis of their plain meaning, as with "seizures" in *Hodari D.* or "reasonable" searches as in *Illinois v. Rodriguez*; or their antecedent common law origins, as in *County of Riverside* or *Minnesota v. Dickerson*. These interpretive approaches, typical of Reasoned Elaboration methodology, have aimed at the rejection of new, experimental, or policy-conscious readings of the amendment. Yet despite his opposition to policy-conscious interpretation of the Fourth Amendment, the exclusionary rule—the critical judicial corollary of, or experiment with, the Fourth Amendment—has not troubled him. Apparently it is established procedure necessary for rational and purposeful criminal decisionmaking, and it is part of his definition of a constitutional criminal law.

FIFTH AMENDMENT ISSUES

The Meaning of *Miranda v. Arizona*

During the Rehnquist Court, the *Miranda* requirement stipulating that police read suspects the Fifth Amendment right against self-incrimination and inform them of the availability of counsel at the time they are taken into custody generated litigation requiring further explication of the requirement. Scalia wrote opinions in three cases in which the Court further explained the *Miranda* rule. In *Minnick v. Mississippi*,[45] Kennedy held for the Court that once counsel has been requested during a custodial interrogation, the police cannot further question the suspect without the presence of counsel regardless of the defendant's later waivers of *Miranda*. Scalia's dissenting opinion challenged the Court's establishment of an "irrebuttable presumption that a criminal suspect, after invoking his *Miranda* rights to counsel, can *never* validly waive the right during any police-initiated encounter, even after the suspect has been provided multiple *Miranda* warnings and has actually consulted his attorney." After noting facts indicating Minnick's voluntary waiver of *Miranda*, Scalia surveyed precedent to conclude that all but one of the previous cases he located had permitted voluntary waiver. Further, he contended that, once police had honored the defendant's request for consultation with an attorney, there was an irrebuttable presumption created against the claim that the confession resulted from ignorance or coercion. He concluded that, in a "protective enterprise . . . beyond our authority under the Fifth Amendment or any other provision of the Constitution," the Court had improperly extended the meaning of precedent so as to bar honest confessions and treat them as "foolish mistakes" in a way that let the admittedly guilty go free.[46] Therefore, his opinion was a classic Reasoned Elaboration criticism of the dangers of what he regarded as creative judicial reading of the text of precedents.

Writing for the Court in *McNeil v. Wisconsin*,[47] Scalia held that McNeil's invocation of *Miranda* rights at a judicial appearance on one charge did not prevent the use of later statements made about other charges without additional *Miranda* warnings. The defendant had made the later statements while in custody on the first charge. Scalia's opinion rested on the principle that the right to counsel during inter-rogation is "offense-specific." The waiver and questioning on the sec-ond set of charges were separable from the initial questioning. If the suspect took advantage of *Miranda* at the initial questioning, this did not create a general ban on future questioning about other offenses. Therefore, Scalia refused to develop new doctrine and create a general ban on police-initiated questioning on any matter once a suspect had invoked *Miranda*. Again writing in the spirit of Reasoned Elaboration, he refused to interfere with an executive agency—the police—and al-low a pragmatic judicial evolution of doctrine.

Finally, Scalia concurred when O'Connor's majority opinion upheld the admissibility of statements made when a defendant had not ex-pressed a clear, unambiguous, and unequivocal request for counsel.[48] However, he took both the majority and the federal prosecutors to task for ignoring the federal statute defining the voluntariness of confes-sions (18 *U.S. Code* § 3501). He indicated that, by ignoring the stat-ute that is the "people's assessment" of proper law enforcement, the federal government allowed prosecutions to be defeated. If federal prosecutors attended to this legal text and followed proper statutory procedures, the federal judiciary might not have to consider so many *Miranda* cases. Thus, his concurrence was a call for procedural reg-ularity as a means for a less policy-oriented and more passive judiciary, in keeping with Reasoned Elaboration jurisprudence.

In a case in which he did not write an opinion, Scalia voted with the Court when it decided that, once a suspect had been informed of *Miranda* rights, his telephone conversations with his wife could still be recorded and used as evidence against him. He also supported an opin-ion that statements the defendant made to police, after requesting counsel but unguided by counsel, could be used to impeach his testi-mony at trial. He backed opinions that allowed the use of corporate records to incriminate an officer of the corporation. He agreed with opinions holding that police did not have to inform suspects about *Miranda* rights during ordinary traffic stops and ticketing of vehicles, or when they used a fellow inmate to elicit incriminating statements from an incarcerated suspect. He supported opinions holding that *Mi-*

randa does not bar the use of statements voluntarily made outside a person's house after a warrantless search of his home, statements made when police depart from the wording of rights set down in *Miranda*, and confessions that are induced by mental illness but are not coerced by police.[49] Finally, Scalia joined opinions written by White and Rehnquist in the splintered decision in *Arizona v. Fulminate*.[50] He voted with White's conclusion that a confession to an informer in a jailhouse, who had promised Fulminate protection from harm, had been coerced. However, he agreed with Rehnquist's conclusion that, since other evidence supported Fulminate's conviction, the admission of the confession at trial was harmless error. In addition, he voted for an opinion that most portions of video and audio tapes of a suspect's behavior when in custody could be used as evidence without posing a problem under the Self-Incrimination Clause.[51] Clearly he has been unwilling to extend *Miranda* to new or unusual circumstances.

The Double Jeopardy Clause

Scalia's opinions about the Fifth Amendment proscription of double jeopardy have attempted to sort out standards for evaluating complicated statutes or prosecutions that appeared on their face to allow more than one trial or penalty for the same incident or criminal act. For example, in *Jones v. Thomas* the issue was whether a defendant's conviction on two crimes—felony murder and attempted robbery—committed during a single incident precluded separate sentences.[52] Thomas was given one sentence for the two crimes. His armed robbery conviction was later overturned on appeal. The state then held a hearing and required him to serve out the sentence for felony murder. For the Court, Kennedy held that the Double Jeopardy Clause only prevented the trial court from imposing no greater punishment than the legislature intended. Consequently, Thomas could be incarcerated until the felony murder sentence expired. Scalia's dissenting opinion, joined by Brennan, Marshall, and Stevens, argued that the Court had ignored precedents that required the imposition of only one of the available lawful punishments for an incident. He rejected three of Kennedy's arguments for distinguishing Thomas's case from precedents prohibiting further sentencing proceedings after the initial sentencing and after the armed robbery conviction had been overturned. Scalia concluded that Thomas should be freed. The Double Jeopardy Clause, Scalia determined, "is and has been, not a provision designed to assure reason and justice in the particular case, but the embodiment of technical, prophylactic rules that require the Government to turn square corners. Whenever it is applied to release a criminal deserving of punishment it frustrates justice in the particular case, but for the greater purpose of assuring repose in the totality of criminal prosecutions and sentences."[53]

Similar themes appeared in Scalia's dissenting opinion in a case on Montana's making individuals who had been convicted on drug charges subject to prosecution for failure to pay a tax on the drugs at a second proceeding. Justice Stevens held that the taxation proceeding was a successive punishment for the same offense and was in violation of the Double Jeopardy Clause.[54] Scalia argued that the clause prohibited separate prosecutions, not separate punishments. He contended that the tax hearing was a civil process. Regardless of whether a second punishment occurred or resulted in a criminal or civil penalty, there had been no second prosecution.[55] Thus, the Montana case differed from *Jones v. Thomas*, wherein a second criminal sentencing effectively indicated a second criminal prosecution. However, in both of these cases and in a later opinion he reiterated his argument that the clause prohibited double prosecutions for the same offense, not double punishments.[56]

In *Grady v. Corbin*,[57] Brennan held that double jeopardy occurred when the prosecution of an offense revealed that a previous prosecution had contained identical statutory elements, or when one prosecution contained a lesser included offense of the other. To determine whether this standard had been met, the critical inquiry was about what the prosecution had tried to prove—its conduct—not whether it had used the same evidence or addressed different crimes. Thus, because misdemeanor charges and felony charges stemming from the same vehicular accident were tried separately, a state had violated the Double Jeopardy Clause. Dissenting, Scalia argued that the defendant was not being prosecuted again for the same offense—"successive prosecutions under two different statutes do not constitute double jeopardy if each statutory crime contains an element that the other does not." Construing the word *offense* in the text of the clause, he determined that the successive prosecutions lawfully might be about the same *"conduct or actions,"* but not the same offense or "element." To buttress his reading of text, he engaged in a lengthy examination of definitions of double jeopardy in precedent cases and treatises from the 1700s forward.[58] His conclusion was that the Court's opinion created a novel standard by ignoring text and longstanding precedent and was unreasonable because it forced prosecutors and courts into the complex and uncertain business of sorting out what a prosecutor had tried to prove in an earlier case.

Returning to the "same elements, same conduct issue" in an opinion for a badly divided Court three years later, Scalia secured the votes to vindicate his *Grady v. Corbin* position. At issue were the prosecutions of two defendants. The prosecutions of each involved multiple charges, including one defendant's drug arrest in violation of a condition of his bail for a murder charge, and a second defendant's commission of assaults against his estranged wife at various times in violation of a civil protection order. Scalia considered the violation of bail and of the protection order to be criminal contempt. In sorting out whether the trial on the contempt charges constituted double jeopardy, Scalia turned to the "same element" standard of his *Grady v. Corbin* dissenting opinion. Although his conclusions about the applicability of the test to all aspects of the two defendants' cases did not win majority support, his use of the "same element" standard did. Then he turned to the *Grady* "same content" test and concluded that the test must be overruled. Rather than reiterating the argument of his *Grady* opinion, he confirmed his reading of text and precedent in *Grady* by refuting Souter's criticism of his use of precedent in *Grady*. Also, Scalia illustrated what he deemed to be "unstable" applications of *Grady's* "same content" rule and the "confusion" it produced.[59] Finally, he voted that there had been no double jeopardy when a defendant was separately tried for manufacturing and distributing the same illegal drugs in two separate federal judicial districts.[60]

Scalia's double jeopardy opinions have all relied on a "plain-meaning" reading of constitutional text and on precedent. In the tradition of Reasoned Elaboration arguments, he has been hostile to perceived doctrinal experiments that he thought led to confusion in law and policy. His message has demanded procedural stability and hostility to pragmatic doctrinal experimentalism.

Other Due Process and Fifth Amendment Issues

Since 1963 the Court has considered that due process under the Fifth and Fourteenth Amendments requires prosecutorial disclosure of evidence that might create a reasonable doubt that otherwise would not exist.[61] To ascertain whether the nondisclosure of evidence prevented the creation of a reasonable doubt, the court had to evaluate the entire record in the case. In *Kyles v. Whitley*,[62] Justice Souter wrote for the Court and held that the cumulative effect of undisclosed evidence created a reasonable doubt about the guilt of the defendant which would not otherwise have existed. Scalia, joined by Kennedy and Thomas, dissented. Most of his opinion addressed whether the undisclosed evidence created the reasonable probability of a different result. He argued that the disclosed evidence, especially eyewitness testimony and physical evidence, could not have been effectively impeached if the undisclosed information had been provided to the defense. Thus, he found no probable different result, and he accused the majority of straining the facts of the case to find one.[63] Although his opinion did not offer a doctrinal alternative, he saw the case facts with greater certainty than did Souter.

In other cases about the Fifth Amendment clauses, Scalia voted for the position of the state. When a defendant violated a plea bargain agreement about a crime, Scalia supported an opinion that the defendant could then be tried for the crime without breaching the Double Jeopardy Clause of the amendment.[64] Also, he joined a Rehnquist majority opinion that held that the Due Process Clause only demands a "good faith" effort, not an absolute requirement, for prosecutors to inform defendants of evidence of innocence.[65]

SIXTH AMENDMENT ISSUES

The Confrontation Clause

The Sixth Amendment grants the accused the right "to be confronted with the witnesses against him." Although the Court made this Confrontation Clause applicable to state judicial proceedings, the clause was seldom litigated prior to the Rehnquist Court era.[66] Invoking the "plain meaning" of the language in the clause and refusing to establish new doctrine, Scalia has written several important opinions about the clause's meaning. His first two opinions about the clause addressed the right to confront out-of-court statements made by a codefendant or coconspirator. He wrote an Opinion of the Court, joined by Brennan, Marshall, Blackmun, and Powell, to ensure that a defendant would be protected against the introduction of a nontestifying codefendant's confession at their joint trial when the confession was inadmissible against the codefendant. The constitutional imperative of the exclusion of inadmissible statements, he argued, was undermined by the introduction of the confession without the possibility of confronting its author to test its reliableness in court. Further, the danger of the confession's admission was the general threat posed to a principle allowing the admission only of "reliable" evidence. Thus, he rejected the dissenting four justices' "common sense" judgment that courts could admit such confessions without confrontation.[67]

However, for a majority including Rehnquist, White, Blackmun, Powell, and O'Connor, Scalia wrote to defend the admissibility of a confession of felony murder by a nontestifying codefendant.[68] In this case, the trial judge instructed jurors not to use the confession against the defendant, and he redacted the confession so that her name and references to her were not presented to the jury. Although Scalia asserted precedent banning the admission of pretrial statements by one defendant against a codefendant, he recognized that in the context of this case the trial judge's measures barred evidence that otherwise should be subject to the confrontation of its source. The limiting instruction thus sufficiently replaced the need for the exclusion of the evidence, separate trials for the two defendants, or the prospect of joint defendants trying to confront each others' testimony and engaging in a kind of joint self-incrimination. In a related issue of confrontation, Scalia permitted the introduction of an out-of-court identification of an assailant by a victim despite the victim's contradiction of the identification when called as a witness.[69] The confrontation right, he reasoned, included the opportunity to inquire into out-of court statements in order to impeach a witness's statements. The right includes the opportunity to confront statements that might be regarded as hearsay because they were not subjected to a prior test of reliability.

Scalia's other opinions about the Confrontation Clause have addressed the juvenile witness issue. He wrote for the Court to prohibit the screening of juvenile witnesses from alleged child molesters during trials. In one case, Iowa law allowed an opaque screen to be placed between the complaining juvenile witnesses and Coy, the accused, to let the children feel less uneasy when testifying. However, Scalia held that the Sixth Amendment simply guaranteed a face-to-face encounter between witness and accused. Although he noted that no prior Supreme Court cases had considered this issue, he inferred from various other cases and historical materials that face-to-face confrontation "is essential to fairness because there is much truth to it." The truth or factual justification for the encounter included, he supposed, the "truth" that "it is always more difficult to tell a lie about a person 'to his face' than 'behind his back.' In the former context, even if the lie is told, it will often be told less convincingly."[70] He marshalled no social scientific evidence to support this assertion that face-to-face encounters made the evidence more reliable. Instead, he simply concluded that the placement of the screen was not harmless error but a direct contradiction of the clause's text.

In another case, Maryland had used closed-circuit television to screen juvenile witnesses from an alleged child molester. Craig, the defendant, could see the witness, but the witness could not see the defendant. O'Connor upheld the practice, reasoning that face-to-face encounter between a witness and a defendant was not an indispensable aspect of the confrontation right. She reasoned that the televised testimony protected the psychological well-being of the victims of child abuse, which was a "sufficiently important" reason to create a narrow exception from the face-to-face encounter rule.[71] Scalia dissented, arguing that the Court had failed "to sustain a categorical guarantee of the Constitution against the tide of prevailing current opinion." Contending that the command of the clause was unmistakably clear, he accused the majority of a pragmatic experimentalism and a capitulation to "currently favored public policy." Specific errors he discerned in the Court's opinion included an "antitextual conclusion" cobbled from "scraps of dicta from various cases that have no bearing here," coupled with a neglect of the Iowa case and other precedent. Especially, the "substantially important reason" test used by the Court upset him. He regarded the test as an erroneous methodology that subverted the text of the clause. The Court, he thought, had also created the potential for the admission of untested evidence and hearsay. He was particularly concerned that the system would restrict efforts by defense counsel to discover the coaching of the testimony of children by other interested parties. He thought that confrontation would diminish this threat to the truthfulness of the testimony.[72] As in his other Confrontation Clause opinions, he tried to read the Sixth Amendment literally and extend existing precedent. Also, he voted in favor of this literal interpretation of the clause.[73] Pragmatic standards excusing face-to-face confrontation to protect the psychological well-being of a witness or to protect children would violate text and threaten the search for truth.

Other Sixth Amendment Issues

In cases about Sixth Amendment counsel issues, Scalia voted for limiting the guarantee of counsel for indigent defendants to one discretionary appeal, even when the defendants were on death row. He also supported the seizure of a defendant's illegally acquired assets even if the seizure of the assets would restrict choice of defense counsel. In cases related to the competency of counsel, he agreed with opinions restricting federal habeas corpus review because a lawyer had not first spelled out facts about the habeas corpus claim in state court and because a party had not shown serious errors affecting a sentence in a capital case. He voted with the Court to allow, in the assessment of a sentence in a later felony conviction, the inclusion of evidence on a person's prior conviction for driving under the influence of alcohol, in a trial in which he had not been offered counsel. His votes in cases about other Sixth Amendment issues included joining Thomas's dissenting opinion that held that a postindictment delay of more than eight years in the trial of a person because he was in another nation did not violate the amendment's Speedy Trial Clause. Also, he supported a Rehnquist majority opinion that, pursuant to the amendment's Jury Trial Clause, allowed a judge to refuse to question prospective jurors about their knowledge of the specific contents of media coverage of a crime.[74]

Scalia's only opinion on jury procedures addressed whether under federal law (18 *U.S. Code* § 1001) a jury had to consider whether evidence was "material" in order to convict a person for concealing or covering up a "trick, scheme, or material fact." Overruling the district court judge, Scalia's Opinion of the Court asserted the principle that the Sixth Amendment demands that "a jury find [a defendant] guilty of all the elements of a crime with which he is charged; one of the elements in the present case is materiality; respondent therefore has a right to have the jury decide materiality."[75] To justify this conclusion, he sorted through numerous prior decisions and the contrary language in one prior case, *United States v. Sinclair*.[76] Finding the reasoning in *Sinclair* to be flawed and partially repudiated in more recent decisions, he repudiated the entire decision.

EIGHTH AMENDMENT ISSUES

Scalia has written extensively about Eighth Amendment provisions against the imposition of "excessive fines" and the infliction of "cruel and unusual punishments." He has addressed whether forfeitures were a form of excessive fine and whether a mandatory sentence and conditions in prisons were cruel and unusual punishment.[77] However, most of his opinions have provided an extensive commentary on capital punishment. Throughout the opinions there are themes drawn from Reasoned Elaboration jurisprudence, especially the postulates that courts should adhere to statutes and precedents, avoid clashes with elected representatives about the proper penalties for criminal actions, and avoid policy experimentalism.

Forfeitures and Fines

To combat crimes involving illegal drugs, various federal and state laws have permitted the forfeiture of the possessions of drug dealers to governments. In two decisions about forfeitures provisions of the federal Comprehensive Drug Abuse and Prevention Act of 1970, the Court considered whether a forfeiture was a fine and how forfeitures might occur. In addressing the issue of the definition of fines in *Austin v. United States*,[78] Scalia concurred with Blackmun's majority opinion, which held that the Excessive Fines Clause of the Eighth Amendment applied to civil forfeitures of property under the act's provisions. Scalia expressed his view that Blackmun's opinion obscured the definition of fines and confused excessiveness inquiry. Using the dictionary and precedent, he wanted a clear definition of fines and forfeitures as a *"payment . . . to a sovereign as punishment for an offense."* However, he disagreed with the majority's apparent belief that the property owner had to be culpable of a crime to be punished with a forfeiture (known as an *in personam* forfeiture). He cited case law holding that *in rem* forfeitures, confiscations of property rights based on improper use of property, also existed. These forfeitures could occur without conviction on an offense, if there were "only probable cause that the subject property was used for the prohibited purpose." An *in rem* forfeiture would be an excessive fine only if "the property cannot be an instrumentality of the offense—the building, for example, in which an isolated drug sale occurs."[79]

In a case about forfeitures decided a few months before *Austin v. United States*, Scalia also issued a concurring opinion. At issue was a statutory exception designed to protect the property of innocent owners from forfeiture when other persons used it for illegal purposes. He agreed with the exception, which had its roots in the common law, but not with its construction of statutory language about the timing of the forfeiture. He supported a reading that prohibited the government's gaining title to the property until after judicial decree of forfeiture. The Court's plurality implied immediate government title dating from the time of the illegal transaction. He also disagreed with the plurality's assignment of the burden of proof of innocence to the property owner, arguing that the issue was not before the Court.[80]

In another case about the definition of fines, Scalia wrote a concurring opinion. During a strike against the Pittston Coal Group, a Virginia state judge imposed $52 million in fines against the United Mine Workers union for contempt of an injunction. The injunction restricted union picketing and required union leaders to police union members and prevent violence and property damage. In later hearings the judge found more than four hundred violations of the injunction and fined the union for contempt. Blackmun held for the Court that the fines were for a criminal contempt, a term he defined on the basis of several existing tests. Such fines could be constitutionally imposed only through criminal proceedings with possible jury trial.[81] Scalia agreed with the majority, noting that under any existing test or standard the contempt was criminal. However, he attempted a clarification of the law. Going to the common law, treatises, and precedents, he argued that criminal contempt was largely a sanction for an identifiable act violating an injunction (e.g., strikers throwing rocks) and that civil contempt was a general prohibition on future acts. However, in modern decrees he found that judges had muddled this distinction. Then, refusing to offer more advice, he indicated that current law made the contempt in this case criminal and not civil.[82] In this opinion, as well as in the other cases on fines, he sought greater clarity, rationality, and purpose in the law. These traits of Reasoned Elaboration analysis, coupled with a Reasoned Elaborationist rejection of doctrinal creativity or pragmatism, dictated his reliance on past doctrine to reason out solutions to the problems of the present.

Mandatory Sentences and the Proportionality Issue

In cases challenging sentences as disproportionate to the severity of the crime, the lack of an individualized sentence for a crime, or the lack of a consideration of mitigating factors, the Burger Court considered whether certain mandatory sentencing laws, such as laws mandating life sentences for an individual's third felony conviction ("three strikes and you're out" laws), might be imposing cruel and unusual punishments. Although badly divided, the Burger Court recognized that some disproportionate sentences violated the Constitution.[83] In *Harmelin v. Michigan*,[84] the Rehnquist Court remained divided on the issue. Scalia wrote an opinion that refused to recognize a constitutional requirement of proportionality in sentencing outside the context of capital cases (because of the special character of the death penalty). However, he could only muster Rehnquist's vote for his position. Marshall, White, Blackmun, and Stevens dissented, arguing that the sentence was disproportionate. Kennedy, joined by O'Connor and Souter, recognized a narrow proportionality principle, holding sentences grossly disproportionate to the crime to be unconstitutional because a series of decisions dating back to 1910 had recognized this principle. He considered it wise to practice stare decisis and recognize that the rule applied in these cases. However, he held that this narrow principle did not apply to the defendant Harmelin. Consequently, these three justices concurred with only one of the five sections of Scalia's opinion.[85] The five-justice majority only agreed that, except in capital cases, it was not cruel or unusual to impose mandatory sentences without the consideration of mitigating circumstances. They determined that nothing in the "text and history" of the Eighth Amendment forbade legislatures from imposing such sentencing practices.[86]

Unlike the seven justices who recognized that some requirement of proportionality in sentences was necessary to avoid cruel and unusual punishment, Scalia has refused any consideration of proportionality. Starting with the proposition that stare decisis was a less rigid requirement in constitutional cases, he has proceeded to use text and tradition in an attempt to overrule all precedents requiring any measure of proportionality or any consideration of mitigating circumstances in noncapital cases. Therefore, he devoted a section of his *Harmelin* opinion to a review of English criminal law practices to reach the conclusion that "it is most unlikely that the English Cruel and Unusual Punishments Clause was meant to forbid 'disproportionate' punishments." Then he examined American case law to determine that "in the 19th century, judicial agreement that a 'cruel and unusual' . . . provision did not constitute a proportionality requirement appears to have been universal." Turning from history, which he treated as evidence against the principle, he presented the core of his argument. The "real function" of a proportionality principle, he argued, is "to enable judges to evaluate a penalty that *some* assemblage of men and women *has* considered as proportionate—and to say that it is not." Thus, the proportionality principle encouraged judicial second-guessing of legislative judgments. He then pointed to history to indicate that this practice was alien to the aims of the Cruel and Unusual Punishment Clause. Put another way, his argument read as follows: English and American legal practice counseled judicial deference to legislative determinations of sentencing practice; courts should only restrict atrocious assaults on bodies under the Cruel and Unusual Punishment Clause. Any additional judicially developed rules about sentencing would violate separation of powers principles and infringe on the legislative role. Further, a judicial rule such as the proportionality principle served as "an invitation to the imposition of subjective values" and could turn the Eighth Amendment into "a rachet, whereby a temporary consensus on leniency for a particular crime fixes a permanent constitutional maximum, disabling the States from giving effect to altered beliefs and responding to changed social conditions." For Scalia, any pragmatic adjustment of sentences was a legislative task, not the province of an unrepresentative judiciary. As for the precedents favoring proportionality which Kennedy had cited, they were "devoid of evidence that this Court had announced a general proportionality principle."[87] As illustrated, Scalia's *Harmelin* opinion rested on Reasoned Elaboration tenets about the judicial role. Text and precedent mattered to him, but they served more as supports for a theory of decisionmaking than as the principle governing the construction of his vision of a functional criminal justice process.

Conditions of Incarceration

After the Burger Court allowed suits by prisoners to challenge, as cruel and unusual, conditions of their imprisonment which were unrelated to their sentence,[88] a large number of suits resulted in state and federal decisions determining that prison and jail conditions constituted cruel and unusual punishment. Subsequently, judges issued decrees to order specific changes in conditions of confinement or prison operations. They even ordered the construction of new facilities. In *Wilson v. Seiter*,[89] the Court considered the criteria for proof of cruel and unusual punishment in cases dealing with the conditions of confinement. Scalia's Opinion of the Court required that a prisoner must show a culpable state of mind on the part of prison officials to prove an Eighth Amendment violation. Evidence of cruel, degrading conditions alone did not prove a violation of the amendment, he claimed. There must be evidence of intentional wanton behavior, official behavior involving deliberate indifference which had created the cruel, degrading conditions.[90] Similar to the intent standard used in equal protection cases, his standard meant that, to establish liability, prisoners needed to do more than show how they were treated. They had to link their treatment to evidence of a deliberate choice of indifference by officials. Evidence of pain and suffering alone did not constitute satisfactory proof of cruel and unusual punishment. Apparently thinking in a similar vein, he voted for an opinion holding that prisoners did not suffer significant Eighth Amendment cruel punishment when exposed to health risks by a cellmate who smoked.[91]

Scalia's standard of proof of cruel and unusual punishment in prison conditions, in the tradition of Reasoned Elaboration, has drawn on a subsidiary principle of judicial practice—the need to provide direct evidence of conscious negligence. However, the result has been a greater burden on the alleged victims. Thus, prisoners can suffer degrading conditions if they are unable to fix blame for those conditions on the deliberate choices of some specific official.

Capital Punishment

In grappling with the constitutionality of capital punishment, the Burger Court justices eventually reached four conclusions. First, as stated in *Furman v. Georgia,* capital punishment was constitutional as long as it was not conducted so as to discriminate against members of discrete and insular minority groups.[92] Second, to ensure that the penalty was applied with due process, the jury was to consider the death penalty separately from the determination of guilt, and then advise the judge on the sentence or select the sentence itself. The jury's advice or sentencing decision and the judge's sentencing decision were subject to judicial review. A state could not mandatorily impose the death penalty without either jury participation and consideration of aggravating and mitigating factors related to the crime and the defendant's character, or alternatively, judicial evaluation of sentencing alternatives, especially when the defendant pleaded guilty.[93] Third, capital punishment was not a proportional penalty for some offenses, notably the crime of rape or the crime of abetting a homicide.[94] Fourth, some classes of persons with diminished capacity, such as juveniles and the insane, could not be executed.[95]

Capital punishment has drawn more opinions from Scalia than has any other specific constitutional issue. Every one of these opinions has supported the procedures used by state courts in the imposition of the death sentence. Additionally, he has never questioned the rationality of death penalty statutes. Whereas some justices regard death as a different kind of punishment, for Scalia the penalty is just another reasonable governmental action.[96]

Racial Discrimination and the Death Penalty

In *McCleskey v. Kemp* Scalia voted for Justice Lewis Powell's opinion that more frequent execution of blacks than whites for murder did not provide explicit evidence of racial discrimination in sentencing in a way that violated the Equal Protection Clause as construed in *Furman v. Georgia*.[97] However, the papers of Justice Marshall contain a memorandum on the case which indicates that Scalia has questioned two aspects of the case: first, whether the statistical evidence of discrimination in the penalty process is "weakened by the fact that each jury and each trial is unique, or by the large numbers of variables at issue"; and second, whether in review of a death penalty, "an effect of racial factors upon sentencing, if it could be shown by sufficiently strong statistical evidence, would require reversal . . . Since it is my view that the unconscious operation of irrational sympathies and antipathies, including racial, upon jury decision and (hence) prosecutorial [ones] is real, acknowledged by the [cases] of this court and ineradicable, I cannot honesty say that I need more proof."[98] The first reservation in the statement, the proposition about statistical evidence, has parallels in his demand for concrete evidence of racial discrimination to justify remedies for school segregation and violations of civil rights laws. However, the second reservation is more powerful, for he has implied that racism so infests the criminal sentencing process that it is "ineradicable." Contrary to the message in most of the *Furman* opinions, he has suggested that judges cannot and need not endeavor to reverse prima facie evidence of racial discrimination in capital sentencing. The statement thus is more than just a challenge to pragmatic liberal efforts to use social-scientific evidence to identify racial discrimination so as to require strict scrutiny of the role of race in death penalty decisions. He has questioned a thesis at the heart of the Equal Protection Clause and *Brown v. Board of Education*—the thesis that law and judicial action can and should eliminate government-sponsored racial discrimination in the United States. However, since he did not publish an opinion using this argument and since he supported the Powell opinion, perhaps he was only offering points for argument rather than stating a position contrary to *Furman*.

Procedures in Capital Cases

Nearly every aspect of death penalty procedures came under scrutiny in cases considered by the Rehnquist Court. These included notice to the defendant of the possibility of a death penalty, the selection of the jury, the evidence of aggravating and mitigating circumstances and other effects of the crime which the sentencer could consider, and the standards used during judicial review of death sentences. Scalia has commented on all of these procedures.

Notice. Scalia has expected reasonable preparation and legal crafts-manship by the defense in death penalty cases. When the Court adopted a standard requiring that the defendant be given adequate notice that a sentencing hearing could result in a death penalty, he dissented. He thought that the notice of charges and penalties at the defendant's initial arraignment was sufficient. Although the Court held that later statements and orders by the judge and a prosecutorial rec-ommendation against the death sentence had confused the situation, and demanded a reassertion of the notice that the charges might carry the death penalty, Scalia found no evidence that convinced him that anyone had misled the defendant or his counsel. Instead, defendant and counsel had unreasonably failed to consider that the death penalty had not been foreclosed in the case.[99]

Jury Selection. Scalia has opposed special requirements on the se-lection of the jury in capital cases. In *Gray v. Mississippi*,[100] he dissented from a plurality ruling that permitted jurors opposed to the death pen-alty to decide capital cases. His argument was that scruples against capital punishment were a sufficient cause for the juror's removal through a prosecutor's preemptory challenge. Echoing the theme of his *Batson* doctrine opinions, but without extensive doctrinal or historical analysis, he could not locate any constitutional restriction on the use of preemptory challenges. The Court's ruling was "a new constitutional doctrine, not rooted in any constitutional provision and contradicted by our prior cases."[101] Therefore, the selection of the jury should follow traditional *voir dire* procedures.

He reiterated this position in his dissenting opinion in *Morgan v. Illinois*.[102] The Court, in an opinion by White, considered whether a defendant could ask jurors whether they would automatically vote to impose the death penalty. The trial judge refused to adopt this mirror image of the *Gray* standard, under a state law permitting the jury to sentence. White reversed the judge's ruling and held that the limitation offended due process by preventing the adequate *voir dire* that is part of the right to an impartial jury. Scalia's dissenting opinion accepted jury sentencing and the propriety of a juror bias to impose the death penalty whenever a defendant is convicted of a capital crime. He argued that jurors with this bias will not always fail to ignore judicial instructions to consider aggravating and mitigating circumstances. Such jurors are not automatically biased persons who should be excluded for cause. Instead, it should be the responsibility of the defendant to select out "merciless jurors" through his challenges; it should not be the duty of the court to impose a blanket ban on jurors who favor imposing the death penalty for murder. Concluding his opinions against special juror selection rules, he lashed out at the Court for constructing a death-is-different jurisprudence that was without "pretense of foundation in constitutional text or American tradition"; that required that "the jury must always be given the option of extending mercy"; and that, in *Morgan,* stipulated, "Not only must mercy be allowed, but now only the merciful may be permitted to sit in judgment." These requirements appeared "not because the People have so decreed, but because such jurors do not share the strong penological preferences of this Court. In my view, that not only is not required by the Constitution of the United States; it grossly offends it."[103]

Evidence of Aggravating and Mitigating Circumstances. Scalia's position has been that few limitations should constrain the evidence considered by the jury or sentencing judge in capital cases. Thus, he held for the Court that a judge cannot instruct a jury to consider only the mitigating factors described in a state statute. Without elaborate analysis, he cited precedent to justify his conclusion.[104] Conversely, he dissented when the majority attempted to restrict the consideration of victim impact statements and evidence of aggravating circumstances. He first set forth his position in a dissenting opinion in *Booth v. Maryland.* He argued that a state could present a victim impact statement as evidence during the penalty phase of a capital case. The majority, in an opinion by Powell, held that the statement had to be excluded because it created a constitutionally unacceptable risk of arbitrary and capricious jury decisionmaking. The statement introduced material that was unrelated to the background and record of the accused or the particular circumstances of the crime and that focused not on the moral guilt of the defendant for the offense but on alleged harms to the

emotions and opinions of persons who were not parties to the crime. In
a terse opinion, Scalia contended that the statement could help the
jury determine both the degree of harm and the defendant's moral
guilt. He argued that courts considered evidence of harm even in
crimes as ordinary as speeding and that the Court itself had considered
the degree of harm in its review of a felony murder rule conviction (a
conviction for participation in a felony resulting in a homicide by a co-
participant). Also, the exclusion of the victim's statement seemingly
made the penalty phase one-sided. Since the Constitution's text did not
preclude the statement, it ought to be available.[105]

In a related case, Scalia dissented when the Court restricted the jury
from considering prosecutorial comments about information considered irrelevant to the decision to kill, including comments about a
religious tract and a voter registration card in the victim's possession at
the time of his murder. Scalia would have allowed the prosecutor's
comments under his *Booth* standard. He thought that by blocking the
statements, the Court had committed an unjustified intrusion into the
democratic process of jury decisionmaking. Thus, *Booth* needed to be
overruled.[106]

He also dissented when the Court overturned a North Carolina rule
requiring a sentencing jury to consider only those mitigating circumstances that it unanimously agreed were supported by a preponderance
of the evidence. For the Court, Marshall ruled that a juror might consider all possibly mitigating evidence.[107] Scalia's argument was that the
state could structure and control discretion in the sentencing process
to prevent arbitrary and capricious decisions and to assure "that death
will not be lightly or mechanically imposed." He thought that precedent did not require any limits on the *manner* of the consideration of
evidence. Rather, precedent placed restrictions on the *kind* of evidence
—such as the victim's statements—that the sentencer could consider.
Considering this to be a crucial distinction, he refused to establish new
doctrine not based on "constitutional text or traditional practice."[108]
He wanted to let the states work out institutional adjudicatory procedures, especially when they reasonably guided jury discretion and
provided for rational collective decisionmaking.

When the Court considered the Arizona capital punishment statute
in *Walton v. Arizona,* the plurality opinion by White moved away from
imposing special requirements on capital sentencing and deferred
to state practice.[109] The opinion let stand Arizona's practice of letting the judge rather than a jury determine aggravating circumstances,

and it upheld the statutory definition of aggravating circumstances against a void-for-vagueness challenge. Scalia's solo concurring opinion launched into a review of the Court's capital punishment decisions, concentrating on the procedures required by the Court. The result of these decisions, he contended, was a contradictory set of standards. "Constraints on the sentencer's discretion to 'impose' the death penalty" were coupled with "a doctrine forbidding constraints on the sentencer's discretion to '*decline* to impose' it." These standards, he argued, "cannot be reconciled." Doctrine, he noted, has required individualized determination of sentences. Because "individualized determination is a unitary concept," the same standard should be applied to all options before the sentencing jury or judge. Otherwise, the decision tends to randomness, inconsistency, and irrationality. The result was more arbitrariness in death sentences, not the diminishment of discrimination which had initially been sought in the early Burger Court decisions about capital punishment. Scalia's alternative was a housecleaning of Eighth Amendment doctrine. He started with the premise that the Eighth Amendment does not give the sentencer unfettered discretion to impose the penalty. However, whereas he wanted to retain constraints on discretion to prevent racial and related forms of discrimination, he wanted to dispose of all judicial doctrine restricting states from establishing rules affecting sentencer's discretion. Thus, judicially mandated restrictions on mandatory sentencing and definitions of aggravating and mitigating circumstances would go, including the doctrines forbidding constraints on the sentencer's discretion to decline to impose the penalty.[110]

The effort of Scalia and other justices to force a reconsideration of sentencing procedures succeeded in part. In *Payne v. Tennessee*,[111] a badly divided Court overruled *Booth* and allowed the consideration of victim-impact statements by a capital case sentencer. The ban on the statements, Rehnquist held for the majority, was based on a misreading of precedent. Again Scalia concurred. His opinion was an assault on the dissenting opinion of Justice Marshall. Marshall had strenuously argued, using the doctrine of stare decisis, for the retention of *Booth*. Scalia replied that he found it difficult to reconcile support for *Booth*— a doctrine resting on "administrative convenience" and not "on the settled practices and expectations of a democratic society"—with ardent support for stare decisis. He indicated that the idea of adherence to precedent demanded adherence to settled, not "novel," rules of law.[112]

Also, Scalia concurred when the Court approved the discretion of a

Florida judge in construing a state statutory definition of aggravating circumstances. However, he dissented from parts of the Court's opinion requiring consideration of mitigating circumstances, citing the argument made in his *Walton v. Arizona* dissenting opinion.[113] In a brief dissent from a per curiam opinion prohibiting Florida sentencers from considering invalid evidence of aggravating circumstances, he confirmed his *Walton* position against interference with state discretion in the establishment of standards about the consideration of evidence.[114] He also dissented alone when the Court overturned, as unconstitutionally vague, Arizona's definition of aggravating circumstances in its death penalty law. Again citing *Walton,* Scalia argued that the Court had, without a basis in "constitutional text or national tradition," imposed a "recently invented" requirement that sentencers consider mitigating evidence. The result of this and related standards, he claimed, would be "an impenetrable complexity and hence a propensity to error that make a scandal and a mockery of the capital sentencing process."[115] In a brief opinion concurring with the Court's decision supporting California's requirement that the sentencer consider special circumstances such as the age of the defendant and his or her past criminal activity, he concluded that the procedure was lawful. The procedure provided guidance to prevent discriminatory application of the death sentence. Also, he appreciated that the Court had created no additional procedural requirements for the imposition of the penalty.[116]

Finally, when Blackmun held for the Court that due process required South Carolina judges to instruct jurors fully on the meaning of legal alternatives to the death penalty, Scalia dissented. He believed that the states, even in capital cases, had devised adequate procedural protection for due process. He perceived no need for the jury instruction rule established by the Court. Joined by Thomas, he argued that the rule went "well beyond what would be necessary to counteract prosecutorial misconduct." Also, the Constitution required no more due process and fundamental fairness in capital cases than in other cases, diminishing the need for the instruction. He feared that the Court was going beyond its previous decisions on aggravating and mitigating circumstances to allow opponents of the death penalty to open "yet another front in their guerilla war to make this unquestionably constitutional sentence a practical impossibility."[117]

Judicial Review. Scalia has disliked defendants' use of procedural rules to initiate multiple appellate reviews of death sentences and delay the imposition of the penalty. Acting as circuit justice for the Fifth

Circuit, he considered requests for extensions of the time period during which a defendant in a capital case was allowed to file a petition for a writ of certiorari with the U.S. Supreme Court. He extended the filing period in three cases. However, stressing that any request for an extension had to meet a standard of "good cause shown," he warned counsel, "I shall not grant extensions in similar circumstances again."[118] Clearly he has desired the orderly and expeditious disposition of capital cases. Thus, he was quite hostile when the Court's majority voted to review a capital case after several lower federal and state courts had reviewed and rejected a "fact-specific claim" made by the defendant and the Court's majority had to strain to find a potential legal error.[119]

Diminished Capacity and Capital Punishment

Despite Burger Court decisions, questions of whether the diminished capacity of juveniles and the mentally ill precluded capital punishment reached the docket of the Rehnquist Court. Scalia dissented from the Court's refusal to allow Oklahoma to impose the death penalty on a juvenile who had been fifteen at the time of the commission of the crime. The Burger Court had vacated a death penalty for a sixteen year old.[120] Building on language in that case, Stevens held that the imposition of the penalty on the Oklahoma juvenile was unusual and abhorrent to the national consciousness. He assumed that the death of juvenile offenders did not contribute to the purposes underlying the penalty. Instead, it sanctioned less culpable individuals with the same sanction used for adult offenders.[121]

In a dissenting opinion joined by Rehnquist, White, and Kennedy, Scalia contended that the majority had failed to provide a historical or rational basis for claiming that the penalty violated a national consensus opposing death sentences for juveniles. First, the text of the Eighth Amendment and its history gave no indication of an age limit on the death sentence. Second, he believed that Oklahoma had given "careful consideration" to social and moral factors before trying the juvenile and imposing the penalty. Citing the choice of many states to adopt statutes allowing death sentences for juveniles, he rejected Stevens's argument that "evolving standards of decency" compelled rejection of the penalty. Being able to locate "no clear line" for an age limit on the sentence, he concluded that the plurality had acted in a "legislative rather than a judicial capacity." He also disagreed with the position of O'Connor's concurring opinion, which argued that the death sentence of the juvenile was a "fluke," and that the state should have adopted legislation specifically permitting juvenile executions. Scalia regarded O'Connor's argument as hoisting "on to the deck of our Eighth Amendment jurisprudence the loose cannon of a brand new principle."[122]

With O'Connor shifting sides, the Court approved the death sentence for sixteen- and seventeen-year-old persons in *Stanford v. Kentucky*.[123] Scalia wrote the Opinion of the Court, making many of the same points about the text and history of the Eighth Amendment and about evolving standards of decency that he had made in the Oklahoma case. "In accordance with the standards of the common law tradition," he found, in earlier eras the execution of persons in this age bracket had not been deemed cruel or unusual. Standards of decency had not evolved to ban the penalty, either. There had been no change in state statutes establishing the penalty to indicate changing standards of decency. The rarity of the application of the penalty to juveniles carried "little significance" as a measure of public attitudes; and public opinion polls, views of interest groups, and positions of professional organizations did not establish a "consensus" against the penalty for youth. In brief comments, he also refused to enter into a proportionality analysis of the sentence because no social consensus indicated a belief in the proportional assessment of the penalty.[124]

The same day as *Stanford*, in a plurality opinion by O'Connor, the Court allowed the execution of a mentally retarded person.[125] Scalia's concurring and dissenting opinion, joined by Rehnquist, White, and Kennedy, contested two points in the O'Connor opinion. First, unlike O'Connor, Scalia saw no need to examine the proportionality of the punishment; as in *Stanford*, he concluded that there was no evidence of a social consensus demonstrating that sometimes the death penalty might be cruel and unusual and hence open to proportionality analysis. Second, he contended that the sentencing of the defendant had been constitutional despite the fact that the jury had not fully considered mental retardation as a mitigating factor. He thought that requiring the jury to consider retardation as a mitigating factor impeded their discretion in evaluating mitigating factors.[126] Later, he reiterated his support of this second argument in a case about whether a state had to give special consideration to the youth of a defendant as a mitigating factor.[127]

Interpretations of the Eighth Amendment: A Summary

Scalia's Eighth Amendment opinions consistently have deferred to standards and procedures established by legislatures. In addition to reiterating this Reasoned Elaboration theme in his opinions, he voted for the death penalty in cases when a defendant participated in a felony resulting in a homicide but did not directly commit the murder; when an appellate court erred and concluded that a trial court had not found mitigating circumstances during the penalty phase of the case; when a defendant was sentenced to death under a statute containing mitigating circumstance criteria subsequently invalidated by the Court; when the defendant alleged that an aggravating factor for imposing the death penalty had been too vaguely stated; when a judge imposed a slightly modified version of the common law reasonable doubt instruction in charging a jury; and when a judge admitted evidence of a prior sentence for another murder during the penalty phase. Scalia's votes indicated satisfaction with most states' definitions and applications of the aggravating and mitigating evidence to be considered during the penalty phase. Consequently, he joined a dissenting opinion by White that argued for a mandatory death penalty rather than special judicial consideration of aggravating and mitigating factors in the imposition of the sentence. In only one case did he vote to reverse a death penalty, joining the Court to hold that Oklahoma's definition of aggravating factors was unconstitutionally vague.[128]

Employing the Reasoned Elaboration technique of relying on text and deferring to statutory choices made by legislative majorities and the presumed popular tradition of the common law, his opinions have rejected any judicial effort to impose limitations on sentences, incarceration, or the death penalty. A caustic tone has often surfaced in his assertion of this logic of Reasoned Elaboration. His tone reflects a hostility to the pragmatism and concern for human dignity found in the opinions of his opponents. To control penalties, especially a penalty of such magnitude as death, the pragmatic liberals have wanted the Court to establish procedures to eliminate arbitrariness (e.g., proportionality analysis and rules associated with the death penalty) and to permit trial judges and juries some guided discretion in the treatment of individual cases. Scalia's Reasoned Elaboration jurisprudence has served as a basis for criticism of this experimentalism, as well as of judicial "lawmaking," and neglect both of text and of social consensus. The result has been his passivity in the face of popular efforts to express moral outrage and exact retribution or revenge against criminals. Ultimately, he has wanted the outcome of a criminal case to be the punishment of the criminal lawbreaker by an efficient legal machinery, under clear procedural rules and popular substantive law.[129]

THE WRIT OF HABEAS CORPUS

In the Habeas Corpus Clause of Article I, section 9, of the Constitution, the Framers designed a protection against arbitrary detention and related police-state tactics. However, as habeas corpus doctrine evolved, the writ became more than the requirement that a detained person be taken before a court to be informed of charges. Rather, the writ served to allow convicted federal and state defendants to be taken before a federal court so that they could challenge the constitutionality of searches and seizures relating to their arrest, the application of Fifth and Sixth Amendment rights during their confinement and trial, and the conditions of their subsequent confinement. When the Warren Court let the writ of habeas corpus become the critical instrument for individual challenges to state court procedures and penalties, the caseload of federal courts exploded.[130] The Burger Court, particularly after its decision in *Stone v. Powell*,[131] restricted the availability of habeas corpus relief for Fourth Amendment claims, thus shifting to the state courts many claims of violations of federal rights. Scalia's opinions have supported this practice.

For example, when a state convict sought federal habeas corpus relief after several failures to gain relief from state appeals courts, Scalia held that the convict had not exhausted all state remedies. Scalia then refused federal relief.[132] Citing federal statutory law and precedents, he concluded that a federal court must ascertain that state relief of the particular claim is procedurally barred and the claimant's state remedies are exhausted. Later, in *Ylst v. Nunnemaker*,[133] Scalia's Opinion of the Court held that a denial of a petition for a writ of habeas corpus did not lift an unexplained state procedural bar imposed on direct appeal of the case. He found that the ban on appeal had to be lifted so that the federal court could determine that all state remedies had been exhausted and that the claim was ready to be heard on its merits in a federal habeas corpus proceeding. In making this decision, he required that the federal court had to look "before" the unexplained decision to the "last reasoned decision." In *Ylst* this last reasoned decision, he discovered, rested on a state procedural default and not the merits of a federal claim. Therefore, the petitioner, Nunnemaker, had to have the state courts offer a decision on the merits of this claim and had to exhaust other relief in state courts before he could ask for a federal habeas corpus hearing about the alleged error.

Also, Scalia has argued that federal habeas corpus relief in capital cases promoted the delay of executions for insubstantial reasons. When the Court, per curiam, granted habeas corpus relief so that a federal court of appeals could consider a newly discovered trial transcript, Scalia concurred. He thought that the judgment of the Court was "correct, but the judgment is also not worth making, serving no purpose but to extend the scandalous delay in the execution of a death sentence lawfully pronounced more than 18 years ago." He argued that the transcript could not possibly support any legal claim requiring the reversal of the sentence, for "it soars beyond the unimaginable, into the wildly delirious" to hold that erroneous assertions by the state in closing arguments had resulted in reversible error.[134]

In a related case in which a defendant sought habeas corpus relief so that a court could consider newly discovered evidence about a capital case, Scalia concurred with Rehnquist's denial of the writ. The defendant had pleaded guilty to the murder of a police officer and, after ten years of proceedings, sought habeas corpus to introduce the new evidence. Rehnquist held that habeas corpus afforded a right to correct procedural errors but not findings of fact. Normally, absent extraordinary evidence of a sort not presented by this defendant, habeas corpus was not to be used to disrupt the finality of findings of fact. Moreover, no due process right or fundamental right rooted in the tradition and conscience of the nation required courts to consider the new evidence. Therefore, the only relief available was executive clemency. Scalia's concurring opinion stressed that "there is no basis in text, tradition, or even in contemporary practice (if that were enough) for finding in the Constitution a right to demand judicial consideration of newly discovered evidence of innocence brought forward after the conviction."[135] Rejecting the defendant's claim as an effort to upset the rules of precedent and practice and place the burden of habeas corpus actions on lower courts, he agreed with all of Rehnquist's argument.

Scalia also voted for Kennedy's majority opinion in a case redefining abuse of the writ of habeas corpus in capital cases. Kennedy's new standard required that, after the filing of the initial writ in the case, all subsequent writs show "cause" for not having raised the claim earlier (and not attribute the omission to attorney neglect), and show "actual prejudice" resulting from the constitutional error during case proceedings.[136] This rule was an effort to control the number of writs and restrict defendant-generated delay of executions. In later cases spelling out the details of the rule, Scalia agreed with opinions that defined "cause" as grave errors by counsel resulting in an unfair verdict, and

that required that the constitutional error resulting in "actual prejudice" had to be proven by clear and convincing evidence, and that—but
for the error—no reasonable juror would have found the defendant
eligible for the death penalty.[137]

When the Court's majority backed off from restrictions on federal
habeas corpus actions and allowed federal habeas corpus jurisdiction
over claims of violations of *Miranda* rights, Scalia concurred and dissented. His primary objection was to the Court's treatment of *Stone v.
Powell*. As an equitable power of federal courts, he contended, habeas
corpus jurisdiction is a matter of discretion for federal judges. *Stone v.
Powell*, he argued, was an application of equitable discretion to hold
that a federal court ought not consider a habeas corpus petition when
the petitioner has had the opportunity to litigate it fully and fairly in
state court. Scalia would apply this principle to all habeas corpus petitions. In enunciating it he challenged the majority's argument about
the specificity of *Stone v. Powell*. More important, he criticized the
"theory" of many habeas corpus decisions by the Warren and Burger
Court. The theory was that "a federal forum must be afforded for every
federal claim of a state criminal defendant." This theory, he explained,
was based on a misreading of precedent and, "worse," inaccurately
presumes that state courts are "second-rate instruments for the vindication of federal rights."[138]

Following up on these themes in another dissenting opinion, he
refused to recognize the Court's standard for the judicial consideration
of second or later habeas corpus petitions in death penalty cases. He
argued that the majority had again used "equitable considerations" to
force federal courts to review successive and abusive habeas petitions
when a claim of some new evidence of innocence of the crime had
been raised. Reading the "plain meaning" of the Finality of Determination section of 28 *U.S. Code* § 2244, he concluded that Congress had
said that federal courts could dismiss the petition without review and
without entertaining evidence of a miscarriage of justice.[139] Thus, prisoners would have to raise procedural error and evidentiary issues in
their first petition, and new evidence of innocence could be ignored by
the courts.

Justice Ginsburg denied relief when a defendant, who had been arrested by federal officers and delivered to Indiana state custody, sought
federal habeas corpus relief after not being tried within 120 days of
delivery, as required by the Interstate Agreement on Detainers. She

held that Indiana's start of the trial 139 days after delivery had not been a "fundamental defect which inherently results in a complete miscarriage of justice [or] an omission inconsistent with rudimentary standards of fair procedure."[140] Scalia concurred, but he argued that the fundamental defect standard was different than Ginsburg suggested. Under her standard, most violations of statutory rights such as the right to be tried within 120 days would not be so fundamental as to allow habeas corpus relief. Because of the rarity of such fundamental defects, he thought that relief ought to be afforded under direct appeal rather than habeas corpus.[141]

Finally, Scalia has favored limitations on the use of the writ of habeas corpus by defendants seeking to challenge state criminal procedures in federal courts, as stated in *Teague v. Lane*.[142] Scalia supported the *Teague* holding changes of rules of criminal procedure did not provide for defendants to use the writ of habeas corpus to secure the retroactive application of a "new rule" of criminal procedure. Although *Teague* permitted two narrowly drawn exceptions to this limitation, Scalia's vote for the limitation signaled his support for efforts to restrict access to the appellate courts and the availability of relief for defendants' criminal due process claims.[143] He joined a dissenting opinion by Souter which argued for the preclusion of the use of the Court's "new rules" of procedures as a reason for habeas corpus review after sentencing in a case. Souter held that the rules lacked a "watershed" character that would allow reconsideration of a case through the granting of a writ of habeas corpus.[144]

Scalia's opinions and votes on the availability of relief through the writ of habeas corpus all would diminish the availability of relief. Driven by adherence to the policy aims of *Stone v. Powell* and a desire for the parsimonious and efficient use of federal judicial resources, he has sought to diminish the federal judicial role in the review of criminal convictions. Like opinions on judicial federalism that have increased state judicial power, Scalia's habeas corpus opinions have placed the defense of many procedural due process rights in state judicial hands. His efforts have rested on justifications rooted in the logic of Reasoned Elaboration, including an unwillingness to upset text and tradition; the desire for a rational, efficient, and orderly scheme of judicial procedures; and a reluctance to experiment with new procedures. He has offered a vision of a federal judiciary that plays a minimal role in criminal justice and leaves the bulk of criminal actions to state courts.

CRIMINAL STATUTES AND COMMON LAW PROCEDURAL STANDARDS

Besides ruling on constitutional claims, Scalia's criminal justice opinions have stipulated that various aspects of criminal procedure are to be governed by established statutory and common law standards and judicial rules of criminal procedure. For example, Scalia declined to create, under the Due Process Clause of the Fourteenth Amendment, a "liberty interest" so that individuals could seek judicial oversight or review of executive branch decisions to prosecute.[145] One category of these opinions reinforcing established standards addressed the meaning of criminal statutes, and another category considered procedural practices.

The Meaning of Criminal Statutes

The plain-meaning approach has governed Scalia's interpretation of criminal statutes. Applying plain-meaning analysis in its most direct form, Scalia used dictionary definitions, the context of usage, and precedent to define the word *conviction* in the federal bank robbery statute. In refusing to use *offense* as a synonym for *conviction*, as apparently sometimes occurred in federal law, Scalia rejected the contentions of defense and dissenters. Finding only that "personal intuition" supported their interpretations, he refused to abandon a literal reading of the text.[146]

Brennan, Marshall, and O'Connor joined his opinion dissenting from the Court's interpretation of the federal mail fraud statute. Relying on precedent, he determined that a section of the statute had to be read narrowly. Therefore, he applied the statute only to mailings in execution of a fraud—not, as the government requested, to mailings that were incidental to the fraud.[147] Also, in interpreting an Arizona felony murder statute, his solo concurring opinion refused to find the law violative of due process. The defendant had argued that the law contained proscriptions of two crimes—killing in the course of robbery, and premeditated killing—and thus offended the due process concept of fundamental fairness. Scalia argued that historical practice indicated that the statute was valid and that due process was satisfied if "the trial is according to the settled course of judicial proceedings."[148] He refused to inquire into the constitutionality of the statute. Due process was fair procedure, not a reason to second-guess a legislature. The same consideration appeared in his solo concurring opinion about the construction of a phrase in the federal statute governing the revocation of probation for drug law violators. He noted that his "straightforward" reading might not be what Congress had intended but that "it is best, as usual, to apply the statute as written, and to let Congress make the needed repairs. That repairs are needed is perhaps the only thing about this wretchedly drafted statute that we all can agree upon."[149]

In addition, Scalia dissented in part from Rehnquist's Opinion of the Court in another case about the meaning of the language of a criminal statute (18 *U.S. Code* § 1503) defining criminal obstruction of the due administration of justice. Citing precedent and dictionary definitions of words in the statute, Scalia argued that the Court had substituted a different meaning for the standard of criminal intent defined in the statute. He then illustrated how the Court's decision put a heavier burden of proof on the government than did his "plain meaning" analysis.[150]

Scalia's concern about the plain meaning of criminal statutes normally has meant that he does not attempt any creative reconstruction of complex statutory provisions. For example, when the Court rejected a federal district judge's construction of a criminal penalty in the Immigration and Nationality Act for due process reasons, Scalia wrote a solo dissenting opinion. The statute provided for the felony prosecution of deported aliens who reentered the country illegally. However, the Court ruled that, because the initial deportation hearing—an administrative action—did not comport with standards of due process, the criminal penalization for reentry could not be imposed. Scalia's opinion was that the standards used at the initial hearing were irrelevant to the later felony prosecution for illegal reentry. Separating the deportation and reentry events, he reasoned that a failure of the deportee to seek judicial review of the violation of due process at the initial deportation hearing could not be used as a defense at a trial for illegal reentry.[151] Thus, when defendants did not take responsibility for exhausting due process guarantees of judicial review at the initial hearing, the statute did not create relief at the second hearing.

Other Aspects of Criminal Procedure

Another category of Scalia's opinions in criminal cases includes considerations of the specific procedural requirements that supplement constitutional due process and are required for a fair trial. Scalia has construed these requirements, either in common law understandings of due process or statutory procedures, in accordance with what he has viewed as "long established" practice. The practices he has treated in this fashion included those found in precedents on criminal intent; the Federal Rules of Criminal Procedure; precedents about offers of immunity from prosecution; precedents about harmless error in jury instructions; and the use of the "beyond a reasonable doubt" standard for conviction by a jury.

Criminal Intent

In a pair of concurring opinions Scalia upheld convictions in cases in which defendants claimed that they had no intent to violate the law. In one of these cases a defendant claimed that his failure to file a federal income tax return had not been willful because he had honestly believed, on the basis of information supplied by others, that the tax law was unconstitutional. Scalia objected to the standard of criminal intent used by the Court's majority. In his solo concurring opinion, he disagreed with the Court's construction of willful behavior. He indicated that the Court had worked "a revolution in past practice" by defining willful behavior as consciousness of the act of not filing the tax return, rather than consciousness of the illegality of the failure to file. However, he agreed with the majority that a jury should consider if the failure to file was criminal—under any standard—or was subject to civil penalties under the Internal Revenue Code.[152] Also, he upheld a statute that did not deem subjective intent to be a necessary condition for the conviction of persons of the sale of items likely to be used in the consumption of illegal drugs. If the statute was drafted so as to require no evidence of subjective intent or willful behavior, it did not violate due process.[153] Thus, Scalia let statutory language, supplemented by common law procedural understandings, guide courts in defining criminal intent. No additional analysis or new judicial standards were necessary.

The Federal Rules of Criminal Procedure

Scalia's construction of the Federal Rules of Criminal Procedure has employed a plain-meaning approach. For example, when considering the hearsay evidence rule he rejected Kennedy's interpretation that would have allowed at trial the admission of more of the defendant's statements to federal agents. He preferred a "narrower definition" of the language of the rule.[154] Likewise, in the construction of provisions of federal sentencing guidelines, his search for a definition of the guidelines' use of the term *stipulation* in relation to statements made as part of a plea agreement focused on the reasonableness of the trial court definition of the word. Reading the defendant's statements in a literal fashion, he concluded that the defendant had not expressly stipulated what the trial court thought he said.[155] Precision in the definition of language led him to his conclusion about the scope of procedural guarantees. In *Midland Asphalt Corporation v. United States*,[156] he employed text and precedent to sort out the meaning of a federal criminal procedural rule on the appellate review of breeches of the secrecy of grand jury testimony. He concluded that the defendant had to await final sentencing before appeal, because no text or precedent allowed a defendant a right not to be tried at all because of the breech of secrecy.

Immunity

American courts commonly permit grants of absolute or qualified immunity from criminal prosecution or civil personal injury action for a suspect's illegal acts, in exchange for evidence against a second defendant. Scalia has written two brief opinions about qualified immunity. In one case, the Court per curiam upheld qualified immunity for Secret Service agents who had, without probable cause and a warrant, arrested a suspect for threatening to assassinate the president. Scalia concurred with Court's assessment that the agents' violation of Fourth Amendment rules was immune from tort action in the special circumstance involving potential of harm to the president.[157] Scalia also concurred with the Court's grant of qualified immunity for prosecutors' alleged false out-of-court statements and fabrication of evidence during a murder investigation. Relying on precedents at common law, Scalia concluded that qualified and not absolute immunity applied to the prosecutors' actions. Immunity from civil rights suit (under 42 *U.S. Code* § 1983) shielded the prosecutors when speaking in the courtroom but not when defaming the defendant by out-of-court statements, he argued. However, he could find no authority to conclude that the preparation—in contrast to the use—of false evidence had harmed the defendant.[158] In neither of these cases did he stray far from established procedural rules.

Harmless Error and Other Issues of Jury Decisionmaking

Errors in jury instructions and the "beyond a reasonable doubt" rule for criminal convictions posed additional procedural problems for the

Court. Since American law recognizes that some procedural errors are harmless, the form of the harmless error rule affects the potential for judicial review of jury instructions. In concurring with the Court's per curiam opinion in *Carella v. California*,[159] Scalia elaborated on the nature of harmless error analysis in jury instruction disputes. The Court held that the Due Process Clause of the Fourteenth Amendment required that the jury be instructed to return a verdict of "guilty" only when the prosecution had proved beyond a reasonable doubt every element of the charged offense. It was not a harmless error to use other standards. Scalia, joined by Brennan, Blackmun, and Marshall, additionally argued that there were two different versions of harmless error analysis. In most cases, a "general" harmless error analysis required judges to evaluate the effect of the evidence introduced by procedural error on the overall body of evidence introduced at trial. If a judicial error resulted in the admission of a fact not established by other evidence, then a harmful error and a due process violation had occurred. With the error in jury instructions, however, the Court required a second and more specific version of harmless error analysis. Because the error in jury instruction reflected a fundamental decision about the exercise of official power, it induced damage to the entire decisionmaking process in a way that could not be rectified.

His interpretation of harmless error precedents also appeared in another concurring opinion. In a case about a robbery that resulted in a homicide by stabbing, a judge's instruction had allowed a jury to infer malice by considering evidence that the defendant carried a gun. Souter found an error in the admission of the gun as evidence of malice. Concurring, Scalia agreed with Souter's test of harmless error. But, unlike Souter, he argued that the instruction to presume malice because of the gun had not been not a general harmless error "for the simple reason that it had no application to the facts of the case."[160] Scalia, however, thought that it was a specific harmful error for juries to be instructed to presume malice because of the unlawful act of robbery, because this error damaged the decisionmaking process in a way that could not be rectified. Again disagreeing with Souter, he saw no reason to examine the entire record of the case to reach this conclusion. He simply thought that the instruction had caused the jury to examine the evidence *"with the wrong question in mind"*—the maliciousness of the robbery and not the stabbing, thus violating due process and denying a fair trial.[161]

Finally, Scalia has tried to define the boundaries of harmless error analysis. In an Opinion of the Court he reaffirmed that the Sixth Amendment jury trial right and due process demanded the use of the reasonable doubt standard for jury assessments of guilt. When this error occurred in a case, it had the effect of producing no lawful jury verdict. Consequently, since the failure to use the reasonable doubt standard vitiated the jury's findings, there was no need for an appellate court harmless error analysis.[162]

Scalia's penchant for commentary on procedures has appeared in opinions clarifying his views on other aspects of jury instructions. Concurring in a case about the instruction of federal juries on entrapment defenses, he argued that the defendant could use the defense even if he did not claim that he had committed a crime. Letting the defendant use the defense, even if by using it he inconsistently implied that he had committed the crime, did no damage to the interests of justice.[163] He also found no damage to justice or due process when a jury failed to specify on which "object," or activities, of a two-object conspiracy it had convicted a person. Relying on common law rules, Scalia held that general verdicts without specification of grounds or charge had long been considered lawful. He then assumed that this practice was a legitimate form of evidentiary evaluation by juries and was encompassed within the meaning of due process.[164] This analysis summed up his loyalty to the idea of procedural stability as the core of a legitimate legal system.

CONCLUSION

In one sense, Scalia's criminal law opinions have been remarkable. He has respected the Warren Court's key procedural innovations. He has not talked of retreating from incorporation doctrine requiring the application of federal standards on the states, or of the elimination of the exclusionary rule or *Miranda*. In opposition to popular sentiment and the version of the criminal process conveyed in the entertainment and information media, he has not regarded all procedural innovations to be evidence of the "softness" of courts on crime. His efforts to repeal judicial criminal procedure doctrine have focused on standards developed during the Burger Court—Eighth Amendment proportionality rules, as in *Harmelin*; and the evidentiary requirements imposed on the penalty phase of capital cases, as best stated in *Walton*.

In another sense, Scalia's criminal law opinions have been less remarkable. In his message about procedural regularity in the criminal process, he has consistently used the methodology of Reasoned Elaboration. In tune with the central aim of Reasoned Elaboration, he has sought to ensure that criminal procedures accord with the popular consensus *as expressed in legislation*. And as best evidenced in death penalty opinions, he believes that the Court should not frustrate a legislative policy by challenging the legislature's values and imposing the justices' humanistic concerns on a legislative majority's policy. Additionally, he has employed other elements of Reasoned Elaboration jurisprudence, including the view that courts should specify clear legal procedures rationally derived from legal principle. Therefore, he has preferred the literal application of constitutional language, as in the Confrontation Clause cases; or the literal application of standards based on precedent, as with "plain view" searches in *Arizona v. Hicks*. He has interpreted procedural standards in a reasonable manner, examining traditional common law practices, precedent, and evidence as a guide to the reasonable, as in *Illinois v. Rodriguez, Minnesota v. Dickerson,* the forfeitures cases, and habeas corpus cases. He has sought to clarify and simplify doctrine, whether about automobile searches, double jeopardy, or harmless error analysis. Experimentalism and judicial creativity have remained anathema to him. Justices arguing for new procedural rules or practices, such as O'Connor's definition of seizures in *Riverside County,* the double jeopardy rule of *Grady v. Corbin,* sentencing proportionality rules in *Harmelin v. Michigan,* and the creation of rules about the penalty phase of capital cases, have received a lecture. Consequently, he has argued for judicial passivity in the definition of criminal procedural rights and processes.

When using Reasoned Elaboration arguments, Scalia has refused to question the discipline imposed by the state on the criminal defendant or convict. He never has questioned the substantive criminal law devised by legislatures. He has assumed that the text written by legislatures, as well as the Constitution, has a singular meaning not subject to pragmatic judicial construction. Thus, confrontation means being in a position to make eye-to-eye contact, not merely being able to hear the words of another person; and the death penalty is a legislative choice not subject to additional, judicially established procedures. He has assumed that text and the state's policies impose a discipline on the criminal, a discipline that is certain and allows little room for discretion. His use of the premises of Reasoned Elaboration has encouraged the judiciary to engage in an orderly enforcement of the criminal law without being distracted into issues of justice. His political vision has let political majorities define the state's instrumental use of criminal law to ensure the prosecution and penalization of lawbreakers. In this sense, his opinions fit with the conservative revival. He has defended traditional procedures and traditional majoritarian values about social and political order, and he has made personal rights yield to the majority's definitions of moral duties and social order.

Chapter Nine

PROTECTING BODIES
AND PROPERTY

Nothing arouses Antonin Scalia's hostility as much as efforts to treat the Constitution as something other than a legal text. Popular or legal citation of the Constitution as a charter of liberties or as an instrument for the alleviation of social problems—the pragmatic use of the document—has incited his most incendiary rhetoric. Judicial efforts to make the Constitution mean what it ought to mean have rankled him so much that he has accused his colleagues of offering a "Nietzschean vision of us unelected, life-tenured judges—leading a Volk."[1] Yet, paradoxically, he has regarded some of the Court's opinions about fundamental liberties of the body to be an example of the Court's deference to the majority, while he has encouraged a back-door defense of fundamental rights to property. The result is an inconsistent mix of moral paternalism and hostility to bureaucratic regulation which fits with the conservative revivalists' effort to moralize the secular state while encouraging private materialism.

For Scalia no aspect of contemporary constitutional law has proved more controversial than the claim that the Due Process Clauses of the Fifth and Fourteenth Amendments protect "fundamental liberties."[2] These liberties, not explicitly stated in the Constitution but "rooted in the traditions and conscience of our people,"[3] are "substantive." They protect the "substance" or liberty of the body from governmental regulation and protect the private property of persons from governmental authority. This attribute distinguishes them from the right to procedural due process, which is seen in the inquiry into whether governmental or judicial regulatory *procedures* are fair or—alternatively—whether they unfairly violate rights to equal protection, freedom of expression, no establishment of religion, fair criminal process, or other statutory and common law liberties. The contention that the Constitution contains specific but unenumerated substantive rights protected by Fifth and Fourteenth Amendment language preventing the deprivation of "life, liberty, or property, without due process of law," and by the Ninth Amendment indication that the "rights retained by the people" include "others" not named in the Constitution, has produced two messages in Scalia's votes and opinions. First, he has not considered most claims of fundamental liberty—such as rights to obtain abortions, to die, or to receive governmental assistance to preserve life—to be violated by reasonable legislation. When the state impedes these liberties, he holds that due process does not require a variety of Fourteenth Amendment heightened scrutiny doctrine. Second, he has respected the right to own and control property, especially real estate, and has stated that public taking or regulation of real estate should follow the Fifth Amendment provision on "just compensation," or due process is violated. Other impediments to the use of property through governmental regulation need only be reasonable exercises of government's police or regulatory powers.

LAW AND TRADITION IN SCALIA'S OPINIONS ABOUT FUNDAMENTAL RIGHTS

Scalia has not recognized a fundamental personal right to control the body—as in abortion cases—or a substantive right to property, but he has recognized some fundamental liberties.[4] In defining these liberties, he has relied on a guiding theme about the generality, or scope, of Fifth and Fourteenth Amendment due process and liberty derived from Reasoned Elaboration jurisprudence. His theme is a respect for *legal* tradition.[5] This means, first, that his conception of tradition in law has not looked at sources of law in ancient customs or general community understandings of fair expectations. As indicated by numerous commentators, Scalia's definitions of tradition have not included respect for general historical traditions. Although some commentators have tried to associate his opinions with an effort to impose an "originalist" reading of the Constitution, Scalia has not been concerned with detailed historical investigation of the Framers' definition of constitutional concepts. Second, he has not relied on an "invented tradition." Eric Hobsbawm has defined an invented tradition as the ritualized practices surrounding substantive action created to symbolize cohesion in a group, the legitimacy of institutions, and allegiance to political beliefs. Fourth of July festivities and the practice of saluting the flag in schools are invented traditions.[6] Except in the Establishment Clause case *Lee v. Weisman*,[7] in which he used a tradition of graduation prayer to offset a claim of disadvantage, Scalia has refused to base opinions on traditional rituals. Instead, he has utilized tradition in a third sense. In his opinions he has used the past at the "most specific level at which a relevant legal tradition protecting, or denying protection to, the asserted right can be identified."[8] His practice has been to define traditional rights and liberty following a criterion set forth by Hart and Sacks, who argued that rights and liberties were not "metaphysical entities, or concepts of the order of nature, or anything else mysterious," and that "traditions were simple characteristic *positions* which people have in authoritative directive arrangements."[9] Therefore, Hart and Sacks's consideration of traditional rights required only a study of the history of authoritative legal positions on rights. Their use of tradition did not demand an inquiry into the general history of, presuppositions regarding, or normative worth of rights. Thus, for Scalia, the use of tradition has become a method akin to Hart and Sacks's use of *custom* to mean "custom in the common law," as distinct from *custom* in the sense of "general community understanding and fair expectation."[10] In the sense in which Scalia uses it, tradition is a technique of interpretation that demands passivity in the face of the longstanding views of the judiciary and legal profession and, only secondarily, reliance on the majority consensus about the legitimacy of historical social or political practices. Nonlegal traditions, minority traditions, and the unrecorded traditions of illiterate or suppressed groups naturally have less value under his practice of following tradition.[11] It is *legal tradition* that matters in his opinions.

By relying on specific legal traditions, Scalia has ignored not only the historical but also the extratextual fundamental rights found in the Court's construction of the "vested right of property" in the early nineteenth century but also the variety of extratextual substantive rights to contract and property recognized by conservative courts in the early twentieth century.[12] Also, he has not accepted Frankfurter's argument that "the ultimate foundation of a free society is the binding tie of cohesive sentiment. Such a sentiment is fostered by all those agencies of the mind and spirit which may serve to gather up the tradition of a people, transmit them from generation to generation, and thereby create that continuity of a treasured common life which constitutes a civilization."[13]

Additionally, Scalia's opinions have not even utilized legal tradition as the sole desideratum in most cases. Rather, he has used it in combination with constitutional language and the concept of judicial passivity. In most respects, his methodology in fundamental rights cases has not been very different from the approach that he has used in many federalism and criminal procedure opinions. In both of the latter categories of cases he deployed series of precedent cases, pre-twentieth-century treatises, and related materials as a legal tradition to guide his reading of the Constitution and statutes. Nevertheless, he has not regarded the Constitution's text as defining tradition. He has not interpreted the Constitution as an open-ended statement of the "spirit" of American values. Rather, he has found that its language limited the use of both general legal traditions and some specific legal traditions, such as dormant Commerce Clause doctrine.[14]

THE QUESTION OF THE SCOPE OF FUNDAMENTAL LIBERTIES

The central postulates of Scalia's evaluation of substantive due process claims surfaced in *Michael H. v. Gerald D.*[15] His plurality opinion, joined by Rehnquist and partly by O'Connor and Kennedy, denied a substantive due process claim to a liberty interest in a parental relationship. Michael H. sued Gerald H. for parental rights to visit his daughter Victoria, who had been conceived when Gerald's wife, Carole, had an adulterous sexual encounter with Michael. California courts denied visitation rights to Michael, but he appealed. At the same time, a petition for his visitation rights was filed on behalf of the daughter. In deciding the case, Scalia first cleared away a procedural due process claim contending that the state had not allowed a hearing to determine paternity. He rejected the claim by holding that California law created an irrebuttable presumption that a child born to married parents was their offspring. This presumption excluded any inquiry into a child's paternity which was "destructive of family integrity and privacy."[16] Only the presumption itself could be questioned, and only then when the effort was to demonstrate that it would not further the policy of family integrity in the California law.

Turning to the substantive due process issue, Scalia recognized that fundamental rights might "be rooted in history and tradition"; however, he sharply curtailed the generality, or scope, of these rights. Examining precedent, he saw the rationale of fundamental rights cases about the family—"They rest not upon such isolated factors but upon the historic respect—indeed, sanctity would not be too strong a term—traditionally accorded to the relationships that develop within the unitary family." But in this case, his review of case facts in light of treatises and common law doctrine led him to conclude that it was "impossible" to recognize a fundamental right "to assert parental rights over a child born into a woman's marriage with another man."[17] "What counts," he asserted, "is whether the States in fact award substantive parental rights to the natural father of a child conceived within and born into an extant marital union that wishes to embrace the child. We are not aware of a single case, old or new, that has done so. This is not the stuff of which fundamental rights are made."[18] Without specific text or legal tradition, the Court could not define a fundamental right.

Scalia then turned to comment on Brennan's dissenting opinion, which offered criticism of Scalia's use of tradition. In footnote 6, Scalia offered a complaint and an explanation. He challenged Brennan's criticism of his definition of tradition. He complained that Brennan refused to acknowledge that a use of a general tradition about fundamental rights left "judges free to decide as they think best when the unanticipated occurs" and was "no rule of law at all." Scalia defended his reliance on "societal tradition" as more rational: "We refer to the most specific level at which a relevant tradition protecting, or denying protection to, the asserted right can be identified. If, for example, there were no societal tradition, either way, regarding the rights of a natural father of a child adulterously conceived, we would have to consult, and (if possible) reason from, the traditions regarding natural fathers in general. But there is such a more specific tradition, and it unqualifiedly denies protection to such a parent."[19] The specific tradition, which he located primarily in common law, was a guide to the generality, or scope, of constitutional rights.

Finally, in footnote 4 of his opinion, Scalia remarked that Brennan had examined the rights of Michael H. without considering the rights of the other parties. "We cannot imagine what compels this strange procedure of looking at the act which is assertedly the subject of a liberty interest in isolation from its effect on other people—rather like inquiring whether there is a liberty interest in firing a gun where the case at hand happens to involve its discharge into another person's body. The logic of Justice BRENNAN's position leads to the conclusion that if Michael had begotten Victoria by rape, that fact would in no way affect his possession of a liberty interest in his relationship with her."[20]

Scalia's criticism of Brennan did more than question the viability of fundamental parental rights. It raised the possibility that rights are not a personal possession or attribute. Rather, fundamental rights could exist only when they did no harm to others. Potentially his argument allowed personal injury actions or statutory law to limit any exercises of rights that proved harmful in the eyes of a judge or jury.[21] However, probably Scalia's argument—unusual for a justice so conscious of text—was intended to mean, along the lines of his argument in *Employment Division v. Smith,* that liberty could be curtailed by neutral, valid criminal laws.[22] Nevertheless, his note implied a narrow scope for any tradition-based fundamental rights developed under the Due Process Clause.

Scalia's opinions in punitive damage cases have further defined his views on fundamental rights. In *Pacific Mutual Life Insurance Company v. Haslip,*[23] his solo concurring opinion considered whether unguided jury assignment of punitive damages was fundamentally unfair and violated the Due Process Clause of the Fourteenth Amendment. Through reasonableness analysis and the use of a balancing test, the Court determined that a punitive damage award in a civil case against the insurance company was not unfair. Scalia made it clear that he wanted a standard more precise than a mere reasonableness test to define due process in punitive damages cases. He also aimed to challenge the balancing formula implied by the majority. He began his search for an alternative standard through a historical analysis of treatises and precedents on the award of damages. Concerned that the Court's opinion dismissed these "legal traditions" and offered a "rootless analysis" of the words *due process* not dictated by precedent, he tried to couple the "traditional historical approach" to the law with the fundamental fairness construction of the Due Process Clause.[24]

The result was his call for a test that, first, determined whether a procedure or rule was traditional in common law or was a longstanding practice, and second, determined whether the procedure or rule was prohibited by the Bill of Rights. A procedure or rule affecting the award of damages, he contended, should not be struck down because of "basic values of our constitutional heritage"; rather, a rule had to violate express Bill of Rights language. The coupling of tradition and text in his *Haslip* opinion also came with a twist on the idea of judicial passivity. Rather than approve the many decisions resting on balancing and basic values arguments, he contended that the policymaking passivity required by stare decisis meant going back to "vigorously alive" traditional interpretations or the constitutional text. However, in an aside at the end of the opinion, Scalia added that constitutional text should trump tradition when the text has a "counterhistorical content" or creates guarantees, such as equal protection or First Amendment rights, that make historical discriminatory practices illegal.[25]

Scalia also concurred in another punitive damages case, *TXO Production Corporation v. Alliance Resources Corporation.*[26] Stevens's Opinion of the Court employed reasonableness analysis to determine that the award of money damages for a common law slander of title (disparagement of title to property) was not excessive. In his brief concurring opinion, joined by Thomas, Scalia reiterated his *Haslip* themes. Contending that the majority had now clearly recognized a substantive due process right to not be subjected to excessive punitive damages, he reacted strongly against the idea that Fourteenth Amendment Due Process was "the secret repository of all sorts of other, unenumerated, substantive rights." As in *Haslip,* his alternative was to treat the clause as protection of procedural fairness. Since the tradition embodied in precedents and in the words of the Bill of Rights did not impede the assessment of punitive damages, he decided to allow unlimited damage awards by juries. Then he added a coda reflecting his commitment to judicial passivity. If there was to be a protection against excessive punitive damages, it was necessary for the "proper institutions of our society to undertake that task." State legislatures should impose any control on awards for damages, he maintained.[27]

In addition to containing an issue of judicial federalism and the jurisdiction of state courts (discussed in chapter 5), Scalia's plurality opinion in *Burnham v. Superior Court of California, County of Marin* included additional commentary on the meaning of due process.[28] To determine the fairness of the service of process by the agent of one state's government on a resident of another state, Brennan's concurring opinion argued for a more pragmatic standard for the determination of jurisdiction. Scalia countered with the assertion that Brennan had reformulated a precedent requiring the use of "traditional standards of fair play and substantial justice" into a test of *"our* [the Court's] notions of fair play and substantial justice." Brennan's approach was subjective and inadequate, Scalia claimed, because it sought a new standard of fundamental fairness when the existing precedent and experience gave evidence of a "continuing American tradition that a particular procedure is fair." Indeed, he argued that what Brennan had established was not a rule that was fair because it could be relied upon by litigants but was rather an ill-defined "totality of circumstances" test of jurisdiction which allowed an arbitrary—or experimental—judicial tinkering with the jurisdiction of state courts in the name of progress. Standing the test of time, traditional due process rules and practice—not "individual Justices' perceptions of fairness"—should define the content of the law.[29]

The minor children who were the defendant parties in *Reno v. Flores* made a substantive due process claim about Immigration and Naturalization Service procedures for the deportation of illegal aliens.[30] INS procedures required that suspected illegal alien children had to be detained unless they could be released to parents, close relatives, or legal guardians. As one aspect of their legal attacks on the INS procedure, the unaccompanied children alleged that this procedure violated their fundamental right to liberty or "freedom from physical restraint" under the Due Process Clause. They sought placement in a "noncustodial setting." Scalia's Opinion of the Court denied this substantive due process challenge to the INS procedure. Addressing the question from the vantage point of tradition, he indicated that he was "unaware" that any court had recognized a constitutional right like that claimed by the unaccompanied alien children. Absent this legal tradition, the right could not be considered to be "rooted in the traditions and conscience of our people," and fundamental. Likewise, he dismissed the argument that the children had a substantive right to an individualized hearing to ascertain what would be in their best interest. He concluded that there was no fundamental constitutional right obligating the government to exercise its custodial responsibilities to serve the substantive best interest of children. Therefore, he decided not to go beyond the absence of the right in precedent and text and create a fundamental right through judicial opinion. The creation of such a right, he indicated, was the province of Congress under its power to control "alien visitors." Having dismissed the substantive due process claim, Scalia concluded that the procedures used for determining custody of the children had to satisfy only lower-tier reasonableness analysis. Thus, he decided the case much as any other case in administrative law, with no disadvantaged class or First Amendment dimensions. After analyzing INS policy choices, he deferred to the rationality of the agency policy with the same spirit of passivity found in his other administrative law decisions.[31]

In very direct language in *United States v. Carlton*,[32] Scalia impugned the entire concept of fundamental rights. Joined in his concurring opinion by Thomas, he criticized a standard adopted by the Court's majority to determine the validity of the retroactive application of an amendment to the federal statute on estate taxes. Writing for the majority, Blackmun held that the retroactive application did not violate the Fifth Amendment Due Process Clause because it was not "harsh and oppressive" or fundamentally unfair. Remarking that substantive due process was an "oxymoron" and that the Due Process Clause guaranteed "*no* substantive rights, but only (as it says) process," Scalia refused to recognize a right that had no foundation in the text of the Bill of Rights. Supplementing this argument, he also noted that the majority had sought to distinguish precedents and modify traditional legal rules about retroactive taxation. The result was an improper use of judicial power, for these practices resulted in the Court "picking and choosing among various rights to be afforded 'substantive due process' protection." He "would follow the text of the Constitution, which sets forth certain substantive rights that cannot be taken away, and adds, beyond that, a right to due process when life, liberty, or property is to be taken away."[33] Yet, here and in *Michael H., Haslip, TXO Production, Reno v. Flores,* and *Burnham* he never identified the substantive rights that he would recognize. Consequently, Scalia's opinions leave their reader asking what the justice would define as a "specific level" of legal tradition which would protect a fundamental right of persons to protect their bodies and material possessions.[34]

Scalia's opinionless votes, like his opinions, conveyed the message that he would not recognize most claims of fundamental rights. He voted to reaffirm the lack of constitutional protection for a claimed fundamental right and liberty interest in personal reputation based on the Fourteenth Amendment Due Process Clause.[35] He supported a unanimous opinion that the Due Process Clause required minimal standards of treatment of confined persons such as the mentally ill, not the protection of the safety of governmental employees. Thus, an employee's heirs had to obtain relief for his death under tort law principles.[36] In *Foucha v. United States,*[37] Scalia agreed with Thomas's dissenting opinion in a conflict about the release of Foucha, who was held because of a condition of criminal insanity. After a hearing determined that Foucha should be released because he was no longer mentally ill, judicial review of the decision resulted in his being confined because of his antisocial nature and his potential danger to society. The Court's majority held that due process required that the state prove by "clear and convincing evidence" that Foucha was a dangerous person whose fundamental "freedom from bodily restraint" had to be restricted.

Thomas's dissent argued that the majority had no constitutional or historical basis for the idea of a fundamental liberty from bodily restraint.

LIBERTY AND THE BODY

Scalia has used blunt words in his opinions about persons' fundamental right to control their bodies. Litigants in these cases have made fundamental rights claims based on inferences of the nature of personal liberty drawn from the Bill of Rights, or the summed implications of the American conception of privacy rights. Their arguments have roused his opposition, and in light of the absence of text and legal tradition to support them, he has roundly refused to recognize their substantive rights claims.

Although judicial opinions about abortion have been lengthy and commentary on the abortion issue has been massive, Scalia's commentary on abortion has been brief—six printed pages in one case, a paragraph in each of two other cases, and one longer concurring and dissenting opinion.[38] Only one abortion case—*Rust v. Sullivan*—has not provoked Scalia to write an opinion.[39] Although the Court considered First Amendment aspects of congressional restrictions on federally funded family-planning services, Scalia joined Rehnquist's Opinion of the Court on both the First Amendment issue and a section concluding that the Due Process Clause did not afford an affirmative right to governmental assistance, even when the aid might be necessary to secure life, liberty, or property against a governmental deprivation of the fundamental liberty.

Scalia's rejection of abortion rights has been clear, but at times it has swelled over banks and turned into a torrent of abuse submerging the ordinarily depersonalized language of opinions. As stated in his brief solo concurring opinion in *Webster v. Reproductive Health Services*,[40] a case about the constitutionality of provisions of a Missouri law barring the use of public funds, facilities, and personnel to assist persons seeking abortions, his goal was the explicit overruling of *Roe v. Wade*.[41] Using pragmatic standards and remedies, *Roe* recognized a fundamental right to choose abortion and permitted restrictions on the right by devising a trimester test to govern the level of judicial scrutiny of governmental regulation of abortion at various stages of a pregnancy. Scalia's reasons for the abandonment of *Roe* paralleled those first stated in the dissenting opinions of Rehnquist and White in *Roe* and its companion case—*Roe* rested not on the language or history of the Constitution but on the Court's creation of a fundamental right contrary to long-standing federal and state statutes.[42] *Roe* was not the product of a passive judiciary reasoning from text and legal tradition. Thus, Scalia's position on abortion paralleled his Reasoned Elaboration argument against fundamental rights in general.

Although his *Webster* opinion offered a rebuttal to the abortion-as-a-fundamental-right argument of Blackmun, Brennan, and Marshall, Scalia especially castigated, "as the least responsible," the arguments of O'Connor. O'Connor's concurring opinion contended that judicial restraint required adherence to the *Roe* precedent at least until a case arose that could not be resolved without reexamining *Roe*. But she then developed an "undue burdens" test and a fetal viability test to evaluate whether or not a law might restrict abortion. All of these "finessing" arguments raised Scalia's ire. In a very direct criticism of O'Connor, he cited instances in which she had spoken more broadly than necessary to resolve a case and thereby bypassed standards of restraint.[43] He also devoted a detailed footnote to illustrating how her undue burdens and fetal viability standards for defining the limit of the fundamental right to an abortion were "irrational." O'Connor's opinion, he concluded, only confused the issue the Court had to confront by making an issue of the "minor problematical aspects of *Roe*." Instead, he wanted the Court to confront *Roe* directly and affirm it or—since he thought that most of the justices thought *Roe* was wrong—overrule it. He clearly did not want to disassemble "doorjamb by doorjamb" the "mansion of constitutionalized abortion law, constructed overnight in *Roe v. Wade*."[44]

In *Hodgson v. Minnesota* and *Ohio v. Akron Center for Reproductive Health* the Court considered Minnesota and Ohio state laws establishing procedures for the notification and consent of parents when their minor children sought abortions.[45] Writing brief solo opinions in both cases, Scalia restated his position that no text and no tradition justified a fundamental right to an abortion. With regard to the standards and distinctions drawn from *Roe* to be used by other justices in these cases, he wrote, "One will search in vain the document we are supposed to be construing for text that provides the basis for the argument over these distinctions; and will find in our society's tradition regarding abortion no hint that the distinctions are constitutionally relevant, much less any indication how a constitutional argument about them ought to be resolved."[46] "[The] Constitution contains no right to abortion. It is not to be found in the longstanding traditions of our society, nor can it be logically deduced from the text of the Constitution."[47] In these cases, Scalia went beyond his usual reliance on text and legal tradition to add social tradition to his opinion.

Scalia reiterated most of these arguments in his concurring opinion in *Planned Parenthood of Southeastern Pennsylvania v. Casey*,[48] an opinion about Pennsylvania's policies requiring, before an abortion, a twenty-four-hour waiting period, provision of certain information about the procedure, notification of a spouse, and parental consent in the case of minors. Joined by Rehnquist, Thomas, and White, Scalia again stated that abortion was not a liberty protected by the Constitution both because "the Constitution says absolutely nothing about it," and because (he backed off from the use of social tradition to the use of legal tradition) "the longstanding traditions of American society have permitted it to be legally proscribed." Thus, using a rational basis test, he deemed the state's regulations a valid exercise of its police powers.[49]

Largely ignoring the position of Blackmun, he turned to disparage the justices who had voted for all or part of a joint opinion to permit states to restrict abortions without overruling *Roe*—O'Connor, Kennedy, Souter, and Stevens. Initially, he attempted to rebut their claim that they had used "reasoned judgment." His criticism made two points. First, their use of reasoned judgment was an inappropriate standard that begged the question. Reasoned judgment, he argued demanded that the Court decide at a "level of philosophical abstraction." Yet, such reasoned judgment took into account only the interest of the woman in the control of her body and the interest of the state in protecting the "potentiality of human life." It ignored the argument of abortion opponents that a fetus is human life. Therefore, the justices' "reasoned judgment" could not be reasoned since it did not include all positions in its balancing of interests and was "bound to be wrong." He added that a decision as to whether a fetus was potential life or was an actual life could not be determined by balancing of interests. It was a "value judgment," not a legal matter.[50]

In the next part of his argument, having decided that the supporters of the joint opinion really had not used reasoned judgment, he noted that they had upheld the central meaning of *Roe* because of stare decisis. Yet he found their reasons for the use of stare decisis incomplete because they never asked the question "'How wrong was the decision on its face?'" They did not confront text and tradition counter to *Roe*; rather, they and "some of the brightest (and most determined) legal minds in the country" could only

> rattle off a collection of adjectives that simply decorate a value judgment and conceal a political choice. The right to abort, we are told, inheres in "liberty" because it is among "a person's most basic decisions" . . . ; it involves a "most intimate and personal choic[e]" . . . ; it is "central to personal dignity and autonomy" . . . ; it "originate[s] within the zone of conscience and belief" . . . ; it is "too intimate and personal" for state interference . . . ; it reflects "intimate views" of a "deep, personal character" . . . ; it involves "intimate relationships" and notions of "personal autonomy and integrity" . . . ; and it concerns a particularly "important [decision] . . ." But it is obvious to anyone applying "reasoned judgment" that the same adjectives can be applied to many forms of conduct that the Court . . . [has] held are not entitled to constitutional protection—because like abortion they have long been criminalized in American society. Those adjectives might be applied, for example, to homosexual sodomy, adult incest, and suicide, all of which are equally "intimate" and "deep[ly] personal" decisions involving "personal autonomy and bodily integrity," and all of which can constitutionally be proscribed because it is our unquestionable constitutional tradition that they are proscribable. It is not reasoned judgment that supports the Court's decision; only personal predilection.[51]

The joint opinion lacked a reasoned elaboration of text and legal tradition and, consequently, could not be a "reasoned judgment."

Despite having tried to debunk the fundamental rights argument in the joint opinion, Scalia directed a third set of arguments at the use of an "undue burdens" test to determine when the right to an abortion might be restricted by the state. Calling it as "doubtful in application as it is unprincipled in origin," he claimed that it was not a standard for decision but a "shell game" to "conceal raw judicial policy choices concerning what is 'appropriate' abortion legislation." An undue burden rule, he claimed, was a rule allowing the use of whatever facts the justices considered important. It was "inherently standardless," inviting the "district judge to give effect to his personal preferences about abortion." The content it had, he thought, was "that a State may not regulate abortion in such a way as to reduce significantly its incidence."[52]

Although the joint opinion held that the trimester test was not part of the "central holding" of *Roe v. Wade* and could be abandoned, Scalia pointed out that the replacement of the trimester test of *Roe* with the undue burdens test altered precedent. This action, he contended, indicated that the joint opinion was not even concerned about following stare decisis on a rule for the application of a fundamental right, a rule that he thought was "central" to *Roe*."[53] This action, he claimed, further undermined the Court's efforts to be "statesmanlike" in settling a divisive issue.

The criticism of the idea of reasoned judgment, the application of reasoned judgment, and the undue burdens test of the joint opinion led to Scalia's conclusion that "the Imperial Judiciary lives." This imperial judiciary, his citations and discussion made plain, was analogous to the Court that had decided that Dred Scott was not a person. It presented a "Nietzschean vision of us unelected, life-tenured judges—leading a Volk who will be 'tested by following' and whose very 'belief in themselves' is mystically bound up in their 'understanding' of a Court that 'speak[s] before all other for their constitutional ideals.' " This image of the Court as akin to defenders of slavery and Nazi dictators of values, he thought, threatened the Court with a loss of legitimacy greater than that which would result if the justices overruled *Roe*. Especially if the Court abandoned *Roe,* he speculated, the justices would be free of overt political pressure such as marches, protests, and mail aimed at getting them to change their opinions. They could get back to "doing essentially lawyers' work up here—reading text and discerning our society's traditional understanding of that text," and Senate judicial confirmation hearings would no longer be "a sort of plebiscite" on favored and disfavored constitutional rights."[54] The Court thus could operate within the confines of its expertise, isolated from the unseemly world of "raw" politics. The status of women's bodies and of fetuses would be left to the politics of majority rule.

Just as Scalia would leave the issue of the right to life to majoritarian politics, he would leave the right to die to popular definition. He premised his solo concurring opinion in *Cruzan v. Director,*[55] a case about the authority of family members to withdraw life support from a terminally ill patient, on the principles

> that the federal courts have no business in the field; that American law has always accorded the State the power to prevent, by force if necessary, suicide—including suicide by refusing to take appropriate measures necessary to preserve one's life; that the point at which life becomes "worthless," and the point at which the means necessary to preserve it become "extraordinary" or "inappropriate" are neither set forth in the Constitution nor known to the nine Justices of the Court better than they are known to nine people picked at random from the Kansas City telephone directory; and that even

when it *is* demonstrated by clear and convincing evidence that a patient no longer wishes certain measures to be taken to preserve her life, it is up to the citizens of Missouri to decide, through their elected representatives, whether the wish will be honored.[56]

Again, control of the body came under the authority of the political majority.

To buttress his contention that the Fourteenth Amendment did not encompass a fundamental right to refuse medical treatment and seek death, Scalia sought support in history and tradition. Again, history and tradition meant the history and tradition of the common law. The common law, he argued, never allowed for assisted suicide, even when pain or illness permanently incapacitated a person. Also, it did not recognize a difference between affirmative steps taken to commit suicide and simple inaction leading to death. Finally, it was lawful under common law for the state courts to interfere with a person's control of her body to prevent a felony suicide.[57]

Concluding with another criticism of Brennan, Scalia challenged his balancing of the state's interest in preserving life against a "person's choice to avoid medical treatment." Scalia claimed that the test proposed by Brennan really meant weighing the state's interest in life against a person's "*choice whether to continue living or to die.*"[58] Thus, Brennan tried to make it "none of the State's business if a person wants to commit suicide." This position, Scalia thought, could be adopted by a state, "but it is not a view imposed by our constitutional traditions, in which the power of the State to prohibit suicide is unquestionable." Thus, absent constitutional text and a common law understanding of due process which included the right to die, he left another issue related to control of the body to political majorities. Then he linked this conclusion, obviously derived via the methodology of Reasoned Elaboration, to a vision of democratic responsibility under a law equally requiring "the democratic majority to accept for themselves what they impose on you and me." Protection of persons ultimately depended on the popular majority's approval of the regulations imposed by the state, not the Court's defense of personal choices about their bodies. Acting as the Jeremiah of the Court, Scalia concluded: "This Court need not, and has no authority to, inject itself into every field of human endeavor where irrationality and oppression may theoretically occur, and if it tries to do so it will destroy itself."[59]

PROPERTY AND TAKINGS

In dicta in *TXO Production* and *Carlton,* Scalia indicated his acceptance of the Court's decisions legitimating New Deal economic policies. In these cases, he agreed with the majority that the Court should not use substantive due process arguments to permit its scrutiny of the constitutionality of economic legislation. Also, he has contended that the review of economic legislation demanded only lower-tier scrutiny to see if it was rationally related to a legitimate governmental purpose.[60] Thus, he has allowed regulation of the market through "reasonable" standards that are the product of the operation of representative politics.

Although Scalia found that the Constitution did not protect substantive economic liberty and that there was no widely shared "constitutional ethos" favoring unregulated markets and absolute freedom in the use of private property, he has stated that legislative intervention in markets normally should be limited to coercive rules.[61] He has not favored the use of most forms of governmental largess, grants, subsidies, and other awards to influence market behavior. He never has supported a fundamental right to governmental largess or "new property." Although he fears mistakes in administrative discretion in the supervision of markets, he has remained even more skeptical of courts' ability to define the economic liberty of market participants in a "sensible" fashion and to craft economic policy that was fair, reasonable, and not subject to interest group pressures.[62]

Although his rejection of substantive due process has opposed special protection for property and other economic interests, his concern for a limited governmental role in the economy and the protection of property rights by the Takings Clause of the Fifth Amendment has influenced his sense of the constitutional protection afforded personal property rights. These concerns have culminated in his arguments to revitalize the Takings Clause as incorporated by the Court into Fourteenth Amendment due process. He has sought a partial restraint on interest group demands and majority factional pressures that threaten owners' control of real estate. Unconcerned with issues of economic inequality or legislative prerogative, he has defended the individual property owner against the allegedly passionate, factional demands of the majority. His opinions have offered a way to protect some rights to the use of real estate without the use of substantive due process and fundamental rights arguments. His opinions thus have tried to provide a qualified autonomy for private choices about the use of property, especially in situations in which the exercise of governments' eminent domain power has supported the ecological concerns associated with contemporary public interest liberalism.[63]

In revitalizing the Taking Clause in land-use cases, Scalia has attempted to shift the post–New Deal boundary between an unconstitutional taking and a constitutionally reasonable regulation, so as to defend rights of property. He directly asserted the nature of this distinction in his Opinion of the Court in *Nollan v. California Coastal Commission*.[64] In *Nollan* he refused to allow California to condition the granting of a permit for rebuilding a house on private property upon a grant of public access across the private property to a public beach. According to his opinion, "no doubt there would have been a taking" that demanded compensation had the state's action been an easement or simple physical occupation of the property by the state. However, the permit process also coerced the owners into allowing a physical occupation of their property. This regulation of beach access by the permit requirement, he argued, was not a valid exercise of a state's police power. Rather, challenging Brennan's dissenting effort to use precedents and California law to define the permit requirement as a valid economic regulation, he stated that there was no "nexus" between the objective of the state's permit process and its requirement of public access across the property.[65] His rule was that a taking occurred when a government, without compensation of private owners, occupied private property directly or coerced its use for transient public occupation under regulations designed to regulate building safety.

More complicated Takings Clause problems concerned the governmental regulation of the value of property or the conditions of its use. In his opinions in cases involving these issues, Scalia had to consider whether a regulation of property was a taking absent governmental occupation or a coercive effort to force public occupation. In *Hodel v. Irving*,[66] Scalia concurred with O'Connor's Opinion of the Court that held that federal prohibitions on the allocation through wills and estate law of small parcels of land held by Indians violated the Takings Clause. Scalia's brief opinion, joined by Rehnquist and Powell, addressed the scope of the impediment to property use and argued for a definition of *taking* which included the loss of control of property resulting from the regulation of some acts of an economically exploitative nature.[67] In *Pennell v. City of San Jose*,[68] his concurring and dissenting opinion, joined by O'Connor, supported the Takings Clause claim of landlords in a dispute over a city rent control ordinance. The ordinance permitted city officials to adjust rent controls to fix rents at a reasonable rate and also to require landlords to keep rents below a reasonable rate of return for buildings in which the "hardship" renters lived. Rehnquist wrote the Court's opinion and postponed a decision on the merits of the takings claim because the economic consequences of the law were not yet clear. Scalia argued that precedent indicated that the case should be decided on its merits because a constitutional harm had occurred. Then he contended that the hardship rent practice violated the Takings Clause because it unreasonably penalized selected landlords and took away their control of rents on their property without compensation. The hardship rent standard, he claimed, used rent regulation "to establish a welfare program privately funded by those landlords who happen to have 'hardship' tenants."[69] In creating this program that disproportionately impeded a property interest of some landlords, the city had not provided sufficient reasons for the hardship renter standard. Rather, the city had offered only rational reasons for a rent control program, not reasons for the "welfare program" of special lower rents for hardship tenants.

His concern with the reasonableness of the consequences of regulation also appeared in his Opinion of the Court in *Lucas v. South Carolina Coastal Council.*[70] On its face, the case appeared to be a dispute about a typical land-use or zoning law regulating the use of real estate on South Carolina's barrier islands. In 1986, Lucas purchased lots on a barrier island, the Isle of Palms, and proposed to construct residences on the lots. In 1988 the state rezoned the Isle and placed Lucas's lots in a no-development zone. Scalia began his opinion by stating that prior cases about the Takings Clause made two categories of regulatory action compensable under the clause: "regulations . . . compel the property owner to suffer a physical 'invasion' of his property," and regulations that deny "all economically beneficial or productive use of land." Using the latter standard, he concluded that "requiring the land to be left in its natural state" left Lucas without "economically beneficial or productive options for its use." This judgment appeared to be based on the assumption if the land were left in its natural state it could have no value to Lucas. Consequently, Scalia deemed that South Carolina's action had been a taking.[71]

Scalia then countered the state's argument that the law reasonably regulated the land. Examining precedents from the law of nuisance allowing regulation of harmful or noxious uses of property, he contended that this law did not serve as reason for departing from "our categorical rule that total regulatory takings must be compensated." Thus, "artful harm-preventing characterizations" for the regulation could not constitutionally survive. Only if provisions allowing a total regulatory taking appeared in a land title or under "background principles" already existing in the state's law of public nuisance could the state be exempted from having to compensate the owner. Other total use restrictions were "inconsistent with the historical compact recorded in the Takings Clause that has become part of our constitutional culture."[72]

More than Scalia's other Takings Clause opinions, *Lucas* coupled Takings Clause text, precedent, and common law and statutory legal tradition to limit the regulation of an economic right.[73] Although he interpreted the Due Process Clause to prevent a front-door entry into the realm of fundamental substantive rights, he used *Lucas* and the other Takings Clause opinions and text and tradition to open a back door to the protection of a substantive right without using fundamental rights language. His decisions protected the market value of property, and free will in the use of land and other real property, while restraining interests that might use property regulation to support the regulation of other supposed social ills. His opinions conveyed the vision that the proper instrumental use of law required a questioning both of public— especially, bureaucratic—restrictions on land use and of the efforts of majorities or interest groups to restrict the independence of the property owner or landlord. Therefore, his opinions connected economic rights to the contemporary conservative hostility to the expanded political pluralism promoted by public interest liberals. The legitimation of the regulatory goals of some emerging interests, including environmentalists, could be controlled by the Takings Clause, and the existing equilibrium in political conflict would be conserved.

In property takings cases in which he did not write an opinion, Scalia voted for more protection of the property owner through more judicial oversight of legislative regulation. In *Keystone Bituminous Coal Association v. DeBenedictis*,[74] he joined Rehnquist's dissenting opinion challenging a decision to uphold a law requiring coal-mining firms to prevent subsidence by leaving 50 percent of the coal when mining below surface structures and cemeteries. Rehnquist contended that the law was a taking and not a reasonable regulation of property to prevent a public nuisance. He argued that the law destroyed an interest in a substantial amount of property by preventing the mining of the coal, and that compensation should be afforded to the firm. Also, in *First Evangelical Lutheran Church v. County of Los Angeles*,[75] Scalia voted for Rehnquist's Opinion of the Court which stated that a temporary denial of the use of the church's recreational property in an "interim" flood protection area was a taking requiring compensation. Scalia also agreed with Rehnquist's Opinion of the Court in *Dolan v. City of Tigard*.[76] Dolan sought a building permit and zoning variance to expand an existing store on her property. The city granted the permit on the condition that she allocate a portion of the property in a flood plain for dedication to public use. Since he judged that the connections between a legitimate state interest in regulating use of the flood plain and the "exactions" on the property owner were insufficient, Rehnquist held that the dedication requirement was not a reasonable exercise of the police power.

Nevertheless, despite increased questioning of the reasonableness of economic regulations, Scalia has supported some regulations against Taking Clause claims. In *Duquesne Light Company v. Barasch*,[77] the Court considered whether a ruling of the Pennsylvania Public Utilities Commission on the rates charged by an electric utility violated the Takings Clause. Rehnquist upheld the ruling as constitutional because the state only disallowed the utility from raising rates to recover its losses from capital investments in generating plants that it planned but did not build. The ruling did not impose an unreasonable regulation unrelated to its legislative objective, as did the ruling considered in *Pennell*, or impede ownership or occupation of property, as did those examined in *Hodel v. Irving* and *Nollan*. Scalia, concurring with White and O'Connor, affirmed the validity or reasonableness of the ratemaking methodology used by the state and indicated that other methods also could be constitutional. However, he noted that the "particular consequences" of ratemaking might raise Takings Clause questions. Thus, he left space for judicial intervention to scrutinize regulation.[78] Although he did not write an opinion, he joined an opinion by O'Connor that refused to address whether a rent control law applying to mobile home lots was a taking, including her statement that the law did not constitute a taking because the landowner did not face a public or private physical occupation of the lots.[79] In addition, he voted for a concurring opinion in a case upholding the transfer of railway right-of-way property by the ICC under provisions of the National Trail System Act. The Court's majority argued that the transfer was a valid exercise of the commerce power and that any claims to compensation for the takings had to be resolved in federal court under statutory provisions. Scalia supported O'Connor's concurring opinion that argued that any claims for compensation related to the transfer should be the province of state courts, which should apply traditional takings doctrine.[80]

In Scalia's pursuit of conservative ends, his Takings Clause opinions have often contradicted a postulate of Reasoned Elaboration. In many of these opinions he has afforded the *judiciary* the opportunity to restrict some aspect of a taking made by the branches of government responsible to political majorities. Some of Scalia's opinions have allowed the justices to add up losses to private persons to determine whether the taking was a "total" governmental seizure.[81] Other opinions have used a test of reasonableness and have provided the justices with an ill-defined tool for measuring the consequence or outcome of regulations of rents, utility rates, and zoning policies. His use of reasonableness has a bite, however. He has afforded the judiciary the power to plow through the evolving common law of nuisance and the justifications of legislatures for a regulatory statute. Even presuming the use of a plain-meaning approach to statutes and a craftsmanlike reading of the legal tradition in precedent cases, the judiciary does not have to defer passively to the legislature. Instead, as indicated in *Lucas*, it has to attend first to the defense of the "bundle of rights" that persons acquire when they obtain title to property.[82] As William Fisher has commented, Scalia's argument calling for a supervision of legislative regulation is cynical about the intentions of "artful" governmental officials who use eminent domain powers to protect the environment or the poor. In its cynicism, it departs from Hart and Sacks's rule that judges should possess a "mood" of "respect" for legislative choices.[83]

SUBSTANTIVE RIGHTS AND REASONED ELABORATION

Scalia's opinions about substantive due process have employed the principles of Reasoned Elaboration to combat efforts to create, using a pragmatic construction of the Bill of Rights and the Fourteenth Amendment, personal rights for the control of the body in times of pregnancy and physical decline. He also has rejected related logic calling for substantive personal liberties related to parenthood and to protect against punitive damage judgments by courts. Like the pragmatists, Scalia has accepted the Court's refusal to afford substantive due process to owners of property; however, he has used the text of the Takings Clause and related legal tradition or history to provide a degree of judicial protection for the substantive rights of property owners.

In the substantive due process cases, Scalia's use of text and legal tradition has followed some of the principles of Reasoned Elaboration. Thus, he has argued that there should be a legal text or legal tradition to justify recognition of most fundamental rights. Judges should act as impartial and neutral arbiters in the interpretation of the text and legal tradition. They should reason out the generality, or scope, of liberties using the classic methods and materials of "lawyer's work." Additionally, he has refused to experiment and develop fundamental rights, and he has called for judicial passivity when text and legal tradition do not provide for a clear statement of a right or liberty. Although the bureaucracy problem was not addressed, his opinions took dead aim at legal standards that expanded political pluralism and encouraged moral discord. His desire to leave to legislatures the issues of parenthood, abortion, and the right to die would empower political and moral majorities and the established interests that influence state policymaking, not legally disadvantaged groups or categories of individuals such as unmarried partners, unmarried pregnant women, or persons in comas and awaiting death. These disadvantaged persons would have to submit to the law made by the majority's or powerholders' representatives, including the criminal law of adultery and suicide. In this paternalistic regime the legislature and the executive could curtail the expression of alternative views of life and the body. Suppression of the potential dangers of alternative or minority ideas related to a personalized control of life could occur. Political and moral choices in these matters would be made uniform and would be directed through the institutions of the state.[84]

However, for Scalia the state's curtailment of private power over the body has not meant the curtailment of private power over the use and disposition of material possessions. Although the state can reasonably regulate private property, Scalia has used the Takings Clause as a device to define a space for the exercise of private power against state regulation. Because the rationale for this distinction was a constitutional clause and a legal tradition about property rights, he was able to claim that his use of the Takings Clause was not an attempt to create a fundamental right. Instead, it was the protection of a right of advantaged persons by judicial interpretation of text and legal tradition. Contrary to the tenets of Reasoned Elaboration, his approach permitted judicial nullification of majority policy choices and a special benefit for a faction. In particular, his ideas about the nullification of environmental regulations indicate that he is placing a specific conservative concern with expanded political pluralism ahead of support for the more general conservative methodology of Reasoned Elaboration jurisprudence. Therefore, as in his approach to content versus contextual regulations of expression, Scalia has modified and adjusted the logic of Reasoned Elaboration to support a policy objective of the conservative revival: protection of property owners from bureaucratic regulation.

Chapter Ten

THE RULE OF LAW AND THE LIMITS OF THE CONSERVATIVE REVIVAL

Antonin Scalia's votes, which for the most part support the national Republican party's political aims, and his opinions, employing his modified version of Reasoned Elaboration, define a political vision that has embraced many of the conservative criticisms of post–New Deal liberal politics. Nonetheless, there is more to his political narrative than the instrumental use of votes and opinions to promote the conservative political revival. He also has engaged in an effort to revive or reinterpret several specific tenets that might justify the American faith in law. His tenets include the obligatory nature of the rule of law, law as a defense for private power, and law as discipline limiting human license.

To understand Scalia's tenets justifying his faith in law, it is important to understand that, in normative terms, Supreme Court justices function within a regime permeated by "Law-thought and legal relations . . . [that] dominate self-understanding and one's understanding of one's relations to others."[1] The justices share, embody, and reinforce the beliefs that define and delimit behavior in their regime. These beliefs are "a distinctive way of imaging the real."[2] Consequently, the analysis of *constitutive discourse* focuses attention on the nature and boundaries of normative beliefs about social, political, and economic power relations embedded in the justices' narrative.[3] Constitutive discourse defines the scope and limits of legitimate political action and interpersonal obligations. Through constitutive messages in their opinions, justices reaffirm cultural understandings of the extent to which persons are legal subjects and everyday social relations are definable in rules of law. Thus, unlike Scalia's instrumental efforts to use case votes and legal arguments to change politics, his constitutive discourse is about his foundational images and political beliefs. These beliefs—core suppositions about politics—are the base of the shared American political faith. As indicated in the third proposition stated in chapter 3, the study of Scalia's constitutive discourse questions the way in which his message sustains a faith that politics can be constructed and controlled by rule of law.

To analyze his constitutive discourse, it is essential to examine Scalia's affinity for the American regime's foundational theory of being. A foundational theory of being shapes citizens' fundamental normative or cultural commitments about the proper meaning of political authority and behavior. Also, a foundational theory of being establishes a perception of security about existence, including a sense of the meaning of life, a self-identity, and principles to govern relations with others.[4] In this chapter I first establish that most Americans assume that politics can be reduced to the development and application of rules and laws, and then describe Scalia's commitment to this "rule-based" or "legalistic" politics. Associated with this commitment are two corollary constitutive ideas—the idea that separate public and private spaces for political life must exist so that individuals might enjoy personal autonomy and material prosperity, and the idea that the discipline of law is necessary to control the irrational use of personal liberty or autonomy.[5] After defining these two ideas, the chapter then discusses Scalia's tenets about the scope of public and private power and the forms of discipline which Americans use to secure this foundational belief in rule-based politics.

THE FAITH IN LAW

As some Rehnquist Court cases indicate, in the United States a powerful faith in the rule of law structures not only state power and market relations but even the intimate relations of husband and wife, the family, sexual conduct, and the personal decision to procreate or to die. In the words of Pierre Bourdieu, the idea of law has a "hegemonic hold on social life." The judiciary only further systematizes and rationalizes the rule of law and imprints it with a "seal of universality." The judiciary and the legal profession provide an "ontological glorification" of the law. They use law to maintain or reproduce social and political relations and ensure civil peace. Again in the words of Bourdieu, in modern regimes "the power of the law is special. It extends beyond the circle of those who are already believers by virtue of the practical affinity uniting them with interests and values fundamental to legal texts and to the ethical and political inclinations of those who have the responsibility of applying them."[6] All Americans, in the words of Stuart Scheingold, "believe that politics *is and should be* conducted in accordance with patterns of rights and obligations established under law."[7] Thus, the public is obligated to follow the law.

The American Commitment to Rule-Based Politics

The American reverence for the Constitution discloses the power of law in American life. The Constitution is a legal plan for the organization of public offices, the constraint of some forms of official power, the creation of authority for the exercise of other forms of official power, the establishment of official accountability to the electorate, and the guarantee of enforceable rights to citizens. The influence of the Constitution, however, goes far beyond its text. The symbolic power of the Constitution, a transcendent faith in the foundational law, permeates American politics. The faith is not a premodern reverence for the body of a sovereign person or the institutions of a religion; it is a modern faith in the legal forms and organizational principles of a text. It is the vision of the Constitution as a legally, normatively, and spiritually higher law. The Constitution has gained its symbolic influence especially because of the Framers' talk of the document as creating a New Order for the Ages, as well as Civil War era talk of a perpetual Union sealed by the blood of dead soldiers, and twentieth-century talk of a charter of human freedom that provides freedom from want and fear at home and serves as a model for liberty across the oceans.[8]

What is the source of the special, almost magical, role of the Constitution in American political practice and belief? The answer is found in the deontological—rule-based—theory of being and political order developed by European thinkers in the seventeenth and eighteenth centuries. These thinkers, identified here as Enlightenment liberals, presented a deontological theory of being that posited a political order drawing on a theory of ideal natural liberty expressed in either an abstract social contract or in obligatory, a priori universal principles about the necessity of rational and autonomous human choices for a moral life. Also, political thinkers with a deontological perspective implied that persons can construct certain truthful moral rules—essential or foundational rules or a rule of law—from the assumed definition of liberty in the contract or from the a priori principles.[9] The derivative principles include the legal duties and rights extracted from the contract or transcendent principles by the individual, using "Reason, which is able to instruct him in the Law he is to govern himself by."[10]

Influenced by Enlightenment liberal philosophers, the American Founders integrated the deontological perspective into American politics. Adopting a contractual model for the foundation of the regime, they drafted a Constitution to order the natural liberty of persons. They regarded the Constitution as a fundamental law containing, by popular consent, the intentions of the people about the control of political power.[11] In formal terms, the Constitution was the objective statement of the social contract's principles. Presumed to be a compact among the people, a document in which the people ceded some of their natural rights, it provided a written text describing in legal terms their agreement on the scope of their natural liberty and the way in which reason could be applied to benefit public affairs and the common good. Within the boundaries of the text and other rules of law derived in conjunction with it, persons could express their natural freedom or interests. Liberty, or exercises of personal autonomy, could exist only within the law; all other exercises of personal choice were "license." Consequently, constitutional argument became the critical methodology for establishing a vision of a good polity and creating appropriate rules to protect personal liberty and civil peace. The government of laws constructed by "reflection and choice" replaced deference to gentry, priests, or "accident and force."[12] The foundational Constitution and its requirement of rule by law was to provide order and reasoned procedures through which human potential might be fulfilled and political action could be directed toward a more enlightened future order.[13]

After the Founding, the definition of American constitutional principles was quickly expropriated by the judiciary. Aided by lawyer-politicians such as Alexander Hamilton and John Marshall, the judiciary developed a hegemony over the interpretation of the Constitution and over the scope of policymaking by all other governmental institutions. To uncover the meaning of the Constitution, they applied the methodologies of the legal craft which were applicable to all legal interpretation. Because of a fear of disorder, other imaginative normative perspectives on politics were excluded from legitimate conversation.[14] American politics came more and more to center on a faith in the political sufficiency and moral efficacy of the rule of law.

Scalia and Rule-Based Politics

Antonin Scalia has signaled his faith in a rule-based politics in almost all of his opinions. As evidenced by opinions laden with comments on the rule of law, he has felt a need to defend the theoretical certainty of law and legal relations. He has stressed an obligation to play by the rules to prevent chaos and ensure civil peace. As he commented in a speech at Rutgers University in Newark, the law would be a "reflection or product" of the values of a "good society." Law would rest on the good society's transcendent rules of moral responsibility, for "laws are more a manifestation and a product of a good society than they are the cause of it," and "legal constraint, the opposite of freedom, is in most of its manifestations a cure for human advice [sic] or folly."[15] However, he has recognized the need for the discipline of liberty to prevent disorder. As he indicated in a speech at Harvard University, "The Rule of Law as a Law of Rules," the task of the judge was to announce a "firm rule of decision."[16] Rules of law, especially the U.S. Constitution, would promote a world free of chaos and a world in which personal liberty and natural autonomy might be achieved. Thus, the first theme in his constitutive discourse has been the requirement that clear legal standards define the scope of governmental power.

Relying on these assumptions about the law, Scalia's separated powers opinions have employed rules to constrain officials of the state and have aspired to extend the rule of law in public sector management and decisionmaking processes. In particular, he has used bright-line legal rules rather than pragmatic judicial adjustment of relations among the branches to signal his commitment to a state disciplined by the rule of law. Although balancing is a discretionary method of judicial choice loosely based on legal rules, it has simply not been legalistic enough for him.[17] Discrete rules of law alone, he has contended, can preserve a functioning political order and preserve freedom. For example, in *Morrison v. Olson* he defended his legal arguments on separated governmental powers as necessary "to preserve individual freedom" from officials exercising uncontrolled power.[18] Unlike James Madison (in Federalist Paper No. 51), he did not offer a normative defense for the distribution of institutionalized political power based on suppositions about the factional nature of political leaders.

In his federalism opinions, Scalia has stated that stable precedent, bright-line legal doctrines, and rules about the role of courts could police the powers of government. According to his opinions, Congress can regulate federal-state relations by specific statutes based on constitutional clauses, and courts should avoid more overtly political pragmatic judgments. Beyond this robust faith in a legally defined politics of intergovernmental relations, Scalia's opinions have conveyed two other normative messages. First, his message of federal preeminence has diminished the potential of state governments to act as independent defenders of public liberties. The lesson of his opinions has been that the primary generation of beneficial policies and the protection of liberties should come from the Constitution and federal law. State governments can create or supplement policies that improve persons' lives, but the ordering of liberty preeminently rests in the hands of Congress. It is the duty of Congress to represent either majority sentiments or the whirl of interest groups that provides the laws and rules that define the regime and that affect the range of judicial authority. If persons sense problems in the operation of the regime, the problem resides with Congress.[19]

Second, Scalia has not conceptualized federalism as a normative statement about the political value of decentralized political power. Rather, in his opinions federalism is a constitutional and legal construct relatively devoid of meaning except insofar as it serves as a means of assigning administrative and legislative duties among governmental units. For example, in both *Agency Holding* and *Union Gas* he offered his views on state sovereignty at length, indicating that division of federal and state governmental power was based on the need to control the authority of courts and not on other political concerns.[20] Thus, despite his attention to the boundaries of judicial power, he has left federal and state governmental institutions free to make policy.

Scalia's opinions about the Equal Protection Clause and civil rights statutes have deployed "neutral" legal standards in an attempt to prevent most alterations in the allocation of power between the majority and racial minorities and other disadvantaged groups. He has scorned minority efforts at an adjustment—and even an application—of the strict scrutiny doctrine to racial classifications, as in *Richmond v. Croson* and *Adarand Constructors*. He has rebuffed gender-conscious readings of Title VII of the Civil Rights Act of 1964—for instance, the majority opinion in *Johnson v. Transportation Agency*—which adopted a more pragmatic attitude about the fit of legal standards and affirmative action programs.[21] He has held that the pragmatic reliance on social facts—such as the general patterns of discrimination by government used to support the affirmative action plans challenged in *Croson* and *Adarand Constructors* or the use of role model theory in *Johnson v. Transportation Agency*—is legally inapplicable or illogical. Scalia's message, restated in his school desegregation remedy and Title VII opinions, has been that individuals are responsible for proving the harms against them by presenting eyewitness or physical evidence.[22] Other facts and normative concerns, including the subtle uses of power to manipulate and induce subjection, have escaped his view of racial and gender relations. His world would feature allegedly neutral laws that ensure that autonomous individuals would rise or fall on their own merit. In a decisive act, neutral law would forget human differences, vanquish history, and erase racist cultural traditions.

Scalia's opinions in cases involving freedom of expression have defended a legally ordered expression of ideas. Nevertheless, by limiting the generality, or scope, of First Amendment rights to a narrowly defined range of expressions, as in *Employment Division v. Smith,* and by refusing to recognize the communicative nature of almost all human actions, as in *Barnes v. Glen Theatre,* Scalia has tried to expand the space for state regulatory actions.[23] His justification for expanded regulatory power has been the law he thought was "clear" in constitutional text and in selected legal precedents. Constitutional text coupled with the political majority's statutes defining the need to control expression has resulted in his definition of limits on expressive liberty. This regulation was in tune with the idea of the rule of law as a device for ordering liberty. Only rules of law that created overbroad restrictions on speech and that penalized some individual's expression because of its content did not survive his analysis.

In his opinions on criminal cases, Scalia has indicated his commitment to the ideas of the rule of law and procedural justice. And in concert with his faith in the rule of law, he has refused to read extra-constitutional principles into the criminal law. Therefore, he has declined to support new procedures about courtroom confrontations, the severity of sentences, prison conditions, and the penalty phase of capital cases. According to Scalia, criminal law has to follow longstanding rules—otherwise, he has implied, arbitrariness will creep into criminal processes and affect both defendants' rights and public interests in civil peace. His criminal law opinions have been not inattentive to defendants' rights. He has supported some bans on warrantless searches, the *Miranda* requirements, the physical confrontation of witnesses, and the protection against double jeopardy.[24] In some opinions he has imposed discipline on the way in which the government can prosecute cases, and he has required police and prosecutorial professionals to respect the privacy and body of the defendant. However, in other opinions he has used rules to teach persons lessons about the evil of license and, indirectly, to promote a retributive regimen of death or incarceration against the criminal.

Although rule-based politics implies a renunciation of unwritten traditions, Scalia's substantive due process opinions have used selected legal precedents and the long-familiar conventions and routines of the legal profession. In his sense, tradition is the rational, modern practice of the judicial construction of opinions that link decisions with normative commitment to the rule of law. For example, the use of the "most specific tradition" sanctioned in the *Michael H.* footnote did more than offer a clear legal rule for the resolution of a case; it contained language about the acceptable normative dimensions of society.[25] For Scalia, tradition, in its "most specific sense," has been little more than the application of longstanding rules of law. This use of tradition has allowed him to avoid visible value choices. He has accepted the idea that existing precedent and law rest on clear, theoretically certain normative principles. He has not bothered with any further search for extralegal normative justification for these principles. He has assumed that the tradition he identified was normatively correct.[26] As indicated by his refusal to use moral theory or pragmatic judgment, he has not questioned the theoretical certainty of law.

Consequently, Scalia has used those precedents that define the protection of property as essential for human self-realization and prosperity and that subject the bodies of women and the dying to the authority of the state. His practice has conserved normative themes about liberty, order, privilege, and patriarchy embedded in historical rules of law and legal procedures. His effort has allowed him to avoid philosophical discussion of the morality of abortion, the right to die, and the meaning of autonomy of the body by stating that legal tradition required someone else to decide the matter or that legal texts already had decided the matter.[27]

Besides confirming the American faith in legalized politics and, consequently, restricting normative debate about the distribution of political power, Scalia has stated two additional tenets that reinforce the constitutive dimension of American law. First, he has advanced a definition of the scope of the public sector and the range of issues subject to political action and governmental control under the rule of law. Second, he has accentuated the discipline that government and private parties should impose on licentious acts threatening the public order and on private liberty provided by the rule of law.

THE DIMENSIONS OF PUBLIC AND PRIVATE POWER

"Ordered liberty," a vision of the political universe, was a central aim of the authors of the Constitution.[28] The Founders desired liberty for social interaction and the fulfillment of individual ends in time, but they also thought that the exercise of liberty outside the law could be dangerous. Their abstract idea of liberty protected by a written constitution presupposed that the formation and self-direction of persons' individuality and sociability—their emotions, intellect, metaphysics, property, art, and culture—occurred only within the boundaries of a political space defined by law. Their Constitution assumed that a well-ordered state would prevent excesses of official power that infringed on individual liberty. Also, it would provide under law the space to search for individual material prosperity and the development of individual moral sentiments.

Constitutional interpretation of rights further contributed to the definition of the public and the private spaces of the regime. The separation of the public and private sectors, validated through a national history of the legal defense of property and personal privacy rights, became a principle of American politics.[29] Because the Constitution concerned itself mostly with laws and rights that limited governmental activity dangerous to natural liberty, the judiciary was often unconcerned with the compulsions arising from private exercises of power. Thus, private persons could exercise power over other private persons in contexts of employment, the family, eleemosynary institutions, and professional, therapeutic, contractual, and casual interpersonal relationships. The Constitution allowed conflicts about the private misuse of power in these settings to be controlled by a framework of political institutions. The regime provided *remedies* against the misuse of private power primarily through the state's criminal, regulatory, and tort law. However, most acts of power by one private person against another demanded that the adversely affected party gain access to a court or an executive agency to adjudicate the dispute; these legal remedies assigned courts and lawyers a central role in the control of private uses of power. Courts and lawyers came to possess important powers to determine whether adverse private uses of power received a public remedy under legislative acts. If the legislature had established no remedy, it could create one, as with the common law of personal injury. More commonly, they would accept the private dominator's claim that his action had been moral, the product of the "laws" of the marketplace or the science of a profession, or of justifiable self-help undertaken to regulate family life or to defend a naturally privileged status.[30] Consequently, the constitutional regime was an incomplete system of rules that left some exercises of power outside of public control.

Scalia has recognized that the rule of law defines the scope and limits of state power and, by default, establishes a zone of private space or liberty. However, the second theme in his constitutive discourse is the need to adjust this boundary. He has been receptive to a greater exercise of state power over private expression and the body. In his opinions on the powers of the branches, he has tended to empower the state because he assumes that it represents the political majority. For example, his treatment of agencies' discretion has expanded the power of administrators to define the scope of private economic choices. His hostility to interest group intervention in administration and possible interest group coloring of legislative history has restricted private participation and influence over the state. Conversely, his pattern of deference to and selective review of legislative actions has encouraged the legislative majority to make precise definitions of state and private power within the confines of the Constitution and legal tradition.[31] These opinions, as well as his opinions on the scope of rights, such as *Employment Division v. Smith, Barnes v. Glen Theatre,* and his substantive due process opinions, have argued for a modification of the differentiation of public and private power appearing in the opinions of many of the justices.[32]

Scalia's federalism opinions have concentrated on the range of federal and state power, not the boundary between public and private power. However, in attending to selected aspects of the way in which race and gender affect life in America he has reconsidered the public-private boundary. In dicta attacking private affirmative action programs and in his *Powers v. Ohio* preemptory challenge opinion, he has proposed limits on public relief for discrimination caused by private uses of power.[33] Also, his opinions have refused to attack private discriminatory decisions, as in cases involving the effect of racial bias in residency opportunities on school segregation. Thus, he has found illegitimate the governmental encouragement of private affirmative action efforts, the creation of third-party standing in the preemptory challenge cases, and governmental efforts to ameliorate the public effects of private discrimination. In his opinions, government is to avoid interfering in private sector choices about human relations, employment, and the education of children. A wall of law can ensure the autonomy of private choices, even if private choices have harmed others through the perpetuation of racial or gender discrimination. For Scalia, drawing a legal line to protect personal autonomy has been more valuable than enforcement of equality by the state.

In fixing the boundaries of expressive freedoms, Scalia has tried to revise the line between expression in public places and expression in private places. He has allowed regulation of expression in public places to prevent the use of fighting words or to serve compelling governmental interests; however, his opinions on content-based expression would permit unregulated "private" personal campaign expenditures. These decisions have respected private expressive choices, but with regard to expression in public places, governments can impose time-place-manner regulations, commercial expression restrictions, and limitations on speech by on-duty public employees. His view of libel and defamation law and the operations of political parties has sought to carve out a space for private persons and organizations to control or at least threaten the expressions of other individuals.[34] His Establishment Clause opinions have encouraged judicial passivity in the face of efforts by private religious organizations to win special rewards from government, a special recognition that sometimes has offended other persons or religious organizations.[35] His opinions have indicated support for both public and private efforts to impose order on expression. Therefore, as he has indicated in his *Austin v. Michigan Chamber of Commerce*,[36] *McInytre v. Ohio Elections Commission*,[37] and Establishment Clause opinions, government and private parties can exercise partial control over the legality of expression.

Scalia's criminal justice opinions have attended to the power of the public sector to protect private rights. Yet, particularly by promoting a greater range of warrantless searches, he has sometimes diminished the constitutionally protected private sphere. However, as indicated by his treatment of the plain view cases and drug testing, he still has tried to affirm at least some private choice free of state power. Thus, he has supported at least some limits on governmental surveillance of private activity.[38] By relying on precedent, Scalia's Takings Clause decisions also have confined the authority of the state. However, his rule-based world has been one in which only selected aspects of human autonomy, such as real property, find a defense in the law. He has left other claims of autonomy, especially autonomy in the control of the body, to definition by political institutions.

Thus, Scalia has tried to reconstitute through law the popular perception of the boundary between public and private power. Although an Enlightenment liberal conception of zones of power is deeply embedded in the way in which Americans perceive and define the political, he wants a different narrative about the scope of law and the roles of persons as subjects of the law—one that conveys a message about the need for the public sector to police the license sought in the rights claims of disadvantaged classes, criminal defendants, pregnant women, and the dying. It is a message about the necessity of conserving public power over traditionally less powerful interests and reinforcing their subjection to the law and to the knowledge possessed by legal elites. It is a message that teaches beliefs about when and in what ways law or private persons are legitimate coordinators of social and political order.

THE DIMENSIONS OF LEGAL DISCIPLINE

It is not surprising that the practice of American constitutional law has been construed as limiting claims to liberty. The idea of legally ordered liberty assumes that disorderly human behavior can abuse political liberty and pose a danger to the fulfillment of individual and social capacities of other persons. Thus, American definitions of liberty have regarded arbitrary political decisions and the irrational display of passion and self-interest as destructive of liberty. Passion and self-interest let liberty degenerate into license and injustice. Injustice is identified as individual suffering resulting from personal license; from irrational institutional procedures or commands for allocating goods and services; or from the unethical or inequitable distribution of valued rights, entitlements, or possessions by others.[39]

The American constitutional faith assumes that injustice can be prevented through rationally designed laws. To control injustice, the regime must impose legal discipline on persons and organizations.[40] Therefore, Americans have come to recognize that liberty can only flourish if political injustice is disciplined by the rules of a written constitution acceded to by popular conventions and, secondarily, by statutes and common law. They have believed that law defends liberty by providing an institutionalized discipline on "the arts of designing men" and on "serious oppressions of the minor party in the community."[41] Also, law serves as a generally applicable body of rules to control or condemn private actions defined as unjust through a representative political process. Thus, law is also a command aimed at the rational ordering of a person's morality, character, social status, or psyche.[42] In the words of Stephen Macedo, a recent defender of a legally constituted regime,

> Law helps impart order to liberty by imposing on all free actions certain general conditions . . . and limits . . . that together create a system of mutual self-restraint harmonizing the freedom of each with the freedom of all . . . Law stands for a certain kind of order: the mutual observance of general, public rules and procedures. Liberal law not only establishes the ends and limits of power, it also provides a setting and structure for public justification. Indeed, the impartial, politically independent institution of the court provides a most promising setting in which to approach the reasoned reflection required by justification.[43]

Like Macedo, many other Americans have assumed that the law employed by independent courts provides an impartial, reasoned, and justifiable solution to conflicts about the nature of personal liberty. The disciplinary character of the law, most evident in the constitutional provision of "police" powers or regulatory powers, implies violence or repression of some personal actions. However, the defenders of constitutional politics assume that the violence of the law or of related repression of behavior is good and legitimate when it is a publicly sanctioned penalty against abusers of ordered individual liberty, and when it "maintains, confirms, insures the permanence and enforceability of the law."[44] Again like Macedo, most Americans have assumed that lawbreaking is an illegitimate effort that offends the liberties of individuals. They assume that law disciplines factional or self-interested behavior. Conversely, a disciplinary law creates legitimate punishments for such disorderly behavior. These sanctions are an "economic" use of violence, or a legitimate, judicious application of violent and coercive force as a technique toward the regularization of human behavior. Such a "responsible," "virtuous," and "normal" use of legal discipline is presumed to prevent more destructive violence and revenge, while purifying the regime of corruption.[45]

Despite the popular assumptions about the benefits of legal discipline, disciplinary acts have another face. Two decades ago, Stuart Scheingold illustrated how the "myth" of American constitutional rights served as a political resource for group efforts challenging the political status quo and pressures for social conformity. He summarized the way in which Americans viewed constitutional rights both as a limit on legislative power and as a resource for use in litigation expanding individual liberty. Although today interest group leaders have accepted the use of constitutional rights as a political resource, Scheingold indicated that interest groups' uses of legal rights as a political resource do not always end with emancipatory political change. Often the judiciary is resistant to group strategies, so he concluded that "law . . . serves the status quo in a kind of dual capacity. Legal processes are closely linked to the dominant configurations of power. At the same time, in its ideological incarnation, the law induces acquiescence in the established order by suggesting that the political system is beneficent and adaptable." John Brigham, elaborating on Scheingold's ideas about law and the politics of rights, found that the language of the Constitution defined the range of political actions and the resources available for political groups seeking greater freedom. Timothy O'Neill concluded an analysis of metaphors in equal protection law by noting that the legal language employed by the judiciary in equal protection cases had narrowed the issues considered in political equality debates, simplified complex political relationships, and impoverished public understanding of political controversies.[46] Thus, constitutional law prevented serious challenges to the existing distribution of power in the American regime. Scheingold, Brigham, and O'Neill sensed that judicial decisions about rights are more often about the creation of stability in the distribution of political power and the discipline of threats to powerholders than about the expansion of political liberty. They asserted that law and judicial interpretations of law supported dominant configurations of political power and limited the agenda of claims about political liberties.

Consequently, a judiciary that responds to powerful or legally adroit claimants can foreclose consideration of injustices through a policy of neglect or through choices harming the normative aspirations and interests of persons.[47] Courts also can refuse to offer public remedies when a person alleges a disadvantage resulting from a private use of power. Judicial definitions of law thus allow the discipline of individuals *both* by the legislative police power and by powerful persons exercising their authority in the private sphere. Thus, when added to the general faith in rule-based politics, judicial discipline constitutes persons as "legal subjects" who think of themselves in ways defined by law and whose human relationships are defined by law, the relatively autonomous power of the courts and the legal profession, and the centers of political power that can direct law to the advantage of a few interests.

The disciplinary nature of American law—which makes conduct a matter of rule following and determines political and moral duties by the explication of rules of law—is embedded in Scalia's opinions. His opinions have reinforced the power of those persons who envision politics as rule-based. Thus, he "resists and disqualifies alternative accounts of social reality."[48] The result is the third theme of his constitutive discourse: deference to the police powers of government and officially sanctioned private exercise of control over other private persons. However, the nature of the disciplinary message in his opinions has varied as he has addressed different issues.

Although Scalia has interpreted the Constitution to defend the rights of some disadvantaged classes, including groups victimized by overbroad restrictions on expression, protestors burning flags, defendants incapable of confronting witnesses against them, and individuals facing double jeopardy, he has often used law to discipline persons and define how they are subjected to the law. His legal attitudes have also inclined him to support the legal discipline imposed by governmental institutions other than the judiciary and by the possessors of real estate and other economic assets. When expressed through the language of Reasoned Elaboration jurisprudence, his cultural and professional attitudes are converted into a legal message favoring majorities even when the majority might be factional or engaged in efforts to vindicate "some common impulse of passion, or of interest, adverse to the rights of other citizens, or to the permanent and aggregate interest of the community."[49] At the same time, both majorities and minorities are made the subjects of laws that identify and discipline their power and liberties in most of their everyday activities.

For heuristic purposes, the messages of Scalia's opinions justifying disciplinary uses of judicial power can be spaced along a continuum that indicates the form of political discipline legitimated in those opinions. Near one end of the continuum are opinions that legitimate the use of power to command, suppress, and manipulate persons, a practice identified here as physical violence and manipulative repression. Nearer the other end of the continuum are opinions that extend legal domination and discipline of persons through the construction of knowledge, ideology, and preference, a practice identified here as symbolic violence and subjection.

Physical Violence

Whether or not justified by law, violence is a means toward the constitution of political order and the definition of political space.[50] As a constitutive process, violence is marked by the imposition of power, power that is colored by the vice of cruelty or inhuman treatment. Physical violence is not necessarily an extralegal activity; it is a form of discipline that disregards the liberty of others. It is the desecration of personal freedom—by the destruction of aspects of persons' physical being or body—in order to impose social and political restraints on personal license. Physical violence thus teaches or reinforces the belief that persons need to be subject to the law.

Physical violence can be a result of the practice of constitutional interpretation and an expression of judicial disciplinary authority. Such violence includes a variety of destructive acts and injurious form of abuses imposed by judges on the bodies of others.[51] When the judiciary employs its power to require capital punishment or to assign physical pain or physical marks that coerce people or deny their liberty, it supports the exercise of physical violence by the state. Robert Cover first described the ways in which the judiciary and others in the judiciary used the rule of law to sanction physical pain or death and to communicate a message about the consequences of deliberate harms of others. He claimed that judges distanced themselves from the use of violence by rigidly separating the act of judicial interpretation of the law of the state from the enforcement of that interpretation through violence, especially the violence associated with criminal sentences.[52] The act of violence thus became justifiable because the proper interpretation of the language of the law demanded it. The interpreter was set apart from responsibility because he or she could blame the regime for the violence and because he or she did not personally commit the violence.

The physically violent but lawful public act today is epitomized by the imposition of the death penalty. It is a tangible tale of the power of law. However, American law also sometimes allows the inscription of public power through physical marks on bodies. For example, according to one federal judge it was lawful for a public institution, the Citadel, in South Carolina, to mark its authority over its first female student by requiring her to have her head shaved.[53] Although the haircut was of temporary duration and was less physically harmful than branding, tattooing, caning, and other acts of public violence that have been inflicted on bodies, it inscribed the authority of the state on the student. The haircut was justified by judicial reference to the demands of equal protection, and was itself a lesson about public authority.[54]

Beginning with these considerations about law and physical violence in the public sphere, Austin Sarat and Thomas Kearns explored judges' efforts to conceal behind a cloak of legal interpretation the physical violence accomplished by some of their choices. The reason for the concealment, they argued, was that the dominant mode of legal interpretation adopts a policy of "forgetting" violence. They found that Anglo-American jurisprudence is so caught up with the identification and explication of rules that create an objective or neutral law that it covers up or ignores the physical pain or marks it permits and validates.[55] The concern with the assurance of a reasonable and consistent normative content to the law, necessary for the preservation of a body of standards by which to assess the conflicts assigned to the judiciary, has obstructed most judges from looking at the physical pain or marks they have inflicted. They have regarded pain as but misfortune caused by the rational solution of legal conflicts; pain was not a product of the force of law.[56]

The forgetting of the physical violence in the disciplinary message of public legal acts also frees private persons to discipline others. For example, in his study of the law of slavery Cover points out how the law sought an autonomy that neglected the private violence of master against slave.[57] Today, the criminal law of the state excuses some acts of private physical violence, including those of parent against child, property occupant against home invader, and teacher against student.[58] Consequently, physical violence is sometimes a lawful expression indicating the disciplinary character of the law and the power of the persons who define the rules. However, perhaps because persons are ashamed of cruelty, the language of due process and legal neutrality camouflages the physical violence and the marks on bodies that law engenders. In the words of Niklas Luhmann, "Physical violence accompanies the law like a shadow."[59]

In tune with the American idea that law is emancipatory and protective, Scalia's treatment of issues such as punitive damages and the *Feres* doctrine has permitted private persons to seek remedies for both state and private sector acts that exacted violence on their bodies.[60] But Scalia's opinions have encouraged the public and private discipline of expression. When he conceded the regulatory power to legislatures in the peyote-eating and nude-dancing cases, it led to probable physical violence against the expressive parties. Persons became prisoners if they participated in a sleep-in protest, ate peyote, or danced without a G-string and pasties. If they used fighting words to express their attitudes about politics, religion, and sex, the harm of incarceration in the physically violent world of an American prison faced them. Scalia would have placed their bodies in jeopardy if not in pain.

Much more bluntly, Scalia's death penalty opinions have presented his message about the capacity of judges to impose physical violence. His opinions have argued for the necessity of the efficient application of physical violence against the convicted criminal, but the opinions have exhibited a normative hollowness. The individual has been forgotten in the discussion in his opinions; the opinions have been discussions of legal texts and traditions to justify the choices of political majorities. Scalia's aim has been the routine and stable application of the law, not the creation of a death-is-different jurisprudence based on moral assumptions about the unique character of capital punishment. Thus, in cases on notice, jury selection, evidence, and judicial review in capital cases, he has spoken of law but not the offender.[61] Indeed, by ignoring the possible relevance of diminished capacity in cases involving the capital punishment of offenders, he has simply disregarded consideration of social facts about the person in favor of what, for him, is a bloodless imposition of physical violence. Also, as revealed in his opinions on the proportionality of sentences and the conditions of incarceration, what has mattered to Scalia is the integrity and reasonableness of the law.[62] Especially because his opinions have said little about the morality of the treatment of convicted persons, his rule-based decisions have forgotten the violence of life in prisons and the effects of exposure to that violence on the bodies and psyches of offenders.

Scalia's judicial passivity sometimes has excused state and private acts of physical violence. In his abortion and right-to-die opinions, he has read the rules of standing and jurisdiction to extend state control over the bodies of persons.[63] Thus, the state can define the pain that pregnant and dying persons must shoulder. In these opinions, he has sought to legitimate the disciplinary norms of the law without inquiry into social facts. He has authorized discipline both by the state and by private persons. For example, his abortion and *Cruzan* right-to-die opinions have disregarded the physical and emotional pain they inflict on persons. His concern has been about the use of judicial power. It has been an antiseptic way of avoiding the real consequences of decisions—letting state governments impose pain on woman and child rather than the fetus. Likewise, his *Cruzan* opinion used texts and precedent to let the states decide when persons should suffer in pain rather than control their pain themselves or through decisions by their families. Again the opinion was antiseptic and inattentive to the emotional dimensions of the pain perhaps experienced by Cruzan and her family.[64] He also has ignored discussion of the social facts of the abortion decision, and he has avoided the messy business of sorting out controversies about the pain to the woman of an unwanted pregnancy, the pain potentially in the future of an unwanted child, and the pain visited on the aborted fetus.

Manipulative Repression

Repression is the process by which the holders of power try to exclude unacceptable desires or impulses from expression in political space. Repression exhibits disregard for the liberty claims of others, but, unlike physical violence, it disciplines the use of political space without coercion of the body. Instead, in the form identified here as manipulative repression, it involves the use of power to manipulate persons so they do not make claims to liberty. Through law they are actively educated or coerced to "accept their role in the existing order of things, either because they can see or imagine no alternative to it, or because they see it as natural and unchangeable."[65] Manipulative repression does not assume the complicity of the subjugated classes. Instead, powerholders attempt to control reluctant classes and induce dependency through active efforts that go beyond the propagation of a myth about the nature of social and political power. The constitutive message is that freedom will be restricted if personal behavior does not conform with law.

Manipulative repression exists in several specific judicial actions affecting the public and private spheres, including exploitation, marginalization, patriarchal restrictions on political participation, and cultural imperialism.[66] *Exploitation* exists when a group is deprived of material benefits or economic status and the deprivation is defended through legalisms employed by the judiciary. The various statutes enforcing involuntary servitude by blacks which flourished in southern states in the late nineteenth century serve as an extreme example of exploitation. These statutes repeatedly denied income to blacks and reassigned it to their white employers or the state government. The courts used the euphemisms of the liberty of contract, the criminal law, and other legal language to mask the inequality of the economic exchange and to justify the exercise of private power and the subsequent suffering of the blacks.[67] The appearance of arguments about possessory rights, contractual duties, future interests, and duties to act reasonably across a range of civil actions also masked the exercise of private power. Their arguments allowed a range of exploitative acts by those holding material resources and permitted private control of employment conditions and of the associated welfare of employees.

Marginalization and *patriarchy* relegate a group to an inferior status. This marked group then faces denial of equal material or political rights. Marginalization and patriarchy, for example, occurred when the Supreme Court upheld a statute denying pregnant women who received Medicaid benefits the opportunity to use their benefits to secure their right to an abortion in the first trimester. When the Supreme Court upheld the constitutionality of the statute it effectively excluded poor women—unless they became dependent on the largess of family, friends, or charities—from full access to a right available to other citizens.[68] Also, poor women were left to suffer the psychic and physical consequences of an unwanted pregnancy, which wealthier women could readily avoid.

Restrictions on political participation create the inability to discuss public policy choices, serve in public institutions, and influence the selection of political leaders. For example, American laws, supported by Supreme Court decisions, long banned jury service by women and rendered them unable to participate in an act of representative government.[69] Disrespect and a feeling of inferiority can result when people are unable to participate in public decisions and realize a sense of civic worth. *Cultural imperialism* is found in laws that perpetuate the culture of one group while restricting the expression of cultural values by other groups. An example is the Supreme Court decision in *United States v. Lee,* which required Amish employers to contribute to the Social Security program despite the claim of the Amish that they should be exempted because of their cultural values requiring mutual assistance and abhorring governmental transfer payments. The Amish suffered psychically because they could not express the unique social relationships and shared values that defined their culture.[70]

The perception of manipulative repression can cause individuals or groups to react with expressions of rage at government or with subversion and insurgency against the politically dominant in the private sphere. To prevent expressions of rage or subversion, the judiciary can make tactical modifications of the law. To quell rage, they can rein-terpret the law, lift the repression, and offer the dominated group the same legal status as the dominant political interests. For example, the Supreme Court eliminated legal disabilities against blacks by the aban-donment of the separate-but-equal doctrine in a series of cases begin-ning with *Brown v. Board of Education*.[71] Nevertheless, the judiciary can reaffirm the domination of the subject group. An example is the continuation of the marginalization of homosexuals which resulted from the Supreme Court's legitimation of state criminal laws against sodomy.[72] American constitutional law provides no sure guarantee against repression because many judges tolerate it or deny its existence.

In opinions about judicial power, Scalia's conception of law has sup-ported some acts of manipulative repression by the state. For example, he has marginalized some claimants, especially ecological interest groups in the *Lujan* environmental standing cases, and he has made it difficult for them to mobilize state power to avert harms to the environ-ment.[73] His opinions limiting standing to sue, enforcing the jurisdic-tional limits on judicial and agency power, and limiting information accessible under the Freedom of Information Act have further limited political participation by some citizens.[74] His FOIA opinions have at-tempted to restrict information that persons might use in political or legal efforts to avoid their marginalization.

Scalia's belief that neutral law can best change discriminatory atti-tudes rests on the assumption that law can discipline or eradicate invidious forms of discrimination. However, his idea of neutral law has fostered a form of manipulative repression that has blunted the efforts of disadvantaged classes to overcome their relative marginalization in the economy. In particular, his efforts to make affirmative action and racial preference programs legally untenable have curtailed the claims of disadvantaged classes to employment and the power that accom-panies financial independence in America. He has failed to help recon-struct racially and sexually constructed political and economic power relationships in the regime. His restrictions on the use of civil rights suits, the introduction of social-scientific evidence of the dependent status of racial minorities and women as classes, and the remedies available to eliminate discrimination (e.g., affirmative action pro-grams) have constrained political and judicial challenges to white or male power in the state and private enterprise.[75] His construction of the Voting Rights Act has not fostered chances for more power for the disadvantaged, especially in the judicial institutions of the public sector.[76] Instead, he has left disadvantaged classes to their own devices in changing the conditions that made them marginalized and incapable of effective political participation.

Scalia's opinions have made it difficult for many parties to challenge the authority of the state to regulate expression. Using the language of legal texts, these opinions have taught lessons about when persons must resign themselves to their fate at the hands of judges rather than express their political interests. In his effort to proscribe speech and other expressive acts that violated neutral criminal laws, reasonable contextual regulations, or libel and defamation laws, he has used legal text and precedent to marginalize or prevent speech and political acts. His obscenity rulings have marginalized the ideas of selected individuals. By relying on the pandering rule, he has failed to demand intensified scrutiny of publications, and he has effectively marginalized the business practices of "adult" enterprises without having to employ an obscenity standard or a strict scrutiny standard. Additionally, Scalia has desired to marginalize offensive but not necessarily harmful acts such as electioneering near the polls, Tupperware parties on public property, and political criticism by public employees. Although his opinions in cases on these issues and others rested on the principles of Reasoned Elaboration, including deference to legislative choices and the will of the majority, they all failed to consider the repression buried in deference to the majority's notion of civic order. In these cases, a public employee's innocent if offensive comments about a political figure and a Tupperware party planned to raise money for college expenses became the subjects of state control.[77] Scalia's opinions, especially those allowing limitations on expression for contextual reasons, have manipulated individuals into suffering because they have required deference to the interests and attitudes embedded in a law. The result of these opinions was that he has deprecated the value of some ideas, especially about drugs and sex, as well as actively repressed their expression.

At the same time he has asserted the legitimacy of expressions of other ideas—cross burning, antiabortion protests, creation science, animal sacrifice, graduation prayers, and separate public schools for a religious organization's children. Although *R.A.V. v. St. Paul* and *Church of the Lukumi Babalu Aye* protected the content of political and moral expression,[78] they did so within a narrow range. However, he supported potentially dangerous expressive acts (in *Madsen v. Women's*

Health Center),[79] indirect tax subsidization of religious publications, the special role of political parties as associations, political patronage, and laws accommodating religious actions in public facilities or providing special public assistance to religious organizations.[80] Thus, Scalia has appeared to be manipulating expression to reward interest groups that he deems to be legitimate speakers. His opinions have legitimated some practices of manipulative repression. For example, his *Austin v. Michigan Chamber of Commerce* opinion allowed private parties the opportunity to use money in an effort to manipulate information and decrease the chance for persons to make informed choices.[81] Because he refused to recognize the effects of economic power on communication, he granted private interests the power to dominate discussion, an essential feature of democracy. Despite the power of corporate political action committees, he assumed that any virtuous citizen should be able to find out about politics. He neglected the way in which the exploitation of communications by economic interests tended to skew information costs and prevented citizens from having ready access to all political discussions. In effect, he converted the strict scrutiny test from a protection of the disadvantaged into an instrument for the exploitation and expropriation of political discussion and the policy agenda by the powerful. Thus, he has sanctioned private efforts to destroy the ability of disadvantaged citizens to make an independent interpretation of the political world.

In cases in which texts and precedents justified it, Scalia's criminal law opinions have left the defendant open to repression by the state. His *Hodari D.* opinion on the scope of seizures, his *Minnick v. Mississippi* and *McNeil v. Wisconsin* opinions on the scope of *Miranda* rules, and his *Grady v. Corbin* opinion on double jeopardy have allowed the state to use evidence toward the prosecution of persons.[82] As indicated by the pragmatic liberal justices' opinions in these cases, his opinions have expressed approval of criminal procedures designed to marginalize and disempower suspects. He has advantaged the state as it prosecuted the suspect.

The *Michael H.* case exhibited Scalia's willingness to allow manipulative repression to seep into the law. In *Michael H.* he marginalized the claim of the natural father and left him incapable of gaining access to his daughter.[83] In *Reno v. Flores* he rendered illegal alien children powerless and allowed their incarceration.[84] In both cases the parties claimed a substantive right, but by excluding this kind of right from his opinions Scalia left the parties with their suffering. The state was allowed to marginalize illegal alien children and the father of an illegitimate child.

Symbolic Violence

Symbolic violence distinguishes a situation in which knowledge of the overt message in the law has turned persons into subjects of politically dominant groups or institutions.[85] It is a situation in which the power of belief in the law prevents people from exercising their liberty. The effort at control originates within the legal profession and private centers of power. Because of efforts by the judiciary to conceal legal discipline through symbolic devices such as the language of legal impartiality and the idea of precedent, members of the subjugated group do not consciously perceive the domination. They are complicit in their own domination because they fail to recognize that the origin of their suffering is inherent in their beliefs. They remain unwilling to challenge myths lodged in rule-based politics, such as the myth of the neutral impartiality of law, because of a fear of uncertainty, internalized attitudes about the nature of reality or legality, or fear of social conflict if the reality of their lack of power is verbalized. They take the world for granted; its politics is legitimate. Drawing on the myth of the neutrality of law and coupling it with an assertion of their own interpretive neutrality, the judiciary can assign blame for unequal liberties and suffering. Through constitutional interpretation, judges can assign blame for restrictions on liberty to misfortune, or to the subjugated group's behavior. For example, a right to free speech is curtailed not because of a judicial decision but because a party threatened immediate civil violence that violated a rule. The myth of the impartiality of the constitutional law provides legitimacy for the hegemony of the state and dominant groups and curtails political discussion about the suffering of the disadvantaged.[86] Moreover, laws and judicial opinions consecrate and reproduce the relationship of domination in new contexts. Symbolic violence thus attempts to destroy the independent interpretation of the world by the subjugated group, it censors any political discussion of their suffering, and it reaffirms their status as legal subjects.

Alexis de Tocqueville first outlined the nature and sources of symbolic violence. He defined it as the subjugation of people to governmental leaders which arises when the people are equal and are interested in the procurement of the "petty and paltry pleasures, with which they glut their lives." In this situation government becomes an "immense and tutelary power, which takes it upon itself to watch after their fate." Through laws the government proceeds to ensure order and economic security in the regime and becomes a "shepherd" that regulates society through numerous rules. Civic virtues slide into decline as government regulates the minor details of life, and the public becomes capable of asserting its interests only at the occasional election.[87] The law of Tocqueville's "government by shepherd" is disciplinary because Tocqueville assumes that disadvantaged classes see their position as natural. Government actively inhibits action; it bends wills toward the goals of the political administration.

Tocqueville thought that the concept of equal rights can prevent rule by tyrants and despots but that equality also strengthens public passivity in the face of a disciplinary law. Equal rights protect people and allow them to satisfy personal material needs, but equal rights also isolate people and make them think of their own interests. This allows governmental officials the space to initiate uniform legal controls in the name of equality, without opposition from an isolated citizenry unconcerned with civic life. People act with little attention to the interests of others, and they leave the amelioration of harms and suffering to the administration and the courts. Justice is defined as "legalisms," and moral conduct becomes a matter of following government's laws.[88]

When legalisms are legitimate, the government, especially the judiciary, can define the language of a right so as to exclude recovery for acts of symbolic violence. The response of affected individuals to their exclusion is *resignation*. They suffer, but they do not rebel. Rebellion would threaten the social peace assured by the state and the habit of dependency. The habit of dependency, the belief that persons should obey the law because it is proper to do so, is a product of the regime's socialization of individuals in the propriety and fairness of the law and the political values it embodies.[89] The nineteenth-century and early-twentieth-century use of the common law standards on master and servant had this effect. According to Karen Orren, the judiciary evolved this law to fit its idea of the role of labor in a liberal regime. The legal rules it developed became a complex scheme for the discipline of workers—through the threat of job loss; employer control of pay and hours of labor; a rule giving an employer a property interest in employees' labor; bans on collective bargaining; the assistance of state officers in the enforcement of contracts; and the imposition of penalties by the state when a worker breached an employment contract. However, employers rarely had to use these tactics of control because many workers internalized the role of "servant" as described in the law. Despite some strikes, many of which resulted in violent suppressive actions by the government or resulted in additional laws to control workers, most of labor was passive. Law allowed the public sector both to "shepherd" labor and to define the legitimacy of private domination of labor. Many workers resigned themselves to the law. Even the unions, already often marginalized by the repressive content of laws, accommodated the law by abandoning confrontational actions against the master-servant rules.[90]

The stories of females subjected to gender discrimination retold by Kristin Bumiller exhibit another dimension of symbolic violence, the way in which law includes control by private persons. For Bumiller, symbolic violence persists not just because of people's habit of deference to the law but because of fear of the law. Despite civil rights laws, her subjects of private acts of gender discrimination failed to achieve any relief from illegal actions. According to Bumiller, the primary reason was that they chose to resist engagement in legal tactics "because they stand in awe of the power of the law to disrupt their daily lives. At the same time, they are cynical about the power of the law actually to help them secure the jobs, housing, and other opportunities they lay claim to. They fear that, if they seek a legal resolution, they will not improve their position but will lose control of a hostile situation."[91] For Bumiller's respondents the superintending power of the law left isolated individuals adrift and in fear of seeking any satisfactory relief for the violent desecration of their lives by discrimination. Fear of submitting their claims to the judiciary shepherded these women into suffering.[92]

Scalia's opinions on the powers of the governmental branches have established extensive discipline through symbolic violence. He has been concerned about ensuring public complicity with the use of power by the judiciary. His arguments for strict textual construction and procedural regularity, and against fundamental fairness precedents, have asserted the stability and neutrality of law. He has indicated that an uncertain law—whether a creation of agencies, Congress, or the courts—undermines faith in the existing legal order and popular complicity with the vision of the public sector conveyed by the courts. Hence, he has urged Congress to draft specific statutes and, in *Chevron* test cases, he has cautioned agencies to abide by statutory text.[93] In addition, he has espoused doctrines designed to induce public complicity with executive actions. He has sustained executive shepherding through a reinforcement of executive powers couched in legal language. He has made it difficult to challenge administrative actions and has sought to free executive policy choice from continuing criticism. His claims about the neutral content of law have been accompanied by the use of legal language to encourage faith or popular complicity in the legal order as defined by the judiciary.

Scalia's equal protection opinions have accepted as given the capacity of governments to make neutral laws, the ability of individuals to make autonomous choices, and the notion that merit defines persons' opportunities in life. As these standards have won acceptance with the Court's majority, he has encouraged popular complicity in legal standards that conceal symbolic violence against disadvantaged groups. Neutral laws alone cannot establish autonomy when race and gender persist as socially imprinted ways of seeing others. Information costs—in the economic sense—prevent autonomy, as do the web of constraints on choice imposed by the influence of others on perceptions, and the demands and discriminations of advantaged classes. Moreover, he has privileged the use of institutional educational attainment and the possession of credentials as measures of merit. He has failed to realize that his own definitions of neutrality and merit are forms of socially constructed knowledge. They are not the truths or principles of the social contract but definitions produced by persons with the power to define knowledge. The power of elites to define merit in this fashion has reduced the chance for equality of those whose disadvantages have retarded their chance to become credentialed. It is symbolic violence against disadvantaged groups.

Another socially constructed standard, "reasonableness," has pervaded Scalia's opinions on the warrant requirement in cases such as *Minnesota v. Dickerson* and *Arizona v. Hicks*; his forfeitures and fines opinions; and his opinions on habeas corpus.[94] His use of reasonableness has shaped the law to conceal behind an impartial language about common sense the symbolic violence done to suspects' autonomy and privacy, and it has forced criminal defendants to resign themselves to the logic of his reading of the law.

In the punitive damages cases *Pacific Mutual v. Haslip* and *TXO Production*,[95] Scalia's opinions did more than enhance the instrumental power of juries, they communicated the constitutive power of judicial decisions. Parties held liable for punitive damages could not challenge the fairness of this act of legal discipline. Rather, there was an act of symbolic violence: the use of legal text and precedent to assert the dominance of the courts and the jury.

Also, because Scalia has indicated a preference for the expression of the ideas of selected interests and for the expression of conceptions of religion influenced by Christian religious institutionalism, and because he has believed that a neutral law constructed by the majority could restrict other expressions, he has sought a law that diminishes the capacity of legally disadvantaged classes to express their beliefs. For example, he has enforced a symbolic violence against expressions of such classes' status. Relying on a legal criterion, Scalia has failed to recognize that the injury caused by denying free exercise of religion might be greater than the harms the expressive act could cause. Indeed, in religious expression cases such as *Smith* his analysis has had three injurious results. First, the denial of the claim has limited the variety of interpretations and expressions of human existence and the choices that all of the public can make about things metaphysical. American society as a whole was harmed because citizens cannot afford the information necessary to educate themselves and make responsible choices about religious exercise from an unregulated list of options. The intelligent search for meaning and order in life by both majorities and minorities—a search with important political consequences for a world of uncertain values—is artificially truncated. Second, the majority of the community has suffered an injury because the exercise of a dissenting view is stifled. American governance assumes that dissent generated by self-interest propels the debate essential for the prevention of tyranny and the evolution of representative public policy. By cutting off some religious exercises as a mode of expression, Scalia has reduced the dynamism of the conflicts that generate the freedom of all persons in the regime. Third, by stating that the exercise of a religious practice did not belong in the regime, he has allowed the state to violate the bounds of decency, respect, tolerance, and obligation to others which is implicit in the American idea of rights. He has permitted the majority to injure itself by engaging in demeaning unethical treatment and inhumane subordination of others. By empowering the majority to impose this injury on itself, he has become an accomplice in political acts that displayed a lack of empathy toward the religious exercises of others or that involved more brutish expressions of hatred and violence toward minority creeds. Also, in his opinions there has sometimes appeared an implicit hostility to the expressions of some specific groups—such as Native Americans—that have a radically non-Western metaphysics or values that do not fit well with Western legal logic. Consequently, the effect of his free exercise opinions has been the reinforcement, through the symbolic power of law, of the message of the dependency of private religious thought on determinations made by the state or private interests.

Subjection

Accountability to the judgments of others, or subjection, recognizes that power exists in interactions and that it is the interactive use of power that defines the normal.[96] Subjection does not involve an authority, such as the judiciary, seeking an objective interest. Instead, power exists as signs and symbols and beliefs about the political and social order. Persons are not subjected to power; rather, power is the internalized discipline of a society, for "power comes from below."[97] In a world of conflict, this practice is less repression or the more subtle domination of persons through symbolic violence than it is the strategy of arranging politics through disciplinary norms.[98] In this context, courts do not wield a dominating power even though they can define the constitutional boundaries of public power. Instead, they are but one of many power centers engaged in a dynamic struggle to define truth and appropriate social behavior. Regardless, the judge and the legal profession have interests and are involved in a strategy to further encourage the arrangement, standardization, and normalization of power relations between the government and citizens, and within the private sphere. The judiciary is trying to use its institutional status and "expert" knowledge to "ensnare" popular justice, "to control it and to strangle it, by re-inscribing it within institutions typical of the state apparatus."[99] Judges and other participants in litigation thus attempt to reduce the danger of everyday political conflicts by interpreting rules as truths that people can silently internalize in their everyday public and private lives. The judge thus assumes that persons are subjects of the law.[100]

As a particular disciplinary use of power, the practice of legal decisionmaking becomes a tactic for marking or inscribing some forms of human behavior as normal and part of the political order. Judges attempt to establish a privileged imagery and rhetoric about rights. When formalized in opinions, their language becomes legitimate and isolates alternative arguments about the power and liberty of persons. Although the establishment and subsequent public internalization of a legitimate law reduces the frequency of occasions on which judges make choices to discipline people, judges still have a single job:[101] they use their special knowledge of law and their hierarchical status to rationalize and normalize new and unsettled power relationships.[102] Thus, they can use law to reinforce the ways in which people are subjects of the state's laws or powerful private institutions. Judicial discipline thus is "not so much punishment but a mix of micro-penalties and rewards" for loyalty to judicial definitions of personal power and status.[103]

Judicial opinions often contain a message of subjection. An example is the Supreme Court's enhancement of gender inequality and female subjection through restricted protection of abortion decisions and less strict scrutiny of discrimination against women. The Court has assisted private discriminatory acts and racial subjection by curtailing redistributive policies such as affirmative action. It has neglected the needs of children and subjected them to uncontrolled parental violence, as illustrated by the justices' treatment of the decision in *DeShaney v. Winnebago County Social Service Department*.[104] It has avoided the concerns of the dying, as in *Cruzan v. Director*, and has turned these persons into the subjects of the power of physicians' choices of courses of treatment.[105] Subjection also occurs when the law allows private choices that subtly but forcefully permit persons to be treated as alien and suspect. For example, the state action doctrine in equal protection law allows some private racist acts and thus reinforces the alienation felt by African Americans.[106]

Scalia has embedded a message of subjection in his separated powers and federalism opinions. He has reinforced, often by incidental remarks, the standards and institutional arrangements that define power in the American regime. The message that human relations can be ordered by law has appeared in his legalist aspirations for governmental management and his efforts to control agency discretion. He has reinforced the authority of the state to order subjection to the executive, he has legitimated the authority of bureaucracy, and he has used legal doctrine to prevent private persons from challenging the exercise of private power against their interests. He has made little effort to let people avoid established governmental power or private power relationships. Instead, his use of rules of law has woven an elaborate fabric of procedural doctrines that enclose individuals in a world in which threats to their autonomy can be offset only when a lawmaking majority is mobilized or when judicial procedures permit a response. His federalism opinions have extended subjection through the legitimation of rules about federal and state governmental power, as in decisions about whether state taxes and regulations interfere with the Commerce Clause, whether federal preemption has occurred, whether federal or state courts have jurisdiction over a dispute, or whether one state or another has control of interstate activity. His opinions have thus tried to conserve a vision of a political order in which governments' disciplinary power rests on law and persons are subject to the wisdom of the law—or of the courts—about the appropriate design of political institutions. Consequently, his opinions have attempted to conserve the written law's disciplinary legal authority and its political power over the general design of the American state and to reinforce the importance of legal order in the minds of the public.

Although Scalia's opinions have curtailed the use of judicial authority to remedy discrimination, they have legitimated private acts that subject minorities and women to the control of majorities. His language about neutral laws, the harm of affirmative action programs to white males, and the improper effect of remedial programs or the pre-emptory challenge cases on majority rule or legal tradition has tried to identify the status quo with justice. Thus, Scalia's equal protection and civil rights statutory opinions have frustrated the greater equalization of power in the United States. His opinions, in tune with the idea of rule-based politics, have used the law to defend the idea of legal neutrality. He has tried to conserve order and the autonomy of those holding the resources of political and economic power. He has not provided power to disadvantaged classes and introduced their interests into political debates. Instead, he has curtailed greater respect for differences and prevented the expansion of political pluralism and moral discord that might result in questions about the subjective status of some persons.

When Scalia privileged certain categories of expression such as flag burning, PAC contributions, and abortion clinic protests, while indicating that the concept of "illegality" could be used to penalize other expressions such as nude dancing, he—like the other justices—made the expressive rights of parties subject to rules adopted by the Court. The justices' special expertise and knowledge was deployed to order and normalize social and political relationships. The rules developed by the justices increased the accountability of individuals to court-imposed boundaries on behavior, and the courts came to shape the identity of persons and define their subjection. Scalia's opinions also have contained messages resulting in the subjection of persons. For example, by restricting the range of constitutionally protected religious exercise, he failed to recognize the "social injury" created by restrictions on constitutional liberties.[107] He has read the law as saying that only concrete injuries to the person are permitted relief. Even if a concrete injury is alleged, as in the *Smith* case, relief often cannot be granted if it contravenes the choices of the majoritarian political institutions or threatens the stability of the social and political order. In addition, Scalia's opinions in freedom of expression cases have relied on the rule of law to make a statement about the normative value of certain ideas. He has privileged some types of expression by shifting them to a certain legal category, as in his *Madsen* effort to read controls on abortion protestors as a content-based rather than contextual bar on expression, and he has deprecated other expressions by placing them beyond the scope of the First Amendment or in a category in which they could be "reasonably" regulated. Freedom to communicate ideas, a central element of free government, became a matter for determination by the courts. And despite the talk of judicial passivity in his opinions, he has communicated the dual power of the political majority's and the Court's values in shaping the liberty of Americans.

His criminal due process opinions also have contributed to the subjection of the community to the judiciary. Through language about the reasonableness of police actions and criminal procedures, he has tried to offset contrary arguments about police bias and about arbitrariness in plea bargaining and the consideration of evidence. Scalia's criminal law opinions thus have contributed to a disciplinary message. In his opinions he has depicted criminal law and procedures as reasonable practices that the judiciary deploys in an effort to order liberty, even if the ordering demands the destruction of the convicted criminal's body. The power of the state to penalize has depended only on law; the morality of crime and punishment has never been in question. So long as he has thought that criminal statutes and precedents were clear, he has left the state free to control persons without appellate court intervention. Only when the law clearly protected rights, as indicated in a few warrantless-search cases such as *Arizona v. Hicks* and *Treasury Employees v. von Raab,* has he prevented the extension of governmental control or surveillance of private lives.

Despite his rejection of most substantive rights that free persons' bodies from public and private discipline, Scalia's use of the Takings Clause has deployed text and legal tradition to defend landowners from the state's discipline. As suggested by John Brigham,[108] Scalia's Takings Clause opinions have resulted in a "double standard" on property rights and other economic rights. The economic interests most commonly held by American workers and the poor, such as jobs and transfer payments, have received the protection of lower-tier rationality analysis. However, real estate has received much greater constitutional protection. Although real estate includes family dwellings, the most valuable real estate is in the hands of corporations, landlords, and the wealthy. Since corporate and investment property is most frequently affected by governmental takings because of its sheer size, its valuable location, and the regulation of its multiple uses, Scalia's effort to revitalize the Takings Clause has been an effort to constitute a regime in which large-scale private property holders receive special protection from governmental control. Indirectly, his opinion defended the power of private property owners, and their ability to subject others—such as their employees, or persons who want to use beaches or enjoy a stable coastal environment—to their interests.[109] Like his opinions on other topics, his Takings Clause opinions have helped to define the subjection of persons to the power relationships in American political life.

In his effort to control license, Scalia has allowed the use of governmental and private political powers to discipline individuals. Most of the time his use of discipline has followed practices approved in laws made by the majority, or past judicial actions. He has thus conserved a rule-based politics that aims at protecting dominant configurations of power. At the same time, his opinions have aimed at inducing acquiescence in the established order by suggesting that the political system is beneficent.[110] Only on rare occasions has he used his votes and opinions to reconstitute politics so that disadvantaged classes might be freed from laws constructed by majority factions. His constitutive message has thus drawn on a dimension of Enlightenment liberalism to conserve the contemporary political order and to discipline interests that might threaten political stability. He has confirmed the hegemonic hold of law—and the interests advantaged by law—on Americans.

CONCLUSION

Antonin Scalia has envisioned a political regime where the future is a consequence of a determinant law. Therefore, in his opinions he has done more than employ law as an instrument to define the future of the

American political order. He also has tried to reinforce a political vision drawn from Enlightenment liberalism which has helped constitute American politics—a vision of a rational political world in which truth is ascertainable and doubt and chaos are banished because of the existence of law. Very much in the American political tradition, his opinions are a vehicle used to delineate a vision of a good society in which law makes for social equilibrium and creates a private sphere to defend individual autonomy and reasonable uses of personal liberty.

However, in his efforts to achieve his good society Scalia has concealed, behind legal language, uses of power that are violent, repressive, and subjective. His good society uses law in a disciplinary manner to conserve the power of those who already own possessions, who benefit from the historical power of their race, who practice mainstream Christianity, who live in traditional families, and who fulfill popular definitions of merit and virtue. People who do not fit into these categories—criminals, social and religious outsiders, exiles, racial minorities—are not to be the objects of public compassion. Rather, if they are to be included in the regime, they have to become the objects of legal discipline. The discipline will either injure their bodies or psyches in order to shepherd them to follow the majority's laws, or, more commonly, will induce them to conform to the moral and political norms that dominant interests in the regime have defined as lawful. Law is not to be a means for the emancipation of the disadvantaged. As a result, he has reinforced the political power of legal elites and the institutions of the state that they have designed to govern America. Apparently, preachers of the conservative revival such as Scalia find a faithlessness or heresy in disadvantaged groups' efforts to reconstitute the law to secure liberty and equality.

Chapter Eleven

THE ARTIFICE OF SCALIA'S POLITICAL MESSAGE

In over two decades of public life, Justice Scalia has articulated a political narrative that has attempted to convey a distinctly conservative and legalistic vision of the future of American politics. He is a legal craftsman devoted to his profession, and a judge whose ideas flow from the American convention of controlling the political world through words. His aim has been to conserve the American faith in rule-based politics and to keep bureaucracy, Congress, and interest groups from generating a more chaotic politics of conflicting interests and—to a far lesser extent—moral discord. His desire for a rule of law that is a law of rules, or a predictable guide for social and political behavior, leads him to conclude that "there are times when even a bad rule is better than no rule at all."[1] However, all of Scalia's talk about the rule of law and reason is an artifice. He offers a narrative that obscures the political aims of his conservative interpretation of the American faith in rule-based politics. But his votes, his opinions—couched in his unique modified Reasoned Elaboration discourse—and his faith in private power and a disciplinary law endorse the vision of American politics favored by the conservative revival: executive policy leadership and a reinforcement of the status of interests that are already powerful.

SCALIA'S INSTRUMENTAL MESSAGE: LAW AS THE CORNERSTONE OF A MODERN CONSERVATISM

Justice Scalia has relied on his conservative political attitudes and used his opinions as an instrument to present a political narrative that supports the three propositions offered in chapter 3. In support of the first proposition, he has sought most but not all of the political ends sought by other contemporary conservatives. He has voted conservatively in a vast majority of the cases before the Court, including almost all cases that he felt were important enough to require his opinion. As suggested in the second proposition offered in chapter 3, Scalia has modified and extended in new directions the principles of Reasoned Elaboration jurisprudence as he has used them to define and defend his conservative political attitudes. He has not simply used Reasoned Elaboration, he has also modified its conservative cast to serve contemporary conservative political objectives. True, Scalia's opinions constantly have reflected on the necessity to protect the institutional settlement process governed by the judiciary, including the idea of the rule of law and the special craft of lawyers as instruments of judicial power. True, his opinions have used the principles of Reasoned Elaboration as a kind of instrument to chart the purposeful nature of the law, the role of judges as umpires in conflicts rather than as policymakers, the necessity of grounding judicial decisions on legal texts and avoiding experimental lawmaking, and the need for judicial passivity in cases about complex policy problems. However, from these postulates about the need to conserve judicial power he has fabricated standards to assail selected post–New Deal and public interest liberal legal doctrines, particularly doctrines resting on pragmatic liberal principles such as flexible scrutiny standards, doctrine about contextual regulation of expression, death penalty procedures, and fundamental rights.

Scalia has rebuilt Reasoned Elaboration principles to serve conservative ends. First, he has tried to construct even stronger partitions to keep the courts out of many kinds of policy matters and to isolate the judiciary from the "raw" world of politics. Beginning with his formalistic conception of the separation of powers, he has tried to erect a high partition between the duties of the federal government's political and judicial branches. His spin on the *Chevron* doctrine has attempted to keep judges out of the administrative process, and his regard for statutory text and his rejection of legislative history have undertaken to keep the courts from revising the policy product of legislative action. In constructing his opinions about these issues, Scalia has established a reverence for the plain meaning of texts which is even more austere than the position of the progenitors of Reasoned Elaboration such as Felix Frankfurter, Henry Hart, and Albert Sacks. He has undertaken a concerted campaign to define the judicial function as the deciphering or translation of text, not as an inquiry into the justice of laws or the exploration of law as a path toward a progressive future. His standards about judicial duty would bind courts into this translator role and would conserve rules of law created by the majority, not the rights of disadvantaged minorities defended by liberals.

Second, for Scalia a limited judicial role in "lawmaking" has not meant an inactive judiciary. Instead, the judiciary has to pursue—actively and instrumentally—the enforcement of law. It has to be a purposeful interpreter of the directive political arrangements in the law for both the present and the future, not simply a rubber stamp legitimating legislative, executive, or judicial policies. Therefore, he has sought the revocation of precedents that he thinks encourage the disregard of constitutional text or longstanding legal traditions. This position has led to his criticism of precedents about the negative Commerce Clause, extensions of statutory borrowing, changes in the *Hans v. Louisiana* doctrine on access to federal courts, the application of equal protection to preemptory challenges of jurors, the intent standard used to prove violations of civil rights, the *Lemon* test, doctrine on proportionality of sentencing, death penalty procedures, changes in habeas corpus standards, and *Roe v. Wade* and the fundamental right to an abortion. Especially in his response to O'Connor in *Planned Parenthood v. Casey,* he has stressed that courts should actively reject precedents not grounded in text and legal tradition. Additionally, his emphasis on texts, legal traditions, and the need to protect the craft of the law has meant that he has particularly disliked pragmatic liberal efforts to expand texts and tradition in an experimental search for a more just regime. Thus, Marshall's special application of intensified scrutiny doctrine in affirmative action cases, the development of procedures in death penalty cases, and most fundamental rights opinions have received Scalia's scorn. Yet Scalia has accepted some of the doctrinal experiments and new legal instruments of the Warren and Burger Courts when they served his conservative ends. For example, he used strict scrutiny doctrine in some equal protection and First Amendment cases. The doctrine dates only from the *Carolene Products* (1938) and *Korematsu v. United States* (1944) cases, and most of its details surfaced during the early years of the Burger Court, but he found it useful in protecting conservative expressions (as in *Madsen*). However, he abandoned strict scrutiny in equal protection cases such as *Croson* and *Adarand* in favor of a racial neutrality rule. His interpretation and enforcement of text, precedent, and tradition almost always has been hostile to liberal justices' political positions such as support for increased federal governmental power, protection for minorities and criminal defendants, and the rigid separation of church and state, and has been more friendly to conservatives.

Third, in trying to focus the work of the Court on text and legal tradition, Scalia has sought to get the Court to do tasks that, in *Planned Parenthood v. Casey,* he called "lawyer's work." He has wanted to isolate the judiciary from politics and to make it appear that juridical craft and reasoning are of a different order than other forms of public debate. The result of this practice, he has intimated, is to secure the legitimacy of the professional role and power of the legal craft. In itself, this has been a political act, an instrumental effort to obscure the political nature of judicial acts from others in the regime. His effort also might be called special interest politics because it seeks a special, privileged role for judicial professionals.

Fourth, Scalia's concern for judicial passivity has encouraged him to employ the traditional rules about standing and the justiciability of cases in an aggressive fashion, as in the two *Lujan* environmental regulation cases. However, he has taken the passivity idea in new directions. His efforts to control the generality, or scope, of rights as an instrument of legal change, as in *Employment Division v. Smith* and *Michael H. v. Gerald D.,* have succeeded in confining the Court's capacity to provide the protection of rights, and they induce passivity in the face of rights claims. Also, his reliance on text, as in his Confrontation Clause cases, has endeavored to keep the Court passive.

However, as indicated by his willingness to challenge precedent and develop a version of separated powers unlike any seen in previous cases and an approach to legislative history not founded in past decisions, his passivity has been selective. The simple conservative definition of Scalia as a good guy using judicial restraint to oppose the bad-guy judicial activism of pragmatic liberalism is too simplistic. He has not avoided active doctrinal development, since he has encouraged passivity in a judiciary that was politically active for two hundred years. He has applied a Catch-22 logic: to have a more passive judiciary you actively have to attack existing legal doctrine and judicial practice, thus violating the techniques of passivity. His *Planned Parenthood v. Casey, Harmelin v. Michigan,* and *Walton v. Arizona* opinions illustrate the application of his logic. Also, the search for judicial passivity in the construction of texts has caused some ironic results. At their extreme these results are exemplified by his effort in *Feres* doctrine cases such as *United States v. Johnson.* In these cases he used text to reject a judicially created standard that, for separation of powers reasons, restricted the adjudication of questions connected to military operations. Consequently, Scalia's concern about passivity has been not solely a function of a belief in judicial restraint. Rather, it has reflected his instrumental search for a proper judicial role. His search has been more pragmatic and less rule-bound than he has claimed.

Scalia's modified application of the postulates of Reasoned Elaboration jurisprudence has indicated the limits of the use of legal language as a control on politics. Although he has retreated to a formal exposition of legal texts time and again in search of theoretical certainty, a clear legal rule, and a rational basis for his decisions, a direct or formal reading of text simply has not always sufficed. Legal and political context has had a bearing on his regard for the directive power of text and legal tradition. Despite efforts to take pragmatic judgment out of legal decisionmaking, Scalia could not completely avoid judgment or deny that his choices had a substantive political meaning and relied on social and political facts as well as the law. All he could do was use words as an instrument to conceal that he was really making choices about policy ends conforming with his conservative political attitudes.[2] His opinions and speeches have contained a vision that politics can be confined to a special space—a relatively autonomous realm dominated by the ideas of law and the practices of the legal profession—so that politics will not affect the translation of the legal texts and tradition that bring order to conflicts within the regime. His vision of the world has assumed a mask of legal impartiality and shows a faith that adherence to the certainty of texts can bury the political subjectivity of decisionmaking, conserve the power of selected interests or factions, and make judging an easy process. Law thus is the cornerstone of his vision of a rational political future.

Scalia and Other Conservative Legal Narratives

Because Reasoned Elaboration is the instrument that Scalia has employed for the expression of his robustly conservative attitudes in cases he has decided, he has been forced to reject the extratextual, moral, philosophical, and historical narratives used by other conservative legalists to justify their inculcation of conservative attitudes into law.[3] His jurisprudence is not in tune with that of legal theorists who rest their argument on extralegal moral principles. He is not a member of the evangelical religious right whose primary political proposition is that constitutional governance should rest on moral principles identical to those discernible by a literal reading of selected biblical passages. He has shown no inclination to use communitarian theories of constitutional interpretation that reject the primacy of legal texts in the construction of political order.[4] He is not a devotee of neo-Aristotelian or neo-Thomist natural rights theories. Although these ideas have influenced scholars such as Judge John T. Noonan Jr., of the Ninth Circuit, their language is absent in Scalia's writing.[5] Scalia has not voiced the belief that constitutional governance should rest on the moral principles of natural law or any other abstract moral philosophy. He also has eschewed any connection to other moralistic theories of the Constitution that have recently surfaced in academic circles.[6] Other than opposing abortion and seeking to protect religious organizations advantaged through Establishment Clause doctrine accommodating religion—actions that he has justified by Reasoned Elaboration arguments—he has avoided even a hint of interest in the religious-cultural criticism of contemporary morality promoted by many conservative revivalists.

Although at the American Enterprise Institute and the University of Chicago Scalia had contact with proponents of the economic analysis of law such as Judge Richard Posner and Judge Frank Easterbrook, few of their concepts appear in his opinions or other writings. Scalia has made no reference to their belief that constitutional governance should be grounded on extraconstitutional utilitarian principles such as the maximization of the wealth of individual citizens. He has not tried to make law mimic the disciplinary norms of the economic theory of the marketplace.[7]

Similarly, Scalia has not evidenced support of the originalist view of former attorney general Edwin Meese III. Meese defended a historical approach to constitutional interpretation based on the belief that constitutional governance rests on loyalty to a literal reading of the original intention of the Framers of the Constitution and its amendments.[8] For Scalia, the rigid originalism of the literalist constitutional theory of Meese and his D.C. Circuit colleague and fellow Reagan judicial appointee Robert Bork was a "lesser evil" than any judicial interpretation of the Constitution not resting on the criteria located in the constitutional text. Nevertheless, Scalia has differed with Bork's notion of fixed constitutional intent in three respects. First, Scalia has been less confident than Bork that the original meaning is knowable and can be correctly applied by busy judges. He has stated that original intent is captured in the words of the Constitution and has to be respected, but he has regarded further exploration of the meaning of language as difficult and sometimes involving discretionary choices.[9] Second, he has accepted that original interpretations of constitutional language should be modified by the doctrine of stare decisis, the legal tradition he has referred to again and again in his decisions. Unlike Bork, he has recognized that some words in the Constitution lack an original meaning and that some clauses are open-ended and contain an evolutionary intent discovered through the consideration of previous judicial decisions.[10] Third, Scalia has deferred to the policies adopted by executives and legislatures in response to majority demands. He has respected recent elections as well as the Constitution as an indicator of acceptable policy values. By defining law as resting on majority sentiment, he has implied that law cannot rest on the "traditional" moral base of the Constitution.[11] Bork has harshly derided the moral relativism of contemporary intellectuals and judges. He has indicated that the Constitution rests on "traditional views of morality" and that the neutral principles or value preferences that he has alleged to exist in the original constitutional text should be applied to contemporary issues. Unlike Scalia, he has never admitted that he would be governed primarily by contemporary majority value preferences.[12] Whereas Bork has dreamt of a world in which constitutional disputes are about law and are disposed of by historical principles of great moral worth never sullied by the crudity of politics, Scalia has been a self-styled "faint-hearted originalist" and a realist who admits that, even if it is distasteful, sometimes the political values of judges affect the content of constitutional law. Thus, Scalia's "faint-hearted" originalism has permitted somewhat more judicial discretion in the interpretation of the Constitution, but his was a discretion that left many difficult choices to other political institutions.[13]

Drawing on some of the same themes as Bork, Anthony Kronman has argued that legal tradition possesses an "authority of its own" as an artifact of human culture. Thus, historical texts and the force of precedent provide a binding guide for instrumental choices. Kronman indicates that legal interpretation and even the construction of new law by legislatures can be grounded in historical texts and traditions.[14] Scalia's pattern of deference to agency and legislature has distanced him from this sort of conservative argument. Legal tradition has mattered to Scalia, but he has used it as an instrument for constructing a vision of a conservative future regime and not as a tool to rebuild the moral order of the past. Unlike Kronman, he has not reverenced the past for its own sake.

Finally, although he is sometimes identified with "new Legal Process" jurisprudence, Scalia's instrumental discourse stands apart from that of some academic descendants of the Reasoned Elaboration of the 1950s and 1960s. Conservative "new Legal Process" theorists such as Richard Ely, a student of Bickel, have proposed a constitutional law designed to reinforce the process of democratic government through judicial efforts to ensure representative government, to open channels of political communication, and to ensure minority participation in political processes. Their constitutional law, however, is in tension with Scalia's modified Reasoned Elaboration. Ely's primary goal was to ensure that courts deal with questions of political participation rather than the substantive merits of political choices. Thus he refused to recognize the pragmatic liberal arguments that the law could help persons realize their potential in a more just regime. Like the Reasoned Elaborationists, he read the Constitution as a purposeful document. However, he was willing to supplement text and legal tradition "to keep the machinery of democratic government running as it should, to make sure the channels of political participation and communication are kept open, . . . and [to] concern [the Court] with what majorities do to minorities."[15] These interpretive practices have distanced Ely from Scalia. Despite the respect for majority choices implicit in Ely's argument, Scalia has not relied on a general notion that the Constitution defined "the general contours" of a process of government; instead, he has employed what he has found in express text and legal tradition, as in *Morrison v. Olson* and other separated powers cases. Likewise, in cases such as *Austin v. Michigan Chamber of Commerce,* Scalia has not deferred to legislative efforts to provide a more open and balanced practice of political communication. Finally, Scalia's view on fundamental rights and extratextual claims of liberties is at odds with Ely's effort to place the court in a "representation-reinforcing role" and to construct rules toward the constitutionally implied but normative objective of facilitating the access of all citizens to politics.

Consequently, Scalia has found himself confronting pragmatic liberal arguments with his own version of Reasoned Elaboration principles. His constitutional arguments, and his interpretation of law more generally, have relied on words and clauses as commands or statements of value that deserve respect. They are the cornerstone of a theoretically certain or determinant law. Other modes of conservative legal argument have mattered little to Scalia. His version of a revived conservatism is majority rule and a state that responds to the power of majorities and vested interests as enshrined in rules of law.

Scalia's Instrumental Modernism

Because he has rejected legal discourses that have a moralistic or philosophical tone, there is an inexorable, machinelike logic to Scalia's instrumental legal discourse. He has assumed that judges can engage in an easy, routine application of law which soothes political problems by the very nature of its uniformity.[16] When this is coupled with passivity and other boundaries on judicial power, he believes that judges can avoid hard questions about the legitimacy of political arrangements, chaotic multiparty political conflicts, and the anxiety of having to decide moral issues. In his vision, courts and law are instruments that buttress order; courts apply law to annihilate the disorder and the anxiety associated with a selected set of conflicts.

Additionally, his opinions have made law into an instrument useful in the construction of a political vision legitimating the politics of modernity.[17] The politics of modernity is secular and rejects any recognition that actions have an intrinsic or transcendent moral value. As indicated by his lack of regard for conservative "New Legal Process" scholars, natural law proponents, and originalists, as well as liberal pragmatists, Scalia has not based decisions on overt use of transcendent moral ideas or pragmatic themes about the moral dignity of persons. His law has not been epic or scripture; it has not been a binding historical statement of transcendent values. And his law has not been an instrument for the enrichment of individual self-worth. His version of the good regime has not rested on morals and natural justice or on aspirations toward a future good regime in which individuals will achieve their potential. Scalia has defined the good regime as the implementation of policies that the majority wants; and what the majority wants is found in secular acts such as the statutes it has approved and the Constitution under which it practices politics. Although the majority has derived its policies from its cultural history or moral principles, Scalia's judge cannot question the cultural or moral basis of majority judgments. From Scalia's viewpoint, the legal texts produced by the majority or the courts are specific instruments that judges should implement without the interference of their personal subjective values.

The politics of modernity endeavors to control "passion."[18] Therefore, a very rational and purposeful or formal law is needed in order to isolate the legal process from passion, emotion, and romantic idealism. Certainly Scalia has expressed dislike of political passion. His *Planned Parenthood v. Casey* opinion described at length how strongly he felt that passionate criticism of the Court was unseemly. Scalia has indicated that politics should be the rational expression of interests through institutional channels. He has contended that emotional appeals via passive resistance (e.g., sleep-ins) and direct action can be

subjected to rules that ensure some degree of order, and he has regarded some expression—such as religious peyote eating, nude dancing, and the sale of obscene materials—as so disorderly that it is beyond
legal defense. Also, procedural rules have been very important for his
effort to control passion. Therefore, he has argued that judges should
define clear and reasonable rules that allow the impersonal evaluation
of conflicts. Because new procedural rules such as death penalty standards or "hybrid" procedures for agency decisionmaking interfere with
reasonable legal decisions, he has stated that judges should avoid developing them. However, as he has indicated by his opinions about laws
changing rules on the confrontation of witnesses or the need for reasons to conduct employee drug testing, governments might be restricted from developing new procedures that could become instruments encouraging the disorderly breech of orderly legal and political
processes.

The politics of modernity values expertise. It assumes that expert
knowledge offers truths to assist the rational governance of the regime.
Scalia's constant reference to the need for judges to practice the lawyer's craft, decipher or translate texts and legal traditions, and avoid
intervention in the expertise of executives, administrators, and legislators has evidenced his commitment to legal expertise. He sees judicial
expertise as knowledge most fitted to traditional two-party adjudication, not to complicated multiparty conflicts. Further, he has argued
that public and interest group interference in executive policymaking
and judicial evaluation of executive policies should be minimized by
rules of standing and other justiciability doctrines.

The politics of modernity values organization and organizational
efficiency.[19] Organization and organizational efficiency mean a leadership that offers direction. The state should deploy effective managerial
technologies to keep peace in the regime. Following this logic, Scalia
has stressed the importance of formal rules as instruments defining the
authority of the branches of government, has tried to defend administrative discretion against some acts of judicial intervention, and has
encouraged the legislature to make precise law.

The politics of modernity values progress. Progress is the result of
the modern understanding of nature as a set of laws susceptible to
human knowledge. By knowing the laws of nature, humans can assert a
mastery of their world. Although a superficial examination might conclude that Scalia has not wanted "progress" that entails a more egalitarian society, a right to die, or a right to an abortion, he has desired

progress in the design of the state to reduce the "quality of 'bads' in the world."[20] For Scalia, progress to betterment of the self and the world demands a politics designed to channel human nature toward a virtuous life in a secular order. In this order, law is the best instrument to ensure a good and virtuous life. Human wickedness cannot be reformed by education or controlled by experimental policies, and cannot be restrained when persons are free to make private choices. Consequently, he has demanded the assertion of legal discipline of the criminal and of ideas that endanger order and social peace in the regime. His idea of progress has led to opinions that emphasize the value of law as an instrument placing limits on the general public's rights of expression, religious practice, and use of the body; restricting the rights of criminal defendants and public employees; and imposing boundaries on remedies for social and political inequality. His is a political vision that values the order induced into the regime by laws promoting the power of executive agencies, organized religion, political parties, legal expertise, and property owners. Without law, Scalia envisions nihilism, the destruction of past progress, and an end to progress toward a more orderly world.

Finally, the politics of modernity values the autonomous individual. Therefore, the law should treat persons without regard to class or status. Thus, Scalia has rejected variations in the use of scrutiny doctrine which permit governmental recognition of class or status differences, such as affirmative action policies, special evidentiary or equitable remedy standards in racial and gender discrimination case or statutory law, the separate consideration of preemptory juror challenges using race or gender criteria, and campaign finance regulations separately treating organized wealth. Racial and gender neutrality is the key, he has argued, to an effective legal order. Thus, he has sought a law that is alienated from communal ties and cultural sentiments and that treats blacks, women, religious peyote eaters, and capital criminals without regard to their group affiliation. Law is not to be an instrument of social distinction.

Scalia's modern law thus has tried to escape the law of the premodern past, especially the ideas of natural law and natural rights that influenced the Framers of the Constitution, judges in early America, and some conservatives.[21] The grounding of his abortion decisions on tenets of Reasoned Elaboration rather than on the natural law tradition of his Roman Catholic heritage, plus opinions that break with Catholic teaching on capital punishment and on concern for the humanity of the poor, minorities, and strangers, illustrates his commitment to modernist ethics. At the same time, he has avoided the relativism or proto-postmodernity sometimes attributed to the pragmatic liberals and pragmatic judges.[22] They have offered either eclectic normative or practical foundations for law which denied the need for legal uniformity, such as Thurgood Marshall's *Bakke* and *Croson* scrutiny of racial classifications, or have repudiated the value of objectivity, pre-established rules and procedures, and traditional standards of rational legal argument, expert knowledge, or progress. Scalia's modern vision of progress defines the good future as a function of legality. He believes that a straightforward, neutral rule of law can be used as a tool to craft a neatly functioning bureaucracy that expresses the majority's unobstructed will.

Scalia's political narrative has used the law as an instrument to construct an austere, dispassionate vision of the world like that depicted in the modern aesthetic. His legal narrative thus is a performance that has similarities with the architecture and painting of modernity. It is akin to the architecture of Le Corbusier and Philip Johnson, to United States Air Force Academy buildings with a clean, neat, ordered, bold, and authoritarian facade, and to the logical efficiency of an expressway; as well as to the rationalized, dehumanized, and formally structured painting of K. S. Malevich, Piet Mondrian, and the Cubists. It has similarities to the cold, mathematical precision of the music produced by Arnold Schoenberg's use of the twelve-tone method, Iannis Xenakis's mathematical musical designs, and the orderly variations of pulsating rhythm in Steve Reich's minimalism. His narrative has similarities with the extreme rationality of analytic positivism in philosophy or in the scientific efforts to examine the human psyche which led to behavioralism in the social sciences. Like modern narratives in the visual arts, philosophy, and the social sciences, Scalia's idea of the role of law has contained the progressive vision of modernity, the view that expert lawyers or writers, builders, artists, musicians, and scientists can help define a more rational regime with less of the chaos introduced by the politics of tradition, the confusion of interests, and claims of rights. Yet, Scalia's narrative has not expressed the progressivism of a pragmatic, public interest liberal avant garde engaged in decentering values. It does not resound with the version of modernism that has produced abstract expressionist painting, the improvisations of jazz, and the architectural eclecticism appearing along the Las Vegas strip.

Instead, as he has presented his vision of the politics of the good or just society, he has striven at every turn to engineer reason and order, to conserve the best of the past, and to confine as "illogical" and "unscientific" the suppositions about human nature associated with humanist idealism. Thus, he has written that "this Court need not, and has no authority to, inject itself into every field of human activity where irrationality and oppression may theoretically occur, and if it tries to do so it will destroy itself."[23] His opinions, as a whole, have constructed precise legal rules that are his instruments in building a legal edifice that shields order from political dangers, chaos, anxiety, conflict, and threats to existing advantaged interests.

SCALIA'S CONSTITUTIVE MESSAGE: REITERATING THE AMERICAN FAITH IN LAW

Ultimately, the modernist instrumental message about law in Scalia's opinions has reiterated and reinforced the constitutive faith in law in a political regime marked by unequal distributions of power and unequal degrees of personal autonomy. He has excluded discussion of the way in which the "social facts" about the distribution of power in American politics challenge the legitimacy of the law. He has often ignored the way in which "fair" procedures fail to eliminate the many faces of violence, repression, and subjection in the American regime. He has pursued theoretical certainty in the law, and he has sought to repress interpretive techniques and doctrines that encourage any recognition of the radically contingent construction of law. His concern has been with palliatives for present-day ills rather than remedies for injustices and the provision of a better life for all persons in the future. Because of this vision, his votes and opinions constitute a vision of the future of American politics that *reproduces* existing power relationships and *simulates* personal liberty.

The Reproduction of Political Power

Because he envisions that the regime can be governed by a rational, purposeful, and neutral law, Scalia's vision has "reproduced" or maintained existing constitutional, legal, and cultural standards about the allocation of political power.[24] He has assumed that judges have a duty to conserve the majority's choices and to reproduce the existing distribution of political power and cultural definitions of truth and liberty. Thus, by reproducing legalized sociopolitical relations, he deprives the law of an aspirational dimension.

Unlike his pragmatic liberal judicial colleagues—Blackmun, Brennan, Marshall, and, to an extent, Stevens—Scalia has not sought a flexibility in the law which encourages a more expansive politics of interests, policies to end racial and gender inequalities, greater protection for the expressions of political and outsiders and criminal defendants, and substantive rights for the pregnant and the dying. His liberal colleagues have believed that pragmatic judging and policymaking, relying on themes of human dignity and equality they associated with constitutional government, was the path to a better America with a more just life for all. To achieve these aspirations, they assumed that the Court could act for the interests of the public.

Despite its aspirations, pragmatic liberalism demands only instrumental adjustments in American constitutional politics. Consequently, pragmatic liberal critiques have attacked Scalia's instrumental discourse, not his vision of a legally ordered politics. The pragmatic liberals have tried to interpret the law to justify different public policies. They leave governmental institutions and private organizations intact but with their power adjusted, redesigned, and disciplined to fit the rules imposed by the new policies. For example, pragmatic liberals have attempted to legitimate affirmative action policy as a legal means of disciplining possible bias toward whites in the employment process, but they do not diminish employers' power over most aspects of the employment process, including the decision to hire, to define the job, and to fix its nonracial qualifications. Thus, pragmatic criticism of Scalia has not fully escaped the distribution of power embedded in law, and it cannot abandon a law that was created with the participation of interests attempting to aggrandize or defend their power in the regime.

The pragmatic liberal criticism of Scalia envisions a political regime that remains concerned about the use of law to conserve or reproduce the distribution of power and the structure of political order. Pragmatic liberalism aspires to engineer greater dignity in the lives of traditionally disadvantaged racial and ethnic minorities, a diminishment of the power of capital and of institutions of the state allied with capitalist interests, and an often ill-defined freer future for Americans. Yet, like Scalia, in his use of Reasoned Elaboration, the pragmatic liberals retain a faith in the presumption that a political world can be constructed and controlled with legal words. Although Scalia has scoffed at the idea that political engineering, a reduction of the power of the wealthy and corporations, or a law that concentrates on alleviating disadvantage will improve America, his constitutive discourse, like that of the pragmatic liberals, relies on a faith in law. His break with the pragmatic liberals is with regard to one canon of that faith. His opinions imply that the pragmatist's legal efforts to improve the conditions of human life never realize their aspirations. His taste is to ignore the political contingencies and commitments of lawmaking and law interpretation in order to present a vision of a hegemonic and theoretically certain law that only aspires to reduce political conflict. Thus, he has decided that any kind of aspirational politics is futile. Law can then only reproduce established political relationships and discipline license. It would not make even the incremental adjustments in the distribution of power proposed by the pragmatists. His opinions thus, by couching political arguments in the discourse of the American faith in law, reiterate the legitimacy of the political values and truths held by those who are politically influential and by legal professionals.[25]

The Simulation of Personal Liberty

Scalia's judicial opinions not only have used the Constitution and law to reproduce the distribution of power and the structure of political order in the United States but also have conveyed a message that simulates personal liberty. Simulation, the replacement of a real thing with its double, results in a confusion of the real and the double. In this vein, Scalia has presented the argument that a disciplinary law, even if inattentive to the differences in political and socioeconomic power among Americans, is the same thing as liberty. His opinions are thus a kind of performance that have tried to convince people that autonomy and social peace result from a theoretically certain or determinant law that permits the application of clear legal rules. He has depicted the law as efficacious in the protection of individual life, expression, and creativity. Law is equated with liberty. It is the image that he has used in an artful effort to construct a system of belief that discourages persons from questioning the justice of the power relationships embedded in an allegedly neutral law and in other "neutral" ideas, such as "merit." His law would devalue political conflict and deploy rules on expression and participation to dissuade the disadvantaged from challenging their subjection.[26] Within the order provided by law, he has assumed that people can engage in reasonable discourse about their political differences. This is the "imagination" of his law.

Scalia's critics charge that in his opinions he envisions a dream world in which political institutions can be made to follow rules and to build a free society without changing inequalities of power and culturally embedded racist and sexist modes of thought. Accordingly, his simulation of liberty through law becomes painfully evident to minorities, women, and other disadvantaged groups. As pointedly revealed in a metaphorical comment by Patricia J. Williams: "The phantom room"—an empty place filled by the unseen presence of "racism as status quo"—"is to me symbolic of the emptiness of formal equality, particularly as expounded by . . . the Reagan Supreme Court. Blindly formalized constructions of equal opportunity are the creation of a space that is filled by a meandering stream of unguided hopes, dreams, fantasies, fears and recollections. They are the presence of the past in imaginary, imaginistic form —the phantom-roomed exile of our longing."[27] Consequently, critics can allege that Scalia's opinions have contributed to an insufficiently inclusive regime of rules that offers little hope for a society with greater personal autonomy or self-realization. His rule-bound political vision has been insufficiently inclusive because it has reinforced the power of the state and ignored the message of frustration voiced by the disadvantaged. He has ignored social facts about sources of inequality and limitations on participation, and he has defended a "neutral" law with a delusional character.[28] His politics parallels the orderly, antiseptic Disneyland version of a nineteenth-century Main Street. The Disneyland street simulates a real main street but disregards its darker aspects, such as dust, piles of horse dung and garbage, Civil War amputees, ragamuffin children, whores, and tubercular beggars. Scalia's politics dismisses the reality of unequal power based on wealth, racism, and sexism with the shibboleth that an individual has the opportunity for success in a world of neutral rules.

By adopting his vision of the linkage of law and liberty, Scalia has revived a faith in the beneficence of rules. Like other preachers in the contemporary conservative revival, he assumes that determinant, universal rules of law or principles such as the law of supply and demand can modify human behavior and produce an orderly if inegalitarian society. However, Scalia fails to consider that the deontological theory of being on which his political vision rests is dubious. An alternative to the American faith in law might be a better way to the realization of the aspirations of all Americans. An alternative ontology or theory of being might avoid the simulation of liberty under law that is the fruit of Scalia's—and most conservatives' and pragmatic liberals'—constitutive discourse by expanding discussions of politics beyond the legal. The alternative would question the Enlightenment liberal presuppositions about law that circumscribe the political consciousness of Scalia and his pragmatic liberal critics.[29]

As a way to an alternative political consciousness, feminist legal scholars recently have developed the concept of "difference" as part of a more encompassing critique of the engendered nature of rule-based politics. The feminist and/or "difference" reconsideration of law has recognized multiple faces of power in the regime.[30] When formalized in law, a gendered definition of power supports legal standards that forbid or isolate contrary arguments about women's power and personal autonomy. The individual who offers the alternative argument is often labeled as "different"—irrational, delinquent, or outlaw. Her different behavior has transgressed the normative basis of truth or reason embedded in the law, and her body is subject to discipline through the legal process.[31] For a more just regime, many feminist scholars want law to include an evaluation of the "discourse of difference." For example, Robin West has sought to "reconstruct" the law so that the "existential and material state of being" of women or other disadvantaged groups is articulated in the law.[32]

Additionally, Martha Minow has tendered a strategy for the acceptance of difference and the articulation of women's unique state of being in law. Minow has not rejected rights but has engaged in "embedding rights within relationships." Especially, she has regarded existing legal rules about difference as unsatisfactory because they treat differences as intrinsic rather than as the product of categorization by legally influential classes. She has refused to admit that people can be neutral or theoretically determinant, that some differences are irrelevant or natural, and that the status quo is good. Thus, she has rejected the legal neutrality postulate of Scalia's modified Reasoned Elaboration jurisprudence. Instead, her "social relations approach" would require a legal decisionmaker to notice people's mutual dependence, to investigate legal constructions of difference, and to question the judgments of persons about difference and, as needed, criticize and challenge them or consider other perspectives on human difference before making a decision. Also, her approach would maintain a "steady inquiry into . . . interpersonal and political relationships," a "suspicion of abstractions," and a concern for the need for difference or equality in particular circumstances. The thrust of her strategy would be to disturb embedded power relations, both hierarchical and dispersed, and related social and legal norms. Her social relations approach sounds like an instrumental methodology of legal interpretation; however, she differs from pragmatic liberals because she is less committed to practical certainty in law. Her approach aims at assuring that the connections and attachments among diverse persons are fairly treated by judges in each case. Her version of equality and rights calls for judges to respect the distinctive differences among people rather than engage in the application of pragmatically developed rules. She also has indicated that legal categories or rules about the treatment of persons are social, mutable, and arbitrary. In making every choice she wants judges to question their partiality and the way in which they assign a priority to an individual's claims. From this practice, she anticipates individualized legal decisions protecting the myriad of differences in society. Although she ultimately relies on legality and a "rescue" of rights for the construction of a fairer regime, she wants legal rules and procedures to be constantly tested and adjusted as instruments for the promotion of substantive fairness and personal autonomy.[33]

Unlike Scalia, difference theorists offer consciousness of outcomes which is extremely attentive to the diversity of the human condition. Their perspective willingly works difference into law and undercuts stable legal rules so long as the differences function toward the goal of legal respect for individuals. Although pragmatic liberals use the categories of legal doctrine instrumentally, difference jurisprudence does more. Also contrary to Scalia's modified Reasoned Elaboration jurisprudence and his pragmatic critics, difference theorists propose not just one legal standard for evaluating constitutional rights and liberties claims, but many.

Because difference theory implies that the American regime cannot rest on a single set of rules, it requires discussion of alternative means of protecting individual liberty. Thus, the idea of difference is a step towards an alternative theory of being, a "hermeneutical ontology."[34] Extending feminist and/or "difference" arguments, a hermeneutical ontology rejects the idea that law with either a theoretical or practical certainty can be derived from the foundational principles of American constitutional politics. A hermeneutical ontology recognizes that the law is simply the practice of argument and the interpretation of written words lacking meaning in a political context.

In contrast to Scalia's view of law, a hermeneutical critique conceptualizes the Constitution as "a kind of institutionalized and formalized site of power struggles" rather than as a set of rules that discipline politics. It adopts the proposition that the Constitution is law, but, differing sharply from the constitutive discourse of Scalia, sees it as mutable law shaped by practical experience, interpretation, and action. The Constitution can offer no certainty; it is only a few lines of text subject to different readings because of the shifting values of readers. Thus, alternative interpretations of constitutional words such as *liberty, equal, protection,* and *speech,* and of the words of legal precedents, are used in interpretation directed toward building a law that recognizes the practical needs of persons with differences for greater personal autonomy and liberty. The hermeneutical critic sees the Constitution as a text that can be co-opted by the less powerful or by voices outside of the courts.[35]

Since law has only a provisional and politically determined meaning, a hermeneutical ontology regards the constant practice of argument as the source of law. Therefore, if law is to address difference, the arguments "internal" to the legal process, such as Scalia's use of Reasoned Elaboration arguments or pragmatic liberalism, must be supplemented by "external" critique of legal professionals' political vision and—contrary to the negativism of critical legal studies—by aspirations for a good society. The external criticism questions the justice of a law that reflects and justifies the interests of the more powerful persons in the regime. It is a critique that must come from persons who suffer disadvantage from legal interpretations establishing "clear" and "neutral" rules and who have aspirations for a better life. It should expose the historical contingency of constitutional and legal standards and of claims that law can be ethically neutral, determinate, and emancipatory.

A hermeneutical critic would begin with a legal and political argument that discloses the power relationships in a "rational" legality.[36] In equal protection law she might question the ambiguity of the distinction between advantaged and disadvantaged classes which is locked into the tiers of scrutiny approach. Thus, the Court's refusal to include poor white persons, gays, or lesbians in the category of disadvantaged classes, or the "intermediate" treatment of gender bias, might be interrogated. She would seek a more flexible, less rule-bound definition of class. Likewise, debate might generate an argument alleging that the remedies for discrimination are inadequate. Alternatively, the argument could begin by asserting that law, rather than being a rule pro-

duced by constitutional politics, is a politically questionable practice
that is not necessarily neutral, principled, certain, practical, or fair.
The aim of disadvantaged persons should be to question—by lawsuit,
direct action, or other means—the rationality of existing rules and to
oppose the reproduction of unequal power and the simulation of fairness that law affords the regime. In its effort at moral education of the
advantaged, a counter-practice especially needs to "exploit" the incomplete dominance of legal arguments about social distinctions. Discussion should be used to try to redeem law and protect the worth of
persons.[37] In the words of Seyla Benhabib, "the purpose is to develop a
model of public dialogue such as to demystify existing power relations
and the current public dialogue which sanctifies them," so that we can
say "what is in the public interest as opposed to the universalization of
what is only in the interest of a particular group."[38]

Consequently, a hermeneutical criticism of Scalia would demand a
partial rejection of the political virtues of reasonable cooperation, bargaining, and rational communication and the call for a politics of order
and equilibrium found in Scalia's opinions. To offer viable alternatives
to the law as construed by Scalia, critics have to argue with passion.
Passion, or a politics of emotion, is fundamentally hostile to the rule of
law.[39] Passion seeks to upset the tradition of orderly analysis and discussion of political options favored by legalists such as Scalia or by
legalists who have sought a much more open discussion of the rule of
law in the United States. When used by disadvantaged parties, it upsets
established normative modes of talking about law and Constitution by
refusing to assume their rationality. Passionate argument has the capacity to induce attention to political inequities by the very shock of its
attack on the reasonableness of the law.[40]

A viable hermeneutical discourse also depends on the critic's recognition that the law has to undergo constant political criticism if it is to
satisfy demands for personal liberty.[41] Existing interpretations of the
Constitution and other law have to be attacked in legal language. Critics of Scalia have to avoid lapsing into the notion that changes in law
can revolutionize power relationships and the treatment of disadvantaged persons in the regime. The strength of cultural values and hostility, and of the fear of revolutions in personal material and social
status, has meant that critics are entering into a long-term conflict in
which the outcome is often no more than marginal gains.

Finally, the viability of a hermeneutical critique of a rule-based political vision such as Scalia's depends on a reconceptualization of liberty.

In the Enlightenment liberal tradition echoed in the Constitution and Scalia's opinions, liberty or autonomy exists in two limited ways. People possess "rational autonomy"; "they are free within the limits of political justice to pursue their (permissible) conceptions of the good; and they are motivated to secure their higher-order interests associated with their moral powers." Also, people have "full autonomy," which is achieved when persons "act from principles of justice that specify the fair terms of cooperation they would give to themselves when fairly represented as free and equal persons."[42] These two definitions of autonomy posit the power of a priori principles of political justice. However, a priori or constitutional principles of political justice restrain action. They establish a normative order that stands beyond political critique. For an alternative politics with a law recognizing difference, all conceptions of order and power have to be questioned. Therefore, autonomy needs to be more broadly conceptualized. What is needed is an autonomy that allows for the interrogation of all arguments about the value of rule-based politics, so that "autonomy does not consist in acting according to a law discovered in an immutable reason and given once and for all" but becomes "the unlimited questioning of oneself about the law and its foundations and the capacity, in light of this interrogation, *to make, to do,* and *to institute* (therefore also, *to say*)."[43] This existentialist conception of autonomy opens up the possibility of radically new conceptions of power which demand more from individuals than adherence to an imposed legal discipline promising personal emancipation. Also, such a conception of autonomy promotes a search for social facts which might justify the inclusion of alternative perceptions of political power in the law.[44] Doubtless, a passionate argument for redefining existing constitutional and other legal standards to establish a radical autonomy speaks in a language that a devotee of the law of rules would find misguided. Like difference theory, it speaks past the concerns of working judges locked into the idea of a regime based on law—a regime that simulates but does not provide liberty.

Because they stand outside the normal constitutive legalistic narratives, difference and hermeneutical criticism of the simulation of liberty in law have not drawn any reaction from Scalia. Scalia and the lawyer-politicians who have great influence over the government of America probably cannot understand the claims of these criticisms. They are an alien narrative, a foreign language. Additionally, the difference and hermeneutical criticisms, by arguing that liberty comes from the moral commitments of persons in community to each other, or from respect for the unique interests of others and action to promote those interests, or from continual assessment of political relationships, assume that a political order based on generally applicable rules of law is insufficient or delusional. The criticisms encourage judges to go beyond a political ontology based on the assumptions of Enlightenment liberalism. Scalia, the modern conservative, only envisions a world governed by and conserving Enlightenment values as enshrined in American politics. Just as he has refused to use natural law and pre-Enlightenment conceptions of tradition, so here too he stands apart from the critics of his ontology. He simply is not of a mind to consider whether liberty is a simulation of autonomous choice when it is redefined in law and legal rights.

SCALIA, THE CONSERVATIVE VISION, AND THE POLITICS OF FEAR

Why has Scalia's vision only sought to reproduce a political-legal order and simulate liberty? Why has he rebuked or neglected criticisms of his political vision? Perhaps he has wanted the certainty of law to serve as an artifice that could mask his anxiety about the uncertain consequences of a regime moving toward greater equality of power and greater representation of interests under the direction of the state. He has recognized that law is dangerous when it offers arguments challenging the multiple interwoven power relationships and the discipline woven into the political practices of the American regime. He has become concerned that the politics of interests could generate an instrumental law that challenges the power of advantaged classes and the legal profession. Thus, his use of law has placed boundaries on the liberty of the less powerful because of his fear of conflict. He apparently believes that American law has created boundaries that (in the words of Jennifer Nedelsky) "keep the threatening others at bay" and protect us from certain dangers imputed to the behavior of others. "But equally (or more) important, our boundary-setting rights protect us from the seemingly overwhelming responsibility that would flow from a recognition of unity."[45]

Through its reproductive and simulative nature, Scalia's law would protect people from the existential fear of having to, in the words of Rodney King, the victim of a racist beating by Los Angeles police, "get along here."[46] Thus, Scalia's law offers progress toward the well-ordered state and the end of the chaos of expanded pluralist politics promoted by the New Deal and public interest liberalism. Yet his political vision offers little prospect for a regime that moves beyond conservative political attitudes about bureaucracy and the dangers of political and moral pluralism, as well as related attitudes about law and the lawyer's craft, toward a culture of civil peace built on inspiring respect for the autonomy of others, and individual responsibility for the welfare of all in the regime. He can only envision the conservation of what he regards as the best of present-day American life through the rule of law. As he stated in a speech, "laws are more a manifestation and a product of the goodness of our society than they are the cause of it."[47] From this perspective, lawmakers should not aspire to create a better world or to free persons from the fears of modern life.

Notes

PREFACE AND ACKNOWLEDGMENTS

1. Mistretta v. United States, 488 U.S. 361, 427 (1989) (Scalia, J., dissenting).

2. Planned Parenthood of Southeastern Pennsylvania v. Casey, 112 S.Ct. 2791, 2875, 2882 (Scalia, J., concurring and dissenting).

3. Judicial Conference, District of Columbia Circuit, "Luncheon Remarks," Federal Rules Decisions 128 (1989): 455.

INTRODUCTION

1. Jeffrey Rosen, "The Leader of the Opposition," New Republic, 18 Jan. 1993, 20. His name is pronounced "SCA-LEE-AH"; see Judicial Conference, District of Columbia Circuit, "Banquet," Federal Rules Decisions 124 (1988): 284–85.

2. See Peter H. Irons, The New Deal Lawyers (Princeton: Princeton University Press, 1982).

3. The term vision is used to describe a way of perceiving political phenomena and of imagining an order among political phenomena, according to a certain rational pattern of order and a transcendent value or association with the Good; a political vision often suggests a transfiguration of the political order for the future realization of human aspirations. See Sheldon S. Wolin, Politics and Vision: Continuity and Innovation in Western Political Thought (Boston: Little, Brown, 1960), 17–21.

4. Antonin Scalia, "Historical Anomalies in Administrative Law," Yearbook of the Supreme Court Historical Society (1985): 106.

5. See the insightful discussion about the New Deal in William E. Leuchtenberg, Franklin D. Roosevelt and the New Deal, 1932–1940 (New York: Harper and Row, 1963), 326–48; and Cass R. Sunstein, "Constitutionalism after the New Deal," Harvard Law Review 101 (1987): 421–510. Michael W. McCann, Taking Reform Seriously: Perspectives on Public Interest Liberalism (Ithaca: Cornell University Press, 1986), 71–121, provides full details on its subject.

6. This summary of conservative thought draws on Alan Brinkley, "The Problem of American Conservatism," American Historical Review 99 (1994): 409–29; Gary Dorrien, The Neoconservative Mind: Politics, Culture, and the War of Ideology (Philadelphia: Temple University Press, 1993); Paul Gottfried,

The Conservative Movement, rev. ed. (New York: Twayne, 1993); Allen Gutt-mann, *The Conservative Tradition in America* (New York: Oxford University Press, 1967), 123–80; Ronald Lora, *Conservative Minds in America* (Chicago: Rand McNally, 1971); George H. Nash, *The Conservative Intellectual Movement in America since 1945* (New York: Basic, 1976); and Clinton Rossiter, *Conservatism in America: The Thankless Persuasion,* 2d ed., rev. (New York: Vintage, 1962).

7. James Q. Wilson, "The Bureaucracy Problem," *Public Interest* 6 (1967): 3–9; idem, "The Rise of the Bureaucratic State," ibid., 41 (1975): 77–103. Key intellectual sources of the antistatist, antibureaucracy position of contemporary conservatism include Friedrich A. Hayek, *The Road to Serfdom* (Chicago: University of Chicago Press, 1944); and Milton Friedman, *Capitalism and Freedom* (Chicago: University of Chicago Press, 1962). The arguments about the inefficiency of bureaucracy and the lack of representative control of agencies surface in economic literature, especially Ronald H. Coase, "The Federal Communications Commission," *Journal of Law and Economics* 2 (1959): 1–40; William Niskanen Jr., *Bureaucracy and Representative Government* (Chicago: Aldine, 1971); Sam Peltzman, "Toward a More General Theory of Regulation," *Journal of Law and Economics* 19 (1976): 211–40; Richard A. Posner, "Theories of Economic Regulation," *Bell Journal of Economics and Management Science* 5 (1974): 335–58; George Stigler, "The Theory of Economic Regulation," ibid., 2 (1971): 3–21; and idem, "The Process of Economic Regulation," *Antitrust Bulletin* 17 (1972): 207–15.

8. The most noted academic political science criticism of pluralism is Theodore J. Lowi, *The End of Liberalism: The Second Republic of the United States,* 2d ed. (New York: W. W. Norton, 1979), 22–63. Economic depictions of the costs of pluralism include Gary S. Becker, "Public Policies, Pressure Groups, and Dead Weight Costs," *Journal of Public Economics* 28 (1985): 329–47; and idem, "A Theory of Competition among Interest Groups for Political Influence," *Quarterly Journal of Economics* 98 (1983): 371–400. In the words of Ronald Kahn, *The Supreme Court and Constitutional Theory, 1953–1993* (Lawrence: University Press of Kansas, 1994), 120, 129–30, 182–85, conservatives accept the existing uneven pluralist dispersal of power within the regime, while many liberals are "critical-pluralists" who seek greater diversity in interest group participation in politics and a more egalitarian dispersal of power.

9. See Brinkley, "Problem of American Conservatism," 419–23. This argument is made differently by conservatives influenced by Edmund Burke—see Russell Kirk, *The Conservative Mind: From Burke to Santayana* (Chicago: Regnery, 1953); by conservatives of a neo-Aristotelian bent—see Leo Strauss, *Natural Right and History* (Chicago: University of Chicago Press, 1953); by conservatives influenced by Roman Catholicism—see Edward A. Purcell Jr., *The Crisis of Democratic Theory: Scientific Naturalism and the Problem of*

Value (Lexington: University Press of Kentucky, 1973), 164–72; by cultural traditionalists—see William J. Bennett, *Our Children and Our Country: Improving America's Schools and Affirming the Common Culture* (New York: Simon and Schuster, 1988), 69–85, 91–113, 167–217; and by cultural and Protestant religious fundamentalists—see Brinkley, "Problem of American Conservatism," 423–29; Pat Robertson, *America's Dates with Destiny* (Nashville: Thomas Nelson, 1986), 173–304; and Pat Robertson, *The New World Order* (Dallas: Word, 1991).

10. Alexander Hamilton, James Madison, and John Jay, *The Federalist,* ed. Jacob E. Cooke (1787–88; Middletown, Conn.: Wesleyan University Press, 1961), paper no. 10 (Madison), pp. 56–65.

11. I define jurisprudence as the normative conceptual apparatus employed to justify the law or legal decisions. See Roger Cotterrell, *The Politics of Jurisprudence: A Critical Introduction to Legal Philosophy* (Philadelphia: University of Pennsylvania Press, 1989), 2–3.

12. See Joyce A. Baugh, "Justice Antonin Scalia and the Freshman Effect" (paper presented at annual meeting of Midwest Political Science Association, Chicago, Ill., 1989); Richard A. Brisbin Jr., "The Conservatism of Antonin Scalia," *Political Science Quarterly* 105 (1990): 2–22; Michael Patrick King, "Justice Antonin Scalia: The First Term on the Supreme Court—1986–1987," *Rutgers Law Journal* 20 (1988): 1–77; Richter H. Moore and Charles B. Fields, "Justice Antonin Scalia in the Criminal Arena" (paper presented at annual meeting of Southern Political Science Association, Atlanta, Ga., 1988); Thea F. Rubin and Albert P. Melone, "Justice Antonin Scalia: A First Year Freshman Effect?" *Judicature* 72 (1988): 98–102.

13. See Richard A. Brisbin Jr., "Conservative Jurisprudence in the Reagan Era" *Cumberland Law Review* 19 (1988–89): 497–537; James G. Wilson, "Justice Diffused: A Comparison of Edmund Burke's Conservatism with the Views of Five Conservative, Academic Judges," *University of Miami Law Review* 40 (1986): 965–69. Bernard Schwartz, *The New Right and the Constitution: Turning Back the Legal Clock* (Boston: Northeastern University Press, 1990), tends to neglect the differences within the "new right" jurisprudence.

14. On ideological description of the Court in the Warren and Burger eras, see Bernard Schwartz, *History of the Supreme Court* (New York: Oxford University Press, 1993), 263–85, 311–36, 362–77; and David Kairys, *With Justice for Some: A Critique of the Conservative Supreme Court* (New York: New Press, 1993). The description is supported by the empirical data on voting in civil liberties cases; see Lawrence Baum, "Policy Change in the Supreme Court," *American Politics Quarterly* 23 (1995): 378, table 2.

15. Richard A. Brisbin Jr., "Justice Antonin Scalia, Constitutional Discourse, and the Legalistic State," *Western Political Quarterly* 44 (1991): 1005–38; Toby Golick, "Justice Scalia, Poverty and the Good Society," *Cardozo Law Review* 12 (1991): 1817–30; Steven R. Greenburger, "Justice Scalia's Due

Process Traditionalism Applied to Territorial Jurisdiction: The Illusion of Adjudication without Judgment," *Boston College Law Review* 33 (1992): 981–1036; Dwight L. Greene, "Justice Scalia and Tonto: Judicial Ignorance, and the Myth of Colorless Individualism in *Bostick v. Florida*," *Tulane Law Review* 67 (1993): 1979–2062; Elizabeth A. Leiss, "Censoring Legislative History: Justice Scalia on the Use of Legislative History in Statutory Interpretation," *Nebraska Law Review* 72 (1993): 568–85; David Schultz, "Legislative Process and Intent in Justice Scalia's Interpretive Method," *Akron Law Review* 25 (1992): 595–610; idem, "Judicial Review and Legislative Deference: The Political Process of Antonin Scalia," *Nova Law Review* 16 (1992): 1249–83; Eric J. Segall, "Justice Scalia, Critical Legal Studies, and the Rule of Law," *George Washington Law Review* 62 (1994): 991–1042; David A. Strauss, "Tradition, Precedent, and Justice Scalia," *Cardozo Law Review* 12 (1991): 1699–1716; and Mark V. Tushnet, "Scalia and the Dormant Commerce Clause: A Foolish Formalism?" ibid., 12 (1991): 1717–43, present variations on the argument that Scalia's method is but a screen to hide a covert political agenda.

16. George Kannar, "The Constitutional Catechism of Antonin Scalia," *Yale Law Journal* 99 (1990): 1297–1357. Compare Donald L. Beschele, "Catechism or Imagination: Is Justice Scalia's Style Typically Catholic?" *Villanova Law Review* 37 (1992): 1329–59. See also George Kannar, "Strenuous Virtues, Virtuous Lives: The Social Vision of Antonin Scalia," *Cardozo Law Review* 12 (1991): 1845–67.

17. William N. Eskridge Jr., "The New Textualism," *UCLA Law Review* 37 (1990): 621–91.

18. See, for example, David B. Anders, "Justices Harlan and Black Revisited: The Emerging Dispute between Justice O'Connor and Justice Scalia over Fundamental Unenumerated Rights," *Fordham Law Review* 61 (1993): 895–933; David Boling, "The Jurisprudential Approach of Justice Antonin Scalia: Methodology over Result?" *Arkansas Law Review* 44 (1991): 1143–1205; Robert A. Burt, "Precedent and Authority in Antonin Scalia's Jurisprudence," *Cardozo Law Review* 12 (1991): 1685–1716; Gregory Cook, "Footnote 6: Justice Scalia's Attempt to Impose a Rule of Law on Substantive Due Process," *Harvard Journal of Law and Public Policy* 14 (1991): 853–93; Michael Herz, "Textualism and Taboo: Interpretation and Deference for Justice Scalia," *Cardozo Law Review* 12 (1991): 1663–83; Bradley C. Karkkainen, "'Plain Meaning': Justice Scalia's Jurisprudence of Strict Statutory Construction," *Harvard Journal of Law and Public Policy* 17 (1993): 401–77; Larry Kramer, "Judicial Asceticism," *Cardozo Law Review* 12 (1991): 1789–98; Jean Morgan Meaux, "Justice Scalia and Judicial Restraint: A Conservative Resolution of Conflict between Individual and State," *Tulane Law Review* 62 (1987): 225–60; Gene R. Nichol, "Justice Scalia, Standing, and Public Law Litigation," *Duke Law Journal* 42 (1993): 1141–68; William D. Popkin, "An 'Internal' Critique of Justice Scalia's Theory of Statutory Interpretation," *Minnesota*

Law Review 76 (1992): 1133–87; Timothy L. Raschke Shattuck, "Justice Scalia's Due Process Methodology," *Southern California Law Review* 65 (1992): 2743–91; Patrice C. Scatera, "Deference to Discretion: Scalia's Impact on Judicial Review of Agency Action in an Era of Deregulation," *Hastings Law Journal* 38 (1987): 1223–60; Edward Gary Spitko, "A Critique of Justice Antonin Scalia's Approach to Fundamental Rights Adjudication," *Duke Law Journal* (1990): 1337–60; Arthur Stock, "Justice Scalia's Use of Sources in Statutory and Constitutional Interpretation: How Congress Always Loses," ibid., (1990): 160–92; Peter L. Strauss, "Comment: Legal Process and Judges in the Real World," *Cardozo Law Review* 12 (1991): 1653–62; Stephen Wizner, "Judging in the Good Society: A Comment on the Jurisprudence of Justice Scalia," ibid., 12 (1991): 1831–43; and Benjamin C. Zipursky, "The Pedigrees of Rights and Powers in Scalia's *Cruzan* Concurrence," *University of Pittsburgh Law Review* 56 (1994): 282–321.

19. Brisbin, "Conservatism of Scalia," 25–29; Peter B. Edelman, "Justice Scalia's Jurisprudence and the Good Society: Shades of Felix Frankfurter and the Harvard Hit Parade of the 1950s," *Cardozo Law Review* 12 (1991): 1799–1815; Nicholas S. Zeppos, "Justice Scalia's Textualism" The 'New' New Legal Process," ibid., 12 (1991): 1597–1643.

20. On the definition of social facts, see H. N. Hirsch, *A Theory of Liberty: The Constitution and Minorities* (New York: Routledge, 1992), 2–3; on the effect of political attitudes on judicial decisions, see Jeffrey A. Segal and Harold J. Spaeth, *The Supreme Court and the Attitudinal Model* (Cambridge: Cambridge University Press, 1993).

21. See Roger Benjamin and Raymond Duvall, "The Capitalist State in Context," in *The Democratic State,* ed. Roger Benjamin and Stephen L. Elkin (Lawrence: University Press of Kansas, 1985), 23–24, 28; Stephen L. Elkin, "Pluralism in Its Place: State and Regime in Liberal Democracy," in ibid., 180, 186–208; and idem, *City and Regime in the American Republic* (Chicago: University of Chicago Press, 1987), 110–21.

22. I use the term *discourse* in a historical as well as linguistic sense. Thus, *discourse* is a "discursive process," or a sociohistorical practice of the use of language to produce a meaning. Additionally, because of the historical effect of organizational forms on language, the existence of a variety of discourses with different meanings is recognized; see Peter Goodrich, *Legal Discourse: Studies in Linguistics, Rhetoric, and Legal Analysis* (New York: St. Martin's Press, 1987), 132–51.

23. A narrative is a story about events. Like any story, it uses selected words to explain the "is" of our current state of affairs and teaches a lesson about what "ought" to be; see Robert Cover, "Foreword: *Nomos* and Narrative," *Harvard Law Review* 97 (1983): 10; and David Luban, *Legal Modernism* (Ann Arbor: University of Michigan Press, 1994), 14–17.

24. This point is stressed, with examples, in Charles Fried, "Manners

Makyth Man: The Prose Style of Justice Scalia," *Harvard Journal of Law and Public Policy* 16 (1993): 529–39.

25. James Boyd White, *Justice as Translation: An Essay in Cultural and Legal Criticism* (Chicago: University of Chicago Press, 1990), 90, and also 101.

26. See W. John Moore, "Tugging from the Right," *National Journal,* 20 Oct. 1990, 2510–15; Rosen, "Leader of the Opposition," 20–21, 24, 26–27; David G. Savage, *Turning Right: The Making of the Rehnquist Court* (New York: John Wiley and Sons, 1992); Christopher E. Smith, *Justice Antonin Scalia and the Supreme Court's Conservative Moment* (Westport, Conn.: Praeger, 1993). Smith has argued that the appointment of Scalia opened a "window of opportunity" for a shift toward a much more conservative Court, but he has concluded that Scalia did not avail himself of the opportunity to rally the votes of other justices to the conservative cause. See also Alex Kozinski, "My Pizza with Ninó," *Cardozo Law Review* 12 (1991): 1585–88, for a discussion of Ronald Reagan's hope that Scalia would lead a conservative Court.

27. On his warm personal relations with judges philosophically opposed to his conservatism, see Patricia Wald, quoted in Judicial Conference, District of Columbia Circuit, "Banquet," *Federal Rules Decisions* 124 (1988): 283; and Abner Mikva, quoted in Ruth Marcus and Susan Schmidt, "Scalia Tenacious after Staking out a Position," *Washington Post,* 22 June 1986, A16. See also Fred Barnes, "Top Gun on the High Court," *Reader's Digest* 139 (July 1991): 91–95; Joan Biskipic, "Justice Scalia: Dynamo on the Court," *Congressional Quarterly Weekly Report* 48 (24 May 1990): 916; Kozinski, "Pizza with Ninó," 1583–1601; and David Seligman, "Supreme Court Poker," *Fortune* 114 (21 July 1986): 107–10. An excellent example of his humor is found in Judicial Conference, District of Columbia Circuit, "Luncheon Remarks," *Federal Rules Decisions* 128 (1989): 452–56.

28. See "Ruing Fixed Opinions," *New York Times,* 22 Feb. 1988, 1, 16.

29. See "Court Critique," *Time,* 1 Aug. 1988, 70; David A. Kaplan and Bob Cohn, "The Court's Mr. Right," *Newsweek,* 5 Nov. 1990, 62, 67; John C. Jeffries Jr., *Justice Lewis F. Powell Jr.* (New York: Charles Scribner's Sons, 1994), 534–35; Savage, *Turning Right,* 60–61, 118–19, 201–5, 255–56; James F. Simon, *The Center Holds: The Power Struggle Inside the Rehnquist Court* (New York: Simon and Schuster, 1995), 137–41; Smith, *Scalia,* 60–67, 69–73; Elder Witt, "Antonin Scalia: Just What Reagan Wanted," *Congressional Quarterly Weekly Report* 45 (4 July 1987): 1433.

30. David Schultz, in "Legislative Process and Intent," 598, and "Judicial Review and Legislative Deference: The Political Process of Antonin Scalia," *Nova Law Review* 16 (1992): 1249–83, has tried, inaccurately, to place my previous publications about Scalia solely in the methodological or legal explanation category. My argument is that Scalia's political attitudes and the politi-

cal values contained in his jurisprudential expositions in opinions are inter-connected—thus, Scalia's political vision is exposed both by his votes and by his "methodology," or use of a mode of jurisprudential argument.

CHAPTER ONE: FROM PROFESSOR TO PUNDIT

1. "Dr. S. Eugene Scalia," *New York Times,* 7 Jan. 1986, D21.

2. Ruth Marcus and Susan Schmidt, "Scalia Tenacious after Staking Out a Position," *Washington Post,* 22 June 1986, A1, A16; Claire Cushman, ed., *The Supreme Court Justices: Illustrated Biographies, 1789–1993* (Washington, D.C.: CQ Press, 1993), 511–15. According to Cushman, Maureen Scalia is active in volunteer work for charitable organizations and in the affairs of her church. The Scalia children are Ann, Catherine, Christopher, Eugene, John, Margaret, Mary, Matthew, and Paul.

3. George Kannar, "The Constitutional Catechism of Antonin Scalia," *Yale Law Journal* 99 (1990): 1297–1302. On social backgrounds and judging, see Neal Tate, "Personal Attribute Models of the Voting Behavior of Supreme Court Justices: Liberalism in Civil Liberties and Economic Decisions, 1946–1978," *American Political Science Review* 75 (1981): 355–67; C. Neal Tate and Roger Handberg, "Time Binding and Theory Building in Personal At-tribute Models of Supreme Court Voting Behavior, 1916–88," *American Jour-nal of Political Science* 35 (1991): 460–80; and S. Sidney Ulmer, "Are Social Background Models Time-Bound?" *American Political Science Review* 80 (1986): 957–67.

4. Kannar, "Constitutional Catechism," 1313–20.

5. S. Eugene Scalia, *Carducci: His Critics and Translators in England and America, 1881–1932,* Paterno Library Collection of Italian Studies (New York: S. F. Vanni, 1937), 71, 90. Giosuè Carducci (1839–1915) was an Italian poet and literary historian. See Kannar, "Constitutional Catechism," 1316n. 100, for references to S. E. Scalia, *Carducci,* 88–90. S. Eugene Scalia, *Luigi Capuana and His Times,* Paterno Library Collection of Italian Studies, vol. 4 (New York: S. F. Vanni [Ragusa], 1952), is a literary biography of a late-nine-teenth-century Sicilian novelist, dramatist, and critic. Kannar's citations of it at pp. 37 and 39 reflect on passages in which indirectly the elder Scalia con-veys his views of language and interpretation in the formation of nationalism. *Philip Mazzei: My Life and Wanderings,* trans. S. Eugene Scalia, ed. Mar-gherita Marchione (Morristown, N.J.: American Institute of Italian Studies, 1980), is a translation of the autobiography of an Italian revolutionary adven-turer. It contains no discussion of the problems of translation or interpretation in its preface (13–22) or "Translator's Notes" (418–20). The same is true of a series of S. E. Scalia's translations of works by modernist Italian writers in *Literary Review* 28 (1985): 201–6, 209–12, 215–19, 227–30, 233–38, 245–48, 253–56, 260–72, 297–300, 312–17.

6. See Kannar, "Constitutional Catechism," 1316–17; George Kannar, "Strenuous Virtues, Virtuous Lives: The Social Vision of Antonin Scalia," *Cardozo Law Review* 12 (1991): 1845–67.

7. Donald L. Beschele, "Catechism or Imagination: Is Justice Scalia's Style Typically Catholic?" *Villanova Law Review* 37 (1992): 1329–59, quotation on 1353.

8. A point made in Richard A. Brisbin Jr., "The Conservatism of Antonin Scalia," *Political Science Quarterly* 105 (1990): 25–29; and Peter B. Edelman, "Justice Scalia's Jurisprudence and the Good Society: Shades of Felix Frankfurter and the Harvard Hit Parade of the 1950s," *Cardozo Law Review* 12 (1991): 1799–1815.

9. Legal Realist writings are excerpted in William W. Fisher III, Morton J. Horwitz, and Thomas A. Reed, eds., *American Legal Realism* (New York: Oxford University Press, 1993). The volume includes excerpts from useful articles by Karl Llewellyn: "A Realistic Jurisprudence—The Next Step" (53–58); and "Some Realism about Realism—Responding to Dean Pound" (68–75). Legal Realism is placed in the larger pattern of twentieth-century American thought in Edward A. Purcell Jr., *The Crisis of Democratic Theory: Scientific Naturalism and the Problem of Value* (Lexington: University Press of Kentucky, 1973), 74–95, 159–78. See also Roger Cotterrell, *The Politics of Jurisprudence: A Critical Introduction to Legal Philosophy* (Philadelphia: University of Pennsylvania Press, 1989), 182–215; Morton Horwitz, *The Transformation of American Law, 1870–1960: The Crisis of Legal Orthodoxy* (Cambridge: Harvard University Press, 1992), 169–246; Laura Kalman, *Legal Realism at Yale, 1927–1960* (Chapel Hill: University of North Carolina Press, 1986); Wilfrid Rumble, *Legal Realism: Skepticism, Reform, and the Judicial Process* (Ithaca: Cornell University Press, 1968).

10. See Horwitz, *Transformation of American Law,* 237–40, 253–68; Gary Peller, "Neutral Principles in the 1950s," *University of Michigan Journal of Law Reform* 25 (1988): 561–622; G. Edward White, *Patterns of American Legal Thought* (Indianapolis: Bobbs-Merrill, 1978), 136–63.

11. Herbert Wechsler, "Toward Neutral Principles of Constitutional Law," *Harvard Law Review* 73 (1959): 19.

12. Antonin Scalia, letter to the author, 20 Apr. 1995, discusses his professors. See also Edelman, "Scalia's Jurisprudence," 1799–1815; and Sanford Levinson, "The Confrontation of Religious Faith and Civil Religion: Catholics Becoming Justices," *DePaul Law Review* 39 (1990): 1074–81; and Brisbin, "Conservatism of Scalia," 25–29.

13. *Martindale-Hubbell Law Directory,* 93d year, vol. and sec. 3 (1961): 4189–93; *Martindale-Hubbell Law Directory,* 99th year, vol. and sec. 3 (1967): 185B–190B.

14. Statement of Erwin Griswold, in U.S. Senate, Committee on the Judiciary, *Hearing on the Nomination of Judge Antonin Scalia, to Be Associate*

Justice of the Supreme Court of the United States, 99th Cong., 1st sess., 1986, 148, in *The Supreme Court of the United States: Hearings on Successful and Unsuccessful Nominations of Supreme Court Justices by the Senate Judiciary Committee,* vol. 13, *Antonin Scalia,* ed. Roy M. Mersky and J. Myron Jacobstein (Buffalo: William S. Hein, 1989), 242.

15. C. Graham Lilly and Antonin Scalia, "Appellate Justice: A Crisis in Virginia," *Virginia Law Review* 57 (1971): 3–64.

16. Antonin Scalia, "The Hearing Examiner Loan Program," *Duke Law Journal* (1971): 319–66, esp. 360–66.

17. Edward H. Levi, *Introduction to Legal Reasoning* (Chicago: University of Chicago Press, 1948), 8–27.

18. Antonin Scalia, "Sovereign Immunity and Nonstatutory Review of Federal Administrative Action: Some Conclusions from the Public-Lands Cases," *Michigan Law Review* 68 (1970): 867–924. Scalia reiterated some of these themes in Antonin Scalia, "Historical Anomalies in Administrative Law," *Yearbook of the Supreme Court Historical Society* (1985): 104–6.

19. See Marcus and Schmidt, "Scalia Tenacious," A1, A16. *United States Government Organization Manual, 1974–75* (Washington, D.C.: GPO, 1974), 88–89, describes the Office of Telecommunications Policy.

20. 47 *U.S. Code* §§ 309(a), 326.

21. Antonin Scalia, "Don't Go Near the Water," *Federal Communications Bar Journal* 25 (1972): 111–20.

22. *United States Government Organization Manual, 1974–75,* 414–16.

23. Administrative Conference of the United States, "Report of the Chairman," *Report of the Administrative Conference of the United States* (Washington, D.C.: GPO, 1973), 1–4. His testimony at appropriations hearings also describes the activities and plans of the conference under his chairmanship; see U.S. House of Representatives, Subcommittee on Treasury, Postal Service, and General Governmental Appropriations of the Committee on Appropriations, *Treasury, Postal Service, and General Governmental Appropriations for FY 1974: Hearings,* 93d Cong., 1st sess., 12 Apr. 1973, 38–75; U.S. Senate, Subcommittee on Treasury, Postal Service, and General Governmental Appropriations of the Committee on Appropriations, *Treasury, Postal Service, and General Governmental Appropriations for FY 1974, Part 1: Hearings,* 93d Cong., 1st sess., 9 May 1973, 813–60; U.S. House of Representatives, Subcommittee on Treasury, Postal Service, and General Governmental Appropriations of the Committee on Appropriations, *Treasury, Postal Service, and General Governmental Appropriations for FY 1975, Part 4, General Government: Hearings,* 93d Cong., 2d sess., 24 Apr. 1974, 155–209; U.S. Senate, Subcommittee on Treasury, Postal Service and General Governmental Appropriations of the Committee on Appropriations, *Treasury, Postal Service, and General Governmental Appropriations, Part 1: Hearings,* 93d Cong., 2d sess., 23 May 1974, 937–66.

24. U.S. House of Representatives, Subcommittee on Courts, Civil Liberties, and the Administration of Justice of the Committee on the Judiciary, *Parole Reorganization Act: Hearings on H.R. 1598, H.R. 978, H.R. 2028*, 93d Cong., 1st sess., 21 June 1973, 163–86, 193–208; U.S. House of Representatives, Subcommittee on Foreign Operations and Government Information of the Committee on Government Operations, *Availability of Information to Congress: Hearings, H.R. 4938, H.R. 5983, H.R. 6438*, 93d Cong., 1st sess., 19 Apr. 1973, 223–52; idem, *The Freedom of Information Act: Hearings*, 93d Cong., 1st sess., 10 May 1973, 274–307; U.S. House of Representatives, Subcommittee on Crime of the Committee on the Judiciary, *Bureaucratic Accountability Act of 1974: Hearings*, 93d Cong., 2d sess., 27 Mar. 1974, 42–67; U.S. House of Representatives, Subcommittee on Legislation and Military Operations of the Committee on Government Operations, *To Establish a Consumer Protection Agency: Hearings*, 93d Cong., 1st sess., 11 Oct. 1973, 515–44, 559–84; U.S. Senate, Subcommittee on Reorganization, Research, and International Organizations of the Committee on Government Operations and Subcommittee on Consumers of the Committee on Commerce, *To Establish an Independent Consumer Protection Agency: Hearings*, 93d Cong., 1st sess., 5 Apr. 1973, 577–600; U.S. Senate, Subcommittee on Consumers of the Committee on Commerce, *Food Amendments of 1974: Hearings*, 93d Cong., 2d sess., 25 Mar. 1974, 165–80; U.S. Senate, Subcommittee on Consumers of the Committee on Commerce, and Subcommittee on Representation of Citizens' Interests of the Committee on the Judiciary, *Adequacy of Consumer Redress Mechanisms: Hearings*, 93d Cong., 2d sess., 13 Nov. 1974, 4–18.

25. Antonin Scalia and Frank Goodman, "Procedural Aspects of the Consumer Product Safety Act," *UCLA Law Review* 20 (1973): 899–982.

26. Antonin Scalia, "Letter to Congressman John Dingell, 23 May 1974," in Marshall Breger, "The APA: An Administrative Conference Perspective," *Virginia Law Review* 72 (1986): 344–45.

27. *United States Government Organization Manual, 1975–76* (Washington, D.C.: GPO, 1975), 306, 308, describes his office. See also Marcus and Schmidt, "Scalia Tenacious," A16.

28. Antonin Scalia, "Remarks," in Section of Administrative Law, "1976 Bicentennial Institute, Oversight and Review of Agency Decisionmaking," *Administrative Law Review* 28 (1976): 684–701, quotation on 689.

29. Buckley v. Valeo, 424 U.S. 1, 257–90 (1976) (White, J., concurring and dissenting).

30. See Scalia, "Remarks," 689–95, quotation on 701.

31. U.S. House of Representatives, Subcommittee on Administrative Law and Governmental Relations of the Committee on the Judiciary, *Congressional Review of Administrative Rulemaking: Hearings*, 94th Cong., 1st sess., 7 Nov. 1975, 373–88; U.S. House of Representatives, Subcommittee on Interna-

tional Security and Scientific Affairs of the Committee on International Relations, *Congressional Review of International Agreements: Hearings*, 94th Cong., 2d sess., 22 July 1976, 163–257; U.S. Senate, Committee on Government Operations, *Improving Congressional Oversight of Federal Regulatory Agencies: Hearings*, 94th Cong., 2d sess., 20 May 1976, 76–137; U.S. Senate, Subcommittee on Administrative Practice and Procedure of the Committee on the Judiciary, *Administrative Procedure Act Amendments of 1976: Hearings*, 94th Cong., 2d sess., 28 Apr. 1976, 87–107; U.S. Senate, Subcommittee on the Separation of Powers of the Committee on the Judiciary, *Congressional Oversight of Executive Agreements, 1975: Hearings*, 94th Cong., 1st sess., 15 May 1975, 167–203.

32. On emergencies, see U.S. House of Representatives, Subcommittee on Administrative Law and Governmental Relations of the Committee on the Judiciary, *National Emergencies Act: Hearings on H.R. 3884*, 94th Cong., 1st sess., 6 Mar. 1975, 88–105. On executive privilege, see U.S. House of Representatives, Select Committee on Intelligence, *U.S. Intelligence Activity and Committee Proceedings, Part 4: Hearings*, 94th Cong., 1st sess., 20 Nov. 1975, 1413–63; U.S. Senate, Subcommittee on Intergovernmental Relations of the Committee on Government Operations, *Executive Privilege: Secrecy in Government: Hearings*, 94th Cong., 2d sess., 23 Oct. 1976, 67–128; U.S. Senate, Subcommittee on the Separation of Powers of the Committee on the Judiciary, *Congressional Access to and Control of the Release of Sensitive Government Information: Hearings*, 94th Cong., 2d sess., 12 Mar. 1976, 98–121. On the Twenty-fifth Amendment, see U.S. Senate, Subcommittee on Constitutional Amendments of the Committee on the Judiciary, *Examination of the First Implementation of Section Two of the Twenty-fifth Amendment: Hearings*, 94th Cong., 1st sess., 26 Feb. 1975, 47–67; reprinted in part in Antonin Scalia, "Testimony before the U.S. Senate Subcommittee on Constitutional Amendments," in "Twenty-fifth Amendment Proposals Aired in Senate Hearings; Association Position Favors No Changes," *American Bar Association Journal* 61 (1975): 600–601.

33. On bankruptcy, see U.S. Senate, Subcommittee on Improvements in Judicial Machinery of the Committee on the Judiciary, *Bankruptcy Reform Act: Hearings*, 94th Cong., 1st sess., 31 Oct. 1975, 197–228. On nondiscrimination see U.S. House of Representatives, Subcommittee on Government Information and Individual Rights of the Committee on Government Operations, *Discriminatory Overseas Assignment Policies of Federal Agencies: Hearings*, 94th Cong., 1st sess., 9 Apr. 1975, 86–102. On the boycott, see U.S. House of Representatives, Subcommittee on Monopolies and Commercial Law of the Committee on the Judiciary, *Arab Boycott: Hearings on H.R. 5246, H.R. 12383, H.R. 11488*, 94th Cong., 1st sess., 9 July 1975, 37–74; U.S. House of Representatives, Subcommittee on International Trade and Commerce of the Committee on International Relations, *Discriminatory Arab Pres-*

sure on U.S. Business: Hearings, 94th Cong., 1st sess., 13 Mar. 1975, 71–111; U.S. Senate, Subcommittee on International Finance of the Committee on Banking, Housing, and Urban Affairs, *Foreign Investment and Arab Boycott Legislation: Hearings,* 94th Cong., 1st sess., 22 July 1975, 159–75. On journalistic privilege, see U.S. House of Representatives, Subcommittee on Courts, Civil Liberties, and the Administration of Justice of the Committee on the Judiciary, *Newsman's Privilege: Hearings,* 94th Cong., 1st sess., 23 Apr. 1975, 6–93. On election law, see U.S. Senate, Subcommittee on Privileges and Elections of the Committee on Rules and Administration, *Federal Election Campaign Act Amendments of 1976: Hearings,* 94th Cong., 2d sess., 18 Feb. 1976, 103–45. On the budget see U.S. House of Representatives, Subcommittee on the Departments of State, Justice, Commerce, and the Judiciary Appropriations, of the Committee on Appropriations, *Departments of State, Justice, Commerce, the Judiciary, and Related Agencies Appropriations for FY 1976, Part 2: Hearings,* 94th Cong., 1st sess., 19 Mar. 1975, 747–55.

34. The label *neoconservative* is applied to this group in Gary Dorrien, *The Neoconservative Mind: Politics, Culture, and the War of Ideology* (Philadelphia: Temple University Press, 1993).

35. For biographical information on this period of Scalia's life, see *Almanac of the Federal Judiciary* 2 (1985–86): 14–15; Sidney Blumenthal, "A Well-Connected Conservative," *Washington Post,* 22 June 1986, A16; Marcus and Schmidt, "Scalia Tenacious," A1, A16; U.S. Senate, Committee on the Judiciary, *Hearing on the Confirmation of Federal Judges, Part 4: Nomination of Antonin Scalia to the Court of Appeals,* 97th Cong., 2d sess., 1982, 90–92. See also Antonin Scalia, "Chairman's Message: Support Your Local Professor of Administrative Law," *Administrative Law Review* 34, no. 2 (1982): v–ix.

36. The lack of consistent scholarly productivity with a theoretical, academic focus apparently led Mark Tushnet to label Scalia as "a second-rank faculty member at a first-rank law school." Tushnet also commented, "Compared to the preappointment scholarship of his academic predecessors on the Court, Frankfurter and Douglas, this [Scalia's scholarship] is thin indeed." See Mark Tushnet, "The Warren Court as History: An Interpretation," in *The Warren Court in Historical and Political Perspective,* ed. Mark Tushnet (Charlottesville: University Press of Virginia, 1993), 30.

37. Antonin Scalia, "Back to Basics: Making Law without Making Rules," *Regulation* 5, no. 4 (1981): 25–28.

38. Antonin Scalia, "Two Wrongs Make a Right: The Judicialization of Standardless Rulemaking," *Regulation* 1, no. 1 (1977): 38–41.

39. Antonin Scalia, "Chairman's Message: Rulemaking as Politics," *Administrative Law Review* 34, no. 3 (1982): v–xi. Scalia's concern with ensuring agencies' flexibility in administration surfaces, with regard to a specific problem, in idem, "Chairman's Message: Separation of Functions. Obscurity Preserved," *Administrative Law Review* 34, no. 1 (1982): v–xiv.

40. Antonin Scalia, "Guadalajara! A Case Study in Regulation by Munificence," *Regulation* 2, no. 2 (1978): 23–29.

41. Antonin Scalia, "A Note on the Benzene Case," *Regulation* 4, no. 4 (1980): 25–28.

42. Antonin Scalia, "The Legislative Veto: A False Remedy for System Overload," *Regulation* 3, no. 6 (1979): 19–26; U.S. House of Representatives, Subcommittee on Rules of the House of the Committee on Rules, *Congressional Review of Agency Rulemaking: Hearing on Various Legislative Veto Bills Introduced in the 97th Congress*, 97th Cong., 1st sess., 28 Oct. 1981, 200–210.

43. He stated much the same set of views in other testimony before Congress during the period 1977–82; see U.S. House of Representatives, Subcommittee on Legislation and National Security of the Committee on Government Operations, *Providing Reorganization Authority to the President: Hearings*, 95th Cong., 1st sess., 1 Mar. 1977, 56–75; U.S. House of Representatives, Subcommittee on Rules of the House of the Committee on Rules, *Regulatory Reform and Congressional Review of Agency Rules, Part 1: Hearing on H.R. 1776*, 96th Cong., 1st sess., 26 Sept. 1979, 524–636; U.S. House of Representatives, Committee on Foreign Affairs, *Amendments to the Foreign Assistance Act of 1961: Nuclear Prohibitions and Certain Human Rights Matters: Hearings and Markup on H.R. 5015, H. Res. 286*, 97th Cong., 1st sess., 8 Dec. 1981, 37–51, esp. 39; U.S. Senate, Committee on Governmental Affairs, *To Renew the Reorganization Authority: Hearings*, 95th Cong., 1st sess., 8 Feb. 1977, 39–52; U.S. Senate, Subcommittee on the Consumer of the Committee on Commerce, Science, and Transportation, *Oversight of the Federal Trade Commission: Hearings*, 96th Cong., 1st sess., 19 Sept. 1979, 246–60; U.S. Senate, Subcommittee on Administrative Practice and Procedure of the Committee on the Judiciary, *Regulatory Reform, Part 2: Hearings*, 96th Cong., 1st sess., 18 July 1979, 129–54.

44. Vermont Yankee Nuclear Power Corp. v. Natural Resources Defense Council, 435 U.S. 519 (1978). Justices Harry Blackmun and Lewis Powell did not participate.

45. Antonin Scalia, "Vermont Yankee: The A.P.A., the D.C. Circuit, and the Supreme Court," *Supreme Court Review* (1978): 345–409.

46. Antonin Scalia, "The Freedom of Information Act Has No Clothes," *Regulation* 6, no. 2 (1982): 14–19, quotations on 18, 19. His testimony before a Senate subcommittee, in U.S. Senate, Subcommittee on the Constitution of the Committee on the Judiciary, *Freedom of Information Act, Vol. 1: Hearings on S. 587, S. 1235, S. 1247, S. 1730, S. 1751*, 97th Cong., 1st sess., 9 Dec. 1981, 953–62, reiterates the "free lunch," or costs, problem and the privacy problems he associates with the FOIA. He also notes (at 961) that the executive response to the proposed amendments of 1974 emerged without his involvement.

47. Antonin Scalia, "The ALJ Fiasco—A Reprise," *University of Chicago Law Review* 47 (1979): 57–80. The article was also presented as a public address, at which time Scalia answered a few questions about it; see David Ginsburg, moderator, "Panel IV: Improving the Administrative Process—Time for a New APA? (Part C)," *Administrative Law Review* 32 (1980): 371–80.

48. Antonin Scalia, "Chairman's Message," *Administrative Law Review* 33, no. 4 (1981): v–x. His general support for procedural change is signaled by his appearance and brief testimony before the House of Representatives regarding American Bar Association recommendations on changes in regulation; see U.S. House of Representatives, Subcommittee on Administrative Law and Governmental Relations of the Committee on the Judiciary, *Regulatory Procedures Act of 1981: Hearings on H.R. 746*, 97th Cong., 1st sess., 1981, 111–21.

49. See Antonin Scalia, "Federal Trade Commission," *Regulation* 4, no. 6 (1980): 18–20; idem, "Federal Communications Commission," ibid., 4, no. 6 (1980): 27–28.

50. Antonin Scalia, "Regulatory Reform—The Game Has Changed," *Regulation* 5, no. 1 (1981): 13–15.

51. Antonin Scalia, "Reagulation—The First Year: Regulatory Review and Management," *Regulation* 6, no. 1 (1982): 19–21.

52. U.S. House of Representatives, Subcommittee on Legislation of the Permanent Select Committee on Intelligence, *The Intelligence Identities Protection Act: Hearings*, 97th Cong., 1st sess., 8 Apr. 1981, 112–30.

53. Antonin Scalia, "The Two Faces of Federalism," *Harvard Journal of Law and Public Policy* 6, special issue (1982): 19–22.

54. Regents of Univ. of California v. Bakke, 438 U.S. 265 (1978).

55. Antonin Scalia, "The Disease as the Cure: 'In Order to Get beyond Racism We Must First Take Account of Race,'" *Washington University Law Quarterly* (1979): 147–57, quotations on 148, 149.

56. Ibid., 154–56.

57. U.S. House of Representatives, Subcommittee on Elementary, Secondary, and Vocational Education of the Committee on Education and Labor, *Oversight on Private Schools: Hearings*, 97th Cong., 1st sess., 13 May 1981, 47–52, 65–67; see also U.S. Senate, Subcommittee on Taxation, and Debt Management Generally, of the Committee on Finance, *Tuition Tax Relief Bills, Part 1*, 95th Cong., 2d sess., 19 Jan. 1978, 284–301.

58. U.S. Senate, Subcommittee on Taxation, and Debt Management of the Committee on Finance, *Tuition Tax Credits, Part 1: Hearings on S. 550*, 97th Cong., 1st sess., 3 June 1981, 243–97, quotation on 250.

59. Thus, he is in some agreement with the assessment of the institutional failure of Congress offered by Morris P. Fiorina, *Congress: Keystone of the Washington Establishment* (New Haven: Yale University Press, 1977), 46–47; this assessment was reconsidered in the book's second edition (New Haven: Yale University Press, 1989), 83–141.

CHAPTER TWO: REWIRING THE D.C. CIRCUIT

1. See J. Woodford Howard Jr., *The Courts of Appeals in the Federal Judicial System* (Princeton: Princeton University Press, 1981), 25–33.

2. U.S. Senate, Committee on the Judiciary, *Confirmation of Federal Judges, Part 4: Nomination of Antonin Scalia to the Court of Appeals: Hearings,* 97th Cong., 2d sess., 1982, 90–92.

3. The D.C. Circuit decided or disposed of many cases without opinion in this period; presumably Scalia participated in some of these actions.

4. The personnel of the D.C. Circuit also changed with the death of Edward Tamm and the assignment to senior status (semiretirement) of Malcolm R. Wilkey. They were replaced by James Buckley, Laurence Silberman, and Kenneth Starr.

5. David H. Willison, "Judicial Review of Administrative Decisions: Agency Cases before the Court of Appeals for the District of Columbia, 1981–1984," *American Politics Quarterly* 14 (1986): 317–27.

6. For other examinations of Scalia's opinions for the D.C. Circuit, see Richard Nagareda, "The Appellate Jurisprudence of Antonin Scalia," *University of Chicago Law Review* 54 (1987): 705–39; and James G. Wilson, "Constraints of Power: The Constitutional Opinions of Judges Scalia, Bork, Posner, Easterbrook, and Winter," *University of Miami Law Review* 40 (1986): 1181–1206.

7. See Scalia's position in KCST-TV v. FCC, 699 F.2d 1185, 1195–1201 (D.C. Cir. 1983) (Scalia, J., dissenting). His earlier writings also rejected the procedural hard look; see Antonin Scalia, "Vermont Yankee: The A.P.A., the D.C. Circuit, and the Supreme Court," *Supreme Court Review* (1978): 345. For the origins and nature of this doctrine, see Greater Boston Television Corp. v. FCC, 444 F.2d 841, 851 (D.C. Cir. 1970); Pikes Peak Broadcasting Co. v. FCC, 422 F.2d 671, 682 (D.C. Cir. 1969); WAIT Radio v. FCC, 418 F.2d 1153, 1157 (D.C. Cir. 1969).

8. See Center for Auto Safety v. Peck, 751 F.2d 1336, 1368–70 (D.C. Cir. 1985); and the commentary in Patrice C. Scatera, "Deference to Discretion: Scalia's Impact on Judicial Review of Agency Action in an Era of Deregulation," *Hastings Law Journal* 38 (1987): 1252–54.

9. He found an abuse of discretion through arbitrary and capricious action, or violations of statutory intent about procedures, in Thomas v. New York, 802 F.2d 1443 (D.C. Cir. 1986); Regular Common Carrier Conference v. United States, 793 F.2d 376 (D.C. Cir. 1986); National Treasury Employees Union v. Federal Labor Relations Auth., 793 F.2d 371 (D.C. Cir. 1986); International Ass'n of Bridge, Structural, and Ornamental Iron Workers, Local 111 v. NLRB, 792 F.2d 241 (D.C. Cir. 1986); Gates and Fox Co. v. Occupational Safety and Health Review Comm'n, 790 F.2d 154 (D.C. Cir. 1986); Rainbow Navigation v. Dept. of the Navy, 783 F.2d 1072 (D.C. Cir. 1986); American

Fed'n of Gov't Employees, Local 3090 v. Federal Labor Relations Auth., 777 F.2d 751 (1985) (Scalia, J., concurring); Citizens for Jazz on WRVR, Inc. v. FCC, 775 F.2d 392 (D.C. Cir. 1985); Electrical Dist. No. 1 v. Federal Energy Regulatory Comm'n (FERC), 774 F.2d 490 (D.C. Cir. 1985); FAIC Securities, Inc. v. United States, 768 F.2d 352 (D.C. Cir. 1985); Department of Treasury, United States Customs Serv. v. Fed. Labor Relations Auth., 762 F.2d 1119 (D.C. Cir. 1985); Maryland People's Counsel v. FERC, 761 F.2d 768 (D.C. Cir. 1985); Carter v. Director, Office of Workers' Compensation Programs, 751 F.2d 1398 (D.C. Cir. 1985); Devine v. Pastore, 732 F.2d 213 (D.C. Cir. 1984); New England Coalition on Nuclear Pollution v. Nuclear Regulatory Comm'n, 727 F.2d 1127 (D.C. Cir. 1984). But he did not find an abuse of discretion in numerous agency actions: see National Fed'n of Fed. Employees, Local 615 v. Federal Labor Relations Auth., 801 F.2d 477 (D.C. Cir. 1986); Natural Resources Defense Council v. Thomas, 801 F.2d 457 (D.C. Cir. 1986); Consumers Union v. FTC, 801 F.2d 417 (D.C. Cir. 1986); Road Sprinkler Fitters Local Union 669 v. NLRB, 778 F.2d 8 (D.C. Cir. 1985); City of Charlottesville, Virginia v. FERC, 774 F.2d 1205 (D.C. Cir. 1985); City of Cleveland v. FERC, 773 F.2d 1368 (D.C. Cir. 1985); National Ass'n of Gov't Employees, Local R7–23 v. Federal Labor Relations Auth., 770 F.2d 1223 (D.C. Cir. 1985); Aluminum Co. of Am. v. ICC, 761 F.2d 746 (D.C. Cir. 1985); Atlanta Gas and Light Co. v. FERC, 756 F.2d 191 (D.C. Cir. 1985); Community Nutrition Inst. v. Block, 749 F.2d 50 (D.C. Cir. 1984); International Union, UAW v. Donovan, 746 F.2d 855 (D.C. Cir. 1984); Association of Data Processing Serv. Orgs. v. Board of Governors, Federal Reserve System (FRS), 745 F.2d 677 (D.C. Cir. 1984); City of Winnfield v. FERC, 744 F.2d 871 (D.C. Cir. 1984); de Perez v. FCC, 738 F.2d 1304 (D.C. Cir. 1984); Port Norris Express Co. v. ICC, 728 F.2d 543 (D.C. Cir. 1984); Sea-Land Serv., Inc. v. Dole, 723 F.2d 975 (D.C. Cir. 1983); Papago Tribal Utility Auth. v. FERC, 723 F.2d 950 (D.C. Cir. 1983); Kansas Cities v. FERC, 723 F.2d 82 (D.C. Cir. 1983); City of Bedford v. FERC, 718 F.2d 1164 (D.C. Cir. 1983); Dunning v. National Aeronautics and Space Admin., 718 F.2d 1170 (D.C. Cir. 1983); Steger v. Defense Investigative Serv., 717 F.2d 1402, 1409 (D.C. Cir. 1983) (Scalia, J., dissenting); National Coalition to Ban Handguns v. Bureau of Alcohol, Tobacco, and Firearms, 715 F.2d 632 (D.C. Cir. 1983); American Trucking Ass'ns v. ICC, 697 F.2d 1146 (D.C. Cir. 1983). See also the mixed results of this mode of analysis in Illinois Commerce Comm'n v. ICC, 776 F.2d 355 (D.C. Cir. 1985); Simmons v. ICC, 757 F.2d 296 (D.C. Cir. 1985); Delta Data Sys. Corp. v. Webster, 744 F.2d 197 (D.C. Cir. 1984); Dana Corp. v. ICC, 703 F.2d 1297, 1305 (D.C. Cir. 1983); Drukker Communications, Inc. v. NLRB, 700 F.2d 727 (D.C. Cir. 1983).

10. Center for Auto Safety v. Peck, 751 F.2d at 1370. See also W. Kip Viscusi, "Regulatory Economics in the Courts: An Analysis of Judge Scalia's

NHTSA Bumper Decision," *Law and Contemporary Problems* 50 (1987): 17–31.

11. Antonin Scalia, "Historical Anomalies in Administrative Law," *Yearbook of the Supreme Court Historical Society* (1985): 106–10, quotation on 110.

12. Ramirez de Arellano v. Weinberger (II), 745 F.2d 1500, 1562, 1566 (D.C. Cir. 1984) (Scalia, J., dissenting).

13. Ramirez de Arellano v. Weinberger (I), 724 F.2d 143, 147–55 (D.C. Cir. 1983).

14. Ramirez de Arellano v. Weinberger (II), 745 F.2d at 1551–66 (quotations on 1555, 1561) (Scalia, J., dissenting).

15. See Bivens v. Six Unknown Named Agents of the Fed. Bureau of Narcotics, 403 U.S. 388 (1971).

16. Sanchez-Espinoza v. Reagan, 770 F.2d 202, 205–10 (D.C. Cir. 1985).

17. Halperin v. Kissinger, 807 F.2d 180 (D.C. Cir. 1986); Smith v. Nixon, 807 F.2d 197 (D.C. Cir. 1986); Ellsberg v. Mitchell, 807 F.2d 204 (1986). Scalia also permitted the government to invoke a state secrets privilege to withhold evidence in a civil trial; see Molerio v. FBI, 749 F.2d 815 (1984).

18. Center for Auto Safety v. Peck, 751 F.2d at 1368.

19. Judicial Conference, District of Columbia Circuit, "Judicial Review of Administrative Action in an Era of Deregulation," *Federal Rules Decisions* 105 (1984): 321–46, quotation on 345.

20. Antonin Scalia, "The Role of the Judiciary in Deregulation," *Antitrust Law Journal* 55 (1986): 192–99.

21. Chaney v. Heckler, 718 F.2d 1174, 1192–1200 (D.C. Cir. 1983) (Scalia, J., dissenting).

22. Chaney v. Heckler, 724 F.2d 1030, 1030–31 (D.C. Cir. 1984) (Scalia, J., statement on the denial of rehearing en banc). See also Nagareda, "Appellate Jurisprudence of Scalia," 715–20. The Supreme Court later unanimously sided with his proposition that FDA inaction was a matter subject to the agency's discretion and was not susceptible to judicial reconsideration. Heckler v. Chaney, 470 U.S. 821 (1985).

23. Center for Auto Safety v. Ruckelshaus, 747 F.2d 1, 4–7 (D.C. Cir. 1984).

24. Illinois Commerce Comm'n v. ICC, 749 F.2d 875, 890–93 (D.C. Cir. 1984) (Scalia, J., dissenting).

25. Ibid., 4. For a critique of his approach, see Cass R. Sunstein, *After the Rights Revolution: Reconceiving the Regulatory State* (Cambridge: Harvard University Press, 1990), 127–30.

26. Center for Auto Safety v. Ruckelshaus, 747 F.2d at 1; Illinois Commerce Comm'n v. ICC, 749 F.2d at 892–93 (Scalia, J., dissenting).

27. Hirschey v. FERC, 777 F.2d 1, 6–8 (D.C. Cir. 1985) (Scalia, J., concurring); see also Hirschey v. FERC, 760 F.2d 305, 311–12 (D.C. Cir. 1985)

(Scalia, J., concurring and dissenting); Antonin Scalia, "Speech on Use of Legislative History," quoted in Daniel A. Farber and Phillip P. Frickey, "Legislative Intent and Public Choice," *Virginia Law Review* 74 (1988): 442n. 64, 445n. 65, 454–55.

28. Hirschey v. FERC, 777 F.2d at 7–8 (Scalia, J., concurring).

29. Center for Auto Safety v. Peck, 751 F.2d at 1350–51; Scalia, "Use of Legislative History," 442n. 64, 454–55.

30. Immigration and Naturalization Serv. v. Chadha, 462 U.S. 919 (1983).

31. Synar v. United States, 626 F.Supp. 1374 (D.D.C. 1986) (per curiam). He is alleged to have written much of the per curiam opinion; see Bernard Schwartz, "'Shooting the Piano Player'? Justice Scalia and Administrative Law," *Administrative Law Review* 47 (1995): 13–15; and Wilson, "Constraints of Power," 1181n. 6, 1201.

32. The most cogent is Antonin Scalia, "A Note on the Benzene Case," *Regulation* 4, no. 4 (1980): 25–28.

33. Synar v. United States, 626 F.Supp. at 1382–91.

34. Ibid., 1391–1403. The argument relies on Humphrey's Executor v. United States, 295 U.S. 602, 632 (1935). Scalia, "Historical Anomalies," 106–10, contains a discussion of this case.

35. Synar v. United States, 626 F.Supp. at 1403. The decision was upheld by the Supreme Court in Bowsher v. Synar, 478 U.S. 714 (1986).

36. See Director, Office of Workers' Compensation Programs v. Belcher Erectors, 770 F.2d 1226 (D.C. Cir. 1985); Center for Auto Safety v. Ruckelshaus, 747 F.2d at 5–6; International Union, UAW v. Donovan, 746 F.2d 855; North Carolina v. FERC, 730 F.2d 790 (D.C. Cir. 1984); Ensign-Bickford Co. v. Occupational Safety and Health Review Comm'n, 717 F.2d 1419, 1423–24 (D.C. Cir. 1983) (Scalia, J., dissenting); American Fed'n of Gov't Employees, Local 2782 v. Federal Labor Relations Auth., 702 F.2d 1183 (D.C. Cir. 1983).

37. Chevron U.S.A., Inc. v. Natural Resources Defense Council, 467 U.S. 837 (1984).

38. He uses *Chevron* criteria that favor the agency's use of discretion in Securities Indus. Ass'n v. Comptroller of Currency, 765 F.2d 1196, 1196–98 (D.C. Cir. 1985) (Scalia, J., dissenting). See also Antonin Scalia, "Responsibilities of Federal Regulatory Agencies under Environmental Laws," *Houston Law Review* 24 (1987): 106–9.

39. Brock v. Cathedral Bluffs Shale Oil Co., 796 F.2d 533 (D.C. Cir. 1986); McKelvey v. Turnage, 792 F.2d 194, 209–10 (D.C. Cir. 1986) (Scalia, J., concurring and dissenting); ASARCO, Inc. v. FERC, 777 F.2d 764 (D.C. Cir. 1985); Reynolds Metals Co. v. FERC, 777 F.2d 760 (D.C. Cir. 1985); Western Union Tel. Co. v. FCC, 773 F.2d 375 (D.C. Cir. 1985); California Human Dev. Corp. v. Brock, 762 F.2d 1044, 1052–53 (D.C. Cir. 1985) (Scalia, J., concurring); National Black Media Coalition v. FCC, 760 F.2d 1297 (D.C. Cir. 1985); Gott v. Walters, 756 F.2d 902 (D.C. Cir. 1985); Interstate Natural Gas

Ass'n v. FERC, 756 F.2d 166, 171 (D.C. Cir. 1985) (Scalia, J., concurring); Thompson v. Clark, 741 F.2d 401 (D.C. Cir. 1984); Chaney v. Heckler, 724 F.2d 1030, 1030–31 (D.C. Cir. 1984) (Scalia, J., dissenting); Chaney v. Heckler, 718 F.2d 1174, 1192–1200 (D.C. Cir. 1983) (Scalia, J., dissenting); KCST-TV v. FCC, 699 F.2d 1185, 1195–1201 (D.C. Cir. 1983) (Scalia, J., dissenting). See also the discussion in Nagareda, "Appellate Jurisprudence of Scalia," 720–26.

40. Antonin Scalia, "The Doctrine of Standing as an Essential Element of the Separation of Powers," *Suffolk University Law Review* 17 (1983): 881, 885.

41. Ibid., 886–89. See also Jean Morgan Meaux, "Justice Scalia and Judicial Restraint: A Conservative Resolution of Conflict between Individual and State," *Tulane Law Review* 62 (1987): 233–37; Michael A. Perino, "Justice Scalia: Standing, Environmental Law, and the Supreme Court," *Boston College Environmental Law Review* 15 (1987): 135–79; Scatera, "Deference to Discretion," 1237–47.

42. See Alexander M. Bickel, *The Least Dangerous Branch: The Supreme Court at the Bar of Politics* (Indianapolis: Bobbs-Merrill, 1962), 111–98.

43. Flast v. Cohen, 392 U.S. 83, 99–101 (1968).

44. Scalia, "Doctrine of Standing," 891. See his application of this principle through provisions of the Foreign Sovereign Immunities Act in Asociacion de Reclamantes v. United Mexican States, 735 F.2d 1517 (D.C. Cir. 1984). Scalia also supported restrictions on the ability of associations to sue the legislative branch unless Congress harmed an individual right or violated its explicit constitutional powers; see Morgan v. United States, 801 F.2d 445 (D.C. Cir. 1986).

45. Scalia, "Doctrine of Standing," 894–97, quotation on 894.

46. On fuel economy, see Center for Auto Safety v. National Highway Transp. Safety Admin., 793 F.2d 1322, 1342–44 (D.C. Cir. 1986) (Scalia, J., dissenting); and the discussion in Scatera, "Deference to Discretion," 1238–42. On the films, see Block v. Meese, 793 F.2d 1303, 1307–9 (D.C. Cir. 1986). On surveillance, see United Presbyterian Church in the U.S.A. v. Reagan, 738 F.2d 1375 (D.C. Cir. 1984).

47. Moore v. United States House of Representatives, 733 F.2d 946, 956–65 (D.C. Cir. 1984) (Scalia, J., concurring).

48. Safir v. Dole, 718 F.2d 475 (D.C. Cir. 1983); Carducci v. Regan, 714 F.2d 171 (D.C. Cir. 1983); Community Nutrition Inst. v. Block, 698 F.2d 1239, 1255–59 (D.C. Cir. 1983) (Scalia, J., concurring and dissenting).

49. Transwestern Pipeline Co. v. FERC, 747 F.2d 781 (D.C. Cir. 1984); Simmons v. ICC, 716 F.2d 40 (D.C. Cir. 1983).

50. Conafey by Conafey v. Wyeth Laboratories, 792 F.2d 350, 354–55 (D.C. Cir. 1986) (Scalia, J., dissenting); Mathes v. Commissioner of Internal Revenue, 788 F.2d 33 (D.C. Cir. 1986).

51. Trakas v. Quality Brands, 759 F.2d 185, 188–91 (D.C. Cir. 1985) (Scalia, J., dissenting).

52. Center for Auto Safety v. National Highway Transp. Safety Admin., 793 F.2d at 1344–45 (Scalia, J., dissenting).

53. American Trucking Ass'ns v. ICC, 747 F.2d 787 (D.C. Cir. 1984).

54. Radiofone, Inc. v. FCC, 759 F.2d 936 (D.C. Cir. 1985).

55. Aluminum Co. of Am. v. United States, 790 F.2d 938 (D.C. Cir. 1986); Northern Natural Gas Co. v. FERC, 780 F.2d 59 (D.C. Cir. 1985).

56. Dozier v. Ford Motor Co., 702 F.2d 1189 (D.C. Cir. 1983).

57. Schultz v. Crowley, 802 F.2d 498 (D.C. Cir. 1986).

58. South Carolina Electric and Gas Co. v. ICC, 734 F.2d 1541 (D.C. Cir. 1984); Air New Zealand, Ltd. v. Civil Aeronautics Bd., 726 F.2d 832 (D.C. Cir. 1984).

59. Romero v. National Rifle Ass'n of Am., 749 F.2d 77 (D.C. Cir. 1984).

60. Beattie v. United States, 756 F.2d 91, 106–30 (D.C. Cir. 1984) (Scalia, J., dissenting).

61. Church of Scientology v. IRS, 792 F.2d 146 (D.C. Cir. 1986); Church of Scientology v. IRS, 792 F.2d 153 (D.C. Cir. 1986); Shaw v. FBI, 749 F.2d 58 (D.C. Cir. 1984); Ryan v. Bureau of Alcohol, Tobacco, and Firearms, 715 F.2d 644 (D.C. Cir. 1983); International Bhd. of Teamsters v. National Mediation Bd., 712 F.2d 1495 (D.C. Cir. 1983); Arieff v. Department of Navy, 712 F.2d 1462 (D.C. Cir. 1983); Washington Post Co. v. United States Dept. of State, 685 F.2d 698, 707–8 (D.C. Cir. 1982) (Scalia, J., statement on denial of rehearing). Compare Washington Post Co. v. United States Dept. of Health and Human Servs., 795 F.2d 205 (D.C. Cir. 1986). See the discussion in Meaux, "Scalia and Judicial Restraint," 238–41.

62. FAIC Securities, Inc. v. United States, 768 F.2d 352 (D.C. Cir. 1985); Maryland People's Counsel v. FERC, 760 F.2d 318 (D.C. Cir. 1985).

63. The model is defined in Richard B. Stewart, "The Reformation of American Administrative Law," *Harvard Law Review* 88 (1975): 1767–1813. See also the discussion in Nagareda, "Appellate Jurisprudence of Scalia," 706–15.

64. His eight criminal justice opinions were in Parker v. United States, 801 F.2d 1382 (D.C. Cir. 1986) (on expert testimony); In re Sealed Case, 801 F.2d 1379 (D.C. Cir. 1986) (on release of grand jury documents); In re Sealed Case, 791 F.2d 179 (D.C. Cir. 1986) (on immunity from self-incrimination); United States v. Foster, 783 F.2d 1082 (D.C. Cir. 1986) (on acquittal motions); United States v. Hansen, 772 F.2d 940 (D.C. Cir. 1985) (on rules of evidence); United States v. Byers, 740 F.2d 1104 (D.C. Cir. 1984) (on admissibility of statements to court-appointed psychiatrists); United States v. Richardson, 702 F.2d 1079, 1086–94 (D.C. Cir. 1983) (Scalia, J., dissenting) (on technical problems with limits on double jeopardy appeals and second trials); United States v. Donelson, 695 F.2d 389 (D.C. Cir. 1982) (on statutory language on sentencing by federal magistrates). None of these cases dealt with

core constitutional issues of procedural due process. Six of his decisions supported the prosecution over the defense, while the advantage in one case was not clear.

65. Antonin Scalia, "A House with Many Mansions: Categories of Speech under the First Amendment," in *The Constitution, the Law, and Freedom of Expression, 1787–1987*, ed. James B. Stewart (Carbondale: Southern Illinois University Press, 1987), 9–19.

66. Ibid., 18–19.

67. Block v. Meese, 793 F.2d 1303, 1311–18 (D.C. Cir. 1986). See also the discussion in Meaux, "Scalia and Judicial Restraint," 247–49; and Nagareda, "Appellate Jurisprudence of Scalia," 734–35. Later, the Supreme Court supported much of the analysis in his opinion; see Meese v. Keene, 481 U.S. 465 (1987). See also the discussion in Paul Siegel, "Antonin Scalia and the First Amendment," *Free Speech Yearbook* 26 (1987): 174–76.

68. Ollman v. Evans, 750 F.2d 970, 994–1003 (D.C. Cir. 1984) (Bork, J., concurring).

69. Ibid., 1036 (quotation), 1038 (quotation) (Scalia, J., dissenting in part). See also the discussion in Meaux, "Scalia and Judicial Restraint," 244–46; Nagareda, "Appellate Jurisprudence of Scalia," 729–33; and Siegel, "Scalia and the First Amendment," 166–67.

70. Liberty Lobby, Inc. v. Anderson, 746 F.2d 1563, 1570–71 (D.C. Cir. 1984), following Gertz v. Welch, 418 U.S. 323, 342 (1974) rather than the "convincing clarity" rule of New York Times v. Sullivan, 376 U.S. 254, 285–86 (1964).

71. Liberty Lobby, Inc. v. Anderson, 746 F.2d at 1571–72, 1577–78 (quotation on 1578). The Supreme Court rejected aspects of his opinion; see Anderson v. Liberty Lobby, Inc., 477 U.S. 242 (1986).

72. In re Reporters' Comm. for Freedom of the Press, 773 F.2d 1325 (D.C. Cir. 1985).

73. Ibid., 1331–32, 1336. See also Meaux, "Scalia and Judicial Restraint," 242–43; Nagareda, "Appellate Jurisprudence of Scalia," 726–28; Siegel, "Scalia and the First Amendment," 176–77.

74. Community for Creative Nonviolence v. Watt, 703 F.2d 586, 622–27 (D.C. Cir. 1983) (Scalia, J., dissenting).

75. United States v. O'Brien, 391 U.S. 367 (1968).

76. CCNV v. Watt, 703 F.2d at 622, 625–27 (Scalia, J., dissenting). Later the Supreme Court reviewed the decision and voted to support the camping ban. Like Scalia's argument, the Opinion of the Court by Justice White upheld the regulation as a valid time-place-manner restriction on expression under similar criteria derived from *United States v. O'Brien*; see Clark v. Community for Creative Non-Violence, 468 U.S. 288 (1984). See also Nagareda, "Appellate Jurisprudence of Scalia," 736–38.

77. See Edward V. Heck, "Constitutional Interpretation and a Court in

Transition: Strict Scrutiny from *Shapiro v. Thompson* to *Dunn v. Blumstein*—and Beyond," *United States Air Force Academy Journal of Legal Studies* 3 (1992): 65–90. Scrutiny is discussed in more detail in chapter 6.

78. United States v. Cohen, 733 F.2d 128, 131–36 (D.C. Cir. 1984).

79. Carter v. Duncan-Huggins, 727 F.2d 1225, 1239, 1245, 1247 (D.C. Cir. 1984) (Scalia, J., dissenting).

80. Toney v. Block, 705 F.2d 1364 (D.C. Cir. 1983).

81. Molerio v. FBI, 749 F.2d 815 (D.C. Cir. 1984); Poindexter v. FBI, 737 F.2d 1173, 1192–93 (D.C. Cir. 1984) (Scalia, J., concurring and dissenting).

82. Antonin Scalia, "Economic Affairs as Human Affairs," *Cato Journal* 4 (1985): 703–9; reprinted with minor changes as idem, "On the Merits of the Frying Pan," *Regulation* 9, no. 1 (1985): 10–14.

83. Antonin Scalia, "Morality, Pragmatism, and the Legal Order," *Harvard Journal of Law and Public Policy* 9 (1986): 123–27, quotations on 123, 125.

CHAPTER THREE: SCALIA AND THE CONSERVATISM OF THE REAGAN ADMINISTRATION

1. Christopher E. Smith, *Justice Antonin Scalia and the Supreme Court's Conservative Moment* (Westport, Conn.: Praeger, 1993), 1–20. Compare "Remarks Announcing the Resignation of Chief Justice Warren E. Burger and the Nominations of William H. Rehnquist to Be Chief Justice and Antonin Scalia to Be Associate Justice," *Weekly Compilation of Presidential Documents* (hereafter *Weekly Compilation*), 17 June 1986, reprinted in *The Supreme Court of the United States: Hearings on Successful and Unsuccessful Nominations of Supreme Court Justices by the Senate Judiciary Committee*, vol. 13, *Antonin Scalia*, ed. Roy M. Mersky and J. Myron Jacobstein (Buffalo: William S. Hein, 1989), 11, source of the quotation in the text. (Hereafter this volume is cited as *Supreme Court of the United States*.) See also "Radio Address to the Nation," *Weekly Compilation*, 21 June 1986, reprinted in ibid., 20; "Radio Address to the Nation," *Weekly Compilation*, 5 July 1986, reprinted in ibid., 32; "Remarks at the Annual Convention of the Knights of Columbus," *Weekly Compilation*, 5 Aug. 1986, reprinted in ibid., 36; "Radio Address to the Nation," *Weekly Compilation*, 9 Aug. 1986, reprinted in ibid., 38; "Remarks at the Swearing-in Ceremony for William Rehnquist as Chief Justice and Antonin Scalia as Associate Justice," *Weekly Compilation*, 26 Sept. 1986, reprinted in ibid., 42–43. David G. Savage, *Turning Right: The Making of the Rehnquist Court* (New York: John Wiley and Sons, 1992), 17–18, relies on unnamed sources and says that Scalia's ethnicity caught the attention of Reagan and contributed to the nomination of Scalia instead of Judge Robert Bork.

2. *Congressional Record—Senate*, 17 June 1986, S7645–46; *Congressional Record—House*, 18 June 1986, H3927, reprinted in *Supreme Court of the United States* 13:53–54, 56.

3. U.S. Senate, Committee on the Judiciary, *Hearings on the Nomination of*

Judge Antonin Scalia, to Be Associate Justice of the Supreme Court of the United States, 99th Cong., 2d sess., 5–6 Aug. 1986, in *Supreme Court of the United States* 13:129–30, 133–36, 157–66, 168–69, 171–72, 177, 200–202; see esp. his reply to Biden (145–46); and his replies to Hatch and Simon (54–56, 190–91).

4. See ibid., 131, for his reply to Kennedy; 131–32, 196–99, on precedent; see also Scalia's responses to Senator Arlen Specter (R-Pa.), in ibid., 177–82; and to Biden, in ibid., 195. Here Scalia stated, "I am deeply mistrustful of my ability, without any guidance other than my own intuition, to say what are the deepest and most profound beliefs of our society." Thus again he seemed to accept moral discord in American life. See also ibid., 139, 152–54, 196, on his refusal to answer questions; ibid., 192, on religion; ibid., 170, 188, on affirmative action; and ibid., 166, in response to Leahy.

5. See ibid., 205–62, for his well-known supporters; ibid., 317–42, for support by conservatives; and 279–96, for the concerns of the AFL-CIO.

6. See ibid., 262–78, 307–17, for the NOW statement; ibid., 297–317, for the Rauh statement; ibid., 342–69, for the Feinberg statement; ibid., 370–406, for other critics; and ibid., 404–36, for the litigant's statement.

7. *Congressional Record—Senate,* 11 Sept. 1986, S12357; ibid., 15 Sept. 1986, S12553, 12570; ibid., 17 Sept. 1986, S12832–42, reprinted in *Supreme Court of the United States* 13:67–70, 72–82. The letters discussed by Senator Levin are reprinted in *Supreme Court of the United States* 13:438–41.

8. On the variables associated with the success of nominations, see Jeffrey A. Segal, "Senate Confirmation of Supreme Court Justices: Partisan and Institutional Politics," *Journal of Politics* 49 (1987): 998–1015; Jeffrey A. Segal, Charles M. Cameron, and Albert D. Cover, "A Spatial Model of Roll Call Voting: Senators, Constituents, Presidents, and Interest Groups in Supreme Court Confirmations," *American Journal of Political Science* 36 (1992): 96–121.

9. See Jeffrey A. Segal and Harold J. Spaeth, *The Supreme Court and the Attitudinal Model* (Cambridge: Cambridge University Press, 1993).

10. See Joyce A. Baugh, "Justice Antonin Scalia and the Freshman Effect" (paper presented at annual meeting of Midwest Political Science Association, Chicago, Ill., 1989); Michael Patrick King, "Justice Antonin Scalia: The First Term on the Supreme Court—1986–1987," *Rutgers Law Journal* 20 (1988): 1–77; Thea F. Rubin and Albert P. Melone, "Justice Antonin Scalia: A First Year Freshman Effect?" *Judicature* 72 (1988): 98–102.

11. The categories are defined in Segal and Spaeth, *Supreme Court and Attitudinal Model,* 243; and Harold J. Spaeth, "United States Supreme Court Judicial Database, 1953–1992 Terms, Documentation" [computer file], 5th release (East Lansing: Michigan State University, Dept. of Political Science [producer]; Ann Arbor: Inter-University Consortium for Political and Social Research [distributor], 1994), 84–87.

12. See Roger Handberg, "Decision-Making in a Natural Court, 1916–1921," *American Politics Quarterly* 4 (1976): 357–78.

13. John D. Sprague, *Voting Patterns of the United States Supreme Court: Cases in Federalism, 1889–1959* (Indianapolis: Bobbs-Merrill, 1968), 21–50; Melinda Gann Hall, "Small Group Influences in the United States Supreme Court," *Justice System Journal* 12 (1987): 362–65.

14. Sprague, *Voting Patterns*, 43–50; Hall, "Small Group Influences," 359, 363–65.

15. On Rehnquist's position, see Sue Davis, *Justice Rehnquist and the Constitution* (Princeton: Princeton University Press, 1989); idem, "Justice William H. Rehnquist: Right-Wing Ideologue or Majoritarian Democrat?" in *The Burger Court: Political and Judicial Profiles*, ed. Charles M. Lamb and Stephen C. Halpern (Urbana: University of Illinois Press, 1991), 315–42. On O'Connor's position, see Beverly B. Cook, "Justice Sandra Day O'Connor: Transition to a Republican Court Agenda," in ibid., 238–75.

16. Smith, *Scalia and Court's Conservative Moment*, 77–134.

17. William F. Harris II, *The Interpretable Constitution* (Baltimore: Johns Hopkins University Press, 1993), 1.

18. Antonin Scalia, "The Dissenting Opinion," *Journal of Supreme Court History* (1994): 40. In M. L. Stein, "Scalia Discusses the Press," *Editor and Publisher* 123 (8 Sept. 1990): 16, Scalia is reported as presenting, in a speech to the Los Angeles World Affairs Council and Pepperdine University, "the view that the language and reasoning behind court decisions are on too high a plane for lay journalists to understand, appreciate, and report accurately."

19. Peter Goodrich, "The Role of Linguistics in Legal Analysis," *Modern Law Review* 47 (1984): 531; Pierre Bourdieu, *Language and Symbolic Power*, ed. John B. Thompson, trans. Gino Raymond and Matthew Adamson (Cambridge: Harvard University Press, 1991), 43–65.

20. Recent judicial scholarship, especially scholarship about Scalia, has attempted to separate conservative political ideology or "attitudes" (extralegal variables) and the influence of "legal methodology" or jurisprudential argument (legal variables) as influences on his judicial decisions. It then has tried to provide evidence that one or the other is the primary influence on how a justice's political vision emerges. Tracey E. George and Lee Epstein, "On the Nature of Supreme Court Decision Making," *American Political Science Review* 86 (1992): 323–37, describes the two explanations and finds, quantitatively, that each contributes to an explanation of death penalty case decisions.

21. Peter Goodrich, "Jani anglorum: Signs, Symptoms, Slips, and Interpretation in Law," in *Politics, Postmodernity, and Critical Legal Studies: The Legality of the Contingent*, ed. Costas Douzinas, Peter Goodrich, and Yifat Hachamovitch (London: Routledge, 1994), 135. See also Austin Sarat and Thomas R. Kearns, "Beyond the Great Divide: Forms of Legal Scholarship and

Everyday Life," in *Law in Everyday Life,* ed. Austin Sarat and Thomas R. Kearns (Ann Arbor: University of Michigan Press, 1993), 23–27.

22. Pierre Bourdieu, "The Force of Law: Toward a Sociology of the Juridical Field," trans. Richard Terdiman, *Hastings Law Journal* 38 (1987): 817. See also Pierre Bourdieu and Loïc Wacquant, *An Invitation to Reflexive Sociology* (Chicago: University of Chicago Press, 1992), 94–115; Rosemary J. Coombe, "Room for Manoeuver: Toward a Theory of Practice in Critical Legal Studies," *Law and Social Inquiry* 14 (1989): 71; Sherry B. Ortner, "Theory in Anthropology since the Sixties," *Comparative Studies in Society and History* 26 (1984): 144–60; and Susan S. Silbey, "Ideals and Practices in the Study of Law," *Legal Studies Forum* 9 (1985): 15–22.

23. For a discussion of the reasons for rules which, unfortunately, conceals the political basis of rules, see Frederick Schauer, *Playing by the Rules: A Philosophical Examination of Rule-Based Decision-Making in Law and Life* (New York: Oxford University Press, 1991), 134–66. See also Judith N. Shklar, *Legalism: Law, Morals, and Political Trials* (Cambridge: Harvard University Press, 1964), on the fit between political values and American legality; and the more general discussion of the linkage of government, law, and discipline offered in the following works: Anne Barron, "Legal Discourse and the Colonisation of the Self in the Modern State," in *Post-Modern Law: Enlightenment, Revolution, and the Death of Man,* ed. Andrew Carty (Edinburgh: Edinburgh University Press, 1990), 107–24; Duncan Kennedy, "Legal Formality," *Journal of Legal Studies* 2 (1972): 351, 358–77; and Carol Smart, *Feminism and the Power of Law* (London: Routledge, 1989), 4–14.

24. The existence of multiple instrumental legal discourses about American constitutional law is not uncommon; see Philip Bobbitt, *Constitutional Fate: Theory of the Constitution* (New York: Oxford University Press, 1982), 3–119; and Mark Kessler, "Legal Discourse and Political Intolerance: The Ideology of Clear and Present Danger," *Law and Society Review* 27 (1993): 559–97. See also the discussion in Beau James Brock, "Mr. Justice Antonin Scalia: A Renaissance of Positivism and Predictability in Constitutional Adjudication," *Louisiana Law Review* 51 (1991): 623–50. To this author, Brock's discussion of the influence on natural law on Scalia (630–31) seems misplaced.

25. Martin Edelman, *Democratic Theories and the Constitution* (Albany: State University of New York Press, 1984), 29–65; Laura Kalman, *Legal Realism at Yale, 1927–1960* (Chapel Hill: University of North Carolina Press, 1986), 3–66; Edward A. Purcell Jr., *The Crisis of Democratic Theory: Scientific Naturalism and the Problem of Value* (Lexington: University Press of Kentucky, 1973), 74–94, 159–78; G. Edward White, *Patterns of American Legal Thought* (Indianapolis: Bobbs-Merrill, 1978), 99–163; Robert S. Summers, *Instrumentalism and American Legal Theory* (Ithaca: Cornell University Press, 1982).

26. See Charles W. Anderson, *Pragmatic Liberalism* (Chicago: University of

Chicago Press, 1990). In *John Dewey, The Middle Works, 1899–1924,* ed. Jo Anne Boydston, see *Reconstruction in Philosophy* (1924), in vol. 12 (Carbondale: Southern Illinois University Press, 1982), 40–59; in *John Dewey: The Later Works, 1925–1953,* ed. Jo Anne Boydston, see *The Quest for Certainty: A Study of the Relation of Knowledge and Action* (1929), in vol. 4 (Carbondale: Southern Illinois University Press, 1984), 40–59; *The Public and Its Problems* (1927), in vol. 2 (Carbondale: Southern Illinois University Press, 1984), 325–72; *Liberalism and Social Action* (1935), in vol. 11 (Carbondale: Southern Illinois University Press, 1987), 1–65; "Authority and Social Change" (1936), in vol. 11, 130–45; and *Theory of Valuation* (1939), in vol. 13 (Carbondale: Southern Illinois University Press, 1988), 191–250. See also John P. Murphy, *Pragmatism: From Peirce to Davidson* (Boulder: Westview Press, 1990); Cornel West, *The American Evasion of Philosophy: A Genealogy of Pragmatism* (Madison: University of Wisconsin Press, 1989); and Robert B. Westbrook, *John Dewey and American Democracy* (Ithaca: Cornell University Press, 1991), 430–39.

27. See William E. Leuchtenberg, *Franklin D. Roosevelt and the New Deal, 1932–1940* (New York: Harper and Row, 1963), 326–48. On Legal Realism and pragmatism, see Kalman, *Legal Realism at Yale,* 3–44; Wilfrid E. Rumble Jr., *American Legal Realism: Skepticism, Reform, and the Judicial Process* (Ithaca: Cornell University Press, 1968); and William Twining, *Karl Llewellyn and the Realist Movement* (Norman: University of Oklahoma Press, 1973), 70–83, 375–87.

28. Some the elements of this paradigm are discussed in David Luban, *Legal Modernism* (Ann Arbor: University of Michigan Press, 1994), 133–41.

29. This point is made particularly by one Legal Realist and pragmatist thinker: see Robert L. Hale, *Freedom through Law: Public Control of Private Governing Power* (New York: Columbia University Press, 1952).

30. Although a critic of legal pragmatism, Gary J. Jacobsohn, *Pragmatism, Statesmanship, and the Supreme Court* (Ithaca: Cornell University Press, 1977), 39–64, presents a straightforward discussion of the ideas summarized in these four postulates. This author believes that Jacobsohn overplays the "relativism" of legal pragmatism and neglects its concern with "practical certainty" (50–51). The first postulate can be described as a "critical pluralist" vision of the political order in the language of Ronald Kahn, *The Supreme Court and Constitutional Theory, 1953–1993* (Lawrence: University Press of Kansas, 1994), 180–98, 254–61.

31. See Edwin W. Patterson, "Dewey's Theories of Legal Reasoning and Valuation," in *John Dewey, Philosopher of Science and Freedom: A Symposium,* ed. Sidney Hook (New York: Dial Press, 1950); and Summers, *Instrumentalism,* 31–34, 41–175.

32. See Patterson, "Dewey's Theories," 119; and Twining, *Llewellyn,* 38, 40, 56, 174, 422–23n. 130. Important though less direct influences on the

development of American legal pragmatism are the writings of Charles Sanders Peirce and Oliver Wendell Holmes Jr.; see Thomas C. Grey, "Holmes and Legal Pragmatism," *Stanford Law Review* 41 (1989): 787–870; Robert S. Summers, "Charles Sanders Peirce and America's Dominant Theory of Law," in *Peirce and Law: Issues in Pragmatism, Legal Realism, and Semiotics,* ed. Roberta Kevelson (New York: Peter Lang, 1991), 153–62; John T. Valauri, "Peirce and Holmes," in ibid., 187–201; and G. Edward White, *Justice Oliver Wendell Holmes* (New York: Oxford University Press, 1993), 378–454.

33. John Dewey, "Logical Method and Law" (1924), in John Dewey, *The Middle Works, 1899–1924,* ed. Jo Anne Boydston, vol. 15 (Carbondale: University of Southern Illinois Press, 1983), 73–76.

34. See Dewey, *Public and Its Problems,* 268–71; Patterson, "Dewey's Theories," 130–32.

35. See United States v. Carolene Products, 304 U.S. 144, 152–53n. 4 (1938). The jurisprudential discourse of Warren, Brennan, and Marshall should not be confused with so-called Warren Court liberalism or other distinctive variants of liberal discourse such as the natural rights liberalism of Justice William Douglas. Also, it is distinctive from the historical positivism of Justice Hugo Black. See Edelman, *Democratic Theories,* 121–208, 245–88.

36. See Brown v. Board of Educ. of Topeka, 347 U.S. 483, 494 (1954); Reynolds v. Sims, 377 U.S. 533, 565 (1964).

37. Thus, they normally fit into a pattern of constitutional discourse that Harris, *Interpretable Constitution,* 152–58, classifies as "transcendent structuralism," in which there is a reliance on values that are beyond the written Constitution but imputed in its language. The reliance on the transcendent value of equality is most apparent in Warren's opinion in Reynolds v. Sims, 377 U.S. at 580; and in William J. Brennan Jr., "The Equality Principle in American Constitutional Law," *Ohio State Law Journal* 48 (1987): 921–25. The same statement appears in idem, "The Equality Principle: A Foundation of American Law," *University of California–Davis, Law Review* 20 (1987): 673–78.

38. The questioning of pluralism, as a theme in the opinions of these justices, is called "critical pluralism" in Kahn, *Supreme Court,* 120. See also the discussion in G. Edward White, *Earl Warren: A Public Life* (New York: Oxford University Press, 1982), 217–49. On human dignity, see William J. Brennan Jr., "The Constitution of the United States: Contemporary Ratification" (address to Text and Teaching Symposium, Georgetown University, Washington, D.C., 1985), 9–16. See also the discussion in Peter Irons, *Brennan vs. Rehnquist: The Battle for the Constitution* (New York: Alfred A. Knopf, 1994), 33–42. On economics, see, e.g., Warren's view in United States v. E. I. Du Pont de Nemours and Co., 351 U.S. 377, 413–426 (1956) (Warren, J., dissenting); Brown Shoe Co. v. United States, 370 U.S. 294 (1961); Fibreboard Paper Products v. NLRB, 379 U.S. 203 (1964); NLRB v. Great Dane Trailers, 388

U.S. 26 (1967); FTC v. Fred Meyer, Inc., 390 U.S. 341 (1968). On rights, see Dandridge v. Williams, 397 U.S. 471, 508, 520–30 (1970) (Marshall, J., dissenting); Cox v. Louisiana, 379 U.S. 536 (1965); Abington Township Sch. Dist. v. Schempp, 374 U.S. 203, 230–304 (1963) (Brennan, J., concurring); Paul v. Davis, 424 U.S. 693, 714–35 (1976) (Brennan, J., dissenting).

39. Brennan, "Equality Principle in Constitutional Law," 921. Nowhere is the value of personal dignity made more clear than in Furman v. Georgia, 408 U.S. 238, 281 (1972) (Brennan, J., concurring); and at 360–71 (Marshall, J., concurring).

40. See Shapiro v. Thompson, 394 U.S. 618, 627, 634 (1969); Dunn v. Blumstein, 405 U.S. 330, 336–37 (1972); Frontiero v. Richardson, 411 U.S. 677, 686–88 (1973); San Antonio Indep. Sch. Dist. v. Rodriguez, 411 U.S. 1, 117–30 (1973) (Marshall, J., dissenting); Zablocki v. Redhail, 434 U.S. 374, 383–88 (1978); Harris v. McRae, 448 U.S. 297, 441–43 (1980) (Brennan, J., dissenting); Cleburne v. Cleburne Living Ctr., 473 U.S. 432, 460–73 (1985) (Marshall, J., dissenting). For detailed commentary see Edward V. Heck, "Constitutional Interpretation and a Court in Transition: Strict Scrutiny from *Shapiro v. Thompson* to *Dunn v. Blumstein*—and Beyond," *United States Air Force Academy Journal of Legal Studies* 3 (1992): 65–90; idem, "Judicial Activism and a Conservative Court" (paper presented at meeting of Southwest Political Science Association, Ft. Worth, Tex., 1990); idem, "Coalition Building and the Development of Constitutional Theory: Justice Brennan and Sex Discrimination Cases from *Frontiero* to *Craig*" (paper presented at meeting of Western Social Science Association, Portland, Ore., 1990); idem, "The Liberal as Bridge Builder: Justice Brennan and the Politics of Strict Scrutiny from *Buckley* to *Bakke*" (paper presented at meeting of Southern Political Science Association, Atlanta, Ga., 1990).

41. See City of Richmond v. J. A. Croson Co., 109 S.Ct. 706, 739–57 (1989) (Marshall, J., dissenting); Bernal v. Fainter, 467 U.S. 216, 219–22 (1984).

42. To protect women, they decided that "important governmental objectives" must be served by a gender classification and that there must be a substantial relationship of the classification to the "achievement of those important objectives"; see Craig v. Boren, 429 U.S. 190, 197–98 (1976). Sometimes, as with the treatment of illegal aliens, they evaluated the reasonableness of governmental action using standards other than strict scrutiny and the compelling governmental interest test; see Plyler v. Doe, 457 U.S. 202, 216–24 (1982).

43. Miranda v. Arizona, 384 U.S. 436 (1966).

44. Milliken v. Bradley, 418 U.S. 717, 781–815 (1974) (Marshall, J., dissenting) (desegregation); Regents of the Univ. of California v. Bakke, 438 U.S. 265, 387–402 (Marshall, J., opinion); United Steelworkers of Am. v. Weber, 443 U.S. 193 (1979); Fullilove v. Klutznick, 448 U.S. 448, 517–23 (1980)

(Marshall, J., concurring); Wygant v. Jackson Bd. of Educ., 476 U.S. 267, 295–312 (1986) (Marshall, J., dissenting); Local No. 93, Int'l Ass'n of Firefighters v. City of Cleveland, 478 U.S. 501 (1986); United States v. Paradise, 480 U.S. 149 (1987); Johnson v. Transportation Agency, Santa Clara County, 480 U.S. 616 (1987); City of Richmond v. J. A. Croson Co., 488 U.S. 469, 528–61 (1989) (Marshall, J., dissenting); Metro Broadcasting Inc. v. FCC, 110 S.Ct. 2997 (1990) (affirmative action); Duncan v. Louisiana, 391 U.S. 145 (1968) (incorporation); Griswold v. Connecticut, 391 U.S. 145 (1965); Roe v. Wade, 410 U.S. 113 (1973); Maher v. Roe, 432 U.S. 464, 482–90 (1977) (Brennan, J., dissenting); Michael H. v. Gerald D., 491 U.S. 110, 136–57 (1989) (Brennan, J., dissenting); Cruzan by Cruzan v. Director, Missouri Dept. of Health, 110 S.Ct. 2841, 2863–78 (1990) (Brennan, J., dissenting) (substantive due process).

45. Brown v. Board of Educ., 347 U.S. at 493–96; Reynolds v. Sims, 377 U.S. at 554–71.

46. Hereafter I use "Reasoned Elaboration" rather than "Legal Process" to describe this mode of jurisprudential discourse.

47. Youngstown Sheet and Tube Co. v. Sawyer, 343 U.S. 579, 593 (1952) (Frankfurter, J., concurring); see also Edelman, *Democratic Theories*, 74–75, 94, 114–20, for an elaboration of this idea.

48. Dennis v. United States, 342 U.S. 494, 525 (1950) (Frankfurter, J., concurring). Compare West Virginia State Bd. of Educ. v. Barnette, 319 U.S. 624, 651–52 (1943) (Frankfurter, J., dissenting); Baker v. Carr, 369 U.S. 186, 280–97 (1962) (Frankfurter, J., dissenting).

49. Felix Frankfurter, "Some Reflections on the Reading of Statutes," *Record of the Association of the Bar of the City of New York* 2 (1947): 221.

50. West Virginia State Bd. of Educ. v. Barnette, 319 U.S. at 670–71 (Frankfurter, J., dissenting). See also Frankfurter's support for judicial passivity in Coleman v. Miller, 307 U.S. 433, 460–70 (1939) (opinion of Frankfurter, J.); Colegrove v. Green, 328 U.S. 549, 549–56 (1946); Joint Anti-Fascist Refugee Comm. v. McGrath, 341 U.S. 123, 149–60 (1951) (Frankfurter, J., concurring); United States v. United Auto Workers, 352 U.S. 567, 567–93 (1957); Burns v. Ohio, 360 U.S. 252, 259–63 (1959) (Frankfurter, J., dissenting); Poe v. Ullman, 367 U.S. 497, 497–509 (1961); Baker v. Carr, 369 U.S. at 266–77 (Frankfurter, J., dissenting); and the discussion in Jacobsohn, *Pragmatism*, 120–21, 131–32.

51. Youngstown Sheet and Tube Co. v. Sawyer, 343 U.S. at 593–614 (Frankfurter, J., concurring); Terry v. Adams, 345 U.S. 461, 472–77 (1953); Gomillion v. Lightfoot, 364 U.S. 334, 346–48 (1960). See also Frankfurter, "Reading of Statutes," 220–24. On misconduct, see Colegrove v. Green, 328 U.S. at 556; and Rochin v. California, 342 U.S. 165, 172–73 (1952).

52. Frankfurter, "Reading of Statutes," 223.

53. See SEC v. Chenery Corp., 318 U.S. 80, 91–94 (1943); Felix Frank-

furter, *The Public and Its Government* (New Haven: Yale University Press, 1930), 157–63; Jacobsohn, *Pragmatism,* 144–48; Sanford V. Levinson, "The Democratic Faith of Felix Frankfurter," *Stanford Law Review* 25 (1973): 438–41. On participation in decisions, see United States v. Morgan, 313 U.S. 409, 415–21 (1941); CBS v. United States, 316 U.S. 407, 429–46 (1942) (Frankfurter, J., dissenting); Polish Nat'l Alliance v. NLRB, 322 U.S. 643, 643–48 (1944).

54. James M. Landis, *The Administrative Process* (New Haven: Yale University Press, 1938), 24, 30–31, quotation on 154–55. For detailed discussion of the "expertise" model of administration proposed by Landis, see Gerald E. Frug, "The Ideology of Bureaucracy in American Law," *Harvard Law Review* 97 (1984): 1318–34; and Thomas K. McCraw, *Prophets of Regulation: Charles Francis Adams, Louis D. Brandeis, James M. Landis, Alfred E. Kahn* (Cambridge: Belknap Press of Harvard University Press, 1984), 152–209. Landis adjusted his views on expertise late in his career; see McCraw, *Prophets of Regulation,* 206–7.

55. Landis, *Administrative Process,* 154–55; for Frankfurter's position, see Tigner v. Texas, 310 U.S. 141 (1940); East New York Sav. Bank v. Hahn, 326 U.S. 230 (1945); American Fed'n of Labor v. American Sash and Door Co., 335 U.S. 538, 545–57 (1949) (Frankfurter, J., concurring); Osborne v. Ozlin, 310 U.S. 53 (1940); Phelps Dodge Corp. v. NLRB 313 U.S. 177, 199–200 (1941); Newark Fire Ins. Co. v. State Bd., 307 U.S. 313, 323–24 (1939) (Frankfurter, J.); Wisconsin v. J. C. Penney Co., 311 U.S. 435, 445 (1940).

56. New York v. United States, 326 U.S. 572 (1946), but note the exception at 582. Compare to Polish Nat'l Alliance v. NLRB, 322 U.S. at 649–51 (Frankfurter, J., dissenting); and Baker v. Carr, 369 U.S. at 284–85 (Frankfurter, J., dissenting).

57. Minersville Sch. Dist. v. Gobitis, 310 U.S. 586, 599 (1940). See also Dennis v. United States, 341 U.S. at 555 (Frankfurter, J., concurring). See Jacobsohn, *Pragmatism,* 144–48.

58. See West Virginia State Bd. of Educ. v. Barnette, 319 U.S. at 667 (Frankfurter, J., dissenting); Milk Wagon Drivers Union v. Meadowmoor Dairies, 312 U.S. 287, 293–99 (1949); Cooper v. Aaron, 358 U.S. 1, 24–26 (1958) (Frankfurter, J., concurring); McCollum v. Board of Educ., 333 U.S. 203, 214–20 (1948); Harris v. United States, 331 U.S. 145, 155–74 (1947) (Frankfurter, J., dissenting); Haley v. Ohio, 332 U.S. 596, 601–7 (1947) (Frankfurter, J.); McNabb v. United States, 318 U.S. 322 (1943); and Niemotko v. Maryland, 340 U.S. 268, 275–89 (1951) (Frankfurter, J., concurring). See also Edelman, *Democratic Theories,* 93–114.

59. Henry M. Hart Jr. and Albert M. Sacks, "The Legal Process: Basic Problems in the Making and Application of the Law," tentative ed. (Harvard Law School, Cambridge, 1958), 161. These materials appeared in mimeo-

graphed form for use by students such as Antonin Scalia. Hereafter citation is made to the published version, Henry M. Hart Jr. and Albert M. Sacks, *The Legal Process: Basic Problems in the Making and Application of the Law*, prepared from tentative ed. by William N. Eskridge Jr. and Philip P. Frickey (Westbury, N.Y.: Foundation Press, 1994), 143.

60. Hart and Sacks, *Legal Process*, 3. See also Kalman, *Legal Realism at Yale*, 220–28; Gary Peller, "Neutral Principles in the 1950's," *University of Michigan Journal of Law Reform* 25 (summer 1988): 561–622; and White, *Patterns of American Legal Thought*, 139–63.

61. Hart and Sacks, *Legal Process*, 143–44.

62. See William N. Eskridge Jr. and Philip P. Frickey, "A Historical and Critical Introduction to *The Legal Process*," in ibid., c–cxiii.

63. Hart and Sacks, *Legal Process*, 143. See also Peller, "Neutral Principles," 568–72, 586–91.

64. See Jacobsohn, *Pragmatism*, 133–97, on Frankfurter, Wechsler, and Bickel. I see somewhat less difference between the positions of Hart and Sacks and those of Bickel and Wechsler than does Kahn, *Supreme Court*, 80–89. As Eskridge and Frickey, "Introduction to *Legal Process*," ci, cviii–cxiii, indicate, Hart and Wechsler published an important casebook that resounded with legal process themes: Henry M. Hart Jr. and Herbert Wechsler, *The Federal Courts and the Federal System* (Mineola, N.Y.: Foundation Press, 1953). The crucial difference between Hart and Wechsler was in their evaluation of the Supreme Court's school desegregation decisions.

65. Alexander M. Bickel, *The Morality of Consent* (New Haven: Yale University Press, 1975), 16, 28–29. He further elaborates his moral relativism, as opposed to the "seductive temptations of moral imperatives," at 112–42.

66. Ibid., 5. Thus, Bickel recognized that sometimes majoritarian values can be embedded in legal procedures—see, e.g., Alexander M. Bickel, *The Supreme Court and the Idea of Progress* (New York: Harper and Row, 1970), 103–16, but see his criticism of the countermajoritarian difficulty with judicial review, in idem, *The Least Dangerous Branch: The Supreme Court at the Bar of Politics* (Indianapolis: Bobbs-Merrill, 1962), 16–23. See a similar position in Paul A. Freund, *The Supreme Court of the United States: Its Business, Purposes, and Performance* (Cleveland: Meridian, 1961), 89–91; idem, "Social Justice and the Law," in *On Law and Justice* (Cambridge: Belknap Press of Harvard University Press, 1968), 82–107.

67. See Hart and Sacks, *Legal Process*, iii, 136, 143–50, 159–61. Harris, *Interpretable Constitution*, 145–48, would call this an immanent positivist mode of interpretation.

68. See Hart and Sacks, *Legal Process*, 3–6. The reliance of Reasoned Elaboration theorists on an "uncritical" perspective on American pluralist politics is elaborated in Kahn, *Supreme Court*, 72–89.

69. See Hart and Sacks, *Legal Process,* 113–14.

70. See Herbert Wechsler, "Toward Neutral Principles of Constitutional Law," *Harvard Law Review* 73 (1959): 1–35.

71. See Hart and Sacks, *Legal Process,* 161; Bickel, *Supreme Court and Idea of Progress,* 94–100; Wechsler, "Toward Neutral Principles," 1–35; and White, *Patterns of American Legal Thought,* 144–48. Originally, Bickel, *Least Dangerous Branch,* 49–65, was skeptical of neutral principles, preferring to see principle as "a universal guide but not a universal constraint" (244). The result was space for the judicial craft of equity (250). However, even the Harvard faculty member Archibald Cox, regarded as a liberal for his role in the Watergate affair and his leadership of the reform interest group Common Cause, stressed the need for judicial restraint when the Court could not offer reasons "in terms of principles referable to accepted sources of law" or "on the basis of conventional legal criteria" for its decisions. See Archibald Cox, *The Warren Court: Constitutional Decision as an Instrument of Reform* (Cambridge: Harvard University Press, 1968), 21–23, 40; idem, *The Role of the Supreme Court in American Government* (New York: Oxford University Press, 1976), 99–118. On the underlying assumption, see Hart and Sacks, *Legal Process,* 6–9, 164–65; Peller, "Neutral Principles," 586–91; Nicholas S. Zeppos, "Justice Scalia's Textualism: The 'New' New Legal Process," *Cardozo Law Review* 12 (1991): 1599–1606.

72. Freund, *Supreme Court of the United States,* 92–115. See also Hart and Sacks, *Legal Process,* 146–48.

73. Hart and Sacks, *Legal Process,* 147. See also White, *Patterns of American Legal Thought,* 148–49.

74. See Hart and Sacks, *Legal Process,* 102–7; Bickel, *Least Dangerous Branch,* 16–23; Peller, "Neutral Principles," 599–606. For more extensive discussion of this point, see H. N. Hirsch, *A Theory of Liberty: The Constitution and Minorities* (New York: Routledge, 1992), 88–91; White, *Patterns of American Legal Thought,* 148.

75. Lon L. Fuller, "The Forms and Limits of Adjudication," *Harvard Law Review* 92 (1978): 366, 369, 381–409. Versions of this article were used in classes at Harvard when Scalia was a student, in 1957–60; see 353.

76. See Bickel, *Least Dangerous Branch,* 50, 58–59; idem, *Supreme Court and Idea of Progress,* 50–100; Fuller, "Forms and Limits of Adjudication," 367; and Wechsler, "Toward Neutral Principles," 1–35.

77. Shklar, *Legalism,* 111.

78. See Hart and Sacks, *Legal Process,* 110–12. For general commentary on the nature of social facts and the Rehnquist Court's use of social facts, see Hirsch, *Theory of Liberty,* 97–193.

79. Hart and Sacks, *Legal Process,* 350–51.

80. Felix Frankfurter, "Some Reflections on the Reading of Statutes," *Rec-*

ord of the Association of the Bar of the City of New York 2 (June 1947): 224–26, 230–35. See also Hart and Sacks, *Legal Process,* 1211–54.

81. Louis L. Jaffe, "The Effective Limits of the Administrative Process: A Reevaluation," *Harvard Law Review* 67 (1954): 1105–35; idem, *Judicial Control of Administrative Action* (Boston: Little Brown, 1965), 10–86, 395–720, quotation on 326. For further discussion of this approach to agency power, see Frug, "Ideology of Bureaucracy," 1334–55. Also see Hart and Sacks, *Legal Process,* 165–67.

82. See Hart and Sacks, *Legal Process,* 171–79, 341–44; see also Fuller, "Forms and Limits of Adjudication"; White, *Patterns of American Legal Thought,* 148–49.

83. See Bickel, *Least Dangerous Branch,* 111–98; idem, *Supreme Court and Idea of Progress,* 45–100; and Henry M. Hart Jr., "Foreword: The Time Chart of the Justices," *Harvard Law Review* 73 (1959): 84–125. See also Hart and Sacks, *Legal Process,* 174–80, on the Reasoned Elaboration view of the lawyer's craft.

84. The concept of "easy cases" is discussed in Frederick Schauer, "Easy Cases," *Southern California Law Review* 58 (1985): 399–440.

85. See Richard A. Brisbin Jr., "Conservative Jurisprudence in the Reagan Era," *Cumberland Law Review* 19 (1988–89): 497–537.

86. See Eskridge and Frickey, "Introduction to *Legal Process,*" cvi–ccxvii.

CHAPTER FOUR: PRESIDENTIAL LEADERSHIP AND THE SEPARATION OF POWERS

1. Antonin Scalia, quoted in David Ginsburg, moderator, "Panel IV: Improving the Administrative Process—Time for a New APA? (Part C)," *Administrative Law Review* 32 (1980): 371.

2. Louis Fisher, *Constitutional Conflicts between the Congress and the President* (Princeton: Princeton University Press, 1985), 326. See also M. David Gelfand and Keith Werhan, "Federalism and the Separation of Powers on a 'Conservative' Court: Currents and Cross-Currents from Justices O'Connor and Scalia," *Tulane Law Review* 64 (1990): 1465–68.

3. Antonin Scalia, "The Limits of the Law," *New Jersey Law Journal* 119, no. 18 (1987): 4, originally a speech of 7 Apr. 1987, contains an apparently contradictory thesis: "Good laws and even a good Constitution are ultimately the reflection or product of a good society rather than its cause." The speech, drawing on the ideas of Lon Fuller, perhaps justifies Scalia's reluctance to use judicial power to counter the preferences of majoritarian institutions. But as a "second best" method of ordering society, "law steps in and will inevitably step in when the virtue and prudence of the society, itself, is inadequate to produce the desired result" (5). Consequently, the survival of a good society depends on the rule of law rather than solely on the norms and virtues of its citizens.

4. Antonin Scalia, address presented at American Enterprise Institute for Public Policy Research, Washington, D.C., 1989, 3; a mimeographed copy of the address was provided to me by Justice Scalia. See also the discussion in Larry Kramer, "Judicial Asceticism," *Cardozo Law Review* 12 (1991): 1789–98.

5. Some of these themes are recounted in Christopher E. Smith, "Justice Antonin Scalia and the Institutions of American Government," *Wake Forest Law Review* 25 (1990): 794–804.

6. See, e.g., on constitutional interpretation, Freytag v. Commissioner of Internal Revenue, 111 S.Ct. 2631, 2646–61 (1991) (Scalia, J., concurring); Granfinanciera, S.A. v. Nordberg, 492 U.S. 33, 65–71 (1989) (Scalia, J., concurring); Texas Monthly, Inc. v. Bullock, 489 U.S. 1, 29–45 (1989) (Scalia, J., dissenting); Morrison v. Olson, 487 U.S. 654, 697–734 (1988) (Scalia, J., dissenting); on the interpretation of treaties, United States v. Stuart, 489 U.S. 353, 371–77 (1989) (Scalia, J., concurring); Chan v. Korean Air Lines, 490 U.S. 122, 134 (1989); and on the interpretation of statutes, Key Tronic Corp. v. United States, 114 S.Ct. 1960, 1968–69 (1994) (Scalia, J., dissenting); Dewsnup v. Timm, 112 S.Ct. 773, 779–88 (1992) (Scalia, J., dissenting); West Virginia Univ. Hosps. v. Casey, 111 S.Ct. 1138, 1146–48 (1991); Firestone Tire and Rubber Co. v. Bruch, 489 U.S. 101, 119–20 (1989) (Scalia, J., concurring); United States v. Taylor, 487 U.S. 326, 344–46 (1988) (Scalia, J., concurring); K Mart Corp. v. Cartier, Inc. (II), 486 U.S. 281, 319–29 (1988) (Scalia, J., concurring and dissenting); K Mart Corp. v. Cartier, Inc. (I), 485 U.S. 176, 191–96 (1988) (Scalia, J., dissenting).

7. On Scalia's definition of plain meaning, see Bradley C. Karkkainen, "'Plain Meaning': Justice Scalia's Jurisprudence of Strict Statutory Construction," *Harvard Journal of Law and Public Policy* 17 (1993): 406–15. On statutory and administrative intent, see Thunder Basin Coal Co. v. Reich, 114 S.Ct. 771, 782 (1994) (Scalia, J., concurring); Wisconsin Pub. Intervenor v. Mortier, 111 S.Ct. 2476, 2497–91 (1991) (Scalia, J., concurring); Chisom v. Roemer, 111 S.Ct. 2354, 2369–76 (1991) (Scalia, J., dissenting); Department of Treasury, IRS v. Federal Labor Relations Auth., 494 U.S. 922, 928–32 (1990); Rose v. Rose, 481 U.S. 619, 644 (1987) (Scalia, J. concurring); Edwards v. Aguillard, 482 U.S. 578, 619–36 (1987) (Scalia, J., dissenting). See also Antonin Scalia, "Judicial Deference to Administrative Interpretations of Law," *Duke Law Journal* (June 1989): 517.

8. On committee materials, see Sable Communications of California, Inc. v. FCC, 492 U.S. 115, 133 (1989) (Scalia, J., concurring); Green v. Bock Laundry Mach. Co., 490 U.S. 504, 527–30 (1989) (Scalia, J., concurring); Blanchard v. Bergeron, 489 U.S. 87, 97–100 (1989) (Scalia, J., concurring). On debates and legislative history, see Sullivan v. Finkelstein, 110 S.Ct. 2658, 2667 (1990) (Scalia, J., concurring); Begier v. IRS, 110 S.Ct. 2258, 2267–69 (1990) (Scalia, J., concurring); Taylor v. United States, 495 U.S. 575, 603

(1990) (Scalia, J., concurring); United States v. Taylor, 487 U.S. at 344–46 (Scalia, J., concurring); Immigration and Naturalization Serv. v. Cardoza Fonseca, 480 U.S. 421, 452–53 (1987) (Scalia, J., concurring); Lukhard v. Reed, 481 U.S. 368, 379–80 (1987).

9. Conroy v. Aniskoff, 113 S.Ct. 1562, 1567 (1993) (Scalia, J., concurring). Compare Felix Frankfurter, "Some Reflections on the Reading of Statutes," *Record of the Association of the Bar of the City of New York* 2 (1947): 224–26; Henry M. Hart Jr. and Albert M. Sacks, *The Legal Process: Basic Problems in the Making and Application of the Law,* prepared from tentative ed. by William N. Eskridge Jr. and Philip P. Frickey (Westbury, N.Y.: Foundation Press, 1994), 1211–54.

10. Edwards v. Aguillard, 482 U.S. at 637–40 (Scalia, J., dissenting).

11. See Lee v. Weisman, 112 S.Ct. 2649, 2678–86 (1992) (Scalia, J., dissenting); Freytag v. Commissioner, 111 S.Ct. at 2659–60 (Scalia, J., concurring); Morrison v. Olson, 487 U.S. at 127–32 (Scalia, J., dissenting).

12. Bowen v. Georgetown Univ. Hosp., 488 U.S. 204, 216–25 (1988) (Scalia, J., concurring). See the discussion in Bernard Schwartz, "'Shooting the Piano Player'? Justice Scalia and Administrative Law," *Administrative Law Review* 47 (1995): 31–33, 39–40, on the origins of his opinion.

13. Dewsnup v. Timm, 112 S.Ct. 773, 787 (1992) (Scalia, J., dissenting). See also Burnham v. Superior Ct., 495 U.S. 604, 619–27 (1990); Grady v. Corbin, 495 U.S. 508, 526–36 (1990) (Scalia, J., dissenting); South Carolina v. Gathers, 490 U.S. 805, 823–25 (1989) (Scalia, J., dissenting); and his comments in a speech: Antonin Scalia, "Assorted Canards of Contemporary Legal Analysis," *Case Western Reserve Law Review* 40 (1989–90): 586–90.

14. Tull v. United States, 481 U.S. 412, 427–28 (1987) (Scalia, J., concurring and dissenting); Scalia's opinion was a reaction to Court's use of precedents about the Seventh Amendment. See also Kaiser Aluminum v. Bonjorno, 494 U.S. 827, 840–58 (1990) (Scalia, J., concurring); Schmuck v. United States, 489 U.S. 705, 723–25 (1989) (Scalia, J., dissenting) (use of precedent for clarification of statute).

15. Kaiser Aluminum v. Bonjorno, 494 U.S. at 840–58 (Scalia, J., concurring).

16. Landgraf v. USI Film Products, 114 S.Ct. 1483, 1572–26 (1994) (Scalia, J., concurring).

17. Harper v. Virginia Dept. of Taxation, 113 S.Ct. 2510, 2520–24 (Scalia, J., concurring).

18. Moskal v. United States, 111 S.Ct. 461, 471–78 (1990) (Scalia, J., dissenting). See also Scalia's additional commentary on the doctrine developed in this case in his opinion in United States v. R.L.C., 112 S.Ct. 1329, 1339–41 (1992) (Scalia, J., concurring).

19. American Trucking Ass'ns, Inc. v. Smith, 110 S.Ct. 2323, 2343–45 (1990) (Scalia, J., concurring); Bendix Autolite Corp. v. Midwesco Enter-

prises, 486 U.S. 888, 895–98 (1988) (Scalia, J., concurring); Tyler Pipe Indus. v. Washington State Dept. of Revenue, 483 U.S. 232, 254–55 (1987) (Scalia, J., concurring and dissenting); Antonin Scalia, "The Rule of Law as a Law of Rules," *University of Chicago Law Review* 56 (1989): 1185. See also Mark V. Tushnet, "Scalia and the Dormant Commerce Clause: A Foolish Formalism?" *Cardozo Law Review* 12 (1991): 1717–30.

20. Scalia, address at American Enterprise Institute, 9. Compare Hart and Sacks, *Legal Process,* 341–44, 642–47.

21. Johnson v. Transportation Agency, Santa Clara County, 480 U.S. 616, 669–77 (1987) (Scalia, J., dissenting).

22. United States v. Johnson, 481 U.S. 681, 692–703 (1987) (Scalia, J., dissenting); construing Feres v. United States, 340 U.S. 135 (1950).

23. Allied-Bruce Terminix Cos. v. Dobson, 115 S.Ct. 834, 844–45 (1995) (Scalia, J., dissenting).

24. Pacific Mut. Life Ins. Co. v. Haslip, 111 S.Ct. 1032, 1046–54 (1991) (Scalia, J., concurring). See also Honda Motor Co. v. Oberg, 114 S.Ct. 2331, 2342–43 (1994) (Scalia, J., concurring).

25. TXO Production Corp. v. Alliance Resources Corp., 113 S.Ct. 2711, 2726–28 (1994) (Scalia, J., concurring).

26. Webster v. Reprod. Health Servs., 492 U.S. 490, 532–37 (1989) (Scalia, J., concurring); Hodgson v. Minnesota, 110 S.Ct. 2926, 2960–61 (1990) (Scalia, J., concurring and dissenting); Ohio v. Akron Ctr. for Reprod. Health, 110 S.Ct. 2972, 2984 (1990) (Scalia, J., concurring). The argument is extended to an assault on the "Imperial Judiciary" in Planned Parenthood of Southeastern Pennsylvania v. Casey, 112 S.Ct. 2791, 2873–85 (1992) (Scalia, J., concurring and dissenting).

27. Michael H. v. Gerald D., 491 U.S. 110 (1989).

28. Cruzan by Cruzan v. Director, Missouri Dept. of Health, 110 S.Ct. 2841, 2863 (1990) (Scalia, J., concurring). See also Robert A. Burt, "Precedent and Authority in Antonin Scalia's Jurisprudence," *Cardozo Law Review* 12 (1991): 1685–1716.

29. Payne v. Tennessee, 111 S.Ct. at 2613 (Scalia, J., concurring). Compare Booth v. Maryland, 482 U.S. 66 (1987); and South Carolina v. Gathers, 490 U.S. at 823–25 (Scalia, J., dissenting).

30. Witte v. United States, 115 S.Ct. 2199, 2209–10 (1995) (Scalia, J., concurring).

31. Hubbard v. United States, 115 S.Ct. 1754 (1995) (Scalia, J., concurring); discussing United States v. Bramblett, 348 U.S. 503 (1985).

32. See Saul Brenner and Harold J. Spaeth, *Stare Indecisis: The Alteration of Precedent on the Supreme Court, 1946–1992* (Cambridge: Cambridge University Press, 1995).

33. Scalia, address at American Enterprise Institute, 4, 6–7.

34. Hoffmann-La Roche Inc. v. Sperling, 493 U.S. 165, 174–81 (1989) (Scalia, J., dissenting) (Article III); Tafflin v. Levitt, 493 U.S. 455, 469–73 (1990) (Scalia, J., concurring); Gwaltney of Smithfield, Ltd. v. Chesapeake Bay Found., 484 U.S. 49, 67–71 (1987) (Scalia, J., concurring) (statutes).

35. Chambers v. NASCO, Inc., 111 S.Ct. 2123, 2140–41 (1991) (Scalia, J., dissenting) (trial conduct); Kokkonen v. Guardian Life Ins. Co., 114 S.Ct. 1673 (1994) (withdrawal).

36. See Hoffmann-La Roche, Inc. v. Sperling, 493 U.S. at 174–81 (Scalia, J., dissenting).

37. Peretz v. United States, 111 S.Ct. 2661, 2667–80 (1991) (Scalia, J., dissenting).

38. Thompson v. Thompson, 484 U.S. 174, 191–92 (1988) (Scalia, J., concurring); and see also his comments in a solo opinion about a statutory private right of action in Franklin v. Gwinnett County Pub. Sch., 112 S.Ct. 1028, 1038–39 (1992) (Scalia, J., concurring). See also Lampf, Pleva, Lipkind, Prupis, and Petigrow v. Gilbertson, 111 U.S. 2773, 2783 (1991) (Scalia, J., concurring) (statute of limitations issue).

39. Houston v. Lack, 487 U.S. 266, 277–84 (1988) (Scalia, J., dissenting).

40. Granfinanciera, S.A. v. Nordberg, 492 U.S. at 65–71 (Scalia, J., concurring). See Schwartz, "Shooting the Piano Player," 17–18, on the potential ramifications of Scalia's argument.

41. City of Richmond v. J. A. Croson Co., 488 U.S. 469, 520–28 (1989) (Scalia, J., concurring); Johnson v. Transportation Agency, 480 U.S. at 657–77 (Scalia, J., dissenting).

42. St. Mary's Honor Ctr. v. Hicks, 113 S.Ct. 2742, 2750–54 (1993); Bray v. Alexandria Women's Health Clinic, 113 S.Ct. 753, 758–67 (1993).

43. Richmond v. Croson, 488 U.S. at 520–28 (Scalia, J., concurring); Johnson v. Transportation Agency, 480 U.S. at 668 (Scalia, J., dissenting).

44. Richmond v. Croson, 488 U.S. at 520–28 (Scalia, J., concurring).

45. Johnson v. Transportation Agency, 480 U.S. at 658 (Scalia, J., dissenting).

46. On finality, see Lauro Lines S.R.L. v. Chasser, 490 U.S. 495, 502–3 (1989) (Scalia, J., concurring); Gulfstream Aerospace Corp. v. Mayacamas Corp., 485 U.S. 271, 290–92 (1988) (Scalia, J., concurring). Compare Shalala v. Schaefer, 113 S.Ct. 2625 (1993) (interpreting statutory language on when a final judgment occurs); Midland Asphalt Corp. v. United States, 489 U.S. 794 (1989). On mootness, see Lewis v. Continental Bank Corp., 494 U.S. 472 (1990). On sovereign immunity, see United States v. Nordic Village, Inc., 112 S.Ct. 1011 (quotation) (1992). On case or controversy rule see Honig v. Doe, 484 U.S. 305, 332–42 (1988) (Scalia, J., dissenting). See also Alexander M. Bickel, *The Least Dangerous Branch: The Supreme Court at the Bar of Politics* (Indianapolis: Bobbs-Merrill, 1962), 111–98.

47. United States v. Munoz-Flores, 495 U.S. 385, 408–10 (1990) (Scalia, J., concurring) (legislative house of origin); Franklin v. Massachusetts, 112 S.Ct. 2767, 2787–90 (1992) (Scalia, J., concurring) (census).

48. See Webster v. Reprod. Health Servs., 492 U.S. at 532–37 (Scalia, J., concurring); Hodgson v. Minnesota, 110 S.Ct. at 2960–61 (Scalia, J., concurring and dissenting); Ohio v. Akron Ctr. for Reprod. Health, 110 S.Ct. at 2984 (Scalia, J., concurring).

49. Torres v. Oakland Scavenger Co., 487 U.S. 312, 318–19 (1988) (Scalia, J., concurring).

50. Bowen v. Massachusetts, 487 U.S. 879, 930 (1988) (Scalia, J., dissenting).

51. Pierce v. Underwood, 487 U.S. 552 (1988). Compare Finley v. United States, 490 U.S. 545 (1989) (Equal Access to Justice Act); and Holmes v. Securities Investor Protection Corp., 112 S.Ct. 1311, 1327–29 (1992) (Scalia, J., concurring) (RICO).

52. Eastman Kodak Co. v. Image Technical Servs., Inc., 112 S.Ct. 2072, 2092–2101 (1992) (Scalia, J., dissenting).

53. Finley v. United States, 490 U.S. 545 (1989).

54. Director, Office of Workers' Compensation Programs v. Newport News Shipbuilding and Dry Dock Co., 115 S.Ct. 1278 (1995).

55. Nixon v. United States, 113 S.Ct. 732 (1993).

56. Office of Personnel Management v. Richmond, 110 S.Ct. 2465 (1990).

57. United States v. Alvarez-Machain, 112 S.Ct. 2188 (1992).

58. United States Dept. of Commerce v. Montana, 112 S.Ct. 1415 (1992).

59. Northeastern Florida Chapter of Associated Contractors of Am. v. City of Jacksonville, 113 S.Ct. 2297 (1993).

60. Quinn v. Millsap, 491 U.S. 95 (1989).

61. See Pavelic and LeFlore v. Marvel Entertainment Group, 493 U.S. 120 (1989) (Rule 11); W. S. Kirkpatrick and Co. v. Environmental Tectonics Corp., Int'l, 493 U.S. 400 (1990) (Nigerian bribery); Republic of Argentina v. Weltover, Inc., 112 S.Ct. 2160 (1992) (bond default); United States Dept. of Labor v. Triplett, 494 U.S. 715 (1990) (black lung benefits); Hartford Fire Ins. Co. v. California, 113 S.Ct. 2891, 2911–22 (1993) (Scalia, J., dissenting) (extraterritorial acts); and Lebron v. National R.R. Passenger Corp., 115 S.Ct. 961 (1995) (Amtrak). See also Mississippi v. Turner, 111 S.Ct. 1032 (1991) (Scalia, Cir. J).

62. Morrison v. Olson, 487 U.S. 654 (1988).

63. Ibid., 733 (Scalia, J., dissenting).

64. Ibid., 711–12 (Scalia, J., dissenting).

65. Alexander Hamilton, James Madison, and John Jay, *The Federalist,* ed. Jacob E. Cooke (1787–88; Middletown, Conn.: Wesleyan University Press, 1961), paper no. 48 (Madison), at 332–33. For an effort to show a "strong affinity" between the separated powers theory of Madison and that of Scalia—

an effort that, to this author, fails to provide convincing evidence—see Price Marshall, "No Political Truth: The Federalist and Justice Scalia on the Separation of Powers," *University of Arkansas at Little Rock Law Journal* 12 (1989): 245–64, esp. 247; however, at 260–62 Marshall admits tensions in his argument and seems to contradict himself. Also see Daniel N. Reisman, "Deconstructing Justice Scalia's Separation of Powers Jurisprudence: The Preeminent Executive," *Albany Law Review* 53 (1988): 58–60, 72–77, 82–89, points out a selectivity and incompleteness in Scalia's evaluation of the perspectives of the Framers on the powers of the branches of the federal government.

66. Morrison v. Olson, 487 U.S. at 710 (Scalia, J., dissenting).

67. Myers v. United States, 272 U.S. 52 (1926).

68. Morrison v. Olson, 487 U.S. at 706 (Scalia, J., dissenting).

69. Ibid., 708 (Scalia, J., dissenting) (quoting majority opinion at 695).

70. Ibid., 709.

71. Ibid., 719–23 (Scalia, J., dissenting).

72. Morrison v. Olson, 487 U.S. at 723–27 (Scalia, J., dissenting); considering Humphrey's Executor v. United States, 295 U.S. 602 (1935). Scalia has read *Humphrey's Executor* as a historical anomaly, a dubious attempt by an anti–New Deal Court to control executive power by limiting the removal power of the president. He would give the holding a narrow interpretation to reduce its limiting effects on presidential control of agencies. See Antonin Scalia, "Historical Anomalies in Administrative Law," *Yearbook of the Supreme Court Historical Society* (1985): 106.

73. Morrison v. Olson, 712–15, 732–33 (Scalia, J., dissenting).

74. Ibid., 728–34 (Scalia, J., dissenting).

75. Ibid., 708–15, 733–34 (quotation) (Scalia, J., dissenting).

76. Young v. United States ex rel. Vuitton et Fils S.A., 481 U.S. 787 (1987).

77. Ibid., 815–25 (Scalia, J., concurring). He restates this position in United States v. Providence Journal Co., 485 U.S. 693, 708 (1988) (Scalia, J., concurring). See also his reluctance to extend judicial supervision of prosecutors in Bank of Nova Scotia v. United States, 487 U.S. 250, 264 (1988) (Scalia, J., concurring). The historical analysis of contempt prosecutions used by Scalia is criticized by Reisman, "Scalia's Separation of Powers Jurisprudence," 78–91.

78. Mistretta v. United States, 488 U.S. 361 (1989).

79. Ibid., 420 (Scalia, J., dissenting).

80. Humphrey's Executor v. United States, 295 U.S. 602. Scalia has questioned the reasoning of this case; see the discussion in Schwartz, "Shooting the Piano Player," 2–5, 15–17.

81. Mistretta v. United States, 488 U.S. at 427 (Scalia, J., dissenting). On his reading of precedent, see the discussion in Reisman, "Scalia's Separation of Powers Jurisprudence," 63–65.

82. Freytag v. Commissioner of Internal Revenue, 111 S.Ct. 2631 (1991).

83. See Ibid., 2654–55 (Scalia, J., concurring). Scalia details his differences with Blackmun, especially regarding whether the chief judge of the Tax Court is a department head.

84. Ibid., 2654 (Scalia, J., concurring). For speculation on the implications of this conclusion, see Schwartz, "Shooting the Piano Player," 8.

85. Weiss v. United States, 114 S.Ct. 752, 769–71 (1994) (Scalia, J., concurring).

86. James B. Beam Distilling Co. v. Georgia, 111 U.S. 2439, 2450–51 (1991) (Scalia, J., concurring).

87. Plaut v. Spendthrift Farm, 115 S.Ct. 1447, 1453–56 (1995).

88. Webster v. Doe, 486 U.S. 592, 606–21 (1988) (Scalia, J., dissenting).

89. Franklin v. Massachusetts, 112 S.Ct. at 2887–90 (Scalia, J., concurring). See the discussion of the potential ramifications of his opinion in Schwartz, "Shooting the Piano Player," 35–38.

90. O'Connor v. United States, 479 U.S. 27 (1986).

91. Chan v. Korean Air Lines, 490 U.S. at 134.

92. United States v. Stuart, 489 U.S. at 375 (Scalia, J., concurring). See also the discussion in Malvina Halberstram, "The Use of Legislative History in Treaty Interpretation," *Cardozo Law Review* 12 (1991): 1645–51. See the discussion in Smith, "Justice Antonin Scalia," 786–94, for a slightly different evaluation of these decisions.

93. Metropolitan Washington Airports Auth. v. Citizens for the Abatement of Aircraft Noise, 501 U.S. 252 (1991).

94. Scalia, "Judicial Deference," 511.

95. See Malcolm L. Goggin, Ann O'M. Bowman, James P. Lester, and Laurence J. O'Toole Jr., *Implementation Theory and Practice: Toward a Third Generation* (Glenview, Ill.: Scott, Foresman / Little, Brown Higher Education, 1990).

96. The fact-law distinction is derived from the Administrative Procedure Act, 5 *U.S. Code* §706.

97. ABF Freight Sys., Inc. v. NLRB, 114 S.Ct. 835, 841 (1994) (Scalia, J., concurring).

98. Antonin Scalia, "Responsibilities of Federal Regulatory Agencies under Environmental Laws," *Houston Law Review* 24 (1987): 107; see also 98–102.

99. Chevron U.S.A., Inc. v. Natural Resources Defense Council, 467 U.S. 837, 842–43 (1984).

100. Ibid., 865.

101. Sullivan v. Everhart, 494 U.S. 83 (1990). See also Reno v. Flores, 113 S.Ct. 1439 (1993); Scalia, "Judicial Deference," 511–12.

102. Pauley v. BethEnergy Mines, Inc., 111 S.Ct. 2524, 2539–46 (1991) (Scalia, J., dissenting); Immigration and Naturalization Serv. v. Cardoza Fonseca, 480 U.S. at 453–55 (Scalia, J., concurring).

103. Scalia, "Judicial Deference," 515–17.

104. A point Scalia stresses, joined by Kennedy, in Crandon v. United States, 494 U.S. 152, 177 (1990) (Scalia, J., concurring).

105. EEOC v. Arabian Am. Oil Co., 111 S.Ct. 1227, 1237 (1991) (Scalia, J., concurring).

106. Scalia, "Judicial Deference," 520.

107. Immigration and Naturalization Serv. v. Pangilinan, 486 U.S. 875, 882–85 (1988); Maislin Indus., United States, Inc. v. Primary Steel, Inc., 110 S.Ct. 2759, 2771–72 (1990) (Scalia, J., concurring).

108. See Department of Treasury, IRS v. Federal Labor Relations Auth., 494 U.S. at 928–34 (Civil Service Reform Act); NLRB v. International Bd. of Elec. Workers, Local 340, 481 U.S. 573, 596–98 (1987) (Scalia, J., concurring) (excessive deference); United States v. Burke, 112 S.Ct. 1867, 1874–76 (1992) (Scalia, J., concurring) (NLRB order); City of Chicago v. Environmental Defense Fund, 114 S.Ct. 1588, 1594 (1994) (Resource Conservation and Recovery Act); MCI Telecommunications v. American Tel. and Tel. Co., 114 S.Ct. 2223 (1994) (long-distance rates); Immigration and Naturalization Serv. v. Cardoza Fonseca, 480 U.S. at 453–55 (Scalia, J., concurring) (immigration); and Babbitt v. Sweet Home Chapter of Communities for a Greater Oregon, 115 S.Ct. 2407, 2421–31 (1995) (Scalia, J., dissenting) (Endangered Species Act). For extended commentary on Scalia's opinion in INS v. Cardoza Fonseca in light of statutory interpretation in general, see William N. Eskridge Jr., "The New Textualism," *UCLA Law Review* 37 (1990): 621–91. Scalia's position is further fleshed out in internal memoranda cited in Schwartz, "Shooting the Piano Player," 47–48.

109. Immigration and Naturalization Serv. v. Cardoza Fonseca, 480 U.S. at 454 (Scalia, J., concurring).

110. Pauley v. BethEnergy Mines, Inc., 111 S.Ct at 2539 (Scalia, J., dissenting).

111. See ICC v. Board of Locomotive Eng'rs, 422 U.S. 270 (1987) (material errors); Mississippi Power and Light Co. v. Mississippi ex rel. Moore, 487 U.S. 354, 377–83 (1988) (Scalia, J., concurring) (ratemaking); and Schwartz, "Shooting the Piano Player," 27–29, on these cases, and 23–27, on the unpublished opinion.

112. Immigration and Naturalization Serv. v. Elias-Zacarias, 112 S.Ct. 812 (1992).

113. Pittston Coal Group v. Sebben, 488 U.S. 105 (1988). Related opinions, not specifically relying on the Chevron case, that illustrate his application of the standard of deference when the issues of the case include abuse of discretion through arbitrary and capricious procedural action include the following: Fort Stewart Sch. v. Federal Labor Relations Auth., 495 U.S. 641 (1990); NLRB v. Curtin Matheson Scientific, Inc., 494 U.S. 775, 801–19 (1990) (Scalia, J., dissenting).

114. Arcadia, Ohio v. Ohio Power Co., 498 U.S. 73 (1990).

115. Immigration and Naturalization Serv. v. Doherty, 112 S.Ct. 719, 728–36 (1992) (Scalia, J., concurring and dissenting).

116. Sullivan v. Everhart, 494 U.S. at 88–93; United Food and Commercial Workers Union, Local 23, 484 U.S. 112, 133–34 (1987) (Scalia, J., concurring).

117. See K Mart Corp. v. Cartier, Inc. (II), 486 U.S. 281, 323 (quotation) (1988) (Scalia, J., concurring and dissenting); and Pauley v. BethEnergy Mines, Inc., 111 S.Ct. at 2539 (Scalia, J., dissenting).

118. See Immigration and Naturalization Serv. v. Cardoza-Fonseca, 480 U.S. at 453–55 (Scalia, J. concurring).

119. NLRB v. International Bhd. of Elec. Workers, Local 340, 481 U.S. at 597–98 (Scalia, J., concurring). See also Michael Herz, "Textualism and Taboo: Interpretation and Deference for Justice Scalia," *Cardozo Law Review* 12 (1991): 1663–83; and Karkkainen, " 'Plain Meaning,' " 459–64.

120. United States Dept. of State v. Ray, 112 S.Ct. 541, 550–51 (1991) (Scalia, J., concurring).

121. United States Dept. of Justice v. Julian, 486 U.S. 1, 15–23 (1988) (Scalia, J., dissenting).

122. John Doe Agency v. John Doe Corp., 493 U.S. 146, 160–64 (1989) (Scalia, J., dissenting). See also Schwartz, "Shooting the Piano Player," 50–56.

123. Defined in Richard B. Stewart, "The Reformation of American Administrative Law," *Harvard Law Review* 88 (1975): 1669. See also Michael W. McCann, *Taking Reform Seriously: Perspectives on Public Interest Liberalism* (Ithaca: Cornell University Press, 1986), 90–105, 111–21.

124. Gulfstream Aerospace Corp. v. Mayacamas Corp., 485 U.S. 271, 290–92 (1988) (Scalia, J. concurring). See also Budinich v. Becton Dickinson and Co., 486 U.S. 196 (1988).

125. ICC v. Brotherhood of Locomotive Eng'rs, 482 U.S. 270. He also favors restrictions on judicial review of agency decisions. See "Remarks of Justice Antonin Scalia before the Fellows of the American Bar Foundation and the National Conference of Bar Presidents," New Orleans, La., 15 Feb. 1987, 8.

126. Thunder Basin Coal Co. v. Reich, 114 S.Ct. at 783 (Scalia, J., concurring).

127. Webster v. Doe, 486 U.S. at 606–21 (Scalia, J., dissenting).

128. Honig v. Doe, 484 U.S. at 332–42 (Scalia, J., dissenting).

129. Boyle v. United Technologies Corp., 487 U.S. 500 (1988).

130. United States v. Stanley, 483 U.S. 669 (1987).

131. Anderson v. Creighton, 483 U.S. 635 (1987).

132. United States v. Johnson, 481 U.S. at 692–703 (1987) (Scalia, J., dissenting).

133. Gwaltney of Smithfield, Ltd. v. Chesapeake Bay Found., 484 U.S. at 67–71 (Scalia, J., concurring).

134. United States v. Fausto, 484 U.S. 439 (1988).

135. Reno v. Catholic Social Serv., 113 S.Ct. 2485 (1993).

136. McCarthy v. Madigan, 112 S.Ct. 1081, 1092–93 (1992) (Rehnquist, C.J., concurring).

137. Federal Deposit Ins. Corp. v. Meyer, 114 S.Ct. 996 (1994); Schweiker v. Chilicky, 108 S.Ct. 2460 (1988).

138. City of St. Louis v. Praprotnik, 485 U.S. 112 (1988).

139. Golden State Transit Corp. v. City of Los Angeles, 110 S.Ct 444 (1989).

140. Lujan v. National Wildlife Fed'n, 497 U.S. 871, 890 (1990).

141. Lujan v. Defenders of Wildlife, 112 S.Ct. 2130, 2137–46 (quotation on 2145) (1992). See also the discussion in Patti A. Meeks, "Justice Scalia and the Demise of Environmental Law Standing," *Journal of Land Use and Environmental Law* 8 (1993): 349–73; Gene R. Nichol, "Justice Scalia, Standing, and Public Law Litigation," *Duke Law Journal* 42 (1993): 1141–68; and Schwartz, "Shooting the Piano Player," 40–45.

142. David Schultz, in "Legislative Process and Intent in Justice Scalia's Interpretive Method," *Akron Law Review* 25 (1992): 595–610; and "Judicial Review and Legislative Deference: The Political Process of Antonin Scalia," *Nova Law Review* 16 (1992): 1249–83, fails to appreciate this distinction.

143. See Harris v. Forklift Sys., Inc., 114 S.Ct. 367, 371–72 (1993) (Scalia, J., concurring).

144. See United States v. X-Citement Video, Inc., 115 S.Ct. 464, 473 (1994) (Scalia, J., dissenting); West Virginia Univ. Hosps. v. Casey, 111 S.Ct. at 1141–43; Moskal v. United States, 498 U.S. at 471–78 (Scalia, J. dissenting); Crandon v. United States, 494 U.S. at 168–84 (Scalia, J., concurring); Chan v. Korean Air Lines, 490 U.S. at 126–35; United States v. Stuart, 489 U.S. at 371–73 (Scalia, J. concurring); Mistretta v. United States, 488 U.S. at 423 (Scalia, J., dissenting); Morrison v. Olson, 487 U.S. at 702–33 (Scalia, J. dissenting); United States v. Taylor, 487 U.S. at 344–46 (Scalia, J., concurring); K Mart Corp. v. Cartier, Inc., 485 U.S. at 190–94 (Scalia, J., dissenting); Lukhard v. Reed, 481 U.S. at 374–77; Immigration and Naturalization Serv. v. Cardoza-Fonseca, 480 U.S. at 452–53 (Scalia, J., concurring); O'Connor v. United States, 479 U.S. at 35. For a critique of his approach, see West Virginia Univ. Hosps. v. Casey, 111 S.Ct. at 1148–56 (Marshall, J., dissenting); Elizabeth A. Liess, "Censoring Legislative History: Justice Scalia on the Use of Legislative History in Statutory Interpretation," *Nebraska Law Review* 72 (1993): 577–85; William D. Popkin, "An 'Internal' Critique of Justice Scalia's Theory of Statutory Interpretation," *Minnesota Law Review* 76 (1992): 1161–87; Cass R. Sunstein, *After the Rights Revolution: Reconceiving the Regulatory State* (Cambridge: Harvard University Press, 1990), 127–30. For an analysis more supportive of Scalia's effort, see Karkkainen, " 'Plain Meaning,' " 405–14.

145. Compare Frankfurter, "Reading of Statutes," 224–26. See the discus-

sion in Eskridge, "New Textualism," 650–56; and Thunder Basin Coal Co. v. Reich, 114 S.Ct. at 782 (Scalia, J., concurring); Conroy v. Aniskoff, 113 S.Ct. at 1567–72 (Scalia, J., concurring); Chisom v. Roemer, 111 S.Ct. at 2368–76 (1991) (Scalia, J., dissenting); Department of Treasury v. Federal Labor Relations Auth., 494 U.S. 922 (1990); United Sav. Ass'n of Texas v. Timbers of Inwood Forest Assoc., 484 U.S. 365, 379–81 (1988); Edwards v. Aguillard, 482 U.S. at 617–34 (Scalia, J., dissenting); Scalia, "Judicial Deference," 517; and Karkkainen, " 'Plain Meaning,' " 432–56.

146. Eskridge, "New Textualism," 646. See also the discussion in Karkkainen, " 'Plain Meaning,' " 414–32.

147. Green v. Bock Laundry Mach. Co., 490 U.S. at 528 (Scalia, J., concurring).

148. Chisom v. Roemer, 111 S.Ct. at 2372 (Scalia, J., dissenting); Asgrow Seed Co. v. Winterboer, 115 S.Ct. 788 (1995). In Frankfurter, "Reading of Statutes," 225, the author states, "And so we assume that Congress uses common words in their popular meaning, as used in the common speech of men."

149. Crandon v. United States, 494 U.S. at 169–176 (Scalia, J., concurring). See also Moskal v. United States, 111 S.Ct. at 471 (Scalia, J., dissenting).

150. West Virginia Univ. Hosps. v. Casey, 111 S.Ct. at 1141–48. Popkin, " 'Internal Critique,' " 1140–52, provides more detail on these practices.

151. Tome v. United States, 115 S.Ct. 696, 706 (1995) (Scalia, J., concurring).

152. United States v. Williams, 115 S.Ct. 1611 (1995) (Scalia, J., concurring).

153. Eskridge, "New Textualism," 642–44.

154. Wisconsin Pub. Intervenor v. Mortier, 111 S.Ct. at 2487–91 (Scalia, J., concurring).

155. On committee materials, see Sable Communications v. FCC, 492 U.S. 133 (Scalia, J., concurring); Green v. Bock Laundry Mach. Co., 490 U.S. at 527–29 (Scalia, J. concurring); Blanchard v. Bergeron, 489 U.S. at 97–99 (Scalia, J., concurring). On debates, see Babbitt v. Sweet Home, 115 S.Ct. at 2427 (Scalia, J., dissenting); Conroy v. Aniskoff, 113 S.Ct. at 1567 (Scalia, J., concurring); Wisconsin Pub. Intervenor v. Mortier, 111 S.Ct. at 2487–91 (Scalia, J. concurring); Begier v. IRS, 110 S.Ct. at 2267–69 (Scalia, J., concurring); Taylor v. United States, 495 U.S. at 603 (Scalia, J., concurring); United States v. Taylor, 487 U.S. at 342–45 (Scalia, J. concurring); Puerto Rico Dept. of Consumer Affairs v. Isla Petroleum Corp., 485 U.S. 495, 501 (1988); Rose v. Rose, 481 U.S. at 640–45 (1987) (Scalia, J., concurring); Immigration and Naturalization Serv. v. Cardoza-Fonseca, 480 U.S. at 452–54 (Scalia, J., concurring).

156. Compare Frankfurter, "Reading of Statutes," 229; see also 227–29, 234. Cautious use of legislative history is also indicated in Hart and Sacks, *Legal Process,* 1235–38.

157. Blanchard v. Bergeron, 489 U.S. at 98 (Scalia, J., concurring).

158. Chisom v. Roemer, 111 S.Ct. at 2376 (Scalia, J. dissenting). See also Dewsnup v. Timm, 112 S.Ct. at 783–85 (Scalia, J., dissenting).

159. United States v. R.L.C., 112 S.Ct. at 1340 (Scalia, J., concurring). See also Sarah Newland, "The Mercy of Scalia: Statutory Construction and the Rule of Lenity," *Harvard Civil Rights—Civil Liberties Law Review* 29 (1994): 197–229, esp. 198, 210–11, 217–19.

160. United States v. Thompson/Center Arms Co., 112 S.Ct. 2102, 2110–12 (1992) (Scalia, J., concurring).

161. Chisom v. Roemer, 111 S.Ct. at 2376 (Scalia, J. dissenting); Moskal v. United States, 111 S.Ct. at 471–78 (Scalia, J., dissenting).

162. K Mart Corp. v. Cartier, Inc. (II), 486 U.S. at 325 (Scalia, J., concurring and dissenting).

163. Sullivan v. Finkelstein, 110 S.Ct. at 2667 (Scalia, J., concurring).

164. H.J. Inc. v. Northwestern Bell Tel. Co., 492 U.S. 229, 251–56 (1989) (Scalia, J., concurring).

165. See the discussion in Liess, "Censoring Legislative History," 573–76; Arthur Stock, "Justice Scalia's Use of Sources in Statutory and Constitutional Interpretation: How Congress Always Loses," *Duke Law Journal* (1990): 187–192; Nicholas S. Zeppos, "Justice Scalia's Textualism: The 'New' New Legal Process," *Cardozo Law Review* 12 (1991): 1614–20, 1637–39. A similar point is made in Frankfurter, "Reading of Statutes," 236–37.

166. James B. Beam Distilling Co. v. Georgia, 111 S.Ct. at 2451 (Scalia, J., concurring).

167. Scalia, "Address," 4.

168. Ibid., 3.

169. See Luther Gulick, "Notes on the Theory of Organization," in *Papers on the Science of Administration,* ed. Luther Gulick and Lyndell F. Urwick (New York: Institute of Public Administration, Columbia University, 1937), 9, 3–47; Lyndell F. Urwick, "Organization as a Technical Problem," in ibid., 49–98.

170. See James Landis, *The Administrative Process* (New Haven: Yale University Press, 1938), 34–46; Thomas K. McCraw, *Prophets of Regulation: Charles Francis Adams, Louis D. Brandeis, James M. Landis, Alfred E. Kahn* (Cambridge: Belknap Press of Harvard University Press, 1984), 152–209.

171. Cass R. Sunstein, "Constitutionalism after the New Deal," *Harvard Law Review* 101 (1987): 422–24, 430–46. See also Peri Arnold, *Making the Managerial Presidency: Comprehensive Reorganization Planning, 1905–1980* (Princeton: Princeton University Press, 1986), 81–117; and Barry D. Karl, *Executive Reorganization and Reform in the New Deal: The Genesis of Administrative Management, 1900–1939* (Cambridge: Harvard University Press, 1963). Distrust of government is more pronounced in the public interest liberalism of the 1970s; see McCann, *Taking Reform Seriously,* 78–79, 90–105.

172. See Christopher F. Erdley, *Administrative Law: Rethinking Judicial*

Control of Bureaucracy (New Haven: Yale University Press, 1990), 6–7, 13–29. On synoptic decisionmaking, see David Braybrooke and Charles F. Lindblom, *A Strategy of Decision: Policy Evaluation as a Social Process* (New York: Free Press, 1963).

173. Hamilton, Madison, and Jay, *The Federalist,* papers nos. 47–49, 51–52 (Madison), pp. 323–43, 347–59.

CHAPTER FIVE: THE TRICK OF HARNESSING FEDERAL POWER

1. See NLRB v. Jones and Laughlin Steel Corp., 310 U.S. 1 (1937); United States v. Darby Lumber Co., 312 U.S. 100 (1941); Wickard v. Filburn, 317 U.S. 111 (1941); Southern Pacific Co. v. Arizona, 325 U.S. 761 (1945); Pennsylvania v. Nelson, 350 U.S. 497 (1956); Dean Milk Co. v. City of Madison, 340 U.S. 349 (1956); Huron Portland Cement Co. v. Detroit, 362 U.S. 440 (1960); Heart of Atlanta Motel v. United States, 379 U.S. 241 (1964); Hunt v. Washington State Apple Advertising Comm'n, 432 U.S. 333 (1977); Philadelphia v. New Jersey, 437 U.S. 617 (1978); Garcia v. San Antonio Metro. Transit Auth., 469 U.S. 528 (1985), overruling National League of Cities v. Usery, 426 U.S. 833 (1976).

2. See Timothy Conlan, *New Federalism: Intergovernmental Reform from Nixon to Reagan* (Washington, D.C.: Brookings Institution, 1988); Richard P. Nathan, *The Plot That Failed: Nixon and the Administrative Presidency* (New York: John Wiley and Sons, 1975), 12–34; and Michael Pagano and Ann O'M. Bowman, "The State of American Federalism," *Publius: The Journal of Federalism* 23 (1993): 1–22.

3. Antonin Scalia, "Regulatory Reform—The Game Has Changed," *Regulation* 5, no. 1 (1981): 13; idem, "The Two Faces of Federalism," *Harvard Journal of Law and Public Policy* 6, special issue (1982): 22.

4. M. David Gelfand and Keith Werhan, "Federalism and Separation of Powers on a Conservative Court: Currents and Cross-Currents from Justices O'Connor and Scalia," *Tulane Law Review* 64 (1990): 1460. See also Stewart A. Baker and Katherine H. Wheatley, "Justice Scalia and Federalism: A Sketch," *Urban Lawyer* 20 (1988): 353–65.

5. Garcia v. San Antonio Metro. Transit Auth., 469 U.S. 528. See also Hodel v. Virginia Surface Mining and Reclamation Ass'n, 452 U.S. 264 (1981); United Transport. Union v. Long Island R.R., 455 U.S. 678 (1982); EEOC v. Wyoming, 460 U.S. 226 (1983); FERC v. Mississippi, 456 U.S. 742 (1982). On preemption in general, see Joseph F. Zimmerman, *Federal Preemption: The Silent Revolution* (Ames: Iowa State University Press, 1991).

6. South Dakota v. Dole, 483 U.S. 203 (1987).

7. South Carolina v. Baker, 485 U.S. 505 (1988).

8. Ibid., 528 (Scalia, J., concurring).

9. Gregory v. Ashcroft, 111 S.Ct. 2395 (1991).

10. New York v. United States, 112 S.Ct. 2408 (1992).

11. United States v. Lopez, 115 S.Ct. 1624 (1995).

12. U.S. Term Limits, Inc. v. Thornton, 115 S.Ct. 1842 (1995).

13. California Coastal Comm'n v. Granite Rock Co., 480 U.S. 572 (1987).

14. Ibid., 607 (quotation), 612–14 (Scalia, J., dissenting).

15. Boyle v. United Technologies Corp., 487 U.S. 500, 504–5 (quotations) (1988).

16. Mississippi Power and Light Co. v. Mississippi ex rel. Moore, 487 U.S. 354, 377–91 (1988) (Scalia, J., concurring).

17. New Orleans Pub. Serv., Inc. v. Council of City of New Orleans, 491 U.S. 350 (1989).

18. Owen v. Owen, 500 U.S. 305 (1991).

19. Wisconsin Pub. Intervenor v. Mortier, 111 S.Ct. 2476, 2487–91 (1991) (Scalia, J., concurring).

20. Morales v. Trans World Airlines, 112 S.Ct. 2031, 2036–40 (1992).

21. Cipollone v. Liggett Group, Inc., 112 S.Ct. 2608, 2632–38 (1992) (Scalia, J., concurring and dissenting).

22. Oregon Waste Sys., Inc. v. Oregon Dept. of Environmental Quality, 114 S.Ct. 1677 (1994); C and A Carbone, Inc. v. Town of Clarkstown, 114 S.Ct. 1677 (1994); Gade v. National Solid Wastes Management Ass'n, 112 S.Ct. 2374 (1992); Fort Gratiot Sanitary Landfill v. Michigan Dept. of Natural Resources, 112 S.Ct. 2019 (1992); Chemical Waste Management, Inc. v. Hunt, 112 S.Ct. 2009 (1992); Arkansas v. Oklahoma, 112 S.Ct. 1046 (1992).

23. Lukhard v. Reed, 481 U.S. 368 (1987).

24. Coit Independent Joint Venture v. Federal Sav. and Loan Ins. Corp., 489 U.S. 561, 588–92 (1989) (Scalia, J., concurring).

25. North Dakota v. United States, 495 U.S. 423, 444–48 (1990) (Scalia, J., concurring).

26. Summit Health, Ltd. v. Pinhas, 111 S.Ct. 1842 (1991).

27. Ibid., 1849–54 (Scalia, J. dissenting).

28. Wisconsin Dept. of Revenue v. William Wrigley Jr. Co., 112 S.Ct. 2447 (1992).

29. O'Melveny v. Myers, 114 S.Ct. 2048 (1994).

30. BFP v. Resolution Trust Corp., 114 S.Ct. 1757 (1994).

31. County of Yakima v. Confederated Tribes and Bands of Yakima Indian Nation, 112 S.Ct. 683 (1992).

32. American Dredging Co. v. Miller, 114 S.Ct. 981 (1994).

33. Parker v. Brown, 317 U.S. 341 (1943).

34. City of Columbia v. Omni Outdoor Advertising, Inc., 111 S.Ct. 2578 (1991).

35. FTC v. Ticor Title Ins. Co., 112 S.Ct. 2169, 2180–81 (1992) (Scalia, J., concurring).

36. See Willson v. Black Bird Creek Marsh Co., 2 Pet. 245, 252 (1829), on its origins. Southern Pacific Co. v. Arizona, 325 U.S. 761 (1945); Bibb v. Navajo

Freight Lines, 359 U.S. 520 (1959); Pike v. Bruce Church, Inc., 397 U.S. 137 (1970); and Kassel v. Consol. Freightways Corp., 450 U.S. 662 (1981), illustrate the development of the balancing doctrine. For commentary on Scalia's dormant Commerce Clause opinions, see Richard B. Collins, "Justice Scalia and the Elusive Idea of Discrimination against Interstate Commerce," *New Mexico Law Review* 20 (1990): 555–83; Richard D. Friedman, "Putting Dormancy Out of Its Misery," *Cardozo Law Review* 12 (1991): 1745–61; Walter Hellerstein, "Justice Scalia and the Commerce Clause: Reflections of a Tax Lawyer," ibid., 12 (1991): 1763–87; Mark V. Tushnet, "Scalia and the Dormant Commerce Clause: A Foolish Formalism?" ibid., 12 (1991): 1717–43.

37. See Baldwin v. G.A.F. Seelig, Inc., 294 U.S. 511 (1935); Hood and Sons v. Du Mond, 336 U.S. 525 (1949); Dean Milk v. City of Madison, 340 U.S. 349 (1951); Hunt v. Washington State Apple Advertising Comm'n, 432 U.S. 333 (1977); Philadelphia v. New Jersey, 437 U.S. 617 (1978); Minnesota v. Clover Leaf Creamery, 449 U.S. 456 (1981); New England Power Co. v. New Hampshire, 455 U.S. 331 (1982); Edgar v. MITE Corp. 457 U.S. 624 (1982); and Maine v. Taylor, 477 U.S. 131 (1986).

38. Complete Auto Transit, Inc. v. Brady, 430 U.S. 274, 279 (1977).

39. CTS Corp. v. Dynamics Corp. of Am., 481 U.S. 69, 94–97 (1987) (Scalia, J., concurring).

40. Tyler Pipe Indus. v. Washington State Dept. of Revenue, 483 U.S. 232 (1987).

41. Ibid., 257–59 (Scalia, J., concurring and dissenting).

42. Armco v. Hardesty, 467 U.S. 638, 644 (1984).

43. Tyler Pipe Indus. v. Washington State Dept. of Revenue, 483 U.S. at 254, 265 (quotation) (Scalia, J., concurring and dissenting).

44. New Energy Co. of Indiana v. Limbach, 486 U.S. 269 (1988).

45. Bendix Autolite Corp. v. Midwesco Enterprises, 486 U.S. 888 (1988).

46. Ibid., 897–98 (Scalia, J., concurring). Later, he refused to apply the majority decision in this case retroactively; see Reynoldsville Casket Co. v. Hyde, 115 S.Ct. 1745, 1752 (Scalia, J., concurring).

47. Healy v. Beer Inst., 491 U.S. 324, 340–41 (1989); compare 491 U.S. at 344 (Scalia, J., concurring).

48. Ibid., 345 (Scalia, J., concurring).

49. Goldberg v. Sweet, 488 U.S. 252, 271 (1989) (Scalia, J., concurring).

50. Amerada Hess Corp. v. Director, Div. of Taxation, New Jersey Dept. of Treasury, 490 U.S. 66, 80–81 (1989) (Scalia, J., concurring).

51. Trinova Corp. v. Michigan Dept. of Treasury, 111 S.Ct. 818, 836 (1991) (Scalia, J., concurring).

52. American Trucking Ass'ns v. Scheiner, 483 U.S. 266, 303–6 (1987) (Scalia, J., dissenting).

53. Quill Corp. v. North Dakota By and Through Heitkamp, 112 S.Ct. 1904, 1909–16 (1992). The opinion applied the bright-line rule of National

NOTES TO PAGES 139–145

Bellas Hess, Inc. v. Dept. of Revenue of Illinois, 386 U.S. 753 (1967), deemed in congruence with Complete Auto Transit.

54. Quill Corp. v. North Dakota By and Through Heitkamp, 112 S.Ct. at 1923–24 (Scalia, J., concurring).

55. Oklahoma Tax Comm'n v. Jefferson Lines, Inc., 115 S.Ct. 1331, 1346 (1995) (Scala, J., concurring).

56. West Lynn Creamery v. Healy, 114 S.Ct. 2205 (1994) (Scalia, J., concurring).

57. Ibid., 2218–21 (Scalia, J., concurring).

58. Japan Line, Ltd. v. County of Los Angeles, 441 U.S. 434 (1979).

59. Itel Containers Int'l Corp. v. Huddleston, 113 S.Ct. 1095, 1106–9 (1993) (Scalia, J., concurring).

60. Barclays Bank PLC v. Franchise Tax Bd. of California, 114 S.Ct. 2268, 2287 (1994) (Scalia, J., concurring).

61. Wyoming v. Oklahoma, 112 S.Ct. 789, 804–10 (1992) (Scalia, J., dissenting).

62. See South-Central Timber Dev. v. Wunnicke, 467 U.S. 82 (1984) (state as market participant); Hinklin v. Orbeck, 437 U.S. 518 (1978); United Bldg. and Constr. Trades v. Camden, 465 U.S. 208 (1984); Supreme Court of New Hampshire v. Piper, 470 U.S. 274 (1985) (privileges and immunities).

63. Chisholm v. Georgia, 2 Dall. 419 (1793).

64. Hans v. Louisiana, 134 U.S. 1 (1890).

65. Welch v. Texas Dept. of Highways and Pub. Transport., 483 U.S. 468 (1987).

66. Ibid., 495–96 (Scalia, J., concurring).

67. Pennsylvania v. Union Gas Co., 491 U.S. 1, 29–30, 36–43 (1989) (Scalia, J., concurring and dissenting).

68. Hoffman v. Connecticut Dept. of Income Maintenance, 492 U.S. 96, 105 (1989) (Scalia, J., concurring).

69. Blatchford v. Native Village of Noatak and Circle Village, 501 U.S. 775 (1991).

70. Erie R.R. Co. v. Tompkins, 304 U.S. 64 (1938).

71. Stewart Org., Inc. v. Ricoh Corp., 487 U.S. 22, 33–41 (1988) (Scalia, J., dissenting).

72. Carden v. Arkoma Assoc., 494 U.S. 185 (1990).

73. American Nat'l Red Cross v. S.G., 112 S.Ct. 2465 (1992).

74. Ibid., 2476–81 (Scalia, J., dissenting).

75. Ferens v. John Deere Co., 494 U.S. 516, 533–40 (1990) (Scalia, J., dissenting).

76. Tafflin v. Levitt, 493 U.S. 455 (1990).

77. Ibid., 470–73 (Scalia, J., concurring).

78. Agency Holding Corp. v. Malley-Duff and Assoc., 483 U.S. 143 (1987).

79. See McCluny v. Silliman, 3 Pet. 270 (1830).

80. Agency Holding Corp. v. Malley-Duff and Assoc., 483 U.S. at 143, 163–64, 166–70 (Scalia, J., concurring).

81. Reed v. United Transport. Union, 488 U.S. 319, 334 (1989) (Scalia, J., concurring).

82. North Star Steel Co. v. Thomas, 115 S.Ct. 1927, 1932 (1995) (Scalia, J., concurring).

83. Besides the opinions discussed in this section, Scalia issued a brief dissent to a single factual determination in a complex opinion filled with findings of fact on the location of part of the boundary between Georgia and South Carolina: Georgia v. South Carolina, 110 S.Ct. 2903, 2924 (1990) (Scalia, J., dissenting).

84. Sun Oil Co. v. Wortman, 486 U.S. 717, 722–34 (1988).

85. Puerto Rico v. Branstad, 483 U.S. 219 (1987).

86. Kentucky v. Dennison, 24 How. 66 (1861).

87. Puerto Rico v. Branstad, 483 U.S. at 2810 (Scalia, J., concurring). Also, in Fex v. Michigan, 113 S.Ct. 1085 (1993), Scalia interpreted language in an interstate compact, the Interstate Agreement on Detainers, that was designed to facilitate Article IV extraditions.

88. Burnham v. Superior Court of California, County of Marin, 495 U.S. 604, esp. 622–27 (1990).

CHAPTER SIX: EQUALITY THROUGH THE PANACEA OF NEUTRAL LAW

1. Antonin Scalia, "The Disease as the Cure: 'In Order to Get beyond Racism We Must First Take Account of Race,'" *Washington University Law Quarterly* (1979): 147–57.

2. Alexis de Tocqueville, *Democracy in America,* trans. Phillips Bradley, 2 vols. (1835–40; New York: Vintage, 1945), 1:56.

3. The Slaughterhouse Cases, 16 Wall. 36 (1873) (protection for African Americans); The Civil Rights Cases, 109 U.S. 3 (1883) (state action).

4. For a history of Fourteenth Amendment doctrine, see Edward V. Heck, "Constitutional Interpretation and a Court in Transition: Strict Scrutiny from *Shapiro v. Thompson* to *Dunn v. Blumstein*—and Beyond," *United States Air Force Academy Journal of Legal Studies* 3 (1992): 65–90; Donald W. Jackson, *Even the Children of Strangers: Equality under the U.S. Constitution* (Lawrence: University Press of Kansas, 1992), 27–216; and Michael Klarman, "An Interpretive History of Modern Equal Protection," *Michigan Law Review* 90 (1991): 213–318. Following Edward V. Heck, "Judicial Activism and a Conservative Court: Balancing Individual Rights and Governmental Power in the 1972–1973 Term" (paper presented at meeting of Southwest Political Science Association, Fort Worth, Tex., 1990), 22–23, I use the term *disadvantaged group* rather than the more common but misleading term *suspect class* or the older and less accurate *discrete and insular minorities.* Russell W. Galloway,

"Means-Ends Scrutiny in American Constitutional Law," *Loyola of Los Angeles Law Review* 21 (1988): 453–55; Richard A. Brisbin Jr. and Edward V. Heck, "The Battle over Strict Scrutiny: Coalitional Conflict in the Rehnquist Court," *Santa Clara Law Review* 32 (1992): 1049–1105; and Klarman, "Interpretive History," 213–318, discuss the scrutiny tests. Washington v. Davis, 426 U.S. 229 (1976); Arlington Heights v. Metropolitan Housing Corp., 429 U.S. 252 (1977); Personnel Administrator of Massachusetts v. Feeney, 442 U.S. 256 (1979); and McCleskey v. Kemp, 481 U.S. 279, 292–93 (1987), define evidence of intentional discrimination.

5. United States v. Carolene Products Co., 304 U.S. 144, 152–53n. 4 (1938); Korematsu v. United States, 323 U.S. 214 (1944) (race); Graham v. Richardson, 403 U.S. 532 (1971) (aliens); Dunn v. Blumstein, 405 U.S. 330 (1972) (voting); Shapiro v. Thompson, 394 U.S. 618 (1969) (travel).

6. See Craig v. Boren, 429 U.S. 190, 197–98 (1976); Mathews v. Lucas, 427 U.S. 495 (1976).

7. On "nondeferential rationality review," see Plyler v. Doe, 457 U.S. 202, 216–24 (1982). On "deferential rationality review," see Galloway, "Means-Ends Scrutiny," 451–53.

8. San Antonio Indep. Sch. Dist. v. Rodriguez, 411 U.S. 1 (1974); Massachusetts Bd. of Retirement v. Murgia, 427 U.S. 307 (1979). See also City of Cleburne v. Cleburne Living Ctr., 473 U.S. 432 (1985).

9. Moose Lodge No. 107 v. Irvis, 407 U.S. 163 (1972); Jackson v. Metropolitan Edison Co., 419 U.S. 345 (1974) (state action); Monroe v. Pape, 365 U.S. 167 (1961) ("under color" of law); United States v. Guest, 383 U.S. 745 (1966); Jones v. Alfred H. Mayer Co., 392 U.S. 409 (1968); Runyon v. McCrary, 427 U.S. 160 (1976) (Thirteenth Amendment); Griffin v. Breckenridge, 403 U.S. 88 (1971) (Fourteenth Amendment).

10. City of Richmond v. J. A. Croson Co., 488 U.S. 469 (1989).

11. See the extended discussion of this point in H. N. Hirsch, *A Theory of Liberty: The Constitution and Minorities* (New York: Routledge, 1992), 194–240.

12. Richmond v. Croson, 488 U.S. at 497–508. Interestingly, O'Connor later voted against the Court, in an opinion written by Justice Thomas that made it possible for a group of contractors to seek relief for the consequences of a minority business set-aside program, similar to the Richmond plan, that a city had terminated. Thomas held that the case was not moot and that the business had established an "injury in fact"; see Northeastern Florida Contractors v. Jacksonville, 113 S.Ct. 2297 (1993). O'Connor read precedents on standing and actions to preclude retrospective relief for the contractors; Northeastern Florida Contractors v. Jacksonville, 113 S.Ct. at 2305–9 (O'Connor, J., dissenting).

13. Richmond v. Croson, 488 U.S. at 518–20 (Kennedy, J., concurring).

14. Richmond v. Croson, 488 U.S. at 521–28 (Scalia, J., concurring). Com-

pare Alexander M. Bickel, *The Morality of Consent* (New Haven: Yale University Press, 1975), 133. A brief review of Scalia's affirmative action opinions, coupled with a defense of the justice, is James L. McAlister, "A Pigment of the Imagination: Looking at Affirmative Action through Justice Scalia's Color-Blind Rule," *Marquette Law Review* 77 (1994): 327, 343–49.

15. Richmond v. Croson, 488 U.S. at 521–25 (Scalia, J., concurring).

16. Ibid., 526–28 (Scalia, J., concurring).

17. Regents of the Univ. of California v. Bakke, 438 U.S. 265, 398–401 (1978) (Marshall, J., opinion).

18. Richmond v. Croson, 488 U.S. at 536–39, 551–52 (Marshall, J., dissenting).

19. Ibid., 539–48, 559 (Marshall, J., dissenting).

20. Ibid., 557–61 (Marshall, J., dissenting).

21. For another view, see Jackson, *Even the Children of Strangers,* 217–36. Contrary to the pragmatists, Scalia thus assumes that equality should aim at individuals and not social segments or blocs. See the discussion of different assumptions about equality in Duncan Rae, Douglas Yates, Jennifer Hochschild, Joseph Morone, and Carol Fessler, *Equalities* (Cambridge: Harvard University Press, 1981).

22. Adarand Constructors, Inc. v. Pena, 115 S.Ct. 2097 (1995).

23. Ibid., 2119 (1995) (Scalia, J., concurring).

24. United States v. Paradise, 480 U.S. 149, 199 (Rehnquist, C.J., dissenting).

25. Metro Broadcasting v. FCC, 110 S.Ct. 2997 (1990).

26. Ibid., at 3028–44 (O'Connor, J., dissenting).

27. Ibid., at 3044–47 (Kennedy, J., dissenting).

28. Martin v. Wilks, 490 U.S. 755 (1989).

29. Heller v. Doe by Doe, 113 S.Ct. 2637, 2642 (1993). In dissent, Justice Souter argued, at 2651–52 (Souter, J., dissenting) for the use of the non-deferential rationality test of Cleburne v. Cleburne Living Ctr., 473 U.S. 432, 446–47 (1985).

30. Nordlinger v. Hahn, 112 S.Ct. 2326, 2331–35 (1992).

31. Kadramas v. Dickinson Pub. Sch., 487 U.S. 450 (1987).

32. See San Antonio Indep. Sch. Dist. v. Rodriguez, 411 U.S. 1 (1973).

33. Burdick v. Takushi, 112 S.Ct. 2059 (1992).

34. Allegheny Pittsburgh Coal Co. v. County Comm'n of Webster County, 488 U.S. 998 (1989) (assessment); FCC v. Beach Communications, Inc., 113 S.Ct. 2096 (1993) (cable television).

35. Clark v. Jeter, 486 U.S. 456, 461–62 (1988).

36. Eu v. San Francisco Democratic Comm., 489 U.S. 214 (1989).

37. Brown v. Board of Educ. of Topeka (I), 347 U.S. 483 (1954); Brown v. Board of Educ. of Topeka (II), 349 U.S. 294 (1955); Green v. New Kent County Sch. Bd., 391 U.S. 430, 439 (1968); Swann v. Charlotte-Mecklenburg

Bd. of Educ., 402 U.S. 1 (1971); Keyes v. Sch. Dist., Denver, 413 U.S. 189 (1973); Milliken v. Bradley, 418 U.S. 717 (1974); Pasadena City Bd. of Educ. v. Spangler, 427 U.S. 424 (1976); Columbus Bd. of Educ. v. Penick, 443 U.S. 449 (1979); Dayton Bd. of Educ. v. Brinkman, 443 U.S. 526 (1979); Missouri v. Jenkins, 110 S.Ct. 1651 (1990).

38. Freeman v. Pitts, 112 S.Ct. 1430 (1992).

39. Ibid., 1452–54 (Scalia, J., concurring).

40. Alexander Hamilton, James Madison, and John Jay, *The Federalist,* ed. Jacob E. Cooke (1787–88; Middletown, Conn.: Wesleyan University Press, 1961), paper no. 10 (Madison), p. 57.

41. United States v. Fordice, 112 S.Ct. 2727 (1992).

42. Ibid., 2746–48 (quotation on 2746–47) (Scalia, J., concurring and dissenting).

43. Ibid., 2749–51 (quotation on 2750) (Scalia, J., concurring and dissenting).

44. Ibid., 2751–53 (quotation on 2752) (Scalia, J., concurring and dissenting).

45. Board of Educ. of Oklahoma City Pub. Sch. v. Dowell, 111 S.Ct. 630 (1991).

46. Missouri v. Jenkins (I), 495 U.S. 33, 58–81 (1990) (Kennedy, J., concurring).

47. Missouri v. Jenkins (II), 115 S.Ct. 2038 (1995).

48. Spallone v. United States, 493 U.S. 265 (1990).

49. National Org. for Women v. Scheidler, 114 S.Ct. 798 (1994). This vote silenced earlier concerns that Scalia might consider provisions in RICO to be unconstitutional because they were "void for vagueness"; see the inaccurate speculation of Joseph E. Bauerschmidt, "'Mother of Mercy—Is This the End of RICO?' Justice Scalia Invites Constitutional Void-for-Vagueness Challenge to RICO Pattern," *Notre Dame Law Review* 65 (1990): 1106–64.

50. Astoria Fed. Sav. and Loan v. Solimino, 111 S.Ct. 2166 (1991).

51. Batson v. Kentucky, 476 U.S. 79, 89 (1986).

52. Griffith v. Kentucky, 107 S.Ct. 708 (1987); Ford v. Georgia, 111 S.Ct. 850 (1991); Trevino v. Texas, 112 S.Ct. 1547 (1992).

53. Powers v. Ohio, 111 S.Ct. 1364 (1991) (different-race jurors); Edmonson v. Leesville Concrete Co., 111 S.Ct. 2077 (1991) (challenges in civil cases).

54. Georgia v. McCollum, 112 S.Ct. 2348 (1992).

55. J.E.B. v. Alabama ex rel. T.B., 114 S.Ct. 1419 (1994).

56. Hernandez v. New York, 111 S.Ct. 1859 (1991).

57. Ibid., 1877 (Stevens, J., dissenting).

58. Powers v. Ohio, 111 S.Ct. at 1374–81 (Scalia, J., dissenting).

59. Miranda v. Arizona, 384 U.S. 436 (1966).

60. Powers v. Ohio, 111 S.Ct. at 1381–82 (Scalia, J., dissenting).

61. Edmonson v. Leesville Concrete, 111 S.Ct. 2077 (1991).

62. Ibid., 2095–96 (Scalia, J., dissenting).

63. Georgia v. McCollum, 112 S.Ct. 2348, 2364–65 (Scalia, J., dissenting).

64. J.E.B. v. Alabama ex rel. T.B., 114 S.Ct. at 1437–39 (Scalia, J., dissenting).

65. Holland v. Illinois, 493 U.S. 474 (1990).

66. The Civil Rights Cases, 109 U.S. 3 (1883); Shelley v. Kraemer, 334 U.S. 1 (1948); Burton v. Wilmington Parking Auth., 365 U.S. 715 (1961); Reitman v. Mulkey, 387 U.S. 369 (1967); Jackson v. Metropolitan Edison Co., 419 U.S. 345 (1974); Blum v. Yaretsky, 457 U.S. 991 (1982); Rendell-Baker v. Kohn, 457 U.S. 830 (1982); Lugar v. Edmondson Oil Co., 457 U.S. 922 (1982).

67. NCAA v. Tarkanian, 488 U.S. 179 (1988).

68. San Francisco Arts and Athletics v. United States Olympic Comm., 483 U.S. 522 (1987).

69. DeShaney v. Winnebago County Social Servs. Dep't, 489 U.S. 189 (1989).

70. Johnson v. Transportation Agency, Santa Clara County, 480 U.S. 616 (1987).

71. 42 *U.S. Code* § 2000e-2(a).

72. Johnson v. Transportation Agency, 480 U.S. at 623–39.

73. Ibid., 658, 660 (Scalia, J., dissenting).

74. Ibid., 664 (Scalia, J., dissenting).

75. See especially United Steelworkers v. Weber, 443 U.S. 193 (1979).

76. Johnson v. Transportation Agency, 480 U.S. at 673–77 (Scalia, J., dissenting).

77. Civil Rights Act of 1991, P.L. 102–166; 105 Stat. 1071 (1991). Scalia did not write opinions in several of these cases: Price Waterhouse v. Hopkins, 490 U.S. 228 (1989); Wards Cove Packing Co. v. Atonio, 490 U.S. 642 (1989); Martin v. Wilks, 490 U.S. 755 (1989); and Patterson v. McLean Credit Union, 491 U.S. 164 (1989).

78. EEOC v. Arabian Am. Oil, 111 S.Ct. 1227 (1991).

79. Ibid., 1236–37 (Scalia, J., concurring).

80. Lorance v. AT&T Technologies, 490 U.S. 900 (1989).

81. Ibid., 904–13.

82. Landgraf v. USI Film Products, 114 S.Ct. 1483 (1994); Rivers and Davison v. Roadway Express, Inc., 114 S.Ct. 1510, 1522–26 (1994) (Scalia, J., concurring).

83. International Fed'n of Flight Attendants v. Zipes, 491 U.S. 754 (1989).

84. Ibid., 780 (Marshall, J., dissenting).

85. United Auto Workers v. Johnson Controls, 111 S.Ct. 1196 (1991).

86. Ibid., 1216–17 (Scalia, J., concurring).

87. St. Mary's Honor Ctr. v. Hicks, 113 S.Ct. 2742 (1993).

88. Ibid., 2746–50.

89. Ibid., 2756–66 (Souter, J., dissenting).

90. Ibid., 2754–56.

91. Harris v. Forklift Sys., Inc., 114 S.Ct. 367, 371 (1993).

92. Ibid., 371–72 (Scalia, J., concurring).

93. For additional evidence, see his votes with the majority in Ward's Cove Packing Co. v. Atonio, 490 U.S. at 642; and Patterson v. McLean Credit Union, 491 U.S. at 164; and his vote for Kennedy's dissenting opinion in Price Waterhouse v. Hopkins, 490 U.S. at 279–95 (Kennedy, J., dissenting). According to one undocumented contention, his statements in conference on Patterson v. McLean Credit Union reflected these commitments, but fear of political consequences caused him to refrain from overruling previous cases that offered a different interpretation of the Thirteenth Amendment and various civil rights acts; see James F. Simon, *The Center Holds: The Power Struggle Inside the Rehnquist Court* (New York: Simon and Schuster, 1995), 30, 57–58. Also indicative of his position is his support of O'Connor's complicated test of causation which must be borne by plaintiffs using "disparate impact analysis"—per Griggs v. Duke Power Co., 401 U.S. 424 (1971)—to prove "subjective" (e.g., psychological) harm as distinguished from "objective" harm (e.g., loss of position or wages) from employment practices, as regulated under provisions of the Civil Rights Act of 1964, Title VII. This test was more difficult to satisfy than the test offered by the dissenting justices; see Watson v. Fort Worth Bank and Trust, 478 S.Ct. 977 (1988).

94. Jett v. Dallas Indep. Sch. Dist., 491 U.S. 701 (1989).

95. Ibid., 738–39 (Scalia, J., concurring).

96. Hewitt v. Helms, 482 U.S. 755 (1987).

97. Heck v. Humphrey, 114 S.Ct. 2364 (1994).

98. West v. Atkins, 487 U.S. 42, 58 (1988) (Scalia, J., concurring).

99. Brower v. County of Inyo, 489 U.S. 593 (1989).

100. Burns v. Reed, 111 S.Ct. 1934 (1991).

101. Ibid., 1945–50 (Scalia, J., concurring and dissenting).

102. Bray v. Alexandria Women's Health Clinic, 113 S.Ct. 753 (1993).

103. Ibid., 758–67.

104. Ibid., 758–59 (quotations), 762–67.

105. Chisom v. Roemer, 111 S.Ct. 2354 (1991).

106. Houston Lawyers' Assoc. v. Attorney Gen. of Texas, 111 S.Ct. 2376 (1991).

107. Chisom v. Roemer, 111 S.Ct. at 2369–76 (Scalia, J., dissenting); Houston Lawyers' Ass'n v. Attorney Gen. of Texas, 111 S.Ct. at 2382 (Scalia, J., dissenting).

108. Hamilton, Madison, and Jay, *The Federalist,* paper no. 78 (Hamilton), pp. 527–29.

109. Growe v. Emison, 113 S.Ct. 1075 (1993).

110. Shaw v. Reno, 113 S.Ct. 2816 (1993).

111. Miller v. Johnson, 115 S.Ct. 2475 (1995).

112. Presley v. Etowah County Comm'n, 112 S.Ct. 820 (1992).

113. Holder v. Hall, 114 S.Ct. 2581, 2592 (1994) (Thomas, J., dissenting).

114. For extensive criticism of Scalia's neglect of the social facts of racial bias, see Dwight L. Greene, "Justice Scalia and Tonto, Judicial Ignorance, and the Myth of Colorless Individualism in *Bostick v. Florida*," *Tulane Law Review* 67 (1993): 1979–2062.

CHAPTER SEVEN: ORDERING THE CHAOS OF EXPRESSION

1. Antonin Scalia, "A House with Many Mansions: Categories of Speech under the First Amendment," in *The Constitution, the Law, and Freedom of Expression, 1787–1987,* ed. James B. Stewart (Carbondale: Southern Illinois University Press, 1987), 19.

2. Gitlow v. New York, 268 U.S. 652 (1925); Fiske v. Kansas, 274 U.S. 380 (1927) (freedom of speech); Near v. Minnesota, 283 U.S. 697 (1931) (freedom of the press); DeJonge v. Oregon, 299 U.S. 353 (1937) (freedom of assembly); Cantwell v. Connecticut, 310 U.S. 296 (1940) (free exercise of religion); Everson v. Board of Educ. of Ewing Twp., N.J., 330 U.S. 1 (1947) (Establishment Clause); NAACP v. Alabama, 357 U.S. 449 (1958).

3. Laurence H. Tribe and Michael C. Dorf, *On Reading the Constitution* (Cambridge: Harvard University Press, 1991), 73. For further perspective on the generality issue, compare the discussion in Bruce Ackerman, "Liberating Abstraction," in *The Bill of Rights in the Modern State,* ed. Geoffrey R. Stone, Richard A. Epstein, and Cass R. Sunstein (Chicago: University of Chicago Press, 1992), 317–48, to Frank H. Easterbrook, "Abstraction and Authority," in ibid., 349–80.

4. Edmond Cahn and Hugo L. Black, "Justice Black and First Amendment 'Absolutes': A Public Interview," *New York University Law Review* 37 (1962): 552–54.

5. Paul v. Davis, 424 U.S. 693, 734–35 (1976) (Brennan, J. dissenting).

6. New York v. Ferber, 458 U.S. 747 (1982); Roth v. United States, 354 U.S. 476 (1957). However, state and federal law has made some other forms of expression subject to regulation. These include agreements, offers, and orders to commit crime; some threats or advocacy "directed to inciting or producing imminent lawless action" with the likelihood of producing such action (Brandenburg v. Ohio, 395 U.S. 444 [1969]); criminal solicitations and conspiracies; and criminal fraud.

7. Employment Div., Dept. of Human Resources of Oregon v. Smith, 494 U.S. 872 (1990).

8. See Smith v. Employment Div., Dept. of Human Resources of Oregon, 721 P.2d 445 (1986); Black v. Employment Div., Dept. of Human Resources of Oregon, 721 P.2d 451 (1986); Employment Div., Dept. of Human Resources of

Oregon v. Smith, 485 U.S. 670 (1988), remand to Oregon Supreme Court to determine if religious use of peyote was legal in Oregon; Smith v. Employment Div., Dept. of Human Resources of Oregon, 763 P.2d 146 (1988). All of these actions are summarized in Employment Div. v. Smith, 494 U.S. at 875–76.

9. Employment Div. v. Smith, 494 U.S. at 876–78.

10. Ibid., 878–79.

11. Ibid., 878–82.

12. Ibid., 886.

13. The cases include Sherbert v. Verner, 374 U.S. 398 (1963); Thomas v. Review Bd. of Indiana Employment Security Div., 450 U.S. 707 (1981); Hobbie v. Unemployment Appeals Comm'n of Florida, 480 U.S. 136 (1987) (Scalia voted with majority); Frazee v. Illinois Dept. of Employment Security, 489 U.S. 829 (1989) (Scalia voted with majority).

14. Hernandez v. Commissioner of Internal Revenue, 490 U.S. 680, 704–13 (1989) (O'Connor, J., dissenting). Scalia did not participate in the important free exercise case of Lyng v. Northwest Indian Cemetery Protective Ass'n, 485 U.S. 439 (1988).

15. Employment Div. v. Smith, 494 U.S. at 884.

16. Ibid., 888–89.

17. Ibid., 900, 905–7 (O'Connor, J., concurring). Compare her opinion in Lyng v. Northwest Indian Cemetery Protective Ass'n, 485 U.S. 439 (1988).

18. Employment Div. v. Smith, 494 U.S. at 886n. 3, 887n. 4, 889n. 5.

19. Ibid., 909–21 (Blackmun, J., dissenting). Scalia's reply to Blackmun is in ibid., 887n. 4, 889n. 5. For further commentary, compare Douglas Laycock, "The Remnants of Free Exercise," *Supreme Court Review* (1990): 1–68; to Michael McConnell, "Free Exercise Revisionism and the *Smith* Decision," *University of Chicago Law Review* 57 (1990): 1109–53.

20. Barnes v. Glen Theatre, 111 S.Ct. 2456 (1991).

21. United States v. O'Brien, 391 U.S. 367 (1968). The four-part test allowed the regulation of speechlike conduct if the regulation was constitutionally created, furthered a substantial governmental interest, indicated a substantial interest unrelated to the suppression of free expression, and did not create greater incidental burdens on First Amendment freedoms than were essential to the furtherance of the substantial interest.

22. Barnes v. Glen Theatre, 111 S.Ct. at 2464–66, 2468 (Scalia, J., concurring).

23. Church of the Lukumi Babalu Aye v. City of Hialeah, 113 S.Ct. 2217 (1993).

24. Ibid., 2239–40 (Scalia, J., concurring).

25. Waters v. Churchill, 114 S.Ct. 1878 (1994).

26. Ibid., 1893–98 (Scalia, J., concurring).

27. See Scalia, "House with Many Mansions," 9–19.

28. United States v. Carolene Products, 304 U.S. 144, 152–53n. 4 (1938); Near v. Minnesota, 283 U.S. at 697 (no prior restraint).

29. See West Virginia State Bd. of Educ. v. Barnette, 319 U.S. 624, 639 (1943); United States v. O'Brien, 391 U.S. 367, 377 (1968); Tinker v. Des Moines Sch. Dist., 393 U.S. 503 (1969); Street v. New York, 394 U.S. 576 (1969); Cohen v. California, 403 U.S. 15 (1971); Buckley v. Valeo, 424 U.S. 1 (1976); Sherbert v. Verner, 374 U.S. 398 (1963).

30. See Scalia's votes for the use of heightened scrutiny in Boos v. Barry, 485 U.S. 312 (1988); Texas v. Johnson, 491 U.S. 397 (1989); United States v. Eichman, 497 U.S. 310 (1990).

31. Austin v. Michigan Chamber of Commerce, 494 U.S. 652 (1990).

32. The applicability of heightened scrutiny analysis in campaign contribution cases was established by the Burger Court in Buckley v. Valeo, 457 U.S. 853 (1976).

33. Austin v. Michigan Chamber of Commerce, 494 U.S. at 679–85 (Scalia, J., dissenting).

34. Ibid., 685–92 (Scalia, J., dissenting).

35. Ibid., 692–95 (Scalia, J., dissenting).

36. For additional criticism of Scalia's opinion, see John S. Shockley and David A. Schultz, "The Political Philosophy of Campaign Finance Reform as Articulated in the Dissents in *Austin v. Michigan Chamber of Commerce,*" *St. Mary's Law Journal* 24 (1992): 173–81, 183–96.

37. R.A.V. v. St. Paul, 112 S.Ct. 2538 (1992).

38. The exception was first established by Chaplinsky v. New Hampshire, 315 U.S. 568, 572 (1942).

39. R.A.V. v. St. Paul, 112 S.Ct. at 2542–49.

40. Ibid., 2549–50.

41. Ibid., 2545.

42. Texas v. Johnson, 491 U.S. 397 (1989); United States v. Eichman, 110 S.Ct. 2404 (1990). Despite the liberal direction of his position on flag burning, Scalia's questions during oral argument in the case suggest that he had already decided that the regulation of flag desecration was a content-based restriction on symbolic speech; see Peter Irons and Stephanie Guitton, eds., *May It Please the Court: The Most Significant Oral Arguments Made before the Supreme Court since 1955* (New York: New Press, 1993), 153–56; James F. Simon, *The Center Holds: The Power Struggle Inside the Rehnquist Court* (New York: Simon and Schuster, 1995), 264–66, 271.

43. Meyer v. Grant, 486 U.S. 414 (1988) (ballot petitioning); Board of Airport Comm'rs v. Jews for Jesus, 482 U.S. 569 (1987) (airport petitioning); Boos v. Barry, 485 U.S. 312 (1988) (embassy protest).

44. City of Ladue v. Gilleo, 114 S.Ct. 2038 (1994).

45. Hurley and South Boston Allied War Veterans Council v. Irish-American Gay, Lesbian, and Bisexual Group of Boston, 115 S.Ct. 2338 (1995).

46. Rosenberger v. Rectors and Visitors of the Univ. of Virginia, 115 S.Ct. 2510 (1995).

47. Riley v. National Fed'n of the Blind of N. Carolina, Inc., 487 U.S. 781, 803–4 (1988) (Scalia, J., concurring).

48. Florida Star v. B.J.F., 491 U.S. 524 (1989).

49. Ibid., 541–42 (Scalia, J., concurring).

50. Butterworth v. Smith, 494 U.S. 624 (1990).

51. Ibid., 636–37 (Scalia, J., concurring).

52. Madsen v. Women's Health Ctr., Inc., 114 S.Ct. 2516 (1994).

53. Ibid., 2534 (quotation), 2537–49 (quotation on 2549) (Scalia, J., dissenting). See also his comments on judicial power and the Madsen decision in Winfield v. Kaplan, 114 S.Ct. 2783, 2783–84 (1994) (Scalia, J., dissent to cert. denial).

54. Rust v. Sullivan, 111 S.Ct. 2720 (1991).

55. Alexander v. United States, 113 S.Ct. 2766 (1993).

56. Wisconsin v. Mitchell, 113 S.Ct. 2194 (1993).

57. Gentile v. State Bar of Nevada, 111 S.Ct. 2720 (1991).

58. Simon and Schuster v. New York State Crime Victims Bd., 112 S.Ct. 501 (1991).

59. Hazelwood Sch. Dist. v. Kuhlmeier, 484 U.S. 260 (1988).

60. Frisby v. Schultz, 487 U.S. 474 (1988).

61. Ward v. Rock Against Racism, 491 U.S. 781 (1989).

62. Roth v. United States, 354 U.S. 476, 484 (1957).

63. Miller v. California, 413 U.S. 15, 24 (1973).

64. Pope v. Illinois, 481 U.S. 497 (1987).

65. Ibid., 504–5 (Scalia, J., concurring).

66. FW/PBS, Inc. v. City of Dallas, 493 U.S. 215 (1990).

67. Ibid., 252–53 (Scalia, J., concurring and dissenting).

68. Ginzburg v. United States, 383 U.S. 463 (1966).

69. Ibid., 467, 470–72.

70. FW/PBS, Inc. v. City of Dallas, 493 U.S. at 258–64 (Scalia, J., concurring and dissenting).

71. Sable Communications of California, Inc. v. FCC, 492 U.S. 115, 131–33 (1989) (Scalia, J., concurring).

72. However, Scalia has not adopted the argument that pornography is a form of gender discrimination; compare Catherine MacKinnon, *Feminism Unmodified: Discourses on Law and Life* (Cambridge: Harvard University Press, 1987).

73. The key cases developing this standard include Lovell v. Griffin, 303 U.S. 444 (1938); Hague v. CIO, 307 U.S. 496 (1939); Cox v. New Hampshire, 312 U.S. 569 (1941); Kovacs v. Cooper, 336 U.S. 77 (1949); Feiner v. New York, 340 U.S. 315 (1951); Edwards v. South Carolina, 372 U.S. 229 (1963); Cox v. Louisiana (II), 379 U.S. 558 (1965); Brown v. Louisiana, 383 U.S. 1

(1966); Adderley v. Florida, 285 U.S. 39 (1966); City Council v. Taxpayers for Vincent, 466 U.S. 789 (1984); and Clark v. Community for Creative Non-violence, 468 U.S. 288 (1984).

74. McIntyre v. Ohio Elections Comm'n, 115 S.Ct. 1511 (1995).

75. Ibid., 1532, 1534 (Scalia J., dissenting).

76. Ibid., 1535–37 (Scalia, J., dissenting).

77. New York State Club Ass'n v. City of New York, 487 U.S. 1, 20–21 (1988) (Scalia, J., concurring).

78. Board of Directors of Rotary Int'l v. Rotary Club of Duarte, 481 U.S. 537 (1987) (all-male clubs).

79. City of Dallas v. Stanglin, 490 U.S. 19 (1989) (juvenile dance halls); Lyng v. International Union, UAW, 485 U.S. 360 (1988) (food stamps); O'Lone v. Estate of Shabazz, 482 U.S. 342 (1987) (prisoner rights). Later, he voted for the same kind of deferential rationality analysis in a case that deemed reasonable prison officials' censorship of incoming mail for prisoners; see Thornburgh v. Abbott, 490 U.S. 401 (1989).

80. Dawson v. Delaware, 112 S.Ct. 1093 (1992).

81. Burson v. Freeman, 112 S.Ct. 1846, 1859–61 (1992) (Scalia, J., concurring).

82. United States v. Kokinda, 110 S.Ct. 3115 (1990).

83. Forsyth County v. Nationalist Movement, 112 S.Ct. 2395, 2405–8 (1992) (Rehnquist, C.J., dissenting).

84. Lee v. International Soc'y for Krishna Consciousness, 112 S.Ct. 2701 (1992); and International Soc'y for Krishna Consciousness v. Lee, 112 S.Ct. 2709, 2710 (1992) (Rehnquist, C.J., concurring and dissenting).

85. The libertarian thesis appears in Peter Irons, *Brennan vs. Rehnquist: The Battle for the Constitution* (New York: Alfred A. Knopf, 1994), 163.

86. See Central Hudson Gas Co. v. Public Serv. Comm'n, 447 U.S. 557 (1980).

87. Board of Trustees of State Univ. of New York v. Fox, 492 U.S. 469 (1989).

88. Ibid., 480.

89. Lakewood v. Plain Dealer Publishing Co., 486 U.S. 750 (1988).

90. City of Cincinnati v. Discovery Network, 113 S.Ct. 1505 (1993).

91. Edenfield v. Fane, 113 S.Ct. 1792 (1993); Ibanez v. Florida Dept. of Business and Professional Regulation, Bd. of Accountancy, 114 S.Ct. 2084 (1994).

92. United States v. Edge Broadcasting, 113 S.Ct. 2696 (1993).

93. Peel v. Attorney Registration and Disciplinary Comm'n of Illinois, 110 S.Ct. 2281, 2297–2301 (1990) (O'Connor, J., dissenting).

94. Florida Bar v. Went for It, Inc., 115 S.Ct. 2371 (1995).

95. Turner Broadcasting Sys. v. FCC., 114 S.Ct. 2445 (1994).

96. Rankin v. McPherson, 483 U.S. 378 (1987).

97. Ibid., 395–401 (quotation on 400) (Scalia, J., dissenting).

98. United States v. National Treasury Employees Union, 115 S.Ct. 1003 (1995).

99. Minneapolis Star and Tribune Co. v. Minnesota Comm'r of Revenue, 460 U.S. 575 (1983).

100. Arkansas Writers' Project, Inc. v. Ragland, 481 U.S. 221 (1987).

101. Ibid., 235–38 (Scalia, J., dissenting).

102. Texas Monthly v. Bullock, 489 U.S. 1 (1989).

103. Ibid., 44–45 (Scalia, J., dissenting).

104. Leathers v. Medlock, 111 S.Ct. 1438 (1991).

105. Cohen v. Cowles Media, 111 S.Ct. 2513 (1991).

106. Jimmy Swaggart Ministries v. Board of Equalization, 493 U.S. 378 (1990).

107. NAACP v. Alabama, 357 U.S. 449 (1958); see also Broadrick v. Oklahoma, 413 U.S. 601 (1973).

108. City of Houston, Texas v. Hill, 482 U.S. 451 (1987).

109. Ibid., 472–73 (Scalia, J., concurring); referring to ibid., 476–81 (Powell, J., concurring).

110. Massachusetts v. Oakes, 491 U.S. 576, 585–90 (1989) (Scalia, J., concurring and dissenting).

111. Tashjian v. Republican Party, 479 U.S. 208 (1986).

112. Ibid., 235, 237 (Scalia, J., dissenting).

113. Norman v. Reed, 112 S.Ct. 698 (1992).

114. Ibid., 709–11 (Scalia, J., dissenting).

115. Rutan v. Republican Party, 497 U.S. 62 (1990). The opinion thus clarified the kind of scrutiny required in cases about patronage dismissals; compare Elrod v. Burns, 427 U.S. 347 (1976); Branti v. Finkel, 408 U.S. 593 (1972).

116. Rutan v. Republican Party, 497 U.S. at 97–115 (Scalia, J., dissenting); compare Brennan at 70n. 4.

117. Lehnert v. Ferris Faculty Ass'n, 111 S.Ct. 1950 (1991).

118. Ibid., 1975–81 (Scalia, J., dissenting).

119. New York Times v. Sullivan, 376 U.S. 254, 279–80 (1962); Curtis Publishing Co. v. Butts, 388 U.S. 130 (1967); Gertz v. Robert Welch, Inc., 418 U.S. 323 (1974).

120. Harte-Hanks Communications, Inc. v. Connaughton, 491 U.S. 657 (1989).

121. Ibid., 696–700 (Scalia, J., concurring).

122. Milkovich v. Lorain Journal Co., 110 S.Ct. 2695 (1990).

123. Hustler Magazine v. Falwell, 485 U.S. 46 (1988) (printed parodies); Campbell v. Acuff-Rose Music, 114 S.Ct. 1164 (1994) (musical parodies).

124. Lemon v. Kurtzman, 403 U.S. 602, 612–13 (1970).

125. See Richard A. Brisbin Jr. and Edward V. Heck, "The Battle over Strict

Scrutiny: Coalitional Conflict in the Rehnquist Court," *Santa Clara Law Review* 32 (1992): 1073–83.

126. Edwards v. Aguillard, 482 U.S. 578 (1987).

127. Ibid., 593.

128. Ibid., 616 (Scalia, J., dissenting). Stephen Jay Gould, "Justice Scalia's Misunderstanding," *Constitutional Commentary* 5 (1988): 1–11, takes Scalia to task for an assumption made in support of this statement—the assumption that creation science has some scientific value and therefore deserves as much legal respect as do theories of evolutionary change.

129. Edwards v. Aguillard, 616–40 (Scalia, J., dissenting).

130. Texas Monthly v. Bullock, 489 U.S. at 1.

131. Ibid., 14.

132. Ibid., 33–44 (Scalia, J., dissenting).

133. Lee v. Weisman, 112 S.Ct. 2649 (1992).

134. Ibid., 2679 (Scalia, J., dissenting). This position might also be in part a response to the statements of counsel during oral argument; see Simon, *Center Holds*, 285–86.

135. Lee v. Weisman, 2683–86 (Scalia, J., dissenting). His opinion thus criticized Kennedy's refusal to abandon *Lemon*.

136. Lamb's Chapel v. Center Moriches Union Free Sch. Dist., 113 S.Ct. 2141 (1993).

137. Ibid., 2149–51 (Scalia, J., concurring).

138. Board of Educ. of Kiryas Joel v. Grumet, 144 S.Ct. 2481, 2505–16 (Scalia, J., dissenting).

139. Capitol Square Review and Advisory Bd. v. Pinette, 115 S.Ct. 2440 (1995).

140. Ibid., 2445.

141. In Widmar v. Vincent, 454 U.S. 263, 275 (1981), the Court held that a state university must not exclude student religious groups from facilities available to other student groups.

142. Capitol Square Review and Advisory Bd. v. Pinette, 115 S.Ct. at 2446–50.

143. Lemon v. Kurtzman, 403 U.S. 602, 612–13 (1971): "First, the statute must have a secular legislative purpose; second, its principal or primary effect must be one that neither advances nor inhibits religion; finally, the statute must not foster 'an excessive government Entanglement with religion.'"

144. County of Allegheny v. American Civil Liberties Union, 492 U.S. 573, 655–79 (1989) (Kennedy, J., concurring and dissenting).

145. Board of Educ. of Westside Community Sch. v. Mergens, 110 S.Ct. 2356, 2376–78 (1990) (Kennedy, J., dissenting).

146. Bowen v. Kendrick, 487 U.S. 589, 624–25 (1988) (Kennedy, J., concurring).

147. Zobrest v. Catalina Foothills Sch. Dist., 113 S.Ct. 2462 (1993).

148. Corporation of Presiding Bishop of Church of Jesus Christ of Latter-Day Saints v. Amos, 483 U.S. 327 (1987).

149. For commentary largely in support of these conclusions, see Jay Schlosser, "The Establishment Clause and Justice Scalia: What the Future Holds for Church and State," *Notre Dame Law Review* 63 (summer 1988): 380–92.

150. David Schultz, "Justice Antonin Scalia's First Amendment Jurisprudence: Free Speech, Press, and Associational Decisions," *Journal of Law and Politics* 9 (1993): 559.

151. Austin v. Michigan Chamber of Commerce, 494 U.S. at 694–95 (Scalia, J., dissenting).

CHAPTER EIGHT: CRIME AND THE POWER OF THE STATE

1. Antonin Scalia, "The Limits of the Law," *New Jersey Law Journal* 119, no. 18 (1987): 22.

2. Miranda v. Arizona, 384 U.S. 436 (1966), which also requires police to give persons in custody information on the availability of counsel to protect against compulsory self-incrimination.

3. On Burger Court criminal decisions, see Bernard Schwartz, *The Ascent of Pragmatism: The Burger Court in Action* (Reading, Mass.: Addison-Wesley, 1990), 320–70; Yale Kamisar, "The Warren Court (Was It Really So Defense-Minded), the Burger Court (Is It Really So Prosecution-Oriented), and Police Investigatory Practices," in *The Burger Court: The Counter-Revolution That Wasn't,* ed. Vincent Blasi (New Haven: Yale University Press, 1983), 62–91; and, for a different view, idem, "The 'Police Practice' Phases of the Criminal Process and the Three Phases of the Burger Court," in *The Burger Court: Rights and Wrongs in the Supreme Court.* ed. Herman Schwartz (New York: Elisabeth Sifton Books, 1987), 143–68.

4. Discussions of Scalia's criminal cases include George Kannar, "The Constitutional Catechism of Antonin Scalia," *Yale Law Journal* 99 (1990): 1320–42; Christopher E. Smith, "Justice Antonin Scalia and Criminal Justice Cases," *Kentucky Law Journal* 81 (1992–93): 199–200.

5. Mapp v. Ohio, 367 U.S. 643 (1961).

6. See California v. Acevedo, 111 S.Ct. 1982, 1992–93 (Scalia, J., dissenting).

7. County of Riverside v. McLaughlin, 111 S.Ct. 1661 (1991).

8. Gerstein v. Pugh, 420 U.S. 103 (1975).

9. County of Riverside v. McLaughlin, 111 S.Ct. at 1669–77 (Scalia, J., dissenting).

10. California v. Hodari D., 111 S.Ct. 1547 (1991).

11. Ibid., 1550.

12. Oliver v. United States, 466 U.S. 170 (1984); California v. Ciraolo, 476 U.S. 207 (1986).

13. United States v. Dunn, 480 U.S. 294 (1987).

14. Coolidge v. New Hampshire, 403 U.S. 433 (1971).

15. Arizona v. Hicks, 480 U.S. 321 (1987).

16. Ibid., 327.

17. Murray v. United States, 487 U.S. 533 (1988).

18. United States v. Matlock, 415 U.S. 164 (1974).

19. Illinois v. Rodriguez, 497 U.S. 177 (1990).

20. Ibid., 184–89.

21. California v. Acevedo, 111 U.S. 1982 (1991).

22. Ibid., 1992–94 (Scalia, J., dissenting).

23. Minnesota v. Dickerson, 113 S.Ct. 2130, 2139–41 (1993) (Scalia, J., concurring).

24. Terry v. Ohio, 392 U.S. 1 (1968).

25. Minnesota v. Dickerson, 113 S.Ct. at 2139–41 (Scalia, J., concurring).

26. New Jersey v. T.L.O., 469 U.S. 325 (1985); Hudson v. Palmer, 468 U.S. 517 (1984).

27. O'Connor v. Ortega, 480 U.S. 709 (1987).

28. Ibid., 729–32 (Scalia, J., concurring).

29. Griffin v. Wisconsin, 483 U.S. 868, 873–79 (1987).

30. New York v. Burger, 482 U.S. 691 (1987).

31. Greenwood v. California, 486 U.S. 35 (1988).

32. Horton v. California, 110 S.Ct. 2301 (1990).

33. Maryland v. Buie, 494 U.S. 325 (1990).

34. United States v. Verdugo-Urquidez, 494 U.S. 259 (1990).

35. United States v. Sokolow, 490 U.S. 1 (1989).

36. Colorado v. Bertine, 479 U.S. 367 (1987); Florida v. Wells, 495 U.S. 1 (1990); Florida v. Jimeno, 111 S.Ct. 1801 (1991). The thrust of these positions became clear in his opinion in California v. Acevedo, 500 U.S. 565 (1991), discussed above.

37. Alabama v. White, 110 S.Ct. 2412 (1990) (anonymous tip); Michigan State Police v. Sitz, 110 S.Ct. 2481 (1990) (checkpoints); Florida v. Bostick, 111 S.Ct. 2382 (1991) (bus and train stops).

38. Illinois v. Krull, 480 U.S. 340 (1987).

39. Skinner v. Ry. Labor Executives' Ass'n, 489 U.S. 602 (1989).

40. Soldal v. Cook County, 113 S.Ct. 538 (1992).

41. National Treasury Employees Union v. Von Raab, 489 U.S. 656 (1989).

42. Ibid., 682–84 (quotations on 683), 687 (Scalia, J., dissenting).

43. Vernonia Sch. Dist. 47J v. Acton, 115 S.Ct. 2386 (1995).

44. Ibid., 2391–95.

45. Minnick v. Mississippi, 111 S.Ct. 486 (1990).

46. Ibid., 492, 495–98 (quotations) (Scalia, J., dissenting).

47. McNeil v. Wisconsin, 111 S.Ct. 2204, esp. 2207 (1991).

48. Davis v. United States, 114 S.Ct. 2350 (1994).

49. See Arizona v. Mauro, 481 U.S. 520 (1987) (recorded telephone conversations); Michigan v. Harvey, 494 U.S. 344 (1990) (impeachment); Braswell v. United States, 108 S.Ct. 1625 (1988) (corporate records); Pennsylvania v. Burder, 488 U.S. 9 (1988) (traffic stops); Illinois v. Perkins, 110 S.Ct. 2394 (1990) (inmate testimony); New York v. Harris, 495 U.S 14 (1990) (statements made outside house); Duckworth v. Eagan, 492 U.S. 195 (1989) (departure from Miranda text); Colorado v. Connelly, 479 U.S. 157 (1986) (mental illness).

50. Arizona v. Fulminate, 111 S.Ct. 1246 (1991). Reportedly Scalia had initially not considered the admission of the jail cell confession to be harmless, but he switched his position before the completion of opinions because he thought it "would be difficult to define 'a limited category of really coerced confessions that alone would be excluded from harmless error analysis'"; see James F. Simon, *The Center Holds: The Power Struggle Inside the Rehnquist Court* (New York: Simon and Schuster, 1995), 198.

51. Pennsylvania v. Muniz, 110 S.Ct. 2638 (1990).

52. Jones v. Thomas, 491 U.S. 376 (1989).

53. Ibid., 390–96 (Scalia, J., dissenting).

54. Department of Revenue of Montana v. Kurth Ranch, 114 S.Ct. 1937 (1994).

55. Ibid., 1955–60 (Scalia, J., dissenting).

56. Witte v. United States, 15 S.Ct. 2199, 2209–10 (Scalia, J., concurring).

57. Grady v. Corbin, 495 U.S. 508 (1990).

58. Ibid., 528–43 (Scalia, J., dissenting).

59. United States v. Dixon, 113 S.Ct. 2849, 2855 64 (1993).

60. United States v. Felix, 112 S.Ct. 1377 (1992).

61. Brady v. Maryland, 373 U.S. 83 (1963); United States v. Agurs, 427 U.S. 97 (1976).

62. Kyles v. Whitley, 115 S.Ct. 1555 (1995).

63. Ibid., 1580–88 (Scalia, J., dissenting).

64. Ricketts v. Adamson, 483 U.S. 1 (1987).

65. Arizona v. Youngblood, 488 U.S. 51 (1988).

66. Pointer v. Texas, 380 U.S. 400 (1965). See also Bryan H. Wildenthal, "The Right of Confrontation, Justice Scalia, and the Power and Limits of Textualism," *Washington and Lee Law Review* 48 (1991): 1327–31.

67. Cruz v. New York, 481 U.S. 186, 193 (1987).

68. Richardson v. Marsh, 481 U.S. 200 (1987).

69. United States v. Owens, 484 U.S. 554 (1988).

70. Coy v. Iowa, 487 U.S. 1012, 1019 (1988).

71. Maryland v. Craig, 497 U.S. 836 (1990).

72. Ibid., 860–70 (quotations on 860, 861, 864) (Scalia, J., dissenting). For criticism of this and other Confrontation Clause opinions, see Daniel Shaviro, "The Supreme Court's Bifurcated Interpretation of the Confrontation Clause,"

Hastings Constitutional Law Quarterly 17 (1990): 383–97; and Wildenthal, "Right of Confrontation," 1331–61, 1380–92.

73. Olden v. Kentucky, 488 U.S. 227 (1988); Idaho v. Wright, 110 S.Ct. 3139 (1990) (direct confrontation). He joined a concurring opinion by Thomas to apply the Confrontation Clause to witnesses at trial and formalized testimonial materials submitted to the court; see White v. Illinois, 112 S.Ct. 736, 744–48 (1992) (Thomas, J., concurring). However, he did support a "rape-shield" law restricting the use of evidence and questioning regarding past sexual conduct by victims; see Michigan v. Licks, 111 S.Ct. 1473 (1991). On physical presence, see Crosby v. United States, 113 S.Ct. 748 (1993).

74. Pennsylvania v. Finley, 481 U.S. 551 (1987); Murray v. Giarratano, 492 U.S. 1 (1989) (appeal limitations); United States v. Monsanto, 491 U.S. 600 (1989); Caplin and Drysdale v. United States, 491 U.S. 617 (1989) (seizure of assets); Keeny v. Tampayo-Reyes, 112 S.Ct. 1715 (1992) (habeas corpus relief); Lockhart v. Fretwell, 113 S.Ct. 838 (1993) (serious errors); Nichols v. United States, 114 S.Ct. 1921 (1994) (driving under the influence); Doggett v. United States, 112 S.Ct. 2686, 2694–2701 (1992) (Thomas, J., dissenting) (postindictment delay); Mu'Min v. Virginia, 111 S.Ct. 1899 (1991) (refusal to question jurors).

75. United States v. Gaudin, 115 S.Ct. 2310, 2314 (1995).

76. United States v. Sinclair, 279 U.S. 263 (1929).

77. He also voted for an opinion that allowed defendants to be held without bail as a "regulatory" measure, his only significant attention to the bail clause of the Eighth Amendment; see United States v. Salerno, 481 U.S. 739 (1987). For an overview of Scalia's Eighth Amendment opinions, see Christopher E. Smith, "The Constitution and Criminal Punishment: The Emerging Visions of Justices Scalia and Thomas," *Drake Law Review* 43 (1995): 593–613.

78. Austin v. United States, 113 S.Ct. 2801 (1993).

79. Ibid., 2814–15 (Scalia, J., concurring).

80. United States v. A Parcel of Land, Bldgs., Appurtenances, and Improvements, Known as 92 Buena Vista Ave., Rumson, N.J., 113 S.Ct. 1126, 1138–42 (1993) (Scalia, J., concurring).

81. International Union, United Mine Workers of Am., UAW v. Bagwell, 114 S.Ct. 2552 (1994).

82. Ibid., 2563–65 (Scalia, J., concurring).

83. Rummel v. Estelle, 445 U.S. 263 (1980); Hutto v. Davis, 454 U.S. 370 (1982); Solem v. Helm, 463 U.S. 277 (1983).

84. Harmelin v. Michigan, 111 S.Ct. 2680 (1991).

85. Ibid., 2702 (Kennedy, J., concurring).

86. Ibid., 2701–2.

87. Ibid., 2686–2702.

88. Estelle v. Gamble, 429 U.S. 97 (1976); Rhodes v. Chapman, 452 U.S. 337 (1981).

89. Wilson v. Seiter, 111 S.Ct. 2321 (1991).

90. Ibid., 2327-28.

91. Helling v. McKinney, 113 S.Ct. 2475, 2482-85 (1993) (Thomas, J., dissenting).

92. Furman v. Georgia, 408 U.S. 238 (1972). This was the position of all the justices except Brennan and Marshall.

93. Gregg v. Georgia, 428 U.S. 153 (1976); Jurek v. Texas, 428 U.S. 262 (1976); Proffitt v. Florida, 428 U.S. 242 (1976); Woodson v. North Carolina, 428 U.S. 280 (1976); Roberts v. Louisiana, 431 U.S. 633 (1977); Lockett v. Ohio, 438 U.S. 586 (1978).

94. Coker v. Georgia, 433 U.S. 584 (1977); Edmund v. Florida, 458 U.S. 782 (1982); but see Pulley v. Harris, 465 U.S. 37 (1984).

95. Eddings v. Oklahoma, 455 U.S. 104 (1982); Ford v. Wainwright, 477 U.S. 399 (1986).

96. See Steven G. Gey, "Justice Scalia's Death Penalty," *Florida State University Law Review* 20 (1992): 67-132.

97. McCleskey v. Kemp, 481 U.S. 279 (1987).

98. Memorandum to the Conference from Justice Antonin Scalia in No. 84-6811—McCleskey v. Kemp of 6 Jan. 1987, Thurgood Marshall Papers, Library of Congress, Washington, D.C., quoted in Dennis D. Dorin, "Far Right of the Mainstream: Racism, Rights, and Remedies from the Perspective of Justice Antonin Scalia's *McCleskey* Memorandum," *Mercer Law Review* 45 (1994): 1036. See also a quotation of Scalia's views at a conference reported in Simon, *Center Holds,* 181, that makes roughly the same point.

99. Lankford v. Idaho, 111 S.Ct. 1723, 1733-37 (1991) (Scalia, J., dissenting).

100. Gray v. Mississippi, 481 U.S. 648 (1987).

101. Ibid., 675 (Scalia, J., dissenting)

102. Morgan v. Illinois, 112 S.Ct. 2222 (1992).

103. Ibid., 2236-42 (Scalia, J., dissenting).

104. Hitchcock v. Dugger, 481 U.S. 393, 399 (1987).

105. Booth v. Maryland, 482 U.S. 496, 519-21 (1987) (Scalia, J., dissenting).

106. South Carolina v. Gathers, 490 U.S. 805, 823-25 (1989) (Scalia, J., dissenting).

107. McKoy v. North Carolina, 494 U.S. 433 (1990).

108. Ibid., 459 (quotation), 464-67 (Scalia, J., dissenting).

109. Walton v. Arizona, 497 U.S. 639 (1990).

110. Ibid., 661 (quotation), 664-67, 669-74 (Scalia, J., concurring).

111. Payne v. Tennessee, 111 S.Ct. 2597 (1991).

112. Ibid., 2613-14 (Scalia, J., concurring).

113. Sochor v. Florida, 112 S.Ct. 2114, 2130 (1992) (Scalia, J., concurring and dissenting).

114. Espinosa v. Florida, 112 S.Ct. 2926, 2929 (1992) (Scalia, J., dissenting).

115. Richmond v. Lewis, 113 S.Ct. 528, 568 (1992) (Scalia, J., dissenting).

116. Tuilaepa v. California, 114 S.Ct. 2630, 2639 (1994) (Scalia, J., concurring).

117. Simmons v. South Carolina, 114 S.Ct. 2187, 2203, 2205 (1994) (Scalia, J., dissenting).

118. Madden v. Texas, 111 S.Ct. 902, 905 (1991) (Scalia, Cir. J.).

119. Kyles v. Whitley, 115 S.Ct. at 1576–78 (Scalia, J., dissenting).

120. Eddings v. Oklahoma, 455 U.S. 104 (1982).

121. Thompson v. Oklahoma, 487 U.S. 815 (1988).

122. Ibid., 863–72, 874–78 (Scalia, J., dissenting).

123. Stanford v. Kentucky, 492 U.S. 361 (1989).

124. Ibid., 368–80.

125. Penry v. Lynaugh, 492 U.S. 302 (1989).

126. Ibid., 351, 353–60 (Scalia, J., concurring and dissenting).

127. Johnson v. Texas, 113 S.Ct. 2658, 2672 (1993) (Scalia, J., concurring).

128. Tison v. Arizona, 481 U.S. 137 (1987) (homicide participation); Parker v. Dugger, 111 S.Ct. 731, 740–46 (1991) (White, J., dissenting) (appellate error); Graham v. Collins, 113 S.Ct. 892 (1993) (criteria later invalidated); Arave v. Creech, 113 S.Ct. 1534 (1993) (vague aggravating factor); Victor v. Nebraska, 114 S.Ct. 1239 (1994) (reasonable doubt); Romano v. Oklahoma, 114 S.Ct. 2004 (1994) (prior sentence); Blystone v. Pennsylvania, 494 U.S. 299 (1990); Boyde v. California, 494 U.S. 370 (1990); Lewis v. Jeffers, 110 S.Ct. 3092 (1990) (satisfaction with state rules); Sumner v. Shuman, 483 U.S. 66, 86–89 (1987) (White, J., dissenting) (mandatory penalty); Maynard v. Cartwright, 486 U.S. 356 (1988) (Oklahoma procedures).

129. See also the comments in Gey, "Scalia's Death Penalty," 120–32.

130. The most important exposition of this principle was Fay v. Noia, 372 U.S. 391 (1963).

131. Stone v. Powell, 428 U.S. 465 (1976).

132. Castille v. Peoples, 489 U.S. 346 (1989).

133. Ylst v. Nunnemaker, 111 S.Ct. 2590 (1991).

134. Dobbs v. Zant, 113 S.Ct. 835, 836 (1993) (Scalia, J., concurring).

135. Herrera v. Collins, 113 S.Ct. 853, 874 (1993) (Scalia, J., concurring). See also Tuggle v. Netherland, 116 S.Ct. 283 (1995) (Scalia, J., concurring) on a related issue.

136. McCleskey v. Zant, 111 S.Ct. 1454 (1991).

137. Lockhart v. Fretwell, 113 S.Ct. 838 (1993); Sawyer v. Whitley, 112 S.Ct. 2514 (1992).

138. Withrow v. Williams, 113 S.Ct. 1745, 1769–70 (Scalia, J., concurring and dissenting).

139. Schulp v. Delo, 115 S.Ct. 851, 874–78 (1995) (Scalia, J., dissenting).

140. Reed v. Farley, 114 S.Ct. 2291, 2296–97 (1994).

141. Ibid., 2300–2302 (Scalia, J., concurring).

142. Teague v. Lane, 489 U.S. 288 (1989). See Sawyer v. Smith, 110 S.Ct. 2882 (1990); Butler v. McKellar, 110 S.Ct. 1212 (1990); Saffle v. Parks, 110 S.Ct. 1257 (1990).

143. See also the same message in his vote with the majority in Coleman v. Thompson, 111 S.Ct. 2546 (1990), a case that allowed states to restrict federal habeas corpus review by applying the state's constitutional right to counsel, a provision with a legal meaning fixed by state courts independent of federal jurisdiction.

144. Stringer v. Black, 112 S.Ct. 1130, 1140–46 (1992) (Souter, J., dissenting).

145. Albright v. Oliver, 114 S.Ct. 807, 814 (1994) (Scalia, J., concurring).

146. Deal v. United States, 113 S.Ct. 1993 (1993).

147. Schmuck v. United States, 489 U.S. 705, 722–25 (1989) (Scalia, J., dissenting).

148. Schad v. Arizona, 111 S.Ct. 2491, 2505–7 (1991) (Scalia, J., concurring).

149. United States v. Granderson, 114 S.Ct. 1259, 1270 (1994) (Scalia, J., concurring).

150. United States v. Aguilar, 115 S.Ct. 2357, 2367–69 (1995) (Scalia, J., concurring and dissenting).

151. United States v. Mendoza-Lopez, 481 U.S. 828, 847–49 (1987) (Scalia, J., dissenting).

152. Cheek v. United States, 111 S.Ct. 604, 613–15 (1991) (Scalia, J., concurring).

153. Posters 'N' Things, Ltd. v. United States, 114 S.Ct. 1747, 1755–56 (1994) (Scalia, J., concurring).

154. Williamson v. United States, 114 S.Ct. 2431, 2438 (1994) (Scalia, J., concurring).

155. Braxton v. United States, 111 S.Ct. 1854, 1858–59 (1991).

156. Midland Asphalt Corp. v. United States, 489 U.S. 794 (1989).

157. Hunter v. Bryant, 112 S.Ct. 534, 537 (1991) (Scalia, J., concurring).

158. Buckley v. Fitzsimmons, 113 S.Ct. 2606, 2619–20 (1993) (Scalia, J., concurring).

159. Carella v. California, 491 U.S. 263, 267–73 (1989) (Scalia, J., concurring).

160. Yates v. Evatt, 111 S.Ct. 1884, 1897 (1991) (Scalia, J., concurring).

161. Ibid., 1840 (Scalia, J., concurring).

162. Sullivan v. Louisiana, 113 S.Ct. 2078 (1993).

163. Mathews v. United States, 485 U.S. 58, 67–68 (1988) (Scalia, J., concurring).

164. Griffin v. United States, 112 S.Ct. 466 (1991).

CHAPTER NINE: PROTECTING BODIES AND PROPERTY

1. Planned Parenthood of Southeastern Pennsylvania v. Casey, 112 S.Ct. 2791, 2882 (1992) (Scalia, J., concurring and dissenting). See also Antonin Scalia, "Common-Law Courts in a Civil-Law System: The Role of United States Federal Courts in Interpreting the Constitution and Laws" (Tanner Lectures at Princeton University, Princeton, N.J., 1995).

2. See Meyer v. Nebraska, 262 U.S. 390 (1923); Pierce v. Society of Sisters, 268 U.S. 510 (1925); Skinner v. Oklahoma, 316 U.S. 535 (1942); Griswold v. Connecticut, 381 U.S. 479 (1965); and Roe v. Wade, 410 U.S. 113 (1973).

3. Snyder v. Massachusetts, 291 U.S. 97, 105 (1934); see also Powell v. Alabama, 287 U.S. 45, 67–68 (1932).

4. Lower-tier procedural due process also affords protection of property.

5. As indicated by his "specific tradition" argument, this is a very limited use of history, one more limited than some of his critics imply. Compare Laurence H. Tribe and Michael C. Dorf, *On Reading the Constitution* (Cambridge: Harvard University Press, 1991), 98–101; and Steven R. Greenburger, "Justice Scalia's Due Process Traditionalism Applied to Territorial Jurisdiction: The Illusion of Adjudication without Judgment," *Boston College Law Review* 33 (1992): 985–97. For a discussion of different uses of history by the Court, see Charles A. Miller, *The Supreme Court and the Uses of History* (Cambridge: Harvard University Press, 1969), 8–38, 189–201. Miller especially draws a distinction between the Court's use of "external," general history, such as the examination of the original intent of the Framers, and the history of legal actions as practiced, for example, by Justices Joseph Story and Felix Frankfurter (20–28, esp. n. 42).

6. Eric Hobsbawm, "Introduction: Inventing Traditions," in *The Invention of Tradition,* ed. Eric Hobsbawm and Terence Ranger (Cambridge: Cambridge University Press, 1983), 1–14; idem, "Mass-Producing Traditions: Europe, 1870–1914," in ibid., 279–80.

7. Lee v. Weisman, 112 S.Ct. 2649, 2679–86 (1992) (Scalia, J., dissenting).

8. Michael H. v. Gerald D., 491 U.S. 110, 127–28n. 6 (1989). See also Gregory C. Cook, "Footnote 6: Justice Scalia's Attempt to Impose a Rule of Law on Substantive Due Process," *Harvard Journal of Law and Public Policy* 14 (1991): 863–66; Timothy L. Raschke Shattuck, "Justice Scalia's Due Process Methodology," *Southern California Law Review* 65 (1992): 2743–91.

9. Henry M. Hart Jr. and Albert M. Sacks, *The Legal Process: Basic Problems in the Making and Application of the Law,* prepared from tentative ed. by William N. Eskridge Jr. and Philip P. Frickey (Westbury, N.Y.: Foundation Press, 1994), 128; see also 429–35.

10. Ibid., 423–30. See also Lon L. Fuller, "The Forms and Limits of Adjudication," *Harvard Law Review* 92 (1978): 378–81.

11. See Raschke Shattuck, "Scalia's Due Process Methodology," 2767–73;

David A. Strauss, "Tradition, Precedent, and Justice Scalia," *Cardozo Law Review* 12 (1991): 1710–15; and, from a different ideological position, Cook, "Footnote 6," 865, 867, 869–78.

12. Edward S. Corwin, "The Basic Doctrine of American Constitutional Law," *Michigan Law Review* 12 (1914): 247 (vested right of property); Meyer v. Nebraska, 262 U.S. 390 (1923); Pierce v. Society of Sisters, 268 U.S. at 510 (extratextual rights).

13. Minersville Sch. Dist. v. Gobitis, 310 U.S. 586, 596 (1940). Also, Scalia has spurned the traditions of " 'English-speaking peoples' " used by Frankfurter; see Adamson v. California, 332 U.S. 46, 67 (1947) (Frankfurter, J., concurring); Rochin v. California, 342 U.S. 165, 169 (1952).

14. See Robert A. Burt, "Precedent and Authority in Antonin Scalia's Jurisprudence," *Cardozo Law Review* 12 (1991): 1694–95. See the somewhat different approach to Scalia's use of tradition as a method of analysis offered in Edward Gary Spitko, "A Critique of Justice Antonin Scalia's Approach to Fundamental Rights Adjudication," *Duke Law Journal* (1990): 1348–52; and L. Benjamin Young, "Justice Scalia's History and Tradition: The Chief Nightmare in Professor Tribe's Anxiety Closet," *Virginia Law Review* 78 (1992): 589–96. For conclusions similar to those offered here, see David B. Anders, "Justices Harlan and Black Revisited: The Emerging Dispute between Justice O'Connor and Justice Scalia over Fundamental Unenumerated Rights," *Fordham Law Review* 61 (1993): 906–8, 924–25, 927; Greenburger, "Scalia's Due Process Traditionalism," 984, 1022–34; Raschke Shattuck, "Scalia's Due Process Methodology," 2765–67; and Nicholas S. Zeppos, "Justice Scalia's Textualism: The New 'New' Legal Process," *Cardozo Law Review* 12 (1991): 1632–33. Bethany A. Cook and Lisa C. Kahn, "Justice Scalia's Due Process Model: A History Lesson in Constitutional Interpretation," *St. John's Journal of Legal Commentary* 6 (1991): 275–84, overrate the dispositive force of general, nonlegal traditions for Scalia.

15. Michael H. v. Gerald D., 491 U.S. 110 (1989). For commentary, see Cook and Kahn, "Scalia's Due Process Model," 263–85; Cook, "Footnote 6," 853–93; Spitko, "Critique," 1337–60; Tribe and Dorf, *Reading the Constitution*, 73–74, 98–117.

16. Michael H. v. Gerald D., 491 U.S. at 120.

17. Ibid., 123–24.

18. Ibid., 127.

19. Ibid., 127n. 6. Scalia also dismissed the case of the child, Victoria, on the basis of the same lack of tradition, noting for unspecified reasons that it was even "weaker" than that of her natural father, Michael. Also, because she was not a member of a legally recognized disadvantaged class, he found no discrimination against the child demanding higher-tier equal protection analysis. Ibid., 131.

20. Ibid., 124n. 4.

21. Tribe and Dorf, *Reading the Constitution,* 107–9, read the note in this manner.

22. Employment Div. v. Smith, 494 U.S. 872, 878–79 (1990).

23. Pacific Mut. Life Ins. Co. v. Haslip, 111 S.Ct. 1032 (1991).

24. Ibid., 1046–52 (Scalia, J., concurring).

25. Ibid., 1052–54 (Scalia, J., concurring).

26. TXO Production Corp. v. Alliance Resources Corp., 113 S.Ct. 2711 (1993).

27. Ibid., 2727–28 (Scalia, J., concurring).

28. Burnham v. Superior Court of California, County of Marin, 495 U.S. 604 (1990). For further discussion of this case, see Greenburger, "Scalia's Due Process Traditionalism," 997–1022.

29. Burnham v. Superior Court, 495 U.S. at 623–27.

30. Reno v. Flores, 113 S.Ct. 1439 (1993).

31. Ibid., 1447–54.

32. United States v. Carlton, 114 S.Ct. 2018 (1994).

33. Ibid., 2026–27 (Scalia, J., concurring).

34. See Tribe and Dorf, *Reading the Constitution,* 101–4, for further criticism.

35. Sigert v. Gilley, 111 S.Ct. 1789 (1991), relying on Paul v. Davis, 424 U.S. 693 (1976).

36. Collins v. City of Harker Heights, 112 S.Ct. 1061 (1992).

37. Foucha v. United States, 112 S.Ct. 1780, 1797–1809 (1992) (Thomas, J., concurring).

38. For a recent introduction to the issues and the literature, compare Ronald Dworkin, "Unenumerated Rights: Whether and How *Roe* Should Be Overruled," in *The Bill of Rights in the Modern State,* ed. Geoffrey R. Stone, Richard A. Epstein, and Cass R. Sunstein (Chicago: University of Chicago Press, 1992), 381–432; and Richard A. Posner, "Legal Reasoning from the Top Down and the Bottom Up: The Question of Unenumerated Constitutional Rights," in ibid., 433–50.

39. Rust v. Sullivan, 111 S.Ct. 1759, 1776–78 (1991).

40. Webster v. Reprod. Health Servs., 492 U.S. 490, 532 (1989) (Scalia, J., concurring).

41. Roe v. Wade, 410 U.S. 113 (1973).

42. Webster v. Reprod. Health Servs., 492 U.S. at 532 (Scalia, J., concurring); citing Roe v. Wade, 410 U.S. at 172–78 (Rehnquist, J., dissenting), and at 221–23 (White, J., dissenting).

43. Webster v. Reprod. Health Servs., 492 U.S. at 532–35 (Scalia, J., concurring); responding to ibid., 492 U.S. at 523–31 (O'Connor, J., concurring).

44. Ibid., 536n, 537 (Scalia, J., concurring). See also James F. Simon, *The Center Holds: The Power Struggle Inside the Rehnquist Court* (New York: Si-

mon and Schuster, 1995), 131–38, 141, on Scalia's participation in oral argument and conference discussions and O'Connor's response in *Webster*.

45. Hodgson v. Minnesota, 497 U.S. 417 (1990); Ohio v. Akron Ctr. for Reprod. Health, 497 U.S. 502 (1990).

46. Hodgson v. Minnesota, 497 U.S. at 480 (Scalia, J., concurring and dissenting).

47. Ohio v. Akron Ctr. for Reprod. Health, 497 U.S. at 520 (Scalia, J., concurring).

48. Planned Parenthood of Southeastern Pennsylvania v. Casey, 112 S.Ct. 2872–85 (1992) (Scalia, J., concurring and dissenting).

49. Ibid., 2874 (Scalia, J., concurring and dissenting).

50. Ibid., 2875–80 (Scalia, J., concurring and dissenting).

51. Ibid., 2875–76 (Scalia, J., concurring and dissenting).

52. Ibid., 2876, 2878, 2880 (Scalia, J., concurring and dissenting).

53. Ibid., 2881 (Scalia, J., concurring and dissenting).

54. Ibid., 2882–84 (Scalia, J., concurring and dissenting). On the Court's internal struggles in this case, see Simon, *Center Holds,* 144–67.

55. Cruzan by Cruzan v. Director, Missouri Dept. of Health, 110 S.Ct. 2841 (1990).

56. Ibid., 2859 (Scalia, J., concurring).

57. Ibid., 2860–62 (Scalia, J., concurring).

58. Ibid., 2862 (Scalia, J., concurring). Compare ibid., 2870 (Brennan, J., dissenting).

59. Ibid., 2863 (Scalia, J., concurring). On this case see also Benjamin C. Zipursky, "The Pedigree of Rights and Powers in Scalia's *Cruzan* Concurrence," *University of Pittsburgh Law Review* 56 (1994): 283–321.

60. TXO Production v. Alliance Resources, 113 S.Ct. at 2727 (Scalia, J., concurring); United States v. Carlton, 113 S.Ct. at 2027 (Scalia, J., concurring).

61. See Antonin Scalia, "Economic Affairs as Human Affairs," *Cato Journal* 4 (1985): 707–9.

62. On new property, see Antonin Scalia, "Guadalajara! A Case Study in Regulation by Munificence," *Regulation* 2 (1978): 23–29. Compare Charles Reich, "The New Property," *Yale Law Journal* 73 (1964): 733–86. On economic policy in general, see Scalia, "Economic Affairs," 706–7. This position does not strikingly differentiate him from most justices of the post–New Deal period, justices who envisioned a corporate America regulated to prevent fraud and malfeasance and protected from market failures by the rulemaking, ratemaking, monetary, and fiscal policies of a positive state. The result is the "desuetude" of the Court in economic matters, a position in tune with the Reasoned Elaboration theme of a passive judiciary; see Arthur Selwyn Miller, *The Supreme Court and American Capitalism* (New York: Free Press, 1968).

63. For details on the idea of property rights and the issue of factionalism, see Jennifer Nedlesky, *Private Property and the Limits of American Constitutionalism* (Chicago: University of Chicago Press, 1990). On public interest liberalism and ecological concerns, see Michael W. McCann, *Taking Reform Seriously: Perspectives on Public Interest Liberalism* (Ithaca: Cornell University Press, 1986), 87, 164–67.

64. Nollan v. California Coastal Comm'n, 483 U.S. 825 (1987).

65. Ibid., 831–38.

66. Hodel v. Irving, 481 U.S. 704 (1987).

67. Ibid., 719 (Scalia, J., concurring).

68. Pennell v. City of San Jose, 485 U.S. 1 (1988).

69. Ibid., 15–19, 22 (Scalia, J., concurring and dissenting).

70. Lucas v. South Carolina Coastal Council, 112 S.Ct. 2886 (1992).

71. Ibid., 2893–95.

72. Ibid., 2898, 2898n. 12, 2900.

73. Importantly, Scalia does not adopt the competing approaches to takings offered by academics. Compare Scalia's view to that expressed in Bruce A. Ackerman, *Private Property and the Constitution* (New Haven: Yale University Press, 1977); and Richard Epstein, *Takings: Private Property and the Power of Eminent Domain* (Cambridge: Harvard University Press, 1985). The argument here rejects implications, as in J. Frietag, "Takings 1992: Scalia's Jurisprudence and a Fifth Amendment Doctrine to Avoid Lochner Redivivus," *Valparaiso University Law Review* 28 (1994): 743–83, that Scalia wanted to resurrect fundamental liberty through the creation of land development rights under the Takings Clause.

74. Keystone Bituminous Coal Ass'n v. DeBenedictis, 480 U.S. 470, 506–21 (1987) (Rehnquist, C.J., dissenting).

75. First Evangelical Lutheran Church v. County of Los Angeles, 482 U.S. 304 (1987).

76. Dolan v. City of Tigard, 114 S.Ct. 2309 (1994).

77. Duquesne Light Co. v. Barasch, 488 U.S. 299 (1989).

78. Ibid., 317 (Scalia, J., concurring).

79. Yee v. Escondido, California, 112 S.Ct. 1522 (1992).

80. Preseault v. ICC, 494 U.S. 1, 20–25 (1990) (O'Connor, J., concurring).

81. See the loose guidance on the nature of total takings in Lucas v. South Carolina Coastal Council, 112 S.Ct. at 2901, which draws not on federal constitutional precedent or legislation but on a scholarly restatement of state tort law.

82. Ibid., 2899.

83. See William W. Fisher III, "The Trouble with *Lucas*," *Stanford Law Review* 45 (1993): 1408–9. For a differing view, arguing that the decisions require legislative accountability (although it is not clear whether this is accountability to courts, landowners, or the public), see Alfred P. Levitt, "Taking

on a New Direction: The Rehnquist-Scalia Approach to Regulatory Takings," *Temple Law Review* 66 (1993): 197, 219–22. Compare Hart and Sacks, *Legal Process,* 1374. This is also noted in Peter B. Edelman, "Justice Scalia's Jurisprudence and the Good Society: Shades of Felix Frankfurter and the Harvard Hit Parade of the 1950s," *Cardozo Law Review* 12 (1991): 1804.

84. A similar argument appears in Zipursky, "Pedigree of Rights and Powers."

CHAPTER TEN: THE RULE OF LAW AND THE LIMITS OF THE CONSERVATIVE REVIVAL

1. Austin Sarat and Thomas R. Kearns, "Beyond the Great Divide: Forms of Legal Scholarship and Everyday Life," in *Law in Everyday Life,* ed. Austin Sarat and Thomas R. Kearns (Ann Arbor: University of Michigan Press, 1993), 29.

2. Clifford Geertz, "Local Knowledge: Fact and Law in Comparative Perspective," in *Local Knowledge: Further Essays in Interpretive Anthropology* (New York: Basic, 1983), 184.

3. In addition to Sarat and Kearns, "Beyond the Great Divide," 27–34, 50–61, the definition of the constitutive nature of law here draws on John Brigham, "Right, Rage, and Remedy: Forms of Law in Political Discourse," *Studies in American Political Development* 2 (1987): 303–7; Kristin Bumiller, *The Civil Rights Society: The Social Construction of Victims* (Baltimore: Johns Hopkins University Press, 1988); Robert M. Cover, "The Supreme Court, 1982 Term—Foreword: *Nomos* and Narrative," *Harvard Law Review* 97 (1983): 4–68; David M. Engel, "Law in Everyday Life: The Construction of Community and Difference," in Sarat and Kearns, *Law in Everyday Life,* 126–35; Michel Foucault, *The Archaeology of Knowledge and Discourse on Language,* trans. A. M. Sheridan Smith (1969, 1971; New York: Pantheon, 1972), 215–37; Geertz, "Local Knowledge," 217–30; Christine Harrington and Sally Engle Merry, "Ideological Production: The Making of Community Mediation," *Law and Society Review* 22 (1988): 709–35; William F. Harris II, *The Interpretable Constitution* (Baltimore: Johns Hopkins University Press, 1993), 7–32; Alan Hunt, *Explorations in Law and Society: Toward a Constitutive Theory of Law* (New York: Routledge, 1993), 301–33; Susan S. Silbey, "Ideals and Practices in the Study of Law," *Legal Studies Forum* 9 (1985): 15–22; Jonathan Simon, "The Ideological Effects of Actuarial Practices," *Law and Society Review* 22 (1988): 771–800; and Lucie White, "Ordering Voice: Rhetoric and Democracy in Project Head Start," in *The Rhetoric of Law,* ed. Austin Sarat and Thomas R. Kearns (Ann Arbor: University of Michigan Press, 1994), 185–223.

4. See Anthony Giddens, *Modernity and Self-Identity: Self and Society in Late Modernity* (Stanford: Stanford University Press, 1991), 35–69.

5. See Rogers M. Smith, *Liberalism and American Constitutional Law* (Cambridge: Harvard University Press, 1985), 18–59.

6. Pierre Bourdieu, "The Force of Law: Toward a Sociology of the Juridical Field," trans. Richard Terdiman, *Hastings Law Journal* 38 (1988): 843–48, quotation on 843–44.

7. Stuart A. Scheingold, *The Politics of Rights: Lawyers, Public Policy, and Political Change* (New Haven: Yale University Press, 1974), 13.

8. On the Constitution as a symbol and faith, see John Brigham, *The Cult of the Court* (Philadelphia: Temple University Press, 1987), 46–59; Michael Kammen, *A Machine That Would Go of Itself: The Constitution in American Culture* (New York: Alfred A. Knopf, 1986); Max Lerner, "Constitutionalism and Court as Symbols," *Yale Law Journal* 46 (1937): 1290–1319; Sanford Levinson, *Constitutional Faith* (Princeton: Princeton University Press, 1988), 9–17.

9. On the derivation of rules from an abstract contract see John Locke, "The Second Treatise of Government," in *Two Treatises of Government,* ed. Peter Laslett (1689; New York: Mentor, 1960), 309–18, 366–400. Smith, *Liberalism and Constitutional Law,* 13–35, summarizes the nature of Locke's values. The alternative Enlightenment definition of a deontological theory of being derived from a priori principles (the categorical imperative) is found in Immanuel Kant, *Critique of Pure Reason,* 2d ed., trans. Norman Kemp Smith (1787; trans. Garden City, N.Y.: Anchor, 1966), 29–33, 41–48, 58–62. For a concise summary of Kant's linkage of deontology to the idea of law, see Gilles Deleuze, *Kant's Critical Philosophy: The Doctrine of the Faculties,* trans. Hugh Tomlinson and Barbara Habberjam (1963; Minneapolis: University of Minnesota Press, 1984), x–xi; and Costas Douzinas and Ronnie Warrington, "The Face of Justice: A Jurisprudence of Alterity," *Social and Legal Studies* 3 (1994): 409–12.

10. Locke, "Second Treatise," 352. The separation of the rule of law from politics was advanced to limit the coercive power of the state by various liberal legal scholars. In the twentieth century the strongest support for this idea has come in the works of classical liberal scholars educated in the German-speaking world: Gottfried Dietze, *Two Concepts of the Rule of Law* (Indianapolis: Liberty Fund, 1973); Friedrich A. Hayek, *The Constitution of Liberty* (Chicago: University of Chicago Press, 1960), 133–61; idem, *Law, Legislation, and Liberty: A New Statement of the Liberal Principles of Justice and Political Economy,* vol. 1, *Rules and Order* (Chicago: University of Chicago Press, 1973); and Hans Kelsen, *The Pure Theory of the Law* (Berkeley: University of California Press, 1967), 1, 279–80.

11. See Alexander Hamilton, James Madison, and John Jay, *The Federalist,* ed. Jacob E. Cooke (1787–88; Middletown, Conn.: Wesleyan University Press, 1961), paper no. 78 (Hamilton), pp. 524–30; Marbury v. Madison, 1 Cranch 137 (1803); McCulloch v. Maryland, 4 Wheat. 316 (1819).

12. See Hamilton, Madison, and Jay, *The Federalist,* paper no. 1 (Hamilton), p. 1; ibid., paper no. 2 (Jay), p. 8. See also Locke, "Second Treatise,"

398–99; Edward S. Corwin, *The "Higher Law" Background of American Constitutional Law* (1928–29; Ithaca: Cornell University Press, 1955); and John Phillip Reid, *The Concept of Liberty in the Age of the American Revolution* (Chicago: University of Chicago Press, 1988).

13. The historical reception of Locke's and other political theories containing a deontological theory of being, and their integration into a American political practice, is recounted in Bernard Bailyn, *The Ideological Origins of the American Revolution* (Cambridge: Belknap Press of Harvard University Press, 1967), 67–93, 175–98. Gordon Wood, *The Creation of the American Republic* (New York: W. W. Norton, 1969), 259–305, 430–63, 519–92, 593–615; and Hannah Arendt, *On Revolution* (Harmondsworth: Penguin, 1965), 232–81, detail the exclusion of other modes of political thought and action.

14. See Harris, *Interpretable Constitution*, 19–29. See Stephen Macedo, *Liberal Virtues: Citizenship, Virtue, and Community in Liberal Constitutionalism* (Oxford: Clarendon Press, 1990), 78–202, for a theoretical justification for these historical events.

15. Antonin Scalia, "The Limits of the Law," *New Jersey Law Journal* 119, no. 18 (1987): 4, 5, 23. See also the discussion in Larry Kramer, "Judicial Asceticism," *Cardozo Law Review* 12 (1991): 1789–98; Stephen Wizner, "Judging in the Good Society: A Comment on the Jurisprudence of Justice Scalia," ibid., 12 (1991): 1831–43.

16. Antonin Scalia, "The Rule of Law as a Law of Rules," *University of Chicago Law Review* 56 (1989): 1175, 1180.

17. Morrison v. Olson, 487 U.S. 654, 711–12 (1988) (Scalia, J., dissenting).

18. Ibid., 727 (Scalia, J., dissenting). However, Scalia's primary emphasis in this and his other opinions is on separated powers as a rule of law rather than as a source of liberty—a point made in chapter 4, above; and in Price Marshall, "'No Political Truth': The *Federalist* and Justice Scalia on the Separation of Powers," *University of Arkansas at Little Rock Law Journal* 12 (1989): 247. Compare Christopher E. Smith, *Justice Antonin Scalia and the Supreme Court's Conservative Moment* (Westport, Conn.: Praeger, 1993), 41, for a different view.

19. See the discussion of specific opinions in chap. 5, above.

20. Agency Holding Corp. v. Malley-Duff and Assoc., 483 U.S. 143, 157–70 (1987) (Scalia, J., concurring); Pennsylvania v. Union Gas Co., 491 U.S. 1, 29–45 (1989) (Scalia, J., concurring and dissenting).

21. City of Richmond v. J. A. Croson Co., 488 U.S. 469, 520–28 (1989) (Scalia, J., concurring); Adarand Constructors, Inc. v. Pena, 115 S.Ct. 2097, 2118–19 (1995) (Scalia, J., concurring); Johnson v. Transportation Agency, Santa Clara County, 480 U.S. 616, 669–77 (1987) (Scalia, J., dissenting).

22. See the discussion of specific opinions in chap. 6, above.

23. Employment Div., Dept. of Human Resources of Oregon v. Smith, 494

U.S. 872, 874–79 (1990); Barnes v. Glen Theatre, 111 S.Ct. 2456, 2463–68 (1991) (Scalia, J., dissenting).

24. See the discussion of specific opinions in chap. 8, above.

25. Michael H. v. Gerald D., 491 U.S. 110, 127 n. 6 (1989).

26. See the discussion of tradition in chap. 9, above.

27. See chap. 9, above.

28. Hamilton, Madison, and Jay, *The Federalist,* paper no. 10 (Madison), pp. 56–65; Reid, *Concept of Liberty.* See also the discussion of the importance of liberty in American thought in H. N. Hirsch, *A Theory of Liberty: The Constitution and Minorities* (New York: Routledge, 1992), 41–51.

29. Hamilton, Madison, and Jay, *The Federalist,* paper no. 10 (Madison), pp. 56–65.

30. See Robert Weisberg, "Private Violence as Moral Action: The Law as Inspiration and Example," in *Law's Violence,* ed. Austin Sarat and Thomas R. Kearns (Ann Arbor: University of Michigan Press, 1992), 175–210.

31. See the discussion of the specific opinions in chap. 4, above.

32. See, for examples, Employment Div., Dept. of Human Resources of Oregon v. Smith, 494 U.S. 872 (1990); Pacific Mut. Life Ins. Co. v. Haslip, 111 S.Ct. 1032, 1046–54 (1991) (Scalia, J., concurring); Barnes v. Glen Theatre, 111 S.Ct. 2456, 2463–68 (1991) (Scalia, J., dissenting); Planned Parenthood of Southeastern Pennsylvania v. Casey, 112 S.Ct. 2791, 2873–85 (1992) (Scalia, J., concurring and dissenting); TXO Production Corp. v. Alliance Resources Corp., 113 S.Ct. 2711, 2726–28 (1994) (Scalia, J., concurring).

33. Powers v. Ohio, 111 S.Ct. 1364, 1374–82 (1991) (Scalia, J., dissenting). See the discussion of specific opinions in chap. 6, above.

34. See the discussion of specific opinions in chap. 7, above.

35. See the discussion of specific opinions in chap. 7, above.

36. Austin v. Michigan Chamber of Commerce, 494 U.S. 652, 679–85 (1990) (Scalia, J., dissenting).

37. McIntyre v. Ohio Elections Comm'n, 115 S.Ct. 1511, 1530–37 (1995) (Scalia, J., dissenting).

38. See chap. 8, above.

39. Judith N. Shklar, *The Faces of Injustice* (New Haven: Yale University Press, 1990), 16–50.

40. *Discipline* is used to describe control on political space because it implies prescription by rules more strongly than does the term *coercion;* compare Michael A. Weinstein, "Coercion, Space, and the Modes of Human Domination," in *Coercion,* Nomos no. 14, ed. J. Roland Pennock and John W. Chapman (Chicago: Aldine-Atherton, 1972), 65.

41. Hamilton, Madison, and Jay, *The Federalist,* paper no. 10 (Madison), pp. 56–65; paper no. 51, pp. 347–53; paper no. 78 (Hamilton), p. 527. See also the discussion in Arendt, *On Revolution,* 141–281; and Sheldon S.

Wolin, *Politics and Vision: Continuity and Innovation in Western Political Thought* (Boston: Little, Brown, 1960), 388–93.

42. This conception of law is stated in Max Weber, *Economy and Society: An Outline of Interpretive Sociology,* ed. Guenther Roth and Claus Wittich (1924; Berkeley: University of California Press, 1976), 729–31. Weber's definition of discipline is found on 1149. Although he recognized the disciplinary nature of law, he was unwilling to break with a deontological theory of being that valued law as the basis for a reasonable political life; see the commentary in Stephen M. Feldman, "An Interpretation of Max Weber's Theory of Law: Metaphysics, Economics, and the Iron Cage of Constitutional Law," *Law and Social Inquiry* 16 (1991): 205–48. Other critical insights into the disciplinary nature of Western law appear in Friedrich Nietzsche, *On the Genealogy of Morals,* trans. Walter Kaufmann and R. J. Hollingdale (1887; New York: Vintage, 1967), 62–79.

43. Macedo, *Liberal Virtues,* 80–81.

44. Jacques Derrida, "Force of Law: The 'Mystical Foundation of Authority,'" in *Deconstruction and the Possibility of Justice,* ed. Drucilla Cornell, Michel Rosenfield, and David Gary Carlson (New York: Routledge, 1992), 31, 31–35. See Leslie J. Moran, "Violence and the Law: The Case of Sado-Masochism," *Social and Legal Studies* 4 (1995): 234–35, for a list of justifications for the violence of the law.

45. The "economy of violence" in Enlightenment liberal thought stems from the arguments of Niccolò Machiavelli; see Wolin, *Politics and Vision,* 220–24.

46. Scheingold, *Politics of Rights,* 204; Brigham, "Right, Rage, Remedy," 306–16; Timothy J. O'Neill, "The Language of Equality in a Constitutional Order," *American Political Science Review* 75 (1981): 626–35.

47. See Derrida, "Force of Law," 24; Austin Sarat and Thomas R. Kearns, "Introduction," in Sarat and Kearns, *Law's Violence,* 5–6.

48. Carole Smart, *Feminism and the Power of Law* (London: Routledge, 1989), 4.

49. Hamilton, Madison, and Jay, *The Federalist,* paper no. 10 (Madison), p. 57.

50. Hannah Arendt, "On Violence," in *Crises of the Republic* (New York: Harcourt Brace Jovanovich, 1970), 52–56; Walter Benjamin, "Critique of Violence," in *Reflections: Essays, Aphorisms, Autobiographical Writings,* ed. Peter Demetz (1920–21; New York: Schocken, 1978), 277–300.

51. See Kenneth Baynes, "Violence and Communication: The Limits of Philosophical Explanations of Violence," in *Justice, Law, and Violence,* ed. James B. Brady and Newton Garver (Philadelphia: Temple University Press, 1991); Newton Garver, "What Violence Is," *Nation* 207 (1968): 817–22; Jan Naverson, "Force, Violence, and Law," in Brady and Garver, *Justice, Law, and Violence;* John Ladd, "The Idea of Collective Violence," in ibid.; Raymond

Williams, *Keywords: A Vocabulary of Culture and Society* (New York: Oxford University Press, 1976), 278–79.

52. Robert M. Cover, "Violence and the Word," *Yale Law Journal* 95 (1986): esp. 1627. See also Lynne Henderson, "Authoritarianism and the Rule of Law," *Indiana Law Journal* 66 (1991): 383, 403–6; Niklas Luhmann, *A Sociological Theory of the Law*, trans. Elizabeth King and Martin Albrow (1972; London: Routledge and Kegan Paul, 1985), 83–90; Austin Sarat and Thomas R. Kearns, "Making Peace with Violence: Robert Cover on Law and Legal Theory," in Sarat and Kearns, *Law's Violence*, 211–50.

53. Catherine S. Manegold, "Judge Allows Head Shaving of Woman at the Citadel," *New York Times*, 2 Aug. 1994, A10; idem, "Judge Rules Again That the Citadel May Shave First Female Cadet's Head," ibid., 11 Aug. 1994, A8, A14.

54. On the use of violence to "inscribe" authority over bodies, see Anne Norton, *Reflections on Political Identity* (Baltimore: Johns Hopkins University Press, 1988), 182–84. For other examples of the physical violence of law against persons, see Patricia M. Wald, "Violence under the Law: A Judge's Perspective," in Sarat and Kearns, *Law's Violence*, 77–100.

55. Austin Sarat and Thomas R. Kearns, "A Journey through Forgetting: Toward a Jurisprudence of Violence," in *The Fate of Law*, ed. Austin Sarat and Thomas R. Kearns (Ann Arbor: University of Michigan Press, 1991), 221–46; see also Cover, "Violence and the Word," 1629; Henderson, "Authoritarianism and the Rule of Law," 410–34.

56. Sarat and Kearns, "Journey through Forgetting," 264–71; see also Thomas L. Dumm, "Fear of Law," *Studies in Law, Politics, and Society* 10 (1990): 31; Austin Sarat, "Speaking of Death: Narratives of Violence in Capital Trials," in Sarat and Kearns, *Rhetoric of Law*, 135–83.

57. Robert Cover, *Justice Accused: Antislavery and the Judicial Process* (New Haven: Yale University Press, 1975).

58. See Weisberg, "Private Violence," 175–210; and Elizabeth M. Schneider, "The Violence of Privacy," in *The Public Nature of Private Violence: The Discovery of Domestic Abuse*, ed. Martha Albertson Fineman and Roxanne Mykitiuk (New York: Routledge, 1994), 36–58.

59. Luhmann, *Theory of Law*, 86.

60. United States v. Johnson, 481 U.S. 681, 692–703 (1987) (Scalia, J., dissenting); Pacific Mut. Life Ins. Co. v. Haslip, 111 S.Ct. at 1046–54 (Scalia, J., concurring); Barnes v. Glen Theatre, 111 S.Ct. at 2463–68 (Scalia, J., dissenting); TXO Production v. Alliance Resources, 113 S.Ct. at 2726–28 (Scalia, J., concurring).

61. See the discussion of specific opinions in chap. 8, above.

62. Austin v. United States, 113 S.Ct. 2801, 2812–15 (1993) (Scalia, J., concurring); Harmelin v. Michigan, 111 S.Ct. 2680 (1991); Wilson v. Seiter, 111 S.Ct. 2321 (1991).

63. See Cruzan by Cruzan v. Director, Missouri Dept. of Health, 110 S.Ct. 2841, 2859–63 (1990) (Scalia, J., concurring); Planned Parenthood of Southeastern Pennsylvania v. Casey, 112 S.Ct. at 2873–85 (1992) (Scalia, J., concurring and dissenting).

64. Cruzan v. Director, 110 S.Ct. at 2859–63 (Scalia, J., concurring).

65. Steven Lukes, *Power: A Radical View* (London: Macmillan, 1974), 24.

66. See ibid., 48–63; and also Anthony V. Alfieri, "Reconstructive Poverty Law Practice: Learning Lessons of Client Narrative," *Yale Law Journal* 100 (1991): 2125–30.

67. See William Cohen, "Negro Involuntary Servitude in the South, 1865–1940: A Preliminary Analysis," *Journal of Southern History* 42 (1976): 31–60.

68. Harris v. McRae, 448 U.S. 297 (1980).

69. Hoyt v. Florida, 368 U.S. 57 (1961); compare Taylor v. Louisiana, 419 U.S. 522 (1975).

70. United States v. Lee, 455 U.S. 252 (1982). Cultural imperialism is somewhat akin to what Alfieri, "Reconstructive Poverty Law Practice," 2129–30, calls "discipline."

71. Brown v. Board of Educ. of Topeka, 347 U.S. 483 (1954).

72. Bowers v. Hardwick, 478 U.S. 186 (1986).

73. Lujan v. National Wildlife Fed'n, 497 U.S. 871 (1990); Lujan v. Defenders of Wildlife, 112 S.Ct. 2130 (1992).

74. See the discussion of specific opinions in chap. 4, above.

75. See the discussion of the specific opinions in chap. 6 above.

76. See the discussion of the specific opinions in chap. 6 above.

77. See the discussion of specific opinions in chap. 7, above.

78. R.A.V. v. City of St. Paul, Minnesota, 112 S.Ct. 2538 (1992); Church of the Lukumi Babalu Aye v. City of Hialeah, 113 S.Ct. 2217, 2239–40 (1993) (Scalia, J., concurring).

79. Madsen v. Women's Health Ctr., Inc., 114 S.Ct. 2516, 2534–52 (1994) (Scalia, J., concurring and dissenting).

80. See the discussion of specific opinions in chap. 7, above.

81. Austin v. Michigan Chamber of Commerce, 494 U.S. at 679–85 (1990) (Scalia, J., dissenting).

82. California v. Hodari D., 111 S.Ct. 1547 (1991); Minnick v. Mississippi, 111 S.Ct. 486, 492–96 (1990) (Scalia, J., dissenting); McNeil v. Wisconsin, 111 S.Ct. 2204 (1991); Grady v. Corbin, 495 U.S. 508, 528–29 (1990) (Scalia, J., dissenting).

83. Michael H. v. Gerald D., 110 S.Ct. at 2335–46.

84. Reno v. Flores, 113 S.Ct. 1439 (1993).

85. Pierre Bourdieu, *Outline of a Theory of Practice*, trans. Richard Nice (Cambridge: Cambridge University Press, 1977), 83–197, 237n. 47; idem, *The Logic of Practice*, trans. Richard Nice (Stanford: Stanford University Press, 1990), 122–34; idem, *Language and Symbolic Power*, ed. John B.

Thompson, trans. Gino Raymond and Matthew Adamson (Cambridge: Harvard University Press, 1991), 50–52; Pierre Bourdieu and Jean-Claude Passeron, *Reproduction in Education, Society, and Culture,* trans. Richard Nice (Beverly Hills: Sage Publications, 1977), 3–11; Pierre Bourdieu and Loïc Wacquant, *An Invitation to Reflexive Sociology* (Chicago: University of Chicago Press, 1992), 167–68; Rosemary J. Coombe, "Room for Manoeuver: Toward a Theory of Practice in Critical Legal Studies," *Law and Social Inquiry* 14 (1989): 100–103; and John B. Thompson, *Studies in the Theory of Ideology* (Berkeley: University of California Press, 1984), 42–72.

86. See Iris Marion Young, *Justice and the Politics of Difference* (Princeton: Princeton University Press, 1990), 96–121.

87. Alexis de Tocqueville, *Democracy in America,* 2 vols., trans. Phillips Bradley (1835–40; New York: Vintage, 1945), 2:334–39.

88. See Roger Boesche, *The Strange Liberalism of Alexis de Tocqueville* (Ithaca: Cornell University Press, 1987), 229–59; Thomas L. Dumm, *Democracy and Punishment: Disciplinary Origins of the United States* (Madison: University of Wisconsin Press, 1987), 128–40; and Judith N. Shklar, *Legalism: Law, Morals, and Political Trials* (Cambridge: Harvard University Press, 1964), 1.

89. This point is made by the psychological literature on procedural justice; see Tom R. Tyler, *Why People Obey the Law* (New Haven: Yale University Press, 1990).

90. Karen Orren, *Belated Feudalism: Labor, the Law, and Liberal Development in the United States* (Cambridge: Cambridge University Press, 1991).

91. Bumiller, *Civil Rights Society,* 109.

92. See Bourdieu and Wacquant, *Reflexive Sociology,* 169–74.

93. Equal Employment Opportunity Comm'n v. Arabian Am. Oil Co., 111 S.Ct. 1227, 1236–37 (1991) (Scalia, J., concurring).

94. Minnesota v. Dickerson, 113 S.Ct. 2130, 2139–41 (1993) (Scalia, J., concurring); Arizona v. Hicks, 480 U.S. 321 (1987). See also the discussion of specific opinions in chap. 8, above.

95. Pacific Mut. Life Ins. Co. v. Haslip, 111 S.Ct. at 1046–54 (Scalia, J., concurring); TXO Production v. Alliance Resources, 113 S.Ct. at 2726–28 (Scalia, J., concurring).

96. The term *subjection* is from Maurice Blanchot, "Michel Foucault as I Imagine Him," in *Foucault/Blanchot,* trans. Jeffrey Melman (New York: Zone, 1987), 83–88.

97. Michel Foucault, *The History of Sexuality,* vol. 1, *An Introduction,* trans. Robert Hurley (New York: Vintage, 1980), 94.

98. For interpretations of power and subjection in Foucault's work, see Anne Barron, "Legal Discourse and the Colonisation of the Self in the Modern State," in *Post-Modern Law: Enlightenment, Revolution, and the Death of Man,* ed. Andrew Carty (Edinburgh: Edinburgh University Press, 1990), 114–20; Gilles Deleuze, *Foucault,* trans. and ed. Seán Hand (Minneapolis: Univer-

sity of Minnesota Press, 1988), 29, 71; Peter Dews, *Logics of Disintegration: Post-Structuralist Thought and the Claims of Critical Theory* (London: Verso, 1987), 144–99; Nancy Fraser, *Unruly Practices: Power, Discourse, and Gender in Contemporary Social Theory* (Minneapolis: University of Minnesota Press, 1989), 17–33; David Couzens Hoy, "Power, Repression, and Progress: Foucault, Lukes, and the Frankfurt School," in *Foucault: A Critical Reader,* ed. David Couzens Hoy (Oxford: Basil Blackwell, 1986); Hunt, *Explorations in Law and Society,* 267–300; Alan Hunt and Gary Wickham, *Foucault and Law: Towards a Sociology of Governance* (London: Pluto Press, 1994); Jerry Palmer and Frank Pearce, "Legal Discourse and State Power: Foucault and the Juridical Relation," *International Journal of the Sociology of Law* 11 (1983): 361–83; Joseph Rouse, "Power/Knowledge," in *The Cambridge Companion to Foucault,* ed. Gary Gutting (Cambridge: Cambridge University Press, 1994), 92–114; Jonathan Simon, "'In Another Kind of Wood': Michel Foucault and Sociolegal Studies," *Law and Social Inquiry* 17 (1992): 49–56; Barry Smart, *Foucault, Marxism, and Critique* (London: Routledge and Kegan Paul, 1983), 73–122; and idem, *Michel Foucault* (Chichester: Ellis Horwood, 1985), 75–107.

99. Michel Foucault, *Power/Knowledge: Selected Interviews and Other Writings, 1972–1977,* ed. Colin Gordon (New York: Pantheon, 1980), 1; see also Foucault, *History of Sexuality* 1:144.

100. Michel Foucault, "Maurice Blanchot: The Thought from Outside," in *Foucault/Blanchot,* trans. Brian Massumi (New York: Zone, 1987), 33–40.

101. For the argument that Foucault tries to "expel" law from modernity because he describes a reduced use of the law when disputes are "normalized" by other institutions or by persons' acceptance of the limits of their power and rights, and for a criticism of Foucault on this point, see Hunt, *Explorations in Law and Society,* 267–300; and Hunt and Wickham, *Foucault and Law,* 55–71. For other readings, see Deleuze, *Foucault,* 29–30; Dumm, "Fear of Law," 34–42; and Simon, "'In Another Kind of Wood,'" 49–56.

102. Palmer and Pearce, "Legal Discourse and State Power," 377.

103. Hunt and Wickham, *Foucault and Law,* 21.

104. DeShaney v. Winnebago County Social Servs. Dept., 489 U.S. 189 (1989).

105. Cruzan v. Director, 110 S.Ct. at 2841. The state also could impose a course of treatment, an act of repression.

106. See Patricia J. Williams, *The Alchemy of Race and Rights* (Cambridge: Harvard University Press, 1991), 3–51.

107. For a discussion of definitions of social injury, see Adrian Howe, "'Social Injury' Revisited: Towards a Feminist Theory of Social Justice," *International Journal of the Sociology of Law* 15 (1986): 423–38.

108. John Brigham, "Constitutional Property: The Double Standard and Beyond," in *Judging in the Constitution: Critical Essays on Judicial Lawmaking,*

ed. Michael W. McCann and Gerald L. Houseman (Glenview, Ill.: Scott, Foresman, 1989), 187–201.

109. See the discussion of specific opinions in chap. 9, above.

110. Thus, his law serves the two ends indicated in Scheingold, *Politics of Rights,* 204.

CHAPTER ELEVEN: THE ARTIFICE OF SCALIA'S POLITICAL MESSAGE

1. Antonin Scalia, "The Rule of Law as a Law of Rules," *University of Chicago Law Review* 56 (1989): 1179.

2. This is a criticism also made of Reasoned Elaboration and other process theories more generally in H. N. Hirsch, *A Theory of Liberty: The Constitution and Minorities* (New York: Routledge, 1992), 115–93; and Laurence Tribe, *Constitutional Choices* (Cambridge: Harvard University Press, 1985), 9–20.

3. See Sotorios A. Barber, *The Constitution of Judicial Power* (Baltimore: Johns Hopkins University Press, 1993), 1–178; Richard A. Brisbin Jr., "Conservative Jurisprudence in the Reagan Era," *Cumberland Law Review* 19 (1988–89): 504–28; Stephen Macedo, *The New Right v. the Constitution,* rev. ed. (Washington, D.C.: Cato Institute, 1987); and the classification scheme in William F. Harris II, *The Interpretable Constitution* (Baltimore: Johns Hopkins University Press, 1993), 144–58.

4. Compare Mary Ann Glendon, *Rights Talk: The Impoverishment of Political Discourse* (New York: Free Press, 1991).

5. John T. Noonan Jr., "The Root and Branch of Roe v. Wade," *Nebraska Law Review* 63 (1984): 668–79, effectively summarizes the principles of his voluminous publications.

6. Moral theories include Hadley Arkes, *Beyond the Constitution* (Princeton: Princeton University Press, 1990); Walter Berns, *Freedom, Virtue, and the First Amendment* (Baton Rouge: Louisiana State University Press, 1957); idem, *The First Amendment and the Future of American Democracy* (New York: Basic, 1976); Michael W. McConnell, "The Role of Democratic Politics in Transforming Moral Conviction into Law," *Yale Law Journal* 98 (1989): 1501–43; and idem, "On Reading the Constitution," *Cornell Law Review* 73 (1989): 359–63. The moral theories influenced by religion include Richard J. Neuhaus, "The Moral Delegitimization of Law," *Notre Dame Journal of Law, Ethics and Public Policy* 4 (1989): 51–61; Michael J. Perry, *The Constitution, the Courts, and Human Rights: An Inquiry into the Legitimacy of Policymaking by the Judiciary* (New Haven: Yale University Press, 1982); modified in idem, *Morality, Politics, and Law: A Bicentennial Essay* (New York: Oxford University Press, 1988); idem, *The Constitution and the Courts: Law or Politics?* (New York: Oxford University Press, 1994); and, from a different Christian perspective, H. Jefferson Powell, *The Moral Tradition of American Constitutionalism: A Theological Interpretation* (Durham: Duke University Press, 1993).

7. See, for an overview, Daniel A. Farber and Philip P. Frickey, *Law and Public Choice: A Critical Introduction* (Chicago: University of Chicago Press, 1991), 38–87, 144–53. Sources of this discourse include Richard A. Posner, *The Economics of Justice* (Cambridge: Harvard University Press, 1981), 48–115; idem, *Economic Analysis of Law*, 4th ed. (Boston: Little, Brown, 1992); Frank H. Easterbrook, "Criminal Procedure as a Market System," *Journal of Legal Studies* 12 (1983): 289–332; and idem, "Ways of Criticizing the Court," *Harvard Law Review* 95 (1981): 802–32. Compare Scalia's position in Antonin Scalia, "Morality, Pragmatism, and the Legal Order," *Harvard Journal of Law and Public Policy* 9 (1986): 123–27; idem, "Economic Affairs as Human Affairs," *Cato Journal* 4 (1985): 706. Scalia's one use of economic analysis is in an antitrust opinion, Business Electronic Corp. v. Sharp Electronics Corp., 485 U.S. 717 (1988).

8. Edwin Meese III, "Our Constitution's Design," *Marquette Law Review* 70 (1987): 381–88; idem, "The Attorney General's View of the Supreme Court," *Public Administration Review* 45 (1985): 701; idem, "The Supreme Court of the United States," *South Texas Law Review* 27 (1986): 455; idem, "The Law of the Constitution," *Tulane Law Review* 61 (1987): 979–90.

9. Antonin Scalia, "Originalism: The Lesser Evil," *University of Cincinnati Law Review* 57 (1989): 854–63; compare Robert H. Bork, *The Tempting of America: The Political Seduction of the Law* (New York: Free Press, 1990), 161–67. Bork's constitutional theory is never directly defined. Instead, he engages in criticism of others to define his jurisprudential ideas.

10. Scalia, "Originalism," 861–62; compare Bork, *Tempting of America*, 155–59.

11. Scalia, "Originalism," 862; compare Robert H. Bork, *Tradition and Morality in Constitutional Law*, Francis Boyer Lectures on Public Policy (Washington, D.C.: American Enterprise Institute for Public Policy Research, 1984), 2–6.

12. Bork, *Tradition and Morality*, 6–11; idem, *Tempting of America*, 241–65. This position clearly puts Bork at odds with Reasoned Elaboration theorists such as Wechsler and Bickel; see Bork, *Tempting of America*, 143–46, 187–93.

13. Scalia, "Originalism," 864. See also Eric J. Segall, "Justice Scalia, Critical Legal Studies, and the Rule of Law," *George Washington Law Review* 62 (1994): 1002–4.

14. Anthony T. Kronman, "Precedent and Tradition," *Yale Law Journal* 99 (1990): 1029–68. See also the commentary in David Luban, *Legal Modernism* (Ann Arbor: University of Michigan Press, 1994), 93–123.

15. John Hart Ely, *Democracy and Distrust: A Theory of Judicial Review* (Cambridge: Harvard University Press, 1980), 76.

16. A point stressed in Toby Golick, "Justice Scalia, Poverty, and the Good Society," *Cardozo Law Review* 12 (1991): 1817–30. On the influence of the

image of law as a machine, see James Boyd White, "Imagining the Law," in *The Rhetoric of Law*, ed. Austin Sarat and Thomas R. Kearns (Ann Arbor: University of Michigan Press, 1994), 32–34.

17. The definition of the politics and law of modernity draws on Max Weber, *Economy and Society: An Outline of Interpretive Sociology*, ed. Guenther Roth and Claus Wittich (1923; Berkeley: University of California Press, 1978), 809–900; Zygmunt Bauman, *Modernity and the Holocaust* (Ithaca: Cornell University Press, 1989); Marshall Berman, *All That Is Solid Melts into Air: The Experience of Modernity* (New York: Simon and Schuster, 1982); Hans Blumenberg, *The Legitimacy of the Modern Age*, trans. Robert M. Wallace (Cambridge: MIT Press, 1983); William E. Connolly, *Political Theory and Modernity* (Oxford: Basil Blackwell, 1988), 1–15; Peter Fitzpatrick, *The Mythology of Modern Law* (London: Routledge, 1992), 44–145; Luban, *Legal Modernism* (Luban overemphasizes the role of the avant garde in modernity); Stephen Toulmin, *Cosmopolis: The Hidden Agenda of Modernity* (New York: Free Press, 1990), 109–17; Roberto M. Unger, *Law in Modern Society* (New York: Free Press, 1976); Robin West, "Jurisprudence as Narrative," in *Narrative, Authority and the Law* (Ann Arbor: University of Michigan Press, 1993), 345–418; and Sheldon S. Wolin, *Politics and Vision: Continuity and Innovation in Western Political Thought* (Boston: Little, Brown, 1960), 352–434.

18. See Albert O. Hirschman, *The Passions and the Interests: Political Arguments for Capitalism before Its Triumph* (Princeton: Princeton University Press, 1977). The best example of the American effort to control political passion is made in Alexander Hamilton, James Madison, and John Jay, *The Federalist*, ed. Jacob E. Cooke (1787–88; Middletown, Conn.: Wesleyan University Press, 1961), paper no. 10 (Madison), pp. 56–65.

19. Wolin, *Politics and Vision*, 352–434.

20. Blumenberg, *Legitimacy of the Modern Age*, 53.

21. Edward S. Corwin, *The "Higher Law" Background of American Constitutional Law* (1928–29; Ithaca: Cornell University Press, 1955).

22. The linkage of pragmatism to postmodernity is made by Richard Rorty; see his *Philosophy and the Mirror of Nature* (Princeton: Princeton University Press, 1979); and idem, "The Banality of Pragmatism and the Poetry of Justice," in *Pragmatism in Law and Society*, ed. Michael Brint and William Weaver (Boulder: Westview Press, 1991), 89–97. See also the commentary in Lynn D. Baker, " 'Just Do It': Pragmatism and Progressive Social Change," in ibid., 99–119; Cornel West, "The Limits of Pragmatism," in ibid., 121–26; Ronald Dworkin," Pragmatism, Right Answers, and True Banality," in ibid., 359–88; and Luban, *Legal Modernism*, 125–78. In J. M. Balkin, "What Is Postmodern Constitutionalism?" *Michigan Law Review* 90 (1992): 1966–90, the concept of the postmodern is cogently discussed, as are the effects of postmodern culture on law; however, the author does not define postmodern legal discourse.

23. Cruzan by Cruzan v. Director, Missouri Dept. of Health, 110 S.Ct. 2841, 2863 (1990).

24. This section draws on ideas presented in Pierre Bourdieu and Jean-Claude Passeron, *Reproduction in Education, Society, and Culture,* trans. Richard Nice (London: Sage Publications, 1977, 1990).

25. Critical legal studies offer another challenge to Scalia's reproduction of legal rationality. Like pragmatic liberals, critical scholars refuse to regard law as a set of theoretically determinant neutral rules resting on popular or moral values. However, they doubt that law can be redesigned to serve aspirations for greater human dignity, equality, or liberty. Rather, they consider law to be an expression of the coercive aspirations of capital, males, or officials of a relatively autonomous state. They argue that faith in law and rights locks persons into debates about political procedures and rules and represses some political claims questioning the real nature of political power. By limiting political imagination and criticism, faith in law and rights has reinforced the hegemonic domination of state officials and capitalists. Also, critical scholars have claimed that law lacks the capacity to transform the repressive conditions in human existence. Indeed, some critical scholars have claimed that rights and other constitutional rules are barriers to the construction of a better regime. Despite their complaints about law, critical legal scholars have offered only a "deconstruction," "destabilization," or "trashing" of law as a way out of the hegemonic domination by state, class, and race embedded in law. In their iconoclastic assault on the theoretical certainty of law, critical scholars have not specified an alternative mode of constitutive discourse, a new vision of the regime, or a clear set of aspirations for the future of American politics. See the criticism in Luban, *Legal Modernism,* 51–92; and the arguments in Alan Freeman, "Legitimatizing Racial Discrimination through Antidiscrimination Law: A Critical Review of Supreme Court Doctrine," in *Critical Legal Studies,* ed. Allan C. Hutchinson (Totowa, N.J.: Rowan and Littlefield, 1989), 120–36; Peter Gabel and Duncan Kennedy, "Roll Over Beethoven," *Stanford Law Review* 36 (1984): 33–34; Peter Gabel, "The Phenomenology of Rights-Consciousness and the Pact of the Withdrawn Selves," *Texas Law Review* 62 (1984): 1586–99; the studies in David Kairys, ed., *The Politics of Law: A Progressive Critique,* rev. ed. (New York: Pantheon, 1990); Mark Kelman, *A Guide to Critical Legal Studies* (Cambridge: Harvard University Press, 1987), 1–14, 300–302; Gary Minda, *Postmodern Legal Movements: Law and Jurisprudence at Century's End* (New York: New York University Press, 1995), 106–27; Mark Tushnet, "An Essay on Rights," *Texas Law Review* 62 (1984): 1363–94; idem, "Critical Legal Studies: An Introduction to its Origins and Underpinnings," *Journal of Legal Education* 36 (1986): 504–17; and Roberto M. Unger, *The Critical Legal Studies Movement* (Cambridge: Harvard University Press, 1986), 15–90.

26. See Peter Goodrich, *Languages of Law: From Logics of Memory to Nomadic Masks* (London: Weidenfield and Nicolson, 1990), 283–88.

27. Patricia J. Williams, *The Alchemy of Race and Rights* (Cambridge: Harvard University Press, 1991), 49.

28. On the underinclusive and overinclusive nature of legal rules, and the suboptimal nature of law, see Frederick Schauer, *Playing by the Rules: A Philosophical Examination of Rule-Based Decision-Making in Law and Life* (Oxford: Clarendon Press, 1991), 31–37, 135–66. See also Michael W. McCann, "Equal Protection for Social Inequality: Race and Class in Constitutional Ideology," in *Judging the Constitution: Critical Essays on Judicial Lawmaking,* ed. Michael W. McCann and Gerald L. Houseman (Glenview, Ill.: Scott, Foresman, 1989), 231–64.

29. I have excluded the ontology of modern communitarianism or civic republicanism from the following discussion because, although it argues for an ontological revolution in a society, its proponents offer few suggestions—other than spontaneous generation—to explain how such a massive change in the public's normative political commitments might transpire. Thus, their abstract arguments have little to offer critics of the legalist constitutive narrative. For an introduction to communitarian and civic republican narratives, see Glendon, *Rights Talk*; Joel F. Handler, *Law and the Search for Community* (Philadelphia: University of Pennsylvania Press, 1990), 83–106; Suzanna Sherry, "Civic Virtue and the Feminine Voice in Constitutional Adjudication," *Virginia Law Review* 72 (1986): 543–616; and Mark Tushnet, *Red, White, and Blue: A Critical Analysis of Constitutional Law* (Cambridge: Harvard University Press, 1988).

30. Mary Jo Frug, *Postmodern Legal Feminism* (New York: Routledge, 1992), 122–45. For a description of difference in comparison to other feminist jurisprudential theories, see Gayle Binion, "Toward a Feminist Regrounding of Constitutional Law," *Social Science Quarterly* 72 (1991): 207–20; Patricia A. Cain, "Feminist Jurisprudence: Grounding the Theories," *Berkeley Women's Law Journal* 4 (1989): 199–214; Leslie Friedman Goldstein, "Can This Marriage Be Saved? Feminist Public Policy and Feminist Jurisprudence," in *Feminist Jurisprudence: The Difference Debate* (Lanham, Md.: Rowan and Littlefield, 1992), 11–40; Minda, *Postmodern Legal Movements,* 128–48; and Robin West, "Jurisprudence and Gender," *University of Chicago Law Review* 55 (1988): 1–72.

31. See Zillah R. Eisenstein, *The Female Body and the Law* (Berkeley: University of California Press, 1988).

32. See West, "Jurisprudence and Gender." See also Patricia A. Cain, "Feminism and the Limits of Equality," *Georgia Law Review* 24 (summer 1990): 803–47.

33. Martha Minow, *Making All the Difference: Inclusion, Exclusion, and American Law* (Ithaca: Cornell University Press, 1990), 15, 53–74, 112–14,

213, 215, 217, 306–11, 371–90. See the criticism in Katherine T. Bartlett, "Minow's Social-Relations Approach to Difference: Unanswering the Unasked," *Law and Social Inquiry* 17 (1992): 437–70. Iris Marion Young has drawn upon Minow's social relations strategy to describe several organizational changes in politics which could "provide mechanisms for the effective recognition and representation of the distinct voices and perspectives of those constituent groups that are oppressed or disadvantaged." See Young, *Justice and the Politics of Difference* (Princeton: Princeton University Press, 1990), 171, 184–91, 226–56.

34. Hans-Georg Gadamer, *Truth and Method*, 2d ed. rev., trans. Joel Weinsheimer and Donald G. Marshall (1986; New York: Crossroad, 1989), 265–71, 438–91. See also Gianni Vattimo, "Truth and Rhetoric in Hermeneutic Ontology," in *The End of Modernity: Nihilism and Hermeneutics in Postmodern Culture*, trans. Jon R. Snyder (1985; Baltimore: Johns Hopkins University Press, 1988), 130–44; Costas Douzinas and Ronnie Warrington with Shaun McVeigh, *Postmodern Jurisprudence: The Law of Text in the Texts of Law* (London: Routledge, 1991), 29–51.

35. Carol Smart, *Feminism and the Power of Law* (London: Routledge, 1989), 138. See also Mark Kessler, "Legal Discourse and Political Intolerance: The Ideology of Clear and Present Danger," *Law and Society Review* 27 (1993): 562–68.

36. Michel Foucault, "Politics and Reason," in *Politics, Philosophy, Culture: Interviews and Other Writings, 1977–1984*, ed. Leonard D. Kritzman (New York: Routledge, 1988), 57–85.

37. The tendency of Enlightenment liberal theories of law to regard rights and equality as things or objects, to "commodify" them, is specified in Valerie Kerruish, *Jurisprudence as Ideology* (London: Routledge, 1991), 139–65; on exploitation of law, see 181.

38. Seyla Benhabib, "Liberal Dialogue versus a Critical Theory of Discursive Legitimation," in *Liberalism and the Moral Life*, ed. Nancy L. Rosenblum (Cambridge: Harvard University Press, 1989), 154. See also Kimberlé Williams Crenshaw, "Demarginalizing the Intersection of Race and Sex: A Black Feminist Critique of Antidiscrimination Doctrine, Feminist Theory, and Antiracist Politics," *University of Chicago Law Forum* (1989): 139–67.

39. On the antipathy of American constitutional practice to passion see Alexander Hamilton, James Madison, and John Jay, *The Federalist*, ed. Jacob E. Cooke (1787–88; Middletown, Conn.: Wesleyan University Press, 1961), paper no. 10 (Madison), pp. 56–65; Hirschman, *Passions and Interests*, 20–62.

40. The use of passion thus differentiates the approach of the external critic from the deliberative discussion, especially by legal professionals, favored in Cass R. Sunstein, *The Partial Constitution* (Cambridge: Harvard University Press, 1993).

41. See William Connolly, *Politics and Ambiguity* (Madison: University of Wisconsin Press, 1987), 14–16, 46–51; Peter Goodrich, *Legal Discourse: Studies in Linguistics, Rhetoric, and Legal Analysis* (New York: St. Martin's Press, 1987), 211; and Boaventura de Sousa Santos, "The Postmodern Transition: Law and Politics," in *The Fate of the Law*, ed. Austin Sarat and Thomas R. Kearns (Ann Arbor: University of Michigan Press, 1991), 105–11, for the sources of this statement. The statement rests on the philosophical argument for ontological relativity defended in W. V. Quine, *Ontological Relativity and Other Essays* (New York: Columbia University Press, 1969), 26–83.

42. John Rawls, *Political Liberalism* (New York: Columbia University Press, 1993), 77. See also the discussion in Stephen Macedo, *Liberal Virtues: Citizenship, Virtue, and Community in Liberal Constitutionalism* (Oxford: Clarendon Press, 1990), esp. 220–21, where the author argues that liberty or personal autonomy is bounded by choices made through public deliberation, especially within the institutions of the law.

43. Cornelius Castoriadis, "Power, Politics, Autonomy," in *Cultural-Political Interventions in the Unfinished Project of Enlightenment*, ed. Axel Honneth, Thomas McCarthy, and Albrecht Wellmer (Cambridge: MIT Press, 1992), 288.

44. These statements are influenced by Emmanuel Levinas, *Otherwise than Being or Beyond Essence*, 2d ed., trans. Alphonso Lingis (1970; Dordrecht: Kluwer Academic, 1991).

45. Jennifer Nedelsky, "Law, Boundaries, and the Bounded Self," in *Law and the Order of Culture*, ed. Robert Post (Berkeley: University of California Press, 1991), 183.

46. Rodney King, quoted in "Rodney King Speaks Out: 'Can We All Get Along?'" *New York Times*, 2 May 1992, A6.

47. Antonin Scalia, "The Limits of the Law," *New Jersey Law Journal* 119, no. 8 (1987): 23.

Bibliography of the Publications of Antonin Scalia to 1 November 1995

OPINIONS FOR THE U.S. SUPREME COURT OR A PLURALITY OF THE JUSTICES

American Dredging Co. v. Miller, 114 S.Ct. 981 (1994).

Anderson v. Creighton, 483 U.S. 635 (1987).

Arcadia, Ohio v. Ohio Power Co., 498 U.S. 73 (1990).

Arizona v. Hicks, 480 U.S. 321 (1987).

Asahi Metal Industry Co. v. Superior Court of California, Solano County, 480 U.S. 102 (1987).

Asgrow Seed Co. v. Winterboer, 115 S.Ct. 788 (1995).

BFP v. Resolution Trust Corp., 114 S.Ct. 1757 (1994).

Blatchford v. Native Village of Noatak and Circle Village, 501 U.S. 775 (1991).

Board of Trustees of State University of New York v. Fox, 492 U.S. 469 (1989).

Boyle v. United Technologies Corp., 487 U.S. 500 (1988).

Bray v. Alexandria Women's Health Clinic, 113 S.Ct. 753 (1993).

Braxton v. United States, 500 U.S. 344 (1991).

Brower v. County of Inyo, 489 U.S. 593 (1989).

Budinich v. Becton Dickinson and Co., 486 U.S. 196 (1988).

Burnham v. Superior Court of California, County of Marin, 495 U.S. 604 (1990).

Business Electronics Corp. v. Sharp Electronics Corp., 485 U.S. 717 (1988).

California v. Hodari D., 499 U.S. 621 (1991).

Capitol Square Review and Advisory Board v. Pinette, 115 S.Ct. 2440 (1995).

Carden v. Arkoma Associates, 494 U.S. 185 (1990).

Castille v. Peoples, 489 U.S. 346 (1989).

Chan v. Korean Air Lines, 490 U.S. 122 (1989).

City of Burlington v. Dague, 112 S.Ct. 2638 (1992).

City of Columbia v. Omni Outdoor Advertising, Inc., 499 U.S. 365 (1991).

City of Chicago v. Environmental Defense Fund, 114 S.Ct. 1588 (1994).

Commissioner of Internal Revenue v. Bollinger, 485 U.S. 340 (1988).

County of Yakima v. Confederated Tribes and Bands of Yakima Indian Nation, 112 S.Ct. 683 (1992).

Coy v. Iowa, 487 U.S. 1012 (1988).

Cruz v. New York, 481 U.S. 186 (1987).

Deal v. United States, 113 S.Ct. 1993 (1993).

Department of Treasury, Internal Revenue Service v. Federal Labor Relations Authority, 494 U.S. 922 (1990).

Director, Office of Workers' Compensation Programs v. Newport News Shipbuilding and Dry Dock Co., 115 S.Ct. 1278 (1995).

Eli Lilly and Co. v. Medtronic, Inc., 496 U.S. 661 (1990).

Employment Division, Department of Human Resources of Oregon v. Smith, 494 U.S. 872 (1990).

Fex v. Michigan, 113 S.Ct. 1085 (1993).

Finley v. United States, 490 U.S. 545 (1989).

Fort Stewart Schools v. Federal Labor Relations Authority, 495 U.S. 641 (1990).

Griffin v. United States, 112 S.Ct. 466 (1991).

Griffin v. Wisconsin, 483 U.S. 868 (1987).

Growe v. Emison, 113 S.Ct. 1075 (1993).

Harmelin v. Michigan, 501 U.S. 957 (1991).

Heck v. Humphrey, 114 S.Ct. 2364 (1994).

Hewitt v. Helms, 482 U.S. 755 (1987).

Hitchcock v. Dugger, 481 U.S. 393 (1987).

Holland v. Illinois, 493 U.S. 474 (1990).

Illinois v. Rodriguez, 497 U.S. 177 (1990).

Immigration and Naturalization Service v. Elias-Zacarias, 112 S.Ct. 812 (1992).

Immigration and Naturalization Service v. Pangilinan, 486 U.S. 875 (1988).

Independent Federation of Flight Attendants v. Zipes, 491 U.S. 754 (1989).

Interstate Commerce Commission v. Brotherhood of Locomotive Engineers, 482 U.S. 270 (1987).

Kokkonen v. Guardian Life Insurance Co., 114 S.Ct. 1673 (1994).

Kungys v. United States, 485 U.S. 759 (1988).

Langley v. Federal Deposit Insurance Corp., 484 U.S. 86 (1987).

Lebron v. National Railroad Passenger Corp., 115 S.Ct. 961 (1995).

Lewis v. Continental Bank Corporation, 494 U.S. 472 (1990).

Liteky v. United States, 114 S.Ct. 1147 (1994).

Local 144 Nursing Home Pension Fund v. Demisay, 113 S.Ct. 2252 (1993).

Lorance v. AT and T Technologies, Inc., 490 U.S. 900 (1989).

Lucas v. South Carolina Coastal Council, 112 S.Ct. 2886 (1992).

Lujan v. Defenders of Wildlife, 112 S.Ct. 2130 (1992).

Lujan v. National Wildlife Federation, 497 U.S. 871 (1990).

Lukhard v. Reed, 481 U.S. 368 (1987).

MCI Telecommunications v. American Telephone and Telegraph Co., 114 S.Ct. 2223 (1994).

McNeil v. Wisconsin, 501 U.S. 171 (1991).

Mertens v. Hewitt Associates, 113 S.Ct. 2063 (1993).

Michael H. v. Gerald D., 491 U.S. 110 (1989).

Midland Asphalt Corp. v. United States, 489 U.S. 794 (1989).

Morales v. Trans World Airlines, 112 S.Ct. 2031 (1992).

Murray v. United States, 487 U.S. 533 (1988).

New Energy Co. of Indiana v. Limbach, 486 U.S. 269 (1988).

New Orleans Public Service, Inc. v. Council of City of New Orleans, 491 U.S. 350 (1989).

Nollan v. California Coastal Commission, 483 U.S. 825 (1987).

O'Connor v. United States, 479 U.S. 27 (1986).

O'Melveny v. Myers, 114 S.Ct. 2048 (1994).

Owen v. Owen, 500 U.S. 305 (1991).

Pavelic and LeFlore v. Marvel Entertainment Group, 493 U.S. 120 (1989).

Pennsylvania v. Delaware Valley Citizens' Council for Clean Air, 483 U.S. 711 (1987).

Pierce v. Underwood, 487 U.S. 552 (1988).

Pittston Coal Group v. Sebben, 488 U.S. 105 (1988).

Plaut v. Spendthrift Farm, Inc., 115 S.Ct. 1447 (1995).

Puerto Rico Department of Consumer Affairs v. Isla Petroleum Corp., 485 U.S. 495 (1988).

R.A.V. v. City of St. Paul, Minnesota, 112 S.Ct. 2538 (1992).

Reiter v. Cooper, 113 S.Ct. 1213 (1993).

Reno v. Flores, 113 S.Ct. 1439 (1993).

Republic of Argentina v. Weltover, Inc., 112 S.Ct. 2160 (1992).

Richardson v. Marsh, 481 U.S. 200 (1987).

St. Mary's Honor Center v. Hicks, 113 S.Ct. 2742 (1993).

Shalala v. Schaefer, 113 S.Ct. 2625 (1993).

Stanford v. Kentucky, 492 U.S. 361 (1989).

Sullivan v. Everhart, 494 U.S. 83 (1990).

Sullivan v. Louisiana, 113 S.Ct. 2078 (1993).

Sun Oil Co. v. Wortman, 486 U.S. 717 (1988).

Town of Newton v. Rumery, 480 U.S. 386 (1987).

Tuilaepa v. California, 114 S.Ct. 2630 (1994).

United Savings Association of Texas v. Timbers of Inwood Forest Associates, 484 U.S. 365 (1988).

United States By and Through Internal Revenue Service v. McDermott, 113 S.Ct. 1526 (1993).

United States v. Dixon, 113 S.Ct. 2849 (1993).

United States v. Fausto, 484 U.S. 439 (1988).

United States v. Gaudin, 115 S.Ct. 2310 (1995).

United States v. Nordic Village, Inc., 112 S.Ct. 1011 (1992).

United States v. Owens, 484 U.S. 554 (1988).

United States v. Stanley, 483 U.S. 669 (1987).

United States v. Williams, 112 S.Ct. 1735 (1992).

United States Bancorp Mortgage Co. v. Bonner Mall Partnership, 115 S.Ct. 386 (1994).

United States Department of Labor v. Triplett, 494 U.S. 715 (1990).

Vernonia School District 47J v. Acton, 115 S.Ct. 2386 (1995).

West Virginia University Hospitals v. Casey, 499 U.S. 83 (1991).

Wilson v. Seiter, 501 U.S. 294 (1991).

Wisconsin Department of Revenue v. William Wrigley Jr. Co., 112 S.Ct. 2447 (1992).

W. S. Kirkpatrick and Co. v. Environmental Tectonics Corp., Int'l, 493 U.S. 400 (1990).

Ylst v. Nunnemaker, 501 U.S. 797 (1991).

CONCURRING OPINIONS IN THE U.S. SUPREME COURT

ABF Freight System, Inc. v. National Labor Relations Board, 114 S.Ct. 835 (1994).

Adarand Constructors, Inc. v. Pena, 115 S.Ct. 2097 (1995).

Agency Holding Corp. v. Malley-Duff and Associates, 483 U.S. 143 (1987).

Albright v. Oliver, 114 S.Ct. 807 (1994).

Amerada Hess Corp. v. Director, Division of Taxation, New Jersey Department of Treasury, 490 U.S. 66 (1989).

American Trucking Associations, Inc. v. Smith, 496 U.S. 167 (1990).

Austin v. United States, 113 S.Ct. 2801 (1993).

Bank of Nova Scotia v. United States, 487 U.S. 250 (1988).

Bankers Life and Casualty Co. v. Crenshaw, 486 U.S. 71 (1988).

Barclays Bank PLC v. Franchise Tax Board of California, 114 S.Ct. 2268 (1994).

Barnes v. Glen Theatre, 501 U.S. 560 (1991).

Begier v. Internal Revenue Service, 496 U.S. 53 (1990).

Bendix Autolite Corp. v. Midwesco Enterprises, 486 U.S. 888 (1988).

Blanchard v. Bergeron, 489 U.S. 87 (1989).

Bowen v. Georgetown University Hospital, 488 U.S. 204 (1988).

Buckley v. Fitzsimmons, 113 S.Ct. 2606 (1993).

Burson v. Freeman, 112 S.Ct. 1846 (1992).

Butterworth v. Smith, 494 U.S. 624 (1990).

California v. Acevedo, 500 U.S. 565 (1991).

California Federal Savings and Loan Association v. Guerra, 479 U.S. 272 (1987).

Cardinal Chemical Co. v. Morton Int'l, Inc., 113 S.Ct. 1967 (1993).

Carella v. California, 491 U.S. 263 (1989).

Cheek v. United States, 498 U.S. 192 (1991).

Church of the Lukumi Babalu Aye v. City of Hialeah, 113 S.Ct. 2217 (1993).

Citicorp Industrial Credit v. Brock, 483 U.S. 27 (1987).

City of Houston, Texas v. Hill, 482 U.S. 451 (1987).

City of Richmond v. J. A. Croson Co., 488 U.S. 469 (1989).

Coit Independence Joint Venture v. Federal Savings and Loan Insurance Corp., 489 U.S. 561 (1989).

Commissioner of Internal Revenue v. Fink, 483 U.S. 89 (1987).

Connecticut v. Doehr, 501 U.S. 1 (1991).

Conroy v. Aniskoff, 113 S.Ct. 1562 (1993).

Crandon v. United States, 494 U.S. 152 (1990).

Cruzan by Cruzan v. Director, Missouri Department of Health, 497 U.S. 261 (1990).

CTS Corp. v. Dynamics Corp. of America, 481 U.S. 69 (1987).

Davis v. United States, 114 S.Ct. 2350 (1994).

Dellmuth v. Muth, 491 U.S. 223 (1989).

Dobbs v. Zant, 113 S.Ct. 835 (1993).

Duquesne Light Co. v. Barasch, 488 U.S. 299 (1989).

Equal Employment Opportunity Commission v. Arabian American Oil Co., 499 U.S. 244 (1991).

Federal Trade Commission v. Ticor Title Ins. Co., 112 S.Ct. 2169 (1992).

Firestone Tire and Rubber Co. v. Bruch, 489 U.S. 101 (1989).

The Florida Star v. B.J.F., 491 U.S. 524 (1989).

Franklin v. Gwinnett County Public Schools, 112 S.Ct. 1028 (1992).

Franklin v. Massachusetts, 112 S.Ct. 2767 (1992).

Freeman v. Pitts, 112 S.Ct. 1430 (1992).

Freytag v. Commissioner of Internal Revenue, 501 U.S. 868 (1991).

Granfinanciera, S.A. v. Nordberg, 492 U.S. 33 (1989).

Green v. Bock Laundry Mach. Co., 490 U.S. 504 (1989).

Goldberg v. Sweet, 488 U.S. 252 (1989).

Gulfstream Aerospace Corp. v. Mayacamas Corp., 485 U.S. 271 (1988).

Gwaltney of Smithfield, Ltd. v. Chesapeake Bay Foundation, 484 U.S. 49 (1987).

Harper v. Virginia Dept. of Taxation, 113 S.Ct. 2510 (1993).

Harris v. Forklift Systems, Inc., 114 S.Ct. 367 (1993).

Harte-Hanks Communications, Inc. v. Connaughton, 491 U.S. 657 (1989).

Healy v. Beer Institute, Inc., 491 U.S. 324 (1989).

Herrera v. Collins, 113 S.Ct. 853 (1993).

H.J., Inc. v. Northwestern Bell Telephone Co., 492 U.S. 229 (1989).

Hodel v. Irving, 481 U.S. 704 (1987).

Hoffman v. Connecticut Department of Income Maintenance, 492 U.S. 96 (1989).

Holmes v. Securities Investor Protection Corp., 112 S.Ct. 1311 (1992).

Honda Motor Co. v. Oberg, 114 S.Ct. 2331 (1994).

Hubbard v. United States, 115 S.Ct. 1754 (1995).

Hunter v. Bryant, 112 S.Ct. 534 (1991).

Immigration and Naturalization Service v. Cardosa-Fonseca, 480 U.S. 421 (1987).

International Union, United Automobile, Aerospace and Agricultural Implement Workers of America (UAW) v. Johnson Controls, Inc., 499 U.S. 187 (1991).

International Union, United Mine Workers of America, UAW v. Bagwell, 114 S.Ct. 2552 (1994).

Itel Containers International Corp. v. Huddleston, 113 S.Ct. 1095 (1993).

James B. Beam Distilling Co. v. Georgia, 501 U.S. 529 (1991).

Jett v. Dallas Independent School District, 491 U.S. 701 (1989).

Johnson v. Texas, 113 S.Ct. 2658 (1993).

Kaiser Aluminum and Chemical Corp. v. Bonjorno, 494 U.S. 827 (1990).

Lamb's Chapel v. Center Moriches Union Free School Dist., 113 S.Ct. 2141 (1993).

Lampf, Pleva, Lipkind, Prupis and Petigrow v. Gilbertson, 501 U.S. 350 (1991).

Landgraf v. USI Film Products, 114 S.Ct. 1483 (1994).

Lauro Lines S.R.L. v. Chasser, 490 U.S. 495 (1989).

McCormick v. United States, 500 U.S. 257 (1991).

Maislin Industries, United States, Inc. v. Primary Steel, Inc., 497 U.S. 116 (1990).

Mathews v. United States, 485 U.S. 58 (1988).

Minnesota v. Dickerson, 113 S.Ct. 2130 (1993).

Mississippi Power and Light Co. v. Mississippi ex rel. Moore, 487 U.S. 354 (1988).

New York State Club Association v. City of New York, 487 U.S. 1 (1988).

National Labor Relations Board v. International Brotherhood of Electrical Workers, Local 340, 481 U.S. 573 (1987).

National Labor Relations Board v. United Food and Commercial Workers Union, Local 23, AFL-CIO, 484 U.S. 112 (1987).

North Dakota v. United States, 495 U.S. 423 (1990).

North Star Steel Co. v. Thomas, 115 S.Ct. 1927 (1995).

O'Connor v. Ortega, 480 U.S. 709 (1987).

Ohio v. Akron Center for Reproductive Health, 497 U.S. 502 (1990).

Oklahoma Tax Commission v. Jefferson Lines, Inc., 115 S.Ct. 1331 (1995).

Pacific Mutual Life Insurance Co. v. Haslip, 499 U.S. 1 (1991).

Patterson v. Shumate, 112 S.Ct. 2242 (1992).

Payne v. Tennessee, 501 U.S. 808 (1991).

Pennzoil Co. v. Texaco, Inc., 481 U.S. 1 (1987).

Pope v. Illinois, 481 U.S. 497 (1987).

Posters 'N' Things, Ltd. v. United States, 114 S.Ct. 1747 (1994).

Puerto Rico v. Branstad, 483 U.S. 219 (1987).

Quill Corp. v. North Dakota By and Through Heitkamp, 112 S.Ct. 1904 (1992).

Reed v. Farley, 114 S.Ct. 2291 (1994).

Reed v. United Transportation Union, 488 U.S. 319 (1989).

Riley v. National Federation of the Blind of North Carolina, 487 U.S. 781 (1988).

Rivers and Davison v. Roadway Express, Inc., 114 S.Ct. 1483 (1994).

Reynoldsville Casket Co. v. Hyde, 115 S.Ct. 1842 (1995).

Rose v. Rose, 481 U.S. 619 (1987).

Sable Communications of California, Inc. v. Federal Communications Commission, 492 U.S. 115 (1989).

Schad v. Arizona, 501 U.S. 624 (1991).

Sisson v. Ruby, 497 U.S. 358 (1990).

Smith v. Barry, 112 S.Ct. 678 (1992).

South Carolina v. Baker, 485 U.S. 505 (1988).

Sullivan v. Finkelstein, 496 U.S. 617 (1990).

Tafflin v. Levitt, 493 U.S. 455 (1990).

Taylor v. United States, 495 U.S. 575 (1990).

Texaco Inc. v. Hasbrouck, 496 U.S. 543 (1990).

Thompson v. Thompson, 484 U.S. 174 (1988).

Thunder Basin Coal Co. v. Reich, 114 S.Ct. 771 (1994).

Tome v. United States, 115 S.Ct. 696 (1995).

Torres v. Oakland Scavenger Co., 487 U.S. 312 (1988).

Trinova Corp. v. Michigan Department of Treasury, 498 U.S. 358 (1991).

Two Pesos, Inc. v. Taco Cabana, Inc., 112 S.Ct. 2753 (1992).

TXO Production Corp. v. Alliance Resources Corp., 113 S.Ct. 2711 (1994).

Union Bank v. Wolas, 112 S.Ct. 527 (1991).

United States v. A Parcel of Land, Buildings, Appurtenances, and Improvements, Known as 92 Buena Vista Ave., Rumson, N.J., 113 S.Ct. 1126 (1993).

United States v. Burke, 112 S.Ct. 1867 (1992).

United States v. Carlton, 114 S.Ct. 2018 (1994).

United States v. Gaubert, 499 U.S. 315 (1991).

United States v. Granderson, 114 S.Ct. 1259 (1994).

United States v. Irvine, First Trust National Association, 114 S.Ct. 1473 (1994).

United States v. Munoz-Flores, 495 U.S. 385 (1990).

United States v. Providence Journal Co., 485 U.S. 693 (1988).

United States v. R.L.C., 112 S.Ct. 1329 (1992).

United States v. Stuart, 489 U.S. 353 (1989).

United States v. Taylor, 487 U.S. 326 (1988).

United States v. Thompson/Center Arms Co., 112 S.Ct. 2102 (1992).

United States v. Williams, 115 S.Ct. 1611 (1995).
United States Department of State v. Ray, 112 S.Ct. 541 (1991).
Virginia Bankshares, Inc. v. Sandberg, 501 U.S. 1083 (1991).
Waters v. Churchill, 114 S.Ct. 1878 (1994).
Walton v. Arizona, 497 U.S. 639 (1990).
Webster v. Reproductive Health Services, 492 U.S. 490 (1989)
Weiss v. United States, 114 S.Ct. 752 (1994).
Welch v. Texas Dept. of Highways and Public Transportation, 483 U.S. 468
    (1987).
West v. Atkins, 487 U.S. 42 (1988).
West Lynn Creamery v. Healy, 114 S.Ct. 2205 (1994).
Williamson v. United States, 114 S.Ct. 2431 (1994).
Wisconsin Public Intervenor v. Mortier, 501 U.S. 597 (1991).
Witte v. United States, 115 S.Ct. 2199 (1995).
Yates v. Evatt, 500 U.S. 391 (1991).
Young v. U.S. ex rel. Vuitton et Fils S.A., 481 U.S. 787 (1987).

CONCURRING-AND-DISSENTING OPINIONS IN THE U.S. SUPREME COURT

Burns v. Reed, 500 U.S. 478 (1991).
Cipollone v. Liggett Group, Inc., 112 S.Ct. 2608 (1992).
FW/PBS, Inc. v. City of Dallas, 493 U.S. 215 (1990).
Georgia v. South Carolina, 497 U.S. 376 (1990).
Hodgson v. Minnesota, 497 U.S. 417 (1990).
Immigration and Naturalization Service v. Doherty, 112 S.Ct. 719 (1992).
K Mart Corp. v. Cartier, Inc., 486 U.S. 281 (1988).
Lehnert v. Ferris Faculty Association, 500 U.S. 507 (1991).
Madsen v. Women's Health Center, Inc., 114 S.Ct. 2516 (1994).
Massachusetts v. Oakes, 491 U.S. 576 (1989).
Pennell v. City of San Jose, 485 U.S. 1 (1988).
Pennsylvania v. Union Gas Co., 491 U.S. 1 (1989).
Penry v. Lynaugh, 492 U.S. 302 (1989).
Planned Parenthood of Southeastern Pennsylvania v. Casey, 112 S.Ct. 2791
    (1992).
Sochor v. Florida, 112 S.Ct. 2114 (1992).
Tull v. United States, 481 U.S. 412 (1987).
Tyler Pipe Industries v. Washington State Department of Revenue, 483 U.S.
    232 (1987).
United States v. Aguilar, 115 S.Ct. 2357 (1995).
United States v. Dunn, 480 U.S. 294 (1987).
United States v. Fordice, 112 S.Ct. 2727 (1992).
Withrow v. Williams, 113 S.Ct. 1745 (1993).

DISSENTING OPINIONS IN THE U.S. SUPREME COURT

Allied-Bruce Terminix Cos., v. Dobson, 115 S.Ct. 834 (1995).

American National Red Cross v. S.G., 112 S.Ct. 2465 (1992).

American Trucking Associations, Inc. v. Scheiner, 483 U.S. 266 (1987).

Arkansas Writers' Project, Inc. v. Ragland, 481 U.S. 221 (1987).

Austin v. Michigan Chamber of Commerce, 494 U.S. 652 (1990).

Babbitt v. Sweet Home Chapter of Communities for a Greater Oregon, 115 S.Ct. 2407 (1995).

Board of Education of Kiryas Joel v. Grumet, 114 S.Ct. 2481 (1994).

Booth v. Maryland, 482 U.S. 496 (1987).

Bowen v. Massachusetts, 487 U.S. 879 (1988).

Brock v. Roadway Express, Inc., 481 U.S. 252 (1987).

California Coastal Commission v. Granite Rock Co., 480 U.S. 572 (1987).

Chambers v. NASCO, Inc., 501 U.S. 32 (1991).

Chisom v. Roemer, 501 U.S. 380 (1991).

County of Riverside v. McLaughlin, 500 U.S. 44 (1991).

Department of Revenue of Montana v. Kurth Ranch, 114 S.Ct. 1937 (1994).

Dewsnup v. Timm, 112 S.Ct. 773 (1992).

Eastman Kodak Co. v. Image Technical Services, 112 S.Ct. 2072 (1992).

Edmonson v. Leesville Concrete Co., Inc., 500 U.S. 614 (1991).

Edwards v. Aguillard, 482 U.S. 578 (1987).

Espinosa v. Florida, 112 S.Ct. 2926 (1992).

Ferens v. John Deere Co., 494 U.S. 516 (1990).

Georgia v. McCollum, 112 S.Ct. 2348 (1992).

Georgia v. South Carolina, 497 U.S. 376 (1990).

Grady v. Corbin, 495 U.S. 508 (1990).

Gray v. Mississippi, 481 U.S. 648 (1987).

Hartford Fire Insurance Co. v. California, 113 S.Ct. 2891 (1993).

Hoffmann-La Roche Inc. v. Sperling, 493 U.S. 165 (1989).

Honig v. Doe, 484 U.S. 305 (1988).

Houston v. Lack, 487 U.S. 266 (1988).

Houston Lawyers' Association v. Attorney General of Texas, 501 U.S. 419 (1991).

J.E.B. v. Alabama ex rel. T.B., 114 S.Ct. 1419 (1994).

John Doe Agency v. John Doe Corp., 493 U.S. 146 (1989).

Johnson v. Transportation Agency, Santa Clara County, 480 U.S. 616 (1987).

Jones v. Thomas, 491 U.S. 376 (1989).

K Mart Corp. v. Cartier, Inc., 485 U.S. 176 (1988).

Key Tronic Corp. v. United States, 114 S.Ct. 1960 (1994).

Kyles v. Whitley, 115 S.Ct. 1555 (1995).

Lankford v. Idaho, 500 U.S. 110 (1991).

Lee v. Weisman, 112 S.Ct. 2649 (1992).

Maryland v. Craig, 497 U.S. 836 (1990).

McIntyre v. Ohio Elections Commission, 115 S.Ct. 1511 (1995).

McKoy v. North Carolina, 494 U.S. 433 (1990).

Minnick v. Mississippi, 498 U.S. 146 (1990).

Mireles v. Waco, 112 S.Ct. 286 (1991).

Mistretta v. United States, 488 U.S. 361 (1989).

Morgan v. Illinois, 112 S.Ct. 2222 (1992).

Morrison v. Olson, 487 U.S. 654 (1988).

Moskal v. United States, 498 U.S. 103 (1990).

National Labor Relations Board v. Curtin Matheson Scientific, Inc., 494 U.S. 775 (1990).

National Treasury Employees Union v. Von Raab, 489 U.S. 656 (1989).

Norman v. Reed, 112 S.Ct. 698 (1992).

Pauley v. BethEnergy Mines, Inc., 501 U.S. 680 (1991).

Peretz v. United States, 501 U.S. 923 (1991).

Powers v. Ohio, 499 U.S. 400 (1991).

Rankin v. McPherson, 483 U.S. 378 (1987).

Richmond v. Lewis, 113 S.Ct. 528 (1992).

Rutan v. Republican Party of Illinois, 497 U.S. 62 (1990).

Schlup v. Delo, 115 S.Ct. 851 (1995).

Schmuck v. United States, 489 U.S. 705 (1989).

Simmons v. South Carolina, 144 S.Ct. 2187 (1994).

Smith v. United States, 113 S.Ct. 2050 (1993).

South Carolina v. Gathers, 490 U.S. 805 (1989).

Stewart Organization, Inc. v. Ricoh Corp., 487 U.S. 22 (1988).

Summit Health, Ltd. v. Pinhas, 500 U.S. 322 (1991).

Tashjian v. Republican Party of Connecticut, 479 U.S. 208 (1986).

Texas Monthly, Inc. v. Bullock, 489 U.S. 1 (1989).

Thompson v. Oklahoma, 487 U.S. 815 (1988).

United States v. Johnson, 481 U.S. 681 (1987).

United States v. Mendoza-Lopez, 481 U.S. 828 (1987).

United States v. X-Citement Video, Inc., 115 S.Ct. 464 (1994).

United States Department of Justice v. Julian, 486 U.S. 1 (1988).

Webster v. Doe, 486 U.S. 592 (1988).

Wyoming v. Oklahoma, 112 S.Ct. 789 (1992).

OPINIONS WRITTEN DURING SUPREME COURT RECESS

Barnes v. E-Systems, Inc. Group Hospital Medical and Surgical Insurance Plan, 112 S.Ct. 1 (1991).

Campos v. City of Houston, 112 S.Ct. 354 (1991).

Edwards v. Hope Medical Group for Women, 115 S.Ct. 1 (1994).

Kentucky v. Stincer, 479 U.S. 1303 (1986).

Kleem v. Immigration and Naturalization Service, 479 U.S. 1308 (1986).
Madden v. Texas, 498 U.S. 1301 (1991).
Mississippi v. Turner, 498 U.S. 1306 (1991).
Ohio Citizens for Responsible Energy, Inc. v. Nuclear Regulatory Commission, 479 U.S. 1312 (1986).

OPINIONS ON DENIAL OF CERTIORARI

Tuggle v. Netherland, 116 S.Ct. 283 (1995).
Virginia Military Institute v. United States, 113 S.Ct. 2431 (1993).
Winfield v. Kaplan, 114 S.Ct. 2783 (1994).

OPINIONS FOR THE U.S. COURT OF APPEALS FOR THE D.C. CIRCUIT

Air New Zealand Ltd. v. Civil Aeronautics Board, 726 F.2d 832 (D.C. Cir. 1984).
Aluminum Co. of America v. Interstate Commerce Commission, 761 F.2d 746 (D.C. Cir. 1985).
Aluminum Co. of America v. United States, 790 F.2d 938 (D.C. Cir. 1986).
American Federation of Government Employees, AFL-CIO, Local 2782 v. Federal Labor Relations Authority, 702 F.2d 1183 (D.C. Cir. 1983).
American Trucking Associations, Inc. v. Interstate Commerce Commission, 697 F.2d 1146 (D.C. Cir. 1983).
American Trucking Associations, Inc. v. Interstate Commerce Commission, 747 F.2d 787 (D.C. Cir. 1984).
Arieff v. United States Department of Navy, 712 F.2d 1462 (D.C. Cir. 1983).
ASARCO, Inc. v. Federal Energy Regulatory Commission, 777 F.2d 764 (D.C. Cir. 1985).
Asociacion de Reclamantes v. United Mexican States, 735 F.2d 1517 (D.C. Cir. 1984).
Association of Data Processing Service Organizations v. Board of Governors of Federal Reserve System, 745 F.2d 677 (D.C. Cir. 1984).
Atlanta Gas Light Co. v. Federal Energy Regulatory Commission, 756 F.2d 191 (D.C. Cir. 1985).
Block v. Meese, 793 F.2d 1303 (D.C. Cir. 1986).
Brock v. Cathedral Bluffs Shale Oil Co., 796 F.2d 533 (D.C. Cir. 1986).
Bouchet v. National Urban League, 730 F.2d 799 (D.C. Cir. 1984).
Carducci v. Regan, 714 F.2d 171 (D.C. Cir. 1983).
Carter v. Director, Office of Workers' Compensation Programs, United States Department of Labor, 751 F.2d 1398 (D.C. Cir. 1985).
Center for Auto Safety v. Peck, 751 F.2d 1336 (D.C. Cir. 1985).
Center for Auto Safety v. Ruckelshaus, 747 F.2d 1 (D.C. Cir. 1984).
Church of Scientology of California v. Internal Revenue Service, 792 F.2d 146 (D.C. Cir. 1986).

Church of Scientology of California v. Internal Revenue Service, 792 F.2d 153 (D.C. Cir. 1986).

Citizens for Jazz on WRVR, Inc. v. Federal Communications Commission, 775 F.2d 392 (D.C. Cir. 1985).

City of Bedford v. Federal Energy Regulatory Commission, 718 F.2d 1164 (D.C. Cir. 1983).

City of Charlottesville, Virginia v. Federal Energy Regulatory Commission, 774 F.2d 1205 (D.C. Cir. 1985).

City of Cleveland, Ohio v. Federal Energy Regulatory Commission, 773 F.2d 1368 (D.C. Cir. 1985).

City of Winnfield, Louisiana v. Federal Energy Regulatory Commission, 744 F.2d 871 (D.C. Cir. 1984).

Community Nutrition Institute v. Block, 749 F.2d 50 (D.C. Cir. 1984).

Consumers Union of United States v. Federal Trade Commission, 801 F.2d 417 (D.C. Cir. 1986).

Dana Corp. v. Interstate Commerce Commission, 703 F.2d 1297 (D.C. Cir. 1983).

Delta Data Systems Corp. v. Webster, 744 F.2d 197 (D.C. Cir. 1984).

Department of Treasury, United States Customs Service, Washington, D.C. v. Federal Labor Relations Authority, 762 F.2d 1119 (D.C. Cir. 1985).

De Perez v. Federal Communications Commission, 738 F.2d 1304 (D.C. Cir. 1984).

Devine v. Pastore, 732 F.2d 213 (D.C. Cir. 1984).

Director, Office of Workers' Compensation Programs, United States Department of Labor v. Belcher Erectors, 770 F.2d 1220 (D.C. Cir. 1985).

Dozier v. Ford Motor Co., 702 F.2d 1189 (D.C. Cir. 1983).

Drukker Communications, Inc. v. National Labor Relations Board, 700 F.2d 727 (D.C. Cir. 1983).

Dunning v. National Aeronautics and Space Administration, 718 F.2d 1170 (D.C. Cir. 1983).

Electrical District No. 1 v. Federal Energy Regulatory Commission, 774 F.2d 490 (D.C. Cir. 1985).

Ellsberg v. Mitchell, 807 F.2d 204 (D.C. Cir. 1986).

FAIC Securities, Inc. v. United States, 768 F.2d 352 (D.C. Cir. 1985).

Gates and Fox Co. v. Occupational Safety and Health Review Commission, 790 F.2d 154 (D.C. Cir. 1986).

Gatoil, Inc. v. Washington Metropolitan Area Transit Authority, 801 F.2d 451 (D.C. Cir. 1986).

Gott v. Walters, 756 F.2d 902 (D.C. Cir. 1985).

Halperin v. Kissinger, 807 F.2d 180 (D.C. Cir. 1986).

Illinois Commerce Commission v. Interstate Commerce Commission, 776 F.2d 355 (D.C. Cir. 1985).

In re Reporters Committee for Freedom of the Press, 773 F.2d 1325 (D.C. Cir. 1985).

In re Sealed Case, 791 F.2d 179 (D.C. Cir. 1986).

In re Sealed Case, 801 F.2d 1379 (D.C. Cir. 1986).

International Association of Bridge, Structural, and Ornamental Iron Workers, AFL-CIO, Local No. 111 v. National Labor Relations Board, 792 F.2d 241 (D.C. Cir. 1986).

International Brotherhood of Teamsters, Chauffeurs, Warehousemen, and Helpers of America v. National Mediation Board, 712 F.2d 1495 (D.C. Cir. 1983).

International Union, United Automobile, Aerospace, and Agricultural Implement Workers of America v. Donovan, 746 F.2d 855 (D.C. Cir. 1984).

Jordan v. Medley, 711 F.2d 211 (D.C. Cir. 1983).

Kansas Cities v. Federal Energy Regulatory Commission, 723 F.2d 82 (D.C. Cir. 1983).

Liberty Lobby, Inc. v. Anderson, 746 F.2d 1563 (D.C. Cir. 1984).

Maryland People's Counsel v. Federal Energy Regulatory Commission, 760 F.2d 318 (D.C. Cir. 1985).

Maryland People's Counsel v. Federal Energy Regulatory Commission, 761 F.2d 768 (D.C. Cir. 1985).

Mathes v. Commissioner of Internal Revenue, 788 F.2d 33 (D.C. Cir. 1986).

Molerio v. Federal Bureau of Investigation, 749 F.2d 815 (D.C. Cir. 1984).

Morgan v. United States, 801 F.2d 445 (D.C. Cir. 1986).

National Association of Government Employees, Local R7–23 v. Federal Labor Relations Authority, 770 F.2d 1223 (D.C. Cir. 1985).

National Black Media Coalition v. Federal Communications Commission, 760 F.2d 1297 (D.C. Cir. 1985).

National Coalition to Ban Handguns v. Bureau of Alcohol, Tobacco, and Firearms, 715 F.2d 632 (D.C. Cir. 1983).

National Federation of Federal Employees, Local 615 v. Federal Labor Relations Authority, 801 F.2d 477 (D.C. Cir. 1986).

National Treasury Employees Union v. Federal Labor Relations Authority, 793 F.2d 371 (D.C. Cir. 1986).

Natural Resources Defense Council, Inc. v. Thomas, 801 F.2d 457 (D.C. Cir. 1986).

New England Coalition on Nuclear Pollution v. Nuclear Regulatory Commission, 727 F.2d 1127 (D.C. Cir. 1984).

North Carolina v. Federal Energy Regulatory Commission, 730 F.2d 790 (D.C. Cir. 1984).

Northern Natural Gas Co., Division of InterNorth, Inc. v. Federal Energy Regulatory Commission, 780 F.2d 59 (D.C. Cir. 1985).

Papago Tribal Utility Authority v. Federal Energy Regulatory Commission, 723 F.2d 950 (D.C. Cir. 1983).

Parker v. United States, 801 F.2d 1382 (D.C. Cir. 1986).

Port Norris Express Co. v. Interstate Commerce Commission, 728 F.2d 543 (D.C. Cir. 1984).

Radiofone, Inc. v. Federal Communications Commission, 759 F.2d 936 (D.C. Cir. 1985).

Rainbow Navigation, Inc. v. Department of Navy, 783 F.2d 1072 (D.C. Cir. 1986).

Ramirez de Arellano v. Weinberger, 724 F.2d 143 (D.C. Cir. 1983).

Regular Common Carrier Conference v. United States, 793 F.2d 376 (D.C. Cir. 1986).

Republic Airlines v. United Air Lines, 796 F.2d 526 (D.C. Cir. 1986).

Reynolds Metals Co. v. Federal Energy Regulatory Commission, 777 F.2d 760 (D.C. Cir. 1985).

Road Sprinkler Fitters Local Union No. 669 v. National Labor Relations Board, 778 F.2d 8 (D.C. Cir. 1985).

Romero v. National Rifle Association of America, 749 F.2d 77 (D.C. Cir. 1984).

Ryan v. Bureau of Alcohol, Tobacco and Firearms, 715 F.2d 644 (D.C. Cir. 1983).

Safir v. Dole, 718 F.2d 475 (D.C. Cir. 1983).

Sanchez-Espinoza v. Reagan, 770 F.2d 202 (D.C. Cir. 1985).

Sea-Land Service, Inc. v. Dole, 723 F.2d 975 (D.C. Cir. 1983).

Sharp v. Weinberger, 798 F.2d 1521 (D.C. Cir. 1986).

Shaw v. Federal Bureau of Investigation, 749 F.2d 58 (D.C. Cir. 1984).

Shultz v. Crowley, 802 F.2d 498 (D.C. Cir. 1986).

Simmons v. Interstate Commerce Commission, 716 F.2d 40 (D.C. Cir. 1983).

Simmons v. Interstate Commerce Commission, 757 F.2d 296 (D.C. Cir. 1985).

Smith v. Nixon, 807 F.2d 197 (D.C. Cir. 1986).

South Carolina Electric and Gas Co. v. Interstate Commerce Commission, 734 F.2d 1541 (D.C. Cir. 1984).

Tavoulareas v. Comnas, 720 F.2d 192 (D.C. Cir. 1983).

Thomas v. State of New York, 802 F.2d 1443 (D.C. Cir. 1986).

Thompson v. Clark, 741 F.2d 401 (D.C. Cir. 1984).

Toney v. Block, 705 F.2d 1364 (D.C. Cir. 1983).

Transwestern Pipeline Co. v. Federal Energy Regulatory Commission, 747 F.2d 781 (D.C. Cir. 1984).

Tymshare, Inc. v. Covell, 727 F.2d 1145 (D.C. Cir. 1984).

United Presbyterian Church in the U.S.A. v. Reagan, 738 F.2d 1375 (D.C. Cir. 1984).

United States v. Byers, 740 F.2d 1104 (D.C. Cir. 1984).

United States v. Cohen, 733 F.2d 128 (D.C. Cir. 1984).

United States v. Donelson, 695 F.2d 583 (D.C. Cir. 1982).

United States v. Foster, 783 F.2d 1082 (D.C. Cir. 1986).

United States v. Hansen, 772 F.2d 940 (D.C. Cir. 1985).

Washington Post Co. v. United States Department of Health and Human Services, 795 F.2d 205 (D.C. Cir. 1986).

Western Union Telegraph Co. v. Federal Communications Commission, 773 F.2d 375 (D.C. Cir. 1985).

CONCURRING OPINIONS IN THE U.S. COURT OF APPEALS FOR THE D.C. CIRCUIT

American Federation of Government Employees, AFL-CIO, Local 3090 v. Federal Labor Relations Authority, 777 F.2d 751 (D.C. Cir. 1985).

Answering Service, Inc. v. Egan, 728 F.2d 1500 (D.C. Cir. 1984).

California Human Development Corp. v. Brock, 762 F.2d 1044 (D.C. Cir. 1985).

Hirschey v. Federal Energy Regulatory Commission, 777 F.2d 1 (D.C. Cir. 1985).

Interstate Natural Gas Association of America v. Federal Energy Regulatory Commission, 756 F.2d 166 (D.C. Cir. 1985).

Moore v. United States House of Representatives, 733 F.2d 946 (D.C. Cir. 1984).

CONCURRING-AND-DISSENTING OPINIONS IN THE U.S. COURT OF APPEALS FOR THE D.C. CIRCUIT

Community Nutrition Institute v. Block, 698 F.2d 1239 (D.C. Cir. 1983).

Fink v. National Savings and Trust Co., 772 F.2d 951 (D.C. Cir. 1985).

Hirschey v. Federal Energy Regulatory Commission, 760 F.2d 305 (D.C. Cir. 1985).

McKelvey v. Turnage, 792 F.2d 194 (D.C. Cir. 1986).

Poindexter v. Federal Bureau of Investigation, 737 F.2d 1173 (D.C. Cir. 1984).

Securities Industry Association v. Comptroller of Currency, 758 F.2d 739 (D.C. Cir. 1985).

DISSENTING OPINIONS IN THE U.S. COURT OF APPEALS FOR THE D.C. CIRCUIT

Beattie v. United States, 756 F.2d 91 (D.C. Cir. 1984).

Carter v. Duncan-Huggins, Ltd., 727 F.2d 1225 (D.C. Cir. 1984).

Center for Auto Safety v. National Highway Traffic Safety Administration, 793 F.2d 1322 (D.C. Cir. 1986).

Chaney v. Heckler, 718 F.2d 1174 (D.C. Cir. 1983).

Community for Creative Non-Violence v. Watt, 703 F.2d 586 (D.C. Cir. 1983).

Conafay by Conafay v. Wyeth Laboratories, a Division of American Home Products Corp., 793 F.2d 350 (D.C. Cir. 1986).

Ensign-Bickford Co. v. Occupational Safety and Health Review Commission, 717 F.2d 1419 (D.C. Cir. 1983).

Illinois Commerce Commission v. Interstate Commerce Commission, 749 F.2d 875 (D.C. Cir. 1984).

In re Center for Auto Safety, 793 F.2d 1346 (D.C. Cir. 1986).

KCST-TV v. Federal Communications Commission, 699 F.2d 1185 (D.C. Cir. 1983).

Ollman v. Evans, 750 F.2d 970 (D.C. Cir. 1984).

Ramirez de Arellano v. Weinberger, 745 F.2d 1500 (D.C. Cir. 1984).

Security Industry Association v. Comptroller of the Currency, 765 F.2d 1196 (D.C. Cir. 1985).

Steger v. Defense Investigative Service Department of Defense, 717 F.2d 1402 (D.C. Cir. 1983).

Trakas v. Quality Brands, Inc., 759 F.2d 185 (D.C. Cir. 1985).

United States v. Richardson, 702 F.2d 1079 (D.C. Cir. 1983).

STATEMENTS ON THE DENIAL OF REHEARING IN THE U.S. COURT OF APPEALS FOR THE D.C. CIRCUIT

Chaney v. Heckler, 724 F.2d 1030 (D.C. Cir. 1984)

Washington Post Co. v. United States Department of State, 685 F.2d 698 (D.C. Cir. 1982).

ARTICLES, ADDRESSES, AND MISCELLANEOUS PUBLIC STATEMENTS

Administrative Conference of the United States. 1973. "Report of the Chairman." *1972–73 Report of the Administrative Conference of the United States*. Washington, D.C.: GPO, 1–4.

Burditt, George, and Antonin Scalia. 1973. "Introductory Remarks." *Food Drug Cosmetic Law Journal* 28:661.

Ginsburg, David, moderator. 1980. "Panel IV: Improving the Administrative Process—Time for a New APA? (Part C)." *Administrative Law Review* 32: 357–81.

Judicial Conference, District of Columbia Circuit. 1984. "Judicial Review of Administrative Action in an Era of Deregulation." *Federal Rules Decisions* 105:321–46.

——. 1988. "Banquet." *Federal Rules Decisions* 124:283–88.

——. 1989. "Luncheon Remarks." *Federal Rules Decisions* 128:452–56.

Lilly, C. Graham, and Antonin Scalia. 1971. "Appellate Justice: A Crisis in Virginia." *Virginia Law Review* 57:3–64.

Scalia, Antonin. 1970. "Sovereign Immunity and Nonstatutory Review of Federal Administrative Action: Some Conclusions from the Public-Lands Cases." *Michigan Law Review* 68:867–924.

——. 1971. "The Hearing Examiner Loan Program." *Duke Law Journal*, pp. 319–66.

——. 1972. "Don't Go Near the Water." *Federal Communications Bar Journal,* pp. 111–20.

——. 1977. "Two Wrongs Make a Right: The Judicialization of Standardless Rulemaking." *Regulation* 1, no. 1: 38–41.

——. 1978. "Guadalajara! A Case Study in Regulation by Munificence." *Regulation* 2, no. 2: 23–29.

——. 1978. "Vermont Yankee: The A.P.A., the D.C. Circuit, and the Supreme Court." *Supreme Court Review,* pp. 345–409.

——. 1979. "The ALJ Fiasco–A Reprise." *University of Chicago Law Review* 47:57–80.

——. 1979. "The Disease as the Cure: 'In Order to Get Beyond Racism We Must First Take Account of Race.'" *Washington University Law Quarterly,* winter, 147–57.

——. 1979. "The Legislative Veto: A False Remedy for System Overload." *Regulation* 3, no. 6: 19–26.

——. 1980. "Federal Communications Commission." *Regulation* 4, no. 6: 27–28.

——. 1980. "Federal Trade Commission." *Regulation* 4, no. 6:18–20.

——. 1980. "A Note on the Benzene Case." *Regulation* 4, no. 4:25–28.

——. 1981. "Back to Basics: Making Law without Making Rules." *Regulation* 5, no. 4:25–28.

——. 1981. "Chairman's Message." *Administrative Law Review* 33, no. 4:v–x.

——. 1981. "Regulatory Reform–The Game Has Changed." *Regulation* 5, no. 1:13–15.

——. 1982. "Chairman's Message: Rulemaking as Politics." *Administrative Law Review* 34, no. 3:v–xi.

——. 1982. "Chairman's Message: Separation of Functions. Obscurity Preserved." *Administrative Law Review* 34, no. 1:v–xiv.

——. 1982. "Chairman's Message: Support Your Local Professor of Administrative Law." *Administrative Law Review* 34, no. 2:v–ix.

——. 1982. "The Freedom of Information Act Has No Clothes." *Regulation* 6, no. 2:14–19.

——. 1982. "Reagulation–The First Year. Regulatory Review and Management." *Regulation* 6, no. 1:19–21.

——. 1982. "The Two Faces of Federalism." *Harvard Journal of Law and Public Policy* 6:19–22.

——. 1983. "The Doctrine of Standing as an Essential Element of the Separation of Powers." *Suffolk University Law Review* 17:881–99.

——. 1985. "Economic Affairs as Human Affairs." *Cato Journal* 4:703–9.

——. 1985. "Historical Anomalies in Administrative Law." *Yearbook of the Supreme Court Historical Society,* pp. 103–11.

——. 1985. "On the Merits of the Frying Pan." *Regulation* 9, no. 1:10–14.

——. 1986. "Letter to Congressman John Dingell," 23 May 1974. In Marshall Breger, "The APA: An Administrative Conference Perspective." *Virginia Law Review* 72:344–45.

——. 1986. "Morality, Pragmatism, and the Legal Order." *Harvard Journal of Law and Public Policy* 9:123–27.

——. 1986. "The Role of the Judiciary in Deregulation." *Antitrust Law Journal* 55:191–98.

——. 1987. "A House with Many Mansions: Categories of Speech under the First Amendment." In *The Constitution, the Law, and Freedom of Expression, 1787–1987*, ed. James B. Stewart. Carbondale: Southern Illinois University Press.

——. 1987. "The Limits of the Law." *New Jersey Law Journal* 119, no. 8:4–5, 22–23.

——. 1987. "Responsibilities of Federal Regulatory Agencies under Environmental Laws." *Houston Law Review* 24:97–109; followed by "Responses to Justice Scalia," *Houston Law Review* 24:111–23.

——. 1988. "Speech on the Use of Legislative History." Reprinted in part in Daniel Farber and Philip P. Frickey. "Legislative Intent and Public Choice." *Virginia Law Review* 74:423–69.

——. 1989. "Judicial Deference to Administrative Interpretations of Law." *Duke Law Journal*, pp. 511–21.

——. 1989. "Originalism: The Lesser Evil." *University of Cincinnati Law Review* 57:849–65.

——. 1989. "The Rule of Law as a Law of Rules." *University of Chicago Law Review* 56:1175–88.

——. 1989. Untitled address. Presented at American Enterprise Institute for Public Policy Research, Washington, D.C.; broadcast on C-SPAN network.

——. 1989–90. "Assorted Canards of Contemporary Legal Analysis." *Case Western Reserve Law Review* 40:581–97.

——. 1991. "Tribute to Emerson G. Spies." *Virginia Law Review* 77:427–37.

——. 1994. "The Dissenting Opinion." *Journal of Supreme Court History*, pp. 33–34.

——. 1995. "Common-Law Courts in a Civil-Law System: The Role of United States Federal Courts in Interpreting the Constitution and Laws." Tanner Lectures at Princeton University, Princeton, N.J. [Tentative draft; not yet available for public release and quotation.]

Scalia, Antonin, and Frank Goodman. 1973. "Procedural Aspects of the Consumer Product Safety Act." *UCLA Law Review* 20: 899–982.

Section of Administrative Law. 1976. "1976 Bicentennial Institute, Oversight and Review of Agency Decisionmaking." *Administrative Law Review* 28: 569–742.

"Twenty-fifth Amendment Proposals Aired in Senate Hearings." 1975. *American Bar Association Journal* 61:599–602.

U.S. House of Representatives. Committee on Foreign Affairs. 1981. *Amendments to the Foreign Assistance Act of 1961; Nuclear Prohibitions and Certain Human Rights Matters: Hearings and Markup on H.R. 5015, H. Res. 286.* 97th Cong., 1st sess. 8 Dec., 31–51.

U.S. House of Representatives. Select Committee on Intelligence. 1975. *U.S. Intelligence Activity and Committee Proceedings, Part 4: Hearings.* 94th Congress, 1st sess. 20 Nov., 1413–63.

U.S. House of Representatives. Subcommittee on Administrative Law and Governmental Relations of the Committee on the Judiciary. 1975. *Congressional Review of Administrative Rulemaking: Hearings.* 94th Cong., 1st sess. 7 Nov., 377–88.

U.S. House of Representatives. Subcommittee on Administrative Law and Governmental Relations of the Committee on the Judiciary. 1975. *National Emergencies Act: Hearings on H.R. 3884.* 94th Cong., 1st sess. 6 Mar., 88–105.

U.S. House of Representatives. Subcommittee on Administrative Law and Governmental Relations of the Committee on the Judiciary. 1981. *Regulatory Procedures Act of 1981: Hearings on H.R. 746.* 97th Cong., 1st sess. 2 Apr., 104–77.

U.S. House of Representatives. Subcommittee on Courts, Civil Liberties, and the Administration of Justice of the Committee on the Judiciary. 1973. *Parole Reorganization Act: Hearings on H.R. 1598, H.R. 978, H.R. 2028.* 93d Cong., 1st sess. 21 June, 163–86, 193–208.

U.S. House of Representatives. Subcommittee on Courts, Civil Liberties, and the Administration of Justice of the Committee on the Judiciary. 1975. *Newsman's Privilege: Hearings.* 94th Cong., 1st sess. 23 Apr., 6–93.

U.S. House of Representatives. Subcommittee on Crime of the Committee on the Judiciary. 1974. *Bureaucratic Accountability Act of 1974: Hearings.* 93d Cong., 2d sess. 27 Mar., 42–67.

U.S. House of Representatives. Subcommittee on the Departments of State, Justice, Commerce, and the Judiciary Appropriations of the Committee on Appropriations. 1975. *Departments of State, Justice, Commerce, the Judiciary, and Related Agencies Appropriations for FY 1976, Part 2: Hearings.* 94th Cong., 1st sess. 19 Mar., 747–55.

U.S. House of Representatives. Subcommittee on Elementary, Secondary, and Vocational Education of the Committee on Education and Labor. 1981. *Oversight on Private Schools: Hearings.* 97th Cong., 1st sess. 13 May, 47–67.

U.S. House of Representatives. Subcommittee on Foreign Operations and Government Information of the Committee on Government Operations. 1973. *Availability of Information to Congress: Hearings, H.R. 4938, H.R. 5983, H.R. 6438.* 93d Cong., 1st sess. 19 Apr., 223–52.

U.S. House of Representatives. Subcommittee on Foreign Operations and

Government Information of the Committee on Government Operations. 1973. *The Freedom of Information Act: Hearings.* 93d Cong., 1st sess. 10 May, 274–307.

U.S. House of Representatives. Subcommittee on Government Information and Individual Rights of the Committee on Government Operations. 1975. *Discriminatory Overseas Assignment Policies of Federal Agencies: Hearings.* 94th Cong., 1st sess. 9 Apr., 86–102.

U.S. House of Representatives. Subcommittee on International Security and Scientific Affairs of the Committee on International Relations. 1976. *Congressional Review of International Agreements: Hearings.* 94th Cong., 2d sess. 22 July, 113–257.

U.S. House of Representatives. Subcommittee on International Trade and Commerce of the Committee on International Relations. 1975. *Discriminatory Arab Pressure on U.S. Business: Hearings.* 94th Cong., 1st sess. 13 Mar., 71–111.

U.S. House of Representatives. Subcommittee on Legislation and Military Operations of the Committee on Government Operations. 1973. *To Establish a Consumer Protection Agency: Hearings.* 93d Cong., 1st sess. 11 Oct., 515–44, 559–84.

U.S. House of Representatives. Subcommittee on Legislation and National Security of the Committee on Government Operations. 1977. *Providing Reorganization Authority to the President: Hearings.* 95th Cong., 1st sess. 1 Mar., 56–75.

U.S. House of Representatives. Subcommittee on Legislation of the Permanent Select Committee on Intelligence. 1981. *The Intelligence Identities Protection Act: Hearings.* 97th Cong., 1st sess. 8 Apr., 102–30.

U.S. House of Representatives. Subcommittee on Monopolies and Commercial Law of the Committee on the Judiciary. 1975. *Arab Boycott: Hearings on H.R. 5246, H.R. 12383, H.R. 11488.* 94th Cong., 1st sess. 9 July, 37–74.

U.S. House of Representatives. Subcommittee on Rules of the House of the Committee on Rules. 1979. *Regulatory Reform and Congressional Review of Agency Rules, Part 1: Hearing on H.R. 1776.* 96th Cong., 1st sess. 26 Sept., 524–636.

U.S. House of Representatives. Subcommittee on Rules of the House of the Committee on Rules. 1981. *Congressional Review of Agency Rulemaking: Hearing on Various Legislative Veto Bills Introduced in the 97th Congress.* 97th Cong., 1st sess. 28 Oct., 200–210.

U.S. House of Representatives. Subcommittee on Treasury, Postal Service, and General Governmental Appropriations of the Committee on Appropriations. 1973. *Treasury, Postal Service, and General Governmental Appropriations for FY 1974: Hearings.* 93d Cong., 1st sess. 12 Apr., 38–75.

U.S. House of Representatives. Subcommittee on Treasury, Postal Service, and General Governmental Appropriations of the Committee on Appropriations. 1974. *Treasury, Postal Service, and General Governmental Appropriations for FY 1975, Part 4, General Government: Hearings.* 93d Cong., 2d sess. 24 Apr., 155–209.

U.S. Senate. Committee on Government Operations. 1976. *Improving Congressional Oversight of Federal Regulatory Agencies: Hearings.* 94th Cong., 2d sess. 20 May, 76–137.

U.S. Senate. Committee on Governmental Affairs. 1977. *To Renew the Reorganization Authority: Hearings.* 95th Cong., 1st sess., 8 Feb., 39–52.

U.S. Senate. Committee on the Judiciary. 1982. *Confirmation of Federal Judges, Part 4, Nomination of Antonin Scalia to the Court of Appeals: Hearing.* 97th Cong., 2d sess. 5–6 Aug., 90–92.

U.S. Senate. Committee on the Judiciary. 1986. *Hearing on the Nomination of Judge Antonin Scalia, to Be Associate Justice of the Supreme Court of the United States,* 99th Cong., 2d sess. 5–6 Aug. Reprinted in *The Supreme Court of the United States: Hearings on Successful and Unsuccessful Nominations of Supreme Court Justices by the Senate Judiciary Committee, Volume 13, Antonin Scalia,* ed. Roy M. Mersky and J. Myron Jacobstein. Buffalo: William S. Hein, 1989, 89–465.

U.S. Senate. Subcommittee on Administrative Practice and Procedure of the Committee on the Judiciary. 1976. *Administrative Procedure Act Amendments of 1976: Hearings.* 94th Cong., 2d sess. 28 Apr., 87–107.

U.S. Senate. Subcommittee on Administrative Practice and Procedure of the Committee on the Judiciary. 1979. *Regulatory Reform, Part 2: Hearings.* 96th Cong., 1st sess. 18 July, 129–54.

U.S. Senate. Subcommittee on Constitutional Amendments of the Committee on the Judiciary. 1975. *Examination of the First Implementation of Section 2 of the Twenty-fifth Amendment: Hearings.* 94th Cong., 1st sess. 26 Feb., 47–67.

U.S. Senate. Subcommittee on Consumers of the Committee on Commerce. 1974. *Food Amendments of 1974: Hearings.* 93d Cong., 2d sess. 25 Mar., 165–80.

U.S. Senate. Subcommittee on Consumers of the Committee on Commerce; and Subcommittee on Representation of Citizens' Interests of the Committee on the Judiciary. 1974. *Adequacy of Consumer Redress Mechanisms: Hearings.* 93d Cong., 2d sess. 13 Nov., 4–18.

U.S. Senate. Subcommittee on the Consumer of the Committee on Commerce, Science, and Transportation. 1979. *Oversight of the Federal Trade Commission: Hearings.* 96th Cong., 1st sess. 19 Sept., 246–60.

U.S. Senate. Subcommittee on the Constitution of the Committee on the Judiciary. 1981. *Freedom of Information Act, Vol. 1: Hearings on S. 587, S. 1235, S. 1247, S. 1730, S. 1751.* 97th Cong., 1st sess. 9 Dec., 953–62.

U.S. Senate. Subcommittee on Improvements in Judicial Machinery of the

Committee on the Judiciary. 1975. *Bankruptcy Reform Act: Hearings.* 94th Cong., 1st sess. 31 Oct., 197–228.

U.S. Senate. Subcommittee on Intergovernmental Relations of the Committee on Government Operations. 1976. *Executive Privilege, Secrecy in Government: Hearings.* 94th Cong., 2d sess. 23 Oct., 67–128.

U.S. Senate. Subcommittee on International Finance of the Committee on Banking, Housing, and Urban Affairs. 1975. *Foreign Investment and Arab Boycott Legislation: Hearings.* 94th Cong., 1st sess. 22 July, 159–75.

U.S. Senate. Subcommittee on Privileges and Elections of the Committee on Rules and Administration. 1976. *Federal Election Campaign Act Amendments of 1976: Hearings.* 94th Cong., 2d sess. 18 Feb., 103–145.

U.S. Senate. Subcommittee on Reorganization, Research, and International Organizations of the Committee on Government Operations; and Subcommittee on Consumers of the Committee on Commerce. 1973. *To Establish an Independent Consumer Protection Agency: Hearings.* 93d Cong., 1st sess. 5 Apr., 577–600.

U.S. Senate. Subcommittee on the Separation of Powers of the Committee on the Judiciary. 1975. *Congressional Oversight of Executive Agreements, 1975: Hearings.* 94th Cong., 1st sess. 15 May, 167–203.

U.S. Senate. Subcommittee on the Separation of Powers of the Committee on the Judiciary. 1976. *Congressional Access to and Control of the Release of Sensitive Government Information: Hearings.* 94th Cong., 2d sess. 12 Mar., 98–121.

U.S. Senate. Subcommittee on Taxation and Debt Management Generally of the Committee on Finance. 1978. *Tuition Tax Relief Bills, Part 1.* 95th Cong., 2d sess. 19 Jan., 284–301.

U.S. Senate. Subcommittee on Taxation, and Debt Management of the Committee on Finance. 1981. *Tuition Tax Credits, Part 1: Hearings on S. 550.* 97th Cong., 1st sess. 3 June, 243–337.

U.S. Senate. Subcommittee on Treasury, Postal Service, and General Governmental Appropriations of the Committee on Appropriations. 1973. *Treasury, Postal Service, and General Governmental Appropriations for FY 1974, Part 1: Hearings.* 93d Cong., 1st sess. 9 May, 813–60.

U.S. Senate. Subcommittee on Treasury, Postal Service and General Governmental Appropriations of the Committee on Appropriations. 1974. *Treasury, Postal Service, and General Governmental Appropriations, Part 1: Hearings.* 93d Cong., 2d sess. 23 May, 937–66.

Index